Principles of Public Economics

Principles of Public Economics

A Public Choice Approach

Francesco Forte

Emeritus Professor, Department of Public Economics,
University of Rome 'La Sapienza', Italy

Edward Elgar

Cheltenham, UK • Northampton, MA, USA

© Francesco Forte 2010

This book is an updated revision of *Principi di Economia Pubblica*, 4th edition updated to the rules and institutions of the Monetary Union, Milan: Giuffrè Editore.
© Francesco Forte 2000
Translated from Italian by Rachel Barrit Costa

Published by
Edward Elgar Publishing Limited
The Lypiatts
15 Lansdown Road
Cheltenham
Glos GL50 2JA
UK

Edward Elgar Publishing, Inc.
William Pratt House
9 Dewey Court
Northampton
Massachusetts 01060
USA

A catalogue record for this book
is available from the British Library

Library of Congress Control Number: 2009940976

Mixed Sources
Product group from well-managed
forests and other controlled sources
www.fsc.org Cert no. SA-COC-1565
© 1996 Forest Stewardship Council
FSC

ISBN 978 1 85898 673 9 (cased)

Printed and bound by MPG Books Group, UK

Contents

Figures

Tables

Acknowledgements

The author would like to acknowledge Rachel Barrit Costa for her competent translation of this work. He would also like to thank Domenico D'Amico for his diligent aid in the editing process.

Introduction: background: some aspects of the history of thought

1 THE CLASSICAL FORMULATIONS: SMITH'S THEORY OF EXCHANGE: RICARDO'S REDUCTIONIST THEORY

The economic theory of public finance has been studied from a number of perspectives since the era of classical economics, traditionally considered to start from A. Smith (Smith, 1776). The school of A. Smith held a conception of the public economy that was based on a systematic approach, in which the public economy is set in relation to the market economy. According to this framework, a well ordered nation is characterized by an exchange between taxation and public expenditure. Taxes are utilized to assure protection of freedom and property and to provide the public works and services, without which the market system cannot function. Furthermore, in this set-up taxes are determined not only on mere exchange but also on the criterion of 'ability to pay', which allows for certain redistributive elements to promote equality of taxation, which are not determined a priori. An additional principle is that taxes should be formulated plainly and with certainty; they should not be inconvenient to pay, and every tax should be designed to cost the taxpayer as little as possible over and above what it yields in terms of revenue for the state. The approach thus outlined did not embody a *systematic* theoretical analysis of the tasks to be addressed by the government with regard to public needs, that is with regard to the public or private nature of the various needs of individuals; rather, it showed a propensity to limit the role of the state.

A different approach, which can be defined as 'reductionist', was adopted by David Ricardo (Ricardo, 1817), who sought to establish it on a scientific basis. His approach essentially consisted of an enquiry into the economic effects of the public revenue, namely taxes and the public debt, taking fiscal decisions and public expenditure as a given. Within this framework, an explanation of the relations between public revenue and the market can be provided, leading to suggestions that may be of use for governments: indeed through an analysis of shifting tax incidence and the public debt, this approach reveals the economic laws that limit the possibility of government influence over the economy. On the other hand, it has nothing to say on decision-making processes within the public economy. Further, by neglecting the various types of public expenditure – and considering all public expenditure as unproductive consumption – this approach risks becoming deceptive.[1] But since this type of economic study of public finance can be carried out rigorously by applying the general theory of micro- and macroeconomics, it has come to be the most widely developed framework in the field of *theoretical* studies of public finance.

2   THE SOCIAL SCHOOL OF WAGNER

In opposition to this perspective, in the mid-nineteenth century a line of investigation arose that can be defined as the welfare approach. Prompted by the phenomenon of industrial development, it became known as the 'social' school of public finance, the earliest and most influential exponent of which was the German economist A. Wagner (Wagner, 1883). Wagner regarded the state as an artificial entity, similar to a public limited company, but with unlimited duration, its activity being exercised by government officials endowed with coercive power. The state is an indispensable entity that satisfies the needs individuals feel as members of their community, in relation to the social nature of such needs. It acts primarily by transforming material resources into services. Starting from this formulation of a principle, Wagner obtained a law of the constant expansion of public expenditure, which in his analysis has both a positive and a normative meaning. However, he outlined no law concerning the limit on this expansion. And after his sketch of the basic premises, theoretically stimulating though his description may be, any further analysis of the activity conducted by the state can be seen purely as applied economics.

3   THE UTILITARIAN-WELFARE SCHOOL OF J.S. MILL AND A.C. PIGOU

A quite different welfare framework, considerably more refined from an analytical point of view, was developed in utilitarian terms by J.S. Mill (Mill, 1871), H. Sidgwick (Sidgwick, 1883), A. Marshall (Marshall, 1920 [1961])[2] and A.C. Pigou (Pigou, 1920; and 1928 [1947]), with the analysis of the defects or failures of the market as compared to its allocational optimality. F.I. Edgeworth (Edgeworth, 1897) and A.C. Pigou (1928 [1947]) completed the work, by focusing attention on the optimal tax revenue in relation to public expenditure. But they did not base the theory of public revenue on the relation between the costs and benefits of expenditure for individual subjects, in contrast to the main strand of Smithian analysis, which was founded on the exchange principle. Rather, they focused on principles of maximization of the welfare of the collective community, starting out from the postulate that the state should pursue this aim on the basis of the algebraic sum of individual utilities. Such a postulate, in turn, was based on the assumption that the utilities of different subjects can indeed be summed together and that they are similar and show a decreasing trend with increasing income. Redistribution is thus justified from the rich to the poor by taxes and public spending. However, according to Edgeworth and Pigou, one should combine the principle of decreasing utility with the negative effects of high taxes on high incomes and wealth because their reduction of savings and their disincentive effects reduce the aggregate income. Thus tributes are based on a principle of ability to pay, understood as the minimum sacrifice, corrected with the above cautions, thus totally sweeping away the Smithian principle of benefit. As compared to the previous approach, this picture has the advantage of providing a general normative theory of the public economy. On the other hand, it can be criticized on account of the method of summing the utilities of different subjects into a single whole, denominated collective utility or welfare, almost as if society were a sort of 'larger than life man', endowed with existence and value in his own right. But it should be noted that while both Edgeworth and Pigou, as said, admit that by reducing incentives and the income available for savings, excessive redistribution reduces national income and thereby hampers the process of maximum collective utility, they provide no analytical criteria for the *limits* on redistribution. Thus ability to pay, which seemed to be determined on the basis of a precise formula of minimum collective sacrifice, remains a blurred concept. Moreover, since this approach is based on the calculations made by an enlightened and omniscient planner, it disregards all problems involved in the decision-making processes of the positive public economy. From this it follows that the investigation based on normative economics represents an artificially enlightened standpoint, inasmuch as it almost takes for granted the assumption that whereas the market may have its failures, the state and its action is subject to no such eventuality.

4   THE MARGINALIST SCHOOL OF ECONOMY IN AUSTRIA, ITALY AND SWEDEN: IN PARTICULAR, SAX, WICKSELL, A. DE VITI DE MARCO, LINDAHL AND EINAUDI

But as early as the closing decades of the nineteenth century a different approach to the economic theory of public finance had arisen in Austria, Italy and Sweden. Its leading figures were E. Sax, F. von Wieser, G. Ricca Salerno, U. Mazzola, A. De Viti De Marco and K. Wicksell,[3] and it focused on maximization of *individual welfare*. In its basic framework the citizens, considered as rational subjects guided by their own subjective utility, distribute their incomes among private and public goods according to their own marginal utility, and taxes are the fiscal price of the public goods thus established. This school, which was later further developed in Sweden by Eric Lindahl (Lindahl, 1919 [1958]; and 1928 [1958]) and, in Italy, by Luigi Einaudi,[4] had the merit of setting tax-paying citizens' choices at the centre of the decision-making and maximization processes undertaken by the public operator, as indeed is the general practice in democratic countries, albeit not necessarily through clear and cogent rational plans. In the Marginalist approach, the *democratic* public economy is coherently linked to the market economy, and the laws of economic value operate in a unitary manner, on the market and in the public economy. For these reasons, the above-described approach, which has been called the 'economic school' of public finance, has opened the way to study the process of public choices by which the individuals reach or fail to reach their ends through this collective action. With Mazzola, and later with Wicksell and Lindahl, this school of thought reached a univocal definition of wants (in reference to goods) of a public nature, as goods supplied collectively and utilized singly by individual subjects. Since individuals have different marginal utilities, they draw different benefits from the goods in question; thus they should pay different fiscal prices as they are demanding different units of the public goods supplied.[5] Wicksell then provided a further elaboration of the concept, arguing that in order to prevent the majority from burdening the minority with the cost of the amounts of consumption which, for the minority, entailed a cost higher than their marginal utility, it was necessary to have a rule of unanimous voting or qualified majority. The Buchanan 'public choice school' starting from this theorem did develop the theory of the fiscal constitution. De Viti De Marco conceived the public economy as a dichotomy of a cooperative model in which the government coincides with the electors-taxpayers who produce and consume the public services chosen by them and a monopolistic model in which the government responds to a class that dominates the others. Luigi

Einaudi, assuming this approach to public finance, developed an analysis of the different effects of taxation in relation to different models of public expenditure supposedly characterized by a lesser or greater degree of coherence with the individual demand for public goods in a market economy, as well as different models of taxation designed to conform to the competitive functioning of a dynamic market economy.[6] But neither he nor those who subsequently pursued the economic approach to fiscal economy in terms of individual choice devoted themselves to an enquiry into the more complex reasons for public intervention underlying the analysis of market failures put forward by the champions of the welfare economy, because such an analysis seemed to form part of a different methodological approach. Thus the theory of public goods developed by the economic school became increasingly incapable of furnishing analytical tools for critical analysis of the expanding range of tasks that the government, in its various different aspects, found itself having to address in democratic industrial countries, even though the theory in question was supposed to apply precisely to such issues. Furthermore, in relation to the model of the democratic state where taxes are the price of the goods an individual obtains through collective action, and where the demand springing from individuals is equal, on the margin, to the individual fiscal cost, as is the case on the market, no attention was devoted to examining the theme, highlighted by Wagner, of the distinction between the state – as an organization with its own personality – and the firms organized as joint-stock companies, a distinction stemming from the fact that the state as a firm operates by a non-market bureaucracy. What is the behaviour of the public bureaucracy, in the De Viti–Einaudi cooperative model, with regard to public goods? Moreover, in a democracy public decisions depend first of all on the citizens' choices, expressed through their vote, whereby citizens make decisions as to who should represent them, but they also depend on the subsequent decisions made by these representatives, who may or may not obtain a majority. And what are the rules that assure that the politicians do not exert opportunistic behaviours and that the majority does not exploit the minority?

Those who championed this methodological approach neglected the decision-making processes through which the law of economic value in the public economy, that is the very law on which they based their approach, may or may not come into action in concrete systems of government.[7] And no answer was offered to the problems raised by Montemartini, who observed that inherent within public finance, in a democracy with universal suffrage and given the principle of 'one man, one vote', there is an *intrinsic* political factor of coactive power of the majorities that interferes with the utilitarian interests of the minorities.[8]

5   THE SOCIOLOGICAL PERSPECTIVE OF PARETO
    AND PUVIANI, THE POLITICAL APPROACH
    OF GRIZIOTTI AND THE SOCIOLOGICAL-
    ECONOMIC LINE OF ENQUIRY ADOPTED BY
    FASIANI AND COSCIANI

A sceptical position can be found in the approach first introduced by W. Pareto (1916 [1954; 1935; 1983]), which rejects the concept of a scientific theory of fiscal economics, because the public finance phenomena are the expression of non-rational sociological factors through which the dominant classes oppress and deceive the citizens. An independent development of financial sociology was also put forward by Amilcare Puviani (1903 [1973]), with his theory of the fiscal illusion. Unsatisfied with these proposals, B. Griziotti[9] contended that the bases for the analysis of the fiscal phenomenon should be sought in interdisciplinary study of the 'political' character of the state. Given its powers of coercion and its almost unlimited duration over time, the state may have different ends and greater economic means than private individuals who are members of it in a given period of time, and it is not affected by the limitations of market economies. Consequently, the fiscal investigation cannot be restricted to the rigid economic paradigm of individual fiscal choices mimicking the market economy of De Viti De Marco or of Einaudi, nor to the paradigms of the maximum of aggregate utility in the manner of Pigou. By modifying the hypotheses on the type of ends of De Viti's state, the entire construct of Devitian arguments could have undergone an inversion similar to that which occurs when one puts the clock hands back.[10] But this could not be accommodated in a simple model of individual or aggregate utility of the various subjects. What was needed was an analysis of the structures and behaviour of the *institutions* of the state, by means of an interdisciplinary study that would include political considerations and the economic analysis of the fiscal legislation. Thus Griziotti championed and developed the economic analysis of law with economic principles of a general nature, concerning the fiscal constitution and the system of taxation.[11]

Other scholars, such as Seligman in the United States (Seligman, 1925) gave preference to developing the analysis of the rationale of different taxation systems, with brief premises on the nature of taxation as a social phenomenon, while others such as Fasiani (1951), influenced by the Keynesian macro economic approach, relinquished the marginalist economic theory of public finance, preferring a sociological-economic approach, which led them to embrace the reductionist Ricardian framework and concentrate their attention on the economic effects of taxation.

6   THE KEYNESIAN REVOLUTION

A major shake-up of these different lines of enquiry, in terms of the fiscal policies they advocated, was triggered by J.M. Keynes, with his 'general theory of employment' (Keynes, 1936). The Keynesian agenda held that the state should address the task of introducing full employment and development policies that the market is unable to achieve on its own. That is to say, by means of fiscal policy the state is able to provide means that are not available to the market, and which are capable of bringing about dynamic macroeconomic equilibrium. But Keynes himself remained silent with regard to an analysis of the decision-making process through which fiscal macroeconomic policy can genuinely correct market choices, *without generating inflation and heavy debts that would weigh on future generations*. Nor could the theory of macroeconomic fiscal policy substitute for the government's task designed to satisfy and finance the need for public goods.

7   MUSGRAVE'S SYNTHESIS OF THE THREE PATTERNS, THAT IS OF THE ECONOMIC, UTILITARIAN-WELFARE, AND KEYNESIAN APPROACH: STIGLITZ'S EMPHASIS ON THE WELFARE APPROACH AND THE AGGREGATE FUNCTION OF SOCIAL WELFARE

A comprehensive synthesis of the three approaches, namely the economic approach with its allocational rules, that of the welfare economy distributive issues and the Keynesian fiscal policy approach was put forward by R.A. Musgrave (1959), who proposed an ideal subdivision of the public budget into three branches, that of production of public goods, the allocation branch, that of distribution, and that of stabilization. Musgrave thus delineated the processes of maximization by an imaginary rational public decision-maker who behaves on the basis of individual microeconomic preferences, shared criteria of fairness and the macroeconomic objectives. But even the Musgravian synthesis disregarded the problems of the real decision-making processes of the public economy. Furthermore, the tripartite division was not sufficient to explain the state of effective welfare. As was noted by Forte (1976)[12] and by Blankart (2008), in actual fact the tasks of public finance must be analysed by means of a four-part subdivision, since the welfare state assumes, as well as the allocative, distributive and stabilization functions, the additional function, which may or may not be well founded, of modifying the demand of goods that individuals

select on the market, by means of an extensive category of public consumption of divisible goods, social security, health care, education and
other goods considered to be meritorious goods. For although Musgrave
presented the category of meritorious goods, he did so in a purely auto-
referential 'paternalistic' profile and inserted them into the allocative
function, neglecting the fact that within the framework of the allocation
approach based on the economic law of value following the preferences of
the individuals, this function refers to a failure of their demand as emerges
in the market.

In effect, Musgrave's line of investigation is actually a continuation,
extended and updated, of the Pigouvian welfare approach. And this same
line was adopted by the authors who formalized the new approach by
means of a welfare function with aggregation of the utilities of the various
subjects into a single total to be maximized, as hypothetically conceived
by the economist. The leading exponent of this new approach is currently
Joseph Stiglitz (2000).[13]

8   THE NEW ECONOMIC APPROACH, IN TERMS OF 'PUBLIC CHOICE': BUCHANAN

The new approach, which expanded the 'economic' analysis of the public
economy to include not only political and institutional factors, but also
the macroeconomic objectives of taxation policy and the results of the
abstract analysis of theoretical welfare economics focusing on the failures
of the market and the state, was developed through the new school of
'public choice'. The leading exponent is J.M. Buchanan,[14] who extended
the theory of decision-making processes from the constitutional level
(Buchanan and Tullock 1962 [1999]) to the subsequent levels of the public
economy, and from thence also to the operative activities of the public
bureaucracies. The school of 'public choice' makes use of background
knowledge from economic science, such as the theory of voting decisions,
game theory, the theory of voting power, agency relations, transaction
costs, and so on, which were only partially mentioned or hinted at above
and will later be developed further. Naturally, the public choice approach
is alien to the argument that maximization of collective welfare can be an
algebraic sum of individual welfare.[15] As we will see, in the public choice
approach, which will be developed here, this axiomatic formulation is
replaced by an analysis of decision-making processes in terms of voting
theory, game theory, agency relations and in terms of the Coasian theory
of the firm and of the transaction costs applied to the governments as
complex firms supplying public goods.

NOTES

1. According to Ricardo, taxes are a quota of the product of the land and of the nation's labour, which the government may dispose of for its own unproductive consumption. Analogously, for J.B. Say (1841 [1848]), taxes serve to sustain the government's unproductive consumption. What can be derived from this is, merely, the suggestion that it is a phenomenon which should be reduced to the very minimum and which deserves no particular analysis.

2. J.S. Mill (1848 [1871]), *Principles of Political Economy with some of their Applications to Social Philosophy*, lists seven cases in which public expenditure is justified by failures of the market: I) the consumer's inability to judge the quality of the good (e.g. education); II) immaturity and mental illness which prevent individuals from judging their own interests; III) cases in which the interest is too far removed in time and individuals cannot achieve clear perception; IV) cases in which by each pursuing greatest achievement of their own particular interests individuals damage the interests of others (monopoly); V) cases where individuals are unable to achieve their own interests due to lack of coordination (e.g. shop opening hours without government regulation); VI) cases in which an individual's own personal interest is not sufficient because the interests of others are also involved (e.g. the poor); VII) cases in which individuals have no interest in conducting that particular activity because it is, for the most part, carried out in favour of others free of charge (e.g. scientific research). Sidgwick, in his *Principles of Political Economy* (1883), was the first to develop the notion of external economies. A. Marshall is recognized as the originator of the statement embodying the fundamental principle that the market is unable to achieve the optimum, even in a regime of competition, on account of decreasing and increasing costs. Erroneously, P. Sraffa argued that the questions Marshall was dealing with concerned situations of imperfect competition. In actual fact, Marshall presented a theoretical analysis in which the overall results generated by an enterprise consisted of reciprocal external economies and diseconomies generated for the industry of its given sector or for the overall economy. See Forte (2003).

3. See Sax (1887), Von Wieser (1889 [1893]), Ricca Salerno (1888), Mazzola (1890), De Viti De Marco (1888); Wicksell (1896 [1958]). On the thinking of Ricca Salerno, in relation to these other authors, cf. Forte (2005a).

4. In particular in *Saggi sul Risparmio e l'imposta* [Essays on Savings and Taxation] (1941 [1958]) composed of a collection of studies conducted from 1912 onwards, and in *Miti e Paradossi della Giustizia Tributaria* [Myths and Paradoxes of Justice in Taxation], (1938 [1959] Chapter XII), and also in *Principi di Scienza delle Finanze* [Principles of Public Finance] (1940 [1956]).

5. This formulation is due to Mazzola (1890), for whom the public needs of individuals concerned indivisible goods that are conditional upon the development of associative life. Lindahl maintained that this conception of public need justified progressive taxation because subjects with a lower income have a higher marginal utility for private goods, and therefore desire smaller amounts of these.

6. See in particular Einaudi (1919); 1938 [1959], Chapters XI and XII.

7. Wicksell, as we have seen, made reference to the mechanism of unanimous or qualified majority voting, but he restricted himself to stating this voting criterion, without further investigation into the achievement of balance in decision-making processes. Pantaleoni (1883 [1938; 1958]) argued that the choices made by parliaments represent the attitudes held by the average voter; he thus hinted at the principle of the decision-making power wielded by the median elector, but he did not elaborate the question further. Luigi Einaudi drew on historical examples and based his arguments on a theoretical analysis of the Wicksellian framework in order to enquire into democratic decisions on taxes in ideal electoral systems, in Einaudi (1938 [1959], chapters XI and XII). The fascist era precluded the possibility of an analysis based on the democracies of the time.

8. Cf. Montemartini (1900 [1958]). This scholar, who belonged to the Pavia school and

subscribed to the marginalist approach, strongly influenced the thought of Griziotti (partly also due to their close personal relationship). That the rule of the majority vote is a consequence of the principle of 'one person, one vote' in the American conception of democracy, for intrinsic reasons of economic democracy and not for purely technical reasons, can be seen very clearly in the analysis by A. de Tocqueville, on which see A.T. Peacock (1992), and F. Forte (2005b).

9. The political theory of public finance put forward by Griziotti draws its origin from his 1909 essay *I principi distributivi delle imposte moderne sul reddito e sugli acquisti di rendite e di incrementi di capitali* [The Distributive Principles of Modern Taxes on Income and on the Increase in Rents and Capital Increases] republished in Griziotti (1956), partial English translation: 'The different fiscal burden of public debt and extraordinary taxation', in Pasinetti (1992), in which Griziotti argued that it is possible to construct a pure science of public finance as a 'political phenomenon with economic effects', and suggested various different abstract models appropriate for an interpretation of actual or hypothetical reality. What was required was to 'examine all the concrete and ideal arrangements of taxation; then, for each of these, construct the system, the crystal-clear model, in conformity with the financial ends the given government seeks to pursue and then examine whether such ends are achievable; and, finally, to highlight objectively the laws and properties of that particular system in a certain environment with respect to the fiscal ends to be achieved, which are, namely, the aim of ensuring coverage for a certain need and sharing out the tax burden in a certain proportion among the different categories of persons [. . .], setting aside any concern to establish which is the fairest system, or which one the most useful and which one imposes the least burden, leaving these issues to be dealt with by other investigations'. On Griziotti's theory of public finance, see Forte (2007).

10. B Griziotti (1935), republished with amendments in Griziotti (1953), pp. 154 ff.

11. Griziotti (1915), (1925), (1939) and in various other later papers republished in the two volumes of Griziotti (1956).

12. Forte (1976), Chapter 3, 'A. Il problema del valore. Nucleo e fondamento dell'economia finanziaria', section 3 'Dimensione del nucleo', [A. The Problem of Value. Nucleus and Foundation of Financial Economics. section 3 Size of the Nucleus], in which I wrote 'The problem of how to apportion resources among the various uses is a question that involves fiscal economics, not only with regard to the opposition between public goods and private goods, but also as regards other pairs of opposites, which are overlaid on the public vs. private good opposition: consumption and investments, primary and secondary consumption, necessary and non-essential consumption, "higher" consumption and material consumption, harmful consumption and consumption regarded as useful, investments in one part or the other, of one type or another and so forth'. Obviously, this 'apportioning' function is different in the framework of an individualistic market economy as compared to a welfare economy that is respectful (partially, in the allocational part) of the market economy, and even more so compared to a dirigiste framework.

13. Stiglitz (2000) Chapter 4, 4.2 and ff). It is amazing to observe that Stiglitz, while embracing a welfare-oriented and (intimate) approach of dirigisme, believes (Chapter I, section 1.3.3) that the branches of the public sector amount to three, as in Musgrave's framework. But numerous authors with a paternalistic approach seek to mask their critical value judgement on the consumption society, with spurious arguments about distributive or allocational 'efficiency', rather than displaying them honestly for what they are.

14. The bibliography of this author is vast. His complete works (up to 1998) are published by the Liberty Fund. A good selection that provides an overview of his writings can be found in Buchanan (1988).

15. Following Pareto (1916 [1954]), Chapter XII, section 2128–2139, Vol. II of the 1954 edn, it is necessary to draw a distinction between the maximum welfare of the collectivity and the maximum for the collectivity. In the former case, the maximum that

is maximized is the aggregate welfare of the community taken as a whole, and the maximum welfare of each individual is included in the aggregate by virtue of the algebraic sum, according to the model *à la* Pigou (1920). In the latter case, the welfare that is maximized is that of individuals considered singly, according to 'Pareto's principle' (on which we will focus attention in Chapter 2, section 2).

1. Decision-making processes and the structures of public finance

1 PUBLIC ECONOMY, PUBLIC FINANCE AND THE ECONOMIC SYSTEM

1.1 The Public Economy in Collectivist Systems, in Systems with Dirigisme and Market Economic Systems, in Authoritarian and Democratic Regimes

In the analysis of the public economy it is necessary to start out by considering the different models of the state, and thus of political regimes. The rationale for this starting-point is that the 'economic' model which posits that choices made in the public economy are based on the same concept of equilibrium between the collective demand curve of individuals and the supply cost as the concept that holds on the market is only one of the possible hypotheses. It implies the existence of a democratic regime and an economic system where the market plays a central role. But the state can be governed with an authoritarian political regime rather than a democratic system. And the role assigned to the market with respect to the public operator may vary. As far as the various types of economic systems are concerned, considerations on the role of the public economy require a distinction between market economy systems, systems with dirigisme and 'etatism' and collectivist systems.

In collectivist systems, the public economy tends to replace the market system almost completely, so that the latter appears as a merely residual phenomenon. In systems with dirigisme and etatism, on the other hand, one finds a coexistence between the public and the market economy, with both playing a significant role. But the laws of the market are pervasively modified by the intervention of the public economy. By contrast, in predominantly market-based systems – *like the system in which we have supposedly been living since the Maastricht Treaty* – the public economy *tends to be subsidiary* to the market economy. It should be noted, however, that the size of the public economy sector may be greater in a market system than in systems with dirigisme. This is because the extent of public revenue and expenditure, as a percentage of the national product, is not the only measure of the degree of interventionism by the public economy. Public interference in the market system may also come about through distorting actions of public enterprises and through distorting regulations and controls of an administrative nature. On the other hand taxation and public expenditure may, even in a predominantly market model, be fairly wide-ranging to provide for civil and social expenditure, but given that the logic of the market is what regulates the entire economic process, public intervention must not interfere with the *productive* processes of the market, except in cases when the market is ascertained to be flawed by imperfections. Furthermore, a (predominantly) market-based economic system cannot have a public enterprise sector outside of limited cases in the public utility area, and even in this framework severe monopolistic problems may arise.

Thus the 'public economy–market' relation and, additionally, the relation between democracy and the system of relations holding between the public economy and the market, present strikingly different configurations in the various models.

An overview of the different configurations is given in Table 1.1, where the columns indicate the two types of political regime – democratic and authoritarian – and the rows the three types of economic regimes – market-based, dirigisme/etatism, collectivism – with some of their fundamental characteristics.

1.2 The Web of Interaction between Democratic and Authoritarian Political Regimes and Collectivism, Dirigisme and Market Economies: the Incoherent Models

First let us consider the boxes that contain no coherent models.

Cell IIIA concerning the democratic regime with a collectivist economy does not contain a coherent model. Since the collectivist economy pervades the whole of the economy, it does not allow those individual freedoms that make a democratic regime possible. That is to say, when private property and private initiative are stifled apart from extremely minor aspects, citizens are not free when casting their vote, because they are dependent on whoever holds the reins of economic power. And, certainly, those in the political sphere who hold the reins of economic power cannot allow citizens to take part in free elections and decide on programs and on those who are to wield power in politics, as this would impair the grip on power held by the existing rulers. If it does actually happen that the balance of authoritarian political power is disrupted, enabling democratic forces to come to power, then the new democratic forces dismantle collectivism in order to increase the freedoms enjoyed by the citizens, who

Table 1.1   Types of economic systems and political regimes

Type of economic system	Democratic political regime A	Authoritarian political regime B
I. Predominantly free market	The public economy is subsidiary to the market economy, but this does not necessarily imply that the public economy has only a very limited size; the model is coherent and allows for different political approaches in the state/market relation	The public economy is subsidiary to the market economy, but the political powers repress non-economic individual freedoms; this renders the model incoherent and unstable
II. Dirigisme/etatism	The public economy is very important and operates by virtue of extensive public finance and/or pervasive regulations and/or a wide-ranging sector of public enterprises; the development of democracy tends to counteract the excesses of dirigisme	As the public economy is very important, by virtue of regulatory action as well as public enterprises and/or extensive public finance, this facilitates maintenance of the authoritarian regime/monopolistic equilibrium
III. Collectivism	The public economy pervades the entire economy; democracy cannot operate; if it does develop then the economic model evolves towards other solutions	As the public economy pervades the entire economy, this facilitates maintenance of the authoritarian regime; however, the efficiency of the system is poor

have become electors. But this may take many years, down a long winding path.

This, in effect, has happened in the economies of the Soviet bloc countries, after the break-up of the Soviet Union. It cannot be taken for granted that this break-up of the authoritarian regime of the collectivist economic system will automatically be succeeded by a normal market economy, as the latter requires good laws and good institutions in order to function.

Let us now consider cell IB: an authoritarian political regime with a free market economy. If the forces of competition operate on the market, in particular on the international market, then this too is an incoherent model; as a result, either the authoritarian regime comes to an end or the free market ceases.

The 1789 revolution that swept away the mercantilist state in France developed when a mercantile bourgeoisie and farming smallholders had already achieved a substantial level of development. Operating respectively in the sector of craftwork, industry and trade on the one hand, and in that of agriculture and related activities on the other, the mercantile bourgeoisie and the smallholders had given rise to a market teeming with operators, whose aspiration was that of freedom of competition.

1.3   Continuation: Coherent Models

The model of cell IIIB characterized by an authoritarian regime and a collectivist economy is, in fact, coherent and may achieve equilibrium. Collectivism places the fundamental reins of economic power in the hands of the political power and the authoritarian regime ensures power of enforcement of the orders through which the collectivist system is managed. Public finance is only a handmaiden of the economic activity, which is almost entirely in public hands, but there are public enterprises that charge other public enterprises or consumers a price according to the rules of the collectivist plan, just as there are also public services financed by taxes, decided by the collectivist political power.

Theoretical analysis, corroborated by historical experience, has however shown that the economic efficiency of this model is poor. And therefore it has a low level of economic and cultural development.

The models of cell IIB – authoritarian political regimes, with dirigisme-etatism – are likewise equilibrium models, at least from the economic point of view. Here too it can be said that the reins of authoritarian political power are extensively influenced by the decisions of the public economic power, and vice versa. Here the market is in existence; its costs and prices are widely influenced by decisions stemming from the central power. Taxes as well as expenditure are established by the central power, either in an authoritarian manner, paternalistically, taking into account what seem to be the needs of citizens, rather in the same way as a father with dependent children, or else in a despotic manner, bestowing favours on certain groups at the expense of others, or with a combination of these two modes of action. As experience has shown, a market system that is coherent with this model is the predominantly monopolistic system, as the intricate link between political and economic power encourages the emergence of enterprises that have a dominant position on the market and the dirigisme constraints of the public economy hinder competition.

> The foremost historical example is represented by the authoritarian political regimes of the seventeenth and eighteenth centuries with a so-called mercantilist economy, in which the government established pervasive regulations and engaged in a broad array of actions partly by means of tax burdens and tax relief and subsidies, and partly by making use of enterprises that were granted privileged public licences, with the aim of favouring the national economy and/or some particular sectors of the latter. But the economic and political balance of this model can be disrupted and swept away by the fact that at a certain point the lack of competition leads to stagnation or economic decline, while the authoritarian political regime does not guarantee that those who hold the reins of power are always going to be enlightened. Capable sovereigns desirous of assuring the wellbeing of their subjects may be succeeded by sovereigns who are totally inept and/or thirsting for power and money, who thus rashly embark on extenuating military adventures; moreover, in authoritarian regimes the question of succession in the framework of autocratic power can give rise to struggles that ultimately culminate in dissolution.

Now let us consider cells IA and IIA, that is those concerning democratic political regimes, focusing on the public economy and its relation with the market economy. Once again, as in the authoritarian models, we find a twofold division between predominantly free market economic systems and economic systems where dirigisme and etatism predominate. It should be added that, often, reality lies midway between the two, with oscillations towards the one model or the other depending on the parties in power. However, in order for there to be political democracy, it is necessary for the economic system not to be characterized by excessively wide-ranging dirigisme. For in this case the citizens would not be truly free. Furthermore, democracies aspire to economic and social welfare and this is possible only if per capita income grows to a fairly high level. Such a rise cannot be achieved, nor can it be maintained, if there is an excess of dirigisme (cf. Sen, 1999; 2003). But neither can it be attained in cases of extreme laissez-faire, where low-income subjects enjoy no social protection and extremes of social imbalance arise. It is precisely in the framework of debate on the merits and demerits of these types of model that the school of 'public choice' has taken shape, addressing the issue of the public economy in terms of individual choices. To the extent to which its analysis in terms of positive economics is valid, dirigisme does not appear to be defensible, since the main choices in the public choice approach, in terms of positive economics, are those which are made on the market, and the public economy integrates and corrects the market choices, yet without dominating them. But the approach of the school of public choice is also valid as a means of examining how and why dirigisme itself develops or persists.

> In democracies, from the nineteenth century onwards, an extensive welfare state has developed, sustained by a considerably extensive system of taxation. At first, this model was pursued even by conservative governments such as that of Bismarck, under the impetus of socialist political movements and the thought of public finance scholars like Wagner (see section 2 in Introduction), whose school was named, accordingly, the school of 'Chair Socialism'. Its continued development gradually led to the great welfare state of the second half of the twentieth century. But in the era of global markets, the public finance systems of market economy countries are losing some of their earlier welfare character, as the enterprises and capital tend to move to where the tax burden is lower and taxes translate into public services rather than being designed for purposes of social redistribution. Thus while the predominant model in the second part of the twentieth century, in democratic regimes, appeared to be that of box IIA, it now seems to be *tending* more towards that of box IA.

1.4   A General Socio-Biological Vision: Predatory, Parasitic, Tutorial and Market-based Public Economy Frameworks

The above-described differences in the type of relation between individuals and the public economy, arising from the various combinations among different political regimes and different economic models, can in a socio-biological framework be classified according to three general situations: one in which the public economy is at the service of the citizens, one in which it exploits but does not oppress the citizens, and one in which it both exploits and oppresses citizens. In the socio-biological classification of Pantaleoni,[1] these three frameworks are respectively 'tutorial', parasitic and predatory. A stylized economic definition of these three frameworks can be given in terms of the well-known concepts of microeconomics, namely the producer's rents and the consumer's rents.[2]

In the predatory framework, the majority of citizens pay tax in excess of the benefits deriving from public expenditure. Consequently, for this group the public economy represents a net loss. This is due partly to the fact that such citizens receive scanty benefit from the expenditure, and also to the fact that the levies are oppressive. The public economy is an obstacle to the market economy. This is the hypothesis that L. Einaudi (1941) designated as the 'hail-tax'.

In the parasitic framework, the majority of citizens pay taxes that do not result in a global burden exceeding the benefits they receive from public services; however, the citizens obtain no net advantage from such services. The consumer's rents and the producer's rents of the public economy go to completely different subjects, who form part of or collude with the ruling class. As occurs in the stable balance between a parasite and the exploited host,[3] the host opts for welfare choices from which the parasite also draws benefit. But while the biological parasite often lives off the exploited host without any interaction that could substantially modify their behaviour, in the case of economic parasitism there is a considerable modification of the market system as compared to the ordinary system, in the sense that parasitic fiscal rent-seeking by private operators tends to distract the latter from productive economic activity and thereby favours the enterprises cleverest – and luckiest – in 'fiscal rent-seeking'.

> According to Douglass North, in nineteenth century Mexico the oppressive, inquisitorial and arbitrary nature of the institutional environment compelled every enterprise, whether urban or rural, to operate according to a strongly politicized manner of proceeding, making use of kinship relations, political influence and family prestige in order to obtain privileged access to favourable credit arrangements, illegally recruit labour, accumulate debt or have contracts enforced, evade taxes or avoid the verdict of law-courts and defend or assert property rights over their land. Small businesses excluded from the privileges enjoyed by large enterprises or from political favours were forced to act in a permanently semi-clandestine condition, always on the fringe of the law, at the mercy of petty officialdom, never safe from arbitrary actions and never protected against the rights of the most powerful.[4] This state of affairs may partly reproduce, albeit with some exaggeration, many of the current parasitic frameworks of developing countries and the situation of some pre-unification Italian States, such as the Bourbon regime, which have left an unfavourable legacy in the South of Italy.

In the tutorial framework, the government aims to promote the welfare of the general population or at least of the majority of the citizens, and average citizens pay taxes that enable them to obtain a net benefit from the public economy. In this framework, the public economy is a factor of development of the market economy, albeit to a differentiated extent, and naturally, in relation to the advantages a citizen draws from it.

> This model is typical of circumstances during the *good government* era of the Roman Empire and in some of the authoritarian States of the Renaissance and the following centuries, when the sovereigns or aristocracies who held the reins of power were oriented towards pursuing the 'happiness' of their subjects. But this is also the ideal type that includes the model of Bismarck's social state, the Beveridge welfare state and the Roosevelt New Deal and the Kennedy–Johnson model of 'great society'.

1.5 The Cooperative and Monopolistic Models: the Maximum of the Collective Community and for the Collective Community

At this point, we can turn to the seminal dichotomy noted by De Viti de Marco,[5] whereby the public economy can, fundamentally, be analysed using two basic models: the cooperative model[6] and the monopolistic model. However, a word of warning is in order: while these themes will initially be addressed with the approach adopted by Luigi Einaudi, we will then develop this approach in a Buchananian public choice frame, but considering the government as a firm, in a Coasian frame. The point of view of the cooperative model adopted here differs from the mere exchange approach of the traditional economic school inasmuch as it focuses on the public choice processes *of governments as firms.*

In the cooperative model, which in effect is none other than the democratic model in the pure state, based on the principle of 'one person, one vote', taxes are the prices that citizens pay, as in a cooperative, for the goods they decide to produce by means of the public operator, in order to satisfy their needs when they judge that such needs cannot be satisfied through the market or that it is not advantageous to do so. The state as a firm identifies itself with the citizens as members of a cooperative. Therefore, citizens manage public expenditure in the same way as individuals who participate in a cooperative that produces goods or services and who are, at the same time, consumers of the cooperative's production, linked to the other subjects of the cooperative in a communitarian manner and on an equal footing with the other members. In this ideal framework, which even in the best of democracies is realized only imperfectly, equilibrium is reached by finding the ideal meeting point between the demand for goods and services citizens believe should be run by the public operator, and the cost of such services, as evaluated by the citizens themselves (cf. the graph in Figure 1.1 below). Choices in the public economy are made in the same way as those on the market, with a general balance between the needs satisfied by individuals (as private individuals and in enterprises) through the public operator, and needs satisfied on the market. The same economic law operates both for the market economy and the public economy. However, it is necessary to take into account the complex decision-making structures of the 'government-cooperative' (GC) that characterize a democratic state. On the other hand, it should also be borne in mind that there is an element of *mutualism* in a cooperative, which is assured by the 'one person, one vote' principle. Therefore, while it is incontrovertible that the average subject chooses a demand for goods of the 'government-cooperative' that equals her marginal cost, such a subject also fulfils the function of integrating the supply in favour of the 'poor' who would be unable to obtain a minimum of certain collective services if they were to rely purely on their own resources. But mutualism has some limits, as we will see.

In contrast to the above-described cooperative model, conducted according to the Einaudian framework of 'public choice', in a Coasian frame as mentioned earlier it is of interest to consider the 'monopolistic' model. In this model, where effective democratic competition is absent, the average tax-paying citizen is exploited by the government in favour of interest groups or political and bureaucratic cliques who wield considerable power, and populist patronage structures. A characteristic of the monopolistic model is that the government and the patronage network tend to absorb the entire rent that the taxpayer might otherwise obtain from the public economy, as occurs in the model of perfectly discriminated market monopoly.[7] But the exploitation can extend further. That is to say, it may also bring about situations hypothesized by Pantaleoni in his concept of the parasitic or predatory regime, summarized in the Einaudian image of the 'hail-tax'. Moreover, it should be noted that the current model of the 'monopolistic' state, as well as many of the historical models, does not involve a decrease in supply, like the classical model of the monopoly market without complete discrimination of prices[8] or with a supply of a size comparable to that of the cooperative model, but instead leads to elephantiasis of the sphere of activity of the public economy. It is worth emphasizing that exploitation of this kind comes into being due to the fact that private operators, in collusion with those in power in the world of politics and the bureaucracy, often seek and obtain fiscal rents which generate and reinforce monopolistic positions on the market.

Thus the monopolistic model takes on numerous different forms and can be considered as a set of deviations from the cooperative model, which arise as a characteristic of the public economy in a competitive democracy with a predominantly competitive market economy.

A word of warning is in order, however. It does not seem appropriate to brand every very large welfare state as a monopolistic state. There can be welfare-oriented public economies which, despite their large size in terms of their share of the national product, do not operate in such a manner as to deprive the average tax-paying citizen of the greater part of the benefit obtainable from public expenditure in favour of subjects who benefit from rents of a social nature, and nor do such economies inevitably induce enterprises to engage constantly in fiscal rent-seeking. To take a concrete example, consider the public economy of the Scandinavian countries, which have succeeded in reconciling the large welfare state with the market economy. In other countries, on the other hand, the welfare state is facing severe difficulties, because it appears to have overstepped the limits of the 'tutorial' model. Its reform aims to bring it back within the limits of the genuine cooperative model. But even in these states, the problem of parasitism, linked to systematic fiscal rent-seeking, has deeper roots elsewhere (see subsection 1.4, with regard to the parasitic set-up).

1.6   Public Goods in the National Product

The system of public finance is composed of flows both of revenue and of expenditure that interact with the market economy product, giving rise to the gross domestic product, GDP. To analyse these aspects in the macroeconomic framework of GDP, it is therefore necessary to consider the flows into which GDP can be decomposed. GDP is the total of goods and final consumption services C and of investment in capital goods IK produced in the given year, in the economy considered, + the new stock of perishable goods SP existing at the end of the given year that have not been processed into final goods, + the goods and services exported during the year EX, decreased by those that have been imported, IM. Therefore we can write

$$GDP = C + IK + S_P + EX - IM, \qquad (1.1)$$

which can be simplified by writing I instead of $IK + Sp$, in such a manner as to consider as investments both those in the form of capital goods and those in the form of the inventory of perishable goods. Thus we can write EI, the balance of payments, instead of $EX-IM$. Therefore:

$$GDP = C + I + EI \qquad (1.1')$$

Consumption and investments are carried out partly by families FA, partly by the market enterprises M (investments only) and partly by the government G. Thus

$$GDP = C_{FA} + CG + IFA + I_M + IG \qquad (1.1'')$$

GDP, in turn, is composed of the sum of the gross value-added VAL produced by enterprises, + VAL_G the gross value-added produced by the government, at its various levels.[9]

The gross value-added of an enterprise[10] VAL is taken to mean the new value, that is the 'additional' value an enterprise obtains by means of its *internal production factors*, on its net revenue, R, calculated before tax, as compared to the cost of the external production factors FE, such factors being purchased from other suppliers. The external production factors are also known as 'intermediate goods and services' (raw materials, semi-finished products, other perishable goods, energy sources, services, but not capital goods purchased by the enterprise and utilized in production, as the latter are considered to be internal production factors).[11] Thus the net revenue R of an enterprise is composed of its $VAL + FE$. To determine the gross revenue F of the enterprise, it is necessary to sum the net revenue

R with the indirect taxes TI, namely $F=R+TI$; consequently the gross revenue F of enterprises is:

$$F = FE + VAL + TI \qquad (1.2)$$

A similar argument can be put forward for the government. The value of the goods and services B_G, which the government provides free of charge, is constituted by FE and by the gross value-added of the government VAL_G. Since the government's goods B_G are provided free of charge, they are not subject to any indirect taxes TI. But since the government purchases intermediate goods that are subject to indirect taxation, the latter form part of FE_G.

$$B_G = FE_G + VAL_G \qquad (1.2')$$

But it should be noted that the sum of $FE_G + VAL_G$ does not correspond to a net revenue (or a gross revenue), given that here there are goods provided free of charge; rather, the sum corresponds to the production costs of B_G.

FE and FE_G are either imported or are produced domestically by enterprises that achieve a gross revenue F as a result of selling their product to enterprises or to the government. These Fs consist of other $FE + VAL$ + imported goods and so forth. In the end, what we find is that the entire market gross revenue F and the entire cost of the goods and services B_G provided free of charge by the government can be sorted into the categories of domestic *value-added*, importations and indirect taxes. Eliminating importations, which do not form part of the national product, GDP consists of the gross value-added of all the enterprises operating on the domestic market and of the gross value-added of the government + all the indirect taxes TI, namely:

$$GDP = VAL_M + VALG + TI \qquad (1.3)$$

Bearing in mind [1.1'] according to which GDP consists of consumption, gross investments and the balance between imports and exports, we can write:

$$VAL_M + VAL_G + TI = C + I + EI \qquad (1.3')$$

that is to say, GDP consists, on the supply side, of the value-added of enterprises + the value-added of the government + indirect taxation, while on the demand side it consists of consumption, investments and the foreign trade balance.

1.7 The Value Added of Enterprises and that of the Government

We will now turn to ascertaining which components make up the value-added of an enterprise or the government. Let us begin by considering an enterprise. It was stated above that the proceeds F of the enterprise consist of payments made for external production factors FE and VAL which are composed of remunerations for *internal production factors*. These consist of: 1) the labour factor; 2) capital goods owned by the enterprise (installations, machinery, equipment, computers, furniture and other furnishings, immaterial goods such as patents, industrial designs and so on); 3) use of immovable, movable and immaterial third-party goods (rent from buildings and land, car hire, royalties from patents and so on); 4) financing; 5) entrepreneurs who organize the production factors and take on the business risk. Thus VAL is composed of payments for the labour factor within the enterprise, which is composed of wages gross of social security contributions WL[12] + payments for interest on the financial capital loaned IF + payments for the use of buildings, movable goods and immaterial goods, denominated as rents, i.e. R + the residue that remains after payments have been made for the other internal and external factors as remuneration for use of one's own capital K and for the entrepreneurial factors, which is denominated as gross profit, inasmuch as it is gross of amortization for the material and immaterial capital owned by the firm, KL. Therefore the total value-added of the enterprises obtained by summing the gross value-added of the enterprises operating on the domestic market VAL_M, consists of:

$$VAL_M = WL_M + IF_M + R_M + KL_M \qquad (1.4)$$

that is to say, wages, interest, surpluses, profits gross of amortization.

The gross-value added of the government VAL_G has fewer components than VAL_M, given the different characteristics of its production factors and the conventions used to calculate it. It consists of remunerations for the labour factor, that is for state employees, gross of social security contributions $WL_G + R_G$ for rent of buildings, car hire and other forms of hiring, use of third-party immaterial goods, but its total does not include interest on the public debt used to finance public investment goods since this interest is difficult to distinguish from other public debt interest. Furthermore, VAL_G does not include the profit consisting of remuneration for the government's own capital or for corporate risk and organization. Profit, by definition, is absent in the case of public goods since they are provided by the government free of charge. Their value is calculated on the cost, net of interest. In any case, since they are public goods provided free of charge, it cannot be known whether they are worth more or less than their cost. Consequently, the method adopted to estimate their value-added can often be regarded as an optimistic estimation.

1.8 Government Expenditure is Composed of Public Goods and Transfer Payments

But it would be a mistake to believe that public expenditure goes no further than B_G: in effect, the government does not supply merely goods and services in the strict sense, but it also provides sums of money without any counterpart of goods or services. Such transfers of money are destined for families and enterprises. Some of the transfers, like pensions financed by social security contributions, do have a financial counterpart, while certain others are given free, without any real counterpart of goods or services, for instance child support allowances, subsidies for investments and loss-making public and private services, and the interest on the public debt which, as we have seen, is excluded from the government's value-added. The provisions not offset by any requirement of purchase of goods and services, denominated transfer payments, do not form part of the value-added of the government and therefore of the GDP. But if we seek to examine the government's entire free-of-direct charge expenditure S_G, it is composed of the cost value of public goods and services + government transfer payments T_G, namely

$$S_G = FE_G + VAL_G + T_G \qquad (1.5)$$

This expenditure is funded in two ways: firstly, with direct taxes TD, social security contributions CS and indirect taxes and dues TI, and with government debt at various levels (central, regional, local). Thus we will have:

$$S_G = TI + TD + CS + D_G \qquad (1.6)$$

1.9 The Circuit of the National Product between Families, Enterprises and Government

The circuit of GDP between families and enterprises and the government, assuming for the sake of simplicity that the foreign balance is zero,[13] is thus composed in the following manner. Families and enterprises use their incomes, deriving from the value-added of wages (including those paid by the government), interest (only that paid by enterprises for their business activities), profits and rents (of rented premises, of mines, patents, brand names and similar immaterial goods of which GDP is composed)

+ transfer payments from the government (for interest on the public debt and transfers as pensions, subsidies to enterprises and families), to engage in consumption and investments which incorporate indirect tax and social security contributions that go to the government. Furthermore, they pay direct taxes to the government. Families and enterprises obtain not only wages and transfer payments, but also public consumption and public investment from the government free of charge. The government, by means of the expenditure to supply these consumption and investment goods and services free of charge, purchases intermediate goods and services from the enterprises and pays wages to families.

2 THE OPTIMAL EQUILIBRIUM OF THE PUBLIC ECONOMY AS A FIRM IN DEMOCRACY

2.1 The Einaudian Equilibrium Model of Democratic Public Finance in the Cooperative State, in Comparison to the Market Equilibrium Model

To understand the laws of pure optimal equilibrium of financial economics in the cooperative model it is helpful to look back at the model of public finance in the ideal democracy, as outlined by Luigi Einaudi, integrating the framework put forward by De Viti De Marco:

> In a democratic or representative or cooperative regime, citizens delegate to their parliamentary representatives the task of calculating the advantages and proper funding of public services, and the representatives decide to set up a new service and the related tax levy if they believe that this would bring greater advantage for the collectivity than the alternative of preserving wealth for private ends [. . .] If wealth is distributed in this manner, it is clear that the tax levy must be considered useful for tax-payers, and must be of a kind suitable to provide them with maximum utility [. . .] At the margin, where infinitesimal differences are involved when the units of wealth considered are extremely small, there may be some doubt as to whether it is more advantageous to adopt the one type of approach or the other.[. . .] Below the margins there can be no doubt as to the choice.[14]

In this optimal model, taxation is the voluntary price of the goods and services citizens have entrusted to the public operator. Einaudi does not specify that in this model even the rules adopted and applied by the governments for the functioning of the market economy, as well as the rules for organization of the public system, are an expression of this calculation of the advantage for citizens. In effect, these rules in the cooperative model aim to ensure optimal functioning of the competitive

market system, based on private property rights and therefore on individual choices.[15] But this is implicit in Einaudi's argument. He also warns
that in a real-world context taxes are not voluntary prices but obligatory dues. In other words, it is not the case that every time citizens pay
a specific tax they receive goods offered by the government in return for
the payment, unlike the market situation, where there is a genuine law of
demand and supply. The situation can more appropriately be compared
to a subscription to a club, which involves payment of annual dues, in a
global service contract. Furthermore, even if one assumes that the politicians whom citizens have entrusted with representing them do genuinely
make the choices citizens would like to make if they had all the necessary
information available and were fully aware of the lack of public goods,
it is equally true, as Einaudi points out, that the actual need for certain
fundamental goods, such as defence, justice, culture and education is felt
when they are perceived to be lacking: but then it is too late to satisfy
them. In addition, as we will see (Chapter 3, section 2), there are cases of
insufficient rationality in day-to-day choices relating to the future, or to
goods the knowledge of which is increased by their repeated consumption. Consequently, sensible politicians have to interpret citizens' true
intentions and desires, not their momentary demand. Finally, even if all
this is taken for granted, there remains the fact that some citizens have
antisocial attitudes and do not aspire to have the public goods of collective justice and defence that the majority wishes to enjoy. This means
that some of the choices made by politicians satisfy only a part of the
demands that may be expressed by well-informed citizens, whereas the
(small) antisocial remainder of the citizens are obliged to pay for public
goods they do not want or desire only to a lesser extent.[16] It should also
be borne in mind that the principle governing democratic public choice,
as also in a private cooperative, is that of 'one person, one vote' and not
that of votes in proportion to the share held in the overall organization,
as would be typical of shares in a commercial joint-stock company. And
the principle of 'one person, one vote' leads to a difference in collective
decision-making with regard to the goods the public operator supplies,
in comparison to decision-making processes on the market. Collective
market demands are determined on the basis of individual demands
which, however, have different weights depending on the income of
the various citizens involved. Thus citizens can be said to 'vote on the
market' on the basis of their income. But in the public economy, citizens'
votes have equal weight. Collective decisions resulting from the votes
cast by the citizens' representatives in democratic assemblies at various
levels of government depend on the number of voters. If majority voting
is adopted, the majority can, through its vote, claim that certain benefits,

not commensurate to taxes, should be granted to those in a more deprived situation. Such a move is not possible on the market. The principle of 'one person, one vote' can, in the absence of constitutional rules to limit majority decisions that are adverse to the minority, divert the path from the concept of taxation as the ideal price suggested by Luigi Einaudi. But a democracy with a market economy involves a constitution that limits redistribution. So the model takes on the configuration of a cooperative, which is based on exchange but also on mutualism. Moreover, regardless of the presence of rules designed to limit redistribution, it is also important to note, as we will see further on, that once redistribution exceeds certain limits, the public economy is no longer coherent with market economy equilibrium and one observes economic effects that make it no longer advantageous to engage in redistribution for those who would be its intended beneficiaries.

The crisis of the welfare state, in the European countries, which have taken the welfare model to excess, is a clear demonstration of the above situation.

Therefore the model of the price tax holds. But real-world public finance differs from the ideal Einaudian model because, as in a large cooperative, it is not easy for the individual member of the community to make her voice and her vote heard. This is especially true in a complex organization which is, of necessity, extensively bureaucratized and where those in a ruling position have considerable scope to bypass the task of fulfilling the desires of those who are officially their 'principals', that is to say, the electors. Representative democracy is a complex machine and the public apparatuses of the state (but also of the municipalities, unless the municipality is very small) are complex public economy firms. Problems such as transaction costs,[17] informational asymmetries, or opportunistic forms of behaviour, may arise in the framework of agency relations between the electors and their representatives and the public administration. These difficulties are compounded by problems stemming from the imperfections of any voting system and the paradoxes of decisions achieved by voting. Furthermore the analogy drawn between the democratic government as a large cooperative firm and a large 'capitalistic' cooperative where similar problems may take place is imperfect. This is so because even if a multiplicity of governments may assure some competition, the right to leave the public cooperative that does not appear satisfactory in order to choose a different one is limited by factors that do not exist with any private cooperative. Several of these issues will be addressed during the course of our investigations (cf. in this regard this chapter, subsection 2.5, ff.). And they are issues that do not allow any ready-made solution.

2.2   The Pure Equilibrium Model of Public Finance in the Democratic Model

Keeping in mind these preliminary comments, we will now turn our attention to the stylized – and indeed idealized – model of the citizen who chooses and pays for public goods, with price-taxes in an Einaudian ideal democracy, which we represent in Figure 1.1. Figure 1.1 pertains to the *problems affecting the great majority of citizens*, represented here by an 'average' tax-paying citizen.[18]

The average individual (elector, taxpayer) to whom we refer here is a stylized figure, a representation of a person (including the market firms represented by their managers and owners) who is humanly rational, by and large honest, taking care of her own and her family's interests to an average extent, but not selfishly egoistic, nor selfishly materialistic, not below the poverty line, and not (particularly) rich. The hypothesis of the 'average individual' as an average of the people of a given community appears to be preferable to that of *homo oeconomicus*, because it is more realistic in the context of positive and normative economics.[19] It will generally constitute our term of reference in this and the following chapters.

Average people have an ethical code, which they would rationally like to respect, although this is often not feasible as it imposes too high a burden.[20] The existence of a shared ethical code is an important factor in economic development.

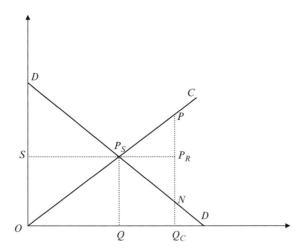

Figure 1.1   The equilibrium of the democratic model

Let us suppose that the average individual *J* operates in a simplified decision-making situation in which her desires, will and aspirations automatically translate into the government's will. Let us also suppose that the individual's choice concerns only two goods, public goods *G* and private goods *B*: for the sake of simplicity, these goods are inclusive of goods and services purchasable with money and of 'leisure time', which the individual *J* gives up when producing the monetary income needed to procure the other goods.

> Leisure time, it should be noted, does not consist only in the twofold aspect of enjoyment of the goods obtained by the monetary purchase and simple rest. It also consists of so-called self-consumption, that is to say, individuals may produce for themselves or for their own family members certain goods or services they would otherwise have to forgo or procure on the market or obtain by means of public finance. For instance, housework and similar chores are alternative to services involving home helps or childminders, or catering staff.

Subject *J* obtains goods B_M on the market and by sacrificing her leisure time, and procures goods *G* – which have a variety of characteristics that may or may not be identical with the characteristics of goods available on the market[21] – by recourse to the cooperative-government, *CG*, which acts as an agent for *J*, as in the case of the 'cooperative-state' model. The price-tax that *J* pays to *CG* is necessary in order to allow *J* to obtain the desired quantity of *G*. Along the *y* axis we will indicate the marginal utilities D and the marginal costs C of *J* for *G*. Along the *x* axis, is the quantity of goods *G* that *J* can produce and consume, by means of *CG* (who is *J*'s agent). We now plot the marginal utility curve *DD*, for *G*, of individual *J*; in accordance with the usual hypothesis of decreasing satisfactions deriving from the various goods; we assume that the curve is decreasing from the top left towards the bottom right, as the quantity of *G* consumed gradually increases along the abscissa. For ease of graphic presentation, we represent it in a stylized form as a straight line, although 'realistic' demand curves generally have other shapes. We now plot the curve relating to the marginal cost that *J* incurs, in producing *G*, as a result of the tax levied on *J* by the 'government-cooperative'. *G*'s *subjective* production cost can be represented by the units of B_M that *J* forgoes in order to be able to afford gradually increasing units of *G*, by means of agent *CG*. The marginal cost curve *OC* starts from the origin *O*, in which it has the value of zero, and then it gradually increases with increasing supply of *G*. Here too, for the sake of ease of graphic presentation, we use a straight line, even though marginal cost curves usually show other shapes. It is important to underline that we are dealing here with marginal costs, and therefore at any point the line of the cost concerns only the additional small unit produced. The marginal cost C of each additional unit is increasing, as it is constituted by the *sacrifice* of units of B_M, a sacrifice that is made in order to obtain G. And the greater the number of units of B_M that J refrains from using as private goods, the greater J's sacrifice becomes. This occurs even though the units of product C that J obtains by sacrificing B_M may not have a decreasing return from a purely technological point of view, that they are not at increasing costs but rather at constant or decreasing costs. Such an outcome is due to the fact that the sacrifice of units of B_M destined to procure additional units of G is increasing for J, because it implies that the quantity of units of B_M still left to satisfy J's private needs is becoming increasingly reduced. The point of optimum equilibrium between the marginal cost curve OC and the marginal utility curve DD is given by the point at which they meet. At that point the marginal cost of public goods G indicated by OC is equal to their marginal utility, indicated by DD (see Figure 1.1). That is to say, as long as the marginal utility of G exceeds the cost, it is advantageous to expand production of G. But when the marginal cost exceeds the marginal utility, the advantage vanishes.

As a result, we have production of the quantity OQ of G at price P_S. This implies, for J, maximization of the triangle DOP_S, which represents the sum of the producer's rent, which is constituted by OSP_S, and by the consumer's rent, which is given by $DS\,P_S$.

2.3 In the Cooperative Model the Public Service Producer's Rent goes to the Taxpayer, Not to the Bureaucracy or to the Political Groups that are Running the Government

Subject J, in our framework, enjoys a producer's rent deriving from the transformation of private resources B into goods supplied by the public operator CG, as J's agent, given by the triangle OSP_S since P_S is not the *fiscal cost* incurred by J for the entire supply of public goods OQ, but only that for the last unit. For each of the previous units, the fiscal cost, represented exactly by the marginal cost, is lower. Furthermore, subject J enjoys a consumer's rent because, for each of the units prior to the one in which the marginal cost P_S is equal to the marginal utility, J has a marginal utility greater than P_S.

The reason why, in our framework, the citizen-elector-taxpayer enjoys a 'producer's rent' for the provision of public services stems from our assumption that such an individual is simultaneously a demander and provider of these services. The individual in question is thus in a situation analogous to that of the cooperator in the cooperative model, which corresponds to a case where the world of politics and the bureaucracy are at the service of the citizen, and have no rents that would accrue from operating in their own interest instead of that of the citizen. We will see later that in reality this situation often is not the case.

2.4 Efficiency of the Government and Redistribution

If the production was increased by the political representatives to OQG, individual J would undergo a welfare loss given by the triangle P_sPN. which represents the excess of the cost of G over the demand of J, which must be subtracted from her rent DOP_s.

It might seem as if this graphic representation is an almost metaphysical exercise, *endowed with no empirical value*, given that for J the area of the 'return' of public goods, which is constituted by J's consumer's rent and producer's rent, arises from the difference between the cost for J in terms of the units of B sacrificed and the marginal utility of G obtained. And the *marginal utility* of G and the *marginal sacrifice* of B could appear to be concepts that are merely subjective.

But, as was noted earlier, for the user firms the 'consumption' of public goods is effectively a component of the production process. For firms the marginal utility of public goods is in fact their *marginal productivity*. But even with regard to private consumption of public goods, as was observed earlier, the notion of 'marginal utility' can often be replaced by that of 'marginal productivity', since they are complementary and/or instrumental to private utilization of human and material resources.

When public goods are a replacement for private goods, as in the case of free healthcare, the consumer's marginal utility of the public good refers to the monetary savings thereby achieved. In other cases, for example with regard to public pensions, J's marginal utility is expressed by means of a financial return, in relation to the amount of social security contributions paid. As far as the cost in terms of the sacrifice of B_M is concerned, it should be borne in mind that in reality, B_M corresponds to a monetary value. Therefore, it consists in the taxes which are expressed in money.

2.5 The Producer's Surplus and the Consumer's Surplus of Public Goods and the Minimum Equilibrium

As can be seen, far from being metaphysical notions, these 'triangles of rents' are the graphic manner of expressing phenomena with regard to which measurements could be carried out, on the assumption that a decision could be made to calculate the costs and benefits of public goods both for the citizens and for the firms that consume them and are subject to taxation.

It follows that the greater the efficiency of public expenditure and its appropriate response to individuals' real demands, and the lower the cost to the taxpayer in terms of taxes and other forms of public revenue over and above what is necessary to cover expenses, the greater will be the rents that the public economy gives to the market economy. It likewise obviously follows that inefficiency in expenditure, poor allocation and bad taxes reduces these rents. Government efficiency allows substantial redistribution, compatible with the market and with economic development. Inefficiency reduces the scope for redistribution. If these triangles are reduced to zero, the citizen-taxpayer reaches the minimum equilibrium.

> In the Scandinavian countries, public finance carries out elevated redistribution, but this does not spark a revolt among the taxpayers, nor does it seem to have hindered growth of the national product or the resulting per capita income, which is among the highest in the world. This is probably due to the fact that in these countries public finance operates very efficiently and respects the preferences expressed by citizens-taxpayers-electors.

2.6   The Principal–Agent Relation

The actual management of the government as a firm, even in the cooperative model, proper to a democracy with a market economy, is for the most part not carried out directly by the citizens but by their democratic representatives, who devote themselves full-time, or almost, to this work. Its activities in the provision of its supply of goods and services (inclusive of transfers) are carried out by specialized bodies which, in the broad sense, are known as the 'bureaucracy' (see Chapter 5, section 1).

> In the current language of economics, which is adopted here, the bureaucracy includes all those who are professionally engaged in running public affairs as permanent employees or self-employed professionals: the bureaucrats strictly speaking, military service personnel, the police, the judiciary, teachers and professors, the technicians working in the various public sector services, such as the corps of public works engineers, public health care workers, the accountants of the public finances, and the tax collectors and so forth.

The overall set of relations between voting citizens and taxpayers and politicians, and between these and the bureaucracy and, by extension, between citizens-taxpayers who cast their votes and the bureaucracy that runs public affairs can be examined (and improved) by analysis and reflection (which also allows for suggestions concerning institutional change) on the agency paradigm which holds between the 'principal' (that is to say, in the broad non-juridical sense of the 'mandatory', i.e. the person who actively is in charge of assigning tasks) and the 'agent' (that is to say, the 'mandatory', the person who is the passive executor, again in the broad non-juridical sense, of the task entrusted to her by the principal) as in the general theory of the firm as a hierarchical organization, in the Coasian approach. Over the entire range that extends from present and future citizens, whose interests are contained in (and guaranteed by) the constitution, that is the charter of the cooperative-government, to the present electors who express their own choices within this 'contract', to their representatives in the assemblies, to the government, to the top managers of the various bureaucracies, to the heads of the various services depending on them, right up to the final executors of the choices, it is possible to view the choices made within the public economy as a chain of agency relations between principal and agent. In this chain each principal conducts her activities by availing herself of an agent, who in turn becomes a principal, and so forth, right up to the final agent who is in a direct relation with citizens.

The user of public goods is, as we know, in principle – in the 'cooperative model' – not only the beneficiary but also the 'principal' of the supply–demand relation, in the sense that within the cooperative the user is identical to the provider.

The crucial issues in the 'principal–agent' relation, generally speaking, as regards the hierarchical organization and the external transactions of the firm, are:

a.   the difficulty of specifying all the clauses of the 'contract' that binds the two parties, and of suspending or rescinding it in cases of malfunction, which involves disrupting public services;

b.   the aim (pursued by both parties) of accessing accurate information on other parties' behaviour and needs;

c.   the task of 'monitoring', carried out by the principal or on the principal's behalf by ad hoc agencies, in order to check the agent's behaviour and to reward agents who perform successfully, while punishing those whose work is poor.

On the other hand, the agency relation of the public economy belongs to the subset of *collective* agency relations between a large number of principals and a single *team* of agents, analogously to the situation holding between the shareholders of a large company and its administrators. But this is not all, for this very fact exacerbates the problems described in (b) above and prevents direct monitoring by the principal. Additionally, it generates a new class of problems of aggregation of the preferences of the various principals.

2.7 The 'Political Market'

Citizens who seek to obtain public goods cannot simply make individual purchases as they would from ordinary market enterprises or from the consumption cooperatives of which they may be members. They act collectively, through their political agents and the bureaucrats, by paying dues, taxes and public charges and taking on other forms of public obligations (public debt, issue of money, personal duties such as military service, and so on) in order to perform the activities through which public goods are purchased in a manner that is apparently free or to some extent free of charge.

'Exchange' in the public economy – if it truly exists – thus has political connotations. And in a democracy it is a 'political market' that is carried out through the institutions of the public economy, leading to noteworthy transaction costs in terms of personal time, information and economic resources and also in terms of material and immaterial things concerning decision-making processes and their enforcement (cf. North, 1990).

Cooperators who go to their own consumption cooperative in order to make some purchases are carrying out market exchange operations with a supply that depends on their own action. However, they delegate the supply of goods to other subjects, through an agency relationship.

Thus a cooperator is not only a user but also the 'principal' of the cooperative's supply activities. The situation is analogous in the case of a citizen – in the cooperative public model – since the citizen acts through the government and the bureaucracy who, in their capacity as representatives acting for the citizen, have been assigned the task of providing public goods.

The meeting between collective demand and provision of public goods takes place through elective assemblies and through the forms of direct democracy: this meeting constitutes the 'political market'.

The public bureaucracy accomplishes the provision of public goods in favour of individuals and enterprises partly by means of its own activities, making use of production factors obtained on the market, partly by using goods produced on the open market and partly also with goods from regulated enterprises. In exchange for public goods the citizens (individuals and enterprises) pay 'fiscal prices' which, in a democracy, are decided through resolutions passed by their representatives or by the citizens directly. And, as we have seen, especially with regard to the cooperative model, in equilibrium, the fiscal prices have a reasonable relation to the benefits received and with the general principles of fairness.

By 'fiscal prices' we mean, in the broad sense, all the payments, in money or in kind, compulsorily or voluntarily, given by the market economy to the public economy. To these should be added the burdens resulting from the regulations (for example constraints on private goods for the protection of artistic and environmental values).

Alongside the complex of 'official' relations of the political market, a para-political market also arises. Here the pressure groups composed of political organizations and economic, trade union-related, religious, cultural, social, sports-related interest groups and lobbies offer favours and advantages of various kinds to the electors and to those who are elected to public office, as well as to those who belong to the bureaucracy, in exchange for personal 'favours' and support for the interests of the category involved (cf. Chapter 5, section 2).

The parties and the interest groups – as such – obtain their power of exerting political influence and their means to do so from the 'services' they give the citizen in exchange for prices, membership dues, voluntary contributions and at times (especially in the case of parties) public subsidies linked to such services. They are the electors' 'private agents'. The suppliers of production factors for the public economy belong, officially, to the economic market, which is instrumental to the political market. But at times they adopt a mode of behaviour that is unlawful or that verges on unlawfulness, in order to manipulate public choices to their own advantage.

2.8   The Cooperative Game and Opportunism, in the Principal–Agent Paradigm

Given a 'well specified contract' (in the broad sense of 'bilateral relation' containing a *do ut des*), with accurate symmetric information (= on both sides) that can be obtained at low cost, and given the possibility of modifying or rescinding the contract without excessive transaction costs, the agent should build up a form of 'cooperative game' with the principal, whereby the principal's aim becomes the most advantageous aim for the agent as well. The advantages and disadvantages resulting from the agent's behaviour will affect both parties, that is the agent as well as the principal. But, unlike in a joint-stock cooperative between the cooperators and their delegates who vote in the assembly, there is no such 'contract' of subordination or mandate holding between electors who cast their vote and their representatives. However, in a genuine democratic parliamentary system, every effort is made to render the relation between the elector and the elected as direct as possible, bypassing the interface of bureaucracies and political parties.

In contrast, those in governing positions have a hierarchical relation towards the bureaucracies, as do the heads of bureaucratic organs towards the apparatuses they preside over, although such relations are different and less direct than is observed in the corporate world.

One cannot expect agents to behave in the interest of principals rather than adopting opportunistic modes of behaviour[22] more advantageous to the agents themselves (for instance, in the case of employees, 'slacking', or in the case of persons in a managerial position who handle money, seeking 'favours' and advantages for their own benefit) if the principal has no clear knowledge of the agent's behaviour. Only a principal who has insight into the agent's behaviour can adopt choices advantageous to the agent in response to positive behaviour by the agent, or choices detrimental to the agent in order to counter non-cooperative behaviour. The cost of information, the power and capacity to exercise control, to grant rewards or mete out punishments, as embodied in the formal or informal paradigm that regulates the agency relation, and the structure of the clauses defining its content, thereby assume crucial importance.

While a loan contract or a property lease is, in itself, almost 'complete', with regard to the interest of the 'principal', this is somewhat less true for the relation between a physician and a patient, or between a skilled worker and the enterprise that employs the worker. It is much less true for the relation of teachers towards the state that employs them.

Additionally, unlike in a consumption cooperative where the top managers derive daily information concerning their consumers' preferences in the basis of their market economy results, in the cooperative-government, the top manager as the agent providing free goods and services faces a special problem of the costs and difficulty in acquiring information concerning the principal's 'real interest'.

2.9 The Various Imperfections of the Paradigm of Political Agency in the Relation between Electors and the Elected, and between the Latter and Governments

We can identify three requirements for a good 'political agency' relation: *efficiency*, that is the ability to provide a fast response at contained cost, with decisions that are certain and non-fluctuating; *effectiveness*, that is the ability to interpret what principals really prefer and to act accordingly; and *equity*, that is 'fairness' with respect for all the preferences of the various principals.

As far as agency relations between electors and the elected are concerned, 'cooperative game' behaviour is made more difficult and imperfect by the fact that:

a. there is no mandate in the formal sense of the term, since the successful outcome of the ballot does not impose on those who have been elected any specific binding mode of behaviour in terms of parliamentary or government choices, nor does it oblige the electors to cast their vote once again in favour of the previously elected candidates when the next election is held, even if such candidates have acted appropriately from the point of view of the electors;

b. principals face high information costs in seeking to understand agents' decisions and mode of behaviour, but the same holds for agents who endeavour to gain insight into the interests and specific desires of their principals (the citizens and the enterprises and associations to which they belong);

c. there are very many principals, some of whom are better organized than others, clustering together in parties and interest groups. Agents, even those who are unbiased, cannot disregard these differences, for if they failed to take them into account they would run the risk of not being re-elected. Therefore the 'population' of the elected is selected in such a manner as to result in a predominance of agents who give greater consideration to the principals most influential in the voting process;

d. the elected will have to give due consideration to the interests of the 'various principals', who include *future subjects not yet endowed with the right to vote as well as the current electors in the future*, while at the same time the elected are subject to voting decisions made by electors who may have a less marked interest in the wellbeing of such future voters, or indeed in their own wellbeing in the future.

Here too, as in point (c), the political agency relation tends to lose fairness.

In agency relations between elective assemblies and governments, reciprocal information is somewhat better. Indeed, unlike in joint-stock companies where the assembly normally meets only once a year and on few other occasions, the parliament meets repeatedly during the parliamentary sessions and works in contact with the members of the government.

Even in the absence of a formal mandate (the governmental programme approved by parliament is often generic, and cannot foresee all future cases), there are moments of an institutional nature – such as the budget forecast – in which the programme can be specified, and appropriate frameworks through which it can be monitored (for example presentation of the budget). Furthermore, an informal 'reciprocity game' develops between government and parliament, based on exchange of advantages and disadvantages.[23] The role of the parliamentary opposition is extremely important for an effective agency relation with citizens. This can be explained by noting that the parliamentary majority has an interest in colluding with the government, which is its agent, in order to engage effectively in opportunistic behaviour vis-à-vis the citizens. The opposition can contribute to 'exposing' such opportunism, for instance by exaggerated criticism which has the effect of 'alerting' public opinion.

Consequently, the distinction between 'competitive' and 'collusive' democracy is decisive. In 'collusive' democracy, the opposition is led to 'associate' itself with the majority, through rules of various types (often unknown to the public at large)[24] which enable the opposition to benefit from favours and take part in the spoils in return for refraining from exercising genuine and effective control over laws or over policies regarding expenditure and revenue, and other public action.

The model is similar to that of a collusive oligopoly in which firms enter into agreements with one another behind the scenes (while pretending to be in competition) in order to share out among themselves the exploitation of consumers.

2.10 The Imperfections of the Agency Relation between the Government and the Bureaucracy

The effectiveness of the agency relation between the bureaucratic powers and the members of the government is hindered by various factors:

a. the rigidity of public employment contracts, a rigidity which originally stemmed from, or at least was justified by, the need to protect public employees from the pressures and manipulative influence of the interests the bureaucracy has to deal with;

b. the informational asymmetry between the bureaucracy, which maintains its administrative function without solution of continuity, and the governments that succeed one another and which, since they do not operate in the field, thus have to face elevated information costs;[25]

c. the related difficulty, for the government in power, in attempting to adopt long-term policies towards those working within the bureaucratic apparatuses, in order to ensure that an effective cooperative game can be developed in conjunction with them;[26]

d. the difficulty, which is characteristic of large-sized hierarchical structures (and this is more likely to affect the bureaucratic apparatuses of the large state and the large municipalities than smaller government agencies), in exercising control over the peripheral agents; furthermore, the results achieved by peripheral agents are difficult to ascertain, since the signal deriving from profit, which would be typical of a large cooperative operating in the market context, is in this case absent.[27]

2.11   The Constitutional Pact as the Charter of the Cooperative-government

In order to ensure that agency relations can come into play as satisfactorily as possible and pursue the goals of democracy, efficiency and respect for citizens' right not to be subjected to arbitrary interference, what is required is a 'constitutional pact'. Such a pact, which has a function similar to the charter of the cooperative with regard to the rights and duties of the present and future cooperators, does not necessarily depend, either wholly or in large part, on a written constitutional text denominated 'constitution' and voted by a purpose-designated assembly, according to Buchanan and Tullock's seminal theorization (Buchanan and Tullock, 1962 [1999]). Rather, the constitution must take shape to a large extent through evolution, with the consensus of the greater part of the community under consideration, through shared general principles, that is to say, the 'primary rules of the game'. These rules are then considered to be at a higher level than the ordinary rules that are passed and implemented over the course of time.[28]

The constitution – in the cooperative model and in the welfarist model that we see in present-day advanced democratic countries[29] – establishes the way the people exercise their 'sovereign powers' through the right to vote and the various freedoms (political, civil, economic) which bring the constitution into force.[30] Additionally, it provides for separation between the power to pass laws and the power to administer public affairs on a legal basis, and also separates the power to make judgements on disputes and to exercise control over the public apparatus and management of public revenue from the other two powers. Further aspects concern the establishment of principles of economic freedom and equality, as well as the principle that tax levies should be commensurate with the benefits deriving from expenditure and with capacity to pay. Equally important are aspects concerning the duties of solidarity towards those who are in a less favoured condition, and the establishment of safeguards protecting the future generations and the 'high values' of culture, science and the environment.

As noted, the executive power cannot exercise legislative power, and vice versa.

In order to enable those in control of management of public affairs to fulfil their task impartially, it is essential for them to be independent of any other power or interest, whether public or private.

Within the economy there should be no individual groups wielding excessive power such as would distort public choices;[31] the power of disseminating information through the media and the press should be independent of economic power, while electoral expenses should be rigidly

limited, in order to avert the risk that politicians may become systematically dependent on the economic powers and that those who espouse an
independent line may be driven out.

2.12   The Budget in the Agency Relation and in Macroeconomic Flows

In a democratic regime, the budget that the government or the Local
Council (or the Regional or Provincial Council etc.) submits every year to
parliament or to the Local Council Meeting (or to the Regional Assembly
or the Provincial Council etc.) for approval in the form of a new law or a
regulation (if the assembly has no power to enact laws) is the 'document'
through which the electors' representatives entrust the executive power
with a mandate to provide a supply of 'public goods'. This is on the basis
of the laws currently in force or of new rulings contained in the budget or
in annexed texts, authorizing the executive power to fund the public goods
by imposing 'fiscal prices' and (conceivably) by the emission of public debt.
When the balance sheet is drawn up at the end of the appointed period,
the government (or the Local or Provincial Council etc.) submits to parliament a detailed account of what has been achieved. This is, theoretically
at least, a moment in which the representatives of the electors' 'principals'
exercise control over the behaviour of the 'agents'. We will return to this
theme in Chapter 6, section 1.

2.13   Political Entrepreneurs, their Aims, Competition among Political
Enterprises in a Democratic Regime, and Economic Development

The picture would be incomplete if we failed to specify that political
parties, with their organizations – which can be defined in economic terms
as political enterprises – should be included among the aspects to be considered in examining the agency relation between electors and their political representatives and administrators. Adopting the definition given by
Giovanni Montemartini,[32] the political entrepreneurs are effectively that
particular set of politicians who create and develop the political enterprise, the latter being understood as an organized movement which offers
citizens a series of programmes and persons with the aim of obtaining a
mandate, so as to manage citizens' interests through the institutions of the
political market, *which enjoys coercive power*.

According to a reductive line of argument, political enterprises are concerned only with maximizing their votes and thus their seats. And since
they are *political* enterprises, their votes and seats are the equivalent of
turnover in economic enterprises. Therefore political enterprises, just like
an insurance company or a bank, may engage in 'opportunistic behaviour'

which is in the interest of whoever controls the enterprise, and they may even resort to deception as part of their opportunistic behaviour. The figure of the politician emerging from this framework might seem to be that of a cynical opportunist devoid of ideals and principles of their own, whose only goal is to achieve power. But in actual fact the political entrepreneur is often inspired by the desire to achieve a reputation. And a reputation can only partially be measured in terms of success seen as maximizing the number of votes received: it is also measured in terms of excellence in other abilities which involve the quality of management of political affairs. As is the case for every enterprise in a competitive market, political enterprises of the public economy operating in a democratic regime characterized by properly functioning political competition find that their success and reputation depend on satisfaction of needs, that is interests, which are expressed through demand. The votes political entrepreneurs maximize are a measure of their success, in relation to the demand they satisfy. And just as in economic terms there exist convenience goods alongside others that are niche or elite products or destined for limited market segments, the goods supplied by political enterprises can likewise address different sectors of the political market. They can maximize the vote in relation to their possible electorate. In a democracy, the party behaves like an economic enterprise, engaging in propaganda and marketing its supply so that it is preferred by the public. They may seek to 'embellish' it in order to achieve greater success, but they cannot do so by systematically deceiving the public. Even more so than is the case for the economic enterprise, the political enterprise is successful if it develops great entrepreneurial figures, given that leadership is a particularly important skill in government decision-making. However, political leaders and politicians in general may display opportunistic behaviour at the expense of the electors, just as occurs with corporate administrators and executives, and also with the administrators and executives of the (large) joint-stock cooperatives. In addition they may seek to further their own interests as well as the public interest. This is favoured by the complexity of the chain of principal–agent relations between the will of the people and the provision of public services. On the other hand, just as in a competitive economic system any enterprises that do not serve the public lose a share of the market, the same holds true for political movements in a competitive democracy. And this can occur even if the 'users', that is the citizens-electors-taxpayers, are affected by continuous problems involving 'information costs' (in terms of time, attention, expenses in obtaining documentation, and so on). To some extent, the aim of an increase in size and power pursued by a political enterprise – that is by political parties and movements – is designed to restrain competition from other political enterprises (political parties and movements). And just like economic enterprises, when political enterprises are not faced with strong competition, they may not supply the quality of goods and services the public actually desires, but rather those they are used to giving and which are best suited to furthering their own interests.

According to De Viti De Marco, over the long term, political competition tends to bring to light the law of economic value in public finance, since discontented electors will turn to representatives who are more likely to satisfy their own preferences. And if this does not happen, in a market economy a situation of disequilibrium arises, generating political movements that give rise to a change in the majority.

This is an optimistic formulation, stated in very general terms, which requires empirical verification in the sense of a demonstration that there is a relation between the democratic character of governments and the level of income and economic growth.

A possible alternative convergent line of argument is proposed by A. Alchian (1950), who claims that efficient systems give rise to growth, while inefficient systems tend towards failure, so that in the end the former prevail and the others are eliminated or become less and less important. This would appear to be confirmed in the studies by D. North.[33]

3   VOTING POWER, OPTIMAL ELECTORAL SYSTEMS, THE VOTING PARADOXES

3.1   Representative Democracy in Governments and in Joint-stock Companies (and Joint-stock Cooperatives)

In an advanced society the most widely prevailing democratic decision-making method is not direct democracy, in which the citizens, *acting on the principle of one man one vote*, directly make administrative and political decisions that concern the community they belong to and which involve the various levels of government (local, regional, central government). Rather, it is representative democracy, in which citizens elect their own representatives who then form the assembly that makes the fundamental decisions for management of public affairs. This is an elementary principle of the division of labour, whereby someone who is active in the world of work does not have sufficient time and information to devote attention to direct management of public affairs as well. The same situation occurs, and for the same reason – limited time and costs and difficulty in learning specialized information – in enterprises, including cooperative enterprises, that have reached a certain size and which decide to form a public company. Shareholders, including those of large cooperatives, do not participate in management of the company but vote in the shareholders' assembly, which elects the board of directors. In joint-stock cooperatives, as in the elections of political democracies, each member of the institution considered has only one vote, while in corporations the votes are based on the shares held by each member. But not even the shareholders' assembly of a public company or, analogously, the assembly of a democratic public organization can run the actual affairs of the enterprise: this requires a hierarchical relationship between those who are in command of the enterprise and those who execute the orders at the various levels. But in an assembly where each member has one vote there exists no hierarchical power that is permanently in position. The powers of the president of the assembly, who is elected by the assembly, by definition are limited to a task of carrying out arbitration: setting the agenda (often together with a select committee elected by the assembly) and regulating debate within the assembly and the ensuing rulings, acting in a (supposedly) impartial manner. The president is assisted by secretaries and deputy presidents, but only for impartial execution of the tasks involved in arbitration.

The problem of executing government activities in a democratic public organization, as in a public company, is solved by nominating a group of persons endowed with executive power, who are chosen from among the members of the assembly itself, while in a cooperative they are chosen from among the cooperators, and at times they may be supplemented by external specialists. In the public organization, this group is headed by the executive power (the mayor, the regional president, the head of the government). A public company, like a large joint-stock cooperative, is headed by the managing director. At times, to avoid the concentration of excessive power in the hands of the head of the executive power, and/or to subdivide decisions, especially with regard to the major overall strategy and other fundamental decisions, the figure of a president is introduced in complex organizations and in those where fiduciary relationships are not very intense; in such cases the president has a position above that of the head of the executive power and acts as the guarantor of the management of the executive power, vis-à-vis the assembly.

But the assembly of a democratic political organization has duties that differ from those of a public company, even those of a cooperative ruled by the 'one member, one vote' principle which embodies elements of solidarity. That is to say, a democratic political organization embodies the sovereignty of the people, that is the public power, which contains elements of legal coercion that are an intrinsic feature of the public organization and are binding both on private organizations and market enterprises. The shareholders' assembly of public companies cannot enact laws or regulations endowed with power over subjects who are external to the employees of the public company. In contrast, the assembly of the state or of the municipality, can indeed enact such laws and regulations which are binding on all the members of the community over which the assembly exercises power (its jurisdiction), within the limits established by a constitution that regulates the powers of the various levels of government.

On the other hand, the assembly of the democratic public organization does have duties concerning the management of the public economy which, as far as economic calculation is concerned, resemble the duties forming part of the market economy companies. Among these, a predominant position is occupied by the duty of drawing up the budget (cf. above, section 2.11), which concerns expenses and revenue that are expected to be part of the organization's activities, generally for the coming year, possibly within the framework of a long-term budget plan. A similar situation is found in a modern public company as a big modern consumption or production cooperative. The budget is the plan of future activities. And planning, that is setting up a plan and then acting accordingly, is the rational method for choice and action in the economy and in general in civil society.

In order to perform these tasks of enacting laws or regulations, approving the budget and checking that it is carried out by the executive power, the assembly is divided up into committees which, generally speaking, should themselves be subdivided analogously to the divisions within the executive power. Each committee will have its president, assisted by secretaries and deputy presidents.

It is clear that in a democratic regime, nominating all these organs requires voting procedures: citizens must vote to elect the assembly (in the public cooperatives organized as public companies it is the shareholders who vote, always with one vote), the members of the assembly must vote to elect its executive organ and the members of the executive organ must likewise vote on decisions, if the regulations and practice establish that its head cannot make purely individual decisions.

3.2 The Principle 'One Elector, One Vote' in the Agency Relation in the Model of Representative Democracy

The principle 'one elector, one vote', which characterizes democratic regimes, implies – theoretically – that citizens' choices on the political market, in matters concerning the economy (and more generally in matters concerning public affairs) are not weighed in terms of purchasing power, but on the basis of the mere status of being an adult citizen. This contrasts with the prevailing procedures for making choices within the economic market, but not with that of the cooperatives operating on the market. However, there is a profound difference between a vote seen as a direct decision-making process performed by citizens (by referendum) as a process whereby citizens choose their own representatives, versus a vote as a decision-making process within the democratic collective bodies.

In assemblies and in the committees of which the assembly is made up it is possible to vote, article by article or even clause by clause, on highly complex laws and budgets full of tables, accompanied by motions that require the executive power to engage in detailed procedures. By contrast, when citizens are called to vote in an election, they only have to choose among different parties (or movements) and among different candidates – with a different predominance of the party over the candidate or the candidate over the party, depending on the electoral system – without the programmes that the parties or candidates support being included as a crucial factor in the voting procedure. Rather, citizens monitor the implementation of programmes by exercising surveillance over the behaviour of their candidates once the latter have been elected, and by expressing their satisfaction or dissatisfaction, with dissatisfaction leading to potential loss of votes.

A greater opportunity for citizens to formulate more detailed decisions is given by the system for referendums, either abrogative or putting forward a proposal. However, the wording of a referendum cannot be too complicated and long-winded, because this would exacerbate the information costs which, for a substantial proportion of citizens, represent a considerable burden, even in a democracy with a highly educated population and broad-ranging competitive information provided by the mass media.

3.3 Electoral Systems for the Formation of Democratic Assemblies: Equitableness, Effectiveness, Efficiency of the Political Agency Relation between Elector and Elected Representative: Majority Principle and Proportional Principle

The problem of implementing an *effective*, *equitable* and *efficient* agency relation between electors and elected candidates in democratic assemblies allows no optimal solution in any 'model', because it involves conflicting aims.[34]

On the one hand the optimum electoral system should pursue *effectiveness* in the agency relation between elector and elected representative, ensuring that the relation is as direct as possible. But on the other hand, the optimum electoral system should also pursue *fairness*, in relation to the postulate 'one elector, one vote', from which it follows that: a) the vote of each elector should be able to have equal weight; b) each elector should be represented; c) the majority should have a greater power to govern than the minority; d) but the latter should have the possibility of becoming the

majority.[35] In addition to being effective and fair, the political agency relation should also be *efficient*: that is by granting agents sufficient time and
authority to take action by means of the collegial organs of the assembly
and of the government. Furthermore, decisions should be certain over
time; that is to say, they should be clearly established, and also certain as
regards their content, i.e. formulated with clarity, so that those operating
on the market and in civil society can take appropriate action in accordance with the decisions, without uncertainty or arbitrary action. A game
where the rules are continually changing or can be interpreted in different
ways depending on who is making decisions is not efficient. Neither is it
fair or effective. Thus efficiency, except for the case of a community of
envious and diffident individuals, should be the primary prerequisite of
any good electoral system. This, as we will see, tends to lead to a preference
for the majority regime as compared to proportional representation. In the
majority system there are as many electoral constituencies as there are representatives to be elected, and for this reason it is also known as the plural
system. In proportional representation, a limited number of constituencies
is established, each with many seats. In the majority system, citizens elect
their representative by means of a simple majority, in each territorial constituency. In the proportional system, different lists, each with more than
one candidate, are chosen in each constituency, and candidates of the different lists are elected in proportion to the votes received by each list.

3.4   The Pure Proportional Method is Fair (Equitable), but its Efficiency is Low and the Effectiveness of its Political Agency is Poor

The pure proportional method implies that each vote has equal weight,
because each list – in each electoral constituency composed of many
seats – has a right to seats in the same percentage as the votes obtained
by the given list, out of the total of citizens eligible to vote or of the total
turnout.[36] An elector's choice is determined first and foremost by the party
the elector votes for, not by a person; therefore the elector may have a
more precise agency relation with the representatives, from the point of
view of ideology and the party programme, than is the case when the
elector has to vote for a person, even if the person belongs to a party, as
in the single-member constituency system. Furthermore, if a preferential
voting method is admitted, electors can indicate their chosen candidate or
candidates from among the names on the list, in which case it is not merely
the party that is chosen but also the persons themselves. However, if each
elector can choose more than one preferential candidate, the party may
influence the votes for the candidates by suggesting that one of these votes
should be given to a candidate indicated by the party.

Thus proportional representation offers the best solution in the quest to achieve equal voting weight for every vote, and to avoid the chafing of minorities against the majority, or frustration of the minorities. But this system interposes the party in the agency relation between electors and elected. It gives rise to inefficiency of the collegial organs, that is the assembly and government, because it favours the birth of political splinter groups and hence the proliferation of lists. Therefore – in relation to the growth of voting power of the various different groups as compared to their voting weights[37] – it makes parliamentary debate and resolutions intricate and long-drawn-out and also results in fluid, overlarge and quarrelsome government coalitions. Consequently, coalitions face great difficulty in trying to devise a coherent line of action and to act on the basis of long-term policies; they are more likely to accept compromises and continuous procrastinations, on account of the difficulty in reaching and maintaining an agreement.

It is also argued that in this system the majorities are unstable because the coalitions may change. This is true in the pure proportional system where the various parties are allowed to stand for election without providing any binding indication of which coalition they intend in future to support on a long-term basis, or any indication of the 'leader' to whom they pledge to commit themselves irrevocably. Moreover, in real life pure proportional systems, to avert the risk that the party may prevail over the agency relation between electors and the elected, there is normally the principle that any representative is free to leave the party in which she has been elected to move to another party or to form a new one or to remain alone and vote without any party discipline.

3.5   The Corrected Proportional System can be Fair and Efficient but the Political Agency is only Partially Effective

To reduce the most striking defects of the pure proportional system it is possible to establish a 'threshold' whereby, for instance, parties which fail to achieve at least 5 per cent of votes at the national level are eliminated.[38]

Furthermore, a principle can be established stating that no elected candidate can defect from the group the candidate chose at the moment of standing for election, and that once government coalitions have been formed at the beginning of a parliamentary term (with a given leader), then either the coalitions should endure for the entire term of parliament, or, if this is no longer possible, then parliament should be dissolved and new elections held. The proportional system may be rendered more suitable for stable coalitions by adding the principle of the coalition (headed by a leader): each list should indicate the coalition to which it belongs and the 'residue' of each list is utilized by its coalition. The indication of the leader of the party or of the coalition of political movements presented to the electorate may add personalization to the proportional system.

To avert the risk that parties may prevail over the agency relation between the elector and the elected, the suggestion could be put forward that the elector should be allowed to express only one preference. But if the party controls a certain number of preferences, and the electoral constituencies are broad – which means a high cost for the electors in obtaining information on the candidates, and for the elected with regard to the electors – then the party may be able to manoeuvre, in the different geographical areas, to get its preferred candidates elected.

By reducing the size of constituencies, the elector's relation with the candidates becomes more effective and the number of parties that can be represented is reduced, but if the reduction is pursued to excess (for example below 15 options) the results may be anomalous from the point of view of fairness,[39] unless there is a procedure of recovering the residue in a national constituency in which the candidates indicated by the parties are elected. But this system compromises the immediacy of the agency relation between electors and the elected.

3.6   The Pure Plurality System Allows Effective Political Agency Relations and Efficient Functioning of the Collective Agents, but it is Unfair Under All Three Aspects of the Precept 'One Person, One Vote'

Interference by the parties in the agency relation between the elector and the elected is drastically reduced with the plurality system, in which each constituency has only one seat and thus the candidate who obtains the relative majority wins the constituency. There is also a drastic reduction in information costs, both for the electors and for the candidates and the winner. Therefore, the political agency becomes more effective. But it is also unfair, under all the aspects considered. The principle which holds that the criterion of 'one elector, one vote' should allow all electors to benefit equally from the political agency relation no longer holds: movements having an electorate that is moderately concentrated in the various areas are favoured as compared to those with an electorate that is widely scattered over the different areas, and also as compared to those with an electorate concentrated in just a few areas. What may happen is that a minority of the electors may prevail over the relative or absolute majority, winning more seats and even the absolute majority.

In general, it can be demonstrated that the system in question favours the middle classes over the working classes or groups of the electorate holding extreme opinions.[40]

Moreover the pure plurality system is unstable as the elected representatives are not bound to any party. However, in order to ensure stable majorities even this system has to prevent the elected candidate of one group from transferring to another group that forms part of another coalition, and it has to establish the principle whereby all candidates declare which leader (of which coalition) they support: either during the elections or as soon as the term of parliament has begun, under pain of being expelled, should they change allegiance.

Finally, this method systematically relegates to the sidelines any minority forces or new movements.[41] But it is worth noting that if it adopts the principle of the 'leader' of the coalition and, in the case of victory, of the government – indicated above – then it favours a bipolar political system, drastically reducing the numbers of parties and thus also favouring the efficient action of collective bodies, that is of assemblies and governments. By virtue of this simplification, it generates a duopolistic competitive model; however, since the predominant feature is the political agency relation of the elected with the elector, the system – without correction by the principle of the leader – could give rise to local interests, patronage relations, or special interest lobbies, instead of policy lines pertaining to general interests.[42]

3.7 The Two-round Plurality System Allows Effective Political Agency Relations, it Facilitates but Does Not Ensure that the Choices Made by the Collective Agency Bodies are Efficient, and it Gives Rise to Reduction of Fairness with Regard to the Criterion of 'One Elector, One Vote'

With the 'pure' plurality system, in the first round citizens of a constituency vote for only one seat, choosing among the candidates of all the lists. Then if in the first round no candidate receives a majority of votes, the two or three (or four) candidates who have obtained the best quotient of votes survive for the second round. But here only two candidates may be voted for. The lists without candidates in the second round are allowed to join forces with one of the two lists that have candidates for the second round. The candidate of the coalition which, in the second round, obtains the relative majority wins the seat.[43] The lists that join forces by supporting one of the two candidates for the final challenge negotiate with one another, reaching a decision based both on affinity with one of the two candidates and on an assessment of which of them has the greatest likelihood of winning, with this additional support. This implies that the given individual's political agency relation will be very substantial. The bargaining process will also take into account the extent to which each list in the various constituencies, in the first and second round, has to forgo one or more candidates and this may result in sacrificing more popular candidates in favour of others who are less popular.

Furthermore, if it is established that only the two candidates who had the greatest quotients in the first round can continue to the second round, then the re-aggregations will be limited to two names, and the outcome of the run-off ends up damaging the intermediate movements and candidates who could win in the second round, even if they came in third or fourth in the first round.

The number of parties is reduced and they are in any case spurred to join forces. But there is no drive to a bipolar political system and there may be cases where no party has the majority. It may also happen – albeit less than in the one-round single-member constituency system (first-past-the-post) – that a coalition obtains the absolute or relative majority of seats even if it does not have the majority of votes on the national level.

Finally, the plurality system may be corrected with the addition of a proportional quota: this mixed system (adopted in Italy from 1994 to 2005) combines the virtues and defects of the two pure systems.

3.8 The Majority Premium and the Leader both of the Coalition and the Government as a Means to Achieve Efficiency of Collective Agencies

None of the systems examined *guarantees* a stable majority. The proportional system, including proportional representation with a minimum threshold, allows a plurality of parties. Unless additional rules are introduced, it can give rise to variable and tiny majorities, with small parties that shift opportunistically from one coalition to another. The one-round plurality system can likewise give rise to tiny majorities, and since in this case what prevails is the personal and particularistic relation between the elector and the elected, individual elected members may seek to blackmail the majority to which they belong. Finally, the two-round plurality system may have the defects of both systems, namely that of opportunistic behaviour and of the 'blackmailing' involving minor political movements belonging to coalitions.

One method to endow both systems with greater compactness is to establish that electors go to the polls not only to vote for parties and candidates, but also to elect a leader, who is to become the head of the (municipal, regional, national) government if her coalition wins the majority.

But if a majority is won only with a very narrow majority, which is therefore unstable, the central governments have to multiply the ministries, and local governments will have to multiply their council departments, and they will have to agree to compromises and contend with cross-veto tactics, which may result in short-term policies and budget deficits.

To avert these eventualities, a majority premium can be established, whether for the proportional or the plurality system (in its one-round or two-round version) system. According to this criterion, parties that have 'joined forces' to try to obtain the 'majority premium' and which, through the resulting sum of their votes, manage on the national level to obtain a given quotient of relative majority that is quite close to the absolute (for example at least 40 per cent), would have the right to an additional number of seats. This would enable them to achieve a substantial margin of absolute majority, and they would thus be safe from blackmail attempts launched by minor groups.

However, this method can prove to be iniquitous if one coalition prevails over another by no more than a handful of votes in a situation where the majority premium is large. To attenuate this risk, the alternative is to establish that:

a. the majority premium can be obtained only by winning the absolute majority of the valid votes cast (excluding from the count the invalid votes and those abstained) and not with a mere simple majority over the opposing coalitions (even in the case of only two coalitions the two types of rule are very different, because the absolute majority of the valid votes is always higher than 50 per cent).
b. the majority premium can be obtained on the basis of the relative majority, but the premium does not come into being if the difference between the votes is too small, for instance it is less than 1 per cent.

But in general no electoral system guarantees the efficiency, effectiveness and fairness of decision-making processes in the agency relation if it is not linked to the principle of determining the leader of the coalition that is destined to govern.

3.9   Voting Rules: Simple Majority, Qualified Majority and Unanimity: Voting Weight and Voting Power: Introduction to the Problem

Decisions in a representative democracy raise complex problems of *collective* agency relations between electors on the one hand and the elected members in the assembly, on the other. Further problems arise in the relations between the electors and the members of the executive power expressed by the assembly. The members are supposed to act in the overall interest of all citizens, but they also have to follow the directives and interests of those who specifically elected them. This is analogous to the problem encountered in public companies, as regards the interests of small shareholders versus the interests of holders of a controlling share in the company; it is likewise analogous to the problems of a cooperative where a compact group of cooperators overrides divided minorities.[44] For instance, it is generally believed that those who are elected to political assemblies (and the same is true for shareholders' assemblies) should, in their general activity, behave without any obligatory mandate *towards their own electors*. The reason is, so the argument goes, that since they are members of the democratic institution that is concerned with the collective welfare of that community, they should pursue the general interest rather than the particular interests of their representatives. But a *literal* interpretation of this principle[45] is inconsistent with a model based on the assumption that the public economy works along the same lines as a market economy, and thus obeys the same laws as a market economy, that is individual advantage, albeit without relinquishing the awareness that in a democratic system the collective action of the public economy has a communitarian nature. Rather, a more appropriate formula is that theorized by Bruno Leoni,[46] in which political representatives are actually entrusted with two mandates when group decisions are involved: one requires them to act in the interests of their own principals, while the other implies acting in the overall interests of the group, that is of the principals taken as a group. And it is precisely this search for an agreement capable of reconciling the two aspects that constitutes the essence of the task of a political representative, who is bound not by a specific but instead by a generic mandate, which concerns the activities of the group. The guarantee that this can be obtained does not reside in a putative altruistic character of those who have been elected, but – as argued by Leoni (1960) – in voting rules capable of attributing equal weight to each elector.

But in the decision-making process, the various voters may have different preferences and opinions, which are expressed with different 'motions',[47] so that it becomes necessary to establish the rule through which it becomes possible to decide which motion should prevail. The best known and most elementary rule is:

1. a simple majority of votes, in comparison to the votes won by any other of the motions that have been tabled.

However, other types of rule also exist:

2. a simple majority out of the total of voters;
3. a qualified majority (e.g. 55 per cent, 60 per cent, 70 per cent) out of the total of voters;
4. unanimity.

Downs[48] (1957) champions the simple majority principle, that is to say, the rule of 50% +1, arguing that 'equal weight of the voters' means that each elector can be added to each of the others in the same way as one would add up the cardinal numbers according to the elementary rules of arithmetic. This would be the only practical tool to achieve a decision, inasmuch as it allows the greater quantity to prevail over the smaller quantity.[49]

> Any rule that requires more than a simple majority in order for a law to be approved allows a minority to impede the action of the majority, thereby endowing the vote of each member of the minority with a greater weight than is attributed to the vote of each member of the majority.

This statement, as we will see in terms of the theory of *voting power*, is wrong, because if, for instance, one were to establish a rule of a qualified majority of 60 per cent, then a minority of 40 per cent would have a voting power equal to zero despite its mathematical weight of 40, while the 60 per cent majority would have a voting power of 100, despite its mathematical weight of 60. Furthermore, with the 60 per cent majority, as we will see, each voter would have a lower probability of ending up in the losing group as compared to the simple majority rule, and this would increase the voting power of groups within an assembly. Such a situation differs from the voting power of the simple majority of the votes expressed for the different motions, particularly when none of the individual groups reaches the absolute majority on its own. And it is important to prevent the minority from being oppressed by the majority.

3.10 Voting Power and Weight: First Theorem: Absolute Voting Power is Greater than Voting Weight, but when Players have the Same Voting Weight then their Normalized Voting Power is Equal to their Voting Weight, whatever the Number of Players

The voting weight of a given group in an assembly is given by the percentage of votes it commands as a percentage of the total votes of the assembly. Voting power, on the other hand, under equal quota or quorum required for a proposal to pass, is given, *according to Banzhaf's index* (Banzhaf, 1965), by the number of cases in which the group in question has the possibility of exerting a crucially decisive influence over the assembly, considering all the possible winning coalitions, which are all those in which the sum of votes reaches the quota required to achieve the majority, according to the voting rules established.

For example, in a simple majority regime, with only three players *A*,

Table 1.2   Winning coalitions with simple majority rule when there are three voters

1.   *A, B*
2.   *A, C*
3.   *B, C*
4.   *A, B, C*

B and *C*, each endowed with one vote, in an assembly *S*, there are four winning coalitions, as can be seen from Table 1.2.

Assuming that each player can enter into an alliance with any or all of the others, *A*, *B* and *C* each have the possibility of being 'swing' players, that is decisive for the majority of *S*, in two out of the four possible coalitions. Let us consider *A*, for example: *A* can be decisive by entering into an alliance with *B* and forming *AB*, or with *C*, forming *AC*. On the other hand, *A* is not decisive in the coalition *ACB* since, even in the absence of *A*, *CB* forms the majority of *S*. *A*'s 'absolute' voting power, for *S*, is thus equal to 2/4, that is to say, $\frac{1}{2} = 0.5$.

If we designate the Banzhaf index of player *i* as B_I, the set of winning coalitions as *W* – given the majority rule for the assembly (or committee) under consideration and given the members of the assembly – and if we designate the number of coalitions in which player *i* is decisive (that is a 'swing' player, meaning that if *i* changes allegiance then the coalition loses) as N_I, and the number of players as *n*, then we have

$$B_I(W) = N_I(W)/2^{n-1} \qquad (1.7)$$

in which 2^{n-1} represents the total number of equi-probable winning coalitions. When there are three players, and each one has a vote, there are four winning coalitions. Therefore we will have 2^{3-1}, i.e. 2^2 coalitions, which is, in fact, 4. When there are 5 players, the formula becomes 2^{1-5}, i.e. 2^4, which is, in fact, 16.

With three players, as we have seen, each player has a voting power of 0.5, in other words 1/2, since each one is a swing player in two out of four possible winning coalitions. But the voting power is only 1.3 given that the total votes of the assembly amount to 3.

The normalized voting power of each player is equal to her voting power divided by the sum of voting powers that are at the disposal of all the players of the assembly under consideration,

$$B_I(W) = N_I(W)/2^{n-1} \text{ divided by } S_J = n\, n_J(W) \qquad (1.8)$$

in which $S_{J=n} nJ$ (*W*) is the sum of the voting powers of the *n* players composing the assembly *W*.

Voting power, as can be seen from the numerical examples, which the reader can verify personally, is always higher than the voting weight. But the normalized voting power of each individual player *i* endowed with the same voting weight is always equal to the voting weight, which by definition is a normalized value, since it is the percentage of the votes of the individual voter out of the total votes of the assembly.

With three players, since each one has a voting power of 1/2, the total of the voting powers is 3/2 and it is evident that 1/2 = 1/3.

The first theorem to emerge is that with any majority rule, the absolute voting power of each player exceeds her voting weight, but if the players all have the same voting weight, their normalized voting power is equal to their voting weight.

Second theorem: with an increasing number of players, the voting power increases more than proportionately to their voting weight and the possible outcomes in terms of a majority of the assembly increase exponentially with an increasing number of players.

As the number of players with the same voting weight increases, while their normalized voting power is always equal to their voting weight, their voting weight and also their voting power decreases, there is an increase in the divergence between voting weight and voting power.

In an assembly with five players, *A,B,C,D,E*, each endowed with equal voting weight definable as 1/5=0.20, and given a simple majority of 3 out of 5, there are now 18 winning coalitions (see Table 1.3).

Let us now consider the voting power of player *A*. It can be noted that *A*'s voting power is decisive only in six coalitions out of 16. *A*'s absolute voting power is 6/16 =3/8, that is to say 0.375. The other four players also have the same voting power. The voting power of each player has decreased, as was to be logically expected, in comparison to the assembly with only three voters, in which each player's voting power was 1/2. But the divergence between voting weight and voting power has not only remained, but it has actually increased. The *voting weight* of the players has gone down from 1/3 to 1/5, in other words it has decreased by 65 per cent. By contrast, the players' *voting power*, which has gone from 1/2 to 3/8, has in fact decreased by 33 per cent, because the number of winning coalitions has increased from 4 to 16, that is by 400 per cent.

On the other hand, the normalized voting power of the individual players is 3/8:15/8=1/5. Once again the normalized voting power is equal

Table 1.3   Winning coalitions with simple majority rule when there are five voters

1.	A, B, C	9.	B, D, E
2.	A, B, D	10.	C, D, E
3.	A, B, E	11.	A, B, C, D
4.	A, C, D	12.	A, B, D, E
5.	A, C, E	13.	A, B, C, E
6.	A, D, E	14.	A, C, D, E
7.	B, C, D	15.	B, C, D, E
8.	B, C, E	16.	A, B, C, D, E

to voting weight, since each player has as many votes as the other voters and the total of voting powers has increased in relation to the increase in number of voters.

The fact that the total of voting powers increases with increasing number of voters indicates that the various players have an increasing possibility of engaging in manoeuvres as they seek to form alliances in order to become part of a winning coalition. This gives us the second theorem, which is of interest here. With an increase in the number of members of the assembly, considered as individual voters, for each of them the possibility of entering into different coalitions increases more than proportionately: therefore the result becomes less certain and more laborious, and potentially less stable, in relation to the possibility of repeated balloting. This means that if there is an increase in the number of parties of an assembly and such parties are not bound by a rigid duty to vote as a single block, there is an increase in uncertainty with regard to the formation and stability of the majority.

3.11   From the Simple to the Qualified Majority, with Players having Equal Voting Weight the Voting Power Exceeds the Voting Weight by More than is the Case with the Simple Majority: Voting Power and Block Power are Identical with a Simple Majority but Diverge with a Qualified Majority

Now, for the assembly with five players, each having one vote, let us consider the qualified majority of 2/3. To reach the quorum of two-thirds =66.666 it is necessary to have four votes, namely 80 per cent of the votes, i.e. 4/5. The voting power of the individual players is greater than with the simple majority, and there are only six possible winning coalitions (see Table 1.4).

A will be a swing voter in four out of six combinations, as is the case for the other four voters. Therefore each player will have a voting power of 4/6, in other words 2/3=0.66, equal to the quorum. Voting power now

Table 1.4   Winning coalitions with qualified majority rule of 2/3 when there are five voters

1.	*A, B, C, D*
2.	*A, B, C, E*
3.	*A, B, D, E*
4.	*A, C, D, E*
5.	*B, C, D, E*
6.	*A, B, C, D, E*

exceeds voting weight (which is 1/5=20 per cent) by more than three times (333 per cent).[50]

According to Anthony Downs the simple majority is a 'fundamental' principle of a democracy. It has been objected (Leoni, 1960) that it is hard to see why this is so, given that 50% +1 vote as compared to just half of the votes is not a magic number, per se better than 51 per cent or 55 per cent and so on. An answer to the objection comes from the theory of voting powers. In an assembly with an odd number of voters, under the simple majority rule of 50%+1, voting power and block power are equivalent. To impede the majority's resolutions it is necessary to shift one vote, exactly what is needed for the assembly to overturn the majority. But under the qualified majority rule, with all those greater than 50%+1 (and in an assembly where there is an even number of votes, with a difference of two votes between majority and minority) we find, in addition to voting power, the emergence of a new decision-making power: the block vote.

Let us consider the case of a qualified majority of one additional vote as compared to the simple majority, assuming an odd-numbered assembly of 101 voters. The majority that is needed in order to get a motion passed is 52 votes (one more than the simple majority). Any minority that succeeds in gathering together 50 votes has block power, even if it has neither the simple majority nor any voting power. In an even-numbered assembly having 100 votes, the majority of 52 votes gives the minority a block power that is greater still, since the minority need only reach 49 votes in order to exert block power. In general, with an increasing qualified majority the minority's block power likewise increases.

So this gives us a third theorem: the qualified majority increases the individual players' voting power, under equal number of voters, and gives rise to block power in addition to voting power; consequently, the qualified majority increases the possibility for the players to undertake strategic action and reduces the effectiveness of the assembly's decision-making power, in the sense of the ability to produce decisions.

3.12   An Assembly with Players who have Highly Unequal Voting Power: The Voting Power of Parties with Unequal Voting Weight Differs, in a Differentiated Manner, from their Voting Weight. Parties with a Different Voting Weight may have the Same Voting Power. Small Parties can have a far Greater Voting Power, in Relation to their Voting Weight, as compared to Large Parties, than could be Expected on the Basis of the Ratio between their Voting Weights

In an assembly where the voting weights are very unequal, the voting powers of the various players will be markedly different. Consider an assembly with 51 members and five parties, in which there are two large parties, *A* with 20 votes and *B* with 22, while *C*, *D* and *E* have three votes each. There are 16 winning combinations, shown in Table 1.5.

Both *A* and *B* are swing players in eight coalitions, and therefore they have a voting power equal to 8/16=0.5; *C*, *D* and *E*, on the other hand, are swing players in four coalitions out of 16, and therefore they have a voting power equal to 4/16= 0.25. The total of the voting powers is 1.75, so that the normalized voting power of *A* and *B* is equal to 0.2857 while that of *C*, *D* and *E* is equal to 0.1428. In contrast, *A*'s voting weight is equal to 0.40, that of *B* to 0.44. However, the voting weight of *C*, *D* and *E* equals 0.06 (rounded) for each of them.

Three interesting results can be observed.

1. The absolute voting power of the large parties is greater than their voting weight, but their normalized voting power is lower than their voting weight; therefore they have a greater strategic capacity than would be expected merely by reference to their voting weight, but in comparison to the other parties they have a lower strategic capacity than would be expected from their voting weight.

Table 1.5   Winning coalitions with simple majority rule in an assembly of 51 members when party A *has 20 votes, party* B *22 votes, and parties* C, D *and* E *three votes each*

1.	*A, C, D*	9.	*A, B, C, D*
2.	*A, C, E*	10.	*A, B, C, E*
3.	*A, D, E*	11.	*A, B, D, E*
4.	*B, C, D*	12.	*A, B, C*
5.	*B, C, E*	13.	*A, B, D*
6.	*B, D, E*	14.	*A, B, E*
7.	*A, C, D, E*	15.	*A, B*
8.	*B, C, D, E*	16.	*A, B, C, D, E*

2.   The voting power of the small parties is much greater than their voting weight, either when absolute power or normalized power is considered; therefore their strategic capacity and their political influence is far greater than could be imagined merely on the basis of their numerical strength. In the present case, whereas the voting weight of the smaller parties is less than one third of that of the large parties, their voting power is half.

3.   The voting power of the parties does not necessarily vary with variations in their voting weight: in the present case, both the party that has 40% of the voting weights and party *B* that has 44% have the same voting power.

We can therefore state the fourth and the fifth theorems:

Fourth Theorem: *Parties with different voting weights can have the same voting power.*

Fifth Theorem: *Small parties can have a voting power which, as compared to the large parties, is far greater than could be expected from the ratio between their voting weights.*

A further corollary can be derived from the above consideration: *a large party and the small parties could, in certain cases, have the same voting power.*[51]

3.13   Since the Difference between Voting Weights and Voting Powers is not Proportionate to Either of these, one may find Cases where, in an Assembly with Unequal Voting Weights and Under the Simple Majority Rule, the Voting Power of a Small Party may be Nil: The Voting Power of the Marginal Vote

Let us imagine another hypothesis, namely that of an assembly composed of 51 members in which party *A* has a voting weight of 16, while party *B* has a weight of 5 and *C,D, E* have a voting weight of 10. The simple majority rule holds (see Table 1.6).

It can easily be seen that *B* is not a swing player in any coalition. Indeed the coalitions with a majority of 31 votes, that is, the smallest winning coalitions, do not need a party with five votes, because without it, they have 26 votes, which are enough for the simple majority. *B* is not crucial for the formation of any majority with *A* alone, nor is *B* sufficient to form a majority with one of the three intermediate parties *E, D, C*, nor even with two of them; furthermore, *B* is of no help in forming a majority composed

Table 1.6   Winning coalitions with simple majority rule in an assembly of 51 members when party A *has 16 votes, party* B *five votes, and parties* C, D *and* E *10 votes each*

1. $A, B, C = 16 + 5 + 10 = 31$	9. $A, B, C, D = 16 + 5 + 10 + 10 = 41$
2. $A, B, D = 16 + 5 + 10 = 31$	10. $A, B, D, E = 16 + 5 + 10 + 10 = 41$
3. $A, B, E = 16 + 5 + 10 = 31$	11. $B, C, D, E = 5 + 10 + 10 + 10 = 35$
4. $A, C, D = 16 + 10 + 10 = 36$	12. $A, C, D, E = 16 + 10 + 10 + 10 = 46$
5. $A, C, E = 16 + 10 + 10 = 36$	13. $A, B, C, D, E = 51$
6. $A, D, E = 16 + 10 + 10 = 36$	14. $A, C = 26$
7. $C, D, E = 10 + 10 + 10 = 30$	15. $A, D = 26$
8. $A, B, C, D = 16 + 5 + 10 + 10 = 41$	16. $A, E = 26$

of *A* and one of the intermediate parties. *B* is not decisive for any majority. From this theorem and the previous ones, there emerges a mathematical concept of the utmost importance: that of the voting power of the marginal vote. *There need only be a tiny shift in the quota of votes for B to shift from an elevated voting power to a nil voting power. In the present case, one additional vote for B with the loss of one vote for C or D or E, makes B decisive in two coalitions. This can come about not only in relation to a small variation in B's own quota, but also in relation to a small variation in the quota obtained by some other party. Suppose that C and D lose one vote, gained by E. Then B again becomes decisive in two coalitions.*

3.14   Increase in Block Power with Increasing Quorum of the Qualified Majority

The block power of the individual parties can be measured by considering, among all the possible unsuccessful coalitions, those coalitions that have block power. Under qualified majority rule, as the quorum increases there is also an increase in the probability of forming part of the block minority, that is to get block power. With a 60 per cent quorum in an assembly of 101 shareholders, the required majority is 61. The minority of 40 is in a losing position from the point of view of voting weight and has no block weight. But a minority of 41 has a positive block power, despite not having sufficient voting power to win. The marginal voter between 40 and 41 (in probabilistic terms, a priori this could be any one among the 61 voters) has block power, but no voting power. This can be calculated on the marginal voter between 60 and 61: in probabilistic terms, a priori this could once again be any of the 61 voters, but with the possibility of forming part not of a coalition of 61, but rather of a coalition composed of only 41 members. The chance for one of them being defeated is smaller.

As regards block power, greater significance should be awarded to the statement, in itself obvious, that the probability of being part of the losing group decreases with an increase in the quota or quorum of votes required for the majority decision. More specifically, this is true not only because the chance of being a swing player in the winning coalition increases, but also because the chance arises to be part of coalitions endowed with block power.

Based on these observations it can be argued that as the quota of the qualified majority increases, the decision-making power of each party that is a member of the assembly likewise increases. Thus, *ceteris paribus*, the decision-making power of the individual parties increases, as does the blackmailing power of individual members of all of the parties, because each vote becomes more important.

Therefore, *the simple majority rule facilitates the production of decisions, while the qualified majority slows the process down. But the qualified majority reduces the danger of exploitation of the minorities by the majority.* As pointed out by Bruno Leoni (1960), the problem of political assemblies is far greater than for public companies. In public companies, those who find themselves in the minority and are exploited can opt to exit from the company, by selling their shares. This possible defection, which is reflected in a fall in the value of the company's shares, should prompt those who control the company to take into account the interests of the shareholding public. Furthermore, the organized minorities can, through their block power, blackmail the majorities. And as the qualified majority gradually increases, there may be a rise in new minorities aiming to maximize, formed not so much with the intent of buying other shareholders' votes at the lowest price, but rather with the aim of selling their own vote at the highest price to their fellow voters, who want a decision to be passed (Leoni, 1960).

3.15   The Theorem of the Median Elector and Optimum Equilibrium of the Public Economy

In the light of the above considerations, it might seem that with regard to the model of the democratic public economy as outlined in section 2.2, the optimum equilibrium of the public economy is a utopian or certainly a remote phenomenon. But it should not be forgotten that in purely abstract terms, not all the possible coalitions identifiable with the theory of voting power are equally probable. One may well find unbalanced situations where players who are dissatisfied with the situation in which they find themselves start looking around for new solutions, until they find a more satisfactory arrangement, beyond which no further advantage is likely to

Table 1.7   Individual equilibrium solutions for the demand and supply of a public good

A	B	C	D	E
1 _____	2 _____	3 _____	4 _____	5 _____

be obtained (or become possible). This can be defined as the equilibrium solution. And in particular, as far as the supply and demand of public goods is concerned, this seems to be the equilibrium solution of the median elector.[52]

To see why this is so, let us assume, for the sake of simplicity, that the electors can be subdivided according to their preferences for public goods, and that they can then be broken down by income levels and grouped from left to right starting from the group (or subsets not contained in any other) of subjects with the lowest income, and continuing up to the groups (or subsets) with the highest income levels. We now identify the subset of median electors, which is, by definition, the intermediate group, and which will have intermediate preferences. The distance, measured in terms of excess or shortfall, between the solution accepted by a given electoral subset or their representatives and the solution they would have preferred, can be defined as that subset's 'frustration'. If we posit that the distances between the solutions accepted by the various subsets are all spaced at regular identical intervals, and assume that in an equilibrium situation there will emerge coalitions capable of minimizing the frustrations, it can be demonstrated that in a simple majority regime – which is the most commonly accepted voting system for public budgets – the winning equilibrium coalitions will be represented exclusively by those that contain the subset of median electors. It follows that this subset will play a decisive role in determining *equilibrium* majorities.

Let us suppose (see Table 1.7) there are five income subsets, each contained in no other, and likewise five subsets of electors' representatives; all five of the subsets, denominated *A, B, C, D, E* according to standard practice, vote in the government assembly under consideration here. Let us further assume that the individual equilibrium demand and supply solutions for the public good *G* considered are represented by five classes arranged in increasing order of quantity demanded and fiscal cost; the five classes will be denominated as I, II, III, IV, V. The first, in subset *A*, includes only the quantity Q_I, with fiscal cost F_I. The second, belonging to subset *B*, includes the quantity $Q_{II} > Q_I$ which involves the fiscal cost $F_{II} > F_I$. The third, in subset *C*, includes the quantity $Q_{III} > Q_{II}$ which involves the fiscal cost $F_{III} > F_{II}$. The fourth, in subset *D*, includes the quantity

Table 1.8   *Winning coalitions with simple majority rule when there are five voters deciding on the supply of a public good*

1.	*A, B, C*	5.	*B, D, E*	9.	*A, B, D*	13.	*A, B, D, E*
2.	*A, C, D*	6.	*C, D, E*	10.	*A, B, E*	14.	*A, B, C, E*
3.	*B, C, E*	7.	*A, D, E*	11.	*A, C, D, E*	15.	*A, B, C, D*
4.	*B, C, D*	8.	*A, C, E*	12.	*B, C, D, E*	16.	*A, B, C, D, E*

$Q_{IV} > Q_{III}$ which involves the fiscal cost $F_{IV} > F_{III}$. The fifth and last, of subset E, which includes the quantity Q_V max, namely the greatest quantity among those demanded, involves the fiscal cost F_V max, namely the greatest fiscal cost among the equilibrium solutions of the various citizen-taxpayer subsets.

Given that the simple majority is three out of five, the possible victorious coalitions are as shown in Table 1.8.

Now, coalition 16 does not satisfy any of the players, since each member of 16 has a different demand for G, with a different supply of F. Therefore coalition 16 maximizes frustrations and is in any case overabundant for achieving a majority. Coalitions 15, 14, 13, 12 and 11, which are formed by four subsets, likewise involve excessive frustrations as compared to those that arise when there is a simple majority. It is therefore more helpful to consider only the minimum victorious coalitions, that is those with a minimum majority necessary for a majority and resulting in the least frustration. As can be seen from Table 1.8, there are 10 coalitions with three subsets each that fit this description. If the five mentioned solutions, namely Q_I, with a fiscal cost F_I of A, Q_{II} with a fiscal cost F_{II} of B, up to Q_V with a fiscal cost F_V max of E, are placed on the horizontal line extending from A to D, as in a way similar to that presented in Table 1.7 where there are only five coalitions, it can readily be seen that only one victorious minimal coalition, B,C,D has only two frustration intervals, respectively of B and of D, while all the others have a greater number; furthermore, only coalitions A,B,C; A,C,D; B,C,E; and C,D,E have three frustration intervals while the remaining five, namely A, D, E; A, C, E; B, D, E; A, B, D; A,B, E all have a greater number. As can be seen, to minimize the frustrations, the coalitions featuring the presence of the median elector are the ones that prevail. It can therefore be argued that the solutions which prevail by minimizing the frustrations all include the one preferred by the median elector.

However, two further aspects should be pointed out. The argument outlined above should not be taken in the sense that each consumption of public goods by the various members of the considered community should have the dimension of that of the median elector. There are public goods that are provided to all citizens indivisibly, in a given extent, but which can be consumed to different extents. In this case, while the provision may be commensurate with demand in reference to the median elector or of the elector with higher consumption, the same does not hold true for consumption (see further on, in Chapter 4). In a situation of optimum equilibrium, this naturally leads to a different fiscal cost, resulting from a difference in consumption. On the other hand, there are certain other types of goods – for instance, compulsory education or obligatory public pension schemes – which, by virtue of their nature or because their manner of functioning requires standardization, are not only supplied to all citizens in a given quantity but are also consumed by all citizens more or less uniformly. When this is the case, one may imagine a bargaining process between the representatives of the median elector and those of the other electors who make up the winning coalition.

Finally, an objection to the above argument should be noted. It can be claimed (and this was argued in particular by Wicksell, 1896 [1958]) that in a simple majority regime those who form part of the winning coalition, in a non-qualified majority regime, will seek to transfer the fiscal cost of public goods to the minority and will therefore vastly expand the provision of such goods, to their own benefit, but without having to bear the corresponding costs. *But this argument does not hold for subjects who choose rationally, in a regime of transparent choices, and within a framework of well-informed public opinion.* For if such subjects are in a position where they can exploit the minority, they will have no advantage in demanding a greater quantity of public goods than they genuinely need, but rather will find it more advantageous to try to ensure that they become the beneficiaries of money transfers to be destined to whatever utilization they prefer. The fact that whoever is part of the majority can indeed, via public finance, obtain redistributions does not mean that such a subject must necessarily resort to excessive consumption of public goods in order to achieve such an aim. This is likely to happen only if the subject tries to disguise ongoing exploitation by resorting to pretexts concerning her lawful right to engage in that particular form of consumption because it is meritorious or advantageous for the collectivity, etc., in other words through a process of financial illusion. These are certainly important phenomena that have an impact on reality, and awareness of such aspects underscores the need to forge the closest possible links between expansion of public expenditure and the payment of taxes, the burden of which falls on those who are the beneficiaries of these public expenditures. But such phenomena do not concern rational choices, in a regime of perfect information.

3.16   The Electors' Voting Power: In a Regime of Representative Democracy the Individual Elector's Power Generally Tends to Zero, Because the Number of Those who Cast their Vote is Extremely High: the Voting Paradox

So far we have considered voting power in an assembly. But it is also interesting to consider voting power with regard to the body of the electorate. Generally, in a representative democracy, the body of the electorate is composed of an enormously large number of individuals. In a state such as United Kingdom, or Italy, with about 60 million inhabitants, the voting population numbers 40 million. And since the Chamber in Italy is composed of 630 members and the Senate of 315, each electoral constituency is composed, respectively, of 63 500 and 31 700 voters. Let us assume that a representative must be elected with a relative majority vote, and that five candidates are standing for election; in the minimum hypothesis, in order to be elected a candidate needs at least 12 701 votes in the Chamber and 6341 in the Senate. Therefore each extra or lost vote is worth *at least* 1/12701 or 1/6341, respectively. This is a totally insignificant voting weight. Therefore, no elector, by definition, can be decisive for the outcome of the ballot. Consequently, no elector, considered individually, has any voting power. So each elector might well feel that not bothering to go to the polling station could represent a considerable saving of time and effort, since her individual vote is not going to change the result other than by an imperceptible fraction. But if the entire population acts on this principle, then no one will go to the polls and the whole system fails. This is an instance of the free rider dilemma (discussed in Chapter 3, section 1). A similar line of reasoning can also be put forward for elections in minor electoral constituencies of the Regions, Local Authorities and Provinces.

> To be sure, a ruling can be issued that would make it 'obligatory' to cast one's vote in elections, as a 'civic duty'.[53] But a person cannot be tried before a criminal court for failing to turn out to the polls, unless one is prepared to violate elementary rights of freedom.

And yet, despite the nil voting power and the non-criminalization of those who do not vote, the electors go to the polls and cast their vote, and the system of representative democracy with large electoral constituencies does work. The explanation resides principally in the mode of behaviour of the cooperative model when very large numbers are involved. All persons know that if they do not behave as if their own individual action was important, the result would be negative and therefore each person performs that act, expecting all the others who likewise desire that collective outcome, to follow the same line of reasoning: if each of the voters 'transports her own small grain of sand', victory will be assured.

In more hedonic terms, electors may in any case experience a feeling of satisfaction in voting for their own favourites, as occurs in sports stadiums when everyone is cheering their side on and the individual clapping turns into collective applause. This means that the individual spectators actually take pleasure in the game itself and are pursuing an 'intrinsic motivation' that they wish to express.

> Political entrepreneurs, who are concerned with maximizing their votes, engage in propaganda for their cause among the electors, trying to arouse precisely these types of feelings: they urge each individual to cast a vote, calling upon people's sense of duty and pleasure in participating, because 'if lots of people do the same', then the desired result will be achieved.

Yet a high voter turnout does not necessarily imply that the system is more 'competitive' and that it therefore gives citizens who are dissatisfied with their representatives a greater opportunity to choose a different party and different persons to represent them. Competitiveness depends on a number of factors: the type of electoral system, the rules concerning the various political and civil freedoms and their actual enforcement, the independence of the media and the press, the transparency of decisions and decision-making processes and of the way in which public affairs are run, the possibility or difficulty of comparing the management style of one's own government with that of different or similar states and regions, the feasibility of relocating one's interests and business activities to a different state or regions, and so on.

3.17   Irrationality and Instability of the Vote: the Black and Arrow Paradox for Majority Resolutions[54]

It can, however, be demonstrated (Arrow, 1951 [1963] and Black 1958) that in an assembly or committee composed of at least three members, when there are three possible packets of choice a univocal majority cannot always be found.

In this connection, Arrow set out several important postulates that form the basis for his theorem which shows that finding a univocal solution is 'impossible':

1.   all individual preferences matter;
2.   positive association between individual preferences and society's preferences;

3. sovereignty of individual preferences (= other preferences or external choices do not count);
4. independence from non-relevant alternatives, that is independence from the relation with goods that are 'different' from those being compared, which excludes the utilization of a yardstick such as money and thus excludes cardinal judgements;
5. no dictatorship: a given person's preferences cannot predominate over those of others.

It can be demonstrated that if voting sessions are conducted simply by expressing a preference among 'different "motions"' (that is choices or options concerning a given subject), that is to say by passing a purely ordinal judgement, if the choices are independent of other alternatives that deal with different subjects, if none of those casting a vote have the power to impose their own preferences or to exclude those of others, and if there is no external power that awards priority to one or the other decision, it is conceivable that the result obtained by means of the majority rule may be non-coherent, unstable and cyclical.

A decision is not coherent (or not 'rational') if, quite apart from anything else, it violates the criterion of transitivity which holds that in cases where there are three possible motions or options *A*, *B*, *C* and assuming that *A* is preferred to *B* and *B* to *C*, then *A* must also be preferred to *C*.

A decision is unstable when a given assembly (or in general a given electoral body), called upon to repeat its vote with the motions presented in a different order, expresses a different decision.

Finally, it is cyclical if a return to the previous order of presentation of the motions leads to a repetition of the previous outcome.

Let us now posit three groups of voters $V_I; V_{II}; V_{III}$ and three options *A*, *B*, *C*, which, considered pairwise, are submitted to the groups. We denote by **P** the preference for one element of the pair over the other.

We will assume that the following preferences are expressed, by the three groups respectively:

V_I *A* **P** *B*, *B* **P** *C* hence by transitivity *A* **P** *C*
V_{II} *B* **P** *C*, *C* **P** *A* hence by transitivity *B* **P** *A*
V_{III} *C* **P** *A*, *A* **P** *B* hence by transitivity *C* **P** *B*

If *A* is put to the vote against *B*, *A* obtains two **P** (of which V_I and V_{III}), in other words the majority. If *B* is put to the vote against *C* then *B* likewise obtains two votes (respectively of V_I and V_{II}), in other words the majority. Now it should be found, by transitivity, that for the majority *A* **P** *C*. However, we note that if *C* is put to the vote against *A*, even *C* obtains two votes (of V_{II} and V_{III}). Thus we have, at one and the same time, A **P** C and C **P** A, which is non-coherent, that is irrational. Only by supposing that from A **P** B and B **P** C we do not derive, by transitivity, A **P** C – but this too is irrational – can this irrationality be avoided.

Now, let us suppose that at the behest of the President of the Assembly, the following ballots are held: first, A against B and then the winning option against C. It is clear that since A **P** B has two votes (V_I and V_{III}), the winner is A. On the other hand, if A is put to the vote against C, since A **P** C has only one vote while C **P** A has two, then the winner is C. Now, if the President decides that no further ballots will be held, the choice can be described as 'dictatorial' because it depends on the order in which the President had the ballots held. That is to say, it he had first put to C the vote against B, since C **P** B has only one vote by transitivity while B **P** C has two votes (of V_I and V_{II}) the winner would have been B; but then in the balloting of B against A, since A **P** B has two votes (of V_I and V_{III}), the winner would have been A. If in the first ballot C has been put to the vote against A, since C **P** A has two votes A would have been eliminated. But in the balloting of C against B, since B **P** C has two votes, the winner would have been B!

But if, at the request of V_I and V_{II}, after C has won against A the President then puts A to the vote against B, the winner will be B. At this point, however, V_I and V_{III} will demand that A be put to the vote against B: and if the President agrees, the winner will be A. Obviously V_{III}, allied with V_{II}, can then ask that a repeat ballot be held, putting A to the vote against C again. And this will enable C to re-emerge. Thus the majority voting system is in this case unstable and cyclical. If a coalition forms that objects to a repeat ballot, the choice becomes stabilized. An analogous outcome is obtained if the President does not hold a repeat ballot. But in the latter case, the choice will be 'imposed' in the sense indicated above.[55] In an ordinary assembly, normally the balloting is not repeated in the same session once a majority has been reached. Also the order in which the different motions are put to the vote is already established by the regulations, with formal criteria: for example, the government's motion or that of the majority is put to the vote first, or voting is held first of all on motions against the government or against the majority, starting from the motions most distant from the government or majority. In this manner a solution of some sort, at least temporarily stable, is achieved. This is not an 'imposed' choice because the order was set a priori without knowing which motion would prevail. Also if the rule endures for a fairly prolonged period of time, no one can be said to be favoured over another because the preferences for the different motions have a different distribution. It cannot be argued that this is irrational, since the non-transitivity does not concern the individual person but rather the group, that is the difficulty experienced by the group in reaching an agreement. The fact that a different solution may subsequently be reached also increases the competitiveness of the system, reducing the possibility of oppression by a given majority.[56] Thus in ordinary affairs the Black–Arrow paradox may be overcome.

However, the Black–Arrow theorem shows that *as far as ethical principles and the basic rules are concerned*, the principle of majority voting does not necessarily imply that what emerges is the community's predominant judgement, since there can be more than one of these judgements. Thus in this case democracy is unable to provide coherent and rational solutions, but only solutions that are reasonable inasmuch as they derive from shared voting rules, applied in a tolerant manner, that is by searching for the greatest possible consensus.

NOTES

1. Pantaleoni (1904). The tripartite division is based on an analogy from biology between 'predators' that actively live off others, with a relationship dominated by the 'struggle for survival'; parasites that live 'at the expense of others' with passive exploitation, which allows them to retain control over the institutions; predators that dominate others, using them as their own tool but assuring them adequate protection, because and to the extent to which this coincides with the interests of whoever is exercising the protection.
2. The consumer's rent or surplus is the difference between the price the subject would be willing to pay and that which a consumer effectively pays, cf. Marshall (1920 [1961], Book 3, Chap. 6, p.1). The producer's rent or surplus is the difference between the remuneration the producer receives, based on the market price, and the production price. In the cooperative the two rents belong to the same subject since the consumer and the producer are one and the same. What is meant by consumer's surplus and that of the producer with regard to public goods can be seen in Figure 1.1 below. Analysis of the optima by means of these two analytical tools will be developed in detail in Chapter 10, on optimal taxation.
3. This corresponds to the model of De Viti De Marco's monopolistic state, on which see subsection 1.5 above.
4. See North (1990), Chapter 12, final section on the consequences, where the author also refers to a 1978 historical essay by J.H. Coatswoth on hindrances to development in Mexico during the nineteenth century (from which the passage cited in the text is taken), in order to explain the different development of North America and Latin America.
5. De Viti De Marco (1934 [1936], Book I, Chapter I, sections 6–8).
6. De Viti De Marco (1934) stated: 'This is reminiscent of the concept of a cooperative, the elementary character of which resides in the personal identity between producers and consumers. Therefore we can consider the democratic state as the type of state that can be likened to the economic figure of the cooperative'.
7. In the market economy, the monopolist takes over the consumer's entire surplus by engaging in complete price discrimination, the so-called first degree discriminating monopoly. De Viti De Marco includes in this model authoritarian governments that

      exploit the governed subjects, but he also seems inclined to consider that democratic states with pronounced redistribution, which finance expenditure in favour of populist popular majorities by imposing progressive taxation, also belong to this category.

8.   Unlike the market economy, where suppliers of goods in a monopoly regime (illustrated in Chapter 10, Figure 10.3) who seek to take possession of a substantial part of the consumer's rents that the purchaser obtains in a competitive regime must, if they are unable to impose price discrimination, act by decreasing the supply. In the public economy a monopolistic government that aims to absorb the consumer's rent, in an authoritarian political regime, has no need to decrease the supply to a level below that which, for the government, represents the equilibrium quantity. This is because such a government, supported by coercive power and free from constitutional constraints, can seize the consumer's rent by means of high taxation. Now, in an authoritarian regime of a predatory type, the government can deprive taxpayers of the greater part of the benefit of public expenditure by providing scanty and poor public goods, as this enables the government to maximize the rents in its own favour. But in this set-up the government can also impose high taxation on its citizens in order to expand the volume of military expenditure and to enact populist redistributive policies, which serve to maintain and increase government power. In a parasitic framework, it is in the interest of the government, as has been noted, to supply tax-paying citizens with a volume of public expenditure that is adequate for their needs, so as to avoid a decrease in the supply of public goods which would damage the market economy. Furthermore, such a government will tend to increase public expenditure in favour of unproductive social groups that live off subsidies, employment in useless state-run, semi-autonomous but state-maintained and local offices, loss-making public enterprises, and so on.

9.   That is to say, the state, the bodies that form part of the state apparatus and depend on the state (national insurance and social security organizations, universities, research institutes, and so on), the Regions, the Local Authorities, the Provincial Authorities and other related bodies.

10.   Including the self-employed and families considered as enterprises run from home, which have employees needed for the 'production' of home services and for care of the sick and the elderly.

11.   Material, personal and immaterial services are a highly important component of intermediate goods. They include transportation and insurance, telephone, postal and media communication services, professional services, tradesmen, technical consultancy, economic, corporate and legal services, cleaning and surveillance services and other miscellaneous services.

12.   The letter W refers to wages.

13.   This holds both for foreign trade and also for transactions involving remittances from abroad and foreign payments.

14.   See Einaudi (1919), pp. 185–8.

15.   This theme is developed by the Ordo-economics of Walter Eucken, Wilhelm Röpke and Alfred Muller Armaci and their followers. See Goldschmidt and Wohlgemuth (2008); Peacock and Willgerodt (1989a) and (1989b).

16.   See Einaudi (1940 [1959]), Chapters XI and XII.

17.   The notion of transaction costs is fundamental for understanding the market economy itself. See Coase (1937; 1960; 1988) and Williamson (1985) as well as North (1990), with a slightly different approach.

18.   The average taxpayer-elector should not be confused with the median elector, the latter being the elector who has the greatest influence on the democratic outcome of decisions. On the concept of 'median elector' see, further on, section 2.15.

19.   On this issue cf. North (1990) Chapter III. Blankart (2008) Chapter I, § 2, centres his investigation on the hypothesis of the *homo oeconomicus* selfishly oriented towards his own welfare, and argues, with a highly persuasive live of reasoning, that this corresponds to the welfare of the average man, as an intermediate figure between that of the altruistic person who pursues other people's welfare, and thus relinquishes his own

satisfaction, and that of the evil-minded or antisocial person who is pursuing the ruination of others, because this allows him to gloat with satisfaction. Yet this ingenious argument does not convince me. Apart from extreme cases, evil individuals are egoists who pursue their own welfare even if this has to be done at other people's expense, and even if this mode of behaviour is wrong according to the prevailing rules: that is to say, evil individuals are totally unconcerned about the 'unjust' harm inflicted on others. This kind of antisocial person does exist, but the entire social organization, from the constitution to the laws currently in force, to evaluation based on personal reputation, condemns such a person and seeks to ostracize the individual in question. In contrast, altruism is praised and encouraged (although often hypocritically, paying lip-service to the concept), because it is regarded as ethically praiseworthy. And the facts suggest that even egoistic persons have an ethical code, which they would rationally like to respect, except that this often proves impossible when it becomes too much of a burden. But the existence of a shared ethical code is a fact of positive economics and it should not be neglected, because it is among the factors of economic development. Therefore, from the point of view of positive economics, it appears to me that the realistic hypothesis of the average man is the one adopted in the text.

20. According to D. Nelson and E. Silberberg (1987), respect for the moral code and shared ideologies, as well as altruism, can be regarded, according to present knowledge, as negatively inclined functions with respect to the price the subject has to pay in order to abide by the code. Willingness to abide by the rules decreases with an increasing price the subject has to pay in order to be observant. Cf. North (1990, pp. 47 and 71).
21. Which will be examined in detail in Chapter 3.
22. On the concept of 'opportunistic behaviour' within an agency relation (and more generally, in a contractual relation), see Williamson (1985).
23. On reciprocity games, in addition to the work by Luce and Raiffa (1957), see Axelrod (1984).
24. A typical expedient of collusive democracy can be observed in the parliamentary voting system, in which there is no limit either on the presentation of amendments to laws or on the time devoted to debate on bills of law. In such cases, the majority is compelled to seek an agreement with the opposition in order to obtain the decision.
25. On relations between politicians and the bureaucratic apparatus and among the various levels of the latter, in terms of cooperative games and opportunistic behaviour, the fundamental work is that by A. Breton and R. Wintrobe (1982).
26. We will see further on (Chap. 3, section 1), that while in the case of a game composed of only one 'hand' it may be advantageous to adopt a line of action like the 'prisoner's dilemma', the advantage is reduced or wiped out in games that are repeated for an elevated number of hands. On the greater efficiency of governments that have a prospect of more prolonged duration, see Grilli et al. (1991).
27. These issues will be taken up again in Chapter 5, section 1, devoted to the theory of bureaucracy.
28. Blankart (2008) points out that two criticisms can be raised against the formulation in terms of a fiscal constitution created by an assembly according to the Buchanan and Tullock formula. First, it can be demonstrated that under the veil of ignorance, different solutions may emerge as compared to the outcome potentially resulting from a decision by an assembly of representatives. Thus it cannot be taken for granted that the outcome is likely to recognized, *ex post*, as satisfactory by all those involved. Second, the constitution has to be interpreted and judges can modify it. This means that the reference framework should be an evolutionary formulation, like that of F. Hayek (1982). Buchanan's constitutional theory is reworked in evolutionary terms in the version by V. Vanberg (1994); see also Forte (1995). On this issue, compare the more extensive treatment by F. Forte and D. D'Amico (2007).
29. Advanced from the civic and cultural point of view and not only from the technological and economic point of view.
30. The question of citizens' constitutional rights is addressed in an extensive range of

literature, linked to the more general issue of the 'rights of man'. Cf., among others, the Universal Declaration of the Rights of Man approved by the United Nations Assembly on 10 December 1948 and the Italian constitution, Arts. 13–28 Rights and Duties of Citizens as well as 41, 42, 43 (Property Rights) and 48, 49, 50 (Political Rights) and 53 (Principle of taxation according to ability to pay). On this point see also Ruffini (1946); Giuffrè and Villani (eds) (1988).

31. On this point see in particular Eucken (1952 [2004]), Book IV, 'Die Wettbewerbsordunung und ihre Verwirklichung'.
32. See Montemartini (1900 [1958]) and Forte (1986).
33. Cf. in particular North (1990) Chapter 12.
34. On the various electoral systems see Fisichella, in *Enciclopedia del Diritto*, Giuffrè, vol. XIV; Grofman and Lijphart (eds) (1984); Fisichella (1970; 1982).
35. On the principle which establishes that the majority has the *right* to prevail over the minority, known as the 'majority principle', cf. Ruffini (1976).
36. For example, a list that obtains 3.3 per cent of votes in a constituency composed of 30 seats obtains one seat. However, the highly complicated problem of the residual votes not sufficient to elect one member then arises. This can be solved by utilizing all the residue in a single national constituency, in which each party has a list of candidates. For each list, as many candidates will be elected with the residue as there are electoral quotients obtained with this residue (the quotients are calculated by dividing the number of persons eligible to vote, on the national level, by the number of total seats at the national level). Alternatively, the residual votes are utilized by attributing them to the parties that have the highest ratio between the votes obtained in a given constituency, and the number of seats (the so-called D'Hont method), or by other expedients.

   In favour of the proportional system, in the purest form that can be achieved, see H. Kelsen, (1920 [1929]; 1924; 1955), and earlier, J.S. Mill, (1861 [1963]), Chapter VII, *Of True and False Democracy; Representation of All, and Representation of the Majority only*.
37. See below, section 3.10 and ff.
38. This is the method adopted in Germany. It has not prevented a Liberal Party from remaining in parliament and being part of the government, nor has it prevented the rise of the Green Party on the parliamentary level. But it has reduced the government coalitions to just a few parties and has made them more stable.
39. For instance, let us suppose there are 15 constituencies: there may be some party that obtains a seat by winning 6 per cent of the votes, just as there may be a party that obtains a seat with 12 per cent. This can come about because, when there are 15 seats, the full quotient is 6.666 per cent and the fractions below this quantity all contribute to the partitioning of the remainders. And so – assuming that the number of seats not directly assigned is three – then 12 per cent of the votes, which have a remainder of 5.666 per cent, cannot have a second seat, being defeated by one with 6.5 per cent, one with 6 per cent and one with 5.8 per cent. This is still tolerable, but if there are 10 seats and the full quotient is therefore 10 per cent, it may happen – if 35 per cent of the votes are not directly assigned – that they will go to four parties, which have roughly 8 per cent while – let us say – two parties which have 7 per cent each are left with a single seat.
40. Breton (1974) argues that with this system, if there are only two parties, then at most 25 per cent of the electors could be represented in the Government, because in every electoral district, on the assumption of uniform distribution, half (minus one) of the votes goes to the defeated minority, while the government will be composed of the majority within the elected, that is at most by half of half (plus one) of the votes of the citizens represented.

   But the dangers of lack of representation, Breton points out, are even greater with three parties: thus if the three parties have an equal weight, 16.6 per cent of the electors will be represented in the Government (based on the above calculation), that is half (plus one) of the 33.3 per cent that elects representatives.
41. On the importance of enabling small parties to emerge in order to counter the tendency

to political massification, which goes hand in hand with economic massification, cf. Koslowski, and the comment by Forte in Koslowski, 1987a, Chapter 3.

42. On the role of the parties, to avoid the risk of politics turning into a clash among particular interests, see Thurow (1980).

43. In France, in the first round, the candidate who obtains the absolute majority of the votes expressed is elected directly, provided that this majority amounts at least to a quarter of the electors registered to vote. Then, all candidates who have obtained at least 12.5 per cent of the votes of the registered electors are admitted to the second round (with 15 per cent of abstentions and of non-voters, it becomes 14.7 per cent). In the second round the candidate who has obtained the relative majority is elected, and in the (abstract) case of perfect parity, the most senior candidate is elected. In the impure two-round system, the so-called run-off voting system, only the two candidates who obtained the most votes in the first round are allowed to go through to the second round. Such a system loses many of the advantages of the system adopted in France. In Italy it is adopted in local and regional elections.

44. Cf. Anthony Downs (1957); Bruno Leoni 'Political decision and majority rule', also published in *Il Politico* in 1960 in the Italian version, edited by Mario Stoppino with the title 'Decisioni Politiche e Regole della Maggioranza' and B. Leoni, (1967 [2009]), dating from 1966, presented at the first national congress of Doctrine of the State, in May 1966, published in *Il Politico*, in 1967. This essay and the preceding one were republished in Leoni (2009b), *Scritti di Scienza Politica e di Teoria del Diritto*, with an introductory essay by Mario Stoppino.

45. Established in the Italian Constitution art. 67. The principle should mean that the elected member cannot enter into contracts with her electors, to act as guidance for her behaviour during assemblies, nor act as if there were a specific tacit contract with some of them.

46. In the 1960 essay.

47. This technical term is to be understood as meaning any kind of proposal that is concerned with articles of law, numbers, appointment of persons, treaties or contracts, decisions to embark on or decide not to carry out works and activities, and so on.

48. In the seminal book (1957), *An Economic Theory of Democracy*.

49. Here Leoni cites Downs (1960).

50. The normalized voting power will be 4/6:20/6 = 1/5 as usual, given that each one has the same vote as the others.

51. Now consider an assembly of 51 members, in which party A has 15 votes, while party B has 6 votes and C, D, and E have 10 votes each. A with 15 votes out of 51 has a voting weight of 0.3; the smallest party, B, having 6 votes out of 50, has a voting weight of 0.12, while C, D and E with 10 votes each have a voting weight of 0.2. We indicate, for each winning coalition, the number of votes, bearing in mind that giving the voting rule, in order to be such a coalition must have more than 25 votes.

These coalitions are:

1. $A, B, C = 15 + 6 + 10 = 31$
2. $C, D, E = 10 + 10 + 10 = 30$
3. $A, B, C, D = 15 + 6 + 10 + 10 - 41$
4. $A, B, C, E = 15 + 6 + 10 + 10 = 41$
5. $A, B, D, E = 15 + 6 + 10 + 10 = 41$
6. $B, C, D, E = 6 + 10 + 10 + 10 = 36$
7. $A, C, D, E = 15 + 10 + 10 + 10 = 45$
8. $B, C, E = 6 + 10 + 10 = 26$
9. $B, D, E = 6 + 10 + 10 = 26$
10. $A, B, D = 15 + 6 + 10 - 31$
11. $A, B, E = 15 + 6 + 10 = 31$
12. $A, C, D = 15 + 10 + 10 = 35$
13. $A, C, E = 15 + 10 + 10 = 35$
14. $A, D, E = 15 + 10 + 10 = 35$
15. $A, B, C, D, E = 51$
16. $B, C, D = 6 + 10 + 10 = 26$

Thus A is a swing voter in 6 combinations, but B too is a swing voter in 6 combinations, and the same holds for each of C, D and E.

52. The original demonstration is due to Bowen (1943); cf. Brosio (1986) Chapter V, 'Processi e regole di decisione collettiva', section 5.5. The graphic formulation of Downs (1957) is displayed in section 5.9.

53. This is the case in Italy, as enshrined in Art. 48 of the constitution, which establishes that 'the vote is cast on a personal basis, and it is free and secret. Exercising the right to vote is a civic duty.'
54. The precursor of this paradox is the French mathematician and philosopher J.A. De Condorcet, whose thought is very effectively summarized in Condorcet (1974). Subsequently, see Black (1958) (re-edition of earlier essays) and Arrow (1951 [1963]). The work by Black antedates that of Arrow, who appears not to have known it at the time he developed his brilliant mathematical theorization of social choices performed by means of voting. While Black's analysis focuses on the point of view of the issue of the rationality and stability of balloting in committees, that of Arrow is more concerned with the issue of how a 'collective will' is derived from the vote of the individual members of the committee. Debate on this theme developed above all after Arrow. In the very extensive literature, see at least Buchanan (1960); McLean (1987, Chapter 8).
55. Further developments in Brosio (1986), Chapter V, sections 5.6 and 5.7.
56. See Buchanan (1954a, 1954b).

2. Individual and collective welfare

1 ECONOMIC AND NON-ECONOMIC INDIVIDUAL WELFARE

1.1 The Individual Welfare of the Average Man Includes Not Only Economic Interests, but also Values: Methodological Preamble[1]

In the first chapter we saw that in a market economy, within the framework of a democratic system, the demand and provision of public goods obey laws of general economic advantage for the individuals belonging to the collective community under consideration. By means of the democratic system, individuals – acting for their own benefit and on behalf of their organizations – make the collective choices of what can be called the 'political cooperative', which integrates and corrects the economic market, towards which the political market is subsidiary. The aim pursued by individuals in making such choices is that of achieving their maximum welfare. But note that since the individuals act collectively, they can achieve their individual welfare only through a process of maximization of the welfare of the whole community they belong to. We will now address the issue of individual welfare and collective welfare, taken to mean the welfare of individuals who belong to the community. This is, at one and the same time, a normative analysis, in the sense that it concerns preferred maximization processes that are to be preferred when starting out from given premises, and a positive analysis in that it explains the laws of long-term equilibrium of a free society which embodies the aim of individuals who are organized politically within a democracy, and shows what obstacles are encountered in the real world.

As we have already made clear, in conducting such an analysis, which involves positive and normative economics, it is not sufficient to refer to an abstract figure of *homo oeconomicus* regarded as completely rational and selfish, and pursuing a welfare consisting essentially of utilitarian satisfactions measurable in money. The point is that we are interested in real individuals. And therefore – apart from specific exceptions – it is necessary to refer to an 'average individual', a figure that has a greater *general* explanatory value. Unlike *homo oeconomicus*, the average individual of a free society who belongs to an advanced market-based democratic community has personal ethical constraints and constraints stemming from the community she belongs to. Moreover, in addition to economic-pecuniary interests the average individual also takes values into consideration. Therefore her welfare is not evaluated only in goods and services that are part of GDP, the gross domestic product, but also in other goods and values, such as the protection of civil and political rights and human rights, ecological values and the artistic and historical-cultural heritage. The average individual of a free democratic society thus agrees to exclude 'anti-social' preferences from the welfare she is entitled to pursue. Such 'anti-social' preferences are viewed as contrary to ethical principles concerning the integrity and rights of other persons, protection of the natural and cultural heritage, and so on. Furthermore, the average individual of a free society is not entirely egoistic, and has awareness of sensitive issues such as justice and injustice, albeit not always in the same manner and not always with identical rationality. For example, the average individual has different and greater rationality when she makes, or delegates to others the task of making, certain fundamental decisions of a constitutional nature pertaining to the society she belongs to, as compared to everyday decisions.

Our analysis will be carried out in three stages. First, we will consider individual welfare, with reference to the average individual in a free society. Secondly, we consider the optimal functioning of the market economy system in which collective choices regarding public goods are also admitted, with the same rules, although collective choices will not be examined here. In the third section we consider the collective welfare of individuals in the way it is achieved through public choices that integrate and modify market choices, in the framework of the 'political cooperative'.

This first section, *concerning individual welfare*, outlines the function of the *subjective* individual welfare of the average person in our society, which is endowed with values as well as economic interests. We also endeavour to identify a measurable, objective concept of the average person's subjective individual welfare. Objectively 'measurable' does not mean only that it allows measurements that are objectively valid for the various subjects, with 'cardinal' numbers on which operations of addition, division, subtraction and multiplication can be performed. To be sure, such objective cardinal measurements of individual subjective economic welfare can sometimes be carried out, while at other times they cannot. But as we will see, the situations of greater or lesser individual subjective welfare interpreted as giving room for choices can also be measured objectively, for the various subjects, by means of purely ordinal numbers, that is to say, simply in terms of an ordering, with judgements of preference and indifference.[2]

1.2 The Function of Individual Subjective Economic Welfare: Purchasing Power as an Objective 'Cardinal' Measure of Individual Subjective Economic Welfare

The function of individual subjective welfare W_J^* that is relevant in the individualistic model considers the preferences of the single individual J who is a member of a community S, excluding preferences considered *illegitimate*. However, there are two formulations of W_J^*, one more restricted and one broader: the former referring *only* to economic welfare and the latter concerning global welfare. Let us consider now the more restricted view, as a fundamental component of the global formulation:

$$W_J^* = U_J^* \qquad (2.1)$$

that is to say, the welfare of individual J of S consists of the *subjective* utility U_J^*, in which the asterisk * indicates that we are dealing here with *subjective* welfare, namely, welfare as evaluated by the *subject considered with choices freely made and regarded as legitimate by the subject concerned*, and U refers to the utility of economic goods and services that can be exchanged by means of money. Individual J makes a calculation of these utilities that includes additions and subtractions, because the utilities can be calculated in terms of the common monetary measurement. Therefore (2.1) includes the sum of all types of economic utilities $U^*a + U^*b . . .:: U^*n$ obtained by J from economic goods and services, in other words utilities that can be expressed in money, with regard to which exchange is legitimate.[3] Therefore

$$U_J^* = (U_{Ja}^* + U_{Jb}^* + \ldots + U_{Jn}^*) \qquad (2.1')$$

From this formula, which is *of a cardinal nature*, expressed in terms of subjective utility, we can proceed to the *objective concept of economic welfare as expanse of choices expressed by purchasing power*, arguing, *as a first approximation*,[4] that J will have a greater economic welfare if she has a greater income, at constant prices, that is a *greater effective purchasing power*, since she can obtain more goods that give her economic utility. If a given subject A's income derives from capital, while that of a subject B derives from labour, it can be said that, under equal net income, A has a greater purchasing power than B. This is because A's income, on the assumption that every year she sets aside the amortization necessary to safeguard her capital, is permanent, while B's income is transitory, because B can work only as long as she is alive and in good health, that is for a limited period of time. If B aims to ensure that the income she derives from labour is permanent, she must set aside a part of it every year in order to build up her assets that will yield the income (net of the amount set aside). It should be noted that this formula does not include, in the economic utilities of A or B, the satisfactions they derive by 'empathy' from the utilities of the other subjects (= empathy) that are likewise relevant in a broader consideration.[5]

1.3   Although the Functions of Individual Subjective Economic Welfare as an Expanse of Choices are Measurable Objectively in a Cardinal Manner, they Cannot be Summed Algebraically in Order to Reach a Collective Economic Welfare Function: the Ordinal Measure: GDP as a First Approximation Indicator of Collective Economic Welfare

In the individualistic conception which characterizes the cooperative model, in the framework of a democracy where everyone has a vote, that is where each person counts as an individual, it is not possible to construct a collective welfare function of S as the algebraic sum of the *functions of individual welfare*. Furthermore, *once property rights have been defined* (in the context of the given institutions of the market system) a collective economic welfare function (significant as a first approximation) can be constructed by merely juxtaposing the individual economic welfare statuses of the various subjects $A, B. . .N$, such property rights being given, under *unchanged public economy conditions*:

$$U_S^* = u_S\,(U_A^*, U_B^*, \ldots, U_N^*) \qquad (2.2)$$

That is to say, S's economic welfare will be a function of the utility of the various subjects $A, B. . .N$, members of S, which these subjects have obtained through their decision-making processes. Among the U^* of the various subjects $A, B. . .N$ who are members of S, we have not placed a plus sign but rather a comma, which stands for the fact that within the individualistic profile of the U_S^*, no inter-subjective cardinal calculation, that is no algebraic sum of the various U_S^* of $A, B, \ldots, N$, is allowed.

Admittedly, we can make a reasonable assessment of other people's economic welfare by reflecting that those who have a greater effective and potential purchasing power, under equal physical, environmental etc. conditions, have more opportunity to pursue their own economic welfare than those who have a lower purchasing power.[6] But *in the formulation of a democracy in which each person has a vote, given that it is a system of ends and values in its own right*, individuals are not considered as 'little containers' of units of utility and disutility, to be aggregated together algebraically in calculation of the 'big container' of collective welfare. The aggregations of (2.1) in (2.2) can therefore be carried out only with *ordinal* criteria. As a result, U^*_S increases with the increasing 'legitimate' economic utility of any subject who is a member of S. But what happens to function (2.2) when the welfare of some subject improves while that of some other subject worsens, remains undetermined. Thus it will be possible to say that collective welfare has increased if the welfare of some subjects has improved and none of the other subjects has undergone a decrease in their welfare (the so-called Pareto principle which will be addressed in section 3). Since we have defined individual economic welfare as purchasing power, in other words as income at constant prices, we can measure welfare or the collective economic welfare by using the gross domestic product (or better the gross national product)[7] as a yardstick. If we suppose that the increase in national product extending over several years implies that everyone or almost everyone has improved or at least retained their income, then we can state that barring exceptions, collective economic welfare in the nation under consideration has increased.

On the other hand, it can be supposed that in a democratic community, when there is a growth in the national product which results in an impairment of the economic welfare of part of the subjects, then an attempt will be made to compensate[8] for this damage in order to facilitate collectively advantageous changes and safeguard legitimate property rights, for reasons of equity and good functioning of the market.

This is the reason why an increase in the domestic gross product, that is to say its growth rate, is usually considered as a good indicator of the increase in collective economic welfare, and it is therefore the first macroeconomic target the public economy should aim to achieve. But in addition to the limitations implicit in this manner of measuring welfare, as mentioned earlier, it should be kept in mind that what is measured is the economic part of welfare, not all of it.

Finally, another point to consider is that the cooperative model implies that each person should be able to aspire, in the medium to long run, to an improvement in economic welfare. This explains why it seems important for the economic resources of S to increase, in other words why the growth rate of the national product is important.

1.4 Anti-social Utilities should be Excluded from the Individual Welfare Function

As pointed out earlier, utilities that illegitimately cause damage to others should be excluded from U^*_i. There are two types of 'antisocial subjective economic utilities', with a different impact on individual 'property rights': first and foremost, antisocial utilities that are in effect only subjectively antisocial. These derive, for example, from A's psychological pleasure in gloating over B's unhappiness without depriving the already unfortunate B of anything in particular. This is rather similar to the malicious pleasure someone who is rich and enjoying good health may derive from reflecting on other people's misfortunes and thinking how much better off she is. These antisocial utilities are not forbidden because they do not inflict damage on third parties. But society is certainly under no obligation to support the pursuit of such utilities. In contrast, B's disutilities, U^*_{BA}, deriving from the intensification or rise of needs prompted by the comparison with A, are a different matter and they are of relevance for (2.2) because they constitute a factor which influences the needs arising in the community S, considered in the context of relations and interaction among its various subjects.

The second aspect concerns the subjective economic utilities that A obtains by means of objectively antisocial activities such as theft, fraud and robbery. In this case A obtains welfare at B's expense, with what could be defined as a zero sum game, or possibly a negative sum game, if A incurs costs in order to carry out those activities that cause harm to B. Not only should A's economic satisfaction, in this case, be excluded from A's welfare function, from the point of view of the collective community, but more importantly, the community should prevent this activity from being carried out. This is because failure to protect property rights[9] reduces the advantageousness of producing, saving, investing or consuming, and tends instead to favour the idea that it pays to steal, commit robberies, fraud and so forth. This issue will be taken up again in Chapter 3, section 1.

However, there is a third type of antisocial activity, the borders of which are less easy to map out: those that do not consist in economic envy or economic damage inflicted on other subjects: instead, they consist in impairing the values other subjects believe in and/or which are shared by the collective community under consideration, as well as in wreaking damage on goods such as nature, the landscape, culture and art belonging to others. These are goods which, in addition to their possible utilitarian economic content, have an existence value 'in their own right' (see Chapter 3, section 1.4). This aspect will be addressed after examining the role of values in individual and collective welfare.

1.5   Non-economic Subjective Welfare: 'Values': the Opportunity Cost Involved in Obtaining Values, which is Measured as the Purchasing Power that has to be Relinquished, Constitutes their Minimal Measure in Economic Terms

The broadest version of individual welfare, which concerns the real average person and not the abstract *homo oeconomicus*, takes into account not merely the utility U_j^* deriving from J's satisfaction of economic needs but also V_j^* obtained from satisfaction of J's non-economic needs. The latter refer partly to 'moral goods', and partly to 'non-market material goods', that is to say, physical entities for which there is no market (given the social rules shared by civilization as we know it), for example use of the air we breathe. Globally, we denominate these 'non-economic needs' and goods that satisfy them as 'values' (from the point of view of prevailing social judgements these can at times be negative values) because, first, there is generally a judgement of ethical value[10] even for non-market physical entities and, secondly, because all individuals acknowledge their validity, through their political representatives, on the occasion of elections of a constitutional or post-constitutional nature. An individual recognizes their value *not only for herself but also for the other members of the community* and, more generally, for any other subject, with a distributional outlook that obeys criteria of utility and equity that is variable from subject to subject.

Among such values, we may list:

1. The right to *freedom* and *personal integrity* (including the freedom to decide whether or not to undergo medical treatment and whether or not to donate one's organs), the absence of physical *handicaps* and *good health*, which are recognized by all individuals as values for themselves and for any other human being and, more generally, for any other member of the community to which an individual belongs.
2. Having *free time* available for leisure and for devoting oneself to *consumption* and non-economic goods.
3. *Common artistic, cultural and knowledge-related values* as well as *environmental and natural goods* such as the landscape, pure air, uncontaminated water, flora and fauna, all of which are regarded not only as goods to be enjoyed personally and as the common material and immaterial heritage of the present and future generations, but also as *values in their own right* over which S has no rights (Forte, 1991, Chapter I);
4. *Private 'human values'* such as physiological, affective or friendship relations with other people, or simple reciprocal acquaintance (having children, a family, the right to one's own 'privacy'), and so on.
5. *Civil and political rights*, considered as personal rights and as the immaterial heritage of civilization in S and if possible beyond S. Among such rights, a priority position is that of the general right to freedom 'L' (above and beyond that which is considered in point 4), and this is further divided into the various non-economic liberties (freedom of the person, of thought, religion, movement[11] and so on) as

well as the economic liberties (and this value is accepted, as 'freedom of choice',[12] even by a convinced utilitarian like J. Harsanyi).[13] But in our civilization other rights-values are also held to be primary values. These include values such as equality before the law, without discrimination based on sex, religion, race or political ideology and justice, democratic rights, the right to vote and to form political organizations, ethnic identity, community (local and national) identity, the right to one's own good reputation.

These non-economic goods do not, however, usually come at zero cost, from the economic welfare point of view. In this respect, it should be noted that although 'values' constitute a 'non-market' form of welfare, for a large part of the 'goods' of categories 1, 2 and 3 there is a monetary value, *albeit not exhaustive, in terms of opportunity costs and conservation and recovery costs.* Thus the satisfactions of free time can be measured monetarily with the opportunity cost of the economic benefits obtainable by forsaking such free time (for example the gain obtained by working overtime). To be sure, our society forbids child labour, as a form of exploitation. Thus it can be said that there is an ethical constraint on the economic value of the opportunity for given non-economic values. By the same token, there is an opportunity cost for the landscape or pure air, and this cost arises by refraining from – or by a prohibition on – bricking over the green belts, cutting down forests, emitting pollution through production and consumption. When the environment is blighted, it is possible to estimate the *recovery cost*, if recovery can indeed be undertaken: recovery often costs more than the individual benefit thereby obtained, resulting in collective damage. However, it is not always estimated that the 'negative value' the community would face due to environmental destruction, *ex post*, appears so elevated as to exceed or at least equal the economic cost of recovery, which can be extremely high, on account of budget constraints. Similarly, for an archaeological good such as the Colosseum, or a work of art like Leonardo's *Last Supper*, it is possible to calculate the hypothetical money that would be obtainable by treating it as a market good, although the concept that the *ethical value* of its conservation which involves the whole of society and the future generations as well[14] constitutes a constraint on the economic calculation. Here too the recovery that would become necessary in the case of destruction could, on account of budget constraints, have an economic opportunity cost for the overall set of individuals of S that would exceed the non-economic value. By contrast, we cannot set an even hypothetical monetary value on the 'cultural ophelimity'[15] that pervades a society in which, on account of the protection and promotion of cultural goods, art and cultural goods are greatly appreciated. But this economic value does exist, and it can be inferred, for example, from the fact that the buildings of Gubbio or some other city rich in art treasures, of equal quality and state of conservation, are worth more than those of a normal municipality with similar economic activities and income. Likewise, 'good health' can in part be preserved and restored with medical treatment that has an economic cost, and although certain diseases are incurable, there is still a cost for the reduction of suffering by palliative treatment of those afflicted with such diseases. A monetary value is set on the loss of an arm or the death of a person, although human life and physical integrity are a value in their own right. Thus overall, non-economic values have a cost, and often, an economic return, but often this is not an adequate measure of their intrinsic value, which decision-makers in the public economy must endeavour to take into consideration in order to maximize citizens' welfare, according to the citizens' *real preferences, expressed in the reflexive phase.*

Therefore, when considering the overall individual welfare function, we can consider 'values' as partly measurable with cardinal magnitudes that can be summed with the other utilities, and partly with merely ordinal magnitudes V that can be assessed by preference and indifference judgements, both among the utilities themselves and in addition to the set of the utilities.[16]

This does not imply that the individual Vs are not measured with quantitative magnitudes – which appear subjectively significant – by the various subjects A, B,. . ., N, who also apply measurements in their reciprocal relations through their reciprocal imaginative empathy, that is through the ability to put oneself in 'other people's shoes'.[17]

1.6 The Conflict between Values and Utility and Values in the Various Individuals' Welfare

It may be the case that N, who is pursuing certain 'moral values' V_a, believes that they can be satisfied, from her point of view, only on condition that M agrees to V_a, either voluntarily or by coercion. N, for whom divorce is a negative value, may feel that she would suffer an offence not only if she herself were obliged to undergo a divorce, but also if others were allowed to initiate divorce proceedings and M thus obtained a divorce. On the other hand, if A considers the *general* freedom of vote v to be a moral value V_v, she will suffer a loss of welfare if B wants to be free to surrender her right to vote in elections or in a referendum in exchange for money, obtaining the utility V_v. It will be impossible to satisfy A's V_V and B's utility U_B simultaneously, as these are in conflict with one another. It is a zero sum game. But here the solution is fairly simple in the cooperative model, because in this model the good v cannot be marketed, and therefore it cannot form part of the functions (2.1′).

The 'interfering' values are only partly similar, analytically, to the antisocial economic goods that give one subject an advantage at someone else's expense, violating property, contracts, and so on. They differ for the reason that while antisocial behaviour implies illegitimate invasion of a sphere of property, the interfering values concern other people's behaviour which takes place outside the framework of their sphere of individual properties.[18]

There are various solutions to this problem. The solution proposed for the cooperative model is based on the principle of *preference for 'freedom of choice' and toleration*, which consists in agreeing that all individuals pursue their values (or absence of values) when decisions do not *inevitably* encroach on other people's pursuit of their own values, and in finding a reasonable compromise if this does not seem aberrant from the point of view of the ethical principles shared by all members of the community. For example, if divorce is allowed only on a consensual basis, it is still possible for B, who does not wish to make use of it with A, to remain true to her own moral preferences. In the case of pornography in the press and on screen, these goods should be 'consumed' privately by persons who are of age; but they should be forbidden when they deal with *aberrations* such as paedophilia or anthropophagy. The question of abortion is different. Let us suppose, for example, that if there is a risk of giving birth to a malformed baby, it may be the case that the mother A wants to have an abortion, while the father B wants H to be born; meanwhile N, unrelated to the couple, holds the same opinion on the basis of her ethical belief that 'life is sacred', while the unrelated M is of the opinion that the decision should be taken by the mother. In this case, H's fate concerns the preferences of A, B, N and M simultaneously, and these preferences involve a subject (H) who cannot make her preferences known. For the interfering values regarding the environment and the landscape (protection of living species, non-destruction of forests, and so on) a compromise can be found by means of the criterion of reasonableness: for example, a 'reasonable balance' could be found between those who demand rigid safeguards and those whose preferences allow economic requirements to be taken into account (Fedeli and Forte, 2001 and further on Chapter 4, section 4). But in other cases the problem may be fairly complex. Thus on the question of capital punishment, N may be against it while M may be in favour. Neither of the two holds this position with regard to themselves, but rather with regard to third parties who commit a heinous crime, and there is no way of solving this problem in such as way as to satisfy both parties.

1.7 From Economic Welfare as Effective Purchasing Power to Overall Economic Welfare as Ability to Choose on Fields of Economic Choice

Now we can build an objective, that is observable, general concept of overall individual welfare. This can be done by means of the concept of *ability to choose on fields of choice*, which is an expansion of the first approximation concept of economic welfare as *purchasing power, that is as expanse of economic choices.* We can denote this concept of individual welfare with the subscript c on the right of W (Welfare), as W_{cJ}, that is to say, subject J's welfare as her *ability to choose.*

The first component of W_{cJ} is purchasing power in money at constant prices, which J has at her disposal. As we have seen in sections 1.1–1.6, for economic goods monetary quantifications are persuasive. In effect, average individuals as mentioned in section 1.1 make calculations and quantitative comparisons in money, *at constant prices*, that is in quantitative units of purchasing power. Exactly what is the utility of the money of the various subjects with different purchasing power is not easy for an outside observer to determine, although such observations are in actual fact quite frequent. But certainly whoever has a greater purchasing power, assuming *given prices*[19] – under equal psychophysical conditions, availability of free time, location – can achieve greater satisfaction of her preferences. To build up the concept of individual welfare as ability to choose on fields of choice, and to arrive at the concept of welfare as effective purchasing power, it is necessary to supplement the concept of existing purchasing power with that of *potential purchasing power. A* is independently wealthy and has a private income, has a greater potential purchasing power than *B*, who derives her income from full-time employment, given that *A* could increase her income by seeking employment, whereas *B* cannot. By the same token, if *B* and *C* have the same income, but *C* obtains her income from a part-time job, *A* can be said to have a greater potential purchasing power than *B*, because *C* could increase her income by working longer hours. But this holds if *C* is in a society where her willingness to engage in extra work is not impeded by the shortage of demand for labour of that type or an overall shortage of jobs. If, on the other hand, *C* works part-time because her unemployment is voluntary, she can only hope to achieve greater economic welfare if she gives up a share of her free time.

All this can be *observed*. Thus there is no need to know the different economic preferences of the various subjects in order to establish that, *given their psychophysical conditions, under equal free time in connection with their family situation and conditions of transport to get to the work place, and so on, the capacity for economic choices* open to individuals is a function of effective and potential purchasing power. The concept of individual economic welfare in terms of capacity of choice on *fields of choice* is thus a concept that can be observed objectively, even though it concerns the subjective point of view of the possibility the various individuals have of satisfying their own preferences.

1.8 Capacity of Choice and Fields of Choice for Non-economic Individual Welfare

In addition to effective and potential purchasing power *as the field of choice* for economic goods, there are *fields of choice* for non-economic goods. Here too, as can be noted from the list of cases presented in section 1.5, the notion of *field of choice* is important, and it can be submitted to objective observation. For categories 1–3, there often exists, as we have already noted, a parametric measure. Thus 'leisure time' is measured in hours and days. For many environmental and natural goods[20] there exist physical measurements of 'degradation' and numerical values of 'situation', which define the fields of choice. For the *rights* mentioned in classes 4 and 5 the quantitative measurements cannot easily be applied, but their *dimension* is observable. Thus here too, the observation of *fields of choice*, which may be quite broad and which may increase or be reduced, under equal capacity to choose, serves to measure objectively the welfare of the various subjects. Thus it is possible to have *global* ordinal preference judgements, for *spheres of rights* that are broader in comparison to others that are smaller.[21] Thus one can expand (2.2), obtaining as a first approximation a social welfare function on an individual basis, in which the welfare of the various individuals is expressed as endowment with purchasing power, and with breadth of fields of choice referring to the various non-economic goods.[22]

With the transition from the concept of welfare as a function of economic and non-economic goods to the concept of fields of choice, there is a reduction, both for economic and non-economic goods, in the amount of information on preferences. It is sufficient to know that a larger field of choice is preferred over a smaller one, and to identify the possible conflicts among the fields of choice of the various subjects. In the individualistic formulation it is not possible to sum the purchasing powers and fields of choice of the various subjects algebraically, to arrive at the calculation of maximum welfare. In this formulation, collective welfare increases if the welfare of any of the individuals increases in one or other of these components while the other components and the welfare of the other subjects remain unchanged. This issue will be taken up again in section 3, in relation to the Pareto principle. But it should be noted that with regard to the political context, even in a democracy these algebraic

sums are often performed by means of the votes of the citizens' representative. Thus collective indifference curves are constructed, each of
which contains different combinations, held to be equivalent, with regard
to the welfare of the various subjects. In these curves some subjects have
greater welfare and others less, analogously to the operation performed
for the consumer's indifference curves, in which greater amounts of good
A and smaller amounts of the Bs or vice versa are maintained, on the same
indifference curve. This is a bold operation, which should be used very
parsimoniously.[23]

1.9 The Role of Preferences, in the Concept of Individual Economic Welfare as Purchasing Power

The approach in terms of purchasing power for measurement of individual economic welfare shifts the analysis to a far more operative level
than the analysis in terms of ordinal preferences. It avoids abstractions
in terms of subjective utilities, but it cannot altogether do without the
various subjects' preferences. For instance, the monetary income of the
various subjects may increase while the price level remains unchanged,
but there may be variations in the relative prices of the various goods,
such that the prices of some goods go up while others go down. Let us
consider two goods X and Y, and hypothesize that the former increases
by 5 per cent from year 1 to year 2, while the latter decreases by the same
percentage from year 1 to year 2. Let us suppose that the price of X and
the price of Y is 10 in year 1. In year 2 the price of X is 10.5, while that of
Y is 9.5. Let us now suppose that production both of X and of Y, which in
year 1 was 100, increases to 103 in year 2. We will posit that in the community, composed of two (groups of) subjects, A and B, this results in an
unchanged price level, because total consumption of X as well as of Y is
100 macro units, and therefore the price variations in terms of increase
and decrease balance each other out exactly in formation of the price level.
Therefore if (group) A and (group) B, who had an income of 100 in year
1, have an income of 103 in year 2, it could be argued that both (groups
of) subjects have experienced a 3 per cent increase in welfare as purchasing
power, since they have had a 3 per cent rise in income and the price level
has remained unchanged. But this could be false. Suppose that (group) A
consumes 9 units of X and 1 of Y while (group) B consumes 9 units of Y
and 1 of X. During period 1, A and B, who have, by hypothesis, an income
of 100, have an expenditure of 100. A spends 90 for X and 10 for Y, while
(group) B spends 90 for Y and 10 for X. Now each of the groups has an
income of 103. But if A, with an income of 103, wants to buy 9 units of X
in year 2 in the same way as in year 1, A will have to spend $10.5 \times 9 = 94.5$,

Table 2.1   Differences in purchasing power for individuals with different consumption patterns when relative prices change

Income/goods	Subject A	Subject A	Subject B	Subject B
Quantity/Prices	Year 1	Year 2	Year 1	Year 2
Income	100	103	100	103
Units of X	9	9	1	1
Price of X	10	10.5	10	10.5
Expenditure for X	90	94.5	10	10.5
Units of Y	1	1	9	9
Price of Y	10	9.5	10	9.5
Expenditure for Y	10	9.5	90	85.5
Total expenditure	100	104	100	96

while 1 unit of Y (the same amount of units of Y as A purchased in year 1) will require A to spend 9.5. In total, in year 2, A should spend 104 to maintain the same consumptions as in year 1, while having an income of 103. A's welfare as purchasing power has worsened. By contrast, if subject B wants to buy 9 units of Y, then B will now spend 85.5 while 1 unit of X (the same amount of units of X as B bought in year 1) will require B to spend 10.5. In total, B will spend 96, and since B's income is 103, B's welfare has improved considerably.

Table 2.1 summarizes the situation in the two years for the two (groups of) subjects.

Naturally, the A subjects will try to reduce consumption of X and to increase that of Y in order to counter the price increase of X and take advantage of the drop in price of Y, but if their preferences have remained unchanged, this will imply that they undergo a loss of welfare. Furthermore, if X and Y are not easily substitutable for each other because they concern markedly different types of expenditure, for example, respectively, food and housing (rent and related expenses), then A and B will be unable to induce rapid changes in their consumption patterns. The B subjects can, in turn, increase their consumption of the Ys and reduce that of X, which is already quite low, and thus further increase their welfare, albeit under the constraint of their preferences and the difficulty of substitution among goods belonging to different sectors.

From what we have seen in these reflections, it follows that if the relative prices of X and Y undergo change, it often cannot be established *prima facie* whether welfare in terms of purchasing power has increased or decreased for individual subjects with preferences different from the average preferences that are used to weight the various goods in calculating the national product, since with different preference curves the *A* subjects will be better off and the *B*s worse off, or vice versa.

Therefore, reference to the growth rate of the national product as an increase in global 'purchasing power' is a good general measure of individual welfare, but it is not always univocal. At times what happens resembles Trilussa's joke about statistics, according to which if Tom eats a chicken and Dick eats none, on average Tom and Dick have eaten half a chicken each.

> For instance, if the price of staple foodstuffs such as bread has risen and the price of a bus ticket has also risen, while the price of beef has remained unchanged and mobile phone prices have gone down, then calculation of the national product may record a net increase in real terms, because consumption of bread and bus tickets has little impact on the total and thus on the rate of inflation, which has to be subtracted from the nominal increase in the national product in order to obtain the real product. But low-income subjects, for whom bread and a bus ticket represent a high component of their expenditure, unlike beef and mobile phone usage, may find that their situation has worsened.

1.10 Economic Goods, Free Goods and Values and Welfare as Field of Choice

It is now time to summarize what has been described so far. Overall individual subjective welfare can be measured through observation of the ability to choose in fields of choice. Some aspects of the individual welfare function in question allow cardinal homogeneous quantitative measurement, in terms of purchasing power. Other aspects are not measurable in terms of purchasing power because they are not intrinsically suited to such a measure (numerous values and many environmental goods fall into this category), but they do allow objective measurements (for instance with physical indicators such as the quantity of pollutants that contaminate pure air or the amount of public parkland and leafy surroundings per inhabitant), while others allow only ordinal judgements that can be given by reference parameters (for example freedom rights). To understand how individual welfare choices are made when what are at stake are economic values and free goods and values not measurable in economic terms, one can consider a subject *J* who, in choosing to live and work in a city *M* instead of another city *R*, chooses between a greater availability of goods *A* and *B* that can be purchased on the market and a lower availability of environmental goods *Z* in city *M*, versus the opposite situation in city *R*, where there are fewer economic goods and a greater quantity of environmental goods. (This issue is described with a detailed graphic representation in the Appendix, Figure A.2.) *J* might prefer to live in Reggio Calabria with 2000 euros a month rather than living in Milan with 3000, not only because she would spend less on rent but also because the climate would allow considerably lower heating bills, and since the city is on the sea she would have no need to undertake the expense of holidaying in a different resort, as she can use the environmental goods of the city where she lives. Furthermore, since the air quality is better, she has no need to travel elsewhere in order to breathe good clear air and free her children from the coughs that afflict them when they live in a polluted city environment.

1.11 Ability to Choose in Fields of Choice: the Differences between Normal Persons' Situations and Underprivileged or Disadvantaged Positions

The judgement of welfare as 'ability to choose' does not consider only the breadth of the fields of choice available to the various individuals. It also includes subjective differences in needs, in relation to the size of the household. Family F, for example, includes only person A, whereas family F' includes persons $B + C$. If the total purchasing power of F = total purchasing power of F', we can argue in general that A is better off than B or C, since the per capita purchasing power of A is double that of B and of C. Further, if the total purchasing power of F' is double that of F, presumably the welfare of B,C is greater than that of A, as their mean per capita purchasing power = that of A, but since they live together they achieve notable dimensional economies.[24] Families with equal purchasing power and equal number of components have different economic welfare in relation to the age of the family members: for example, young people of high school age have greater needs than children of primary school age. Also, the sick have greater needs than those who enjoy good health, and the same holds true for those who live at a considerable distance from their place of work as compared to those who work not far from home. All this is true for normal persons, those whom we have considered in the figure of the average person. But it is also necessary to take into consideration the differences in needs arising from positions h of 'personal disadvantage', such as those who suffer from chronic disease or a disability. In such cases, it should be considered that in order to reach the same level of welfare, in terms of ability to choose, as that enjoyed by normal subjects, those who suffer from a disability need to have greater availability of resources. The question of whether these subjects, on account of their handicap, have a lesser or greater subjective utility, in the sense of their awareness of needs satisfaction, could obviously lead to the paradoxical conclusion that, say, someone affected by paralysis has fewer subjective needs than someone who has good legs and arms, because they cannot go for mountain walks or swim in the open sea.

2. OPTIMAL FUNCTIONING OF THE MARKET ECONOMY SYSTEM

2.1 Conditions of Maximum Welfare for the Market Economy System

The market economy system with a market that tends to be competitive – supported to compensate for its inadequacies and corrected in its imperfections by the public economy according to the cooperative model – is the principal means for achieving maximum individual and collective economic welfare in a democratic free society, and for expanding the sphere of possibilities for non-economic welfare. Maximum welfare can, as a general rule, be achieved:

1. if, given ethical and environmental constraints, the production factors are fully utilized and with optimal combinations in the private and public economy, to obtain the given products on the basis of their marginal productivity (*optimal utilization of productive factors and maximum of efficiency of productive factors*);
2. if, given the optimal combinations and full utilization of the productive factors, the enterprises and the public economy produce the maximum national product on the basis of the relation between costs and demand prices, that is utilize in an optimal manner their production capacity in an optimal manner (*maximum of productive efficiency*);
3. if exchanges between enterprises operating on the domestic market and those on the international market, and between enterprises and consumers, take place with equality between marginal costs and prices (maximum efficiency of exchanges) in such a manner as to maximize the national income and maximize consumer satisfaction, under the given demand;
4. if the national income is allocated among the various private utilizations and between private and public utilizations in the best possible manner, in relation to the demand arising from the members of the community and expressed in presence of adequate information (maximum *allocative* efficiency or maximum effectiveness);
5. if the relation between consumption and savings, between savings and investment, and between innovation and other investments is oriented towards growth of the national product over time from the point of view of a reflexive medium and long-term position (maximum dynamic allocative efficiency).

This does not guarantee a distributive optimum from the point of view of the distributive criteria that the various subjects believe they

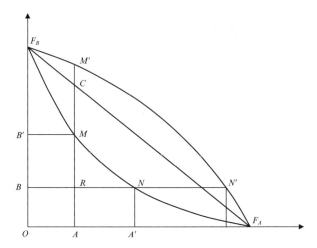

Figure 2.1   The production frontier in a closed economy

have agreed to on the constitutional level. Therefore it will be necessary to introduce corrective public redistribution, on the basis of democratic collective preferences, which will differ according to which majority is in power, within the limits of the constitutional pact of the cooperative model, on the basis of the different criteria of justice and related criteria of social polices (this theme will be addressed in part 3 of this chapter and in part 3 of Chapter 3).

2.2   The Production Frontier

First of all, therefore, it is necessary to identify the conditions of maximum production for the economy. We thus plot the 'production frontier' in Figure 2.1, for the universe of the operators of system S, which has only one production factor, F, and produces two goods, A and B, with the enterprise I and the public operator G. Point F_B on the ordinates indicates the maximum product of B, when the whole of F is destined to maximizing the production of B. Point F_A on the abscissae indicates the maximum product of A when the whole of F is destined to maximizing the product of A. The three lines $F_B M' N' F_A$, $F_B C F_A$ and $F_B M N F_A$ indicate three possible hypotheses of the frontier of production, depending on whether the productions of A and B are, respectively, at rising, constant or decreasing costs. In all three cases, at each point of the frontier there is a possible combination of product A and product B such that the production of A cannot be increased except at the expense of B and vice versa. The three production frontiers are individuated as the set of points of *A* and *B* which have this property.

But in the case of *production at rising costs*, that is with decreasing returns (line $F_B M' N' F_A$) the frontier of production is concave towards the origin of the Cartesian axes because, starting out from the point F_B in which all the resources are devoted to *B* and reducing the resources devoted to its production, product *B* is reduced by less than the increase in product *A*. This continues until an increase in product *A* at the expense of product *B* generates a reduction in product *B* equal to the increase in product *A*. From this point onwards, the transformation curve from *B* to *A*, on the frontier of production, falls fairly sharply downwards towards the right.

The second line, $F_B C F_A$, corresponds to the hypothesis of *production at constant costs*. The frontier of production is now a straight line, whose slope is given by the ratio between the quantity of product of *B* (marked on the ordinates) and of *A* (marked on the abscissae) achieved with one unit of resources, *F*.

The third line, $F_B M N F_A$, convex towards the origin, *corresponds to the hypothesis of production at decreasing costs*, that is at increasing returns, which is the most significant hypothesis in capitalist economies[25] in a dynamic view through time. By taking resources away from production of *B*, which is maximum at point F_B, and shifting them to production of *A*, the loss of product of *B* is greater than the increase in product of *A*, as *B* is in the low-cost phase due to economies of large-scale production, while *A* is still in the high-cost phase as it is produced on a small scale. But as production of *B* is gradually reduced in order to increase that of *A*, the relation between the scale of production of the two goods changes, until a reduction in product *B* generates an equal increase in product *A*. Subsequently the curve slopes downwards more gently towards the bottom right, as it is the production of *A* that benefits from the economies of scale at the expense of production of *B*.

The point *R* inside the frontier of production (of any one of the three considered), which allows production of *OA* and *OB*, is not efficient, *from the point of view of production of A and B*, in the sense that it is always possible to increase production of *B* without reducing that of *A* and vice versa, or even to increase the production of both.

If we consider the frontier $F_B M N F_A$, from *R* it is possible to reach *N* by increasing the production of *A* from *PA* to *OA'*, without reducing production of *B*, which is *OB*. In addition, from *R* it is possible to reach *M* by increasing the production of *B* from *OB* to *OB'*, without reducing production of *A*. Finally, from *R* one can reach a point on the frontier included within the segment *MN* in which there is an increase of product *A* and of product *B*, as compared to *OA* and *OB*.

2.3   The Frontier of Production and Maximum Static and Dynamic Production Efficiency

It should be noted, however, that the frontier of production $F_B F_A$ is not wholly a frontier of maximum efficiency, in contrast to statements that can be read in works by eminent authors. This is because on various points of the frontier the amount of product obtained may turn out to be of lower worth than the resources utilized to produce it. Nothing can assure, a priori, that OF_R is worth more, technologically as well, than the quantity of F destined to it.

For instance, if we measure the product in units of factor F, we might well find that there are points on the frontier of production in which the units of A and B are worth less than those of F utilized to produce them.

> If, for example, A and B are fish, the quantity obtained in the catch may be lower than the quantity of fish that could be obtained at a later date if the resources in the catch had been allowed to continue their growth in water rather than being prematurely caught. Admittedly it can be argued that the catch of three months or a year later is worth less, economically, inasmuch as it is a future good, as compared to the value of fish available at the present time. But if, for example, the maximum interest rate is 5 per cent a year and the catch of three months later contains twice the present amount, it is clear that the decision to lower the nets immediately is not efficient. The same can be said as regards wood obtained by felling trees and more generally with regard to all goods for which the same physical measure of the factors utilized to produce it can be used.

Only a part, albeit a fairly extensive part, of the production frontier is a maximum efficiency zone: the segment included between the two extremes, where the goods produced are technologically worth at least as much as the production factors utilized to produce them.[26] Moreover, the frontier of production cannot be identified unless one takes into account the calculation of maximum individual welfare with regard to the choice between free time and work time, and between free goods, the environment and other values and economic goods. The 'maximum utilization of available production factors' implies maximum utilization of the labour force; however, in an ethically motivated country, child labour and the labour of the sick do not form part of the labour force. The maximum bearable work rhythm and the longest working hours adoptable are the object of individual preferences that are expressed in collective evaluations, placing a constraint on the concept of efficiency. Similar considerations can be put forward for maximum use of natural resources, in relation to the environment and the protected cultural heritage.

It should also be borne in mind that the frontier of production is not a fixed given. If the economy is dynamic in the accumulation of savings and investment, in the formation of human capital, in technological development, in the development of entrepreneurial energy and the search for new markets, then the production frontier tends to shift forwards year by year.

2.4 The Reasons that Determine Whether the Situation is Inside the Production Frontier Instead of on it in the Maximum Efficiency Zone

Apart from the manipulations involving international trade, fundamentally there are four possible reasons for situations inside the production frontier. Some of the national resources may be inactive; the amount of resources used may exceed what is necessary for the production in question; 'too much' may be produced relative to the cost of productive factors; production may be carried out with the wrong type of organizational set-up.

1. Not all the productive resources are utilized.
2. The operators in question utilize an excess of resources compared to the amount usually necessary to produce the given units of product, due to organizational defects, administrative and trade-union constraints, bad management (so-called x inefficiency, which as far as the public bureaucracy is concerned will be addressed in Chapter 5, section 1);
3. The operators in question produce a volume of product which, if measured in terms of productive factors utilized to produce it, are worth less than these factors (this issue was addressed above), because the calculations are wrong or the operators use free goods for which they do not bear the cost or which enjoy public subsidies, or because the costs are (partially) not borne by the operators themselves but by third parties and the latter are unable to pay compensation to the operators in such a manner as to induce them to cease or reduce that particular production. This may happen even though they cause an aggregate burden greater than the benefit they can draw from the operators in question, due to the elevated transaction and information costs (cf. Coase's theorem in subsection 2.8 below);
4. The operators in question make use of a mistaken combination of the various productive factors (this aspect will be addressed in the following subsection) because they make the wrong calculations or because some factor has a heavy fiscal cost that does not weigh on the other factors, or because there is some factor for which the operator in question does not pay all the costs involved (see point 3), or because of organizational inadequacies or rigidity.

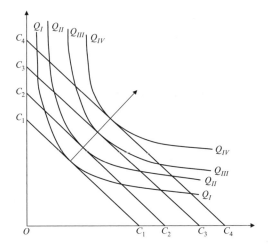

Figure 2.2   Optimal combination between productive factors

2.5   To Achieve Maximum Productive Efficiency, it is Necessary to Ensure the Optimal Combination among Productive Factors: the Tangency between Isocosts and Isoquanta

In order to identify the optimal combination among productive factors, the relations among different productive factor costs must be examined and compared with the relations between the different units of factors required to produce a given unit of product. Let us suppose that we have only two large categories of factors, such as labour and capital, to process a given raw material. If the labour units are increased, under equal units of capital, the amount of product obtained can be increased, using the same amount of raw material. But the same result can be obtained by increasing the units of capital under equal units of labour. Let us now consider the use of increasing units of two production factors F_L and F_K, to obtain product Q with costs $C_1, C_2, C_3, \ldots, C_N$, which increase with increasing Q (Figure 2.2).

The use of two productive factors for each quantity of Q produced will be optimal if it is impossible to increase production of Q by increasing the units of one of the two production factors and decreasing the other, with unchanged overall costs, and it is likewise not possible to produce that unit of Q by means of a different combination of the two productive factors that would allow a reduction in costs. This means that in terms of the product of each of the two productive factors, the marginal cost is equal to the marginal yield, and that the marginal yield of the productive factors, when these are divided by their cost, is equal.

Here we have equality between the marginal yield of the two productive factors in terms of product and the respective marginal cost, or price in a regime of competition, that is

$$F_{Lma} = C_{Lma}$$
$$F_{Kma} = C_{Kma}$$

(2.6)

It is not possible to produce that quantity of product with a lower cost of one or the other of the two productive factors.

Furthermore, in this point there is equality between the marginal yields of the two productive factors, divided by their marginal cost (price), that is

$$F_{Lma} / C_{Lma} = F_{Kma} / C_{Kma}$$

(2.6′)

Competition on the market tends to drive towards optimal productive factor combinations. If there is an excess of labour, which could be reduced by means of a machine performing the same task at a lower cost, an entrepreneur who wants to stay in business will try to adopt this solution. If an increase in use of a specialized labour factor would allow better use of a costly material, with a more sophisticated production process, an entrepreneur who wants to stay in business will try to adopt this solution. Furthermore, Q can be increased in value rather than in physical quantity, by giving a better quality product, if specialized labour is utilized under equal amount of material used. But one can point to a number of reasons that give rise to inefficiency springing from a mistaken combination among production factors:

a. one of the productive factors is underutilized because it is more expensive than its real cost, as it faces disproportionate expenses due to monopoly prices, inequality of taxation, trade union constraints, deficiency in the infrastructure on which the productive factor relies (for example roads and port infrastructures);
b. the cost of one of the productive factors is lower than the real cost because part of the cost is offloaded onto the community or third parties through public subsidies, environmental damage, damage to uncompensated third parties (external diseconomies), and so on;
c. bad organization and mismanagement or constraints and rigidities prevent any improvement in production organization, resulting in an excess of labour over what would be optimal for that quantity of product, or an excess of capital or of raw material, and so on;

d. the organization of the company in question suffers from generalized inefficiency, because it has grown old and wastes capital, materials and labour, as compared to what would be required to produce a unit of the given product under good organization and good management. At times such a company stays in business because it is protected by excise duties and regulations or subsidies that it obtains through its political influence.

2.6 To Achieve Maximum Productive Efficiency it is Vital to have Optimal Allocation of Production Factors among the Different Utilizations and Full Employment

To reach the production frontier, taken as the frontier of maximum efficiency for the system S under consideration, it is not sufficient to ensure optimal combination of productive factors in production of individual units. It is also necessary for the various productive factors to be fully employed and for this to be carried out with equal marginal yield in all productions. If the labour factor F_L is not fully utilized and savings do not fully translate into investment, and the available natural resources are left partially unproductive, then the production frontier is not reached. And if the production factor F_L has a marginal yield greater in product A than in product B in which it is utilized, it is more advantageous to shift it from product B to product A, as this leads to an increase in production, under equal amount of given productive factors utilized: that is to say, this leads to greater efficiency and a shift towards the frontier of production. But such an aim also requires efficiency in trading, which may be impeded by the existence of monopolies, by inadequate transport infrastructures and by uncertainty concerning contracts due to inadequate functioning of the institutions in the legal system (cf. the graphic representation with the Edgeworth-Bowley box of Figure A.2 in the Appendix). Perhaps the latter aspect is the main factor causing inadequate production factor allocation, unemployment and failure to re-employ savings in investments (preferring, when property rights are uncertain and contracts are not respected, to hoard savings in the form of precious metals, jewels and safe foreign investments).

2.7 Optimal Utilization of the Complex of Resources among the Different Products: The Problem of External Economies

It might seem that once production efficiency has been identified, on the basis of the conditions outlined in the previous subsection, the problems of efficiency will have been solved.

But this is not the case. What is necessary is for the frontier, in its maximum efficiency zone, to be correctly plotted, *from the point of view of the production operators*. In other words, the frontier should at all points record the entire product obtained with the factors under consideration, net of the costs required to produce them. But this does not always occur, because technological external economies are generated.[27]

Technological external economies consist in material or immaterial economic resources that go directly to members of the community, without the possibility of being sold at a price by the subjects that produce them (the enterprises, for the external economies of production, and private individuals for the external economies of consumption). In this chapter we will limit discussion to considering them from the point of view of the allocative inefficiency their presence may give rise to. Let us consider an economy with only two products, *A* and *B*, obtained with a homogeneous production factor, *F*. *A* is the class of products that have external economies, *B* represents all the other products. Therefore, for production of *B*, the enterprises will obtain all the return they produce, while for production of *A*, this will not be the case. It will thus be more advantageous for enterprises to produce less of *A* than would be correct if we also considered the external economies, and the resources not utilized in *A* will go into *B*. Consequently, there will be an allocative distortion at the expense of *A* and in favour of *B*.

In Figure 2.3 we indicate production *Q* of *B* on the ordinates and production *Q* of *A* on the abscissae. In the presence of external economies that reduce the advantageousness of *A*, the transformation line between *A* and *B* is given by *TT'*. The equilibrium point *E*, at which the transformation curve *TT'* is tangent to the highest indifference curve *II*, indicates the production of the two goods, which is, in this case, respectively OQ_B and OQ_A. But if the return obtained by *A* is taken to include the external economies of its production, then the transformation line between the productions of *A* and *B* changes and shifts rightwards, to *T''*, since production of *A* is now greater. Consequently a new equilibrium is reached, indicated here by *E'*, given by the tangency of *TT'* to a higher indifference curve, in this case *I'I'*. This implies a situation where production of *A* is $OQ'_A > OQ_A$, and a production of *B* that is $OQ'_B < OQ_B$.

To obtain this result, the public operator may grant enterprises that produce *A* a subsidy or tax relief of an equivalent amount, or offer favourable credit terms or benefits in kind, such as imposing no charge for use of public land equipped for productive activities, and so on. Assuming that the subsidy or similar does indeed match the value of the external economies produced, then the allocative optimum will be reached, in theory at least, although in practice interventions for external economies, as we

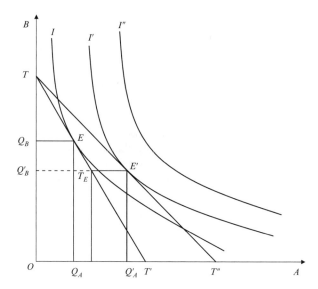

*Figure 2.3	Allocative inefficiency due to external economies and diseconomies*

will see in Chapter 3, sections 1 and 2, should be carried out with greater caution.[28]

## 2.8	Optimal Utilization of the Complex of Resources among the Different Products: The Problem of External Economies and Diseconomies

We can now consider the opposite case, using the same analytical technique. This concerns the case where part of the production cost of A does not enter into the budget of the enterprises which produce the good, but is instead borne by third parties. This phenomenon is known as 'external diseconomy'. When external diseconomies regarding A are present, the transformation curve can be represented (see Figure 2.3 above) by TT'', with the equilibrium point E' in which A supplies OQ'_A and B supplies OQ'_B. By offloading onto A the cost of external diseconomies, the transformation curve becomes TT' and the equilibrium point becomes E; the quantity of A decreases from OQ'_A to OQ_A and that of B increases from OQ'_B to OQ_B. When there are external diseconomies of production of A, the market product is greater, for the enterprises that produce it, than the benefit for the community, and this cost should thus be subtracted from the benefit. But usually the cost is not borne by the buyers of A, but rather by other subjects, with the result that the buyers will have a benefit that corresponds to the return obtained by the producers of *A*, but someone in the community will have a cost without any benefit.

Ronald Coase[29] showed that in a world where transaction costs do not exist, property rights are perfectly defined, the income effects are irrelevant, and the only method for removing external diseconomies that cause damage to the affected parties, *C* consists of subsidies to the damagers, *A*, inducing them to cease or reduce the production of *Q* that generates the diseconomies; the only remaining external diseconomies produced by *A* and damaging *C* are those resulting from a smaller production of *Q*, for which the *C* does not find it advantageous to pay *A* as a means of inducing *A* to cease production of such diseconomies. Obviously this result holds if *A* has a right to produce these diseconomies that affect *C*. The results will be identical if *C* has the right not to be damaged by the external effects of *A*'s action. In fact *A* will cease to pay *C* for the damages inflicted to her when the cost of compensation to *C* added to the cost of producing *B* exceeds the revenue derived from selling *Q*. Let us suppose that an enterprise *A*, for instance the proprietor of an intercontinental airport, causes night-time noise pollution, *K*, which adversely affects the surrounding buildings of *C*s. The airport obtains gain *G* from the airport, while those adversely affected suffer from damage, *D*. Let us assume that *G* is greater than *D* and that the *C*s have the right not to be disturbed by the unpleasant night-time external diseconomies, *K*. Since *G* is greater than *D*, it will be advantageous for *A* to compensate *C*, so that the night flights can continue. Thus the night flights will take place and the noise pollution, *K*, of the buildings of *C*s will persist. But the flights will cost more and there will be fewer passengers. Now let us suppose that *A* has the right to inflict night-time noise pollution on the buildings of *C*s. Since *G* is greater than *D*, the *C*s are unable to pay *A* in order to get the noise pollution *K* stopped, and the night flights will take place in exactly the same way as in the previous case. But there will be no increase in the cost of flights and there will be a greater number of passengers compared to when *A* is responsible for causing the damage to *C*s. Let us now suppose that *D* is greater than *G*. Assuming that *A* does not have the right to pollute with *K*, *A* will now be unable to compensate *C*s in order to continue night-time use of the airport that causes the emissions, *K*. Thus the night-time flights will not take place. Now suppose, instead, that *A* can legally emit *K*. Since *D* is greater than *G*, it will be advantageous to the *C*s to pay *A* for not emitting *K*; in this case, the night flights will again not take place.

But all this presupposes that the only way to eliminate (or reduce) the noise pollution is to eliminate (or reduce) the activities that produce it. But if we suppose that investments can be made to eliminate the damage of pollution, then the effects in the two cases of A's responsibility for pollution or A's legal right to pollute are different. Suppose that special double glazing on the buildings of Cs can eliminate the damage. If A is responsible for the damage to Cs, due to the night flights in question, and assuming that the damage resulting from cessation of the flights is greater than the cost of investing in double glazing in the buildings of Cs, then it will be advantageous for A to make this investment and continue with the flights, but A will thus have an increase in marginal costs that will have to be transferred in the form of higher prices for the flights in question. But when the price of tickets goes up, passenger demand will decrease. If, on the other hand, the Cs do not have the right to be free from pollution, they will not find it advantageous to compensate A for stopping the flights. But they can still invest in double glazing to avoid the damage of noise pollution. In both cases the price of A's night-time flight tickets will not go up and passenger numbers will not shrink. At first sight the result is identical to that which comes about when A is responsible for the damage. But if A is not legally responsible for the pollution damage, the Cs will have two options: either to compensate A so that A stops the flights, or install double glazing. Also, if, as is likely, installing double glazing is less costly, the Cs will decide to install double glazing at their own expense, and some of the night-time flights will continue. Thus, except in the case of the restrictive hypothesis that there is no way of eliminating (or reducing) the external diseconomies generated by A and adversely affecting C, the conclusions that must be drawn are not the symmetrical ones derivable from Figure 2.4.

When, as very often happens, transaction costs are high because the rights are not clearly defined and because it is difficult, from a technical point of view, to identify who generated the diseconomies and who is adversely affected, and it is also difficult to evaluate them, then there will be no heated questioning between the parties and no agreement between A and C in the search for a solution to the problem. The public institutions may try to correct the suboptimal situation with measures aiming to reduce or eliminate the damage affecting those who generate the external diseconomies or measures in favour of those who are adversely affected.

2.9 Allocative Efficiency in Trading on the Market: Ricardo's Theorem on Comparative Costs and Marshall's Theorem on Decreasing Cost Industries

In the market economy, as well as production and its exchanges that we have already considered in relation to productive factors, there are also trading exchanges among the products of enterprises within the domestic economy and with the other economies, and also trade between enterprises

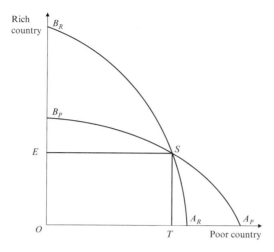

Figure 2.4   Expansion of the frontier of production with international trade

and the final purchasers of goods and services, who utilize them for their own consumption and investments. The issues to be addressed are similar. Here too, allocative inefficiency on the domestic market can depend on three groups of factors:

a.   monopolies and legal obstacles to trade;
b.   lack of transport and communication infrastructures;
c.   weakness of the institutions forming part of the legal system with regard to protection of contracts.

But the important aspects to consider at this point are those pertaining to international trade that involve a drastic change in the frontier of production.

The production frontier expands with international trade (see Figure 2.4), since trade makes it possible to obtain goods that other countries, or the other market areas, produce at lower relative costs, in exchange for goods that we produce at higher relative costs. The phrase 'relative costs' refers to the relation between the costs of the goods in question in the area where they are produced; it does not refer to the relation between costs in the two market areas considered with regard to that particular good. The advantageousness of the trading exchange exists if the relative costs in the two areas are different: this is the so-called theorem of comparative costs developed by David Ricardo.[30] If, as determined by free competition on the market, 10 units of cost are required in the market area R (a rich country), in the best case, in order to produce good B, and 5 units to produce good A, with a trading ratio of $2A=1B$, whereas in the market area P (a poor country) it takes, in the best case, 24 units of cost to produce good B and 6 to produce good A, with a trading relation $4A=1B$, then it will be advantageous for R and P to engage in the trading exchange, since the shape of their frontier of production is different. P, by selling to R, initially can obtain $2B$ in exchange for 1 if R renounces any benefit from the bilateral trade in good A; and R, by selling to P, could obtain $4A$ initially in exchange for B if P renounces any benefit from this trading. It is likely that they will go on trading up to the point in which they have the same ratio of exchange as at point S or will stop at an intermediate level, depending on their contractual power. Additionally, in the case of P the frontier will be more rigid in the transformation of A into B than in the case of R. This will be true even if R has a frontier which, both for B and for A, exceeds that of P. In effect, when P trades slightly more than 2 units of A, it obtains from R slightly less than 1 unit of B. R gains a margin by selling B to P, and P gains a margin by selling A to R. If the production costs of A and B are decreasing, this margin could also be achieved with a quasi even exchange in the amount of $4A$ for $3.5B$, as the unit costs of A and B have decreased.

It was shown by A. Marshall that each market area can, by means of the specialization of its industries, produce at decreasing costs. And the more the area of market expands, the greater the decrease in costs.[31] Consequently, international trade is notably more advantageous than is suggested by a static conception of Ricardo's theorem.

Figure 2.4 represents the expansion of the frontier of production of country R, a 'rich country' and of country P, a 'poor' country, achieved through international trade. The first frontier is given by $B_R A_R$ and the second by $B_P A_P$. But it should be kept in mind that the value scales of the two frontiers may differ, because we are dealing here with comparative costs. The two frontiers intersect in such a manner that the frontier of the rich country, for its own area, is internal to that of the poor country in the area $OESA_R$, while that of the poor country is internal to the frontier of the rich country for the area OB_PST. The frontier of R, the rich country, is expanded by the portion $SA_R A_P$, while that of P, the poor country, is expanded by the portion $B_R SB_P$.

But it need not necessarily be the case that trading exchanges between R and P take place in a framework of equality. R is powerful and could impose a trading monopoly on P for its hi-tech goods, which P intensely desires, whereas P sells goods A at rock bottom prices since P desperately needs currency to buy B, which it badly needs. Customs barriers may distort trade between *R* and *P* by means of import or export duties or export subsidies, depending on whether the aim is to increase or reduce the price of exported goods, in order to more successfully exploit the other party's market.

2.10 Allocative Effectiveness on the Market and between the Market and the Public Economy, and Optimal 'Consumers' Choices'

Efficiency concerns the possibility, for the subjects of the economy under consideration, to reach the frontier of production, in the maximum efficiency zone. But this does not yet imply optimality. To obtain optimality it is necessary to identify the most advantageous utilization of the product from the point of view of the preferences of the subjects considered. How this can be achieved is shown in Figure 2.5.

In this figure we consider the transformation curve between two goods, *A* and *B*, and the family of indifference curves deriving from the demand for the two goods that is expressed in the given society. Under the hypothesis that this family of indifference curves is the 'correct' one (we use a deliberately imprecise term, the meaning of which will be clarified further on, particularly in Chapter 3, subsection 2.2 ff.), the optimum equilibrium will be given by meeting point *E* between the transformation curve between *A* and *B* and the indifference curve I_R tangent to the curve. Thus the utilizations of the two goods are OA_E and OB_E. But it cannot be ruled out that a 'wrong' indifference curve may prevail, such as I_G with

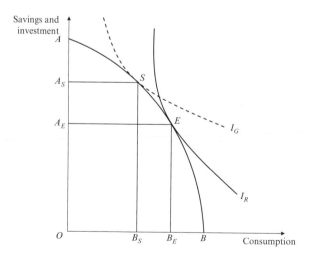

Figure 2.5   Optimal allocative effectiveness

equilibrium in S, in which the utilizations are, respectively, OB_S and OA_S with $OB_S < OB_E$ and $OA_S > OA_E$.

It should also be noted that even on the assumption that there is no 'incorrect' interference by the public economy, if the market is left to its own devices it rarely succeeds in expressing the correct indifference curve when A and B are considered, respectively, as present goods and savings in the form of an entity that represents future goods. This is because present citizens tend to be 'short-sighted' with regard to the future, whenever the issue concerns future citizens. Moreover, they are often 'short-sighted' with regard to their own future as well. So it may well happen that what prevails in the economy is a situation such as S, where there is an excess of consumption (hypothetically represented by A) and an insufficiency of savings (hypothetically represented by B). Additionally, the public economy may distort preferences between present and future goods by means of a public debt which has no correspondence in investment goods that offer an advantage for the future. Therefore, although it is difficult to establish exactly what constitutes the present citizens' 'duty' to accumulate savings for future citizens, it can be stated that generally the equilibrium arising between present goods and savings is incorrect, as compared to the optimum, and it disfavours savings. This provides a good argument in support of a public policy in favour of savings (see also Chapter 3, section 3.7).

There are also other goods which, on account of phenomena of imperfect rationality, find themselves in an unfavourable position in the allocation that takes shape in the economy, and this may justify corrective action by the public economy. A more detailed treatment of this question will be given in Chapter 3, section 2.4 ff. with regard to want and merit goods.

But above all, Figure 2.5 is important for a representation of the theme of optimality (assuming this can ever be reached) in the relation between the market economy and the public economy. We can indicate public goods as A and market goods as B.

As we have seen, the question of satisfying public wants, when individual welfare is pursued rationally in a democracy with a market economy regime, is subject to a general law of maximization of satisfaction, as is the case for other wants. This process involves citizens as private individuals and as enterprises.[32] We pointed out earlier that citizens do not perform this directly, but instead indirectly, through their political representatives. The *optimum general equilibrium* with regard to wants manifested on the market, and the wants and public goods that emerge in the democratic processes of the public economy in question, can be analysed by means of a diagram like that shown in Figure 2.5, for allocation on the market, which can serve to represent the allocation between market goods and public economy goods. In this manner, the model for an individual's optimum choice of public goods, with utility and cost curves, which was shown in Figure 1.1, becomes part of general economic equilibrium, with the cautions pointed out in Chapter 1, section 3 and those to be pointed out in Chapters 5 and 6. But even this passage is still a first approximation, since, as will be seen in the treatment given in the next chapter, there are various different types of wants and public good, and consequently, the democratic choices involved tend to be diversified, in the different models, in relation to their different indivisibility or divisibility. This will be examined in closer detail in Chapter 4, devoted to equilibrium and imbalances in the demand and provision of public goods.

Point E indicates the quantities of B and A which, depending on the average citizen J's preferences, are going to be produced and consumed, respectively, in the community under consideration. As far as consumption of A is concerned, this must coincide with consumption of G indicated in Figure 1.1.

> And in effect the cost curve OC of G in terms of giving up increasing amounts of B_M, in Figure 1.1, is none other than the transformation curve between goods B and goods A, shown in Figure 2.3, expressed in terms of subjective utility. Furthermore, the map of the indifference curves of Figure 2.3 expresses the equivalence of the various amounts of marginal utility of A, with varying amounts of good B and therefore it corresponds to the marginal utility curve of G indicated in Figure 1.1.

The equilibrium between public goods A and private goods B, in the cooperative model, and assuming the preferences of the average representative subject – whether a private individual or an enterprise – is therefore given by the following formula:

$$\frac{\text{marginal utility of } A}{\text{marginal cost in terms of } B} = \frac{\text{marginal utility of } B}{\text{marginal cost in terms of } A} \tag{2.7}$$

From (2.7) we move to the following formula (2.8) in which we replace the units of B with money, although it should be borne in mind that this is a partial formula as it does not include the non-monetary component that was summarized earlier in the notion of free goods and values. But (2.8) is useful because it concerns the optimal partitioning between the public economy and the market, in relation to the national product, the latter being measured in money.

$$\frac{\text{marginal utility of } A}{\text{public revenue (fiscal prices)}} = \frac{\text{marginal utility of } B}{\text{price for dose in question}} \tag{2.8}$$

In other words, the average citizen J's budget is in equilibrium if:

$$\frac{\text{marginal quantity of public goods}}{\text{fiscal prices}} = \frac{\text{marginal quantity of private goods}}{\text{market prices}} \qquad (2.8')$$

An excess of public goods may be due, fundamentally, to

a. the fact that the bureaucracy produces more public goods than citizens would like to have, or with a greater cost as compared to the (maximum) efficiency cost, and the bureaucracy then obliges citizens to pay for such goods (see also Chapter 5);
b. the fact that the majority lays the burden of the cost of public goods on the minority, but does not pay for them;
c. the fact that the pressure exerted by interest groups induces the political representatives to vote in favour of expenses that are not genuinely desired either by the majority or by the minority.

The fact that voting takes place with the majority voting system may lead to an amplification of expenses, going beyond what would be prompted if one were to compare the sum of their marginal utilities with their marginal cost. This may occur because the representatives of the majority can concentrate expenditure in favour of their own proposals while offloading the costs onto the minority.[33]

But the majority may not so much wish to amplify expenditure, as to reduce the tax burden that it would otherwise have to shoulder for the provision of public goods. The majority may seek to achieve this aim by maintaining or reducing consumption of public goods.

The solution depends on what type of majority currently prevails and what type of government it adopts. Often governments engage in fiscal illusion practices partly in order to deceive not only the minority that has lost the elections, but also their own electors, in favour of interest groups who exert a powerful influence over the majority and partly also to promote their own interests and those of the public bureaucracy.

The abstract framework that will be presented in the next chapter focusing on the equilibrium of the public economy in the cooperative model indicates the economic tendencies that express equilibrium from the point of view of efficiency and allocative optimality. If such tendencies genuinely come into being, they give rise to public economy situations corresponding to the preferences of citizens and enterprises. And these are tendencies which, presumably, would be favourable to development of the economy. But in addition to efficiency problems, there are also problems of equity, which will be addressed in section 3, including a comparison between the cooperative model and alternative models, relevant in a democracy oriented to the market economy.

3. MAXIMUM COLLECTIVE WELFARE ON AN INDIVIDUAL BASIS

3.1 The Welfare of those who are not Represented: the Future Generations and Nature

If we consider only the preferences of present voting citizens, this does not necessarily provide assurance of safeguards for the subjects of future generations and for nature, that is for categories that do not have a vote.

The younger generations are systematically under-represented, especially if elections are not held every year. The parliament of the various years following the elections will not represent those who have come of age in the intervening period but were not eligible to vote when the last election was held.

If elections are held every five years, a class of young electors loses four years of the right to be represented, another three years, another two and another one.

Moreover, there is no guarantee that the current electors will want to shoulder the responsibility for protecting nature, given that this involves a sacrifice of some of one's own utilities in favour of future generations and of values that the current electors are often insensitive to, even if they concern an entity which – ethically – should be fully entitled to respect (Forte, 1991).

Clearly, then, there should be a place, at least an ideal place, where the rules of the game can be formulated for pursuit of maximum collective welfare, on an individual basis, in a democracy in which every generation is represented and in which shared values of the highest order come to the fore.

3.2 The 'Original' Contractarian Constitutional Position, as a Source of Rational and Unbiased Calculations of Welfare

It is generally asserted that those who are entrusted with drawing up a constitution for a set of generations of subjects whom they ideally represent, setting aside any reference to their own particular case, are led to make impartial choices when establishing the rules of the game, in such a manner that their choices are characterized by efficiency and will be perfectly fair in bringing advantage equitably to the various future players in the social games (Buchanan and Tullock, 1962 [1999]).

At a more abstract, philosophical level, this 'impartial' position can be idealized as a *mental experiment, which an individual, hypothetically called upon to chart the great choices for society, performs under the veil of the most complete ignorance concerning her own position* and thus concerning that of her loved ones (Rawls, 1982). There remains the problem of what values the individual performing the experiment should hold: her own or those prevailing in the society on behalf of which the mental experiment is being conducted? But some values cannot fail to be accepted by all members of society, once the democratic model of an advanced civilized society has been embraced.

However, the two points of view outlined above can be unified by viewing the economic and political constitution as composed of two parts: one that is extremely general, valid for any democratic model, and the other, more specific, which regulates a given society, in a given era.

Among the principles valid for every constitution oriented towards the cooperative democratic model, there emerges the principle – derived from the postulate of equality among all citizens inasmuch as all the citizens are contracting parties within the social pact – which holds that each individual, *including future citizens who are currently unrepresented*, has the right to pursue her own welfare, but in full compliance with the concept that each individual, together with all other individuals, has undertaken a commitment to respect this same set of rights with regard to all other individuals. The other basic principle of all constitutions associated with the cooperative model is that each player involved in trading exchanges and in the public economy accepts shared rules of the game of a given (fair) relation between costs and advantages, with the one and only exception in favour of those who find themselves in a severely disadvantaged situation within society and thus have the right to special solidarity (see subsection 3.9, ff).

3.3 The Right to Pursue One's Own Welfare W_j^*, and Pareto's Criterion for Maximum Collective Welfare

Thus in a free democratic society every individual has the right to pursue her own welfare, in a relation of private and public exchange based on shared rules of the game concerning the relation between costs and returns, within the framework of the constraints imposed by ethical and environmental values, respect for the future generations and commitment towards those who are in a less favoured position. Therefore, from the point of view of the intervention of the public operator, it is possible to uphold

Pareto's criterion, according to which the welfare of society is considered
to have increased every time someone's welfare has increased without any
reduction in the welfare of others. To be sure, a reduction in the welfare
of subjects *J*, accompanied by an increase in that of subjects *I*, may indeed
take place within the above-stated rules of the game, either by free choice
or as a result of action by the public operator. The private actions on the
market and public actions, however, are phenomena with profoundly different implications from the point of view of Pareto's criterion, as a rule
for *maximum collective welfare*. Actions freely performed on the market
by the various subjects that increase certain subjects' welfare and reduce
that of others do not imply any violation of the above criterion, in that
they form part of the free market game, carried out spontaneously (if by
my own decision I make a bad financial investment, if I gamble on horses
and lose, for instance, I pay the consequences, while others benefit from
my loss; conversely, by a reduction in the price of my goods made possible
by my costs I may increase my own sales while those of some of my competitors decrease). But the same does not hold for the actions of the public
operator or of other subjects who, endowed with power outside the framework of the free market game, increase the welfare of certain subjects at
the expense of that of others. These are violations of Pareto's criterion.

In order to clarify the different aspects of this criterion, which is simple
in appearance, we construct the diagram in Figure 2.6 in which the transformation curve $\bar{P}_B\bar{P}_A$ indicates, in reference to a community composed of
two persons only (representative of two large social groups), the Pareto
frontier, that is the maximum welfare of (the group represented by) subject

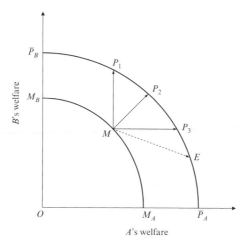

Figure 2.6   The Hicks–Kaldor criterion

B and of (the group represented by) subject A. At the (hypothetical) point $\bar{P}_B$ every resource and all rights go to B, who thus enjoys maximum welfare. At the (hypothetical) point $\bar{P}_A$ every resource and all rights go to A, who thus enjoys maximum welfare. The curve joining the two points $\bar{P}_B$ and $\bar{P}_A$, which we denominate the Pareto frontier, indicates all the possible situations of maximum welfare of A and B: as A's welfare gradually increases with the downward movement towards the right, B's welfare decreases because, by definition, on the frontier it is impossible to increase A's welfare unless it be at the expense of B, and vice versa. The Pareto frontier is (usually) represented by a curve that is concave towards the origin of the Cartesian axes, because the presumption is that the subjective law of decreasing marginal utility holds for each of the two (groups of) subjects. Thus in the transition from the maximum for B, the increase in goods provided to A, which reduces the provision for B, generates for A an increase in welfare, which is greater up to an intermediate point in which the decrease in B's welfare leads to a loss of welfare for her that is equal to A's increase in welfare. Subsequently, when moving further down towards the right, the Pareto frontier becomes steep because B's decrease in welfare results in a smaller increase in welfare for A.

We now consider a point M, situated inside the Pareto frontier $\bar{P}_B\bar{P}_A$, on the curve $M_B M_A$. Point M, and more generally any point of $M_B M_A$, is not in a Pareto-optimal position because it is possible to move from that point to other points, such as P_1, which can allow an increase in B's welfare while leaving that of A unchanged, or such as P_3, which can allow an increase in A's welfare while leaving that of B unchanged, or such as P_2, which can allow an increase in the welfare both of A and of B.

Therefore there are two versions of this criterion:

a. collective welfare increases if, by moving from a given position to another, some subject achieves an increase in welfare while the other subjects suffer no loss (weak Pareto criterion): the moves proceed at least along MP_1 or MP_3;
b. collective welfare increases if, by moving from a given position to another, all those who are involved obtain an advantage (strong Pareto criterion): the moves proceed inside $MP_1 \, MP_3$.

The State, which seeks to improve citizens' *general* welfare through the public economy, will have to operate by means of criterion b) which has better chances of obtaining general approval by A and B (therefore we have defined it as 'strong') and, in its absence, according to criterion a). This means it will have to attempt to remove the inefficiencies and distortions affecting *resource allocation* and will have to minimize its own distortions. It will have to endeavour to produce the public goods and cover their costs in whatever manner is instrumentally most efficient (that is at the lowest costs for any given results) and most effective[34] (that is satisfying the given wants through the best result that can be obtained with the given means, utilized in the most efficient manner).

3.4 The Compensation Criterion: the Theory of Hicks and Kaldor

However, in considering Pareto's criterion with regard to the public economy, a substantial difficulty emerges, highlighted as early as in the work of the British economists Hicks (1939) and Kaldor (1939 [1960]) and later refined by De Scitovsky (1941).[35] There may be situations in which a certain public choice would theoretically be capable of achieving an improvement for some elements of the population while also allowing the possibility of compensating others for the damage suffered. Let us suppose, in Figure 2.6, that subject A, who by hypothesis is in M, succeeds in moving to point E, on the Pareto frontier. Subject B suffers a loss of welfare in comparison to point 3, since E is lower than M, and B's welfare is measured in height, on the axis of the ordinates. But A, in the horizontal rightward movement, which measures A's welfare on the abscissae, obtains an increase in welfare to an extent which, theoretically, could compensate B, by moving to P_3, and A would still be left with a substantial net benefit, equal to MP_3. In fact, the increase could even overcompensate B, by moving toward P_2, in such a manner as to give B an advantage, while A would still retain a good net benefit. According to Hicks and Kaldor, even positions such as E should be pursued by the government, because although they do allow A an advantage, theoretically they would make it possible for the Government to compensate or overcompensate B, the subject placed at a disadvantage. And this holds true even if the compensation is not genuinely provided. This is accounted for by noting that A's benefit exceeds B's loss and therefore, 'collectively', in principle an advantage emerges. But this formulation, which involves algebraically summing A and B's welfare, is a re-edition of the principle of maximum global welfare as the algebraic sum (discussed in subsection 1.1), and it violates Pareto's principle, which forbids this algebraic sum. The violation of this principle is not without consequences: it may lead to non-cooperative behaviour by those who are not compensated and may also induce their political representatives to vote against the policy measure, and this would make it difficult to obtain democratic and operative consent to the measures in question.[36]

We have countless examples of this phenomenon. Take for instance the decision to set up a power station, or to drill a railway tunnel in a given area, which will inflict environmental damage on the local inhabitants. The community, which draws a notable net advantage from the works, should ensure that adequate compensation is provided for this damage, thereby also enabling the populations of the area where the work is undertaken to obtain a net advantage.

3.5   The Hypotheses of Validity of the Hicks–Kaldor Criterion

Therefore, if the compensation is not paid, the result may be contradictory. Furthermore, since everyone has the right to pursue their own interest, as long as the precept of social solidarity is honoured, when its cause is just, the principle of 'hypothetical' compensation decided by a majority resolution is, per se, unacceptable as a general constitutional rule.

But there are a number of important exceptions:

a.   First, the question of a valid title. The damage may concern the loss of a form of welfare to which *B* could make no valid claim, such as that deriving from a 'privilege' *B* had managed to obtain from the community, for example a customs duty or a waiver, which violates the criterion of horizontal equity[37] or a job obtained through political string-pulling, and so forth: nobody can ethically claim compensation for the loss of what the subject 'has no right' to have.

b.   The second aspect concerns the principle of reciprocity. There are general rules of the game which in certain cases involve a burden for some subjects *B*, but on the other hand grant subjects *A* or society taken as the sum of all individuals a greater advantage, which everyone accepts because anyone could find themselves in the condition of *B*, but also in that of *A*. Numerous obligations to do and tolerate things, and many prohibitions, rest on this principle. One need only think of the rule on helping to rescue someone who has had an accident: this involves a burden for the rescuer but saves the physical integrity and the life of the accident victim. Or consider the rule establishing that a person cannot refuse to testify as a witness in a trial: while this may inconvenience the witness, it is based on the principle that anyone might find themselves needing evidence in court from someone who has information about the case that is being tried. Road signs specifying no overtaking or no right or left turn, or speed limits, stop signs, result in a burden for drivers who have to slow down, or stop, but they provide an advantage for traffic in general; therefore everyone has to wait their turn.

The same holds if it can be foreseen that the immediate damage is likely to be compensated by future benefits deriving from other forthcoming government actions through which *B* rather than *A* will gain an advantage: in the public economy, choices must be viewed globally because the public economy is a continuous global process.

c. In the third place, consider the principle *de minimis non curat praetor*. Here the damage, technically, cannot be compensated, without excessive transaction costs and it is only minimal if assessed in reference to the subjective loss of utility as compared to the vast amount of benefit. Each individual is obliged, by virtue of the social contract, to bear small sacrifices if these grant society as a whole an enormous advantage.

But although these cases are extremely important, there are other no less important cases in which the failure to pay compensation generates not only iniquity but also pronounced operational hindrances to economic efficiency.

We have already seen that if compensation is not paid, many large infrastructures of great collective importance encounter a serious obstacle, as the local populations who suffer the damage reject the presence of the infrastructures in question.[38] Similarly, macroeconomic policies can also be thwarted by failure to pay compensation. Take the case of inflation: in order to combat inflation, the state may decide to adopt a 'deflationary' policy, by means of the public economy. According to the Hicks–Kaldor model, the state could adopt a brutal deflationary policy by making large numbers of workers redundant and leaving them penniless without (adequate) indemnification. The line of reasoning we put forward above implies that this is unacceptable. Either a solution has to be found in order to offer workers who have lost their job something in return, such as unemployment benefits compensating for the job loss, or other tangible benefits, albeit perhaps not immediately, or else the deflationary policy should not be introduced. Often, the way out consists in a gradual, non-traumatic treatment that doles out burdens and benefits.

3.6 From the Paretian and Hicks–Kaldor Approach to a Procedure in Terms of Game Theory: Nash Equilibrium

Even when the rule of paying compensation is adopted, a question still remains: what should the amount of the compensation be? Is it reasonable to suppose that if A obtains a large benefit from an action that damages B, the latter will content to be indemnified so that B can be authorized to perform that action? More generally, in the activities of the public economy that grant advantages to a number of subjects, how should the advantages be shared out? The answer can be given in terms of positive and, at the same time, normative economics, with analytical frameworks derived from game theory concerning bargaining equilibrium among the various parties, as a reasonable manner of sharing out the advantages and

Principles of public economics

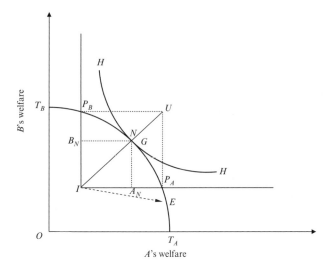

Figure 2.7   Nash and OSFOB equilibria for the apportionment of Paretian improvements

disadvantages that come to the fore in the constitutional context, where unanimity (or quasi-unanimity) voting procedures generally prevail.

In Figure 2.7, which partially reproduces Figure 2.6, we can endeavour to identify a certain point on the welfare frontier between A and B in the segment $P_A P_B$, corresponding to the 'Paretian' improvements from I, namely a point between them that gives rise to a game equilibrium like that of Nash (1950). This implies that the shares of utility the two players forsake at the equilibrium point through their reciprocal concessions are equivalent to one another, so that neither of the two players can stake a claim to have a greater concession from the other one. Following Nash's rule, which will be explained below in further detail, each player threatens not to vote for the common action (rule) under consideration unless she obtains a satisfactory benefit: the threat is likely to be credible, presumably, until the point where her sacrifice at the margin is, proportionately to her benefit, greater than the sacrifice made by the other party. When the opposite case holds, it will be the other party who can issue a credible threat of not subscribing to the common action (rule). It is obvious that for mathematical reasons, if this equivalence of the value of the concessions comes about, one also has the maximum product possible among the various combinations of utility of A and B that can be achieved, as a result of the movement from I to the frontier of welfare in the segment of Paretian improvements $P_A P_B$. Consequently the maximum benefit for B

shall be given by IB_N and the maximum benefit for A shall be given by IA_N which give origin to rectangle $I\,B_N\,N\,IA_N$, the maximum rectangle between I and the frontier on the segment $P_A P_B$, which indicates the maximum product among the residual utilities of A and B. It should be noted that if the point on the frontier really possible had been E, which reduced B's welfare, then what interests us, in relation to determination of the amount of compensation that will have to be paid to B at the expense of A, adopting the Nash equilibrium, is the N point in the segment of Paretian improvements.

In geometric terms, the Nash equilibrium point N, which corresponds to the maximum product of the two variables constituted by the gain in welfare that has to be given to A and B in the area of Paretian improvements from I to $P_A P_B$, is obtained with the tangency to $P_A P_B$ of the maximum equilateral hyperbola inscribable on the Cartesian axes with origin I. This is so because we know that in each of its points the equilateral hyperbola has a constant product. It can be seen that in our case the Nash equilibrium gives A a benefit A_N that is greater than the benefit B_N which B manages to obtain, and this is due to the fact that A's maximum utility from the movement in question is greater.

An alternative apportioning criterion (the result of which in Figure 2.2 is identifiable with that of Nash, due to the peculiar shape of the Pareto frontier) is the contractarian criterion of the constraints of the Minimax of relative concession, or MMCR, which involves reciprocal proportional sacrifice,[39] denominated here as OSFOB,[40] that is 'one step forward, one step backward'. This indicates the dynamics of reciprocal concessions by which the game proceeds. In sharing out the reward or the benefit and/ or the cost and/or the sacrifice that makes the common action possible, *according to this principle*, each of the subjects grants concessions to the other according to her own maximum. The *contractarian* criterion OSFOB thus suggests a division proportional to the maximum advantage each player could obtain by excluding any advantage for the other, net of the costs in obtaining it.

In the hypothesis shown in Figure 2.7, subject A and subject B must share between them a common reward consisting in the segment $P_A P_B$ on the Pareto frontier which, for example, derives from forming a packet of two groups of liberalizations that are of interest, respectively A and B. Each group of liberalizations can be carried out fairly broadly, but it is not politically possible to have all the liberalizations of both groups approved by parliament (or the regional or municipal assembly). Thus there has to be a choice between the advantages of A and those of B. The starting point of A and B, in Figure 2.7, is equal, since it is at point I within the Pareto frontier. The maxima of A and B are at the two extremities of the segment

P_A P_B on the Pareto frontier. And, for the reasons given above, they are incompatible with each other. To reach a convergence on an arrival point, A and B will make concessions to each other with regard to the two groups of liberalizations that interest them. B shifts from point P_B towards point P_A, assuming that P_A will take a proportional step towards P_B. Once this has come about, P_B takes another step towards P_A, which will be followed by a proportional step of P_A towards P_B. And so it will continue until they converge at point G, which involves a sharing out of the global reward and individual renunciations, in proportion to the maximum advantage of the two subjects, which is found at P_B for B and at P_A for A.

Before point G, A can credibly give a warning to B by threatening not to vote for the solution they are both interested in, because A's *total* sacrifice of advantages as compared to her maximum advantage is greater than that of B as compared to B's maximum advantage. Once the proceedings have moved beyond G at the expense of B, it will be B who can credibly launch a warning against A by threatening not to vote in favour of the solution they are both interested in. Geometrically, G is reached by starting out from U, the 'utopian' point at which both A and B obtain all the improvement in question, and then moving back to I, the latter being both players' starting point. This movement involves plotting the bisector UI which meets $P_A P_B$ at point G, a point that is identical to N. The bisector has the evident geometric property of sharing out the benefit of the improvements in question between A and B in proportion to their maximum benefit, indicated respectively by IP_A and IP_B.

The formula to put this principle into practice is simple. Since what is required is to give each subject a share of the reward proportional to her maximum advantage, the share of the reward attributable to each subject will be equal to the percentage of the subject's advantage out of the sum of the advantages of the various subjects. Therefore, in our example, the share P_B of the reward for B will be:

$$P_B G = IP_B / (IP_B + IP_A) \qquad (2.9)$$

It can be argued that for long-term rules, equality in the proportion of the concessions as suggested by the contractarian principle counts more strongly than equality at the margin of the Nash equilibrium. This argument is supported by noting that it satisfies a criterion of *global equity* in sharing out the advantages, while the Nash equilibrium satisfies this criterion only unintentionally, inasmuch as it simply embodies an equilibrium due to matched relations of strength among the contracting parties or among the electors with the unanimity rule.

But the results of the two consensus procedures may coincide if the curve of transformation of A's welfare into that of B has a suitably uniform trend, as in Figure 2.7. And in any case it is the tension between these two types of equilibrium in the ongoing game that dominates the public economy, in the cooperative model.

If the reward is divided up without (significant) cost, the maximum, for each subject, is given by the totality of the undivided reward. Obviously, the subjects cannot all have the maximum of the reward, since the maximum reward is a single lump sum. Each subject will have a share proportionate to her maximum advantage obtained without (significant) cost.

The example of liberalizations is instructive with regard to cases in which there is no obligation to offer compensation inasmuch as the claimant's appeal is actually based on a privilege rather than genuine entitlement. The utilitarian approach, based on an aggregate social welfare function, would tend to focus efforts only on the major liberalizations which give maximum utility. By contrast, in the OSFOB approach the minor liberalizations should not be disregarded, as liberalizations, like other policies, are based on the consensus of those involved. And, discounting the consensus of those who do not have a valid claim, it is unreasonable to expect the rest of the citizens to support operations that create discontent among protected categories, unless the citizens receive some benefit in exchange – assuming the action in question is indeed capable of generating any. Admittedly, it can be argued that if the liberalizations increase GDP, everyone will benefit. But this is a weak argument, to justify only those liberalizations that give the maximum aggregate advantage but with direct benefit going only to particular subjects, who will also enjoy the general benefits deriving from the growth of GDP. The OSFOB principle, in this version, aims to give every individual an opportunity, which each one can then use according to her merit or ability.

3.7   The Contractarian OSFOB Principle in the Case of Sharing out the Advantage of a Common Action that Involves an Individual Cost for Each Player

We will now consider the apportioning of advantages, according to the contractarian principle, in the case of an action that brings Paretian improvements to a group of subjects but an unjustified decrease in the welfare of others. This case can be examined by means of the more general hypothesis of the partitioning of the advantage of a common action that involves an individual cost for each player. Subjects B, who are the ones that have suffered damage, have to be 'compensated' in reparation for the cost inflicted on them by the action of other subjects A, who, incurring a cost of their own, obtain an advantage that should also work to the benefit of the Bs, since it would not have been possible without the Bs' 'sacrifice'. Thus what we are dealing with here is the OSFOB criterion designed to give 'to each one according to her own contribution, or cost'. This is similar to the typical case of power stations, petroleum refineries and railway, which cause severe external diseconomies to a given *local community B* when they are installed. On the other hand subjects A, composed both of those who make the investment and also of the users, all of whom form part of the *national community*, obtain an economic benefit. The contractarian criterion OSFOB (further explained in Chapter 4, section 3) suggests that the benefit of the investment, which we can denominate as T, should be shared out between A and B in proportion to the costs they have shouldered, which we will denominate as C_A and C_B respectively. Therefore the share of the total benefit that should go to B, namely T_B, will be

$$T_B = C_B / (C_A + C_B) \qquad (2.10)$$

By adopting the principle of actual compensation, the B subjects would obtain only a compensation equal to the damage.[41] The solution in terms of maximum aggregate welfare could lead to a very similar result if B is a fairly small fraction of the population of the nation considered A, which draws substantial advantage from the investment. In contrast, the contractarian solution OSFOB involves not only compensating those who have suffered the damage but also giving them part of the advantage of the investment.

Let us now examine the paradigms for the great constitutional rules on welfare, in the interaction between power and equity.

3.8   The Maximum of Utility, in a State of Ignorance Concerning One's Own Personal Position, according to Harsanyi, as the Paradigm of 'Utilitarianism of the Rules' that Satisfies W_S

We saw above that one of the general criteria for maximizing collective welfare on an individual basis is the reciprocity criterion. Certain rules and modes of behaviour are shared by all members of the community as they give each individual, turn by turn, a burden, in exchange for an advantage given to others, but overall they give greater efficiency, with an advantage for everyone. In this regard, it is interesting to consider the formulation proposed by J. Harsanyi (1977 [1982]; 1955; 1975; 1985), which is even more general. Harsanyi formulated a criterion of maximum individual welfare on the basis of a set of rules that maximize the total utility of the overall community. We thus consider a subject J who, under the veil of the most total ignorance concerning her personal real present and future situations as well as those of her current and future loved ones, chooses the optimal situations. *Thus J represents every real subject forming part of the game*, and will tend to make choices that bring advantages to each of the other players, since *J* is in a disinterested position or, as Harsanyi (1977 [1982]) puts it, in a 'moral position'. Every *J* that is a rational subject, *risk-neutral* (that is neither having a propensity to risk nor being risk-averse) will choose the system of rules which, *in the long run,* gives the maximum of aggregate W_S^* with a calculation of the utility or disutility of the various situations that may happen to the various real subjects *A, B,...M, N,* multiplied by the probability of such situations being realized. *J* will therefore choose institutions that give rise to a 'cardinalist' maximum W_S^* determined in such a manner that if divided by the number of individuals considered, it maximizes the overall average per capita welfare of the members of *S* over time. There is no reciprocity principle in Harsanyi's criterion because one part of the set of persons could be systematically sacrificed to the welfare of the other part, on the basis of the probabilistic principle.

A choice of rules of this kind, above all if considered in their functioning *ex post*, therefore clashes against the postulate of the equal right of citizens to pursue their own welfare of W_S^*, which is taken as the premise. But Harsanyi's mental experiment of utilitarianism of the rules is not the only one possible. It can be modified to incorporate the principle of reciprocity and likewise to introduce into this framework the principle of the maximin, with regard to the extreme risks: each one could choose not to sacrifice the unfortunate individuals in favour of the others, to avoid finding herself in a similar situation. However, it is rational to establish a framework of rules based on utilitarian criteria founded on probability and reciprocity, within which each individual judges by herself, occasion by occasion, how to pursue her own preferences in relation to other individuals.

Two rules can be derived from the economic principle of reciprocity. These are rules concerning good legislation, and they are generally presented as self-evident rules of justice: first, the concept that laws should, as far as possible, have a general character, and secondly, the rule that all individuals are equal before the law. In effect, reciprocity might not come about, or might perhaps come about only in a very imperfect manner, if the rules are not general and if some individual is treated very unfairly with regard to the rules.

3.9 Rawls' Approach, in terms of the Priority of Freedom and Alliance between Merits and Needs by Means of the 'Principle of Difference' as Equity

According to the approach put forward by J. Rawls (1971)[42] and followed by Salvatore Veca (1989), with interesting variants, a person who makes the great choices pertaining to the institutions that concern the organization of society does so under the *veil of ignorance* concerning herself and her loved ones, and aims to achieve a social set-up in which each individual is considered as an entity in her own right, endowed with intrinsic moral value. Moreover, such a person does not believe that it is possible to sum different satisfactions of a given individual and merge them into a homogeneous whole, denominated utility. Rather, such a person singles out a *list of main goods* pertaining to *economic resources* and *values*, with the further assumption that the fact of being endowed with a greater or lesser quantity of these goods implies greater or lesser individual welfare, although they cannot be assessed by a unitary and overall cardinal quantification. All individuals should be endowed to an equal degree with the various liberties, and lexicographic precedence should be given to freedom over the other main goods; additionally, all individuals should have equal right to their own dignity and self-respect and equal chance to hold office in various spheres of life, equal access to the professions, and all should enjoy equality of economic opportunity. Whilst equal right to freedom, dignity, respect, access to office and the professions springs directly from the postulate that each person has equal value, the principle of equality of opportunity is less easily derivable from this principle. It could require corrective action at considerable cost in order to remedy the different economic and personal endowments of an individual's parents, or the different social and geographic environment. Rawls is aware of this, and admits attenuation of the rule of equality of economic opportunity, but he introduces the principle of difference, as fairness towards those less favoured. Economic and social inequalities have to be accepted, including those concerning difference in economic opportunity, but on condition that the positive economic results for society arising from such inequalities are used to provide a *differential benefit for the less favoured*, that is to the subjects that have a very low index of main goods. Viewed in terms of a slogan, this is an 'alliance between merits and needs', that is between the meritocracy of the market and solidarity in favour of the underprivileged. In Rawls' eyes, the principle of difference as fairness towards the less favoured is recognized by every citizen who is endowed with a sense of justice as her own main good, in a 'well ordered' society. But it remains to be seen whether this is true not only when a citizen acts under the veil of ignorance, but also *ex post*, in the phase in which each individual comes to know her own fate.

According to the original formulation in Rawls (1971), which he later rejected (Rawls, 1982), the principle of difference is justified as a maximin game strategy, that is maximization of the minimum positive result, when faced with the great ethical risks that involve the inequality of the 'social lottery'. After the criticisms levelled by Harsanyi (1977 [1982]), according to whom it is not logical for society to pursue a maximin rather than a maximax, Rawls reworked the basis of the principle of difference, arguing that it derives from the ethical criterion according to which each person has a value in her own right, and thus potentially has the right to the same fate as all the others. In effect, for safeguards against the extreme risks, on the basis of a principle of reciprocity chosen under the veil of ignorance about the future, those who are well off and the middle classes will have to undertake not so much to maximize advantages for the less favoured, compatibly with the inequalities that continue to arise in society, but instead to guarantee them a minimum: thus not a maximin, that is not maximization of the minimum, but a leximin, namely the guarantee of the minimum. And this involves aiding the community against severe misfortune represented not only by poverty but also, for instance, a permanent physical handicap or a painful and costly disease, which can generate an acute state of need even for a person who is not defined as poor. To defend his principle, Rawls argues that the inequalities in the various levels of income, one's personal estate and social position tend to decrease automatically in a society whose institutions are oriented towards the principle of difference.[43] But this is hardly very convincing. It may well happen that the burden of taxes used to sustain expenditure on behalf of the less favoured falls on the middle classes and/or the working classes instead of falling on the most wealthy, and that measures intended to support the less favoured are not conditional on commitment by the latter to work towards becoming active members of society but depend, rather, on whether or not they are seeking assistance. As a result, extensive application of the principle of difference does not give rise to an alliance between merits and needs, but to an alliance between economic oligarchies and the benefit-dependent welfare state. Ideally, however, Rawls' theory, which awards priority of place to the principle of liberty and supplements it with that of difference, constitutes the synthesis of efficiency and justice[44] of the model of a democratic public economy with a predominantly market economy, of a welfare type such as is found in the Scandinavian social-democratic countries.

3.10 Buchanan: Priority to the Rules of Efficiency over those of Fairness

Buchanan (with Tullock 1962 [1999], as well as 1977; 1971 [1979b]; 1979a; 1986, and with Brennan 1985 [2000]) comes to virtually the opposite conclusion as compared to Rawls, embracing the point of view of an *original constitutional contract*, adopted with the rule of (quasi) unanimity, and assuming subjects that operate for an uncertain future in which the positions of their representatives could change: and therefore not with a veritable veil of ignorance. Buchanan's founding fathers, unlike the person considered by Rawls, who chooses the optimum society under the veil of ignorance, are not influenced by value systems. Agreement is facilitated by so-called log rolling, that is the exchange of 'a bit of help' (just as woodcutters in the mountains come to one another's help, when they have to roll heavy trunks and cannot manage on their own) in order to settle conflicts over preferences concerning rules on which they have different preferences. Buchanan also postulates the right for a contract to be rescinded in the future, and this substantially reduces the hypothesis of agreement on principles of very long duration, giving rise to a predominance of efficiency criteria over equitableness and also reducing the tasks of the public economy to very limited levels. Buchanan argues that each individual will agree to be compensated according to the productivity of what she possesses and will opt to try to obtain a yield from her activities, with the criterion of benefit, as evaluated in a competitive market. The costs of public goods are shared out with the criterion of benefit, repeating the model of a competitive system. Fairness is achieved in two ways: by guaranteeing a minimum of opportunity through the action of the public economy, which increases efficiency and enriches competition, and by assuring that if individuals were to undergo failure they would be guaranteed a minimum, as an 'insurance' against the risks of fate. But according to Buchanan each individual is to be considered responsible for her own choices. Therefore those who voluntarily descend into poverty because they do not wish to work or because they recklessly devote their time to consumption or waste their money unproductively in risky operations or on drink or drugs should not have the right to that 'minimum'. However, he admits that society may grant the individual such an amount because it is worthwhile in 'Hobbesian' terms for purposes of law and order, hygiene, quiet neighbourhoods, social decorum, in order to avoid the damage that could be wrought by those who are in a less favourable situation.[45]

3.11   The Great Rules of the Equilibrium of the Constitutional Game in the Cooperative Model between Rawls and Buchanan, in a Perspective of Normative Equilibrium Founded on Economic Laws

The constitutional agreements in the cooperative model of the public economy can be imagined as rules of the game that move between the two polar paradigms of Rawls and Buchanan, both governed by the principle of freedom, which is awarded first place. And this should not be taken as referring to the abstract point of view of a person who chooses under the veil of ignorance or of the fathers of a constituent assembly who draw up an original constitutional contract, for there is nothing to guarantee *ex post* that when each individual is better informed on what concerns her and what could happen to herself and her immediate descendants, she will be prepared to respect agreements made in abstract conditions. The proper point of view, which holds for normative economics as well, as regards the positive principles of the economic constitution would seem to be that of a constitution capable of being shared not only *ex ante*, but also *ex post*, when it is in force. Such a situation takes shape in the context of a constitutional set-up that acquires its content gradually over time, with the emergence of rules institutionally endowed with a constitutional standing in the economic sense, inasmuch as such rules impose constraints and orientations for the ordinary rules that will be bound by these constitutional rules, and also with the emergence of other rules that acquire this standing by common consent (on the economic concept of constitution see Chapter 6, section 1).

In order to achieve *ex post* effectiveness, Rawls' system of rules seen in the guise of an economic constitution lacks the principle of *'do ut des'*, as clear-cut reciprocity (of exchange) and as reciprocity over time and space that assures consensus in the cooperative bargaining game. As far as Buchanan's constitutional set-up is concerned, the consensus of the parties involved is assured by the right to rescind the contract. But this involves constantly reinitiating the bargaining process and thus clashes with the requirement that the constitutional rules should be endowed with stability. Indeed, 'reversible' constitutional rules appear to be debatable as rules for an extremely long-run game in which the aim is to achieve a set-up that is as enduring as possible, and efficient for the long-term economic choices that characterize a 'developed' economy. The right to rescind from the state is not a realistic hypothesis for persons, but it is for joint-stock societies. Thus it can be argued that the threat of the right to rescind involves a model of 'minimal state', as in fact seems to be suggested by the Buchanian model. The latter thus appears more plausible than that of Rawls, in the relation between *ex ante* and *ex post* choices. But it does not necessarily seem to be the model that leads to greater long-run efficiency, as compared to the concepts of individual welfare that are shared by the greater number. In particular, the scanty attention to equality of starting points, as is characteristic of the minimal state, does not necessarily correspond to greatest production efficiency. The minimal state is indifferent to the contributions of knowledge, art, culture and environmental values, these being left to the destiny meted out to them by the market and to the munificence of non-profit associations and foundations – of which there do actually tend to be a large number in the real world, since they benefit from tax relief. This leads to possible distortions in the market system, which are appraised critically in Buchanan's formation as 'opportunistic rents' (see

Chapter 5, section 2). If Rawls' approach which holds that justice should be entirely regulated *according to the equity principle* of *'difference' for the less favoured* appears unilateral, Buchanan's principle of 'indifference' with regard to values, both in reference to justice as equitableness in redistribution and also in reference to the cultural and environmental heritage, appears unrealistic for a real life community which pursues individual welfare in a regime of free choice.

Buchanan, who is personally highly committed to ethical values, asserts that the economist's personal value judgements should not be introduced into the analysis. He thus expunges from his theoretical model a series of values and conflicts among values that are genuinely present in societies and which affect decision-making processes within the public economy. The idea of taking widely shared values into account, and of trying to gauge whether the potential equilibria emerging in the conflict among values could prove to be the optimal equilibria, given the shared premises, does not imply a value judgement, but a statement of fact. And the economist cannot disregard values pertaining to justice such as equitableness, or the safeguarding of the cultural or environmental heritage, which concern real choices within the public economy.

In the democratic cooperative model based on the principle of 'one person, one vote' the deficiencies of the market with regard to the distributive profile and shared values are corrected in order to reinforce the model itself and increase the consensus around it among the majority of persons. The choice of a constitutional set-up based on a market economy is made and accepted by overwhelming majority agreement, on the condition that all persons have an opportunity within the economic system, in accordance with their merits. Such an accomplishment is brought about through the public economy, giving everyone basic opportunities, the burden of which is to be borne by all members of the society. This meritocratic redistributive principle has a basis of mutualism, because the opportunities provided to the individual at the starting point by the collective community enable her to be of use not only to herself but also to the welfare of all other members, through her contribution to growth of the national product and to the cultural capital of the society. By paying taxes, the successful individual will be able to give back to society what society gave her when she was provided with those basic opportunities free of charge. But even in this framework the market economy still generates notable inequalities, in relation to the principles of property and private initiative which lie at its base, and it involves risks that can lead to severe imbalance between needs and available economic means. In the cooperative model, a remedy to these imbalances between personal economic means and needs is devised through the leximin clause, which involves:

1. Protection of the average citizen against the most severe risks;
2. Guarantee of a minimum for the less favoured.

Thus in this model, redistribution is based, at least theoretically, on principles that conform to the market economy.

3.12 The Problems of the Welfare State in the Cooperative Model

From the operational point of view, however, substantial problems arise, namely:

a. The principle of basic opportunities requires education free of charge for compulsory education up to high school and partly free of charge or semi-free for higher education. This in turn implies or at least effectively justifies a large public bureaucratic apparatus in the sector of education.
b. The principle of the leximin, in the fluctuating relation between economic means and needs, involves mechanisms of public insurance for old-age pensions and a public health service. Although in the cooperative model this is based on a leximin principle, in actual fact there is a tendency for these public bureaucratic apparatuses to be extended towards a maximax.
c. The principle of the leximin for the less favoured involves old age pensions to avoid poverty in the elderly, permanent allowances for the disabled and the unemployed, assistance for the victims of alcoholism, substance abuse and mental illness. And this list could be extended.

This once again raises Buchanan's arguments concerning the 'demerit' of the less favoured, as a reason for not helping them. Systematically subsidizing them may encourage irresponsible behaviour. But an even more fundamental point is that the concept of 'less favoured' is labile, and lends itself to extension in two ways: 1) by including among the less favoured subjects those who were previously in this condition but now no longer are; 2) by broadening the circle to include those who are 'less well-off', that is by shifting from a concept of lack of the minimum to one of insufficient welfare.

3.13 The Problems of the Welfare State in the Rawls Model

The problems outlined above increase in the Rawls model, because the principle of basic opportunities in this model appears (almost) as a principle of equality of opportunities at the starting points. It follows that education should be free of charge at all levels, including at higher levels, for all those who belong to families that are not wealthy enough to be able to afford it. Also, there could be no criterion of merit as a discriminating factor when faced with the aspirations of less favoured subjects. Furthermore, assistance for the less favoured, in this model, does not consist in the guarantee of a minimum, that is a leximin, but in its maximization. This also implies an amplification of government action, which is further aggravated if, due to electoral pressures, the concept of 'less favoured' is not restricted in some way. That is to say, if the less favoured are a minority, their voting power could be insufficient for protection of their rights. This may have the consequence that instead of the welfare state acting for their benefit, it ends up acting not for the benefit of the less favoured but for the benefit of the politically organized sections of society who have a medium–low income and are considerably more numerous. Moreover, although Rawls' paradigm involves acceptance of inequalities, with action to benefit the less favoured, the principle of providing aid for the less favoured without any consideration for the criterion of merit or demerit leads to a lack of efficiency. In particular, the greater the endeavour to reduce their position of disadvantage through redistributive policies, the greater the loss will be, as such policies have a cost, the burden of which is borne by all the other subjects, reducing the overall motivation and ability to save. The functioning of Rawls' model of the welfare state requires:

a.   great endogenous efficiency within the economic system, to counterbalance the exogenous impulse towards the inefficiency of the principle of difference as the dominant principle of equitableness;

b.   great ethical consciousness on the part of the middle classes, to enable them to shoulder the burden of the fiscal costs of the model, and of the medium–low classes to prompt them to accept the principle of selectivity to the benefit of the less favoured, which involves a welfare state characterized by broad-based solidarity towards the less favoured.

3.14   The Crisis of the 'Classical' Welfare State Model of the Pigou–Mirrlees Type

The greatest difficulty in implementing the constitution of collective welfare of the cooperative model or the Rawls model does not, however, reside in the defects of their functioning or in the danger of distortions stemming from opportunistic rent-seeking, with regard to which these models undeniably leave the door ajar. Rather, it resides in the fact that the dominant theoretical structures of the welfare state are those that developed on the basis of utilitarian theory, which starts out from a collective welfare function founded on maximization of the sum of individual utilities, in a hypothesis of isomorphism, that is of individuals who, in similar personal and environmental conditions, have similar utility curves but – in the Mirrlees formulation – different capabilities. The formulation of collective welfare as the (algebraic) sum of the individual curves, which is ruled out by the present author as it is incompatible with the individualistic principles of the cooperative model and therefore with a public economy that conforms to the market economy, is widespread among economists. Note, also, that economists pride themselves on the formal elegance of models that can be built up on this basis. It is a formulation that has the support of the political tradition of progressive movements that arose to improve the conditions of blue-collar workers, who once represented the most numerous social class. In this formulation:

a. redistribution among subjects, in the endeavour to generate a tendency towards a levelling among the various income classes as a means of maximizing aggregate marginal utility,[46] is limited merely by a reduction in efficiency attributable to its negative effects on production. Such effects are then alleviated by the public economy interventions, for example with taxes destined to finance investment, in order to make up for the fact that redistribution induces a reduction in saving or in the private advantageousness of investing;
b. redistribution is effected by means of a complex planned system of provision free of charge, or semi-free of charge, with regard to specific goods such as education, health care, assistance to underprivileged persons or families, and a detailed system of transfer payments in favour of persons and households that find themselves in the various circumstances of facing an excess of needs over available resources, taking into account the variations in welfare in the different circumstances.

The model in question involves high taxation to finance an extensive public economy and a large public bureaucracy. In order to be able to function with an efficient market economy, it requires an elevated ethical conscience and high endogenous economic efficiency in the system. Moreover, given the model's greater tendency towards levelling, these requirements are considerably more pronounced than in the Rawls model. Generally it turns into dirigisme of the economy, as has been the case in history. But this does not appear to be suitable for sustained economic growth. This leads to the dilemma between growth and equity. The dilemma often fails to be solved, plunging the public economy into deficit, with adverse effects as regards the possibility of sustaining the welfare state and of freeing the economic energies of the market from the fiscal costs of the model.

NOTES

1. For a presentation of welfare economics, see Arrow and Scitovsky (1969), Bator (1958), De Van Graaff (1957). From the point of view of collective decision-making processes, see (in Italian) Forte and Mossetto (1972). For the relation between efficiency and social welfare function, see especially Rowley and Peacock (1975), and Sen (1982).
2. As is known, the ordinal numbers, unlike the cardinal numbers, cannot be subjected to the four operations of addition, subtraction, multiplication and division, but can only be 'ranked', with judgements of equal, greater or smaller and with the possibility of identifying equal intervals between one position and another on the ranking scale.
3. Thus (2.1′) should not include the U^* pertaining to goods which cannot legitimately be traded, such as sale of one's own body organs. There remain grey areas such as prostitution, which is 'tolerated'. See further on, section 1.6.
4. Some reservations and further specifications can be advanced in connection with this concept. These will be touched on in sections 1.7–1.10.
5. Cf. on this theme the pioneering essay by Hochman and Rodgers (1969) on 'Paretian optimal redistribution' (i.e. that which corresponds to i's altruistic preferences for j) and the anthology of writings edited by Hochman and Peterson (1974), which takes up the topic again and extends it to collective decision-making processes. But it should not be presumed that this necessarily gives rise to markedly 'altruistic' distributions. A distinction should be drawn between '*empathy*', which stands for the fact that a subject A feels the increases and decreases in utilitarian and non-utilitarian welfare experienced by another subject B as if they were her own, and '*empathic imagination*', which concerns the situation of a subject A who succeeds in 'putting herself in B's shoes', perceiving B's gains and losses of utility and, in general, the improvements and deteriorations in B's welfare just as if they were happening to herself, A, but without (necessarily) feeling such needs to be genuinely her own.
6. According to widespread opinion, which seems to spring from Lionel Robbins (1932 [1935]), interpersonal comparisons of utility and welfare are not possible, because each person is a sphere to herself, an entity separate from the others: 'there is no bridge between them'. But three concepts are mingled together in this concept: 1) that it is not possible to carry out measurements of subjective utility among different goods and there is no quantifiable personal index of 'global utility'; 2) that it is not possible to compare the utility of the various subjects, either in relation to overall provision of the means available to them (aggregate utility) or in relation to delivery of the final unit of a given action (marginal utility); 3) that it is not legitimate to make such measurements in the attempt to take decisions concerning society in general, and more specifically, to pursue maximum collective welfare. On the first point, we have seen that the measurements are possible, if welfare is conceived as room for choice, even though they are quantitative (and cardinal) only for the economic part, while they are ordinal for the remaining part, with or without judgements of intensity. The assertion that the utilities of different subjects can never be subjected to comparison, because they deal with different worlds, appears excessive. We should in fact admit Harsanyi's postulate (1977 [1982]) of 'imaginative empathy', namely psychological affinity among the various human beings, which can be reciprocally perceived. If we were to reject the postulate, we would also have to abandon the attempt to predict other people's behaviour, whereas the entire market economy is structured around forecasts each individual makes concerning the behaviour of others, based on imagination of what their advantage is likely to be. But if we base our outlook on reciprocal rational behaviour, this means that we 'understand' one another with regard to our utilitarian calculations.

    Furthermore, the assertion that nothing is known on the total utility curves and on the shape of individuals' marginal utility curves is contradicted through the analysis performed by Von Neumann and Morgenstern (1944) and Friedman and Savage (1948) concerning the behaviour of gamblers and those who take out insurance against risky events characterized by mathematical probabilities. A low-income subject who places a bet or buys a lottery ticket, paying a small sum with the mathematical probability of a large pay-out which, however, is not equitable (that is such that when multiplying the probabilities of winning by the established jackpot one has a lower sum than the cost of the ticket), evidently estimates the marginal utility of the greater income she hopes to win to be greater than the income she has lost in placing her bet. If such a subject insures her own small home against the risk of fire, by paying an insurance premium that is greater than the compensation she would have a right to, given the – mathematically estimated – probability of fire, this implies that she estimates the marginal utility of the greater income she would be left with after the fire to be considerably greater than the income she forgoes in paying the premium.

7. The national product as the product of the nation may differ from the domestic product as the product in the nation, because some part of the domestic product may belong to (members of) other nations, while the national product may include products obtained in other nations.

8. On the compensation principle see section 3.

9. Including, naturally, those concerning persons.

10. W. Pareto uses the term 'ophelimity' to indicate the satisfactions individuals draw from non-economic factors, while reserving the term 'utility' for economic factors. Therefore subjective welfare, in the Paretian sense, can be defined as that which includes both economic subjective satisfactions and non-economic satisfactions.

11. Some non-economic freedoms, such as that of being a free person and the freedoms of thought and movement themselves, naturally also have a substantial economic content.

12. 'Freedom of choice' for U^* and V^* is more limited than the 'freedom of thought' they enjoy.

13. Cf. Harsanyi, in Sen and Williams (1982), where a cardinal and basically economicist version of utility is adopted (cf. beyond subsection 3.11), but arguing at the same time that in addition to the satisfactions obtained from goods it is also necessary to insert that pertaining to the variable 'L', *freedom of choice*.

14. One could try to estimate it with the so-called method of contingent evaluation. Cultural goods have not only a use value but also an existence value and an option value. On these issues and on the methods for evaluating cultural goods cf. Forte and Mantovani (1954), Part III, Chapter III and Chapter IV, see also Chapter 2, Part 1, section 4.

15. In the Pareto sense. See note 10.

16. Thus we can write

$$W_j^* = w_j \left[(U_{jU}^* + U_{jV}^*), V_j^* \right] \tag{2.3}$$

where U_j^* are variables endowed with a monetary economic dimension, U_{jV}^* are variables endowed with a partial monetary economic dimension (in terms of alternative economic costs lower than or equal to the benefit), relating to value-goods V^*. On the other hand, V_j^* are variables that are not measurable in monetary terms, relating to the same value-goods or to other goods. We have placed commas between the $(U_{jU}^* + U_{jV}^*)$ and the V_j^* of (2.3), in order to indicate that they cannot be summed, but only placed in an ordinal relation, due to the lack of a homogeneous measurement criterion.

17. See above, note 5.

18. Cf. the paradox of Sen in 'The impossibility of a Paretian liberal' (1970 [1982]), according to which a libertine would be willing to eschew the reading of a book with erotic overtones in order to compel a prude to read it, so that the prude could experience new sensations, and the prude prefers to accept the exchange and read the book, in order to avert the need for the libertine to do so. Thus each individual accepts, in order to increase her own welfare in terms of value, the concept of depriving herself of her own freedom of choice, that is of a value which she regards as less important. Sen's demonstration is perfect. But what he does not demonstrate is that preference for maximum 'Paretian' welfare can contrast with the preference for freedom. In effect, what the

libertine and the prude forgo is only their own individual freedom of choice. But they do so by a free choice, which forms part of their non-economic welfare, and they do so – in this case – to increase their non-economic welfare.

19. We refer here to the *relative* prices of the various goods, since variations in the absolute price level are dealt with by means of the concept of (unit of) 'purchasing power'. On the problem of price change in relation to the concept of economic welfare as capacity for choice, see subsection 1.9 below.

20. Thus water and atmospheric contamination by polluting substances is measured in units of pollutants per cubic metre, the size of forests in square kilometres of ground cover, noise in decibels, the fauna population in units of the various species and number of species, and so on.

21. Thus one can write

$$W^*_{CJ} = c(PA^*_J, V^*_{Ja}, V^*_{Jd}, V^*_{Ji}, h) \qquad (2.4)$$

in which PA indicates purchasing power, Va the endowment of environmental and artistic-cultural goods, Vd the endowment of human, civil and political rights, Vt available 'free time' and h the situation with regard to any psycho-physical disabilities that may impair capacity for choice, with the value 0 indicating the absence of any such disabilities.

22. The social welfare function W^*_S concerning individuals 1, 2, . . ., N, can be expressed (by means of the symbols specified in the previous note) through the following formula:

$$W^*_S = w\,[(PA^*_1; V^*_1; h^*_1);\ (PA^*_2; V^*_2; h^*_2);\ \ldots;\ (PA^*_N; V^*_N; h^*_N)] \qquad (2.5)$$

This is a limited formulation, of first approximation, which does not hold when there are situations of *conflicting interference among individual welfares*. As in (2.2), there is a comma between the components of the various individual functions, rather than a plus sign, because they cannot be summed algebraically, and the same is true among the various individual functions.

23. Arguing – on the basis of the hypothesis of subjective decreasing marginal utility – that it may be fair to take means away from those who have more and who thus, presumably, *ceteris paribus*, have a lower marginal utility, and instead, to give to those who are in a state of need, *independently of an evaluation of the capacity for choice on fields of choice, leads to results which are often eccentric*, because the hypothesis of a decrease in subjective marginal utility is debatable. Those who have a larger income usually also have a more elevated subjective utility, because they have a more refined awareness of the concept of satisfying the various needs. Thus a low-income subject may buy lottery tickets or scratch cards, that is not give up the idea of gambling with a small bet in the hope of winning a large sum. Such a sum, multiplied by its mathematical probability, is actually considerably lower than the money spent, because what the subject has in mind is the utility of the income he could obtain if he were to win. And this income – seen as he imagines himself in the rich man's shoes, endowed with 'a rich man's needs' – seems to him to be considerably higher than the marginal utility that he sacrifices – in his limited horizon of needs. In contrast, the same low-income subject will insure his own small home against the risk of fire, paying a mathematically higher premium than the likely compensation pay-out, because his expectation is that if fire breaks out the utility of his income, on the margin, will be so high – given his low income level – that it will exceed the utility of the amount of income he forgoes in paying the premium, now that he owns his home as well. Friedman and Savage (1948) therefore hypothesized a total income utility curve with a variable trend that implies portions having decreasing marginal utility and portions with increasing marginal utility. Furthermore, the point of view of the algebraic maximum of interpersonal collective utility based on the capacity to measure cardinally the process of achieving pleasure and pursuing desires – as pointed out by the father of the Chicago economic school H. Simons (1938) – is

debatable. This would require collecting less tax from whoever, for whatever reason, has a greater capacity for material and moral enjoyment, that is from those who are more efficient utility-producing machines, than from those who have limited desires and pleasures given their modest life horizons.

24. Their dwelling is not double that of *A* because they do not need two kitchens and two living rooms, and perhaps not even two bedrooms. If *A* has two bathrooms because she is 'affluent', then *B*, *C* – who by hypothesis are endowed with the same per capita purchasing power – certainly do not need three bathrooms to achieve the same condition of affluence, and so on.

25. In Stiglitz (2000, Vol. I, section 2.3), the production frontier is presented only with the curve that is concave towards the origin, thereby giving a completely wrong idea of the current economy, which is dominated by the law of decreasing costs.

26. See further on in this volume, in Chapter 5, section 1, the application of this principle to the economy of the bureaucracy, in Niskanen's model.

27. Not all the external economies are technological externalities. There may exist external pecuniary economies. On the distinction between technological and pecuniary external economies see Chapter 3, subsection 1.12.

28. Public wants connected to external economies will be given special treatment in Chapter 3, section 1, with regard to the external economies of production, in the framework of wants and public goods linked to market failures on the supply side, and in section 2, with regard to the external economies of consumption in the framework of wants and public goods linked to market failures on the demand side.

29. For Coase (1960), with nil transaction costs it is indifferent whether *A* has the right to pollute *B* with *K* or whether *B* has the right not to be polluted by *A* with *K*. The result, if property rights are not defined, will depend on the relation between the monetary benefit of *K* for *A* and its monetary cost for *B*. The situation changes with substantial transaction costs and *with different costs for A and C of removing the external diseconomy*. According to the prevailing interpretation, Coase's theorem is a mere equivalence theorem. But in the true Coasian view, according to the present author, Coase aimed to show that in some cases it is better, from an allocative efficiency point of view, to let the damaged pay the damaging party to stop or reduce the damage. See Forte (2003).

30. Cf. Ricardo (1817 [1947, 2005]). For a systematic treatment see Salvatore (2007), Part I, Chapter 2. My graphic representation assumes decreasing returns as in Ricardo. However, increasing return production frontiers would be more appropriate for the developed and developing countries as well, at the present stage of the global economy.

31. Cf. Forte (2003).

32. See above Chapter 1, subsection 2.2.

33. A unanimity voting system, like that imagined by Wicksell, of whom Lindhal is a follower, is affected by the problems described in Chapter 6, section 2.1.

34. The concept of effectiveness refers to satisfying the subjects' most important preferences, by means of given products. On the intermeshing between the concept of efficiency and that of effectiveness, see further on.

35. The three essays by Kaldor, Hicks and Scitovsky are reprinted in the anthology of Caffè (1956).

36. Van De Graaff (1957) takes the argument a step forward, arguing that compensation by the majority in power should be recognized, whenever possible, if the option of not awarding it would 'worsen distribution'.

37. This will be clarified further on, in the discussion on the treatment of the constitutional principles of taxation.

38. This is a case of the well-known 'NIMBY' 'not in my back yard' argument, that is the proposed work is fine, but 'I don't want it in my back yard'.

39. See Gauthier, 1986, Chapter V and the bibliography referred to therein. Cf. also the elementary discussion in Graham (1988, Chapter III), as well as the critical and corrective observations by Barry (1989) from the point of view of justice as impartiality.

40. See Forte (1993), Forte (1995), Fedeli and Forte (2001) and Fedeli and Forte (2002).
41. Naturally a correct interpretation of Coase's theorem does not suggest this result, given that it is not determined in his theorem how much the perpetrator of the damage has to give to the injured party, in cases where the injured party can prevent the perpetrator from carrying out the action that is advantageous to the latter, and the benefit deriving to the perpetrator from this action is (much) greater than the damage to the injured party.
42. For additional clarification and further developments on Rawls' theory of justice, see Forte (1995), *Etica Pubblica e Regole del Gioco*, Chapters XI and XII and Fedeli and Forte (2001; 2002). The literature on Rawls is extremely vast. See, among others, Wolff (1977).
43. Rawls (1971), in actual fact, omits to analyse this issue in detail, to simplify his treatment, which is already highly complex in its own right.
44. Rather precarious, according to the present author, in the current historical era, but perhaps more realistic in developed Western civilization, in the second half of the twentieth century.
45. This criterion is also defined by Buchanan (in 'A Hobbesian Interpretation of the Rawlsian difference principle', in Buchanan (1976 [2001]) as a 'Hobbesian' minimum.
46. On the assumption that individual utilities are decreasing with increasing income, that all subjects are isomorphic with one another, and that they do not change their supply of labour, savings and enterprise in relation to variations in income, then the sum of the marginal utilities will be maximum when everyone has the same income. In other words, the wealthy have gone down, and the poor have gone up, to the same income level. Thus if A has a bigger income than B and their utilities are decreasing and isomorphic, then A's marginal utility of her income will be lower than that associated with B's income. If A's bigger income is moved from A to B, then total marginal utility increases. This holds true up to the point when B's income is equal to that of A and therefore their marginal utilities are equal.

3. Public wants and public goods

1 GENERAL FRAMEWORK OF THE RELATION BETWEEN PUBLIC AND PRIVATE WANTS AND GOODS: PUBLIC WANTS AND GOODS DERIVING FROM SUPPLY SIDE MARKET FAILURES

1.1 Wants and Goods Public in the Individualistic Models and in Paternalistic and Authoritarian Models[1]

Public wants in the pure controlled economy system are wants of the state as an organic entity set on a higher plane than individuals. The governing class, flanked by the technocracy, acts as the authorized interpreter of such needs. A different approach is adopted in the cooperative model, on which we will dwell here: in the cooperative framework, although public wants are satisfied by action taken on the political level jointly with the public bureaucracy, they are reduced to the wants of persons and enterprises as perceived and evaluated by themselves. Such wants are satisfied through the state, in so far as persons and enterprises are not capable of satisfying them adequately on the market. We can therefore analyse public wants and goods with regard to *market deficiencies*, or rather, as is also said, 'market failures':[2]

a. on the supply side, in relation to the different type and degree of indivisibility of goods and the particular nature of the wants;
b. on the demand side, in relation to external economies and diseconomies of consumption and also to merit wants and goods;
c. and on the issue of the interlacing of supply and demand, in relation to redistributive and macroeconomic aims.

But as we saw in Chapter 2, section 3, a glance at the various theories of collective welfare shows that there are various different approaches to the model of a democratic public economy, and these involve different assessments of market deficiencies and different roles assigned to the public economy, with different emphasis on redistributive policies.

Moreover, it is clear that market deficiencies with regard to the macroeconomic perspective, in the model where the public economy is subsidiary to the market, concern the corrections introduced to increase GDP in a regime of monetary stability, with the aim of improving the functioning of the market. But in a controlled economy system, the action is aimed at overcoming the market equilibria.

1.2   Failure of the Market and Failure of the State

It should, however, always be kept in mind that while there may be deficiencies, or 'failures' of the market system and of the individual choices made on the market, there are, equally, deficiencies and disastrous failures of public choices and action that were supposed to correct the market. The voting systems adopted for collective decisions are all flawed, as described earlier.

A democratic and, at the same time, bureaucratic society that endeavours to bring about the various corrections is operating in a regime of 'bounded rationality', with collective choices that are by their own nature imperfect. A society of this nature is unable to cope efficiently and effectively with a 'task overload'. The expanding size of the public economy reduces the efficiency of public action: after the decreasing cost phase obtained from the economies of scale associated with its large size, the public economy enters into the phase of increasing cost due to diseconomies caused by the rising cost both of information and of decision-making processes, as occurs in all large structures. It should also be borne in mind (as will be seen in Chapter 10) that the funding of public expenditure through taxation leads to distortions in the economic system, because in the real world the optimal tax actually does not exist. And as fiscal requirements gradually increase, it becomes necessary to resort to less acceptable forms of taxation – a situation that could be likened to the case of truffles: the really good ones are a rarity, and therefore when the demand is magnified but still has to be satisfied, quality declines.

In any case, in a free market economy there are ethical limits on the action of the state, in the sense that an elevated share of public finance in the economy reduces individuals' ability to choose in matters concerning their own individual sphere.[3]

The proper approach to the theme of public goods and wants, from the point of view of the cooperative model of the public economy, is that of a prudent comparative assessment between 'market failures' and 'failures and/or increasing difficulties of the public economy' that is called upon to correct the market.

1.3 Classification of Public Goods According to Indivisibility in Units of Use and/or Units of Sale

Market failures on the supply side can be analysed in relation to the nature of needs and the goods supplied. In the overwhelming number of cases, the cause of the market 'failure' lies in a situation of pronounced or absolute indivisibility which concerns the nature of the goods or the possibility of ceding them in exchange for payment, that is the so-called exclusion principle. But as we will see, there are also cases of market failure on the supply side, which concern goods that are divisible or for which indivisibility does not truly constitute the most severe problem. This situation can be better understood with the analytical chart shown in Table 3.1, which refers to goods in relation to their indivisibility.

The two large conceptual categories of indivisibility of goods that we consider in this double-entry table, which gives us four classes of goods, are:

I. intrinsic, that is objective, indivisibility, consisting in the fact that a given unit of the good can be used simultaneously by more than one subject;
II. transactional indivisibility, consisting in the fact that the good cannot be ceded on the market because whoever does not wish to pay for it cannot be excluded (the principle of exclusion does not hold).

There are (Class I) goods that are intrinsically and transactionally divisible and therefore the market can supply them efficiently. At times, however, even in the cooperative model, they are held in the public hand for valid reasons, and therefore the public economy cedes them on the market. Among such goods we can list, first, those that belong to the environment – beaches and river banks, some forests and nature reserves, and so on, which are protected by virtue of a value judgement of individual welfare that we saw in Chapter 2, section 1. The public operator is generally called upon to protect these goods, in order for there to be a correct relationship between man and nature. But the public operator can rent out a part of such goods. Other similar goods are those that belong to the state by the theory of sovereignty rights as enshrined in the constitution: the sea, the airwaves, the deep subsoil.[4] The state can cede limited rights on the use of these goods, in such a manner as to prevent anyone from holding a monopoly over them. Class I may also include the goods of public enterprises, which in a public economy with a market regime are an exception. Other goods (Class II) are intrinsically divisible; therefore the market could supply them and does indeed do so, but

Table 3.1   The different types of indivisibility of public goods

Intrinsically and transactionally divisible goods	Goods intrinsically divisible but transactionally non-divisible or not suitable for sale on the market
I	**II**
Intrinsically and transactionally divisible goods = market goods and certain goods of the public economy when the latter operates on the market (e.g. renting out the airwaves and seaside beaches, forestry timber, certain public enterprises)	Intrinsically divisible goods, which are often preferably left undivided into units of sale, e.g. state education, health care, or which should not be divided into units of sale, e.g. assistance to the needy and the victims of calamities, public drinking fountains; intrinsically divisible goods that satisfy indivisible wants such as law courts and police.
Intrinsically indivisible, transactionally divisible goods	**Intrinsically indivisible goods for which division into units of sale is inappropriate or which are transactionally indivisible**
III	**IV**
Goods of an indivisible nature that can be divided transactionally, and which it is not disadvantageous to divide: e.g. certain types of lighthouse services, discoveries and innovations protected by patents, uncongested roads	Goods of an indivisible nature which are transactionally divisible but which should more appropriately be supplied via non-market operations, either because they satisfy indivisible public wants such as long-range missile defences and the Space Shield (Strategic Defence Initiative), or to avoid waste of resources. Pure indivisible, or Samuelsonian, goods, e.g. a discovery which 'by its very nature' is unpatentable (e.g. knowledge of the law of gravity) or the general principles of private law.

often it is regarded as improper to divide them into units of sale, because application of the principle of exclusion appears unacceptable, for various reasons. Thus they are supplied by the public hand using non-market methods. This category includes merit goods and redistributive goods, which will be addressed in sections 2 and 3 of this chapter, but also public drinking fountains, public conveniences and rest rooms, street benches in pedestrian precincts. Such goods – street benches, for instance – are supplied free of charge although technically it would be possible to impose a charge in the form of a ticket or a coin machine, but this is an extremely unfriendly proposal as the nuisance caused to the user in exchange for a small price appears excessive, for various reasons. In certain cases, selling these goods instead of providing them even to those who do not wish to pay for them may appear inappropriate because they satisfy indivisible public wants (for instance, justice and public order services). Various other goods (Class III) are intrinsically indivisible, in the sense that they can be enjoyed simultaneously by large numbers of subjects. Goods in this category could, however, be divided into units of sale, and this may appear appropriate in spite of their intrinsic capability of giving a service to those who are not willing to pay the established price, or because their non-division into units of sale might imply an unacceptably severe waste of resources; therefore they enter Class IV and become public goods that are free of charge or semi-free. Intrinsic indivisibility, as can be seen from the examples in Table 3.1, is extremely widespread. But the goods in question, as in fact shown by the examples given, are often the fruit of massive public investment and technological progress, with regard to which the market is far more efficient than the public economy. What is required, therefore, is to reconcile static efficiency, which points in favour of non-application of the exclusion principle, with dynamic efficiency, which points in favour of applying it and leaving these goods up to the market as far as possible. Class IV consists of two types of goods: those that are intrinsically indivisible and transactionally divisible but whose division is undesirable, and other goods that are intrinsically and transactionally indivisible. Therefore the market cannot supply the latter type unless they are linked to advertisements through which the market obtains a gain from the subjects who advertise themselves. These are public goods *par excellence*. Their class is theoretically important. But most goods supplied by public finance even in a model which follows the principle that the public economy needs to intervene only in case of important market failures, as in the model followed by the present author, do not belong to this category.

1.4 Pure Intrinsically and Transactionally Indivisible Public Goods, or Samuelsonian Goods

Intrinsically and transactionally indivisible goods have two characteristics that allow them to be defined as *pure public goods*:

a. one unit of such goods can be enjoyed simultaneously by an indeterminate number of subjects;
b. subjects that do not wish to pay for this use cannot be excluded.

The most typical class of such goods, which we denominate as 'Samuelsonian'[5] consists in knowledge goods: both the goods of scientific and technological knowledge and also those concerning legal and ethical knowledge consisting in the rules that regulate or can regulate the life of society, and in cultural and heritage goods (art treasures and the historical heritage, as well as design) and ecological goods whose value consists in their existence also independently from their use. These are pure Samuelsonian goods. Everyone can enjoy them, and if certain individuals are unwilling to pay a price for the pleasure, they nevertheless cannot be excluded from enjoyment. On the other hand, those who do not appreciate them can simply avoid using them. The case is similar to that of an unencrypted television show: whoever does not wish to watch the programme changes channel or turns the set off. It is well known, however, that these goods, which are public by nature, can be ceded by enterprises, and their utilization is then accompanied by advertisements, for which the enterprises are paid by the advertisers.

If the goods of scientific, technological and cultural knowledge are protected by patents and copyright royalties that prohibit their reproduction and free utilization, and if they are excludable because they are embodied in a material form (as is the case with statues, paintings, antiquarian books, and so on), then they do not belong to the category of Samuelsonian goods. But copyrights and royalties have a limited duration and can never entirely cover the creations of the human creative mind. Anyone who has read a poem, listened to a musical composition or observed a patented good has learned a form of knowledge that generates further knowledge. Moreover, the fact that cultural goods embodied in a material object are excludable does not imply that they are not, for part of the value, Samuelsonian goods. For instance, many people have never seen Leonardo's *Last Supper* and the Leaning Tower of Pisa unless it be as a reproduction, but they would feel unhappy if these goods of the cultural heritage were destroyed. This can be explained by the fact that the existence of these cultural goods has a value independently of their use, for all people who have any love or respect at all for cultural values. A similar argument holds for the landscape and for living species as goods of the environmental heritage.

Among Samuelsonian goods one can also list the general expenses for the functioning of the *democratic* government, which are to the advantage indivisibly of all members of the community under consideration (the State, the Region, the Local Authority of one's place of residence). Democracy, as such, is an indivisible public good, which is to the advantage of all citizens, without the possibility of exclusion of those who do not pay. This contrasts with defence, which could be supplied on the market, as will be seen in the next subsection. But it should be noted that democracy is not a pure Samuelsonian good, as there can be different and conflicting preferences in this regard: some would wish to have a presidential republic, others a parliamentary republic, and yet others would prefer restoration of the monarchy. Therefore some subjects obtain a lesser utility from democracy than others, as they have to put up with other people's preferences. On the other hand, the preferences of those who do not favour democracy but would prefer an authoritarian state are irrelevant, in our formulation, as these are antisocial preferences which do not form part of legitimate welfare. Everybody will have to pay the cost of democracy, *pro quota*, even if it is not to their liking, because belonging to the public cooperative is compulsory in the democratic government model, in contrast to the choice of belonging to a cooperative in the market economy.

As far as divisible goods are concerned, for each quantity demanded by a subject i, there is a specific average unit cost and a marginal cost. But the situation is different with regard to intrinsically indivisible public goods. With one unit of the given good it is possible to satisfy a plurality of subjects $a, b, . . ., m, n$. There is no marginal cost for its utilization by an additional subject b as well as a or by m in comparison to its use by n.

A distinction can be made between goods that are intrinsically indivisible and that have no limit, in the sense that each person can utilize them without any marginal cost, and those whose utilization is vast but not unlimited. These goods can be defined as imperfectly Samuelsonian in contrast to the pure Samuelsonian goods described earlier.

> With regard to their use value many goods of the cultural and landscape heritage are *imperfectly* Samuelsonian in the sense that they can be enjoyed simultaneously by a large number of subjects, but not an indeterminate number of subjects. The Colosseum can be freely admired from the road that leads from the EUR district of Rome to the centre of the city, and from countless windows, balconies and terraces in the surrounding area, but it would not be possible for a colossal crowd to admire it because such sites have a finite capacity. The same holds true for the landscape that can be admired, for instance, by looking towards the beaches or the roads or the buildings facing the strait between Calabria and Sicily, on either side of the water.

Also, there is a certain degree of conflict with regard to goods of the cultural and landscape heritage because some subjects would like to have a more leafy landscape while others would prefer to have a greater number of historic buildings. Different attitudes are also found with regard to restoration works.

> Some would like Scilla to be preserved as a nineteenth-century fishing village whereas others aim to reconstruct it as a medieval town. But in either case, the result of the restoration is a cultural good, that can be enjoyed:
>
> - as a value in terms of its existence, by all those concerned;
> - as a use value, up to congestion point, by those who travel to the location.

City streets may often be considered as quasi Samuelsonian goods: their divisibility into units of sale is not feasible except with prohibitively high transaction costs because this would impede trading exchanges and civil life; and they have an intrinsic limited indivisibility, consisting in the absence of marginal costs for utilization by additional users; however, intrinsic indivisibility was a much more frequent hypothesis in the era when motorized vehicles did not exist and there was less traffic than at the present day.

1.5   Utilization of Samuelsonian Goods as Compared to Market Goods

We can in any case compose a diagram, as in Figure 3.1, to represent the simultaneous utilizations of a Samuelsonian good by subjects *a, b, m, n* with absence of marginal costs as is characteristic of these goods. The situation can be represented by means of the simplified hypothesis of two subjects *A* and *B*, with demand curves $D_A D$ and $D_B D$. First, we plot the curve $D_A D$, which goes from D_A on the ordinates to *D* on the abscissae. Then we plot the curve $D_B D$ which goes from D_B on the ordinates to *D* on the abscissae. Now we sum the two curves, *putting one of them on top of the other, since they both use the same units of supply.* To do this we start out from the curve $D_B D$, which is the higher one, and then, on the ordinates, proceeding from point D_B we add the stretch of the demand of *A*, that is

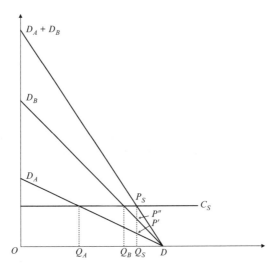

Figure 3.1   Intrinsically indivisible demands for public goods are to be summed vertically

to say, $D_A O$. We thus obtain, on the ordinates, the segment which is indicated at its summit by $D_A + D_B$, in Figure 3.1, and which arrives at O. Now we have to sum the demand curves of A and B, at their termination, on the abscissae. Since both of them terminate in D (but this is only a simplified hypothesis; in general they will terminate on the abscissae at points spaced at different distances) the sum always gives us D. And consequently, since the demand curves of A and B were straight lines, which converge on the same terminal point on the abscissae, the aggregate demand curve for this Samuelsonian good will be represented by the straight line that starts from D and arrives at $D_A + D_B$.

If we suppose that the marginal cost curve for the good S is given by the straight line C_S, then the point of equilibrium in supply of this public good, assuming that each would-be consumer of the good reveals her preferences, will be given by P_S, in which the aggregate demand composed of the line $D_A + D_B D$ meets the cost curve. There, subject A enjoys good S in so far as concerns the *quantity actually demanded by A herself*, $Q_S P'$; this quantity corresponds to the segment $P'' P_S$, due to the way the demand curve is constructed. At the equilibrium point, subject B enjoys good S in so far as regards the quantity that B actually demanded, $P' P''$. It can be observed that if the good were not characterized by a Samuelsonian supply, but were instead a good with normal supply, subject A would only enjoy the quantity OQ_A, on the cost curve C_S, whereas subject B would enjoy the quantity OQ_B. But since the good in question is characterized by a Samuelsonian supply, both A and B enjoy the quantity OQ_S. The Samuelsonian nature of the good, under the same cost curves, generates a dilation of its utilization. And the supply of additional units of this will appear to be extremely advantageous, since many subjects can be satisfied by each one of the units. Given that every individual can utilize these goods without any possibility of excluding those who do not wish to pay the cost, citizens are made to bear the cost through taxation.

However, there is likely to be a tendency to refuse to pay by attempting to dodge tax payments, legally or illegally.

1.6 The Indivisible Public Wants of Law and Order of the 'Protection State' as Conflicting Independent Individual Wants that can be Satisfied Only Through Uniform Provision with Obligatory Consumption Throughout the Community

If one excludes the rules belonging to the sphere of the general principles of law, which may be defined as Samuelsonian public goods inasmuch as they are knowledge goods, only a small part of the other goods that serve to satisfy needs of justice, public order, defence – that is the need for 'protection of persons, their goods and the national territory' – are intrinsically and transactionally indivisible. A large part of such needs is constituted by goods that are perfectly divisible into units of sale but satisfy indivisible wants (see Table 3.1 above, class III), with the possibility of excluding those who do not wish to pay the cost. Many of these goods are intrinsically divisible: for instance services used in the lawcourts as part of criminal cases and civil litigation suits, or law enforcement agency services. Many goods forming part of military defence are intrinsically divisible: tanks, cannons, aircraft, cannot perform their service other than in a circumscribed space. It can be contended that goods such as missiles fitted with long-range nuclear warheads perform intrinsically indivisible services because the threat they pose generates the protection of a very extensive area of land, both close and distant. But their services could, in principle, be provided only to those who are willing to pay, thereby excluding the territories of the communities which decline to pay. Indeed, if one examines the real situation it becomes clear that they serve to defend only the nations that belong to a given alliance and not others, even though the latter might be within easier range of foreign attack. Large numbers of military services, even at the present time, are supplied by private organizations.[6] And in the past the private supply of goods and military services, as well as services in support of the judiciary and of law enforcement, was surprisingly extensive: suffice it to think of the private armies and police forces, and the courts of law, of lords and barons in the feudal era. As argued by Nozick (1974), abstractly considered, the need for protection could be satisfied on the market by armed 'protection' agencies, which would 'insure' those who joined the organization, making them pay membership dues commensurate to the cost of the protection of that person or groups of persons and their respective possessions and estate. Anyone who opted not to pay the 'insurance premium' would not be protected. And it is of no avail to object that the poor would thus be left devoid of protection, for this problem arises for any market good. The fact the poor and needy cannot afford bread and milk and decent housing is not sufficient to support the argument that these goods should be produced by the state itself. The state or the municipality will provide the poor with the means to procure these goods on the market.

Even in the present day and age, in well-ordered democratic states, private supply from the market exists side by side with public provision: for example, there are private security guards for the protection of banks and armoured cars, and forms of private arbitration for conflict resolution among enterprises or for 'sports justice'. Moreover, it is also worth bearing in mind that in our legal systems the cost of the public services of justice and public order is often paid for by those who effectively avail themselves of the services, in the form of official court charges, or charges imposed when administrative authorizations and certificates are issued, passport renewal charges, remuneration of court officers for delivery of writs, summons or notices or for execution of seizure warrants. Also, fines are not only a punitive matter: when it is a question of offences against state and local laws and regulations they also act as a compensation for the law enforcement services and the state and local legal systems.

However, these services are entrusted to the public operator because

a. the supply of the good defined as protection, discussed above, involves the use of force, to coerce those who damage the protected territories and 'persons' into not adopting certain modes of behaviour;
b. the supply of the good defined as 'protection' is enjoyed also by those who would prefer not to have it because they do not wish to bear its cost;
c. the supply of the good defined as protection involves the use of force; this implies that those who demand it trust those who supply it;
d. as protection concerns a relation among subjects, it implies that these subjects will trust that those who are empowered to deliver it will do so impartially.

Simplifying this framework, given three subjects A, B, C, in order for A's protection to be satisfied it is necessary for:

1. C not to damage A and B (*active defection* from admissible behaviour);
2. B to accept to defend herself from C, who is damaging B (passive defection, from defence of her own rights);
3. A, B, C to entrust a subject D with behaving impartially in cases 1 and 2 and with not using her power to exploit or oppress A, B or C.

The need for protection experienced by the various subjects is interdependent, and interferent, that is conflictual, and based on trust.

It is *interdependent* in the sense that protection of subject B provides an advantage for subject A, and that of subject A provides an advantage for subject B. That is to say, a large proportion of citizens feel not only the need to protect *themselves, in a specific manner, against such violations, but they also feel the need for protection, in an equal manner, for the entire territory of the community in which they live and for all its members.*[7] It is necessary to provide the good known as 'protection' to everyone, even to those who cannot pay for it or those who would prefer not to pay because they are not individually affected (enough), or those who would prefer to disobey.

This individual need *is intrinsically interferent and conflictual* in the sense that if those who do not abide by the rules remain unpunished, they often draw advantage from their behaviour, and also in the sense that ideas about justice, defence, law and order can differ sharply in relation to different values, and therefore they require a solution *super partes.*

It is a need for trust-based goods, because supply of this protection cannot be entrusted to private individuals, who might make an attempt at achieving a dominant position to their own advantage or to the advantage of some third party. Therefore citizens entrust the public subject with carrying out the service, subscribing to a pact of submission in exchange for which the public subject is assumed to perform the function of an impartial sovereign. In a democracy, this public authority, *trusted by the citizens*, that is supplying *trust-based goods*, is the expression of the will of the citizens.

All this holds not only for conflicts of interest and principles with regard to international politics or for the 'high' conflicts of domestic policy,[8] but also for the 'low' conflicts involving economic policy, concerning the various rules that regulate the market and property rights. Precisely in order to avert the risk that force, the rules, and the activity of the judiciary are not supplied in a biased manner, they are 'publicized', that is removed from the sphere of private and semi-private groups, reserving them to the sphere of the state as the 'impartial' holder of violence of the last resort.[9]

In a democratic regime, decisions concerning these public needs of *law and order* that are binding on all citizens are subject to vote, according to the majority voting procedure. In the case of 'great principles' this will be a question of 'constitutional' choices that should require a qualified majority (see Chapter 1, subsection 2.1 and Chapter 6, section 1). In some cases agreement is possible by means of reciprocal concessions (see Chapter 4, section 4).

So far, we have drawn a distinction between public wants involving Samuelsonian goods, the supply of which satisfies a number of subjects simultaneously, on the basis of their individual marginal utility, and the want for protection involving defence, justice, order and security, which is public – even if the goods to satisfy it are divisible intrinsically and transactionally – because it is interdependent, conflictual and trust-based. But it should be underlined that this distinction is not academic. These needs can be defined as institutional needs, with reference to the institutions of civil society and the market. Solid institutions of external security, domestic order and security and justice are essential for economic development. They should not be considered in terms of the vertical sum of demands or in connection with the difficulty of ascertaining and catering for individual preferences whenever the exclusion principle cannot be applied, as is the case for Samuelsonian goods: rather, they should be examined in reference to the critical issues that emerge in connection with the above-described characteristics of such needs. Here below we present some theorems that help to address these matters.

1.7 The Collective Need for 'Rules' and for 'Public Protection' of the Market Rules and the Prisoner's Dilemma

To understand why it is necessary to have rules *that are enforced by means of efficient institutions* in order to achieve good functioning of the market, it is important to introduce the fundamental game-theory theorem concerning the public economy, namely what has now become the celebrated 'prisoner's dilemma'.

Let us consider (Table 3.2) the two prisoners *A* and *B* who are each kept in solitary confinement and who have apparently committed a crime jointly.[10]

The Public Prosecutor subjects them to interrogation, informing them that if one of them tells the truth before the other does so, the former will be offered a plea bargain with the recommendation of a substantially lighter sentence, assuming the prisoner in question is effectively guilty.

Obviously, if they were innocent or the crime they committed could not be proven, they would have nothing to worry about by keeping silent. But if they did commit the crime and if the Public Prosecutor can, on the basis of their statements, gather evidence to prove their guilt, they will find themselves facing the following dilemma.

If *A*, abiding by a mafia pact of silence he has agreed to with *B*, keeps his mouth shut and is certain that *B* is doing likewise, the situation is optimal for both. Neither of them squeals and the Public Prosecutor fails to 'get a

Table 3.2   The prisoner's dilemma

A DOES NOT CONFESS, NOR DOES *B*	*A* DOES NOT CONFESS, *B* CONFESSES
Box I	Box II
A and *B* are released from prison shortly thereafter	*B* is soon released and *A* is given the maximum sentence
A CONFESSES, *B* DOES NOT CONFESS	*A* CONFESSES, *B* CONFESSES
Box III	Box IV
A is soon released and *B* is given the maximum sentence	*A* and *B* are both given half the maximum sentences

conviction'. Therefore, they are both released from jail shortly afterwards for lack of evidence. But A receives a visit from the Public Prosecutor who informs the prisoner that if he turns state's evidence he will be offered a plea bargain with the promise of a far lighter sentence, and will in fact soon be released from jail; he is further informed that another Public Prosecutor is already on her way to B or has perhaps already started interrogating B and is making the same proposals, and only the one who is the first to confess will receive the benefit in question. Both of the prisoners now have only two pieces of information: 1) as regards each one of them, what it would be advantageous to do if the other one does not do this; and 2) as regards each one of them, that fact that the same choice paradigm is offered to the other one. Neither of the two has or gives the information that he is most strongly interested in, which consists in knowing at each moment (regime of complete and perfect information) what the other is doing and telling the other what he himself is doing.

Therefore the two have to choose according to the 'paradox of isolated choices'. A knows that if he keeps silent and B squeals, A will be given the maximum sentence. B knows that it he keeps silent and A squeals, B will be given the maximum sentence. Each of them knows that the other party does not know what the first of them is doing, but each of them knows what he has to do to save his skin, namely be the first to squeal. Each of them is well aware that if both of them confess, the sentence will be lighter as compared to what it would be if he himself did not confess whereas the other did. Thus both confess in order to prevent the other from 'getting in before him'. This enables both of them to benefit from a somewhat lighter sentence in return for cooperating with the criminal justice system, but not the 'far lighter sentence' that had been promised to whoever would be the first to squeal. The result is that of Box IV, which is worse for both than if neither had confessed.

It is thereby demonstrated that if the two prisoners are considered as the whole of society, the isolated action can produce individual actions which, despite being rational – in the given circumstances – are damaging to both of them and therefore to the society as consisting of them, and therefore are basically irrational.[11]

If society lacks rules for respect of persons and contracts, or if such rules exist but there are no institutions to enforce them because they are over-elaborate and too inefficient, the market cannot function because bilateral situations of the prisoner's dilemma type arise. It becomes advantageous for each individual not to respect the agreements entered into or the rules currently in force, because this bad behaviour is not sanctioned adversely by the institutions. Therefore no one has trust in others: trading exchanges, investments and productive activities thus become very risky.

Tom enters into a contractual agreement with Dick whereby Tom undertakes to rent out a piece of land to Dick in return for a monthly rental fee. But the rules concerning the obligation to pay are not clear and are not enforced. Furthermore, the rules concerning Tom's obligation to leave his land to Dick, without occupying it or harvesting the fruits or taking some of the harvest when it suits him are not clear and are not enforced. Thus Tom is not certain that Dick will pay the rent, and fears that Dick may refuse to pay, basing his refusal on the grounds that Tom has violated the rules establishing that full use of the land should be granted to Dick. And Dick is afraid that Tom will not respect the obligation establishing that (full) use of the land should be granted to Dick, because – so the latter fears – Tom will be racked by the worry that Dick may not pay the rent. Therefore each member of the pair, each believing that the other one will fail to abide by the agreement, will do exactly as occurs in the prisoner's dilemma, namely be the first to make their confession, that is violate the trust-based agreement. Fearing that this may happen, the rental contract will not be undersigned. In the absence of good rules, the market economy will not thrive.

But it is worth noting that the advantage the prisoner may derive from betraying the conspiracy of silence agreed upon with his mate, and thus from confessing, in other words from not abiding by the rules when the other party is actually respecting them, is dependent on the game being played once only. Suppose that subject *A* has confessed, and after having been freed he decides to join up with some others in order to carry out another robbery. But he is unlikely to find anyone that wants him in their gang, given his *reputation* as an opportunist prepared to betray his mates. In contrast, a subject *M* who has not confessed will, after release from jail, easily be able to find a gang willing to take him on for new criminal undertakings, because he has acquired the *reputation* of a reliable person. The situation is similar for economic operators. Those who repeatedly deceive their counterparts acquire a bad reputation and forsake the chance of clinching a good deal. Instead, those who do not deceive their opposite parties acquire a good *reputation* and can thus increase their volume of business. Furthermore, it is far easier for such a situation to come about in a small community, where *information* circulates easily, than in a large community where there are *difficulties in obtaining information*. There also exist activities involving business, finance and specialized trade in which information on correct and inappropriate behaviour does not easily emerge, given the informational asymmetry between those who manage business affairs and the opposite parties. Finally, in a global market economy each operator virtually finds himself facing all the markets of the whole world. But precisely for this reason, if one does not want a given area to lose its reputation for economic reliability, it is necessary for the institutions to function efficiently and for there to be authorities entrusted with market surveillance, and such authorities should not only enforce the rules but also acquire and transmit information.

1.8   The Theorem of 'Free Riding' and the Economic Efficiency of Public or Private Property Rights; the Paradox of 'Big Numbers'

The theorem of 'free riding' demonstrating the role of property rights and of the efficiency of institutions for protection of such rights in economic development, and the need for their public protection by means of adequate institutions, is a further version of the paradox of isolation. However, it differs from the 'prisoner's dilemma' in that it does not presuppose just a few subjects, but instead a very large number. Here, each subject, engaging in an action that undergoes no punitive sanction from the social group, generates such a tiny damaging external effect that it is irrelevant for the overall scenario that involves all the other players. But taken together, all these tiny effects deriving from the actions of a very large number of subjects generate a highly damaging result, for the overall body of subjects. And when they realize what has happened, it is too late.

Devising an agreement to avert these actions is very tricky because of the large number of subjects among whom agreement has to be reached. Violations are hard to uncover because the group is extremely large and the damage deriving from limited violations is small. Moreover, it is difficult to transmit information privately concerning violations of any agreements that have been reached, as the group is not only enormously vast but also fluid (many subjects are in that location only temporarily).

A good illustration of this game paradigm is given by the case of woodcutters who have free rein to exploit a vast forest that is free from property rights. Each of them can gather wood just as they like, by burning the trees if they so desire, in order to reduce the effort required. Each of them knows that even if she does not act in this way, others she may not know at all most certainly will. But by so doing, these 'free riders', taken together, will rapidly destroy the whole forest, as they will fell a greater number of trees, day by day or month by month, than the quantity that should be left standing to maintain the capital intact (considering the natural growth rate of trees). Anyone who abstains has a smaller amount of timber, and since the others are effectively felling trees, a person who abstains will certainly not be in a better situation, but rather will find herself in a worse condition if she persists in her restrictive behaviour.

Looking at Table 3.3, let us suppose that A is the group of the a subjects, who amount to 50 per cent, and B is the other 50 per cent, composed of the b subjects. The situation that emerges if the A group refrains from felling too many trees but the B group fells too many, or, alternatively, if A fells

Table 3.3   The theorem of the 'free rider'

A FELLS FEW TREES, *B* FELLS FEW TREES	*A* FELLS FEW TREES, *B* FELLS TOO MANY TREES
Box I	Box II
The forest supplies a permanent source of timber	*B* grows rich for two years but by then the forest has been destroyed
A FELLS TOO MANY TREES, *B* FELLS FEW TREES	*A* FELLS TOO MANY TREES, *B* FELLS TOO MANY TREES
Box III	Box IV
A grows rich for two years but by then the forest has been destroyed	*A* and *B* grow rich for one year but by then the forest has been destroyed

too many trees and the *B* group holds back, is a doubling of the time in which the forest is destroyed as compared to Box IV (where all subjects fell as many trees as they can).

We will now focus on *a* as a member of *A*: when all the *A* subjects fell 'too many trees' and the *B* subjects do likewise, then *a*'s decision to refrain from felling 'too many trees' will be so irrelevant that *a* will in any case be faced with destruction of the forest by the time a year has gone by, without having even grown rich from her actions. In other words, *a* will be in an even worse situation than that sketched in Box IV, which is of the 'prisoner's dilemma' type.

If the situation contemplates the presence of property rights and it is genuinely enforced, each subject will act according to her own advantage with regard to felling trees in the forest she owns. If the forest is government property and the government intends to make it available for public use, then the government can introduce regulations to 'ration' use of this good and safeguards to enforce them. Alternatively the government may allow the forest to be divided into individual properties *and protect them* so that each family will have an interest in felling the amount of trees that suits them best.

The theorem of the free rider described above is useful in gaining insight into the 'need for rules' concerning the right to use free environmental goods. Thus a theorem that basically demonstrates the need for private property and for state protection of property rights, which are fundamental for the market economy, actually also applies to the state as the 'protector' of nature.[12]

There are goods (as we saw in Chapter 2, subsection 1.10) that do not derive from the hand of man, but are instead part of nature: for instance 'space' and birds flying in the atmosphere, rivers, lakes, seashores, forests and so on.

Table 3.4   The theorem of abiding by the traffic regulations

Those coming from the right have priority and proceed onwards / those coming from the left have to stop

A AND *B* CONFORM TO THE RULE *A* and *B* gain 10 each *A* CONFORMS TO THE RULE BUT *B* DOES NOT *A* loses 5 and *B* loses 10	*A* DOES NOT CONFORM TO THE RULE BUT *B* DOES *A* loses 10 and *B* loses 5 *A* AND *B* DO NOT CONFORM TO THE RULE *A* and *B* both lose 10

These goods – in an advanced democratic society – are left for common use and since they are not available for private appropriation, they are considered as 'free goods'. But a situation that satisfies all citizens' need to have a *habitat* in which to spend time and live freely and have access to natural resources, in a regime where anyone's opportunity for access is potentially equal to that of any other citizen, also generates problems of wastefulness.

> This is the case regarding fishing in free waters, a case that has been known since it was presented in the nineteenth century by H. Sidgwick (1883): if each individual fishes freely, even during the reproduction period, capturing small fish as well, the fish stocks may fairly soon be depleted.

1.9   The Theorem of the Rule of Driving on the Right or on the Left and Conventions as a Reciprocity Game

It should however be borne in mind that the prisoner's dilemma and that of the free riding discussed above are not the only game paradigms theoretically possible, in the hypothesis of interdependent behaviour of two or more subjects facing two possibilities. We can modify the chart shown in Table 3.2 and assume that when subjects *A* and *B* adopt different modes of behaviour with regard to the rules, whoever fails to respect them does not obtain a benefit but instead suffers greater damage than whoever abides by them. Consequently, this prompts a tendency to respect the rules. Let us hypothesize two travellers *A* and *B*, driving along two roads that cross each other. We will further suppose that by convention, a rule of priority for the driver coming from the right has been established. *A* and *B* have, as usual, four alternatives, which can be represented with Table 3.4, concerning respect for the rules. We will suppose that in the case of a collision the subject who does not respect the rules has to pay for the damage. But let us now also suppose that the injured party does not always succeed in demonstrating that the other party is responsible for the damage, and thus the injured party may fail to obtain compensation. We will further hypothesize that whoever violates the rule of granting priority to those coming from the right and is involved in a collision with a subject who exercises this right of priority suffers greater damage, amounting to, let us say, 10, as compared to the injured party, whose damage amounts to, let us say, 5. When both subjects fail to respect the rule, because the subject coming from the right jams her brakes on and stops instead of going forward and then they end up colliding, their damage amounts to the maximum, let us say, 10.

In this case, as can be seen, violating the rule does not lead to an advantage for whoever is guilty of the violation, and at the same time it causes a damage, presumably of a lesser degree, to the other party. If, in a given community, the rule of driving on the right prevails and thus the related rule of priority awarded to those coming from the right also prevails, then it is very likely to be respected because those who try to get round the rule obtain no particular advantage from so doing. It is also worth noting that this is a reciprocity rule, as each individual has the same probability of coming either from the right or from the left, and therefore each individual will sometimes have to grant priority to someone else, but on other occasions will have the right to priority. Thus each individual is willing to accept this rule. Therefore there exist rules that people abide by, when it is their turn, and there is no advantage in violating them. But, as we have seen, if the game is repeated and there is plenty of information on who defected, there is still no advantage in violating the rule. Therefore it can be stated that with regard to the rise and development of rules and constant respect of the rules, to a large extent they become established by a form of spontaneous order when it is a question of reciprocity rules: they are 'conventions' that arise little by little, and all individuals find it advantageous to recognize and respect them. Consequently, for precisely the reasons described above, they become more solid than the written law books of the states and thus become Samuelsonian goods available to any civilized society. However, 'spontaneous order' is not sufficient for the necessities of advanced states, which operate in a regime of democracy, even though it is true that the rules regulating property rights, exchange of goods, enterprises and business, loans, the employment relation and performance of personal services, as well as rules governing marriage, kinship ties, inheritance and so on have to a large extent developed without any need for specific activity by the state, on the basis of jointly accepted precepts that are interpreted by experts.[13]

This is indeed the process that gave rise to commercial law, in the era of ancient Rome and throughout the greater part of the Middle Ages. It arose as a 'set of conventions', mainly produced by society itself. And with the emergence of commercial law the various customs and institutions that regulate the market also took shape, developing by evolution and selection, starting from the systems of weights and measures, the figure of notaries, and so on.

But in order for rules to be characterized by certainty and to be equal for all persons, they have to be codified, and many of the rules of the game, such as those pertaining to the safeguarding of competition, the Stock Exchange, consumer protection and so on have to be built up by means of ad hoc specialized knowledge. Moreover, their enforcement requires an adequate institutional apparatus.

A highly developed state cannot do without codes, public law courts to settle civil controversies, public officials for protection of contracts and the property of enterprises and so on.

1.10   Dupuit's Indivisible Goods, or Intrinsically Indivisible Goods, which Allow for Transactional Divisibility, and which are Partly Dividable into Units of Sale and Partly not Dividable

As we have seen, there are goods which could be transactionally divided into units of sale, but which are still characterized to a high degree by the capacity to satisfy many different subjects simultaneously (up to saturation point). Although exclusion of those who do not wish to pay is in this case often (not always) technically possible, it is – prior to congestion point – economically inefficient.

The theoretical analysis of these goods as potentially public goods dates back to Dupuit, who, in the very early nineteenth century, was dealing with the question of roads and bridges. On the assumption of fairly light traffic (as was the case at the outset of the nineteenth century), these goods can give a benefit simultaneously to all those who want to travel on them, without any additional cost for the community.[14] One could extend this list to include such goods as tunnels, ports, navigable canals and lighthouses.

In the case of a lighthouse, its owner-operator could impose a toll on each user, for instance by using remote-controlled reconnaissance systems and patrol boats to block those who do not pay. However, this would not necessarily imply that the optimal solution, from the social point of view, would be for such a service to be supplied as a private good and with an individual price determined by the market.

> Why not? Because society would have an additional cost, equal to zero in allowing every additional ship to use the service; consequently every ship that would be discouraged from entering into those waters due to the presence of an admission charge would (prior to congestion point) cause an economic loss to society.[15]

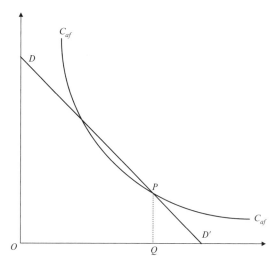

Figure 3.2   Dupuit indivisible semi-public goods

But there also exist lighthouses that perform a market service, charging the ship's crew a fee.[16]

'Dupuit type' goods (Figure 3.2) that are divisible into units of sale can be enjoyed simultaneously by n subjects (but not by an unlimited number of subjects) without the unit consumption of the ith subject leading to a (substantial) decrease in the utility of the unit consumption of the $n - i$ subjects. In such goods, the occurrences of demand are summed vertically as in Samuelsonian goods. However, the fact that a charge can be made for such goods distinguishes the way they are treated in public finance from the way Samuelsonian goods are treated. And since we are concerned here with examining how advantageous it may be not to apply the charge, in Figure 3.2 we present a graphic representation that focuses not so much on the characteristic of the *demand*, which consists in the fact that n subjects can utilize the very same unit of supply simultaneously, but rather on the characteristic of the *supply*, which consists in allowing many utilizations (that is satisfying many users) simultaneously with the same unit of cost. We can define this unit of cost as the 'total fixed cost'.

On the x-axis we indicate the usage units (or utilizations) and on the y-axis the average fixed cost of each quantity of usage. Since many quantities of usage can be provided by a single unit of supply, this means that as the quantity of u gradually increases, the average fixed cost of each usage decreases, *and this reduction is proportional*: that is to say, the fixed cost of each usage decreases by the same proportion as the increase in number of usages. This is due to the simple fact that the cost pie is divided into as many slices as there are usages: if there are two usages, there are two fixed cost slices for each usage, and therefore each usage has an average cost of 50 per cent (100:2); if there are three usages, then there are three fixed cost slices and each usage has an average fixed cost of one-third; if there are 30 usages, there are 30 slices and the average fixed cost of each usage is one-thirtieth of the total fixed cost, and so on. Since the height of the unit average cost is shown on the ordinates and the number of units on the abscissae, their product is always identical, inasmuch as it is the total fixed cost. The curve which has a constant product, at each point individuated by the Cartesian axes of the abscissae and the ordinates, is an equilateral hyperbola.

We can thus plot the curve of the average costs of good D, of Dupuit type, with the shape of an equilateral hyperbola, which draws ever closer to the Cartesian axes. On the y-axis, at the origin, the entire cost is on the first unit of consumption. On the x-axis, as one moves gradually towards the right, the unit cost decreases, (almost) up to vanishing point, as the units of consumption gradually increase.

A private firm may try to maximize profits by selling a quantity lower than OQ which gives a price equal to average costs, that is zero profits. The quantity up to D' is wasted. If the aim of the regulator of the market is to balance the budget, it is necessary to choose quantity OQ, with price P which still results in 'wasteful' utilization of the good, for the whole of the part QD' up to the point where we find 'interested' users i intent on amplifying their unit consumption: in our Figure 3.2, point D', on the assumption that there is never any 'congestion'.

> Thus a motorway with toll charges that aims to cover the costs should 'exclude' all the potential users that are included in the segment PQD', who have a potential utility PQD' with the resulting 'wastage' of this 'consumer's rent'. To avoid this 'wastefulness', the motorway corporation should lower the price to zero, so that the entire demand can be satisfied. But at zero price it can survive only if the state (or the local authority) shoulders the cost. However the latter may increase, with an excess of staff and various types of wastefulness, because 'anyway it's the state that pays'. Since the corporation does not have a market revenue, but lives on public subsidy, it will not have any interest in improving the service, unlike a business which, to obtain a revenue, has to rely on paying customers. Roadworks for ordinary maintenance and road extensions will be slow, because the corporation has no interest in completing the works rapidly in order to expand its customer base.

In addition to these objections, one has to consider that financing the supply of Dupuit goods as free goods implies that somebody other than the consumers has to bear their costs. Also, any system of taxation which provides public services free of charge also generates distortions which reduce consumer and producer rents.

Therefore it is necessary for the 'rents' in question to be extremely significant, qualitatively and quantitatively, in order to justify public provision free of charge.

A compromise solution could consist in setting a lower price than the average cost, that is a so-called subsidized 'political' price (see Chapter 12).

1.11 Hotelling Goods, as a Sub-class of Dupuit Goods and Public Utility Enterprises with Subsidized Prices

A sub-class of the category of Dupuit-style goods is constituted by Hotelling-type goods. The latter type of goods not only have substantial fixed costs but also important variable costs;[17] but at the point of equilibrium between such costs and the demand curve they do not have sufficient revenue to cover the fixed and variable costs. Hotelling demonstrated that if one follows the rule of price equal to the marginal cost, then the enterprise finds itself facing a deficit. Let us consider the graph in Figure 3.3. In this figure a public utility enterprise required to pursue a balanced budget because of the constraints imposed by the public authority would tend to fix the price at level P', the point of encounter between average costs (fixed + variable) and the demand curve where the demand price is

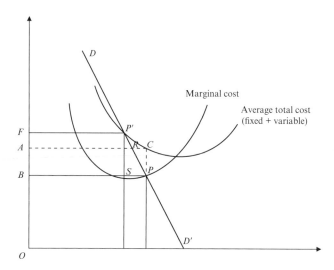

Figure 3.3   Hotelling semi-public goods

equal to the average cost. In this hypothesis, such a situation gives rise to
a waste of productive capacity amounting to SP', the segment of demand
in which marginal costs are lower than the marginal price of demand. The
extent of this waste can be seen by observing the segment of the demand
curve $P'P$ in which demand clearly lies above marginal costs and therefore
the demand price is greater than the marginal cost. But if there is only a
single demand price and it cannot be differentiated, for the portion of the
demand curve that is higher than average costs and for the portion of the
demand curve that is below average costs, then fixing the price at P, for the
quantity OQ for which the marginal demand price is equal to the marginal
cost, involves a deficit. This is because at this point the demand curve has
now gone below the average cost curve, and therefore, while price P does
cover the marginal costs, it does not cover average costs. Naturally, this
depends on the weight of fixed costs with respect to average costs. This
observation brings us back to Dupuit's theorem, with the difference that
now the enterprise operates both with fixed costs and also with variable
costs, and at the equilibrium price that is optimal from the allocative point
of view the enterprise covers variable costs but not (all) fixed costs. Price P
generates a deficit which, in the conditions of our figure, is equal to $PCAB$,
and it is a pronounced deficit, as shown by the rapid drop of demand in
the segment expressing the gap between average costs and marginal costs.
The deficit $PCAB$ could be covered by the public economy with a subsidy
to the enterprise under consideration on the basis of the theorem of the
optimum allocation of resources, which holds that prices should equal
marginal costs. Almost the whole of the subsidy, that is $ARBP$, translates
into the consumer's quasi-rent, while RCP constitutes a marked loss from
the point of view of collective welfare, that is an expense borne by the
exchequer that does not give rise to a producer's rent. However, RCP
is less than $SP'CP$, of which it is only a particular portion, namely the
increase in consumer's rent referring to 'new' usages, which are achieved
with the rule of price at marginal cost rather than at average cost. To this
should be added the gain in consumer's rent obtained by the 'old usages'
which would have continued to exist even with the rule of price at average
cost and which now pay a lower price amounting to $FPBS$, so that their
benefit exceeds the subsidy concerning this particular segment of production $FP'AS'$. Therefore both new and old usages have a net benefit higher
than the subsidy they enjoy. Assuming that the beneficiaries tend to be
identified with the taxpayers who shoulder the burden of the subsidy, the
operation is advantageous even in an individualist non-redistributive perspective, as that of the cooperative model tends to be. Furthermore, if the
marginal usages, which come onto the scene with the price decrease, refer
to low-income subjects, for consumption that taxpaying citizens consider

to have top priority, then the subsidy is justified in the cooperative model as well. Considering the likely perverse effects of the subsidies on the behaviour of the subsidized enterprises, as already seen for firms supplying Dupuit goods, this may hold for public utility services that give a *widespread benefit* such as rail transport and also city and suburban transport in areas where too many cars may cause congestion.

The subsidy could be awarded to enterprises of the given sector so as to cover part of their fixed costs, which would be established a priori by calculating standard costs. However, the enterprises would have to adopt prices equivalent to the marginal costs calculated with the criterion of standard costs. This would be necessary in order to ensure that such enterprises could be run advantageously in terms of the market economy, rewarding enterprises that succeeded in being efficient and managed to operate with costs not exceeding the above-mentioned standard costs. It is not necessary for the enterprises offering the service to be public: they could be private or public enterprises selected by the public operator (for instance the local authority for city public transport) by means of a call for tenders through a public procurement offer. But in order to assess whether such public action is appropriate or not, two factors that set limits on public intervention should be kept constantly in mind, as they have a bearing on the issue of the 'failures' of the public economy. Namely, subsidies have to be financed through taxation, and the taxes may themselves cause distortions: in fact, they sometimes have adverse distributive effects that exceed the positive effects generated by the subsidies they are designed to allow. Deficit-based public management often triggers irresponsible behaviour by the public bureaucracies and thereby generates inefficiency. Consequently it may be advisable to establish prices that ensure a balanced budget,[18] with recourse to tariff discrimination if necessary (see Chapter 12, section 3 ff.).

1.12 Semi-public Goods Consisting of Market Goods that Generate External Economies

As well as the issue of subsidies and political prices for public enterprises controlled by the government or enterprises selected through public procurement, in order to overcome the market failures shown by Dupuit's theorem and Hotelling's theorem, there is the question of subsidies and of the adoption of 'political' prices designed to take into account the 'external economies' generated by ceding goods on the market (which was addressed in Chapter 2, subsection 2.7).[19]

External economies can be analysed with a classification (Table 3.5) that is similar, although not identical, to that adopted in Table 3.1 for goods,

Table 3.5   External economies, real and pecuniary, specific and of the atmosphere kind

I	II
Specific pecuniary external economies An enterprise that purchases given production factors at decreasing costs (e.g. air transport, gas pipeline) benefits from the fact that other enterprises in the same district utilize them, and this may lower the prices. In this example the external economies are reciprocal.	*Specific real external economies* The enterprises of a given sector and/ or district acquire technological know-how and economic knowledge from other enterprises of the same sector and/or district, given that unpatented inventions and information not covered by copyright can be used without payment.
III *Atmosphere pecuniary external economies* The enterprises of a given specialized district obtain at a low price the specialized intermediate goods and services that interest them because of the economies of scale and the reduced transactions costs of their supplier, and they can supply their products, at a lower price. Firms that are part of the same district belonging to the production cycle, upstream or downstream, enjoy similar benefits. This leads to decreased costs and prices and to a new division of labour due to the increased size of the market. These too are reciprocal external economies.	IV *Atmosphere real external economies* The enterprises, the workers and the persons offering professional services who live in a certain district that has specialized in a certain production obtain, free of charge, various types of technological and cultural information and know-how that are part of the 'shared knowledge' of the district. At the same time, they act as drivers of this body of information and know-how, contributing to maintenance and development of the technological/cultural 'atmosphere' of the area.

with regard to intrinsic indivisibility and divisibility or indivisibility (or non-division) into units of sale.

In effect, from the point of view of indivisibility or divisibility, external economies can be distinguished into atmosphere external economies, that is indivisible external economies, which give a benefit simultaneously to *n* subjects, and specific external economies, that is divisible external economies, which go to the benefit of specific subjects taken singly. From the point of view of the users one can distinguish technological external economies, which consist in a benefit free of charge, and those that consist in price reductions for given goods: the latter external economies are denominated as pecuniary external economies. Specific and atmosphere technological external economies can themselves also be distinguished (we omit the illustrative table for the sake of simplicity) into tangible and intangible, in relation to their material or immaterial nature. Plantations on hillsides give tangible technological external economies to the surrounding areas of land, which are thus protected against landslides and mudslides. Enterprises that engage in new production processes or produce innovative goods generate intangible technological external economies of information for the other enterprises that imitate them.

The dichotomy of technological and pecuniary external economies distinguishes benefits of a real nature from benefits consisting in more favourable purchase prices for goods and services, inclusive of transportation costs and transaction costs deriving from extension of the market and increased competitiveness. Thus if an enterprise sets up in a nearby location to supply goods and services that previously had to be brought in from a more distant location, this constitutes a 'pecuniary external economy'.[20] Furthermore, real external economies can be distinguished into two categories. On the one hand there are so-called 'atmosphere' real external economies, which are to be considered as indivisible advantages that are enjoyed objectively free of charge, simultaneously, by a multitude of subjects (typically, information and knowledge, and thus everything that concerns scientific and technological progress and business innovation in production processes and products, market information, and so on). On the other hand there are specific real external economies of the 'unpaid factor' type, for which the externality may arise from prohibitive 'transaction costs' or legal prohibition[21] (for example a workforce that was trained in enterprise A can be hired by other enterprises B which are not obliged to pay A a fee for the training because slavery is forbidden). By contrast, pecuniary external economies are often of the atmosphere kind, because they arise from extension of the market and of market competitiveness (a 'broader financial market', or a market that is more competitive, is a 'good' that can be enjoyed 'free of charge' by a large number of subjects, simultaneously). A further possibility is that of specific external pecuniary benefits, such as overland, air, river or maritime freight transport at decreasing costs, in cases of increasing demand for transport.

In principle, in order to bring about the allocative optimum – in the presence of externalities, as seen in Chapter 2, subsection 2.7 – it would be necessary to expand supply beyond the point where private demand equals marginal costs, up to the point inclusive of the externalities; however, private demand only takes into account the benefits for the purchaser and does not consider the additional aspect of the external economies generated by the supply. In the case of specific benefits a good argument can be made for passing the burden on to the beneficiary. But in the case of indivisible benefits, concerning technological and pecuniary external economies, the cost of the expansion of the supply should be borne by the community on the basis of the principles we saw earlier for intrinsically indivisible goods, with Dupuit's or Samuelsonian characters. However, it must be taken into account that as well as market failures there are also government failures. Also, nothing guarantees that state aid by means of subsidized prices, favourable credit terms and tax relief motivated by the presumed existence of external economies will not, in turn, distort the market under the pressure of fiscal rent-seeking interest groups (see Chapter 5, section 2). It should be kept in mind, also, that there are limits on the expansion of public expenditure arising from the negative effects of taxation on the economy (see above, subsection 1.4).

> Although the so-called industrial policies (obviously) receive a rapturous welcome from market enterprises that benefit from such measures as well as from their organizations, these policies often represent a damaging distortion of the market economy.

Furthermore, not all external economies have an adverse effect on the margin of decisions taken by subjects who produce the external economies; therefore they do not always require public intervention in their favour as a means of achieving supply optimality. There are goods that private enterprises or private individuals may wish to produce in a greater quantity than the amount corresponding to an economic gain because they obtain a 'moral' return that compensates for part of the costs (this is frequently the case with the immaterial services offered by scholars and artists).[22] However, since the resources available to such private parties are limited, their possibility of generating external economies altruistically is limited.[23]

Another possibility concerns cases where the external economies are reciprocal and individuals obtain more from them than they give to third parties; as a result, *once the process is launched*, there is no need for subsidies.

> This situation can be observed, for instance, as regards the external economies that arise in the so-called 'industrial districts'. Italy, in particular, features an abundance of thriving industrial districts. They were theorized by Alfred Marshall at the turn of the nineteenth century on the basis of the English experience of his day, with policy inferences that are far from unambiguous.[24]

The theme of how external economy-generating processes may be triggered – with or without Government incentives – is addressed in the next subsection.

1.13 The Triggering of the Generation of Reciprocal External Economies: Sen's Reassurance Theorem and the Reciprocal Pecuniary and Real External Economies of Investments in New Sectors and Areas

In principle, a situation might arise where, since everybody *would be sure* they were going to receive as many external economies from others as they themselves would generate, everybody would end up producing and investing up to the amount corresponding to the hypothesis of obtaining the full return from their own activity. But the opposite situation may also come about, whereby each individual fears that the others are not going to invest, and therefore no individual makes an investment.

These problems were pointed out by A. Sen (1987) with his 'theorem of reassurance' (see Table 3.6). The situation, as Brennan and Buchanan (1985) subsequently demonstrated by adducing new arguments, tends to lead to a systematic underestimation of investments that refer to the

Table 3.6   The theorem of interdependencies for reciprocal external economies

I	II
A INVESTS IN *Z*, BECAUSE *A* BELIEVES THAT *B* WILL FOLLOW THE EXAMPLE / OR *B* INVESTS IN *Z* BECAUSE *B* BELIEVES THAT *A* WILL FOLLOW THE EXAMPLE AND THIS DOES HAPPEN	*A* INVESTS IN *Z* BECAUSE *A* BELIEVES THAT *B* WILL FOLLOW THE EXAMPLE, BUT THIS DOES NOT HAPPEN
A and *B* invest, and after a little while they gain a good return, others follow them and *Z* develops	*A* invests and does not gain a return, and after a while *A* closes down
III	IV
B INVESTS IN *Z* BECAUSE *B* BELIEVES THAT *A* WILL FOLLOW THE EXAMPLE, BUT THIS DOES NOT HAPPEN	*A* DOES NOT INVEST IN *Z* BECAUSE *A* BELIEVES THAT *B* MAY NOT FOLLOW THE EXAMPLE. *B* DOES NOT INVEST IN *Z* BECAUSE *B* FEARS THAT *A* MAY NOT FOLLOW THE EXAMPLE
B invests but does not get a good return, and after a while *B* has to close down	*A* and *B* make no investments. Neither of them gains a return and neither of them makes a loss, but *Z* does not develop

future. And this is all the more true when their potential yield is likely to be delayed to a later date.

Who makes the first move? Any individual player who ventures to make the first move but is not followed by other players risks failure. Moreover, if the one who makes the first move is successful and the others do indeed 'follow the leader', the first player will nonetheless find she has run a risk and has had to shoulder certain initial expenses that the others, who came afterwards, have not had to face to the same extent. And nobody is going to compensate the first player for this sacrifice.

The situation is illustrated in Table 3.6. Subject *A* is willing to undertake a certain project (for instance investment in a given business, in a new area *Z*), on condition she can be sure that *B* will follow with a similar initiative. But *B* finds herself in exactly the same position. If the two subjects *A* and *B* both invest in the area or sector *Z*, their enterprises will be profitable by virtue of the technological and pecuniary reciprocal external economies they generate. But let us further hypothesize that the area or sector *Z* is not yet sufficiently developed. And whoever is the first to set up a business there will be isolated, and could face operating at a loss or in conditions of great difficulty. If *A* and *B* adopt a cautious approach, given the risk that the other 'may not follow', then the investment will not be made even though it would later have become advantageous. If *A* invests and *B* does not follow her example, fearing that *A* will not persist long enough or fearing her own inability to resist long enough to make a good return, or if *B* is unable to obtain credit from the banks, which are sceptical, then *A* loses out and after a while has to give up the undertaking. Now, if we suppose that *B* invests first and *A* does not follow the example, for the reasons just stated, then after a while *B* will have to close down. If both of them invest, because they provide each other with credible information on their own intentions and banks are willing to finance them, they will both achieve success. Many others follow them and the area or sector *Z* develops.

But the enterprises that are needed for *Z* to take off can be extremely numerous. Exchange of information concerning the behaviour of those involved may be difficult and may have a low degree of credibility. Furthermore, when it is a question of investments, the problem of 'credibility' becomes more complex, because decisions depend on a series of circumstances both internal to the enterprises and also external (for example, the willingness of banks to finance the undertakings, or of the Stock Market to respond positively to a given issue of stocks). Additionally, the decisions may depend on forecasts concerning factors that are beyond the control of the set of operators considered (such as the international economic situation and the worldwide market trend concerning the new initiatives considered).

This theme is crucial in public choices for the promotion of the economic development of backward regions and nations. In the hypothesis considered, even limited public action could generate a development which not long thereafter becomes capable of fuelling itself and thus of repaying – in terms of benefits – the cost of the public aid implemented in the form of subsidies, favourable credit conditions, concession of land free of charge in equipped industrial areas, services free of charge or below cost and tax relief. Thus there may emerge a role for the state to intervene with inducements and incentives of various kinds (for example tax relief, favourable credit conditions, protective tariffs), or to carry out direct investments in Z through its public enterprises, thereby acting as a 'promotor'. Such investments furnish real and pecuniary reciprocal external economies and since the individual enterprise A receives from $N-A$ enterprises a greater quantity of such economies than the quantity A itself gives to $N-A$, a virtuous circle is created, similar to the vicious circle developing in the theorem of the free rider, but operating inversely. And public aid will have no need to become permanent.

1.14 Marshall's Theorem on Decreasing Cost Industries

According to the great early nineteenth-century economist Alfred Marshall, in principle the state has a good reason to subsidize decreasing cost industries or to protect them with import tariffs. Figure 3.4 (which is in accordance with that of Marshall on this subject),[25] contains the hypothesis of a subsidy that lowers the cost curve from SS to $S'S'$. While the subsidy generates a cost for the state amounting to $RP'TC$, it increases the consumer's rent by $cCTKP$, which is far greater, in the hypothesis considered – that is the hypothesis of an elastic demand curve and notably decreasing costs – than the burden shouldered by the State. In effect, since the two triangles $KP'T$ and KEP, above and below the demand curve, are virtually equivalent to each other, there remains a net benefit of $cPER$ for the consumers. It should be noted that here the movement is towards a lower point that is not on the same curve, but on a lower $S'S'$.

However, in Marshall's view this drop in the cost curve concerns not only the individual enterprise, but rather the entire branch of industries and the district considered.[26] This can be explained by the interdependence of investments and the related gradual emergence, over time, of 'irreversible' and 'localized' cost reductions due to the external economies of the technological atmosphere and pecuniary external economies, connected with the presence of a multiplicity of enterprises of a certain sector or of different sectors, which are linked to one another by intermeshed market relations over a given district. These enterprises gradually generate and

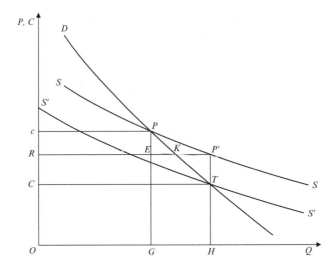

Figure 3.4   Marshall's theorem on decreasing cost industries

absorb specialized knowledge and technological progress by means of interdependent reciprocal actions, and they reciprocally supply an ever broader range of markets, with lower costs thanks to 'economies of scale' in production. This cost trend of an industry or of a specialized district (the so-called 'industrial' district, where 'industrial' embraces not only the manufacturing sector but every branch of production) is not incompatible with the neoclassical hypothesis, accepted by Marshall himself – of increasing costs *for individual enterprises* – in presence of increasing amounts produced. In this context it must be kept in mind that *at each subsequent time*, there is a *lower* curve of increasing costs corresponding to any given scale of production; furthermore, the greater the production scale of the subsequent periods, the lower is the curve, since a greater quantity of fixed capital can be more advantageously utilized, as J. Viner showed (Viner, 1931 [1952]). But naturally, the theorem can be applied to single enterprises as well, as long as they are decreasing-cost enterprises and are induced by potential competition from other enterprises to modify the price up to the point where average costs cross the demand curve.

As far as single enterprises are concerned, the reasons underlying this situation are to be found in Hotelling's theorem in which average unit fixed costs gradually decrease with increasing production. However, equilibrium at the point of encounter between the demand curve and the marginal costs gives rise to a deficit, because the average costs exceed marginal costs at this point. This is the case in many public utility services such as rail transport, airports, ports and also new technology enterprises that require substantial initial investments. It follows that in the beginning these enterprises are making a loss when demand is sluggish. But when demand begins to intensify in the wake of economic development of the area considered, they may begin to obtain a return on their investment because their demand curve meets the total average cost curve at a point where it is by now suitably low. This offers a justification for policies in favour of developing areas and of infant industries, including the option of customs tariffs to protect them from foreign competition. Such tariffs do not involve a cost for the treasury – on the contrary, they provide it with revenue. But they give rise to a hidden additional tax on the domestic purchaser from the price increase of the products in question on the domestic market. A subsidy would imply a cost for the treasury but would not lead to this hidden tax on domestic purchasers and would only benefit the marginal areas or enterprises. On the other hand, it would involve a discretionary power of the government authorities in choosing the district and enterprises supposedly entitled to that public aid. The most delicate problem of policies involving subsidies or protection through customs tariffs that could be justified with Marshall's theory lies in that fact that it is not clear when an industry or an infant district has reached adulthood and therefore no longer needs protection, and when the time has come to stop artificially favouring a developing area and instead leave it to find its own way to cope with market forces.

Moreover, subsidies and protections can give rise to monopolistic structures that provoke market distortions, which then tend to become protracted as a result of their accumulated power. Nor is it always easy to ensure that enterprises which have developed in a climate where they have continually been granted favourable conditions will acquire structures capable of operating effectively once the public aid has ceased.

In short, the satisfaction of this public want can give rise to extremely adverse effects and costs which, in some cases, may turn out to be excessive when the pros and cons are carefully weighed up. Thus it may be more appropriate not to carry out these interventions or substantially to reduce their scope and intensity.[27]

1.15 External Diseconomies of Production and Provision of Public Goods

External diseconomies of production can be classified with the same criteria as external economies. Thus they can be distinguished into technological and pecuniary diseconomies and also into atmosphere and specific diseconomies. In addition, technological external diseconomies can be distinguished into tangible and intangible technological external diseconomies. Fumes from power plants, petroleum refineries and other factories are typical examples of tangible technological external diseconomies. They are cases of atmosphere-external diseconomies, not only in the sense of everyday vocabulary, but also in the economic sense of external diseconomies that indivisibly concern a certain area, and more generally the planet. Pornographic films screened on television without time band limitations can, according to widespread public opinion, generate intangible technological external diseconomies that adversely affect under-age citizens. The external diseconomies produced by traffic congestion are, per se, reciprocal specific technological diseconomies for car users, whose journey costs and time spent on the road are increased, and atmosphere-related technological diseconomies for the inhabitants, who suffer the effects of motor vehicle pollution. But traffic congestion also generates pecuniary external diseconomies (and economies) because prices shoot up within the city areas, in particular housing prices, especially for buildings located near the centre of the city, as the cost of travelling from one place to another rises. These external diseconomies can be said to be generic because they involve the whole of the congested city. But they are, also, specific with regard to the areas that are hardest to reach due to lack of public transport, or with regard to areas that represent a nerve centre of business and working activities (for example presence of universities, law courts, markets, railway stations).

In the case of technological external diseconomies generated in production processes (which we saw in Chapter 2, subsection 2.8), should the parties be unable to reach an agreement, the first approximation method to remedy the inefficiencies arising from the presence of such diseconomies consists either in imposing a charge on those responsible for perpetrating the damage in favour of the damaged party or, alternatively, to let the damaged party pay the other party to cease causing the external diseconomy (cf. Coase's theorem in Chapter 2, subsection 2.8). It can be supposed that the offending party obliged to pay the charge may seek to avoid payment by endeavouring to avoid the external diseconomy through the installation of plants and facilities which prevent the damage or with the adoption of other substances in replacement of the source of pollution. But often the transaction costs involved in this manner of proceeding are prohibitive. Consider, for example, the pollution generated by use of motor vehicle petrol. Adoption of non-polluting or low-pollution fuel such as biofuels (for example ethanol) can reduce these external diseconomies. If one adopts the principle that cars have the right to pollute and it is up to damaged citizens to subsidize the cessation of external diseconomies that affect them, then in theory the inhabitants of cities polluted by the excessive circulation of petrol or diesel-fuelled vehicles should subsidize drivers for the use of non-polluting fuel. But the transaction costs make this impossible. It is more efficient for the state to provide a subsidy (which may take the form of exemption from the manufacturer's sales tax) for production of ethanol and biodiesel destined to automotive use or for promotion of the use of 'green fuel' within urban areas. The cost of these fiscal benefits will be borne by the general taxpayer.

On the other hand it could be established that it is up to those who are damaged by the atmospheric pollution and water contamination from industrial sources to set up purification plants as a means of putting an end to pollution or reducing these external diseconomies as far as possible, since industry has the right to produce them. But even in this case it is practically impossible for citizens to arrange the kind of organization needed to carry out such investments. The local or regional operator can undertake to do so on their behalf, by setting up purification plants the cost of which will be borne by all local citizens through taxation. A similar argument can be put forward for cases in which the polluting enterprises themselves are required to set up purification plants to eliminate or minimize pollution of rivers, lakes and seas. If each firm has to set up water pollution purification plants, this will have to be done with individual investments, which may prove to be inefficient because they do not adequately exploit economies of scale; furthermore, if procedures are undertaken by means of consortium agreements, these may give rise to lengthy contractual negotiations and elevated transaction costs for investment and management. Thus another alternative is for the state or the local or regional authority to undertake the task of setting up and managing such plants, on behalf of the industries that are obliged to eliminate the external diseconomies, passing on the costs to the industries through obligatory charges.

External diseconomies deriving from discharge of solid or liquid wastes from buildings onto roads, land or waterways cause damage to the environment and persons. The damage can be prevented by means of the collection, destruction and/or recycling of solid waste and by means of sewerage for liquid waste. However, elimination of these external diseconomies through refuse collection undertaken by enterprises or consortiums of enterprises, and through their use of collective private sewerage systems, may encounter insurmountable transaction costs and diseconomies of scale. Thus the public operator governing that particular area will have to intervene where the market fails, by means of its own refuse collection and disposal systems and the public sewer mains, passing on the burden of the cost to the users with obligatory charges and tariffs commensurate to the service. *A fortiori* the public operator will have to step in with its own supply of a public good to remedy the 'market failure' in the (unlikely) assumption that it is not up to those who produce waste to put an end to these external diseconomies, but rather that it is up to the damaged community itself. Under such an assumption, the burden of the cost should be shouldered by the entire (local) community, through taxation.

> Notice that if the good is public this does not imply that the public operator is the one that actually produces it: the public operator may use the services of companies chosen on the market by competitive tender.

Not all external diseconomies can be eliminated by government action at reasonable cost. Thus the excessive presence of cars on roads generates external diseconomies for other vehicle users. The expansion of built-up areas raises the value of these areas and generates pecuniary external diseconomies for other users. Noise and some of the atmospheric pollution generated by production activities and trade cannot be eliminated but only abated. One may argue that because the costs of external diseconomies in congested areas will tend to rise, not only for private individuals but also for enterprises, both these categories should choose other areas for their residences and activities. However, there is no guarantee that this process will be optimal. Indeed the presence of external diseconomies may not discourage new enterprises from setting up in such areas, if the benefits of the 'external economies' generated by enterprises already operating in the area exceed these diseconomies. But if they do choose to set up in these areas they may generate new external diseconomies without giving equivalent external economies. It can also be demonstrated that since there are external economies, which in any case attract new enterprises to intensely developing areas, the flow of activities tends to cease at a stage later than that of allocative optimality[28] which comes into being when the additional aggregate external diseconomies equal the aggregate external economies. Optimality can then be accomplished by appropriate urban zoning plans, reducing the space allowed for establishing industrial plants within cities.

1.16   Intervention by the Public Operator to Combat Damage Caused by Monopolies

If a monopoly arises in production, damage of a twofold nature is caused to the economy. First, there is damage due to price rises as compared to a regime of competition; such a phenomenon can be viewed as a sort of consumption tax in favour of the monopolist. Not only does this amount to an unjustified subtraction of purchasing power, but it also artificially reduces utilization of the good or service that has undergone a price rise.

Secondly, in a monopoly, there is a weakening of the incentive regarding product quality improvement, cost reduction and innovation which constitutes an intrinsic aspect of a competitive market. This results in a tendency towards inefficiency. However, at times it has been argued that widespread competition does not make it possible to make use of the economies of scale that spring from decreasing costs, or of the external economies enjoyed by large enterprises, which tend towards a monopoly.

The atomistic enterprise cannot capture the economies that are external to the enterprise itself but internal to the overall industry: instead, these can be captured by the monopolist acting as the only operator of the whole of a given industry. Moreover, the monopolist may decide that the profits accumulated through the monopoly can most advantageously be utilized precisely to carry out the appropriate innovations that will in any case boost the monopoly's profits and can at the same time avert potential competition from new enterprises.[29] Notice, however, that such a situation may come about if the monopoly does not take the form of a monopoly established by law.

But what is difficult to demonstrate is that a monopoly may be more favourable to economic optimality than a situation of competitive oligopoly, which – in turn – may be more efficient than atomistic competition, in the presence of substantial economies of scale and substantial industry external economies.

This points to a potential role for the public economy by anti-monopoly laws and by rules for the public utilities that tend towards the so-called natural monopoly, in such a manner as to prevent monopoly and foster oligopolistic competition.

On the other hand, an artificial tendency towards monopoly could arise from the state's purchasing policies, in cases where the state is induced, for reasons of security, standardization, simplification and confidentiality, to turn to a single supplier or one of a very limited number of suppliers, as is the case with military enterprises. These government procurement policies, which may appear favourable in the short run, can be damaging in the long run.

If the state is unable to regulate the private monopolies in question effectively, it may decide instead to operate by public enterprises. These should in any case be run according to rules comparable to those of an enterprise operating in a competitive regime, and should also have comparable prices. This principle of economic efficiency is currently enshrined in European competition law. On the other hand, to avert the dangers of monopoly, at times there is no need to have recourse to a public enterprise, as it is sufficient to ensure that licences for use of public goods which belong to the state are given to a multiplicity of operators.

This holds in the case of licences granted for use of the airwaves in voice, image and data transmission, air spaces for aircraft flight paths, and for costs involved in use of the sea and the soil and subsoil belonging to the public domain. Einaudi's argument that the state is often the cause of a monopoly is true to a large extent,[30] even if it does not imply that there will always be a valid reason for eliminating or changing public intervention in order to remove the monopoly that derives from state action.

2   THE FAILURES OF THE MARKET ON THE DEMAND SIDE

2.1   External Effects of Consumption and Merit Goods in the Cooperative Model and in Paternalist and Controlled Economy Models

Many public goods, as was seen earlier in the comments on Table 3.1, are not indivisible as regards supply, but they are the object of divided individual consumption and, in principle, they may involve payment of a price capable of covering the cost.

Schools, health care and hospitalization, the world of entertainment, certain museums, old-age pensions, and so on could be paid for on the market by those who benefit from them. In effect, there are private institutions that supply these goods (and services) on the market, in parallel with those that supply such goods (and services) as public goods.

In many of these cases it cannot be said that there are compelling 'failures' on the market *supply side* and that it is these putative failures which justify public provision to satisfy the need. Rather, a rational explanation for the action of the public economy – assuming that there is indeed a rational explanation – should be sought on the demand side (or at least – at times – not only on the supply side).

In this regard, two conceptual categories may be rationally invoked: consumption externalities and merit and demerit goods.[31] But as regards the latter, there is a fundamental difference between the cooperative model and the paternalistic or controlled economy model.

In the paternalistic model, the class of merit goods is amplified and modified, in accordance with the concept that a superior rationality of the state acts as a substitute for the citizens' will and desires. This translates into pursuit of what appears right to the public decision-maker rather than pursuit of citizens' subjective preferences, even if such preferences can be shorn of their irrationality and deficit of information. If there is a variety of choices, these are provided for citizens by the public decision-maker, and they do not result from citizens' different individual preferences.[32]

In the cooperative model, the public economy's action in satisfying merit goods is based on preferences citizens express in their capacity as electors, on the constitutional or post-constitutional level. And since this approach rests on the individualistic postulate of the 'sovereignty of the consumer', it implies that a) in order to enable citizens to satisfy these needs for merit goods, in the framework of the public economy, citizens should genuinely have the widest possible range of choices; b) public provision should be only a component of aggregate provision; c) public provision should whenever possible be done by transfers and tax incentives to private provision.

2.2 The External Economies of Consumption: their Interlacing with Merit Consumption and the Role of the Public Economy

The classification and the issues concerning the external economies of consumption are very similar (and at times identical) to those already noted with regard to the external economies of production. A typical example of 'atmosphere' external economies is that of private gardens that improve the environment. But private gardens also generate specific technological external economies for the nearby houses, which benefit from the pleasant view and the environmental enhancement.

There also exist pecuniary external economies that are peculiar to families, in relation to the demographic factor. If a nation has a low birth rate, families that generate children make a positive contribution to the labour supply and to global demand, thereby contributing to economic growth. This explains why favouring families by providing kindergartens, daycare centres, tax relief, monetary subsidies (child allowances), and so on is based on a sound economic reason and is not merely a question of social fairness.

External economies of consumption are widespread, and the arguments in support of a role for the public economy in favour of the external economies of consumption become more solid when the external economies have a relation with merit goods.

Those who go into higher education after leaving school give themselves an advantage but they also bring benefits to others in the sense that they provide the market with a supply of more highly qualified labour and contribute to spreading and increasing the capital of knowledge and culture in society. They also act as a driver of technological progress and contribute to expansion of the frontier of production.

> Those who purchase and protect cultural goods engage in a superior form of consumption that elevates their own personality towards higher perspectives, but they also generate external economies in the field of the arts and knowledge. They are similar to those who protect nature by enhancing their property with gardens and plants. And if these are goods supplied at decreasing costs, the effect contributes to price decreases, which can be categorized as 'pecuniary external economies'.

The existence of external economies of merit consumption (and of investment in merit consumption goods such as buildings of historic and artistic value) can justify public subsidies, tax exemptions, credit facilities, provision of service free of charge to those who are engaged in such activities.

2.3   External Diseconomies of Consumption

External diseconomies of consumption can be addressed with the same theoretical treatment as those of production. Thus they can likewise be distinguished into technological and pecuniary external diseconomies, and specific and atmosphere external diseconomies. Also, many external diseconomies of consumption are analogous to those of production.

> Household heating systems and private cars generate atmosphere technological external diseconomies for the habitat of cities where they are produced as well as for the air of the country and the planet as a whole, similar to those generated by factories and industrial vehicles. Private cars generate specific technological external diseconomies affecting other vehicles, as well as both generic and specific pecuniary external diseconomies resulting from traffic congestion. Household solid and liquid waste generate technological external diseconomies similar to those of solid and liquid waste deriving from productive activities. And with regard to the external diseconomies of consumption it is likewise possible to distinguish two hypotheses, depending on whether the burden of cessation of the diseconomy is to be borne either by whoever produces it or by whoever is adversely affected.

In the case of external diseconomies of consumption there may be a better reason for supplying public devices designed to reduce them, than is the case with external diseconomies of production. This is because private individuals are more numerous than enterprises and their specific external diseconomies are less easy to identify and eliminate through market methods.

> One method for reducing the technological and pecuniary external diseconomies deriving from private road transport (automobile and motor vehicle traffic) consists in the development of subsidized means of public transport. As can be seen, this is the method of subsidizing the subjects who generate external diseconomies, to induce them to cease engaging in this behaviour. To some extent, this can also be considered as a case of external diseconomies of production as many of these travellers are people going to or coming back from work.

Private individuals may produce tangible and intangible external diseconomies through use of substances that generate harmful external effects, such as tobacco, alcohol or hallucinogenic substances. Consumption of these substances generates material external diseconomies in the form of damage to the welfare and health of passive smokers and road accidents, respectively. It also causes intangible external diseconomies due to the imitation effect, especially among those who are easily influenced (young people). These intangible external diseconomies can give rise to tangible internal diseconomies in the form of damage to the health of those who become addicted to this type of consumption.

In general, the remedies adopted to deal with these external diseconomies consist in taxing the substances and introducing prohibitions. But Coase's principle that it may be preferable to subsidize the cessation of external diseconomies rather than to pass on the cost to those who generate them suggests the additional possibility of the public subsidy policy, by means of detox centres for substance abusers and alcoholics.

2.4 Classification of Merit Wants and Merit Goods of Public Interest in the Cooperative Model

In an individualistic economic system, the public role in merit goods can be justified only in relation to

a. goods the private individual is unable to choose to an optimal extent and in an optimal manner on the market, on account of *imperfect rationality*;
b. *empowering (or functioning-related)* goods to assure some equality of starting points and to provide a safeguard against the major risks of the social lottery that the average citizen may face;
c. *empowering goods*, in order to provide for the needs of the less favoured individuals.

The needs of the less favoured will be addressed in section 3 below, with regard to redistributive needs. Here we will now turn to merit needs, which concern the imperfect rationality of normal individuals, that is of the subject we have defined as the average person.

2.5 Merit Wants as Need for Foresight: The Paradigm of 'Ulysses Tied to the Mast'

The theme of imperfect rationality can be considered, fundamentally, in terms of two paradigms: one referring to present perception of future needs and one referring to the relation between a sequence of choices:

1. merit wants as the need for 'foresight', that is, the need to anticipate what is likely to come about and to provide for future welfare;

2.   merit wants as superior needs, which can be appreciated more deeply after having assuaged them.

There are three possible approaches to the first issue of imperfect rationality:

a.   weak willpower, in other words acrasia, which induces a subject to make a choice different from the promptings of reason;
b.   a short-sighted view of the future and a selfish attitude towards future generations;
c.   uncertainty about the future, which generates a risk that is not (easily) insurable.

Here, one may cite the myth of 'Ulysses tied to the mast' of his ship to prevent his succumbing to the siren's song, in other words to overcome his anticipated acrasia, his weakness of will, at the crucial moment of choice, in a situation of a strong external impulse.[33]

When this line of argument is put forward as a justification for merit goods, on the basis of an anticipation of weak willpower, in conjunction with the principle of the 'irreversible choice' (that is a decision that cannot subsequently be changed at the moment when the state of need arises), this does not mean a *deficit* of information on the part of whoever decides to 'bind herself' to consumption of such goods. On the contrary, the assumption is that there is extensive and vivid information on the favourable ratio between their cost and the benefits that they will bring.

The crucial point of this analytical foundation of merit goods that justifies expenditure and obligatory insurance for health care, accidents in the workplace, pensions, job losses (that is for so-called social welfare and social security), and expenditure for education up to school-leaving age – from an individualistic point of view – resides in the distinction between immediate preferences versus rational plans, or strategies, based on 'true preferences'. Such plans are decided in a phase that is not only reflexive but also formally 'constitutional' and therefore 'irreversible'.[34] Taxpayers – in the constitutional phase – can rationally decide on education up to school-leaving age free of charge, the expense of which will be covered by taxation, in order to avert the risk that the superficial desire not to study expressed by one's offspring may combine with parents' desire, in the immediate circumstances, not to make a sacrifice destined to provide their offspring with an education. This leads to the irreversible choice in favour of compulsory education as a public good (not necessarily supplied by the public hand).

Similarly, obligatory insurance for health care and as a safeguard against the risk of unemployment or accidents, and to provide for one's old age, with the money to be paid out when the established circumstances arise (for example in the event of illness, or in cases of unemployment, or a severe accident, and upon reaching retirement age), can be decided according to this paradigm.

It is self-evident – Elster argues – that individuals are free to be tied up (by the laws) so they tie themselves up (with these seat belts) and protect their 'basic' values against more superficial values. The real problems arise when these restrictions are imposed on individuals against their preferences *ex ante facto* (or perhaps also against their *post facto* preferences).[35]

2.6 Continued: Merit Wants as Needs for Foresight: Shortsightedness vis-à-vis One's Own Future and that of Future Subjects

The assumption that the present individual, looking at things in a 'well informed' and 'cool, calm and collected' way, considers the future in the same way a future subject would consider it, in what would be the present time of the putative future subject, can by no means be taken for granted. This observation holds not only with regard to future subjects, but also for present subjects in the future. When it is a question of 'oneself' in the future, the psychological connection is attenuated. Thus there is a philosophical approach which goes so far as to deny the identity of the individual person who lives, feels, thinks and puts forward arguments, chooses, acts at the various moments before and afterwards.[36] Instead, this approach merely conceives of a relation between the different 'selves' of the individual person at different times, this relation being closer when the times are nearer to the present, in the same way as relations among different people of the same nation.

As D. Parfit (1984) argues, the interest we have in our future could correspond to the degree of connection between our self now and our self in the future. It may be rational to have a less strong interest when one of the foundations of this interest makes itself felt in a less intense manner. Since the connection is almost always weaker when it links more prolonged periods of time, we can rationally take less interest in our more distant future.[37]

Given this framework, the fact that we observe that the individual person usually tends to prefer present welfare to that of the future, and the welfare of the near future to that of the distant future, would appear to be perfectly rational.

But while this may appear rational, at any moment, for any self, it does not appear to be fair, among the different selves, on the basis of the principle of equality of treatment, which requires an 'agent-neutral'[38] mode of behaviour. That is to say, behaviour by those who make choices both for themselves and others should be impartial among the various beneficiaries.

Here there is a form of agency problem between the various selves as principals and the present selves as agents who are empowered to decide for them.

Parfit (1984) argues that our future selves are something like future generations. We can make their fate worse, and since they do not yet exist, they cannot defend themselves. Similarly to the future generations, future selves do not have the right to vote, and their future interests need to be safeguarded.

If those who vote do not have a fair and caring attitude to the future, the paradigm of Ulysses tied to the mast is not easily applicable to rational ordinary choices concerning social security, with regard to the advantage of future generations.[39] In fact it is conceivable that the present generations may be excessive in providence pertaining to the future for themselves, and may vote for it without adequate present funding, thus laying a burden on the future generations which the latter may come to regard as excessive.[40]

This raises the need for constitutional constraints on opportunistic choices by those who have the power of choosing both for themselves and others, so that such choices do not privilege the present generations at the expense of those who will live in the future (myself and generations).

2.7 Continued: Merit Wants as Needs for Foresight: Informational Asymmetry with Regard to Future Needs

The 'market failures' on the demand side that arise from the attitude of 'present selves' towards 'future selves' and future subjects do not merely concern weak willpower and opportunism. They may also concern lack of information on future needs, and this may be true with regard to exactly the same class of goods.

Two distinct issues have to be addressed:

a. informational asymmetry regarding risks, between individual subjects and the State;
b. informational asymmetry between consumers and specialized suppliers, which leads to a category of 'trust goods':[41] the rise of this category is similar to the case of goods whose use may cause great (and irreversible) damage, due to the fact that the user lacks specific knowledge and thus has to 'place trust' in the suppliers' competence and good faith.[42]

Point a) includes private risks that are not (easily) insurable. A typical example concerns damage caused by natural calamities which is only partially covered by insurance. The State has a great capacity to foresee such disasters and can contain the damage through the action of civil protection and national disaster planning and response systems. Furthermore, the State has no spatial and temporal limits, unlike individuals and even joint-stock companies. Also, because the risks of natural calamities tend to balance one another out over time, the State may take care of the damage caused by them through public expenditure financed by general taxation to a far greater extent than is possible with an insurance scheme, however extensive it may be. Generally speaking, given the State's greater dimension, it can be considered the risk-taker of last resort.

Point b), the second aspect of informational asymmetry, concerns trust goods such as those relating to medical treatment and other health services, or (compulsory) education services where the damage of inadequate supply may be considered too severe to be left to free-market demand and supply interaction. The reason why in these cases citizens tend to prefer public rather than market provision is thought to be attributable to greater trust in the political representatives and their ability to exercise control over the technical officers of the public bureaucracy. Yet this argument is highly debatable. Health care may be a good example. We could consider that it is easier for a relationship of reciprocal trust to arise with a private physician who can be seen as the 'agent' of the 'principal' citizen than between the national health service doctor – who is paid on the basis of a fixed quota per citizen – and the citizen herself (on the agency relationship between citizens and public bureaucracy, see Chapter 1, subsection 2.7 ff.).

A more plausible case of trust goods is given by the educational system. A private educational institution may have an interest in passing all its pupils even if they have not reached the appropriate objectives, because the private institution draws its revenue from school fees. The heads and teachers of state-run schools may draw their motivation from the task they have been entrusted with, because proper fulfilment of their task is crucial for their reputation.

> But if the public educational system is funded above all on the basis of the number of pupils enrolled and not on the basis of other parameters (for instance, in the case of schools attended mainly by pupils drawn from the surrounding local area, the reference may be to the population and its characteristics), this argument may be weakened. In fact, as we will see, the public bureaucracy aims to maximize its volume of activity, in order to be awarded more resources. Also teachers and the other permanent staff working in the school system receive a monthly salary independent of the number of pupils in their school.

And then one may argue that the trust in the government for these merit goods does not necessarily imply a public supply of these goods. A public certification of the supplies by private profit and non-profit supplier in competition with public suppliers may enhance the quality of the supplies.

2.8   Superior Merit Goods: Culture, Art, Research: Preference Asymmetry *ex ante* and *ex post*: Adaptive Preferences

The second issue concerning merit goods which may justify the action of the public economy with regard to imperfect rationality, concerns the formation and knowledge of superior merit goods.

> Superior merit goods and needs should not be confused with the class superior consumer good (and needs), defined as those who have a positive elasticity to income so that their consumption (and satisfaction) increases when income increases.

Superior merit goods and needs are those that belong to superior cultural consumptions and investments such as the world of culture, the arts and humanities and scientific research. One may argue that only prolonged consumption and investment in these goods allows true appreciation of their worth, because it is only through extended experience of these spheres of activity that the person 'is formed' and becomes endowed with higher intellectual and perceptive abilities. On this point, two approaches can be outlined.

For the first approach, there is a scale of ranking in utilitarian preferences. 'True' preferences are acquired in the framework of a higher cultural background. Those who acquire such preferences may actually be less happy than a simple person, but this by no means implies they would like to return to that stage of simplicity. A value judgement precludes them from this choice.[43] In the second approach, the preferences emerging at a higher stage cannot be distinguished from other preferences on the basis of value judgements, but only on the basis of a greater capacity to obtain 'utility' as subjective satisfaction of the given ends.

Socrates, Hare wrote,[44] prefers philosophy to tossing a coin, because his capacity to experience utility is greater than that of the proletarian, and the former gives greater satisfaction than the latter, to those who have developed their sensibilities and intelligence.

Socrates has, on the margin, a higher marginal utility because he has a greater capacity for enjoyment, and therefore he obtains an overall greater total utility.

Therefore his marginal dissatisfaction does not prevent him from preferring the state in which he currently finds himself, because it gives him globally more.

With a subsidized supply of superior cultural goods, which are those that give greater utility and develop the capacity to become aware of utility, provided they are adequately practised, global consumers' satisfaction increases.

This outcome – remaining within the assumptions of the paradigm – which consequently increases the demand for these goods, also causes an expansion of their market. If expansion comes about in decreasing cost regimes, then it reduces unit costs, and the subsidies may eventually no longer be necessary.

However, this approach has two severe weak points: the claim according to which it is only through the consumption of (or investment in) so-called superior goods that their utilities increase, and the claim that those who are familiar with superior goods can, should they so desire, even experience the pleasures of the proletarians who are tossing a coin, as well as their own pleasures, which give greater utility. That is to say, education would not imply a shift in preferences, but would only lead to an expansion of preferences. In this line of argument the superior level incorporates within itself the lower level, and it is preferable, on the basis of the simple criterion that a certain set is better than another one when the first contains the second as a subset of the first.

However, this twofold argument is confuted or viewed as open to doubt by the theory of 'adaptive preferences'.[45] Not only do the preference maps expand, but they are modified little by little as the subject gradually engages in the given kinds of consumption, in relation to the environment and the habits the subject has acquired by exercising these preferences. In other words, the preference maps respond to and react upon the subject's interests and values.[46]

As subjects engage in making choices, day by day, moment by moment, such choices generate an accumulation of specific sensibilities that act upon and indeed modify subsequent preferences.

We may at times consider certain needs, described as superior because they are endowed with the above characteristics, to be intrinsically meritorious, based on a judgement that we assume to be made from the point of view of impartial observers having adequate information and an adequate period of time to reflect and decide. However, this judgement is influenced by the 'common values' proper to our society. Such goods may include devoting oneself to knowledge of art, 'classical' music or scientific research. Now, it may be true that those who become accustomed to these 'superior' goods may gradually undergo a subtle shift in their needs and sensibilities, and may conceive a desire for in-depth exploration in these fields. It may also be true that they specialize their preferences and that this reduces their capacity for enjoyment that characterizes 'simple souls'.

However, it is by no means demonstrated that the forms of enjoyment Socrates would consider to be rather coarse are actually any less intense than those of an elevated cultural level, for those who specialize themselves in coarse forms of enjoyment.

It cannot be asserted that the pleasures experienced by those who play simple card games are low-intensity pleasures. Yet, in our society, these card games are hardly considered as a 'merit good' of a superior nature.

As a rebuttal, one may argue that there is a fundamental difference between the 'superior' needs 'of the spirit' and other needs. Satisfaction of the superior needs of the spirit does not generate satiation, but greater desire, because it refines perception of such needs and heightens the ability to enjoy them, so that the marginal utility does not decrease, while global utility increases without the saturation that comes about with the other types of need. Thus it may be said that these are goods with superior marginal utility.

On the other hand, knowledge is not ethically neutral, and each species of knowledge, involving different technological spin-offs, generates different adaptive preferences.

2.9   Value Judgements and Preferences on Adaptive Preferences

On balance, it seems impossible to decide on goods with superior marginal utilities as merit goods merely because they are characterized by adaptive preferences, unless one engages in value judgements, that is 'preferences on preferences', in reference to the various needs of the spirit. Starting out from the individualist point of view, it will prove necessary to reach an agreement on what constitute the 'shared preferences' on preferences.

Merit goods, as superior goods, according to this new position, can be identified only by making reference to 'common values' considered to be superior and correlated to culture, art and knowledge; and generally such values should emerge from democratic processes of free choice.[47]

In the cooperative model, the first common value will in all cases be that of freedom of choice on the part of operators working in the sphere of culture, science and art, but also freedom of choice for the public: favouring classical music through the granting of public subsidies does not imply that the Ministry itself establishes the concert programmes. What is called for is pluralism of institutions and the predominance of (non-profit) private free institutions over public institutions.

2.10   Merit Goods in the Cooperative Model should be Satisfied through Freedom of Choice: the Role of Private Supply

Those who, in a democratic society, with a public economy merely subsidiary to the market economy, experience a public want for the various kinds of merit goods considered above, will aim to obtain them without losing their freedom of choice. Therefore the supply of these goods should conform to the following principles:

a. Maximum outsourcing by the public sector, in order to reduce to a minimum the bureaucratic and paternalistic aspects of the public supply. For instance, museums and public theatres should be run as far as possible by private foundations and also by profit-making firms. This may be particularly the case for collateral activities, which may be run separately from the cultural activities, for example the museum or theatre bookshop or gift shop. Public health services can be supplied by private medical clinics and biomedical laboratories.

b. Greatest possible plurality of subjects working for a given public operator under an outsourcing contract, considering the quality of the service to be performed and the optimum size of the firms in the given sector. For example, this may take the form of competition between doctors working on contracts for the national health service and between clinics and private laboratories performing biochemical analyses. Thus citizens who have the right to public health care services free of charge or at a subsidized price should have a voucher giving them the opportunity to choose the suppliers they deem to be preferable, and the latter will have an incentive to operate with efficiency and efficacy, taking the citizens' preferences into account.

c. Greatest possible competition among the different public operators entitled to supply these goods at the different levels of government. For instance, there could be competition among the hospitals belonging to the various health districts and to the various medical universities. This would broaden citizens' choice of their preferred public operator.

d. The greatest possible variety in the public supply of merit goods, whenever the principle of the citizen's freedom of choice also corresponds to intrinsic differences in value judgements and interests. Not all museums and public theatres, or facilities funded by the public hand, should hold collections or exhibitions of contemporary art, because there are some citizens who prefer classical art. Neither would it be acceptable for the supply to be directed exclusively towards the kind of art that is favoured by the political forces in power, as occurs in authoritarian regimes. Similarly, it is not acceptable for all citizens to have to face compulsory retirement at a given age: freedom of choice will be accompanied by a public pension commensurate with their years of social security contributions and with the residual age of those approaching the retirement age, so that this does not come about at the expense of the pension rights of other citizens. Nor will it be logical to increase the school-leaving age excessively, because not everyone – in their *a priori* irreversible choices – contemplates the 'necessity' of becoming holders of a degree in engineering, philosophy or music: people may, *ex post*, have an ambition to become a good plumber. This does not, however, mean that the government should take no interest in the supply of higher education free of charge or semi-free, as it can be demonstrated that higher education likewise concerns high-value merit goods and that both higher education and vocational training are also associated with important external economies.

e.   The minimum supply of merit goods on a public want basis, consistent with the imperfections of individual rationality. This minimum still involves a substantial dimension of the welfare state, as it is impossible to do without a public social security system, a public health care system, or a public education system. But even if the welfare state remains large in the cooperative model of public economy, its size should be minimized in conformity with the principles of the model. Thus the public economy in this model is subsidiary to, and not a substitution for, the market. Therefore the public pension system should not cover the entire need for pensions, but only a portion, thereby retaining the option for each individual to build up a private pension to integrate with the public system. The choice as to whether or not to continue to higher education will be left up to each individual, in addition to compulsory schooling that guarantees a dignified starting point on the labour market. Provision for public health care should not guarantee against minor illnesses, such as headaches, which are not part of the future risks against which safeguards may be desired by rational average individuals.

3   FAILURES OF THE MARKET ON THE SUPPLY AND DEMAND SIDE AND REDISTRIBUTIVE PUBLIC NEEDS

3.1   Failure of the Market on the Supply and Demand Side of the Private Insurance Scheme for Old Age Pensions

If an old age pension system is merely entrusted to private insurance enterprises, this may be extremely risky, as shown by the USA system, because these enterprises may not be able to pay the promised pensions. With the system of pensions paid to the retired by means of social security contribution levied on the working generation, by a sort of intergenerational constitutional contract (see Chapter 6, section 9, ff.) citizens can be assured that the pension will be paid, since the state is, by definition, the creditor of last resort, possessing the tax revenue and the power of issuing public debt.

3.2 Redistributive Public Needs

In principle, it could be argued that if an individualist function of social welfare is accepted, then to remedy the lack of income of the 'less favoured' – on the basis of the 'constitutional contract' (see Chapter 2, subsections 3.9–3.11) – needy individuals should be given a sum of money that is inversely proportional to their income, and which is greater in relation to family and personal difficulties, which presumably increase the marginal utility of the sum.

This proposal, of a so-called 'negative income tax', is presumed not to interfere with the sovereignty of individuals because the 'less favoured' can destine the money received to whatever goods they prefer.[48]

However, this formulation is simplistic.

First, one of the main principles of justice in a society based on free initiative and individual responsibility is that concerning merit. This principle does not imply giving a 'result' but rather an opportunity. Those who are more enterprising and industrious will achieve a greater result. Thus in the model of the public economy that adopts market economy principles, one of the things to emerge, as we have seen,[49] is the principle of basic opportunities, which involves providing everyone with (compulsory) education free of charge up to school-leaving age and subsidizing forms of higher education for the most deserving.[50] This can be beneficial for society, on account of the external economies of knowledge that education can generate. Thus this principle of fairness also has an important economic base.

But on the other hand, if poor citizens receive a free income from the collective community, they may lack any motivation to work or adopt provident behaviour.

Furthermore, it has been seen that in the cooperative model one of the aims is to furnish safeguards against risks deriving from an imbalance between incomes and needs that may occur due to unforeseen circumstances involving illness, accidents and various types of disabilities. In such cases specific health care provision and payment transfers are required, and these are not commensurate with the poverty of the affected person but to the person's particular need.

In addition, measuring the state of need of indigent 'less favoured' families, in order to ascertain exactly how much income is necessary to guarantee the indispensable minimum satisfaction of their needs, is far from easy. Interventions directed to act on the individual 'enabling' goods is more convincing.

Finally, those who have to shoulder the tax burden (or the obligatory contributions of social insurance) to the benefit of the less favoured may desire to shoulder this burden only if they can rest assured that this measure is genuinely going to achieve the goal of allowing the less favoured and their offspring to satisfy the needs which, according to the average man, appear to be the 'enabling' basic needs. What taxpayers want is for these means not to be 'wasted' by those who receive them, for example not to be frittered away on goods which, according to prevailing opinion, are seen as frivolous or even 'damaging' (such as gambling, alcohol, narcotics).

This outlines a theory of the supply of insurance goods and 'empowering' goods,[51] or 'functioning' goods, which should be as 'non-paternalistic' as possible (cf. subsection 2.10). A theory of this nature holds even if it obviously involves a value judgement on the needs that have to be satisfied in order to assure all citizens of a basic starting point and a minimum of dignified entry into society.

A similar approach – a fortiori – can be adopted in connection with aid by 'rich nations' to 'poor nations', and the so-called developing nations.

Specific action with goods such as vaccinations, medical treatment, educational facilities, water supply and so forth, which correspond to the theory of empowering goods, may thus appear rational even if one starts out from the individualist postulate.[52]

3.3   Hobbesian Redistribution

According to a hypothesis mentioned earlier (Chapter 2, subsection 3.10), formulated by J.M. Buchanan,[53] one reason why those who are comfortably off accept redistribution in favour of the less favoured is a self-seeking desire to avoid any harm that may arise from the social discontent of the needy and from the poverty and associated lack of hygiene and decorum that adversely affects social coexistence.

This 'Hobbesian' redistribution[54] differs from the kind of redistribution framed in terms of empowering goods, and its content is likewise different. The 'Hobbesian' version seeks above all to provide the less favoured with the goods that can contribute to averting the damage that the less favoured may inflict on the community of 'the comfortably off'. For instance, one of the aims will be to prevent the presence of beggars and those who sleep rough: 'tramps' can be provided with dwelling places and soup kitchens at a considerable distance from the main urban areas and the centres of business and social intercourse. Particular attention will be devoted to the treatment of infectious diseases among substance abusers, the poor, and so on.

3.4 Altruistic Paretian Redistribution

Why should one bother to provide assistance to the 'less favoured', apart from the considerations of advantages for the more favoured?

Either because this forms part of the cooperative constitutional pact or because it is felt to be a moral duty, which springs from our reasoning and sentiment.[55]

We can – additionally – argue that such assistance is based on a function of 'empathetic' utility, motivated by the moral sympathy for other people's satisfaction. This formulation is also known as 'Paretian redistribution', because it does not lead to a reduction but rather an increase in the utility of whoever agrees to provide it (Hochman and Rodgers, 1969; Hochman and Peterson, 1974).

Against this view, the objection can be raised that if empathy is genuinely present, each person can satisfy Paretian redistribution through voluntary donations. Why have recourse to the public economy?

A possible counter-argument makes reference to 'task assignment' with regard to 'trust goods': if one works on the assumption that extensive and complex activity will be required in order for this assistance to be effective, and that it will have to be organized and carried out on a certain scale and in a certain way, then the task can be better performed if it is delegated to the public economy, placing trust in politicians and bureaucrats.

More realistically, it may be the case that this 'empathy' is felt by the majority of people but not by all: if this is so, then the redistribution in question will not be 'Paretian', even though it has a utilitarian base.

3.5 Irrationality of Individual Redistributive Decisions: the Theorem of the 'Good Samaritans'

It might seem that in a community where each social group has a given redistributive preference (for example, some groups prefer advanced health care for the most severe diseases, or adequate assistance for the low-income elderly, or training courses for the unemployed), their attitude is more likely to emerge at the level of individual rather than collective preferences. However, here one encounters a particular paradox of decision-making strategy, which may lead to 'underproduction' of some interventions and 'overproduction' of others as compared to shared preferences, which we will call the 'theorem of the good Samaritans'.[56]

Table 3.7 illustrates this theorem. Let us suppose that a person *C* has an accident, on a road that is a long way from places where a person can receive treatment, and that she is unable, by herself, to call for help. Another two people, *A* and *B*, drive along the same road; they are both

Table 3.7   The theorem of the good Samaritans: redistributive deficiencies and inefficiencies

	B thinks that A is going to stop, but stops anyway	B thinks that A is going to stop and therefore does not stop
A thinks that B is going to stop, but A stops anyway	I *C has 'too much assistance'* Fairness with allocative wastefulness	II *C is given first aid and assistance by A, who behaves as a good samaritan* Fairness and efficiency
A thinks that B is going to stop, and so A doesn't stop	III *C is given first aid and assistance by B, who behaves as a good Samaritan* Fairness and efficiency	IV *C receives no assistance and dies* Iniquity and inefficiency

in somewhat of a hurry and, after passing the scene of the accident, they proceed on their separate ways.

The sequence of events is as follows. Both *A* and *B* know that the other is just going to pass or has just passed the scene, and they each think the other has a kindly character. But neither *A* nor *B* knows at exactly what moment the other actually passes the scene of the accident. *A*, seeing *C* severely injured and in need of help, feels solidarity for the victim. But, being in a great hurry, *A* does not stop because she thinks that *B*, having 'a kindly character', will surely stop. And anyway, if *B* had already passed this point, *A* reflects, then *B* would already have stopped. So, noting that *C* has received no help, *A* imagines that *B* has not yet reached the place. *A* feels great empathy for *C*, but supposes that the 'need' for solidarity with *C* that she genuinely feels will certainly be satisfied by *B*. However, *B*, who is likewise in a hurry, follows the same line of reasoning with regard to *A* (Box IV). Naturally, if both *A* and *B* were to decide to stop to help, even though they are both in a great hurry, there would be an excess of assistance, that is a waste of cost, in other words, inefficiency (Box I).

One of the two would have stopped 'pointlessly', and the emergency relief would have been excessive.

This theorem shows that coordinated action supported by altruism can operate better than aid prompted by mere individual initiative, given the fundamental role of information for effective distributive policies. Whose task is it to provide assistance for the elderly? Should it be up to private individuals with spontaneous donation? Is it up to the state or the local authority? The municipal elector may suppose that it is up to the state, and vice versa for the state elector. Who should intervene to retrain the unemployed?

3.6 Macroeconomic Public Wants: Incomes Policy, Countercyclical Fiscal and Monetary Policy

Traditionally, the theory of macroeconomic fiscal and monetary policy concerning action against inflation and action designed to moderate expansion, and action against depression in order to support or correct the accumulation process, is considered as being distinct from the theory of public goods. It is therefore treated with different analytical goods. But this view is mistaken.

Macroeconomic public policy is a chapter of the theory of public goods.[57] The theme of the public coordination of games played by individual operators who, if left to themselves, would stray from optimum equilibrium,[58] applies to macroeconomic public theory as well. This perspective is indispensable, both in order to avoid overestimating the role of such policies (as was the case in the 'old Keynesian school') and also in order to analyse the problems of coordinating the action of the various governments and central banks, on the international level.

Action against inflation, either on the cost or the demand side, can correctly be seen as a public good of the 'Samuelsonian' type.

Sen's 'reassurance' theorem, mentioned earlier, can be applied to such action, as can be the related paradigm of reciprocal external economies, which – in actual fact – is configured as a relinquishing of reciprocal external diseconomies.

Similar arguments can be put forward with regard to policies designed to correct the economic cycle, which set themselves the aim of moderating investments and curbing purchases of stocks of supplies during periods with an inflationary trend, and promoting investments when, in contrast, there is a recessive trend.

3.7 Public Policy in Favour of Accumulation

Action to support the accumulation rate belongs within the theory of public goods. Savings can be considered as a 'merit good' as the need for saving experienced by individuals may be less than what should emerge from choices made by individual operators who are not affected by 'short-sightedness' with regard to the future or by uncertainty with regard to other people's behaviour.

But in any case, the individual calculates the benefits that accrue to herself from her acts of savings and investments, not the external economies which, by saving and investing, she generates through greater capital accumulation and the related development of productivity, or through the progress of a certain sector or economic area.[59]

3.8 Policy of Correcting the Distribution Produced by the Market, to Improve its Functioning

A society in which the gap between the wealthy and the poor is too accentuated may give rise to a market system with insufficient economic exchange, a tendency towards crystallization of the existing centres of power and very scanty inventiveness. Therefore, it may be more advantageous for all concerned to set up rules on the constitutional level in order to avoid excessive concentration of wealth and to allow correction of the 'summits'.

This is a public good that only the state can supply, as an expression of the 'power' that establishes the rules in inherently conflictual situations.[60]

We thus conclude the chapter with the same paradigm of 'subsidiary government' that was introduced at the outset, but with the warning that what is being justified now is not a task of 'neutral subsidiary activity', but rather of 'intervention conforming to the free competitive market and to 'true' individuals' preferences. And this, in the cooperative model, should always be viewed with extreme prudence.[61]

NOTES

1. The question of public needs and public goods has sparked an enormously vast bibliography, because it involves defining what should most appropriately be catered for by the public economy rather than by the private economy. See among the fundamental works, Smith, 1st edn (1776); De Viti De Marco (1888) and Puviani (1901); Musgrave and Peacock (eds), 1958 (in particular, the texts by E. Barone, R. Goldsheid, H. Ritschl, F. Von Wieser); Sax (1887) (an abridged passage is also found in Musgrave and Peacock (1958); Einaudi (1942); Fasiani (1951); Musgrave (1959) and subsequent edn; Buchanan (1968 [1999]).
2. We will make frequent use of the expression 'market failure' despite the veiled prejudice against the market the term conveys, as it is now in current use among economists.
3. Graham (1988) convincingly argues that if one adopts the point of view of 'political individualism', it is also necessary to accept the principle of self-determination, according to which individuals have the right to pursue their interests as they think best, simply because they have the right to choose, even if they are less capable of pursuing their own interests than could be achieved by others entrusted with safeguarding

them paternalistically. Additionally, Graham argues, *unlimited* states are not justi-fied because there are some aspects of human life that necessarily have to be left to individuals.

4. According to Italian law the mineral ore-bearing subsoil does not belong to the owners of the surface soil; this is not the case in American law, which allows greater scope for the rights of private property.

5. Samuelson (1954) was the first to theorize mathematically the characters of these goods, contrasting them with privatistic goods by including them in the theory of general eco-nomic equilibrium, with particularly incisive arguments. Therefore we will call these goods 'Samuelsonian' even though the Samuelsonian theory of public goods includes other categories of goods as well, as we will see. See E. Lindahl, a Swedish economist, follower of Wicksell; Lindahl published his major work on this topic in German, in 1919 (1919 [1958]).

6. The army organized by the Hezbollah, who launch missiles against Israel, is to all effects and purposes a private army.

7. Nozick maintains that if protection is entrusted to private companies, the very substan-tial fixed costs would eventually result in the presence of a single monopolistic 'protec-tion agency', and it would not be advantageous for any normal citizen to be subjected to such an agency in a 'privatistic' regime. This is because the agency would exploit them to the utmost and they would have no means of resisting it. The state, on the other hand, supplies this 'protection' in a general manner, because 'defence of the law' and – in a democracy – extensive civil liberties eliminate the forms of exploitation that derive from the above-described monopoly of power, albeit – in the 'physiological' situation – on condition that it should respect the property rights it was set up to protect. However, Nozick's argument is inadequate. The non-democratic state may exploit citizens, just like Nozick's privatistic agency, and possibly even more so. The need for protection by the public power does not spring from the danger of a monopoly exerted by a private protection agency, but from its nature as an interdependent and intrinsically conflict-ing want, and this kind of want can be satisfied only by the political power, which in a democracy is exercised by the citizens.

8. Schmitt (1927 [1932, 1976, 2007]), p. 354, see in particular the essay on the concept of 'politic'.

9. See Weber (1922 [1976] [1978]), vol. II, Chapter III, section IV, n. 2.

10. The version that Sen (1973b) presents is slightly different.

11. G. Brennan and J.M. Buchanan (1985 [2000]) develop a game paradigm analogous to that in the text, with the exception that they assume one strong subject and one weak subject. This complication does not modify the conclusion, according to which, the best solution is that whereby each subject abides by the rules. It should also be noted that the two authors insist on the rules, but neglect the role of institutions that have to enforce them.

12. Forte (1991).

13. This argument, in particular, was developed by Hayek, above all in 1982, especially the first two chapters of the first volume. See also the essay by Leoni (1961). I would like to take this opportunity, in the present note, to express a tribute to the distinguished Italian scholar of political science and philosophy of law, who, during my university years, shaped my approach of political individualism that constitutes the basis of my thought on the role of the state with respect to individual welfare.

14. In addition to metropolitan roads, many other goods which used to be of the 'pure' Dupuit type are ultra-saturated today on account of congestion phenomena. It is no longer true that all subjects can enjoy Venice *simultaneously*. The throngs of would-be visitors are at times so tightly packed together as to pose a danger for themselves and even for the integrity of Venice itself. Rationally, therefore, one could suggest imposing a charge for an entry ticket to be paid by non-residents, and this would be feasible due to the fact that there are only a limited number of access routes into the city.

15. The citation is from the handbook of *Economics* (Samuelson, 1970).
16. A.T. Peacock, building on the contribution of R. Coase (1974), points out that by obtaining a monopoly, lighthouse owners were able to run their lighthouse as an enterprise, imposing charges on ships that called at nearby ports and which were therefore the greatest (albeit not the only) users of the lighthouse. Peacock adds that at present, the fee can be charged as compensation 'for assistance to navigation' as well as simply for the mere fact of providing illumination. This assistance is provided by more complex lighthouse installations; a price can be set for these special services and the user ships can be identified electronically. See Peacock (1979a).
17. Hotelling (1938) demonstrated that if one follows the rule of price equal to marginal cost, which is constituted by variable costs, then it may be necessary to accept the burden of a deficit. This arises from the fact that in order to cover not only variable costs but also average fixed costs, and to do this with prices equal to marginal costs, it is necessary for the marginal costs to be in their increasing segment at the point of equilibrium; it is also necessary for the increasing segment to be very high, so that it can also cover all variable costs. Naturally, enterprises with constant or decreasing variable costs, which do not benefit from monopoly positions, will be unable to cover the fixed costs. Notice, however, that Hotelling supposes that the enterprise is unable to adopt discriminate tariffs for high demand users as compared to low demand users. In Figure 3.3, if we consider the extreme hypothesis that it is possible to apply as many different prices as there are segments of the demand curve, then it becomes possible to utilize the entire productive capacity below the demand curve.
18. The critical literature on this theme, prompted by 'Hotelling's theorem', is extremely vast.
19. The first to maintain that when there are external economies there is a justification for public action designed to subsidize the activities that produce them, in order to ensure that the marginal costs of the producers are equal to the entire 'social' marginal revenue was A.C. Pigou, in the two works *The Economics of Welfare* (1st edn 1920), and *A Study in Public Finance* (1947). Coase, in 'The problem of social cost' (1960), contended that in many cases this is superfluous because the presence of external economies will induce those who benefit from them and those who produce them to reach an agreement in order to establish systems that include them. On Coase's theorem see Chapter 2, subsection 2.8.
20. T. Scitovsky applied these concepts to the theory on development of less developed areas. This essay was reprinted in Arrow and Scitovsky (1969). (In his earliest writings, Scitovsky appears under the name T. de Scitovsky.)
21. J.H. Meade (1952), reprinted in Arrow and Scitovsky (1969).
22. J.M. Buchanan and C. Stubblebine (1962 [1999]), in Arrow and Scitovsky (1969) demonstrated that not all external economies have relevance on the margin of decision-making.
23. On these issues, with regard to music, cf. Peacock and Weir (1975) and, with regard to complex artistic goods such as Venice, see Mossetto (1992), as well as the more general discussion in Frey and Pommerehne (1989); Villani (1988); Brosio and Santagata (1992).
24. See Forte (1971).
25. See Marshall (1920) quote in the following note.
26. Marshall (1920, Book V, Chapter XIII, pp. 4 ff). The subject is examined in Forte (2003).
27. Even Marshall himself, in expounding his theorem, warned against such dangers, suggesting quantitative and temporal moderation of policy measures; see Forte (2003).
28. A.C. Pigou (1922), in a polemical argument with J.H. Clapham. I analysed this issue in *Le migrazioni interne come problema di economia del benessere*, in AA.VV. (1962).
29. Schumpeter (1942 [2006]).
30. Cf. Einaudi (1938 [1959]), with regard to income tax and taxation of excess earnings and capital gains.

31. The concept of a merit good and merit consumption is due to Musgrave, who sought thereby to reconcile the individualist viewpoint with corrective public action in the area of consumption. (Musgrave also mentions the category of 'demerit goods', which are the opposite of 'merit goods'.) See Musgrave and Musgrave (1973); cf. also Forte in Chiancone and Osculati (1993).

32. The most coherent and tenacious interpreter of this line of thought is R. Titmuss; Titmuss (1970). See, also, on 'paternalism' in relation to public choice, Bariletti (1993).

33. Cf. J. Elster (1979). The author draws on a famous argument put forward by the celebrated philosopher B. Spinoza in his (poorly known) *Political Treatise* available in Italian, ed. by L. Chianese, 1991 [2001].

34. This issue is treated in greater depth by Elster in *Sour Grapes* (1983), where he gives an even more subtle and penetrating analysis than in the 1979 work.

35. J. Elster (1979, p. 151). I have inserted the word 'these' before 'seat belts' in order to make it even more clear that there is a link with the welfare state's supply of goods, to which Elster refers explicitly in this argument.

36. See Parfit (1984), especially Chapter VIII 'Attitudes to time' and Chapter XIV 'Personal interest and rationality'.

37. Parfit (1984 Chapter XIV, p. 400).

38. This terminology is taken from T. Nagel (1988, Chapter VIII, *Value*, from paragraph 4 onwards and Chapter V, *Ethics*). The 'agent-neutral' point of view is also, correctly, known as the 'objective' point of view. However, the term 'objectiveness' could be misleading, in the sense that it is not a question here of observations on real subjects, but of assessments made by an individual 'from no particular place', but who is recognized as having the 'introspective' ability to enter into all real individuals.

39. The inadequacy of Wicksellian unanimity as a rule to ensure that collective decisions do not damage anyone, on account of the fact that the right to vote does not concern all those involved, has been repeatedly pointed out by A.T. Peacock, in particular in the Mattioli Lectures, 1992. See the following note.

40. The issue of the hidden public debt created by the fact that social security is based on the relation between the generations is addressed several times by Peacock in the Mattioli Lectures, 1992.

41. Blankart (2008) developed the concept of 'trust goods' to define goods that are held to be more appropriately provided (also) by the State, on account of the technical difficulty in checking the quality of similar goods that can be supplied by private enterprise. The analysis draws strongly on Forte (1967). The quality of a merit good may decline precisely because it is provided by a state bureaucracy rather than by free private bodies and associations. But not all trust goods are merit goods. The 'trust goods' *par excellence* are the institutional goods pertaining to justice, defence, security, and public law and order, mentioned earlier in section 1 of this chapter.

42. J. Tirole (1988) uses the term 'credence goods' to express this concept.

43. This is the argument put forward by J.S. Mill (1863), for whom it is better to be an 'unhappy Socrates' than an uncouth but happy ignoramus. Even if Socrates is less happy, he does not envy the ignoramus, because he knows that his *status* has greater value.

    Recently, some economists have advocated a 'soft paternalism'; on their proposal and the ensuing debate; see Sunstein and Thaler (2003); Camerer et al. (2003); Sugden (2007, 2008).

44. See Hare (1985), in Sen and Williams (eds) (1982).

45. See Elster (1982). On the effects of satisfying certain preferences, and on the characteristics and intensity of subsequent preferences, see Stigler and Becker (1977); Becker and Murphy (1988).

46. See C. Von Weizsäcker (1971).

47. See Maffettone (1989). But one should not overlook Arrow's theorem, which highlights the difficulty of making sure that value judgements can emerge coherently in society and appropriately express the value of the majority of the population.

48. See Friedman (1962); Martino (ed.) (1977).
49. Which has a central position in Rawls' theory of justice and in the cooperative model, where it is also justified as a criterion for the promotion of collective economic welfare.
50. This can be beneficial for society, on account of the external economies of knowledge that education can generate.
51. On the theory of empowering goods, Cf. Peacock (1991, pp. 46–50) and on that of 'functioning' goods, cf. Sen (1985), and also E. Granaglia (1993).
52. On this theme, see in particular the writings of Sen, which are concerned above all with poor countries rather than the problems of the less favoured in developed countries (Sen, 1985; 1987) (with other authors).
53. Buchanan (1976 [2001], pp. 194–211).
54. The term 'Hobbesian', from T. Hobbes, who put forward the theory that every man is 'a wolf' towards other men and that public order is achievable either with force or through the joint advantage of opposing parties.
55. In the Kantian framework the duty to help others is based only on the rational principle which holds that each individual should behave according to a rule that is potentially 'universalizable'. By contrast, in D. Hume's conception this duty is based first and foremost on a feeling of 'benevolence' towards others, which leads to justice conceived as impartiality. The two approaches are less distant than it might seem: if we love our fellow men because we recognize in them the humanity that is in us, implicitly we admit the Kantian criterion that we should adopt a mode of behaviour that 'is valid for all men': for others, as for us. See A. Alchian, and W.R. Allen, G. Tullock, A.J. Culyer, M.H. Cooper and A.J. Culyer, in Alchian et al. (1973).
56. The paradigm of the text is drawn from the paradigm of the game of the 'levite' and the 'priest' described by McLean (1987), in Chapter 7, section 7.3.2.
57. For a seminal treatment of macroeconomic theory from the point of view of the theory of public goods and of external economies and diseconomies see Baumol (1965). Obviously, the seminal text on fiscal policy for macroeconomic equilibrium is Keynes (1936).
58. The need for such coordination is denied by the so-called 'rational expectations' school developed by Lucas and others. See Lucas (1972); (1981); Lucas and Sargent (1981). But the criticisms of this approach, the ideological foibles of which are directly proportional to the formal complexity of the mathematical models that seek to dress it in scientific garb, appear to be destructive (Vicarelli, 1983).
59. Cf. Buchanan (1992), and, also, the considerations put forward in subsection 1.2.
60. On redistributive policies designed to 'moderate the summits', cf. Einaudi (1949, Part Three *Concetto e limiti della eguaglianza nei punti di partenza*, p. 125 ff.)
61. On the theory of 'market-conforming measures', the reader is referred to the thought of W. Röpke (1944 [1948]).

4. Equilibrium and disequilibrium between demand and supply of public goods

1 PUBLIC WANTS: THE TWO EQUILIBRIUM MODELS: FOR INTRINSICALLY DIVISIBLE AND INTRINSICALLY INDIVISIBLE GOODS

As will have become clear from the analysis of public wants and public goods conducted in the previous chapter, and as will be shown more clearly in the various following sections, the formulas of individual equilibrium for public goods can be divided into two large categories, depending on the intrinsically divisible or indivisible nature of such goods. In the former case, the two demands are summed horizontally, because subject A's enjoyment of an amount of good G excludes that of subject B, while in the latter case they are summed vertically, as each amount of good G allows enjoyment by subject A but also that of subject B and of the nth subject, up to saturation point which, in certain cases, is indeterminate. In both cases, the demand for the public good exercised either by private individuals or by enterprises, implies renouncing other goods.

2 CONSUMPTION AND FISCAL PRICE FOR PUBLIC WANTS DIVISIBLE INTO UNITS OF SUPPLY THAT ARE SPECIFIC FOR EACH OF THE VARIOUS USERS

Let us start out from the simplest case, that of divisible public goods, on the analogy of divisible private goods. The public good in question could be represented by services, for example to satisfy wants involving public transport, waste disposal, crèches and child daycare centres, for the various groups of subjects present in the local area. Satisfying such wants may require different quantities, characterized by prices and levies commensurate with the demands. The demand curves are formed by summing horizontally the quantities demanded by the political representatives of the various subjects, which are added one after another on the axes of the abscissae, specifying the quantities required for each of the prices marked on the ordinates.

We will now examine the – deliberately simplified – case of goods with constant marginal and average unit costs C_m (naturally, constant marginal costs imply marginal costs equal to average unit costs), and supply divisible into separate units. Each group of subjects will have its own demand curve and its own supply curve. We show the curves for two groups in Figures 4.1a and 4.1b. On the basis of the demand curves hypothesized for the two groups of subjects a and b, the quantities they consume at price $P = C_m$ are OQ and OQ', respectively. In Figure 4.1c we have the aggregate demand of a and b expressed on the political market as the sum of the two individual demands at each price. The quantities consumed of a and b are summed on the axis of the abscissae, giving rise (in Figure 4.1c) to a quantity demanded amounting to OQ_T. On the assumption that the constant cost C_m remains unchanged, it becomes possible to have the price P, and therefore to consume the quantity OQ_T, which is the sum of the individual quantities of a and b at that price.

Now we will hypothesize that the cost goes down to C'_m, which is also constant. The demand for a and b increases to $OQ_S + OQ'_S > OQ + OQ'$, so that the quantity consumed in 4.1c rises to OQ_{TS}.

However, in the hypothesis of increasing marginal and average costs, the situation becomes more complicated: while the demand curves of a and b are summed horizontally as previously, the equilibrium price differs from the result that would emerge if the demands for the individual groups a and b were considered separately. This is because the marginal cost for OQ_T is greater than the marginal cost of OQ alone or OQ' alone. It follows that now the aggregation of the demand for a and for b gives rise to a lower consumption than would be found if each could have a separate demand with a separate supply.

3   DIVISIBLE PUBLIC GOODS WITH OBLIGATORY UNIFORM CONSUMPTION BUT DIFFERENT DEMANDS

Certain divisible or semi-divisible public goods involve merit goods, the consumption of which is, for various reasons, generally expected to take place in a uniform manner within the community considered, even though individual citizens might desire different quantities. Examples include compulsory education, obligatory national insurance to provide for old age, the health service free of charge.

We will consider two (groups of an equal number of) individuals a and b

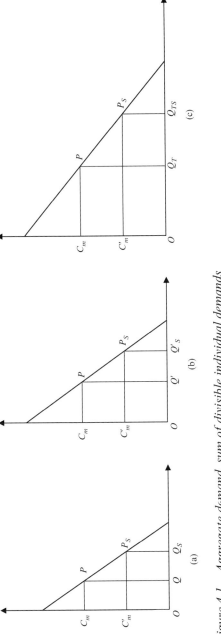

Figure 4.1   Aggregate demand, sum of divisible individual demands

197

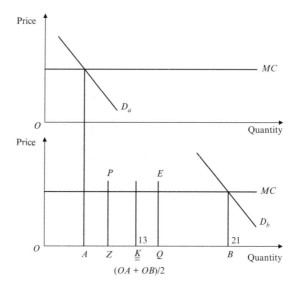

*Figure 4.2   Equilibrium for divisible public goods with uniform provision
and different demands*

whose quantitative preferences for good G, compulsory education, intrinsically divisible, are distinct, but within the community considered, this
good is to be provided in a uniform measure, by virtue of a shared principle
of equal dignity and equality of basic opportunities for all citizens. The
preferences of *a* and *b* are represented by the demand curves *Da* and *Db*
in Figure 4.2, where *MC* represents the marginal production cost.[1] Given
MC, if *G* were provided on the basis of the preferences of *a* and *b*, on the
market, *a* would consume the quantity *OA* and *b* the quantity *OB*. But if *G*
must be provided in equal measure with regard to the years of compulsory
schooling, how can the allocative choice in question be effected by means of
a vote? Let us suppose that *a* prefers, for all citizens, only five years of compulsory schooling, therefore *OA* = 5, while *b* prefers 21 for everyone (right
up to a PhD!), in other words *OB* = 21. The quest for durable consensus on
this allocative choice implies 'loyal' behaviour, whereby there is no deceit-
fulness concerning reciprocal preferences: on the contrary, each individual
tries to imagine herself in other people's shoes, so as to ascertain to what
extent they genuinely agree with her. If the voting procedure is carried out
according to the majority principle, the result could be either *OA* or *OB*,
allowing for the possibility that one of the groups (due to absences at the
voting session or 'defection to the other side') could prevail over the other.
This – by hypothesis – does not appear acceptable for a long-term allocative

decision, in which unanimity voting would appear to be preferable. Under this new voting hypothesis, group *a* might ask group *b* to change their mind, arguing that five years of *G* will certainly give *b* some satisfaction, although to a lesser degree than truly preferred by *b*. Certainly, *b* could hardly use the same line of argument to ask *a* to act in favour of level 21, because this is not contained within *a*'s preference map, but rather goes beyond it. At this point *b* could try offering *a* the solution of the simple arithmetic average, so that the years of *G* to be provided would be $OK = (OA + OB)/2 = 13$, which some believe to be capable of satisfying a criterion of equity (Stiglitz, 1986 [2000]). But with the simple arithmetic average, as can be seen in Figure 4.2, *a* has to move away from her preferences proportionally much more than *b*: thus for *a* the increase from five to 13 years of *G* implies an almost threefold increase in the number of years preferred, whereas for *b* the decrease from 21 to 13 years involves a reduction of less than one-third compared to the preferred level. The agreement on the long-term allocative choice requires a less simplistic bargaining process. Let us now return to the locus of the 'overlapping preferences' of *a* and *b*, which consists of those of *a*: on this level, *b* can reasonably and credibly 'threaten' to refuse to vote in *a*'s favour unless *a* makes concessions because otherwise *b* would be the only one that would have to sacrifice her preferences. Thus *a* will have to 'take a few steps towards *b*', thereby enabling the latter to 'step back a little' so as to move slightly closer towards *a*'s preferences. But how far? If the concessions *a* is asking for appear 'excessive', *b* will be the one that will credibly be able to threaten that she will not vote in favour of *a*'s position. We will use the term *OSFOB, one step forward, one step back*, to refer to this procedure of trying to find a balance by means of reciprocal concessions, backwards and forwards, in the interval of disagreement. There will be a point *y* at which *b*'s threat of refusing to vote for *G* counterbalances *a*'s threat of doing likewise: this point is reached when the sacrifice *a* is prepared to make with respect to her own objective of *G* is proportional to that which *b* is willing to make with respect to hers.

As can easily be demonstrated, equilibrium in the bargaining process along the distance $OA-OB = AB$ (in our case 16 years of school education) will be reached with a division of *AB* between *a* and *b*, which implies that they will undergo the same proportion of sacrifice affecting their respective demand. And since *a*'s demand is much smaller than *b*'s, *a* will take a smaller number of steps forwards than the number of steps *b* will have to take backwards. To find the proportion of sacrifice assignable to *a* and *b* we sum *a*'s demand with that of *b*, obtaining $OA + OB$. Then we divide *a*'s demand, which is *OA* for $OA + OB$, and *b*'s demand, which is *OB* for $OA+OB$, obtaining the two percentages of sacrifice of *a* and *b*. But since by adding the two shares of sacrifice we necessarily obtain the value 1, that is the entire sacrifice, b's share of sacrifice can be determined by simply subtracting from 1 the percentage representing a's sacrifice. Having found the shares of sacrifice to be borne by a and b, now we apply them to the aggregate sacrifice to be divided between them. To find the sacrifice that will be borne by a we multiply the aggregate sacrifice AB by $OA/OA + AB$:

$$AB \times OA/(OA + OB) \tag{4.1}$$

The sacrifice to be borne by b can be found with

$$AB \times OB/(OA + OB) \tag{4.1'}$$

or by merely subtracting a's share of sacrifice from AB.

Since in our example $OA=5$ and $OB=21$, the sum $OA + OB=26$, the share borne by a, can be expressed as 5 over $26= 5/26= 19.23$, and b's share is $21/26 = 80.77$. Now, to determine a's share of the aggregate sacrifice of 16 we multiply 16 by 19.23 and obtain 3.08, which we round down to 3. The share borne by B will be $16 \times 80.77 = 12.912$, rounded up to 13. Thus a must accept an increase of three years of schooling and b a reduction of 11.The equilibrium point will be found at eight years of schooling.

4 PUBLIC REVENUE FOR DIVISIBLE PUBLIC GOODS, WHEN COSTS ARE DIVIDED

A substantial portion of public goods are divisible, and a substantial portion of public revenue is in effect constituted by payments that have (or claim to have) a direct relation with the public good or service provided. As we will see in greater detail further on, there are:

I.   Public prices and fees for certain divisible public goods that are provided by the public operator in return for a monetary payment, often – albeit not always – below cost (for instance, public transport fares, tickets for entry into museums, medical tests and analyses, university fees);

II.   Public prices and fees with a coercive element, for services and goods characterized by compulsory consumption or pertaining to an institutional service (legal fees, fees for certifications and administrative authorizations, 'stamp duty' and registry taxes for the transfer of immovable properties);

III. Compulsory contributions for 'compulsory' or 'semi-compulsory' social insurance: national insurance contributions for pensions, in cases where the latter stand in a relation with the contributions paid;

IV. Special taxes, levied in relation to public expenditure which is expected to give benefits to those who pay them, such as the tributes for refuse collection, the urbanizing contributions destined to cover expenses by the local authorities; on infrastructures for private buildings;

V. Taxes that have a specific link with a benefit or a cost of the public economy, such as car road tax and fuel tax, which, inasmuch as they are connected to road use, could more appropriately be set up as 'earmarked taxes' destined to road expenditure, in so far as they are justified for this utilization.

In the cooperative model these payments for divisible public goods should be applied to the greatest possible extent. However, this cannot always be done, and is not always advantageous, not only for distributive reasons pertaining to equity, but also for reasons of efficiency regarding the goods in question themselves. With regard, for instance, to expenditure for compulsory schooling, considered earlier in the framework of merit consumption, payment of fees to cover the cost of the service does not appear feasible, as this good is provided for everyone in a measure that is intended to be equal, in order to accomplish the principle of equality of starting points. This principle would be violated if the good were delivered in return for payment to be borne by the parents of those who benefit from the service. It can instead be assumed that each individual, apart from the less favoured, will pay the cost of the compulsory education received by means of the tax on the income obtained from their job (housewives who do not work outside the home repay it with the contribution they make to bringing up the new generations and their contribution in kind to the persons in the family who have an outside job). In the case of expenditure for defence and public order, as we have seen, since the want is interdependent and the compulsory consumption generates a benefit that spreads throughout the community, it is impossible to determine the cost for each individual, and these goods are treated as if they were Samuelsonian goods. For health care services, solid arguments could be advanced for applying social contributions commensurate with the personal income of those who benefit from such services, but at times this does not occur.

Or alternatively, as in Italy, it is carried out through financial illusion processes, by means of the Regional Tax on Production (IRAP), which is a tax on the value-added of labour, and of profits and interest on capital produced by private and public entities; the revenue goes to the Regions, where it is mostly utilized to finance their health care services.

Naturally, in many cases, a different approach is adopted: instead of imposing obligatory contributions and tributes linked to the service provided, or public prices that cover the costs, financing by means of general taxes is often preferred, under the pressures of interest groups and for electoral convenience.

5   INTRINSICALLY INDIVISIBLE PUBLIC GOODS: THE CHOICE OF 'QUALITY' IN THE CASE OF DEMANDS WITH DIVERGENT PREFERENCES

The OSFOB model described in section 3 can hold – *for the choice of quality in relation to divergent preferences* – even as regards indivisible or semi-indivisible public goods for which the demands, in a given community, are summed vertically up to a saturation point, but which may be present in different quantities depending on each individual user. For Dupuit and Hotelling goods, which are supplied free of charge or with a public subsidy, individual consumption can vary but the quality of the provision cannot vary. A typical case is that of roads: some users would like to see better road maintenance quality for their vehicles while others would be satisfied with a lower quality, but this is not possible as the service, subsidized by the public hand, is supplied in a uniform manner. *A fortiori* this holds true for public goods that are indivisible in terms of consumption, and which correspond to institutional interdependent individual wants, such as the good consisting of the armed forces, and pure Samuelsonian public goods. By definition, for intrinsically indivisible goods the quality cannot but be equal for the n 'consumers'. Allocative decisions, as far as their quantity is concerned, as has already been seen and as will be noted further on in section 6, could be made by a unanimity procedure, summing the different demands vertically, in order to reach equilibrium between marginal cost and total demand for the different 'consumption' units. But since the choice of uniform quality will imply a search for an agreement among different preferences that cannot be summed, and which must instead 'balance one another' in the model with unanimity voting, the equilibrium solution can be found through the OSFOB procedure described above.

6   CONSUMPTION AND THE FISCAL PRICE FOR INDIVISIBLE PUBLIC WANTS: LIMITS OF VALIDITY OF SAMUELSON'S THEORY

For all intrinsically indivisible goods supplied free of charge, optimum equilibrium can be achieved by means of the formula presented in the previous chapter with regard to Samuelsonian goods (see Samuelson, 1954 and 1955), as demands in this hypothesis are summed vertically. If, as is usually the case, the hypothetical demand curves of the *n* individuals and social groups are different, then at the equilibrium point, referring to marginal demand, the fiscal prices each individual is willing to pay will be different, as has already been observed in Figure 3.1. This condition, which is also valid for a community composed of *n* individuals, highlights the peculiar characteristic of intrinsically indivisible goods supplied free of charge which distinguishes them from private goods. For the latter, Paretian optimal equilibrium is achieved when the marginal substitution rates of each subject are equal to one another and are equal to the marginal transformation rate or price. Here it is the sum of the marginal substitution rates of all subjects that must be equal to the marginal cost.

The political representatives of the various groups of electors may, however, attempt to lead people to believe that the marginal utility obtained from the public goods by their representatives is low, hoping to offload the costs onto others. Therefore usually, in order to cover the expense of these public goods by means of taxation, reference is made to the incomes and other economic parameters to determine the marginal uses of these goods.

But once the price for marginal use has thus been established, there still remains the question of how to share out the cost of the supra-marginal amounts in the community under consideration. Given their characteristic of goods that are provided free or semi-free of charge, the adoption of levies based on the benefit or cost, or on payments of charges of one kind or another, is in many cases impossible or extremely inconvenient and bothersome. Therefore the alternative is often chosen of taxes levied on economic phenomena pertaining to citizens and enterprises. In a non-paternalistic enterprise these levies are 'fiscal prices', that is to say, they refer to presumed consumption of public goods and not to mere capacity to pay. Therefore they make reference to income, assets and one's personal estate, business and trade, and profits that can plausibly be considered as indicators of the benefits of public goods.

The Samuelsonian argument that the sharing out of the cost of indivisible public goods, provided and demanded by a given community, should be determined by the marginal utility of each user, at the equilibrium point between supply and demand of such goods,[2] can lead to the absurd result whereby a substantial portion of the users of public goods should pay nothing at all or only very small charges as compared to the actual amount of consumption, since the goods in question are (mainly) supra-marginal.

To illustrate this paradox, consider a community of only two (groups of) subjects, *A* and *B*, in which there is a given supply of indivisible public goods G_S, at the constant cost 4. Subject *A* has a demand of indivisible public goods which is twice that of subject *B*, although the latter also has

Table 4.1 *Equilibrium for indivisible public goods with fiscal prices on the marginal cost*

Line		1	2	3	4	5	6	7	8	9	10
1	Progressive number of units supplied of the indivisible good G_S	1	2	3	4	5	6	7	8	9	10
2	Number of units Marginal and mean cost per amount of the indivisible good G_S	4	4	4	4	4	4	4	4	4	4
3	A's utility for G_S	10	9	8	7	6	5	4	3	2	1
4	B's utility of B for G_S	5	4	3	2	1	0	0	0	0	0
5	Total utility of G_S for $A+B$	15	13	11	9	7	5	4	3	2	1
6	Equilibrium utility for G_S net of costs	11	9	7	5	3	1	0	no	no	no
7	A's gross rent for G_S	10	9	8	7	6	5	4	no	no	no
8	Gross rent of B for G_S	5	4	3	2	1	no	no	no	no	no
9	Fiscal price per Samuelsonian amount for A	4	4	4	4	4	4	4	no	no	no
10	Fiscal price per Samuelsonian amount for B	0	0	0	0	0	no	no	no	no	no
11	Net rent per amount for A with Samuelsonian price	6	5	4	3	2	1	0	no	no	no
12	Net rent per amount for B with Samuelsonian price	5	4	3	2	1	no	no	no	no	no

a fairly substantial demand. A's marginal utilities for successive amounts of G_S have positive values decreasing by 1, from 10 to 1 (Table 4.1, line 3). B's marginal utilities have positive values decreasing by 1 from 5 to 1 (Table 4.1, line 4). Thus the aggregate marginal utility of A and B, for the successive amounts of G_S, displays the trend shown in line 5 of Table 4.1. Given the constant marginal cost of 4, equilibrium will be achieved with a supply of 7 units, as the aggregate utility of $A+B$, at this point, is 4. But at the point in question, there is no marginal utility of B, because B's marginal utility ceases to have a positive value for the 6th unit, so that there is only a marginal utility of A. It follows that according to the paradigm of Samuelsonian equilibrium fiscal prices, based on equality between the supply cost and the sum of the marginal utilities, A will have to pay a levy of 4 (Table 4.1, line 9) for each amount consumed, whereas B will not incur any charge. A's net rent (obtained by subtracting, for each box, the values of line 9 from those of line 7) will thus be that indicated by the sum of the values of line 11, amounting to 21 units. B's net rent (line 12) is 15 units, and this corresponds to the sum of the values of line 7, which pertain to the gross rent, since B incurs no fiscal charge. Whereas before the tax, A's gross rent is 55 and that of B is 15, i.e. 27.27 per cent of that of A, after the tax A's net rent is 21 and that of B is still 15, i.e. 71.42 per cent, as B does not have to pay anything for consumption of public goods. It is evident that such a distribution of the fiscal burden does not correspond to any logic of equity, nor even of responsibility, for if it were applied it would induce B to take no interest at all in the efficiency of production of public goods G_S. In addition, A would have no interest in the common action, because she would derive no advantage from the fact of G_S being produced by the government. Private production would be more advantageous for her, because she would in any case be paying for B's no-charge part as well, but she could exert better control over the production cost.

7 ALLOCATION OF THE COSTS OF INDIVISIBLE PUBLIC GOODS ACCORDING TO THE PARADIGM OF THE CONTRACTARIAN GAME OSFOB UNDER THE HYPOTHESIS OF INCREASING CONSUMPTION WITH INCREASING INCOME: THE RESULT COINCIDES WITH THAT OF LINDAHL, WHICH LEADS TO PROGRESSIVE TAXATION

These arguments indicate that in real communities different rules from those of the marginalist approach will be worked out for apportioning the cost of intrinsically indivisible goods if application of the exclusion principle is not desired or not wanted, and such goods are therefore freely utilized. This occurs even if the principle of overall equilibrium between demand and supply is followed – albeit with approximation – by means of equality between the marginal cost and *the sum of the marginal utilities* of the various users of the marginal unit of the good considered.

In a community based on the principle of responsibility the apportioning of the cost of indivisible public goods will be determined by the proportion of presumed consumption attributable to each member of the group. In a contractarian cooperative model in which each member of the community has a contractual power based on her interest in the common action, application of this criterion will be based on the principle of sharing the costs in proportion to the expected benefit. Given that the different subjects obtain a different level of consumption and benefit from the public goods of common use, the apportioning of the costs will tend to be determined according to the criterion 'everybody contributes to the common cost in proportion to their share of the cost and benefit of the common action'.

In Chapter 2, subsection 3.6, Figure 2.7, reference was made, for a common action pursuing a Paretian optimum, to two paradigms of the contractual games: Nash equilibrium, and OSFOB. In the Nash paradigm the equilibrium point depends on the equilibrium of the bargaining power of the parties, while in the contractarian model (OSFOB) the division depends on the equilibrium among interests in a reciprocity game, in which each individual renounces a share proportional to her utopian maximum. Since all the participants have an interest in the common actions of the given community, each one, in turn, takes a step backwards, proportional to her maximum, allowing others to take a step forward proportional to their (different) maximum. The good reasons underlying this principle were discussed earlier in this chapter, with regard to choice of the quantity and quality of the public goods that must be consumed uniformly.

To sum up, the apportioning of the cost of the common action, that is the tax price of the indivisible goods, will be determined in proportion to the extent to which every individual or business enterprise forgoes their maximum advantage, gross of their consumption cost. Thus subject *B*, whose consumption is small, has a smaller interest in reaching an agreement than subject *A*, who is a large consumer. *A*'s threat that she may, if she (*A*) has to bear too high a share of the cost, withdraw from the common action aimed at obtaining *G* is more credible than *B*'s, since in some cases (such as that considered in the previous section) *B* might have no less an interest in consuming *G* even if *A* was defecting. On the other hand *A* could exert adverse influence over *B* by threatening to defect from the common action and at the same time warning that if *B* pays no share of the cost she may act privately to try to exclude *B* from consumption of *G*. In actual fact, for some Samuelsonian goods this, as we have seen, might appear (almost) impossible. However, *A* could abandon the community in question. In the simplified case of Table 4.1, what was considered was not the benefit of *G*'s consumption of *A* and *B* but only the amounts of their consumption, measured by some conventional parameters. In the real world, the utilities the various subjects draw from the public goods cannot be determined because, as Samuelson observes, no subject wishes to declare the utility she draws from a public good if this gives rise to a tax burden. Also, different subjects have different preferences and different subjective sensibilities regarding the various goods. Despite this, the consumption of indivisible public goods may be determined by referring to the activities of production, investment and consumption, to which they are complementary. And one may argue that with increasing income, individuals' consumption of indivisible public goods grows more than proportionately, as does consumption of other goods that are to a large extent immaterial. On the other hand the benefit of the consumption of given units of indivisible public goods may differ for the different consumers.

Subject M, with 5 units of G_S, can produce and enjoy more income than subject N, but M has a different combination of production factors and employment of her income as compared to N.

The subjects that obtain greater benefits from indivisible public goods as expressed by their greater incomes may be assumed to have a greater interest in the agreement than subjects who draw a smaller benefit from the common action. Therefore the apportioning of the cost of G_S will be carried out in proportion to the cost and incomes of the different subjects. Notice that for the indivisible public goods, the sum of the values of unit costs of the consumptions of all subjects is a multiple n of the unit cost of the supply G_S, because its supply is used simultaneously by n subjects.

In Figure 4.3 we consider two (groups of) subjects A and B, having a different advantage from indivisible public goods – the advantage being

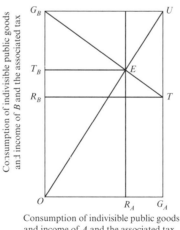

Figure 4.3 Apportionment of the burden in relation to income and to consumption of (totally or partially indivisible) public goods and wants designed for collective use

measured by their incomes – and consuming the goods to a different extent. Subject A, whose income and consumption are indicated on the abscissae, has an income of OR_A, while subject B, considered on the ordinates, has an income of $OR_B > OR_A$. Subject A has a consumption of indivisible public goods amounting to $R_A G_A$, which accounts for a third of her income, while subject B, who has an income much greater than that of subject A, has a consumption of the indivisible public good amounting to $R_B G_B$, which accounts for more than half of her income on the assumption that consumption of public goods is an increasing proportion with increasing income (the proportion has been deliberately exaggerated in this example, for explanatory purposes). The 'Utopian' point U joins the ordinates with the abscissae, at the top right-hand corner. Starting from U and plotting the bisector with origin O, one obtains the relation between the two relevant parameters for sharing out the tax burden between A and B: their income + their consumption of the indivisible public good considered, which are indicated, respectively, by the segment OG_R on the abscissae and by the segment OG_B on the ordinates. The total levy to be paid is $G_B R$. The diagonal $G_B T$ which gives the ratio between A's income and consumption and B's income and consumption indicates, at all its points, the possible apportionment of the fiscal burden between A and B in proportion to their respective income and consumption of public goods. It cuts UO at E, which gives the relation between A's income and costs and B's income and costs, thus allowing the tax burden to be shared out in proportion to these. The levy B has to pay is $G_B T_B$, while A has to pay $T_B R_B$. It should be recalled that $R_A G_A$ is a component of $R_B G_B$ because the good whose cost has to be shared among its consumers–taxpayers is intrinsically indivisible.

The formula for determining the share of the tribute to be borne by B is given by

$$G_B T_B = OG_B / (OG_B + OG_A) \qquad (4.2)$$

In our case, the result is a tax of 50 per cent on B and of 43 per cent on A, while A's income is 37 per cent of that of B, that is there is progressivity in the distribution of the tax burden. This derives logically from the fact that A's consumption of indivisible public goods actually amounts to a third of her income while B's consumption is more than half. In other words we have posited a substantial progressivity to income in the consumption of public goods.

It is interesting to note that the conclusion we have reached here by applying the paradigm of the contractarian bargaining game, on the assumption of an objective phenomenon, that is the consumption of public goods in relation to income, is the same as that proposed by Eric Lindahl (1919; 1928) with the assumption of a marginal utility of public goods that is more than proportional to income. This assumption may be criticized both for its subjectivistic character (we have no psychoscope to ascertain these marginal utilities) and also because it requires the assumption that all subjects have an equal quantity of consumption of public goods, but with different marginal utility. However Lindahl's intuition retains its validity in its statement that those who have more income have a more than proportional interest in production of the indivisible public goods because they draw a greater benefit from them.

The above analysis applies to individuals, not to business enterprises. For the enterprises it can be presumed that consumption of public goods as production factors of a general character is proportional to their income, and this is also the measure of the benefit they derive from such goods. Therefore for the enterprises the appropriate conclusion should be proportional taxation. Returning to Figure 4.3, when $R_B G_B / R_A G_A = OR_A / OR_B$, the division of the tax burden between B and A will be the same, considering either the ratio between the consumptions $R_B G_B / R_A G_A$ or the ratio between the incomes OR_A / OR_B and the ratio between incomes and consumptions by B and A.

The formula for the share of the tax burden of A will become

$$G_B T_B = OR_B / (OR_B + OR_A) \qquad (4.3)$$

8   THE MEASURE OF INEQUALITY: GINI COEFFICIENT AND LORENZ CURVE

We have already noted that the individual welfare function includes empathy and distributive and equity values.

Since income (or welfare) inequality is a *distribution*, a concise definition of this concept cannot be given, nor can it be evaluated in a manner devoid of ambiguity.

It can, however, be examined (and represented graphically) by subdividing the given population into quintiles, deciles or ventiles, starting out from the group with the lowest per capita income and moving gradually up to the higher income groups, and observing the relation between the share of global income and the share of the population considered. The curve thereby obtained, under the hypothesis that 100 per cent has the same distance from the origin both for the population and the income – known as the Lorenz curve,[3] named after the American economist who first addressed the issue – expresses income inequality.

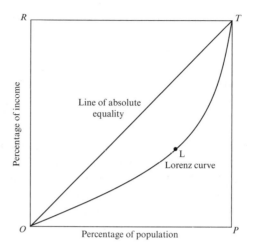

Figure 4.4   Measure of inequality with the Lorenz curve

To clarify this situation, let us consider Figure 4.4.

On the ordinates we indicate the share of global income as a function of the increasing number of persons considered, while on the abscissae we record the 20 quintiles, starting (from left to right) from that with the lowest per capita income and proceeding towards that with the highest per capita income. The share of global income is, naturally, zero when zero population is considered, at the beginning on the axis of the abscissae. It is 100 per cent at the end of the 20 quintiles, indicated on the abscissae, since at this point the entire income of the whole population has been aggregated.

Since we attribute to 100 per cent of the population marked on the abscissae the same distance from the origin as is attributed to the 100 per cent income marked on the ordinates, the box enclosing the curve under examination, delimited by the points *RTPO*, is square.

The diagonal from *T* to *O* divides the box exactly into two, and has the property that all the points of the axis of the ordinates have the same value as those on the abscissae (since the angle *TOP* is = *RTO* = 45°).

In the limit hypothesis of every subject having the same per capita income, obviously the Lorenz curve of income distribution will coincide with the diagonal *OT*, as the percentage increase in the population, considered on the x-axis, will have the same value as that of the income considered on the y-axis.

But since income distribution is unequal, the Lorenz curve will be under *OT*, and the greater the inequality, the more concave the curve will be.

A concise – albeit somewhat ambiguous, as we will see – indicator of the inequality in question is given by the so-called Gini coefficient,[4] which consists in the arithmetic mean of the absolute gap between the two income classes. In simple geometric terms it is equal to the area contained between the Lorenz curve and the line of absolute equality (that is the sum of all the deviations of each point on the Lorenz curve from the line of equality), divided by the area under the line (that is half of the 'Lorenz box').

Therefore

$$G = TLO / TOP \qquad\qquad (4.4)$$

9 INSUFFICIENCY OF THE GINI COEFFICIENT AND AMBIGUITY OF THE LORENZ CURVE

However, if the analysis is taken no further than the synthesis given by the Gini coefficient, it is not always possible to establish in a non-contradictory manner whether the corrective action undertaken by the public economy, which modifies the Lorenz curve, has reduced or increased or left unchanged the inequality in the parts that are of importance for public intervention. For instance, such action could at times consist of deregulations, which remove privileges adversely affecting the less favoured.

Consider, for example, in Figure 4.5, a Lorenz curve referring to welfare as 'purchasing power' such as *OSVLMT*, which is modified – through corrective action undertaken by the public economy – and thus gives rise to *OS'VL'M'T*. The new curve, in terms of the Gini coefficient, would appear to have generated greater inequality, because the area under the curve, between the line of equality and the new curve, is greater than that of the old curve. But for the segment *OV*, the new curve involves a reduction in the inequality given by the area *OSVS'*, whereas for the segment *VU* the new curve presents an increase in inequality given by the area *VLMUM'L'*. This area is greater, geometrically. But in an ordinal judgement it is perfectly possible for the reduction in inequality of the less favoured, which is represented by *OSVS'*, to be more substantial than the increase in inequality that impacts on the medium and medium-high income classes, represented by VLMUM'L'. Such changes may come about, for example, because of deregulation in the economy, which leads to a fall in the unemployment rate of less favoured subjects and a reduction in the 'rents' of intermediate classes, as well as an increase in the profits achieved by the high classes.

The final judgement is left to the aggregation of preferences in collective choices.

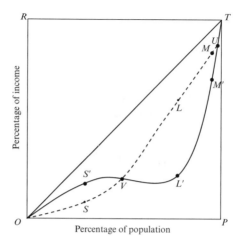

Figure 4.5   Ambiguous Lorenz curves

10   GROWTH OF GDP AND THE FRONTIER OF PRODUCTION: CROSS BETWEEN ALLOCATIVE AND DISTRIBUTIVE EFFECT

Let us suppose production of three goods, X, Y and Z; Goods X and Y are destined to consumption while Z can be either consumed or destined to investment. On the OZ axis of the three-dimensional diagram of Figure 4.6 we measure the quantity consumed, while the residual amount is destined to investment: thus if the whole of Z is consumed, investment is zero, while in the opposite hypothesis the investment is OZ.

It is clear that the more Z is consumed, the less capital is available for producing X and Y; consequently, when there is an elevated consumption of Z, only a small quantity of X and Y can be produced. Therefore, the lower the consumption of Z, the more the frontier of production for X and L will tend to move rightwards.

This representation shows that the aim of growth may be in contrast with distributive equity preferences for the apportionment of GDP between consumption and investments, in particular with regard to choices involving public expenditure and taxation (high tax on enterprises and elevated progressivity on income may reduce the process of accumulation and enterprise development).

Depending on the *type* of accumulation process, the frontier of production may shift more for certain activities than for others. Figure 4.7 shows 'non-neutral' shifts which may be caused by a growth-oriented fiscal policy.

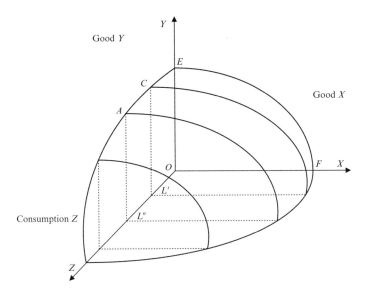

Figure 4.6   *Relation between accumulation, growth and the frontier of production for two groups of goods*

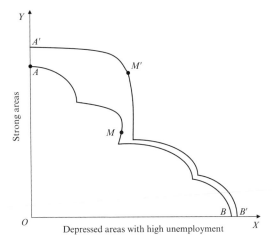

Figure 4.7   Growth policy without equity

11 ALLOCATIVE AND DISTRIBUTIVE GOODS AND THE FISCAL DUTIES 'GAME'

As we have seen, public goods concern two types of wants: 'allocative' and redistributive wants. The latter, in simplified terms, refer to 'duties' toward the 'less favoured'.

The balance that needs to be achieved between fiscal duties and the fiscal rights of normal citizens N therefore concerns a twofold relation between private and public utilities and between 'allocative' public wants and redistributive 'duties', which, for the overall community, can be represented as in Figure 4.8.

In the right-hand quadrant we plot the collective transformation curve RR – which emerges in society with the majority voting rule – between the share of the income RR to be devoted to private utility and the share to be utilized for allocative public goods. The meeting point V between RR and PP, expressing preferences between private and public goods, identifies the equilibrium between private (OU) and public (OD) utilities.

Segment OD thus identifies the *quantum* of fiscal duties which, moved to the left-hand side, generates the frontier DD, in the left-hand quadrant. In the latter quadrant, by means of the tangent of redistributive and allocative preferences FF expressed by majority voting, the share

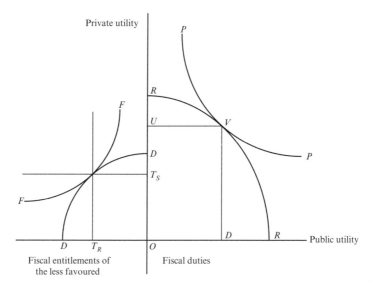

Figure 4.8   Fiscal duties and rights: equilibrium

OT_R for the less favoured (or the 'Rawls share') is identified, and also the OT_S share of 'exchange' for public goods with the private goods of normal citizens N.

In order for the operation to give rise to a level higher than the 'minimum equilibrium' for normal citizens,[5] what is required is that the 'rents' of public goods for 'normal citizens' generated by OD should exceed the share for the less favoured. But if the share for the less favoured is established by a majority vote that does not necessarily reflect the preferences of the well-off portion of the population, while the above-mentioned 'rents' are dependent on the efficiency of the public machine and on the extent of respect for fiscal duties – both of which are rather limited – then there may be a negative disparity.

If, by doing their fiscal duty, many 'normal' citizens have a benefit that is lower than the cost, then the impulse to make a joint move towards defection increases. This is the 'tax revolt' model.

12 'VOTING WITH ONE'S FEET' AS A RATIONALE OF 'LOCAL FINANCE' AND OF FEDERALISM: TAX COMPETITION FOR ENTERPRISES

Individuals who happen to find themselves in a community or a group S_I where their own preferences are 'oppressed' may decide to migrate to another area or another group: they may redistribute themselves, searching for a group whose preferences are akin to their own, as is observed in clubs composed of members with identical or complementary tastes who choose to consort with one another. But the comparison with a club should not be taken literally. People who leave a real club in order to join a different one do not have to move home or go to work in a different city in order to join their club, as would be implied by shifting from one particular public finance unit to another. On the other hand, I individuals may themselves decide against migrating to S_{II} and may for various reasons opt to remain in S_I despite being in a perpetual minority. Such reasons include:

a. because jobs are easy to find in S_I but not in S_{II} (in fact, a subject i might migrate from S_{II} where she is in the majority and move to S_I in order to find work, despite being in the minority in the S_I community and being segregated into a 'ghetto');

b. because she likes the climate, the natural environment and the language of S_I (in other words, its free goods) much more than the corresponding aspects in S_{II};

c. because living space in S_{II} is limited or there are dysfunctions affecting the economic system so that housing and accommodation costs are extremely high;
d. because moving her business to S_{II} raises serious problems in terms of complications affecting logistics and customers.

Reflection of the pros and cons relating to these 'difficulties' may offer a theoretical starting point for the development of broad-based local and federal finance. We may begin by noting that while relocating from one state to another involves considerable complications and is often impossible and 'frustrating', this argument does not apply to voluntary internal migration from one locality to another provided that the constitution protects freedom of movement, that the nation or federation of states is culturally united and its finances and associated urban planning policies are sufficiently 'open', and the labour market is mobile.

This hypothesis gave rise to Tiebout's theorem (Tiebout, 1956), according to which a citizen who becomes 'frustrated', either from the point of view of the mechanisms adopted in a given community for payment of collective goods or on account of the allocative choices adopted for public goods (type, quantity and quality of the individual public goods provided, global volume of the supply and tax burden), can improve her choices by moving to another locality where, in association with other subjects who have like-minded preferences, a solution close to the optimum can be obtained.

However, this mechanism of 'voting with one's feet' conceals a paradox. Theoretically, it functions most satisfactorily in situations of elevated low-cost mobility. But in cases of maximum mobility, an individual i may find it more advantageous to 'split up' her participation in the financing of public goods, by engaging in 'strategic' behaviour which consists of living in a locality that offers the greatest provision of public goods for herself and her family, spending and investing (and supplying services) in a place characterized by maximum provision of productive public goods, and paying taxes where the burden is lowest. The principles of taxation may seek to curb this tendency through fiscal 'harmonization'. But there is a limit on such action, implicit in the model of free fiscal choices applied to the federal system. Thus the conclusion is that the impulse towards 'defecting' without resorting to genuine tax evasion or tax revolt represents a powerful force in an open and pluralistic economy, and this sets a major limit on fiscal action.

The above-described problems affecting individuals who wish to relocate from one place to another in order to obtain the best fiscal regime are not, however, replicated in the same manner in the case of enterprises, above all with regard to firms belonging to larger enterprises that are or can be divided into different units, for example production, management, commerce. Joint-stock companies can 'vote with their feet' by localizing branches of their business in places having the best fiscal regime in relation to public service provision. In particular, for foreign companies whose owners have no right to vote in the community considered, 'voting with their feet' is a highly effective weapon. This may lead to fiscal competition among states that wish to attract businesses to their territory. Such a situation is unexceptionable as long as the taxes imposed on inward companies cover the costs of the public expenditure they benefit from. Given that foreign enterprises localized in the territory of a given community do not usually have fewer benefits from public goods than is the case with domestic companies, the reduction in the tax burden should concern all enterprises. Reductions granted only to foreign enterprises constitute a distortion of the competition market. As can be seen, although the theory of equilibrium between fiscal prices and the average and marginal benefits of public goods is difficult to apply, it is by no means irrelevant from the operative point of view.

NOTES

1. The treatment in the following section refers to the essays by Fedeli and Forte (2003).
2. Which emerges from the theoretical analysis by Samuelson (1954; 1955).
3. On the Lorenz curve, cf. Lorenz (1905); Gini (1912); Atkinson (1970; 1975); Sen (1973).
4. On the Gini coefficient, see the references cited in note 3.
5. See Chapter 1, subsection 2.2.

5. Bureaucracy and interest groups

1 THE MODELS OF BUREAUCRATIC BEHAVIOUR AND THE AGENT–PRINCIPAL RELATION

1.1 The Public Bureaucracy: Structure and Functions

The government is the 'principal' of the implementation of public decisions. The public bureaucracy – in the broad sense of the term, which includes teachers, doctors, the army, the police, and the organs of the legal system and surveillance – constitutes the overall set of 'agents' (or agencies) which carry out, safeguard and control these decisions.[1]

The bureaucracy, in turn, generally appears as a chain of 'principals' and 'agents', from its top down to the intermediate levels and to the base of the apparatus.

The top is sometimes twofold: general directors, and those who are in charge of the function of the given apparatus, or 'functional bureaucracy' (typical of the health care system, where in addition to the bureaucrats of the administration one also finds doctors and 'consultants').

1.2 Difference between Property Rights of the 'Principals' in the 'Agency' Relation of the Public Bureaucracy and in Joint-stock Companies

The problem of property rights together with that of the (lack of) information on the value of the product, in the absence of market prices, is crucial for the difference that distinguishes this 'agency' relation with regard to the heads of the public bureaucracy from that concerning managers of enterprises.

In the case of public services that form part of the state administration or other state-run organizations, the owner is not, unlike in joint-stock companies or in joint-stock cooperatives, a group of individual subjects, but the collective community taken as a whole, and the product is not expressed in turnover and profit but in non-market 'social return'. Thus while individual shareholders who may not be satisfied with the performance of the company they invested in can decide to opt out and sell their shares, citizens belonging to the community whose government owns the organization that provides the public services in question cannot sell their ideal shares (abstractly computable on the basis of taxes paid to the government), which in any case have no market value.[2]

Moreover, in contrast to the citizen who decides to sell underperforming shares, the disappointed taxpayer cannot take with her any portion of the assets of the public service provider, to whose capital the taxpayer previously made a contribution.

By the same token, a saver who sees that a certain company listed on the stock market is doing well can purchase some of its shares, and this goes to the advantage of whoever already possesses shares in the company. The CEOs and the top company managers may then bask in the reflected glory of the company's performance.

In contrast, the managers of the public bureaucracy, unlike private managers and the holders of majority share packets of stock companies or joint-stock cooperatives – or the political representatives in a well-functioning competitive democracy – are not subject to evaluation by others who hold some of the property rights.

In a joint-stock company that achieves no profits or declines on the market, the directors are subject to pressure from the shareholders to whom they are accountable: the majority shareholders, who are their immediate principals, and the broader public of smaller shareholders, who can sell their shares if things are not going to their liking.[3]

In a joint-stock company and cooperative that is performing successfully, the CEOs and top management staff are generally rewarded by the majority shareholders, who see a rise both in the profits and the value of the company's assets, in the sense that other subjects also become interested in acquiring property rights of the company. If the owners do not reward these managers, the latter can still move elsewhere and demand a higher salary on the basis of the success they have achieved.

In a public bureaucracy there are no such signals of information because the community's citizens, as pointed out above, cannot sell their shares in that service. Nor are they capable of putting an economic value on public goods as they do with the market values produced by enterprises, and of linking an increase in the value of the property they possess in a certain community with the success of that particular public management: that is to say, they cannot reward its performance by specific requests to acquire property rights over that public service.

Furthermore politicians, who represent the citizens, are unable to control and check the efficiency of the bureaucracy, in contrast to the controlling procedures that would be put in place by the heads of an enterprise with respect to their apparatus and the managers of such an enterprise.

In short, what we have observed implies that the managers of joint-stock companies and of joint-stock cooperatives have 'property rights' pertaining to their companies, in the sense that when they make a profit their actual or potential remuneration increases, and when a company under-performs their remuneration decreases;[4] but this state of affairs generally does not apply to the public bureaucracies, since there is no market for the products and ownership of public goods.

1.3 Indirect Measures of Efficiency and Effectiveness of the Value of the Product of the Bureaucracy

Efficiency is the optimum relation between costs and result, in the sense that maximum efficiency is achieved when the maximum result is obtained with the given factors, at a given cost. An alternative definition of efficiency is the minimum cost to obtain a given result. If one considers the graph of the frontier of production (in Figure 2.1), maximum efficiency is seen to lie on the frontier of production, because it is here that the given resources are employed in the best manner and it is not possible to reduce the product of good A without reducing that of good B. This means that both A and B are produced at minimum cost, and that the given factors have allowed achievement of the maximum result, a point on the frontier. Effectiveness, on the other hand, concerns the relation between what is produced and what is useful. Maximum effectiveness is achieved when the product obtained satisfies demand in an optimal manner. A product created with maximum efficiency, that is with the minimum cost, may nevertheless have scanty effectiveness: for instance it may be possible to produce a certain medicament with maximum efficiency but the product may have scanty effectiveness for a given therapy or for the entire range of therapies in which it can be utilized. Ineffectiveness also arises when there is product wastage. Figure 2.5 considered, with point E, the allocative effectiveness, which concerns the right amounts of the various products. Giving too little or too much of a given product, as compared to the demand for it, or its marginal utility, leads to ineffectiveness. Late deliveries of supplies are also flawed from the point of view of effectiveness. The public bureaucracies often tend to give an excessive quantity of certain products, as compared to the demand for such products or to what is genuinely useful. Thus public bureaucracies frequently also end up giving a provision that is not adequate to cater for the demand, for example giving an inadequate provision of what is useful. Also they are often creeping bureaucracies, which provide their services at a snail's pace, with the consequence that the service provision often arrives too late.

In principle, the 'ideal' method for evaluating the efficiency and effectiveness of the action of the bureaucracies is the so-called *cost–benefit analysis*, with recourse to shadow prices to estimate the public goods.[5] And as far as investments are concerned, this involves the further problem of having to adopt a discount rate to value in current terms the future flows of benefits, in order to compare them with costs, likewise defined in current terms.

> The reference to shadow prices is riddled with pitfalls. For example, if the cost of the services of public doctors is estimated in reference to the fees charged for medical examinations by private physicians, there is a risk of overestimating the value of the benefit, if the public service free of charge is of poor quality.
>
> And how should one assess 'collateral benefits', the value of which is open to doubt, as in the case of a 'sink' school, when it is a question of evaluating the external economies of education?
>
> In addition to these problems, there is also the tricky problem of gathering information. What guarantee is there that in estimating the benefit of hospital services in monetary terms, there might not be the risk of using as a yardstick the charges of elite clinics that offer different forms of treatment as compared to a state-run hospital?

1.4 Measuring the Productivity of the Bureaucracy and Efficiency Costs by Means of Cost-effectiveness Analysis

Given the above scenario, it may by appropriate to resort to *cost-effectiveness* and *cost-efficiency* analyses,[6] making use of physical measurements of output indicators and, if possible, of results indicators (of which an exemplification is given in Table 5.1). Taking $_AQt_l$ as the volume of output or result of activity A in period $t1$, the productivity in this period will be given by

$$_AQ_{t1} / _AS_{t1}$$

that is by the quantity of product in $t1$ divided by the volume of resources employed (input) $_AS$. Furthermore, on the assumption that the volume of intermediate goods purchased remains unchanged, the specific productivity of the considered productive factors F, for A, will be given by

$$_AQ_{t1} / _FS_{t1}$$

that is by the quantity of product Q in $t1$ divided by the value of the productive factors L_B (labour of the given bureaucracy) and remunerations of the capital (including amortizations and actual or figurative leases) that have been employed. Taking factors different from L_B as given, and considering not the value but the units of L_B, we can have a measure of *physical* productivity of the considered bureaucracy.

Table 5.1   Index of productivity of the bureaucracy

Supply of services and real goods by the bureaucracy	Productivity indexes of the bureaucracy
Personal and material services	*Measure of the units supplied Q*
Law court services	Number of trials and/or sentences
Military services	Power of deterrence
Regulatory activities and controls	Number of standard procedures processed
Administrative and law enforcement services	Number of licences issued, inspections carried out, etc.
Material technical services	Tonnes/km transported, kg of parcels delivered, km^2 forest protected against wildfires
Personal technical services	Number of actions performed (medical examinations, X-rays and chemical analyses, hours of teaching)
Housing or urban planning services	Number of rooms or premises subjected to hygiene inspections, m^2. granted planning permission
Real goods	
Consumption goods	Units of medication at their market prices, at constant price level, units of textbooks measured in pages, units of vaccine for vaccinations
Buildings for dwellings and offices	m^2 per type of building
Buildings for educational or medical services, etc.	m^3 per type of school, hospital facility, etc.
Various public works	km of roads, bridges, etc.
Conservation services	km^2 of reclaimed land, number of trees planted, number of artworks restored

Naturally, these measures of productivity are, at one and the same time, evaluations of efficiency and effectiveness, because the greater the efficiency in use of resources and production factors, the greater – *ceteris paribus* – the effectiveness.

Certainly, the number of trials a Court completes does not illustrate the effectiveness of this office, but at most its efficiency, for the trials could be 'flawed'.

On the other hand, if the various types of trials are not classified, including through use of a complexity index, this item of data could be illusory. Some trials are by their very nature fairly simple, concerning petty crimes such as car theft, while others are considerably more complex, such as trials for armed robbery.

1.5 Bureaucratic Control: The Breton–Wintrobe Models for 'Control'

The productivity of the bureaucracy can be improved and its 'agency' relation rendered more efficient and effective by gathering information on the inputs S and outputs Q of X (where efficiency is the relation between the factors and the product, effectiveness is the relation between the physical units of the product and the utilities that generate it, see subsection 1.3).

Breton and Wintrobe (1982) present an elementary framework outlining the extent to which it is advantageous to carry out checks and undertake controlling measures, and the results of the bureaucracy in terms of cost of the checking activity and the benefits deriving from greater productivity of the bureaucracy. Their framework can be taken as a good starting point for a more sophisticated analysis, in terms of 'the control game'.

At this point we can complicate the framework by considering the reactions of bureaucrats who feel that tabs are being kept on them and who therefore modify their opportunistic behaviour, adapting their behaviour to the type of controlling measures enacted. Thus in the field of health care they will try to fill the available beds, if this is considered by those exercising the supervisory function to be a positive index of activity carried out, and so on. But on the other hand, if the supervisors reduce their inspections, on the assumption that those who have tabs kept on them feel they may still be subjected to severe monitoring, then the members of the bureaucracy, upon perceiving the more lenient approach, will cease to engage in diligent behaviour.[7]

The political principal of the bureaucracy should:

a. try to mimic as far as possible the procedures of control and of marketing of the market enterprises: this, obviously, would be resisted by the top directors of the bureaucracy who fear they may lose their special power based on authority rather than on capability of giving results;
b. introduce as far as possible conditions of competition among the various 'agencies': this implies devoting particular attention to forms of regional autonomy and of competition between public and private services;
c. develop an effective 'agency' relation by means of ad hoc rewards and punishments. This, however, cannot always be done in the manner characteristic of business enterprises because agency relations in the public economy present elements of mobility asymmetric to those of the private economy. For instance, the *managers* of private enterprises are subject to high mobility while the 'ownership' – that is the controlling group – is normally a stable entity. In contrast, the political principals

of the bureaucracy are mobile because they hold office by virtue of the electoral system, while the bureaucratic apparatus is stable.

Let us now examine the various models of 'opportunistic behaviour' of the bureaucracies.

1.6 Niskanen's Model of the Maximization of Expenditure by the Individual Bureaucracy: Its Validity for the Top Levels of the Bureaucracy

According to Niskanen,[8] the bureaucracy tends to maximize the budget in its favour, so as to spend up to the point where the total utility of services provided to citizens is equal to their total cost.

The bureaucracy tends above all to increase its own product, because its power, prestige, career advancement of its staff, pay levels and so on are linked to its product. Therefore the public bureaucracy, in the various services, will tend towards an expansion of the volume of public expenditure, constrained, however, by the citizens' reaction. Niskanen pessimistically supposes that a reaction will emerge only when the total cost exceeds the total utility of the service provided, that is when the service, from the point of view of the user's utility, operates at a loss. It is more logical to suppose that since the bureaucracy needs the consensus of the government, and the latter needs the consensus of the citizens, then it will have to provide a 'minimum profit', just as a big (cooperative) company is expected to do vis-à-vis its shareholders. That is to say, the public bureaucracy will have to provide a 'satisfaction',[9] albeit not a 'maximization', W_s (see subsection 1.7 on the managerial model).

According to theory espoused by Niskanen, the bureaucracy exerts a distorting effect on public expenditure levels, as its maximization is not on the point of intersection between demand and supply of public goods, T, in which consumer demand for public services DD' equals their marginal cost C_m[10] but rather towards point $\overline{T}$ (see Figure 5.1). At this point the users have no further consumer's rent, as the triangle DCT which constitutes the net benefit, in excess of cost C_m for the quantity OQ, is compensated exactly by the loss $TC'\overline{T}$ caused by the excess of cost over returns.

The bureaucracy tends to drive the volume of activities up to the level $O\overline{Q}$ corresponding to point T, because up to this point it still succeeds in globally satisfying consumers' demand for public services. It does not go beyond the level $O\overline{Q}$, and therefore not beyond $\overline{T}$, because from this point onwards the loss incurred by the consumers on account of the excess of costs over benefits would exceed the rent achieved for the quantity OQ.

The emphasis on the bureaucracy's tendency to increase its own product appears to be unilateral, except for the top echelons.

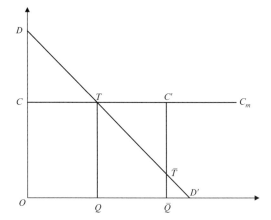

Figure 5.1   The equilibrium of Niskanen's bureaucracy

It would be a mistake to draw the inference from this observation that the top-ranking bureaucrats can succeed in producing efficiently and effectively so as to avoid exceeding the total volume of the consumer's rents. On the market, this comes about through the effect of competitive pressure.

Instead, since the bureaucracy is not subjected to 'competition' or to labour mobility, it shows a tendency, due to a convergence of interests of the base and the top levels, to:

1. persevere in working methods already applied and make excessive use of production factors; thus it tends towards 'X inefficiency';[11]
2. analogously, supply only products that it was already supplying: this is a peculiar form of ineffectiveness, particularly damaging 'in a dynamic world';
3. misrepresent increased utilization of production factors (inputs) as increases in production (outputs);
4. believe that public organizations should function in the interest of the staff instead of the public, with adverse effects on efficiency in utilization of *inputs* as well as on output effectiveness.[12]

1.7   Interaction of the Niskanen Model with that of the Constrained Managerial Model

Niskanen's model, as described above, appears to be greatly simplified: it is excessive to suppose that behaviour of this type on the part of the bureaucracy would fail to trigger any reaction by consumers or consumers'

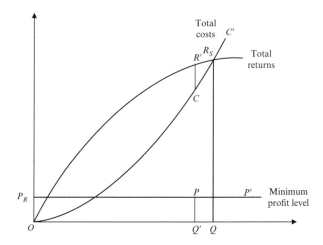

Figure 5.2   The equilibrium of the constrained model of bureaucracy

representatives. We can reinterpret it using the behaviour of the enterprise proposed by Baumol[13] in which the executives aim to maximize turnover and shareholders are interested in maximum profit, and a middle ground between the two aims is found according to the paradigm of maximization of turnover with the constraint of a minimum profit.

We can interpret the new curve of total returns OR'_SR_S determined in this model, represented in Figure 5.2 as the curve of 'returns', in terms of benefits for the users of the public goods. In the case interpreted here, the total cost OCC', which meets OR'_SR_S in R_S, is the production cost of public goods. The line P_RPP' gives the minimum profit level OP_R, which in our case is the 'rent' of the consumer of public goods. In R_S this quasi-rent is zero, because here total returns and total cost are equal (as in $\overline{T}$ in Figure 5.1, where the consumer's global rent is wiped out).

Assuming that the bureaucracy should safeguard the consumer's minimum rent of public goods, equal to OPR, production will thus cease at OQ', which allows this 'quasi-rent' with a global volume of activity R' that is lower than the previous R_S.

In effect, in R' the difference $R'C$ between 'returns' and costs of public goods $= PQ'$.

Notice that this model highlights another aspect of the tendencies of bureaucracies that aim to expand provision: namely, the advantage that resides in thereby covering the maximum share of the 'market' (consisting, for the bureaucracy, in citizens' demand for the goods in question, outside of the market), eliminating as far as possible any competitors who could be more efficient.

1.8 Equilibrium in the Case of Inefficiency in the Provision of Public Goods: X Inefficiency

In fact it would be a mistake – as pointed out earlier – to suppose that the only distortion the bureaucracy tends to bring about, in provision of public goods, resides in the 'volume of activities', taken to mean the quantity of goods supplied. There is an additional tendency, namely that of increasing the production cost as compared to the cost that would arise with a medium-efficient market enterprise. It is also the case that the more the bureaucracy in question has a legal situation of monopoly over that particular provision, the more this second tendency is exacerbated. Four types of cost excesses can be identified. First, an excess of production factors, above all an overabundance of staff, attributable to pressure to expand public-sector employment.

Secondly, lower levels of staff performance, due to the fact that public-sector staff show less dynamic activism than workers in private enterprise, as those who work for the public administration have fewer career incentives and are less controlled with regard to absences from the workplace, proficiency in dealing with the various procedures, and so on.

Thirdly, higher payments to production factors, under pressure from the supplier firms involved.

Fourth, organizational inefficiency, that is imperfect production combinations, due to rigidity of regulations, fear of innovation, and so on.

The first two factors can, properly speaking, be subsumed under the concept of so-called X inefficiency (see note 11), so named because they concern the production factors that are indicated on the x-axis of normal diagrams. The third can be termed Xp inefficiency, inasmuch as it refers to the prices (p) of these production factors. The fourth is T inefficiency (organizational and technological delays) (see Figure A.3 in the Appendix).

X_p inefficiency can be combated partly by containing the weapon with which the bureaucrats' trade unions exert the power of blackmail, namely the threat of strikes. In the public sector, if a strike is conducted with 'wildcat' methods, serious inconvenience is caused to citizens as well as a severe disruption of the functioning of the public machine. An alternative strategy is to enact policies that bind public-sector salaries to productivity.

1.9 The Weberian Forte–Di Pierro Model for 'Offices'

In the model of bureaucratic behaviour theorized by Forte and Di Pierro (1980) on the basis of Max Weber,[14] there are, simultaneously, X_Q and X_Y

and T inefficiencies, that is in the utilization of production factors and in the volume of supply, as compared to what would be their optimum utilization, considering the expected 'social return' and thus the value citizens attribute to that particular supply on the basis of their own organizational and functional paradigm. Forte and Di Pierro (1980) formalized this model, working on the following assumptions: on the cost side, there is assumed to be an excess of factors because of risk aversion or distaste for innovation; there is further assumed to be, again on the service provision side, an overexpansion due to the fact that the criterion to which this bureaucracy conforms is that of respecting the established rules concerning public service, without taking into account any comparison between costs and returns.

This approach should naturally not be confused with the Niskanian framework. We can, in general, contrast the two models of bureaucratic behaviour: that of a 'managerial' type, in which there may well be a Niskanian tendency towards overexpansion of the provision X_Y in order to occupy – for purposes of power – a larger slice of the public economy, versus that of Forte–Di Pierro (1980) of a Weberian type. In this second model, the provision will not have this tendency towards dilation for purposes of acquiring economic power, but it will be accomplished at higher costs X_a and in a greater volume X_Y with organization $\overline{T} < T$ than would be the case for the activities of a market enterprise. The underlying aim, in this second model, is to be able to fulfil the assigned task by means of the bureaucratic 'routine' without any risk of imperfections.[15]

> The Weberian model may also respond to criteria of fairness and political considerations, setting aside efficiency. For instance, this may prompt the concept of maintaining postal and rail services that operate at a severe deficit, in order to provide all citizens with the same service and, more generally, to maintain the prestige of the State (which is a different criterion from the power of bureaucrats).

1.10 Reciprocity Games in Bureaucratic Behaviour and Migué and Bélanger's Theory of the Discretional Margin

The formulation offered by J.L. Migué and G. Bélanger (henceforth M-B)[16] hinges on the concept of 'discretional margin', that is to say a margin that is added to the optimal costs of public goods as X inefficiency or in the form of an increase in supply beyond the equilibrium volume, or as the sum of both deviations from the optimum. This margin is distributed among bureaucrats, politicians and enterprises that work for the Public Administration. M-B consider a set of 'reciprocity games' between the bureaucracy and other subjects, within and outside of the public agency relation.

The implication, here, is that types of collusive behaviour can be found in the 'agency' relation:

1. exchange of favours between politicians and bureaucrats;
2. exchange of favours between bureaucrats and suppliers of the public economy;
3. exchange of favours between politicians and suppliers of the public bureaucracy (as a consequence of the first two points).

The discretional margin of M-B, together with the indirect benefits obtained by bureaucrats in the form of office cars, expenses for dining out, and so on, includes veritable 'economic rents' in money or professional and social positions,[17] not all of which are lawful, in favour of all three of the above-mentioned categories – bureaucrats, politicians and suppliers of the public economy.[18]

But the ordinary bureaucrats of M-B cannot maximize the 'discretionary margin' that allows them to engage in the 'collusive games', if they have to take into account their departmental heads' interest in maximizing production.

1.11 Lessons to be Drawn from the Models Examined

Faced with these problems, the first important point would be to adopt the measures described in subsection 1.5, which arise from reflection on the Breton–Wintrobe model.

Furthermore, every effort should be made to privatize the supply of public goods, by entrusting it to the private sector. This can be done first by outsourcing the activities not strictly characterizing the public service (for example cleaning operations, canteen catering services, the IT centre, security surveillance, equipment, often even actual school buildings, hospital and local council office buildings). However, this raises delicate problems concerning the method for obtaining such goods and services on the market. The system of a call for tenders is often proposed, but tenders may be rigged or manipulated and their transaction cost may be too elevated in terms of time and contractual procedures. This can be addressed drastically by entrusting non-characterizing services globally to a private firm.

> This, for instance, manages all the services, except those of doctors and paramedics and stretcher-bearers, of a hospital which the firm itself has built and equipped with the technical facilities, with regard to which it is also responsible for maintenance.

Furthermore, the entire management of the public provision can be entrusted to market enterprises. This holds in particular (but not necessarily) when such enterprises can finance their activities by obligatory prices or contributions.

> Motorway and local public transport services, for example, can be run by private firms holding a concession, with fares that take into account the problems relating to Dupuit and Hotelling goods. As was observed earlier, for Dupuit goods it is possible to resort to the compromise of fare exemptions for marginal or meritorious users. For Hotelling goods, discriminatory fares can be contemplated, with a reduced price for marginal users and an additional charge for supra-marginal users. Thus in the case of toll roads or motorways, if they are Dupuit goods one could establish that the company holding the concession should not bear the entire cost of amortization, but only a certain portion. If, on the other hand, they are Hotelling goods, then the company should limit itself to demanding a tariff discrimination that will allow optimal utilization of the goods.

2   INTEREST GROUPS, THE PARA-POLITICAL MARKET, FISCAL QUASI-RENT SEEKING

2.1   Interest Groups and Public Goods

In a democratic society that enjoys freedom of thought, of the press, of assembly and association, the right to strike and that of engaging in public demonstrations and protest, provided this is done peacefully, the right to hold *referendums* and petitions, it is normal for there to be 'interest groups' with varying degrees of organization, whose activity – as the term suggests – involves promoting specific interests of various types.[19]

I.   First and foremost, 'ideal' interests (more properly definable as 'values'). Among these, one may list protection of the landscape, the environment, nature, the historical and cultural heritage, promotion of the arts, scientific research, the different religious faiths, patriotic ideals, the country's language, and so on.

II.   Additionally, interest groups have social, humanitarian and empathetic ends. These include assistance and care for less favoured groups such as the disabled, neglected and abused children, the aged and infirm, those affected by particularly severe and widespread pathologies,[20] refugees, the victims of natural calamities, and so on.

III. Furthermore, groups having a recreational function, such as sports, entertainment, tourism: these may pursue group interests and/or have empathetic ends.

IV.   Economic-social and empathetic groups. Examples of this category concern aid for developing countries, protection of emigrants and immigrants, retraining of the unemployed, skills training for the workforce, development of the cooperative movement, student welfare, and so on.[21]

V.   Groups pursuing essentially economic and technical ends concerning the interests of a given group or category. Here one may include protection of the interests, information and technical assistance of such groups as workers, industrialists, associations of the various sectors, merchants and businessmen, farmers and smallholders, craftsmen, credit institutions, the various categories of freelance professionals and pensioners, and so on.[22]

VI. Finally, groups who pursue the end of championing 'civil rights' and 'political rights' that have been contested. In particular, feminist movements, movements in favour of electoral reform, anti-prohibitionists, movements in favour of divorce, gay rights, for or against abortions, and so on.

The organizations that support these values and interests are mainly upholding and providing collective goods which are, to a large extent, and in a technical sense, 'public'. That they are 'public' is due either to the fact that they cannot be divided into units of sales, and individuals who are not willing to pay their share of cost as established by the proprietor cannot be excluded from their enjoyment, or to the fact that imposing a charge on those who obtain the benefit would destroy the distributional nature of the service.[23] In effect, the groups concerned with values and interests, categorized under I, II, III and IV, provide 'public' goods of the Samuelsonian type or 'redistributive' or 'merit' goods. The public goods in question may go to the benefit of some rather than of all members of the collective community, but they generally cause no damage to any subjects.

In contrast, the organizations falling under category V, by their very nature, supply goods which, despite being to a large extent public, can be denied to whoever does not subscribe to the group or can be associated with material and moral sanctions imposed on whoever draws advantage from the goods in question without accepting the costs.[24]

Furthermore, a considerable part of the goods provided by the interest groups of these classes are of an eminently conflicting nature, in the sense that while they give subjects *i*, their intended recipients, an advantage, on the economic plane they damage subjects *j* who oppose these goods.

A classic example consists of the advantage that collective bargaining provides for public and private employees and professionals, and for those who purchase foodstuffs and produce to be processed, and also for employers with regard to the supplies of such goods (agricultural goods, mineral ore and so on) and the supply of labour. This situation has given rise to monopoly powers of buying and selling.

Without the action of the workers' trade unions, it is likely that wages would have undergone a much lower rate of increase during the period of industrial development, generating a lower impetus towards productivity and a smaller market of mass consumption goods.

Additionally, the workers' and employers' trade unions are useful to establish standard contracts that can be of advantage to everyone, including the 'non-enrolled'. But there are risks of a monopoly in cases where obligatory validity of the contracts is enforced even on those who do not belong to the organizations that have set up the contracts in question, as has been the case in Italy for the national labour contracts since the corporative era and up to the present day.

As far as the interest groups of category VI are concerned, the goods they provide are of an eminently conflicting nature, but it would not be accurate to state that the benefit of one of the groups corresponds to damage inflicted on other groups. In this case the conflict of interests and the values they promote frequently act as a driver of progress.

2.2   Interest Groups and 'Public Bad': Fiscal Rents

However, organized interest groups may exploit the pressure they are able to exert as a means to obtain privileged advantages, that is 'fiscal rents', thereby distorting the range of choices.[25]

Within the sphere of the public economy, 'rent-seeking' can be defined as investment in activities in order to obtain benefits in money or in kind (premises free of charge or with a purely symbolic charge, donations of money or possessions, secondment of personnel paid by others, licences, permits and concessions for engaging in business activities, and so on), advantageous waivers on tax liabilities and on constraints that should apply in the absence of such activities. 'Fiscal rent-seeking' includes such aspects as investment in activities designed to influence public choices in one's own favour on matters of revenue and expenditure, or tax avoidance and tax evasion and fraud with reference to tributes, public prices and illegitimately acquiring public benefits.

2.3   Rent-seeking and the Activity of Interest Groups in General: Positive Sum Games or as the Loss of Collective Welfare

There are activities of interest groups that generate 'public goods' of which the benefits are greater than the costs borne by their members and by the collective community. In this case, the fiscal rent obtained by the interest group is the reward for a positive sum game. But there are other activities that generate benefits lower than the costs, and therefore create 'public ills', giving rise to misallocation of resources. Finally, still others merely generate a shift in welfare from one group to another.

The second case, obviously, is a zero sum game; the third is more complex because if distribution improves, it can be stated, in utilitarian terms, that it is a positive sum game, even though in 'resourcist' terms it is a zero sum game.[26] But even in the case of what appears to be a positive sum game for the community – that is the community's gain is greater than the cost it incurs – there may be a net loss for some members of the community and a benefit for others. And there is no guarantee that this allocationally satisfactory result is also equitable.

A result can be allocationally satisfactory, yet distortive, if it improves resource allocation while not leading to a better distribution.[27] Also, if the action of an interest group results in the funding of public good *A*, which otherwise would not have been funded even though its social benefits are greater than the costs, it can be argued that the allocation improves, even if public good *B*, which has social benefits that even more substantially exceed its costs, is not funded because no interest group is concerned with it. This gives a so-called *sub-optimal* or second-best result.

2.4   Laws on the Trend of Organized Interest Groups

We can thus identify some laws on the trends of interest groups with respect to the public economy.

1.   Large enterprises may act as interest groups in their own right, because their 'gain' from associative services tends to cover almost all of the costs of the group. Consequently, they often guide organizations that also involve the interests of smaller operators, as they can in any case shoulder a large share of the costs and inflict damage in various ways on those who, despite enjoying the 'public goods' of the organization, do not wish to join it. For instance, those who opt not to join may find themselves excluded from governmental, parliamentary and bureaucracy-related 'favours' (that is fiscal rents from the government, from parliament and from the bureaucracy).

2.   Organizations of widespread and pervasive interests are costly and their impact tends to be all the greater when the public economy becomes increasingly all-encompassing and subject to manipulation. This is due to the fact that the gain such organizations can provide to their members through specific fiscal rent services will be correspondingly greater, and therefore the excess of their gain over costs will, by the same token, become similarly more likely.

3. Since interest organizations are endowed with a large bureaucracy, an extensive organization and a great number of paid-up members, they have an elevated cost (which cannot always easily be passed on to the beneficiaries), in relation to actions undertaken on the political and semi-political markets (and it is not always advisable to grant members an insight into the detailed accounting linked to these actions). Therefore the more pervasive are the regulations around which their apparatus has been built up, the greater is the power these organizations exert over public choices. Also, non-members will consequently be increasingly at a disadvantage as compared to members.

2.5 The Non-distortive Functions of Interest Organizations

All this does not deny that interest organizations may also have non-distortionary economic functions and therefore that their action may be positive. In particular, such action is positive:

a. when they act as intermediation groups furnishing information, consultancies, and so on, in order to give scope to the preferences of those to whom they offer their patronage and, accordingly, to submit representations to the political operators and to the bureaucracy;
b. when they act as a counterbalancing power, which countervails the distortive effectiveness of adverse pressure exerted against them by other interest groups;
c. when they act as voluntary organizations in the management of common goods to avoid their wastage, making unnecessary the direct intervention of the government with its bureaucracy.[28]

In this perspective, there is some truth in the argument that the multiplicity of interest organizations on the political market and the semi-political market has a positive influence as compared to a world dominated by relatively few interest groups, and a small number of large enterprises endowed with notable contractual power. But it can be said that pervasive regulations tend to boost the number of interest groups at the expense of the proper relationship between politics, the public economy and the market.

2.6 Some Legal Institutes for Improvement of Public Economy Decision-making Processes, in Relation to Distortionary Pressures Exerted by Interest Groups

Binding collective contractual powers and extensive regulatory frameworks pave the way to rent-seeking. Therefore every possible effort should be made to devise rules that forestall these rent-seeking activities. A typical rule is that taxes (and, more generally, public interventions) should be characterized by *legal certainty* (that is to say, formulated with absolute clarity), *simple* (that is with few structural complications), *universal* (with few exceptions), easily *understandable*, and open to *public control by the common citizen*. This approach limits their theoretical perfection, but also the deformation of public economy policies brought about by manipulation on the part of interest groups. In general, the more the rules of the economy are characterized by legal certainty, and are simple, universal, easily understandable and known to the public, the less a) interest organizations will be able to bear choices that contrast with the general needs felt by the citizens; and b) citizens will need interest organizations to protect themselves against discrimination (negative fiscal rents) that may damage them.

NOTES

1. A very extensive theoretical and empirical literature on the economy of the bureaucracy has been developed. See in this regard Breton and Wintrobe (1982); Niskanen (1971); Peacock (1979a) etc; Migué and Bélanger (1974); Forte and Di Pierro (1980); Fedeli (1992; 1999).
2. See on property rights and market organization Alchian and Demsetz (1972).
3. It will, however, be necessary to bear in mind that there is an analytical difference between, on the one hand, an enterprise where the centre of control is constituted by a limited group of shareholders, who are effectively the 'principals' of the managers, and on the other, an enterprise where there is a large range of shareholders (public company). In the public company, whoever holds control could aim to build up the turnover with the constraint of a minimum profit. Generally, though, when the company is listed on the stock market and is owned by a broad collection of shareholders, the joint-stock company – through the investment funds that participate in it – exerts control over its success or failure by means of the gains it makes from sales of its goods and services and by means of the related valuation of its holdings, the shares in which can be ceded and, potentially, purchased, either by assignment of pre-existing shares or by issuing new shares.
4. On the model of the managerial enterprise in which the main aim is turnover while profit acts as a constraint, see note 13 below.
5. On cost–benefit analysis, see in the vast literature on this topic, Musgrave (1969, n.3).
6. On cost-effectiveness analysis, see Forte (1984, vol. I, Part IV), Forte (1983 [1984]) and, in greater detail, J.M. Wolfe (ed.), 1973; Bondonio and Scacciati (1990). The bibliography on this topic, on the international level, is vast and growing. The above citations of the Italian empirical studies are intended simply as illustrative examples.
7. At this point the 'principals' will have to resume the controls. This is a cyclical game.
8. See Niskanen (1971). Niskanen in his more general formulation maintains that bureaucracy maximizes its level of activity, that is the volume of its budget, with the constraint of the users' satisfaction.
9. On satisfaction as an alternative to maximization, see H.A. Simon (1957, Part IV and 1972).
10. Notice that because of the assumption of constant costs, the marginal cost curve is a straight line that coincides with the average costs curve.

11. X inefficiency is defined as excess utilization of production factors as compared to the minimum volume required for the product considered. The 'ratio' of actually utilized volume to the minimum required is the measure of X inefficiency. See, on theories of X efficiency, the work by H. Leibenstein (1978). The term 'X efficiency' is used to distinguish this problem of efficiency from that of 'effectiveness'.

12. This observation contributes to highlighting a certain ideological 'bias' shown by Niskanen, who leans towards the argument that the public apparatus systematically tends to expand public goods beyond the will manifested by citizens; however, it can be demonstrated that in certain cases it tends to 'provide too little' in some crucial sectors such as justice: for instance, at least in Italy, the provision of public goods is insufficient, even if expenditure in relation to effectiveness of supply is elevated.

13. See Baumol (1959) and Williamson (1964). The elaboration with regard to public bureaucracy is owed to the present writer.

14. See Weber (1922 [1976, 1978]), vol. 1, *Conceptual Exposition*.

15. This model, like the two that follow, applies more substantially to the 'offices', that is to the operative middle managers.

16. Migué and Bélanger (1974, pp.27–43), takes up again the seminal work by Williamson (1964) (concerning both the bureaucracy of the managerial enterprise and also the public bureaucracy, with emphasis on the former). On 'reciprocity games', see Axelrod (1984).

17. A typical case is that of the so-called 'revolving doors', namely the fact that the high-ranking bureaucrats who have taken early retirement subsequently find positions in enterprises that work for the government or which operate in a public regulatory framework, and which were previously supervised by such bureaucrats when they were in service, or received numerous orders commissioned by the various government departments.

18. To which one can add the economic operators subject to the various regulatory powers and tax powers.

19. The literature on interest groups or pressure groups can be classified roughly into three types: the optimistic, the realistic and the pessimistic assemblage. On the first of these, see the classic work by Bentley (1908), where it is argued that interest groups exert a positive effect on democracy because the multiplicity of interest groups gives rise to a sort of 'competition' with regard to who can influence political choices. Such choices can thus be interpreted as the expression of a homogeneous aggregation of minorities (namely, the interest groups), which compete with one another and give rise to different majorities whose structure varies on different occasions.

  A typical description of the second type can be found in the work by M. Olson (1965 [1971]), who attributes the decline of nations that have a prolonged democratic history to the consolidation of interest groups that have become stratified over time in such nations.

  The main exponents of the third type are J.M. Buchanan (1980 [2000]) and G. Tullock (1980b), who believe that democracy consists of comparison and contrast among interests, but condemn 'rent-seeking' as perverse. See also Congleton et al. (2008a, b).

20. In the past there was tuberculosis, now cancer and AIDS. These 'interests', which are highly altruistic and aim to alleviate suffering and save the life of unfortunate persons, are also classified as 'values', although they concern material welfare.

21. Although the main aim in this case is above all the protection of economic interests, one cannot deny the presence of altruistic and ideological beliefs in associations pursuing these objectives that are motivated by ethical concerns. Often such beliefs are intense at the origins, whereas – subsequently – the associations in question little by little acquire increasingly pragmatic characteristics and goals.

22. But even here one cannot exclude disinterested, altruistic and cultural motives, associated with fee-charging professional services (accountancy and tax consultancy services, market analysts, loan and credit consultancy services, public authorizations, and so on).

23. Those who support the battle against cancer by promoting prevention and the search for effective therapies and a cure provide advantages even for those who do not belong to the association or those who make no contribution to the movement. Besides, such an association would fail to be true to its humanitarian ends if it systematically made those lacking adequate financial means pay the full price, for example the cost of early diagnoses or of innovative and costly drugs. But if cultural and artistic events are charged at cost price, often it becomes difficult to ensure that their impact on society is appraised as the provision of higher goods; consequently, imperfect perception of their value results in inadequate appreciation of their worth.

24. Thus those who are not trade union members, and likewise 'scabs', can derive advantage from union action without directly paying the costs. But non-members can be censored and expelled from meetings, resulting in exacerbated segregation. Naturally, the stronger and more wide-ranging the trade union organization, the more these 'sanctions' exert a significant effect.

25. The theory of 'rent-seeking' for activities that produce no public good has been examined in depth by G. Tullock, by whom see, in particular, *Rent-seeking as a Negative Sum Game* (1980b) and *Efficient Rent-seeking* (1980a), both published in Buchanan et al. (eds.) (1980). A particularly well-developed strand of the theory of rent-seeking concerns customs tariffs, and in general public policy for control of foreign trade (importation licences, and so on); see A.O. Krueger (1974). From an examination of the theory of rents obtained from economic crime, it is but a short step to the theory of rents deriving from tax evasion and tax fraud.

26. The purely 'resourcist' point of view should be distinguished from the utilitarian perspective of the game. If the pay-off is equal to the amount lost, then, in the 'resourcist' sense what one has is a zero sum game, but if the winner's utility is greater than the loser's, the zero sum game is transformed, in the utilitarian perspective, into a positive sum game. The point of view we have denominated as 'resourcist' is, in actual fact, the allocative perspective: if the resources transferred to the winner are equal to those suffered by the loser, in allocative terms we have a zero sum game. If the utility of these resources is greater for the winner, this concerns distribution and not allocation.

27. Typically, 'rent-seeking' by non-profit organizations that are active in the sphere of art, music, protection of the historical, cultural and religious heritage, is a positive sum game if, in the community concerned, the absence of this kind of activity by such non-profit organizations would result in a lower level of provision of these public goods as compared to what a community composed of well-informed and culturally aware citizens would wish to have. But if the users of these low-cost or virtually free goods are affluent, then this – from the distributive perspective – may be open to criticism.

28. On the last issue, see Ostrom (1990) and (2005), and Ostrom et al. (1994).

6. The fiscal constitution and the rules governing the budget

1 OVERVIEW

1.1 The Institutions and the 'Constitutional Rules'

In order for the public economy to work to the best advantage of citizens belonging to the various social groups and categories, in the framework of a market economy, it is essential to have appropriate institutions and 'rules of the game', through which decision-making processes can take shape and be implemented while respecting criteria of allocative efficiency and effectiveness, as well as equity. The economic institutions and 'rules of the game' that are endowed with a general permanent character and a higher validity than that of individual ordinary rules or laws can be termed the 'Economic Constitution'.

> This concept, which has now become common parlance among economists and is debated jointly among philosophers, economists and scholars of political science concerned with public ethics, does not necessarily coincide with the *juridical* concept of a Constitution. It is quite possible to imagine general rules of the game, destined to become permanent, which are not contained in the Constitution in the formal sense of this term. For instance, rules regulating debate in the two Houses of Parliament on budgetary expenditure and revenue, that is on the budget law for the coming financial year, may be of this type. Similarly, the rules embodied in the Maastricht Treaty and the Stability Pact approved by the Council of Europe in 1997 with regard to Monetary Union are partial elements of a constitution of the public economy in relation to the market, even though it cannot be defined as a 'constitution' in the formal sense.[1]

1.2 Negative, Positive and Intermediate Rules

A certain asymmetry in the rules of the game concerning 'non-agenda' and 'agenda' aspects of the public economy can be observed. Thus on the one hand, there are rules for protection of the so-called negative liberties, to be safeguarded against prohibitions and constraints ('freedom of', for example freedom of enterprise, freedom of property), and on the other, protection of so-called positive freedoms that are obtainable by the attribution of fields of choice and which must be safeguarded through means of various kinds ('freedom from', from want, from malaise and from ignorance). *Prima facie*, it is easier to issue a statement establishing that a tax not laid down by the law but, say, merely by an administrative act is null and void, than to set up a genuinely functioning right to health, which involves a complex and efficient public health care organization.

However, not even the rules of the negative game – if they are general – are easy to guarantee. Thus the protection of the national currency and savings, a task that forms part of the duties traditionally assigned to the state, has over the centuries systematically and dramatically failed to live up to expectations. This failure occurs because violations are extremely difficult to ascertain precisely, and it is even more difficult to guarantee freedom from a heavy burden of taxation by setting a limit on fiscal burden and on public expenditure that does not benefit those who pay for it.

This offers an explanation for the transition from rules concerning general ends – negative or positive – to rules of the game concerning so-called parametric objectives.

> Thus the Maastricht rules establish that the general budget deficit must not exceed 3 per cent and (according to the subsequent Stability Pact) must subsequently go down to zero, and the ratio between the public debt and GDP must tend to 60 per cent, if the debt is higher, and not exceed 60 per cent, if it is lower. However, to prevent the violation of the basic principles of a public economy conforming to market principles, the Maastricht requirement should be supplemented with rules limiting the fiscal burden or public expenditure, although these are much harder to apply.

It is clear that while the general objectives, including the parametric objectives, can be stated in what could become the genuine 'constitution', this is far less easy for the intermediate ends.

> One could establish in the constitution that the tax burden should not exceed, for instance, 50 per cent of GDP, but in order to make this rule operative it is necessary to formulate intermediate principles concerning the tax rates of the individual levies. And as regards the rule that the deficit cannot exceed 3 per cent of GDP, it is necessary to define the subjects of the public budget, specifying what forms part of the budget in the sphere of expenditure and revenue, and how it is to be calculated.

1.3 The 'Disinterested' Position or the General Interest Position of a Constitutional Type: Reciprocity

We would appear to be caught up in the loop of a vicious circle: how can rules be established, without having prior basic rules available to determine how to establish them? How should a general agreement be reached concerning the manner of deciding on constitutional rules in a community that is not necessarily unanimous?

From the theoretical point of view an answer has been found, by assuming that the decision makers do not know either the identity of the rules or their specific destiny, nor that of the subjects they represent and for whom they are supposed to provide safeguards. In this *impartial* situation, the decision makers can, by unanimous vote, reach an agreement on rules of the game which are likely to be best in terms of efficiency and equity. They would probably choose rules which, while allowing subjects to pursue their advantage most successfully, consistently with other individuals' pursuit of their own advantage, would guarantee each individual a minimum, both in terms of rights considered to be essential and also in terms of means of subsistence.

This is, basically, the 'contractualist' formulation, seen earlier[2] (see Chapter 2, subsection 3.8 ff: in particular the theories of Rawls and Buchanan and the principles to be derived for the cooperative model, with their limits).

But the transition has to be made from the mental experiment to the real world. Let us imagine ourselves in the position of a 'founding father' in the Constituent Assembly, making choices on behalf of the electors, their children and grandchildren. The founding father does not know what will happen to these future generations, and therefore only very general interests can be considered. But it cannot be ignored that the founders nevertheless impersonate the preferences of certain social groups, who cherish certain values and interests.

In order for the constitution to be respected *ex post*, after it has come into force, it must be regarded as an equitable and efficient contract among real subjects who hold different interests and values. Therefore it must induce them to cooperate with one another and to abide by the laws; consequently, it should reflect the principle of the unanimous vote.

This 'contract' can consist of two kinds of rules that are generally advantageous *ex post*. First, rules the respect of which is in the interest of all parties – provided that all parties do then respect them – because in the fullness of time and in an overall perspective such rules provide everyone with a (moral or material) benefit. Secondly, rules that equitably share out the costs and advantages deriving from cooperation, and that do not ignore the presence of different preferences and positions, yet seek to ensure a balanced view, according to principles that no one could reasonably reject. Indeed, such principles could hardly be rejected, as they aim to introduce fair regulations for a range of opposite types of situation that anyone might be quite likely to find themselves facing – as a debtor or creditor, supplier or consumer, young or old, male or female, saver or investor of savings, and so on. What is more, these potential situations could equally well concern an individual's children, grandchildren or great-grandchildren. Rules of the first type enjoy unanimous consensus *ex post* as well, as long as the game is repeated. Individuals' impartiality towards their own interests derives not so much from knowing what social status they may or may not enjoy as, rather, from knowing that the rule will apply in all cases, both in those which may prove to be disadvantageous to the individuals involved and also in those felt to be advantageous to them, or towards which they are indifferent. Thus even though the rule may not *always* – in every hand of the game – be appreciated, it is nevertheless recognized and embraced as valid by *each* player in the overall set of hands making up the game.

> If the rule which lays down that taxation must respect criteria of equality of treatment, without granting privileges to one group or another (a criterion established by constitutions, but often violated by the ordinary laws), is respected by all individuals, then it brings advantages to all concerned, because a system in which everyone has their own special privilege is worse than one in which nobody has any privilege. And the same holds true with regard to the rule that there must be monetary stability because prolonged inflation damages the entire community (D'Amico, 2007).

With regard to the problem of sharing out the costs and advantages of public goods (on which see Chapter 4, sections 3, 4 and 7), and the relation between one's own *merits* recognized by the market and obligations linked to the *wants* of others, which must be considered in terms of mutuality obligations (see Chapter 2, subsection 3.8) or obligations towards less favoured subjects (see Chapter 2, subsection 3.9 ff.), the rules should reflect 'game equilibrium' or rather 'supergame equilibrium' (repeated game), such as that of proportional sharing. The latter, which we denominated OSFOB, appears to be the most general and non-discriminatory contractarian rule.

1.4   Rules For the Game and Rules in the Game

The rules of the game are of two types:

1. *the rules for the game*, which concern both the entitlement to conduct the institutions and the procedures to conduct and implement decision-making processes;
2. *the rules in the game*, which concern distribution of the costs and the advantages of the game.

The fundamental rules for the game of the public economy in the cooperative model – in relation to the individual social welfare function (analysed earlier in Chapter 2, especially subsection 1.5) – are:

1. 'one person, one vote';
2. people's or one's own votes are not saleable;
3. recognition and equality of the basic 'moral rights' of all citizens (personal
    integrity, freedom, civil and political rights, and so on) and safeguards
    against damage to natural, environmental and cultural goods, whenever
    these are acknowledged to be endowed with intrinsic value, such as the
    seas and oceans, the ecosphere, the multiplicity of living species, works
    of art, the important archeological and historical heritage;
4. respect for contracts and other agreements;
5. respect (apart from constitutionally delimited exceptional cases) for
    property acquired with a 'valid title', through: a) one's own labour (in
    the broad sense); b) original occupancy (with the exception, in certain
    cases, of natural and environmental goods endowed with intrinsic
    value); c) the fruit of one's own capital; d) free cession by contract or
    by virtue of the liberality of third parties holding a valid title;
6. the obligation to pay taxes for public expenditure within the rules of
    the fiscal constitution, which will be seen further on.[3]

(The issue of the rules of the game for apportioning the cost of public
goods was addressed in Chapter 4, while the rules on welfare in particular
were dealt with partly in Chapter 2, subsection 3.8, ff., and they are partly
touched on again above.)

Among the rules of the game there are the rules concerning the institutions through which citizens in a democracy engage in an (efficient,
effective and equitable) agency relation with the political representatives,
as well as the rules to be adopted in order to establish the institutions of
the legislative and executive bodies and of the judiciary, and the associated rules governing their functioning. They include the electoral rules,
the presidential or parliamentary form of the State, and their duties and
the procedures by means of which they operate, in particular in public
expenditure and revenue.

1.5   The Generality of the Rules: Horizontal Equity of Taxation

To avert the risk that the economic and social game may lend itself to abuse,
and to ensure that it is as advantageous as possible for all citizens, the constitution must establish fixed *general rules in the game*, which leave no loopholes for misuse by majorities who are looking for a way to *discriminate*

against or even iniquitously *exploit* the minorities. In addition, such rules must be objectively ascertainable and therefore they must be clear and endowed with legal certainty, even if they are not absolutely perfect in their application to individual cases: *summum ius, summa iniuria*.

The so-called principle of horizontal equity of taxation forms part of this body of rules. This principle is laid down by Articles 3 and 53 of the Italian Constitution, which establish that citizens are equal before the law, and also lay down the obligation for all citizens to contribute to public expenditure in relation to their individual ability to pay. It follows from these Articles that each individual must pay the same levy, under equal ability to pay. The latter is generally identified in reference to their economic capacity indices, some of the most significant of which are, naturally, their income, their assets and personal estate, and consumption, the latter being taxed in Italy, as in the other European countries, by means of value-added tax (VAT) on consumption. All persons, if their conditions are equal in terms of the taxable base on which they will be assessed (income, for personal income tax, and profit, for corporate tax, the added value taxable in VAT, and so forth) are to be treated equally.

No exemptions are allowed for those who, inasmuch as they belong by law or de facto to the national community, benefit from public expenditure, in contrast to widespread practices in previous eras that applied to members of the clergy, the nobility and the high ranks of the army.

Horizontal equity is not merely a distributive concept, designed to prevent injustices in favour of *A* or at the expense of *B*. Rather, it is also a principle of non-discrimination, in a regime of competition. The Italian constitution is integrated in this regard by the European Union Treaty, which forbids indirect taxes whose structure would generate distortions in trade among the member states (such as, say, a higher tax on beer than on wine in states with an extensive wine-making industry, and a higher tax on wine than on beer in countries with a strong brewing industry). The European Union Treaty further establishes, in an even more general manner, that apart from certain well-defined exceptions, no 'state aid' that would be likely to distort competition on the European markets is admissible in any form whatsoever. For example, a tax exemption in favour of given enterprises that operate in a certain area or production sector is a form of state aid. The same holds true for a tax on an economic activity or entity considered to be a rival of a similar activity or entity that the state in question wishes to favour.

In general, tax incentives in favour of less developed areas are admitted only for certain specific objectives of employment and investment, but not as a general principle.

However, there is also the problem of incentives for those who generate external economies through particular production processes or through particular modes of employment of their income. In such cases it cannot be asserted that total or partial tax exemption is a form of 'state aid'. It is a remuneration for a service rendered to the community as a whole. This is the case, for instance, for tax incentives for environmental protection – for example by means of energy-saving measures or non-polluting energy sources – or for the protection and enhancement of the historical and artistic heritage, or for expenses pertaining to scientific and technological research (see Chapter 3, subsection 1.12 ff. and 2.2–2.3).

1.6   Vertical Equity of Taxation in Relation to the Various Different Benefits of Public Expenditure and the Different Wants

In addition to the principle of horizontal equity, there is also the principle of vertical equity. This principle affirms that as a general rule, those who have greater economic means should contribute to the burden of public expenses to a more than proportional extent, that is in the form of progressive taxation. As such, this principle, in the cooperative model in which taxes are the fiscal prices of public services, is highly debatable.

> Article 53 of the Italian Constitution, clause 2, states that the tax system is based on the criterion of progressivity in taxation. But it is related to the first clause which asserts that it is everyone's duty to contribute to the public expenditure. The reference to the tax system excludes application of the principle of progressivity to social insurance contributions.

In the tax system it is possible, on the basis of this principle, partially to derogate from the principle of horizontal equity by allowing exemptions and reduced consumption tax rates for consumption that constitutes a large share of the expenditure of low-income subjects but not of medium or high-income subjects, as in the case of certain staple products that satisfy primary needs, considered by consumers to be 'basic necessities'.

It may be argued that consumption of public goods, as a percentage of income, tends to increase progressively with a gradual increase in income, from minimal levels to medium levels, subsequently becoming proportional for medium-high and high incomes. If such an assumption is held to be true in a model where the public economy is market-conforming, which involves predominance of the principle that taxes are the fiscal price of public goods, then this justifies moderately progressive taxation, in so far as taxation of income and consumption is concerned. However, what the correct formulation should be in this perspective depends on the distribution of public expenditure among the various subjects and geographic areas.

Determining the appropriate formulation would require cost–benefit analyses of the tax system broken down by different incomes and areas of the country. This would not represent a difficult enquiry for the official statistical services. But such analyses are hardly ever carried out, perhaps because this appears highly unpopular.

However, vertical equity in the system of taxation does not only concern the issue of progressivity of tax on income and consumption. It also concerns differences among wants of the various persons and families, under equal income and expenditure of (potential) contributors. In this context, vertical equity interferes with the principle of horizontal equity, giving rise to a broad range of opportunities for discrimination based on somewhat vaguely worded distributive principles.

There may be a lower tax-paying capacity due to specific indexes of need, such as family responsibilities and child care expenses, expenses for medical treatment and disabilities. In Italy, the empathy-oriented conception traceable at several places in the text of the Italian Constitution may authorize this approach.

The greatest threat undermining vertical equity resides in the fact as a measure of inequality; it lends itself to a plethora of arithmetical concepts, unlike horizontal equity, which, under ascertained equal conditions, admits only one, namely equality. The problem occurs in particular with regard to evaluating which states of need are to be considered relevant for progressive income tax. What weight should be assigned to a given disability or to the fact of having dependent children, for the purposes of tax relief? Medical expenses for health care are deductible, so why not those for children's daycare centres?

How should savings utilized for buying one's home be assessed for the purposes of tax relief? The principle is explicitly mentioned in the Italian Constitution. But should it be applied in the same measure to all types of dwellings?

The question of how to measure wants becomes even more complicated when considering tax on consumption. By how much should the rate be reduced for expenditure on basic needs involving education or medication?

As can be seen, despite the national and European 'constitutional' rules that provide for horizontal equity, once the principle of vertical equity is accepted there is considerable scope for fiscal rent-seeking by various interest groups. A number of loopholes and exceptions come onto the scene. And by interfering with horizontal equity, vertical equity gives rise to outcomes which, by their very nature, are notably discretionary.

1.7   Fiscal Federalism, and the Principle of Taxes as the 'Marginal' Fiscal Price of Public Goods

One important way to implement the principle of taxation as the fiscal price of public services is so-called 'fiscal federalism', that is devolution of the task of satisfying the public needs to regional and local governments, in other words to democratically elected governments of a lower level than central government. Each of these lower-level governments, endowed with its own independent budget for expenditure and revenue, can in a sense be viewed as a club, potentially in competition with the others for the localization of the activities of families and enterprises. The electors, composed of the residents, will decide on the relation between expenditure and taxation, for each class of the resident population and for enterprises. Non-residents and enterprises will take part in the economic and civil activities of the community in question, taking into account the tax burden and the benefits of public expenditure that this will involve. On the other hand, theoretically, electors – residents – who have found themselves in a minority with regard to policy decisions in the local public economy or who in one way or another are not satisfied with the way their local community is run by the public body will have a chance to choose another 'club', that is a different regional or local community, that operates in a different territorial area with what appears to be a better relation between public services and taxes. But as was noted in Chapter 4, often this 'rescission clause' is not a feasible alternative for the electors, because the community in which they reside is not a genuine club. 'Voting with one's feet', by relocating to a local authority or region that gives a better ratio between quantity and quality of public goods and fiscal cost, can generate considerable inconvenience in terms of moving house, putting one's children in a different school, finding a job in a different city, and so on. But even so, examination of the behaviour of the different governments does allow citizens to draw some comparisons among the different ways of running public affairs, and this may be useful for informed critical awareness of the efficiency, effectiveness and equity of their local government in the various fields of activity and in relations with the various classes of subjects. Furthermore, communities with a better government will be able to exert a greater power of attraction over non-residents, encouraging them to move to these communities and acting as an impetus for businesses to start up or open branches in the area. This will bring advantages, not only to the newcomers but also to the communities in question, by means of more lively business activities and external economies of various types. But although it may be desirable to multiply the levels of government and the number of governments at each level in order to enhance the capacity to respond to the needs in the given area and expand the range of alternatives, this clashes with two limits: the structural costs that each government has, and the costs to be faced by the taxpayer-elector who has to engage with a multiplicity of public institutions and acquire the necessary information on their tax liabilities and the various regulations.

In order for the fiscal constitution to give rise to a system of regional and local governments conforming to the ideal model outlined earlier, it is therefore necessary to take the above costs into account and thus to limit the governmental levels and the number of governments at all levels.

However, in particular, there is one condition that is crucial in determining whether it is genuinely possible to bring about the model of effective and informative competition among regional and local governments, conceived as clubs that provide residents and would-be newcomers with services in exchange for fiscal prices, as well as a 'rescission clause'. This condition is that the budget of each of these governments presents a real link-up between expenditure and revenue, in the sense that the most important shares of expenditure decided by the various governments must be financed by these governments themselves, with an increase of revenue levied on residents or on those operating within the community, and conversely, that a reduction in expenditure must result in a reduction of this tax burden.

This is the fundamental problem the federalist fiscal constitution has to address and solve. The link-up must be effective above all *on the margin*, with regard to variations in public expenditure and revenue, and must operate symmetrically, both in the sense that greater expenses undertaken by a given regional or local government must be financed with greater revenue raised by the government in question, and also in the sense that a reduction in expenditure must translate into a lower level of taxes levied by this government on its own tax-paying citizens and users of its services. The higher government may then make a substantial contribution to the costs of the lower-level governments, but it will be required to allow them scope for independent action on the margin, so that they are called upon to be responsible for their own fiscal choices.

1.8 The Rules of the Federalist Fiscal Constitution

But even once the above defined principles are established, further problems remain.

The first concerns the most appropriate structuring of fiscal federalism tools on the revenue side, in order to avert strategic behaviour on the part of taxpayers, who might try their luck simultaneously in several different communities so as to obtain in each one the maximum of services with the minimum tax burden. For instance, if local authorities obtain their revenue with an income tax, a taxpayer could register as a resident in a small municipality which has a light tax burden because it offers only residential services. Such a taxpayer might at the same time get a job in a large municipality that engages in fairly substantial expenditure to cover the services provided for productive and consumption activities and for social services destined to assist the less favoured members of the community. On the other hand, if the local authorities impose their own taxes on consumption and businesses, the above type of strategic behaviour will be fruitless. But if one supposes that the local authorities are not allowed to levy important taxes on the income of their residents, but must instead mostly rely on taxes on consumption and production, then the residential municipalities could find themselves facing an excess of costs as compared to the available financial means that have to be raised by apportioning the costs among those who benefit from their services.

The second difficulty arises in connection with the rules involved in formation of the fiscal prices of public services. With simple majority voting, as will be shown below, it cannot be ruled out that the majority may offload the fiscal costs onto the minority. Therefore it is imperative to establish rules for a fiscal constitution, in order to specify the powers of expenditure of lower-level governments and delimit their power to levy taxes. The principle according to which the regional and local governments are empowered to decide on expenditure in all fields that are not assigned by the central government – sponsored by some advocates of fiscal federalism – is in contrast to the principle that public needs arise specifically in relation to 'failures of the market', and not simply whenever the bureaucracy and those who hold the reins of political power opt in favour of a given expense. Indeed, with this principle, those in power can exploit the strategic effects of majority voting in which one section of the electorate resolves to provide certain services and the rest of the electorate pays for them.

Another aspect of the potential oppression of the majority over the minority at local level can be observed when the local government fulfils tasks characteristic of an enterprise: in such a case the local government has a large number of employees who, when the occasion arises, in their capacity as electors cast their vote in favour of the administration that assures them the best regime.

The third problem can be found in regard to what J. Buchanan (1975) called the dilemma of the Samaritan (not to be confused with the theorem of the good Samaritans described in Chapter 3, subsection 3.5). It is quite possible that a lower-level government *B*, which provides services considered to be essential or highly meritorious, such as health care or grants for university education, may find itself overspending its predefined budget and moving into deficit. *B* may thus suspend services supposed to be provided for citizens *C*s, 'blackmailing' the higher-level government *A* with the argument that if *A* does not intervene to pay off *B*'s debts, *B* will be unable to ensure continued service provision to the *C*s. And the *C*s, 'through no fault of their own', will be the ones who will suffer even though they have every right to benefit from those services. *A* thus faces the dilemma of whether to refrain from helping *B*, who 'does not deserve to be helped because government *B* should have stayed within its budgetary limits', and it's not right 'to give a bad example by rewarding governments that don't stay within their budgets, because otherwise all the governments will overspend in order to obtain the reward', or whether to intervene so that no damage is inflicted on the *C*s, who 'don't deserve to be ill-treated'.

In Italy the central government has the habit of systematically paying off the deficit of the Regional Health Care Authorities and the Universities (and it hardly seems likely that if INPS, the social security entity, had insufficient funds to pay pensions it would baulk at taking action and would refuse to intervene with its own fiscal resources or by issuing public debt).

The solution that J.M. Buchanan proposes is that the central governments should 'bind themselves' constitutionally, in such a manner that the lower-level governments cannot blackmail them. But this solution cannot solve the problems of the so-called blameless injured parties. It thus seems necessary to establish that when *B* overspends its predefined budget, *B* itself should be obliged, by constitutional rules that the central government cannot manipulate, to introduce levies, charges and prices so as to assure that the onus for the service falls on its own electors. The latter will thus have to bear the burden of having chosen irresponsible administrators.

1.9 The Principle of Benefit in Social Security as 'Social Insurance'

It is impossible to exclude from public finance the principle of benefit. Also, if this is done systematically, profound imbalances are generated in the structure of public finance and the economy which are difficult to rectify. This axiom emerges very clearly when one observes the finance of obligatory social insurance, denominated as social security in the phase of detachment from the principle of benefit, and as 'social insurance' in the phase characterized by the search for a new balance, partly restoring that principle. Social insurance (of the obligatory type) is an expression of the theorem of 'Ulysses tied to the mast' (see Chapter 3, subsection 2.5). Following this principle it becomes compulsory for the working citizen to be insured against the risks of old age, illness, infirmity, unemployment and sometimes against the various costs connected with child-bearing and family responsibilities arising at different stages during a person's lifetime. This insurance is designed to guarantee the citizen, through her own means, against her own lack of providence that could derive from 'inadequate sense of responsibility' towards herself in the future, or towards her family and towards society, which would otherwise be called upon to come to her aid – with inevitably inadequate means – as a belated remedy for this lack of foresight. All individuals, in the constitutional phase, when considering the matter in a cool, calm frame of mind, will be in favour of the social insurance choice, and there is no need for this to be based on the idea that citizens are 'in ignorance of their own future status': citizens simply need to be aware that each person has a life cycle containing (a large part of) these events. There may be some people who believe they will never face the risk of being unemployed, but who nevertheless wish to have a job-seeker's allowance for the eventuality of deciding to change jobs, so that the transitory period would be covered. And each of us is destined to become old, or sick, or face the risk of accidents, or may want to start a family. This is why the choice of compulsory social insurance is fully rational, for all individuals, except for a tiny minority of the very wealthy whose future is already provided for. In fact compulsory social insurance is implemented not only for the above-mentioned circumstances, but also for automobile accidents. In this compulsory insurance, the relation between the policy premium and the services delivered is based, by definition, on insurance principles. These are of two different types, depending on whether the insurance concerns one's pension or the other risks. In the former case, all the services provided by the insurance derive from the income obtained from the invested assets. In the latter the services derive from the premiums that have been paid up, with the safeguard of reserves which, through the returns they generate, guarantee the system against imbalances between the 'premiums' currently paid to the insurance provider and the services delivered. But why, one may ask, should the system require citizens to comply with compulsory public insurance rather than obliging each individual to obtain cover by means of a market insurance, possibly a mutual insurance of a cooperative nature? The argument that private insurance is too discriminatory – it subjects individuals to medical examinations and assesses their specific risks – is not fully convincing, given that mutual insurances do not adopt such practices. The argument that private insurance companies may not be reliable or may be cowboy operations also does not seem plausible, because it is possible to set up a professional register and introduce surveillance of operators working in this sector, as is the case for investment funds and market-based pension funds. Even the argument that such an insurance system does not cover the risks of the less favoured or special non-insurable risks (such as catastrophes cause by earthquakes, exceptional flooding, and so forth) is not very persuasive, because provision could be made for the less favoured by means of public social services, with regard to insurable risks, without the need to set up public social insurance for normal subjects.

Enterprises, on the other hand, can indeed engage in something of this kind, for their own workers, by means of pension funds that may also include shares in their own corporate assets, but only if they are structured as joint-stock companies. Since revenues from capital fluctuate, pension funds run by enterprises would need to have a trend towards non-decreasing employment, as this ensures they have an excess of young members of their workforce as compared to those close to retirement. An additional condition is that the financial market should be well developed so that firms have no difficulty in weathering temporary liquidity imbalances between pension obligations and employee pension funds. As far as concerns the hypothesis of compulsory insurance arrangements among self-employed workers, on a basis of mutuality, here too there are a number of organizational problems. Thus the provision of compulsory public insurance, in countries lacking a highly developed financial market, may supplant the alternative of the arrangement among the self-employed based on mutuality and the hypothesis of firm-based insurance schemes, because it is 'more efficient'. But it does not necessarily mean a shift to a compulsory public insurance system based on the revenue of the social insurance contribution invested in financial products and in real estate.

The 'positive' reason for a constitutional choice adopting public economy systems, in particular with regard to pension insurance, is that a government can set up a compulsory insurance of a mutual nature without the need to accumulate the capital required to those entitled to a pension, that is by a huge public compulsory insurance similar to the private old age pension insurances. In fact the government can achieve aggregate equivalence between services provided and premiums paid through the contributions it collects and can, through its power to levy taxes, offer a guarantee against the risk deriving from the fact that there are no assets which guarantee the pay-out. A private cooperative movement cannot act in this manner. The public system has been able to become extremely popular because, at its outset, only a tiny fraction of workers belonging to the nation to which the new system is applied have many years of contributions when they retire and are thus entitled to a substantial pension. Therefore the state has no need to pay pensions with the income from invested capital, but it can adopt for pensions as well the system of setting aside reserves, which risk insurances utilize as a guarantee against ordinary risks of accidents. This leads to development of the *'aggregate balancing'* system, or Pay As You Earn (PAYE), and in the eventuality of imbalance between contributions and pensions, it is possible to have recourse to the reserves. If this is not enough, the difference between contributions paid in and incomes from reserves and pensions delivered will be covered by increased contributions. If the resulting burden appears to be excessive, the difference will be covered by the state through disbursements that increase on the basis of James Buchanan's theorem of the Samaritan. Thus the relation between contributions paid and pensions received becomes increasingly tenuous, and the right to a pension arises from the mere fact of having paid one's contributions, but it is not individually commensurate to the contributions paid. But this is possible, globally, when the body of current pensioners represents a limited portion of the overall workforce, as the number of those in work is rising and the national product growth rate is elevated, so that the assemblage of taxed contribution-paying incomes is increasing.

In addition to the PAYE model of compulsory social insurance, with its inherent degenerations, one also finds, on the theoretical – and positive – plane the model of social security based on the distributive principle 'From each one according to his capacities, to each one according to his needs'. This model does not start out from principles of responsibility, like social insurances, but from the criterion of the maximum collective utility by means of the sum of individual utilities, in the hypothesis of decreasing marginal utilities and isomorphism of the various subjects, which makes it possible to compare and sum their utilities. It follows that whoever has financial means also has the duty to come to the aid of those who do not, independently of criteria of merit and demerit, limited only by the disincentive effects on formation of the national product. In this model it is possible, indeed it is quite logical, to waive the principle that social security is paid through specific contributions on the beneficiaries, in that the model requires each subject to pay with her general economic means. This brings about a structural change. The fact that the social security model becomes detached from the relation between contributions paid and services delivered also implies its distancing from the insurance principle, which holds that services are provided mainly on the basis of the current or expected proceeds from the reserves in which the contributions have been invested, rather than on the basis of public expenditure supplied by public transfer payments. There the social security model begins to break down due to its disincentive effects on the national product, as people little by little become accustomed to preferring the situation of leisure to that of developing capacities, on account of the effects of the fiscal system. However, even before that stage is reached, the ideal model is distorted by the fact that once social security is detached from criteria of responsibility and thus of appropriate compensation, it turns into a never-ending realm of chasing after privileges, with a murky web of interactions among interest groups, politicians in search of consensus and bureaucracies managing the immense bureaucratic machine thereby built up.

Meanwhile, PAYE-based systems also begin to break down if the population has ceased to grow and therefore the overall numbers of retirees has risen, under equal numbers of persons retiring every year, and if the national product growth rate has declined and therefore the overall mass of contributions, under equal tax bands and number of persons in work, has a very low growth. With a GDP growth rate lower than the interest rate, the PAYE system becomes less remunerative than a capitalization system, even under the hypothesis that each individual has a pension in proportion to contributions paid, with stable employment and total salaries growing only in relation to the national product. Thus at this point it is of interest to take a fresh look at the criterion of a connection between contributions paid by an individual and the individual's rights, and the system based on the returns of a huge public pension fund, that is the capitalization model, like the original model of compulsory social insurance. In order to bring about the principle of benefit, we should ask: is this model possible and preferable, or would it be preferable to have a constitutional contract based on a 'contributive' model, based on the reciprocity principle, that respects the same relation between contributions and services on the individual level, but which is achieved by means of revenue collected from present workers in favour of the retired? The latter model involves a pact between generations, so that when present workers reach retirement they will receive from future workers the same treatment – based on their present contributions – that they have given to the retired workers, on the basis of the contributions they paid in the past.

1.10   The Intra-generational and the Inter-generational Constitutional Pact for Social Insurance: Choice between the Capitalization-based Public Model, the Contributive Public Model and a Mixed Model Conceived as Contributive in the Public Pillar and Capitalization-based in the Private Pillar

The problem can be distinguished into two groups of questions, depending on whether the constitutional 'contract' is seen as a pact between generations or within the same generation. The capitalization system of public pensions involves an intra-generational pact, because retirees are paid a pension by means of the return on the aggregate capital accumulated through investing their contributions. The 'contributive' public pension system, evoked above, involves a pact between generations, as the present workers pay contributions to a system from which they will benefit, as pensioners, when they have reached old age. In a society with a large number of old age pensioners, the latter may, in the absence of constitutional rules, appropriate themselves of pension rights at the expense of the younger generations, who are in a minority in the sense that some of them do not vote, some of them do vote but are not politically organized or unionized, and some of them are neither particularly interested in these specific choices nor equally well informed concerning (their) distant future. The empirical verification of a possible violation of the pact between generations is not immediate, because current workers who, through their contributions, pay the pensions of retirees cannot find out now, *by examining the facts*, what is likely to happen to them in the future when they approach retirement. Therefore the reaction to violation of the principle of reciprocity, aiming to redress the violation, cannot come into play as promptly as occurs when the effects of the violation are immediately perceived. When the violation does emerge, the situation has already become irreversible. In this regard the insurance system, based as it is on the principle that pensions are paid through the aggregate proceeds of contributions paid, seems to give greater guarantees than the contributive system, in which the correspondence between contributions and pensions is assured not by the capital which has been invested, but by the respect for rules which could perhaps be violated. No such problem arises for unemployment insurance or insurance against other forms in which a worker is temporarily out of work (such as being laid off, in which case wages may be paid by the 'integration fund'), or is on sick leave, or is off work due to an accident in the workplace or work-related disability, or on maternity leave or has health care needs. The reason is that in these cases the contributive system does not involve a pact between generations, but within generations, and any exception made in favour of one group and at the expense of others leads to an immediate empirical verification and the possibility of reaction on the basis of violation of the principle of reciprocity. Precisely for this reason, when it is necessary to guarantee payment of the services by means of reserves, which are needed for cover of risks that do not compensate one another automatically, the public system can operate correctly, also on the basis of a reciprocity pact which, on the constitutional level, is generic.

One then may argue that the contributive system for the public pensions is worse than the capitalization system because the intergenerational pact is much less stringent than an intra-generational pact. But if the aim is to guarantee integrally the constitutional pact on pensions, by means of the invested capital, two difficulties arise that render this system unacceptable, as a general solution, except in small nations. The point is that in a country with a tendency toward ageing, even when the retirement age is fairly elevated, such as 65 years of age, if one makes the assumption that pensions cover at least 70 per cent of final salary and can increase over time at a rate equal to the mean increase in GDP, then pensions will have to reach a share amounting to 12–13 per cent of the gross national product, which translates into a 15 per cent share of the *net* national product. Any financial subject that possesses a capital giving an income equal to 15 per cent of the national product and that invests it in the national economy controls the national economy. Therefore only in a small country, where the capitalization-based public pension system invests only minimally in the national economy, is this system compatible with the market system and sustainable. In a large country, if the system with integral capitalization of the pension system aims to offer adequate pension provision, this involves a risk of insolvency due to the difficulty in finding secure remunerative investments, and a risk of nationalization of the economy, through the overweening power of this gigantic social insurance subject on the financial investment market. The only general solution compatible with the market economy is that of the contributive system, based on a constitutional pact in which it is established that:

a. each pensioner receives a pension commensurate with her expected residual life, by an amount determined on the basis of the contributions paid, so that the percentage of the pension as compared to final salary grows as a function of years of paid contributions and of their annual amount, and decreases as a function of years of residual life, so that those who retire later obtain a larger pension through the effect of the interplay between these two variables;
b. every pensioner receives not merely a pension that is commensurate with the total of contributions paid, but something more, which can be called 'the return of the contributions', because it is proportional to contributions paid and is equal to the rate of growth rate of the wages and other remunerations of those who are in work, whose contributions, levied on them at given rates, pay the pensions to those who have retired.

In order for the system to remain in equilibrium, it is necessary that:

a. the gradual extension of average life expectancy should be periodically monitored, in order to calibrate pension rights in relation to contributions paid;
b. periodic monitoring should be carried out on the parameter adopted for the 'return' on the contributions paid, in order to take into account

the variations in the growth rate of the labour income, subject to the social insurance contributions. The revenue thus obtained determines the amount through which the social insurance institution can pay pensions yearly to those who have entered retirement and can at the same time maintain the 'pensions' budget in equilibrium.

In order for the social insurance contributions to bring a return capable of achieving equilibrium between revenues and pension payments in the social insurance budget, it is by no means necessary for the number of people in work to increase. All that is required is for there to be a growth in global taxable income from labour, and this can come about even if the number of people in work remains constant or decreases. But when the number of people in work remains constant, the return depends exclusively on the growth of the overall labour income of this body, that is to say, on its growth per working person year by year. In the case of a decreasing body of workers, the return depends on this growth, net of the effect of the decrease in number of persons in work.

The social insurance constitution should therefore have obligatory rules on the correct initial determination and periodic assessment of the above parameters. It should also contemplate a type of social insurance budget with rules of constitutional ranking prescribing that each year an estimate should be drawn up outlining the budgets for revenue and outgoings of the future decades, so that any pension-related debt of future years can be highlighted.

However, adopting a gigantic contributory system as the only solution for old age pensions presents risks of malfunctioning and excessive pressure of the contributions necessary for a high pension. Furthermore, it destroys savings, to the extent to which it substitutes a current income financing system for the system of saving for one's old age. This is a good reason for not forcing Ulysses to tie himself *entirely* to this mast of public social insurance for future pensions, but of constraining him instead to supplement his public pension by investing part of his income in private pension funds of his own choice, so that he can directly manage the capitalization-based system through which he will receive a portion of his pension. This two-pillar system, as the reader will readily comprehend, is particularly in line with the cooperative model of the public economy, in which the individual is at one and the same time a supplier and beneficiary of public goods.

1.11   The Public Budgets and Democracy

The public budget (see Chapter 1, subsection 2.6) can be examined in terms of the agency relation between parliament and the government, and can be viewed as the global tool for the financial choices that parliament (the principal) entrusts its agent (the government) with making. Therefore it is an accounting document (endowed with the juridical value of law for the State), which can be considered as the agency relation 'contract' between the two above-mentioned public decision-makers. It contains the indication of the revenue and expenditure of the public operator during the period under consideration, and includes the balance sheet of assets and liabilities (less used) and the income account, that is the revenues and expenditures budget. In the former, the real and financial assets possessed are shown on the asset side, while the financial liabilities of the public operator in the period considered are shown on the liabilities side. The balance sheet of assets and liabilities normally is not designed to form part of the budget *ex ante* but only of the budget *ex post*. It is little discussed and furthermore it is technically incomplete because it usually does not contain the full inventory of the real goods owned by the public operator. The income accounts constitute the public budget *par excellence*, and it is this aspect which normally represents the focus of debate. It may be *ex ante* or *ex post*. Of these two, the more important is the *ex ante* budget which contains the authorizations granted by parliament to the government through the budget law, on matters of expenditure and revenue collection. If, at the end of parliamentary debate, the budget is rejected, the government that presented it may fall.

> In Italy the budget law is preceded by the financial law that contains the legislative innovations concerning revenue and expenditure that have to be introduced into the existing financial legislation. So the debate on the budget law actually becomes a discussion on proposed changes in the financial legislation that modify the items of the overall budget.

1.12 Structure of the Agency Relation in the Stages of the Central Government Budget

The central government's budget estimate – and the related financial law, if any – is formulated through a procedure that can be subdivided into five stages:

1. *Preparation by the organ of the executive power.* This is the most critical aspect of the agency relation regarding the budget, because the bureaucracies of the various branches of the public administration systematically claim increases on their budgets in order to pursue maximization of their activity. The Minister of the Treasury has the difficult task of placing a limit on their requests, risking unpopularity.

In Italy, on the level of central government, the bill containing the budget and the associated yearly financial law that introduces variations in the legislation determining revenues and expenditures is preceded by an Economic and Financial Planning Document (DPEF), which is submitted to Parliament by the government before the beginning of the budget session.

The DPEF is a three-year estimate that works according to a scroll-down method, in the sense that every year the immediately preceding year is removed (and published only as an *ex post* record, not to be discussed) and a further year is added, in order to recompose the three-year span. Thus, in reference to the state and the state-run sector, the DPEF contains the state budget and that of the public bodies which form part of the state (excluding the national insurance bodies, the railways and the postal system, because these have a plc structure). This budget includes the aggregate of current spending and capital spending, that of current receipts and capital receipts, the balance between current spending and revenue, the balance of current spending net of interest, the balance between overall revenue and expenditure. It also gives a consolidated account of the general government (state-run sector and regional and local governments and bodies that fall under their authority), with the above described classifications. It is this latter statement of account which (with only a few variants) is the document of relevance at European Union level, in conformity with the Treaty of Maastricht and the subsequent Stability Pact.

In other countries there is only one law concerning the financial legislation and the budget law, which contains both the legislative variations and the budget accounts after them.

To put a brake on the claims for budget increments put forward by the various branches of the public administration, a 'heroic' rule has been suggested, namely that of 'zero budgeting'. Under this principle, for each branch of the public administration the entire budget has to be discussed every financial year. Thus all the budgetary items must be reviewed, every year – an enormous task. A different, simpler rule may be adopted: a general principle that with regard to current expenditure each branch of the public administration is allowed to claim no more than an increment equal to the likely inflation rate.

For investment expenditures the inflation rate plus the likely rate of increase in GDP could be allowed. If any given public administration asks for a greater increase of its current expenditures it has to provide the Treasury with a detailed explanation of the reasons for the increase. But apart from very exceptional cases, no administration is allowed to exceed a given rate, set at a much lower level than the likely increase of GDP in real terms. The rule, for example, could be the likely real GDP growth rate divided by two. The public revenue, in normal times, increases at a yearly rate equal to the rate of inflation plus the rate of real GDP growth (plus something more, if the tax system is progressive). Following the above rule, therefore, the Minister of the Treasury will be left with room for a reduction of the budget deficit or the tax burden, or even for additional investment expenditures.[4]

2. *Approval by the decision-making organ* (parliament, the regional assembly, the municipal assembly). For central government, in Italy the budget is likewise presented on a scroll-down basis, but the parliamentary approval concerns only the next year and is only in relation to the central government.[5] This approval is preceded by the approval of the DPEF in the two Houses (Chamber of Deputies and Senate), with a motion that is binding only for the large aggregates and the balance of the first year of the three-year period.

    The balances previously approved through the DPEF place a gag rule on discussion of the budget, This prevents the approval of amendments that would increase expenditures or reduce taxes. without reduction of expenditures or increase in taxes.

3. *Implementation and possible correction by the assembly upon request by the executive power, with 'settlement budget' laws* in the case of variations from the estimated budget. According to the 'Stability Pact' introduced following the Treaty of Maastricht, modifications can also be requested by the European Union if the deficit and debt ratio to GP agreed with the EU has been overstepped.

4. *Ex post* controls to ensure that the actual items of expenditure and revenue are in conformity with those set out in the budget law (and in the financial law which has merged with the budget law, changing it). Such controls are to be performed by the appropriate organs. If, as in Italy, the inspection is carried out by the General Accounting Office of the Treasury, one cannot be sure that the control is effective. It is naive to assume that a bureaucracy of a given government can genuinely control the other bureaucracies of the same government: the possibility of a collusive (log rolling) game not infrequently looms on the horizon.

5. Ex post *balance sheet that includes the statement of assets and liabilities* (drawn up in Italy in skeletal form) by the executive power, presented to Parliament together with the judgment by an autonomous external control authority (in Italy the Court of Audits, whose powers are at this stage rather limited). *This ex post document is then approved by the representative assemblies.*

1.13 The Principles of the Budget

The rules for the budget game, as a periodically updated 'basic contract' of the electors' agency relation with their representatives, are defined from the point of view of the efficiency and effectiveness of this relation and of the relation between the politicians and the bureaucracy.

1. *The principle that the budget is annual* implies that the budget is approved year by year so that the electors of the level of government involved can annually manifest, through their representatives (in the state parliament, the regional council or the local council), their choices regarding the financial management and their trust in the agents who conduct it. The annual budget is, however, supplemented by a multi-year budget so that the medium-term effects of the various policies can be taken into account, as well as any reforms that have been adopted. The multi-year budget and the annual budget complement each other. However, if the spending authorizations derive from the yearly budget, the multi-year budget is a mere 'estimate' without incisive effects. If, on the other hand, the spending authorizations derive from the multi-year budget, the annual budget of every year becomes a binding estimate, in which only limited alterations can be introduced. The principle of the annual budget is then lost.

2. The *universality principle* implies that all the revenue and expenditure are included in the budget: if this is not the case, and the budget includes only part of the public operations, then the citizens' right to exercise control over the executive and to give their prior consent to the State's revenue and expenditure becomes severely limited.

> In Italy the principle of universality is currently violated with regard to the State, due to the existence of numerous 'off-balance-sheet' administrative operations through which the authorized action of 'separate bodies' takes place. This is the case for instance of the national insurance organizations, which collect contributions and the gains on their assets, and deliver services on the basis of budgets that are distinct from the state budget and are not even annexed to the latter.

3. *The unity principle* requires all expenditures to be set against the overall body of revenue. This rule, introduced to combat 'sectionalism', prevents individual items of revenue from being reserved for funding of specific expenses. However, in the case of levies based on a particular benefit, it is logical that this should be managed through a separate financial account to avert the risk of such levies being destined to cover other forms of expenditure, and to ensure that what is spent is commensurate with the amount collected, and vice versa. The principle of unity is correctly waived in the case of social insurance financing, in which the different national insurance contributions due from employers and employees and the self-employed are put

in separate funds with separate accounting for their pensions, sick leave benefits, maternity leave, unemployment benefits, and so on. The management of each such insurance should be separated for the different categories of subject – employees, craft workers, merchants and shop-keepers, agricultural smallholders, and so on – to respect the benefit principle and to foster responsible conduct.

> The *coverage principle*[6] according to which 'every law that results in new and greater expenditure or a lower amount of revenue must indicate the means by which the procedure will be funded', connects the expenditures with the revenues as required by the cooperative model of the public economy and does not contradict the principle of unity of the budget. This is because it does not imply that for any new expenditure there should be a specific item of revenue, but rather that if there is an increase in expenditure, there should also be an increase in revenue.

4. *According to the principle of analyticity* of the budget (or of its specification) the budget must set out all its items analytically: if this were not required, then it would be far easier to circumvent the close control of parliament (or the regional or municipal council). The traditional classification criterion is the administrative classification, which distinguishes the various items in relation to the different laws that authorize them and also in relation to the individual subjects who, in the various branches of the public administration, are entrusted with carrying out the various different operations. At present it is considered useful to group together this myriad of items into basic units, with reference to the operational units that carry out the various activities involving expenditure and collecting the various types of revenue. In addition to the administrative classification there is also the economic classification, according to homogeneous national accounting categories (current expenditure for goods and services, for wages and salaries, for current account transfers and capital expenditures of these categories). A further classification can be made by function: the general organs of the state (or of the region), defence, law and order, justice, production objectives, education, scientific research, culture and art goods, health care, social security, social services of assistance, all of which can be sub-classified (for instance, primary school education, compulsory high school, superior high school education, university education, professional training).[7]

5. The *economic principle* is in a sense the specification of the previous principle. On the basis of this principle, the costs and outcomes of each action involving public expenditure are set side by side. The costs are distinguished into public spending for: personnel, purchase

of goods and services, depreciation of equipment and facilities, transfers, and costs to be borne by other components of the system. The outcomes are measures with physical success and activity indicators: pupils educated and square metres of road built or maintained, and so on constitute indicators of success; hours of teaching and applications or files processed constitute indicators of activities (see Chapter 5, section 1.4).[8]

6. The *principle of clarity* consists in easy readability of the budget, and therefore it implies there should be no 'tricks', like the presence of certain 'omnibus' funds, or certain off-the-books liabilities such as a state guarantee for private loans, certain debts of past financial years recognized in subsequent years to mask or undervalue the expenses of the past budgets, and certain settlements of deficits of autonomous subjects connected to the State such as the Local Health Care Units (ASL). These operations are recorded as expenses for capital movements, below the budget line, arguing that they are expenditures to extinguish debts so that the net result is zero (but in actual fact these debts were never indicated in the previous state budget).

7. The *principle of publicity* implies a public vote on amendments and on the articles of the budget law and related financial laws, and also implies that the state budget should be published so that it can be made accessible to citizens.[9]

1.14 The Principle of the Division between the Current Account Budget and the Capital Account Budget

In a system of public finance that seeks to achieve the maximum of the allocative principles that we have seen, with regard to the equilibrium between supply and demand of public goods for enterprises and individuals, it is important to devise a coherent structuring of the budgets to ensure that the fiscal prices of public goods and the other public revenues are linked to the corresponding expenses.

The first criterion to be adopted in pursuing this goal is that of the subdivision of the budget into current expenditure and capital expenditure. Current expenditure should be covered by current sources of revenue, consisting of levies and public prices, to be borne by present subjects inasmuch as current expenses concern the present users of public goods. Capital expenditure, on the other hand, to the extent to which it takes the form of investments, could be covered by revenue also to be obtained from future subjects, via the public debt, given that the benefits of these expenditures will extend into the future. Similarly, the revenue for the investment budget could be constituted partly by alienation of assets in addition to the public debt. However, on the basis of the principle of the linkage between the benefit from public goods and the financing of such goods, it does not seem appropriate to conceive of covering the investment budget with these sources of revenue alone, given that the expenditure in question also gives present benefits.

> The division between the current account budget and the capital account budget has long been acknowledged and incorporated into the budget legislation of advanced governments, as a rule of good government. Use of the public debt exclusively for funding investment expenditure is defined as the 'golden rule' and it is included in some constitutions, like that of Germany. In Italy, the prohibition on using the public debt to finance current expenses, i.e. the obligation to balance the current account budget, is limited to regional and local finance.

1.15 'Earmarking' Revenues

By contrast, controversy still surrounds the principle of setting up separate accounts of revenues devoted to expenses with which the revenues in question stand in correspondence as the charges are borne by those who benefit from – or in various ways are the cause of – the expenditure. A classic case is a motor vehicle tax designed to cover road construction, use and maintenance, or legal fees to cover the costs of the judiciary. The ruling class and the bureaucracy do not appreciate this limit on their spending power.

> But this principle, given its economic basis, is gradually becoming more widely accepted, through the development of separate budgets, of autonomous entities. And, in Italy, health care charges (the so-called 'tickets' for medical tests and prescriptions) are destined to the separate budgets of the Local Health Care Units (ASL) providing the services, before their confluence in the regional budgets.

2 THE CONSTITUTIONAL RULES FOR PARLIAMENTARY CHOICES

2.1 The Wicksellian Rule of Unanimity for Allocative Public Expenditure

One of the ways in which a drive towards expansion of public expenditure may imply allocative distortions consists, as was seen earlier, in the possibility, for the majority, both to make decisions that go to the advantage of the whole community, the costs of which, however, are not borne by the majority, and also to make spending decisions that are particularly advantageous for the majority itself, although the latter does not bear the greater part of the costs.[10] This is rational for the majority, but not for the community as a whole, as for some of the subjects this results in a net damage that the majority may not be able to compensate.[11]

To avoid this situation, according to the paradigm of Wicksell as stated by the author himself, voting decisions concerning public expenditure, *in the case of allocative rather than redistributive expenditure*, should be made by unanimity voting.[12] This will guarantee the result of the marginalist criterion discussed in Chapter 1, subsection 2.2.

2.2 The Problem of 'Blackmail' by Small Groups

There are, however, two orders of difficulty that work against this voting rule. First, it is very difficult to separate purely redistributive choices from those that are intended to be allocative.

Purely redistributive choices, in the welfare state, often do not appear as problems of mere transfer of monetary sums from the wealthy to the less well-off, but rather as problems of supply of social services of a general nature, which contain in their structure certain measures that give a particular advantage to the less favoured.

The second, more severe, difficulty, as noted by Wicksell himself, is that if one admits the unanimity principle, this paves the way for blackmail by small minorities, who block a given expense even though it would be useful to them, because they want to try to extract a 'rent' from those who are interested in the proposed measure. This leads to severe delay or paralysis of decision-making processes, which by their very nature already proceed at a slow pace within the public economy.

2.3 Qualified Majority

To overcome this difficulty, Wicksell proposed the empirical rule of 'quasi unanimity', that is 70 per cent or 80 per cent of the votes. But what percentage should be chosen? And are we sure that the problem of 'blackmail' is identical in its negative effects for every type of decision?

Buchanan and Tullock (1962, especially Chapter VI) made another seminal contribution to this issue by relying on the two concepts of 'exploitation' of one part over the other, and of the cost or inefficiency of the decision-making process.

While the capacity for exploitation, according to their formulation, decreases gradually with an increasing percentage of voters required for a resolution to be valid, declining to zero for a unanimous vote, the cost and inefficiency of the decision-making process increase with a gradual increase in the percentage of voters required for approval of decisions.

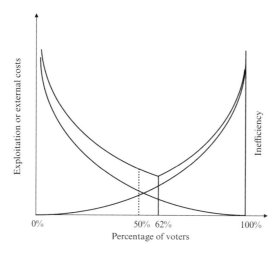

Figure 6.1   Qualified majority: Buchanan and Tullock model

But it should be noted that distributive choices, which were excluded from
Wicksell's paradigm, are hereby reintroduced, in a predominant position.

In Figure 6.1 the number of voters whose assent is required, from 0 per
cent to (obviously) 100 per cent, is shown on the abscissae. The left-hand
ordinates show the 'exploitation' or external cost that decreases with an
increasing number of voters, while the right-hand ordinates show the cost
or inefficiency of decisions, which increases with an increasing number of
voters whose assent is required. The higher curve is none other than the
sum of the two, namely the total cost curve which makes it possible to
choose, at its minimum, the optimal majority *quorum* following the general
economic rule of minimizing the total cost when the result is a given.

In the example illustrated here, there emerges a qualified majority of
62 per cent. When making constitutional decisions, which are valid for
prolonged periods of time, the external costs become rather high, whereas
the time taken to reach a decision is of less relevance than is the case
for immediate decisions, as constitutional decisions involve momentous
choices concerning principles. Here there tends to emerge a rule of 'quasi
unanimity'. The situation changes when it is a matter of current decisions,
especially those concerning the annual budget. In this regard, given the
importance of reaching a timely decision, a steep decision-making cost
curve is hypothesized, and a lower majority may be preferred.[13]

In addition to the relation between constitutional choices and post-
constitutional decisions, in particular as regards the budget, this dichotomy
can also be utilized to explain the foundation of the European Council's

Principles of public economics

unanimity and quasi unanimity rules, which have been composed by the governments of the EU member states, and the predominance of qualified majority rules in the European Parliament on certain decisions that are likely to have momentous consequences.

> The Buchanan and Tullock theorem is also relevant in judging the merits and demerits of a bicameral system: if the two chambers have a different composition, because of the different system of election or appointment of their members, the double voting of the two assemblies will act as a qualified majority.

2.4 The Principle of Approving the Budget due to Expiry of the Approval Deadline provided that the Budget contains no Pathological Increases

If the budget is not approved within the appropriate time limit, in accordance with the constitutional rule that parliament has the right and the duty to approve the budget every year as a rational synthesis of the entire revenue and the entire expenditure, and as a condition the government must meet in order to exercise its fiscal and monetary power, then 'extremely high' costs are incurred. To overcome this risk the government must have the power to obtain approval of the budget by a vote of confidence based on a simple majority, provided that some basic rules are respected.

Indeed, Wicksell himself excluded from the scope of his rule any decision-making situations in which an agreement *must* necessarily be reached: that is to say, cases in which not reaching an agreement leads to paralysis of the state, so that some form of choice will be inevitable. Therefore it is more rational to establish the principle that once a certain deadline has passed, the budget originally proposed by the government should be considered as approved provided that it respects the pre-established rules on the deficit and the public debt and does not contain, within its wording or concepts, any increase in public spending above the 'natural' minimal expenditure.[14]

2.5 Quantification of the Rule in Relation to GDP

Let us now consider how the above rule may be applied. When a government operating in an economy with a certain real growth of GDP submits its annual budget, generally it cannot avoid presenting increases in public expenditure, regardless of whether there may be any variation in the purchasing power of the currency.

For example, expenses already approved in the past may increase because they are linked to the general growth of productivity, which leads to wage increases, in the public sector as well, even though the same increases in productivity may in this case not take place. Other reasons why expenses may rise are related to population growth, the increase in the old age population or the circumstance that public expenditure is instrumental to greater production and greater private consumption.

A good operative rule could consist in considering that whenever expenses listed in the budget exceed the 'natural' growth rate of expenditure, the latter being estimated at half the growth rate of the gross national product, then the entire volume of expenses above this ceiling should be considered as 'new expenses'. An exception could be made for circumstances where public expenditure exceeds 40 pre cent of GDP, in which case the 'natural' growth should be estimated, say, at two-thirds lower than the rate at which GDP grows.

2.6　A Qualified Majority for New Allocative Expenses does not Guarantee Rational Containment of Expenditure

At this point, however, it is important to note that Wicksell's doctrine may – with regard to the budget – be valid for approval of new allocative expenses but not for their abrogation, nor for all the other measures contemplated. The point is that a parliament which introduces budgetary measures while relying on a qualified majority can become a collusive decision-making organ, and since collusion is a bond sealed by exchange of favours, it generates increased spending.

The greater the majority required for governing and for approving the measures the government considers to be of vital importance, the lower is the competition to which the 'political enterprise'[15] (or the coalition of political enterprises) is exposed. The analogy with the oligopoly operating on the economic market[16] is incomplete because costs in the political enterprise, in contrast to costs in a large-sized economic enterprise, decrease over a certain stretch, only to show a subsequent increasing trend, due to the fact that acquiring consensus involves a mounting array of concessions to interest groups peripheral or extraneous to the political enterprise in question. In a sense, the analogy can be viewed in the paradigm of monopolistic competition, according to which an enterprise that seeks to maximize its turnover (the corresponding element, for the political enterprise, being the mass of votes) incurs rising 'sales' costs that lead it into the increasing cost portion of the curve.

Now, if the political enterprise has rising average costs, it follows that establishing the requirement of a qualified majority in the framework of the exercise of executive power means establishing a higher average cost level of the political enterprise than the minimum level needed to achieve a stable 'democratic' decision, that is to say the minimum rule of a simple majority.

2.7 'Exploitation' of the Political Enterprise according to the Model of Political Oligopoly

The 'qualified majority' rule is 'more costly' in terms of favours granted on the budget as compared to the simple majority rule because it increases the proportion of those who participate in the 'political enterprise' and who thus seek a share in power, hoping to obtain a 'remuneration' which – from the point of view of the management group, that is the political entrepreneur – takes the form of an increase in cost. This cost is then transferred to the community, either through taxes, or financial burdens of other types (the public debt, the deficit, price restrictions, and so on).

All this is accompanied by an increase in expenses for the apparatus that 'creates consensus'. But on the other hand, the tendency of the political enterprise that exercises its power to obtain a 'value-added' in favour of its members (or supporters) is restrained to the extent to which it is exposed to competition from other political enterprises. In other words its 'political market' can be contested.[17] It thus becomes clear that the lower the majority required for managing the political enterprise in power, the greater the likelihood that the enterprise in power will be supplanted by others that are completely different.

Buchanan and Tullock's statement that increasing the required majority reduces the degree of exploitation and thus, presumably, also curbs the tendency towards an overloaded budget appears to be a first approximation formulation, which can be shown to be unrealistic if two key concepts pertaining to the above-described political enterprise are introduced. Namely, when the political enterprise's need for votes increases, there is a parallel increase in the cost of building up consensus, a cost it offloads onto the community; moreover, when its 'contestability' by other rival members is curtailed, then its 'power' in the political market goes up.

2.8 Asymmetric and therefore Anticollusive Voting Rules

Wicksell's 'quasi unanimity' principle can be utilized effectively only with a structure that neither determines nor stimulates 'collusion' between political parties in power and those in the opposition, but instead discourages any such tendency to collusion.

It should be established that a simple majority may always come to an agreement on a reduction in the individual expenses voted by qualified majority, but without it being possible to introduce – by simple majority

– new expenses in place of such reductions. Instead, only tax reductions should be introduced by the Wicksellian rule (provided that the budget respects the rules on the relation between deficit and GDP and the stock of debt and GDP).

2.9 The Constitutional Rule of a Balanced Current Account Budget or Budget Surplus for the Aim of Containment of the Capital Account Deficit within the Level of the Maximum Consented Budget Deficit

Faced with the multiplicity of objectives of the various groups, the government may be driven to propose a deficit budget, of gargantuan size, in which the various requests of the different groups and also of the opposition are piled up together, with an *overload* for the future generations as compared to rationally available resources.

Hence the need for the constitutional rule that limits the annual deficit to a minimum and/or requires a balanced budget in the medium term.[18]

A public budget that has a capital account deficit not exceeding, say, 3 per cent should not be considered as having an abnormally sized deficit if the growth rate of GDP is elevated and if the debt thereby incurred is matched by public investments that will provide an advantage for future generations. However, this may be acceptable on condition that the future generations are not already laden with the task of servicing the interest on a debt that generates a disproportional tax burden, which is what happens when the debt is considerably over 60 per cent of GDP. Beyond this level, transferring the burden of capital expenditure to the future is no longer feasible without producing future financial crises, even if the proposed expenditure promises to be advantageous for the future.

It should in fact be noted that when starting out from a debt/GDP ratio of 60 per cent, a 3 per cent budget deficit rate can be financed 'in perpetuo' with new debt – without the 60 per cent figure ever rising – provided that the growth rate of GDP is at least 5 per cent, composed, for instance, of a 2.5 per cent nominal increase due to the 2.5 per cent inflation rate, and a 2.5 per cent real growth rate without variation in the interest rate. In such circumstances, in order to maintain the debt/GDP ratio unchanged, it will be possible to increase the mass of public debt by a percentage equal to the GDP growth rate, multiplied by 0.60 through the effect of the issue of debt, which gives precisely 3 per cent of GDP.

But if the average *aggregate* growth rate is only 3–4 per cent (2–2.5 per cent of real growth and 1.5 per cent of inflation), the deficit at which the debt/GDP ratio of 60 per cent is not exceeded goes down to 1.8–2.4 per cent (see Chapter 13, section 1.10).

2.10   The Assumptions of the Theorem according to which Public Expenditure Increases in the Absence of the Deficit Constraint

The validity of the hypothesis that financing by means of the public debt rather than by taxation does not reduce the popularity of political decision makers among electors is based partly on the fact that citizens prefer their own present interest to that of their own future and of the future generations; but it is also based on the information-related asymmetry in the principal–agent relation that holds between citizens and political representatives. For instance, if adequate information is disseminated on the advantages of expenditures, then the benefits are immediately perceived by the electors, at times even to an exaggerated extent, while the present financial burden of the public debt, connected to complicated reactions on interest rates, on the volume and the yield of investments and thus on the GDP growth rate and employment, is not perceived in its specificity and intensity. On the other hand the future burden of the flow of taxes needed to finance the debt may be undervalued by the present electors (see Chapter 13, sections 2 and 3).

With regard to taxation, on the other hand, even if every effort is made by the government authorities to moderate the tax burden, the impact of taxation is immediately felt by the taxpayer. This is partly due to the fact that when the tax burden is high and the system involving the many different levies is extremely complicated, this results in distortions and disincentives, which generate an excess burden.

2.11   The Tendency to Deficit through the Effect of 'Decision-making Blockages' and Collusive Democracy

Thus, in the absence of the deficit constraint, expenditure tends to increase, together with the indebtedness, in an 'irrational' manner.

In addition to the above described factors, there may be a third aspect that should be taken into account, one which – in a sense – multiplies the two previous points. This is the existence of a system of collusive rather than competitive democracy, which may be made possible by the *pure* proportional electoral system and by rules on decision-making processes – like the bicameral system and the possibility of filibustering by minorities who submit an unlimited number of amendments – which require a more or less unanimous vote. Each group elected by the proportional system seeks to achieve the maximum possible advantage for its own interests concerning expenditure (and tax exemptions), but at the same time it also tends to veto decisions involving an increase in revenue that adversely affect its own group. Opting for the deficit, which implies an agreement on expenditure while postponing to the future an agreement over revenue, thus appears as the preferable result (even though it may be a 'second-best' solution) for each group, as compared with giving up their own expenditure proposals or their own veto on taxes. This comes about because of a 'free-riding' type of situation. For instance, an individual group, in isolation, might conceivably realize that in an overall perspective the elevated deficit with its negative macroeconomic effects will prove to be a greater burden – even from the point of view of a 'short-sighted' calculation by present electors – as compared to a budget with a lower rate of indebtedness that allows greater economic growth. Nevertheless, in the absence of binding rules that place a limit on the budget, each individual group knows that its abstention from asking for new expenditure and tax exemption will be of no avail in curbing similar activities by the other groups.[19]

The collusive coalition among the various groups will try to carefully manipulate the information circulated in this regard so as not to disclose to their representatives that the problem of 'fiscal adjustment' has been transferred into the future. Such a ploy enables the colluding groups to increase their representatives' feeling that the measures proposed are advantageous for them. This once again highlights the issue of informational asymmetries concerning the benefits of expenditure and the fiscal costs.

Naturally, these defects can be overcome by rules such as relinquishing pure bicameralism and adopting time limits for illustration of amendments, as well as abandoning electoral systems like proportional representation not corrected by minimal thresholds, since such systems allow fragmentation of the parties represented in elected assemblies. These defects may also be overcome with the constraints on excessive deficits as embodied in the Maastricht rules.

2.12   Decision-making Decentralization as a Cause of the Tendency towards going into Deficit

In a coalition government deriving from an agreement among various parties, none of which is able to form a majority with a dominant voting power (which often, albeit not necessarily, occurs with proportional representation), the Ministers who are the expression of the coalition are all eager to be rewarded with a good assignment of expenditure, and they endeavour to get around the coverage constraint by means of taxes that are difficult to collect in an amount adequate for the purpose.

These defects are attenuated if the electoral system favours the emergence of a non-polycentric majority and of a leader who can keep all the strands together, for example by direct election of the head of state, or of the mayor, and so on and/or by election of the leader of the predetermined coalition of parties.

2.13   Institutional Reforms to Curb the Tendency to go into Deficit

These factors prompt a number of suggestions – in addition to those already seen – concerning the constitutional rules on the budget. Some refer directly to the budget itself, while others have a broader scope, involving voting systems and the Government institutions.

I.   Adoption of an electoral system such as the plurality system or pro-portional representation with a minimum threshold for the award of a seat, and coalition leader, as this would encourage rather than discourage competition among the political groupings.

II.   Creation of a parliamentary decision-making system that prevents delaying tactics and 'surprise' balloting. This would allow even a limited majority to ensure that its decisions prevail without collu-sion with the minorities.

III.   Establishment of a framework which ensures that the govern-ment in power takes the main responsibility for the revenue- and expenditure-related aspects of the budget, in order to reduce the power of the interest groups expressed in parliament. By enabling the government to veto amendments that contrast with the overall deficit voted by a previous motion,[20] such a framework would avoid bargaining on the budget itself. Additionally, responsibility for revenue and expenditure with predetermined rules should be unified, in the context of the government, under the control of the Ministry of Finance and the Treasury (in Italy currently denomi-nated Ministry of the Economy) (see above Part One, subsection 1.12, item 1). As a further measure, either direct election of the Prime Minister, by appointment of the leader of the winning coali-tion or a Presidential Government should be introduced, to avoid or reduce the perverse effects of 'decision-making decentralization' (see above, subsection 1.12).

IV.   Avoidance of the tendency for governments to have a short term of office, by establishing 'crisis' procedures to cope with situations where the government is facing a non-confidence vote and is likely to fall. Ideally, every effort should be made to prolong the term of office of parliament to its full duration and to achieve correspond-ence between the term of office of a government and that of parlia-ment. This would be further aided by the creation of rules against 'variable majorities' such as a rule by which an elected member of parliament who defects to another party automatically loses her parliamentary status.

V. Requirement that new multi-year expenditures should be matched by corresponding multi-year sources of revenue and that *the assessment of the correspondence* should be performed by an external unbiased organ.

2.14 Cyclical Balancing of the Capital Account Budget

The criterion of a budget deficit in periods of depression, with the obligation of balancing the budget in the mid-term, say, over a five-year period, as a sign of 'reliability' was proposed by Swedish economists such as Lindahl, in the 1930s, for capital expenditure, provided that the current account remains balanced.

This criterion, which the 'Stability Pact' originally established for the European Monetary Union as an objective, in consideration of the elevated debt of some countries, appears too rigid in the long run. On the one hand, there is no reason to suppose that during periods of expansion it is suitable to have a budget surplus – achieved by raising taxes – in order to moderate the economy, since it would suffice to increase the interest rate and restrict the volume of public investments funded with loans. On the other hand, the arguments concerning consumer short-sightedness and the generational egoism considered in Chapter 3 warn against adopting constitutional rules that excessively discourage the tendency of governments to spend on investment in infrastructures, environmental protection and research, provided that the deficit is contained within a limit that prevents excessive growth of the debt. Thus what can be suggested is that the rule of the percentage constraint on the public debt for such investments in the overall set of public budgets (state, other bodies of the state sector, Regions and Local Authorities and other local sector bodies) should not be considered by year but could instead be considered for four-year or three-year periods, while maintaining a ceiling on the deficit (see subsections 2.17–2.18).

The reform of the European Stability Pact has introduced the principle of the cyclical budget, but has not earmarked the investment budget for this purpose.

2.15 'Coverage of Expenses' with the Constraint that Taxes and Expenses should be General

Wicksell – as we have seen – believed (and Buchanan and Tullock have followed this line of thought) that in a simple majority regime it may be possible for the majority to offload the fiscal costs of public expenditure onto the minority and to approve expenses that favour the majority. But this can be made far harder by establishing constitutional rules of horizontal and vertical equity that thwart any attempt to introduce discriminations in the sphere of taxes and expenses.

> These constraints are contained – albeit in a generic manner – in Arts. 3 and 53 of the Italian Constitution, which prescribe, respectively, the principle of equality among citizens and the criterion that public expenses are to be shouldered by all citizens according to (under equal conditions) ability to pay.
>
> Special taxes, for example an excise tax, and graduations of rates of general consumption taxes are allowable, but not in a way that endows them with the character of charges imposed on particular social classes or groups. The Constitutional Court is empowered to establish when this general rule is violated.
>
> For instance, the Court could decide that taxation at a rate reduced to 2 per cent on cheese versus 18 per cent on salami and ham constitutes a discrimination in favour of certain producers and an unfair advantage for others who are in competition with them on the market and do not appear to have greater capacity to pay.

Often there are forms of expenditure that cannot be general: for instance the bridge over the Strait of Messina would give a particular benefit to Sicily and Calabria.

However, decision-making processes can be improved by modifying the decision-making procedures adopted in public expenditure voting to require a link-up among expenditures pertaining to the same theme, as for instance the national programmes of investments in infrastructures.

This should also be done for current account expenditures. To take an example, if debate concerns a salary increase for top civil servants or, say, primary school teachers, this would have to be linked to the general salary policy for civil servants. Similar 'rules of the game' concerning the new expenditure can act as a 'brake' on irrational increases in expenses backed by interest groups.

2.16 The Constitutional Limit on the Personal and Business Tax Burden

The maximum limit on personal and business income tax rates follows logically from the principles of respect for property and the freedom of economic initiative, enshrined in the Constitutional Charters of democratic market economy countries. Implicitly, if there is a limit on the deficit, the limit on the fiscal burden signifies a limit on the increase in expenditure. This also ensures that expenditure does not increase beyond its utility for the taxpayers, fuelling unsustainable redistribution (see Chapter 4, section 11).

It is difficult to specify the maximum marginal rate in precise terms, but – to take an example – the constraint of not exceeding 50 per cent in the marginal tax rate appears reasonable, as an 'equitable compromise' between the state and the taxpayer with regard to the maximum rate at which the state can tax citizens' income. But the greatest problem is not that of the ceiling on the maximum rate: rather, it is that of determining which band of high income is subject to that marginal rate. An income of 100 000 euros taxed at 50 per cent becomes 50 000 euros and it is obvious that this would lead to a flattening of qualified labour incomes and discourage saving (see also Chapters 8 and 9).

Also in order to set a global limit on the global tax burden on individuals and on business it is necessary to establish what is a levy or a contribution to be assimilated to the levies.

If a limit is set on the income tax rates and as well on business taxation and on wealth taxes, then the increase in expenditure will have to be financed with consumption taxes that affect all income classes. This will be acceptable only if the great majority of citizens believe the increased expenditure to be worthwhile.

Furthermore, as is the case for the tax limits in terms of the tax burden on GDP, it is also necessary to set very clear criteria with which to establish the size of GDP. There may be a temptation to inflate the statistical sources in order to avoid exceeding the constitutional limit on the tax burden.

In Italy the limit on the tax burden is laid down by the constitution in two ways, both of which are imperfect.

Article 23 establishes that no capital tax can be levied unless it is established by a law. This means that a parliamentary majority is necessary to institute a tax or to increase the corresponding tax rates or expand their taxable base. But there is no rule of qualified majority to do so.

Article 53 establishes that all citizens are expected to contribute to public expenses on the basis of their ability to pay and that the taxation system is characterized by progressivity. Therefore taxes are set in relation to the benefits deriving from public expenditure, but in a generic manner. There is no specification of the limit beyond which there is no ability to pay. Progressivity is not delimited either upwards or downwards, or at the intermediate levels.

2.17 The Debatable Effectiveness of the Fiscal Constitution Rules on the Deficit in Independent States

The only organ that can enforce respect of the fiscal constitution of an independent state is the one that enacts laws (in Italy, the Head of State).

If this organ is elected by parliament, it may experience embarrassment in vetoing laws that violate the fiscal constitutions voted by parliament itself (Forte, 1998). There remains the power of audit of an autonomous national audit court (in Italy the Court of Audit, as in other European countries), which can ascertain the violation and enjoin the government and parliament to take appropriate measures to rectify the situation. However, if, during the year, the corrective measures are slow in coming, what can the national audit court do to induce the institutions to take action?

Furthermore, if the rules on revenue and expenditure lend themselves to accounting manipulations because they lack a detailed connection with the national accounting system or the latter was not conceived in such a manner as to apply also to public budget accounting, it is possible that ways may be found to circumvent the rules on the deficit and those on the debt (Forte, 2001).

Therefore, proper functioning of the fiscal constitution rules on the deficit and the public debt require there to be:

a.   a careful definition of the accounting criteria of the budgets at the various levels of government for the various types of bodies that are to be aggregated in the consolidated budget of the 'general government', inclusive of the entire sector of public finance;

b.   prompt appraisal by an organ that acts *super partes* and is endowed with sufficient authority to prevent violations and induce prompt correction if any violations have been committed.

> At the European level this control is now performed by Eurostat, which is a statistical office of the European Commission, with the cooperation of the Courts of Audit of the member states, not by the Court of Audits of the European Union.
>
> Reference is made, in this matter, to the European System of Integrated Economic Accounts (ESA), as officially established in 1995, which defines in detail each relevant item by government 'sector', as well as all items relevant for accounting in the market sector. However, the interpretation of doubtful cases is entrusted to the Statistical Office of the European Union (Eurostat), and not to the corresponding offices of the member states. Consequently the latter cannot engage in any 'creative finance' manipulations without the consent of Eurostat, which answers to the overall set of EU member States, through a complex game of political jockeying.
>
> The future pension-related debt is not included in the public debt according to the official definition. This solution has been politically justified by the fact that the calculation is debatable, if it is a question of trying to represent the future debt in terms of the present context. But this is a weak excuse, because the debt can be calculated for the future, without

relating it to the present context. In actual fact, the calculation in relation to the present context had seemed impracticable because the trade unions of the various European countries would have opposed the Maastricht rules.

2.18 The Rules of the Fiscal Constitution in the Case of Monetary Union among Sovereign States

An Economic and Monetary Union needs, in any case, to have rules standardizing its own economic and fiscal accounting system, in order to acquire homogeneous indicators on the trend of the economic and monetary variables throughout the area of the Union, which will then be available to guide the Central Bank's monetary policy.

In a EMU characterized by reciprocal diffidence, the strict limit on the budget deficit of member state governments may appear preferable to discretionary evaluations concerning the merit of proposed expenditure and the various policies enacted, as it can be argued that the benefit of the deficit expenditure goes to the residents of the individual member states, while the burden is distributed throughout the community. However, this may result in blocking investment expenditures, anti-cyclical policies and the lowering of tax rates with temporary budget deficit, all of which generate economic growth which spreads from the individual state where the measure was enacted to the whole community.

This calls into question the rigidity of rules such as that of Maastricht on the maximum allowed deficit/GDP ratio of 3 per cent and on the percentage reduction of the public debt/GDP ratio when the debt ratio exceeds 60 per cent. The deficit/GDP ratio, and similarly the public debt/GDP ratio, may be misleading with regard to the actual state of health of a public economy and its capacity to cope with future debt servicing commitments. For as we have seen, investment expenditure may generate benefits in terms of growth of GDP whereby the debts incurred to finance such expenditure become more sustainable. Furthermore, the lowering of tax rates can generate income growth, so that the increase in taxable income makes up for the temporary loss of revenue (see below, Chapter 8, section 8 ff. on the Laffer curve).

However, the real question is that if it is true that there is a need for a fiscal constitution of a *monetary nature* in order to achieve the aims of monetary stability and address future monetary and fiscal responsibilities, it is also true that before taking such a step, in a competitive market economy that seeks to grow, there is a need for a fiscal constitution of a *fiscal nature.* Such a constitution should leave it up to the market to see to the primary task of economic growth and, in this framework, conceive of taxes as the fiscal prices of public services delivered to families and enterprises. The pivotal element of such a constitution is the limit on the tax burden borne by individuals, and on the overall sum of taxes, and the relation between revenue and expenditure. The limit on the tax burden and that on the deficit implies a limit on expenditure. The quantity and quality of government spending is of interest to individuals, since they are the beneficiaries of the expenditure for which they pay taxes.

NOTES

1. On the relation among conventions (that is rules on which there is overall agreement) that emerge during observance and constitution of the rules, see Forte (1995).
2. See Forte 1995, especially Chapter II; Barry (1989), which develops the concept of justice as impartiality.
3. The modern approach to the theory of 'valid entitlement' with regard to property rights, from the point of view of original individual rights, is to be found in Nozick (1974). It would be beyond the scope of this note to survey the limitations of this theory, which involve the distributive and allocative aspects. Cf. Maffettone (1989, Chapter III and IV); Granaglia (1988).

    The expression 'respecting contracts and promises' is intended to refer – following the formulation by D. Hume (1740 [2003]), Book III, Part II on *Justice and Injustice* – to all bilateral and unilateral acts that private individuals can carry out in conformity with the laws in force (drawing up wills, marriages, dowry promises etc., as well as sale, rental and labour contracts etc.). According to the principle of the 'rule of law' taxes can be levied on citizens only if such taxes are *based on the law* which, in turn, is limited by the principles regarding individual rights and the market economy, laid down in the constitution.
4. The above rule was suggested by the author in Italy, in the programme put forward by the autumn 1983 Craxi Government. However, that Government did not apply the rule and the ratio of public debt to GDP increased rather than diminished. The rule, which I had explained in the press, was then applied in Britain, in a slightly different manner by the Labour government, and has become known as the Brown Rule.
5. In Italy, an Act was passed in December 1977 which provided that the three-year budget should be introduced together with the annual budget.
6. Stated by Art. 81 of the Italian Constitution.
7. In Italy, the functional classification is still inadequate, especially as for the sub-classifications.
8. In Italy cost centre accounting is being developed systematically. Outcome and activity indicators are only sporadically used.
9. In Italy the state budgets are published yearly in a special supplement of the Official Gazette. No clarification is given to render the contents accessible to the non-initiated. The budgets of the other bodies and governments and their overall results are not easily accessible.
10. See F. Forte, 'Control of public spending growth and majority rule' in Forte and Peacock (1985).
11. For an examination of Wicksell's unanimity principle according to Wicksell, see Forte (1985a), in Greenaway and Shaw (1985).
12. On these themes see also the discussion in Chapter 1, subsection 3.9, ff.
13. A careful reading of Wicksell (1896) shows that his suggestion of financing through loans rather than taxes concerned only capital expenditure and special war expenditure. On the latter point he admits simple majority voting, in relation to the necessity of the

financing. For any other fiscal choices implying public debt carried he always requires a qualified majority.

14. An alternative solution is automatic approval due to expiry of a deadline, when the budget does not foresee new (laws enacting an increase in) taxes and the overall budget of revenue and expenses is balanced (balance being achieved with the 'natural' increase in revenue associated with growth in GDP).

15. The concept of 'political enterprise' and 'political entrepreneur' dates back to the neo-classical economist G. Montemartini. On the theory of the political entrepreneur see Chapter 1, subsection 2.13.

16. Modigliani, *New Developments on the Oligopoly Front* (1958), shows that the possibility of new oligopolistic enterprises entering the market, and therefore the limit on the 'exploitation margin' deriving from higher-than-cost prices set by enterprises already on the market, is all the greater if such enterprises are more efficient because they can minimize fixed costs. This theme was further developed in the theory of 'contestable markets': see Baumol et al. (1982).

17. In analogy with contestable (oligopoly) markets: see Baumol et al. (1982).

18. The three rules – a) that the only sector of the budget in which a deficit is allowed should be that of investment expenditure; b) that the deficit in question cannot exceed 3 per cent of GDP; c) that the stock of debt cannot exceed 60 per cent of GDP – are the rules which, according to the Maastricht Treaty of the European Monetary Union, were supposed to be adhered to in the public budgets of the member states, in 1997. However, in 1997 the Amsterdam Stability Pact established the balanced budget rule as a long-term rule. Later on the pact was amended, introducing the principle of flexibility in relation to cyclical fluctuation. See below subsection 2.14.

19. This seems to be one of the causes of the huge rise in the public debt in Italy from the 1970s to 1988, when the DPEF, fixing a limit on the deficit, was introduced. See above subsection 1.12, item 1 and below, subsection 2.13. On these issues see in particular Persson and Tabellini (2003).

20. In Italy this is done through the motion of approval of the DPEF. See note 19.

7. Public expenditure

1 ANALYSIS OF EXPENDITURE BY ECONOMIC CATEGORIES

1.1 The Value-added of the Public Administration in the Framework of the Gross Domestic Value-added and of GDP

As will be recalled from section 1 of Chapter 1, government spending S_G is composed of i) goods and services B_G and ii) transfer payments T_G, that is to say:

$$S_G = B_G + T_G \tag{7.1}$$

The government goods B_G are, in turn, composed of purchases of intermediate goods FE_G and of gross value-added VAL_G, namely:

$$B_G = FE_G + VAL_G \tag{7.2}$$

The government's value-added VAL_G is itself composed of consumption, wages and, to a very small extent, depreciations.

The government's transfer payments and also its goods and services can go to consumption C_G and/or to investments I_G. Therefore we can write:

$$S_G = C_G + I_G \tag{7.3}$$

The national government's value-added is summed with that of the market enterprises $M\ VAL_M$, giving rise to the total value-added which, when summed with the indirect taxes TI on products of the enterprises M, composes GDP, namely:

$$GDP = VAL_M + VAL_G + TI \tag{7.4}$$

It should also be recalled, from equation (1.1'), that GDP consists of consumption C, gross investments I and the balance between importations and exportations EI. Therefore we can write:

$$VAL_M + VAL_G + TI = C + I + EI \qquad (7.5)$$

that is to say, GDP consists, on the supply side, of the market value-added (which consists in the value-added of enterprises + the value-added of the domestic services of families' employees) + the government's value-added + indirect taxes, minus government transfers to enterprises or to families in relation to their expenses for consumption and investments. The sum of the added values of the market and of the government is known as the gross national product at factor cost. By adding indirect taxes and payment transfers to families and enterprises for consumption and investment, one obtains GDP at market prices. When market depreciations (of enterprises with regard to all real durable assets, that is estates and movables, and of families with regard to real estate only) and government depreciations (with regard to the assets with a market value for which depreciations are required) are subtracted, what is obtained is the net national product, respectively at factor cost and at market prices.

Let us now take a look at national expenditure, in consumption and investments, which is equal to the national product plus the algebraic balance of the current accounts for goods and services of the balance of payments. It can be seen that consumption is partly carried out by families, FA, and partly by the government, while investments are undertaken by enterprises, families (for homes) and by the government. But it should also be kept in mind that the role of government in consumption and investment is twofold. One aspect concerns its own consumption and investments, while the other concerns the sum composed of its transfers to families and enterprises for consumption, summed with transfers for investments to families and enterprises. If the expenses for the government's investment and consumption are summed together with the expenses of families and enterprises, a double calculation is made, because the consumption and investments of families and enterprises include the government transfers. Therefore these must be excluded from the total aggregate of consumption and investment.

1.2 Classification by European Functions of Governments

At the European and international level a standard classification of the functions of the public economy has been formulated, to be integrated with that commonly adopted in the various national accounting systems. It is denominated COFOG (Classification of the Functions of Governments) and it is here presented for disaggregation on two levels. However, in order to be operative it needs further subdivision into at least another two levels, so that the classification is sufficiently detailed to allow specific measurement, by means of ad hoc indicators (as described in Chapter 5, subsection 1.4). This operation is needed in order to pursue adequately the aim of evaluating the efficiency and effectiveness of public action, although this is a form of control deeply disliked by the public bureaucracy, which mounts stiff opposition to it by invoking accounting difficulties. Many of these functions, as can be noted in Table 7.1, do not concern provision of public services, but activities designed to regulate the market economy. This is particularly clear with regard to Division 4, which concerns Economic Affairs. The classification has some debatable elements, such as the fact that 'Defence' includes the heading 'Civil Protection Services', which should more properly be included in Division 5, 'Environmental Protection', because it concerns the protection of persons, their places of settlement and the environment in which they live, from natural damage, not from enemies. Another debatable criterion is that expenditure on research is split up into basic research, which appears among the general services of the Public Administration, and applied research, which is listed as a sub-class of every Division, with a clearly artificial classification (omitted here), so that there is R&D for Public Order and Safety, R&D for Education, R&D for Recreation, Culture and Religion, R&D for Social Protection as well as R&D for Defence, for Health, for the Environment, for the various productive and Economic Affairs. Thus research areas that do not exist are intermingled with others for which there is a complex body of work.

In the Italian public administration the classificatory framework in question has so far been established on the central level and for the macro divisions, and has not been subdivided into the specific functions of governments, either in terms of geographic areas, with regard to the action of the central government, or for the regional and local governments. Theoretically, with this structure the public bureaucracy of the central government in Italy could exert broad control both on itself and on the bureaucracies of the lower-level governments, to which the central government gives substantial transfer payments as well as holding ultimate responsibility over their budgets. This form of control could serve for formulation of the general government's budget, which is the consolidated budget account for the public budgets at all levels of government and which is relevant for measuring the deficit/GDP and the debt/GDP ratios (discussed in Chapter 6, on fiscal constitution, especially in subsections 1.12 and 2.9 and also dealt with further on in Chapter 13 on public debt and fiscal policy).

But public bureaucracies, as already noted, do not appreciate having to exert control over themselves and over the lower-level public

Table 7.1   The macro functions (divisions) of the COFOG budget

1.	*General services and services of the public administrations*
1.1.	Executive and legislative organs, financial and fiscal affairs and foreign affairs
1.2.	Economic aid to developing countries and economies in transition
1.3.	General services
1.4.	Basic research
1.5.	Public debt transactions
1.7.	General transfers between different governmental levels
2.	*Defence*
2.1.	Military defence
2.2.	Civil defence
2.3.	Foreign military aid
3.	*Public order and safety*
3.1.	Police services
3.2.	Fire-fighting
3.3.	Law courts
3.4.	Prisons
4.	*Economic affairs*
4.1.	General economic and commercial affairs and labour affairs
4.2.	Agriculture, forestry, fisheries and hunting
4.3	Fuel and energy
4.4.	Mining, manufacturing and construction
4.5.	Road, water, rail, air and pipeline transport and other transport
4.6.	Communication
4.7.	Other activities: tourism, commercial distribution, storage and warehousing
4.8.	Research and Development for the economy
5.	*Environmental protection*
5.1.	Waste management
5.2.	Waste water treatment
5.3.	Pollution abatement
5.4.	Protection of biodiversity and the landscape heritage
6.	*Housing and community amenities*
6.1.	Housing development
6.2.	Community amenities
6.3.	Water supply
6.4.	Street lighting
7.	*Health care*
7.1.	Pharmaceutical products and other medical and therapeutic appliances
7.2.	Outpatient services
7.3.	Hospital services
7.4.	Public health services

Table 7.1 (continued)

8.	*Recreation, culture and faiths*
8.1.	Recreational and sporting services
8.2.	Cultural activities
8.3.	Broadcasting and publishing services
8.4.	Faith services and other community services
9.	*Education*
9.1.	Pre-primary and primary education
9.2.	Secondary education
9.3.	Post-secondary non-tertiary education
9.4.	First and second-level university education
9.5.	Subsidiary services to education
10.	*Social protection*
10.1.	Sickness and disability
10.2.	Old age
10.3.	Survivors
10.4.	Family and children
10.5.	Unemployment
10.6.	Housing

Note: For each division there are also research expenses and other non-classifiable expenses.

Source: Forte and D'Eugenio (2005).

bureaucratic apparatuses, because they would suffer a loss of power and would no longer be able to engage in opportunistic modes of action. Parliament, on the other hand, could have greater interest in adopting this technique of analysis of public expenditure for regulations and for goods and services than is the case with the public bureaucracy, since parliament is supposed to exert control over the bureaucracy. And as far as central government is concerned, on the one hand it clearly has an interest in this tool, with its subdivisions. On the other hand, it has to take into consideration the power of its bureaucracy and that of the lower-level governments, on which it in fact relies for its electoral consensus. The problem is how to induce the bureacracy to cooperate in this task.

This caveat having been stated, it remains true that the analysis by functions of governments concerning public expenditure, with a uniform classification for all governments and their subdivisions, is – on paper – a precious public economy planning tool, which can be of aid for public choice and for monitoring the outcome of public action.

1.3 Financial Transfers and Real Expenses, or Transformations

The transfers–transformations dichotomy is frequently encountered in public expenditure.[1]

National accounting customarily, as seen above in section 1.1, distinguishes public goods in terms of the factors utilized, dividing them into net value-added (that is salaried employment income), depreciations, purchase of intermediate goods and services, transfers. Grouping together the first three of these categories, the value of the 'real products' supplied by the public administration is obtained. Such products can also be denominated as 'public services' or, with a more neutral term, 'public transformations', indicating that these are supplies coming from the fiscal economy through its transformation of market economy resources, which thus become unavailable for other uses.

'Transformation' expenses, which embody provision of 'real' goods, stand in contrast with transfers, which are financial disbursements, that is the passage of sums of money from the financial economy to the pockets of market subjects, or to the coffers of other governments.

A careful consideration of the actual content of this dichotomy is of the utmost importance. In some cases the financial economy does not provide the public services directly, but rather it supplies them indirectly, availing itself of the market, according to different gradations of competition and free choice.

We can, therefore, distinguish two major classes of hypotheses.

a. The public operator purchases on the market – preferably in a framework of competition – the goods or technical service which the government itself then provides to users, managing only the intermediary phase;
b. The public operator empowers a private operator to obtain a given service free of charge, or with reimbursement, and the service is of a preestablished type, to be obtained either strictly only from a given list of private operators or with freedom of choice of the service providers.[2]

In the second hypothesis, when the user of a service has the right to choose the supply and does not face the obligation of paying the sum in advance, then it can be said that she has the right to a 'voucher' for the compulsory or optional purchase. The voucher can be 'in nature', as in the case of a medical prescription, which entitles the user to obtain certain types of medication from any pharmacist, or it may be monetary, such as a voucher entitling the bearer to obtain refreshments or food from a university catering service, free of charge up to a certain amount.

Thus the coupon (and the same holds true for entitlement to reimbursement) can allow freedom of choice. This may be a 'subjective' freedom, in the sense that with regard to a certain good or service the choice may be made among various different suppliers, or 'objective' in the sense that there is freedom of choice among various different goods provided by a specified supplier, or alternatively, the freedom may be understood in a broader sense, with both types of choice allowed.

These public services are not classifiable as 'transformations', if one considers the point of view of the public operator as a producer, as in the national accounting perspective. But they are indeed transformations if the public operator is considered as a supplier that corresponds to the cooperative model of the public economy, in which the public operator is subsidiary to the market and makes the greatest possible use of it. Such a criterion is based on the principle of the efficiency of competition and of free choice for the user of the public services. However, the term 'spurious' or 'indirect' transformations could be used here, to indicate that in the national accounting view these are transfers, which must be cancelled in calculation of GDP, to avoid double counting with the value of the market production at market prices.

1.4 Transfers that are Generic or Specific, Free of Charge or Imposing a Charge

The term 'specific transfers' is used here to refer to the broad range of contributions by the public operator to specific activities by various other subjects (families, enterprises, lower-level and higher-level governments, international institutions), such contributions being designed to cover part of their costs in recognition of the fact that these are merit consumption or investments that generate external economies or Hotelling goods and so on.

Specific transfers stand in opposition to generic transfers, such as state contributions to the European Community or to the Regions or the International Cooperation Agencies, for their expenses considered globally.

While in the case of specific transfers, the operator that carries out the transfer interferes in decision-making processes carried out by the subjects that receive the transfer; this does not occur in the case of generic transfers. In the latter case, the beneficiary is, in principle, free to choose. A generic transfer from one government to another of a higher or lower level is logical only if the beneficiary cannot, alone, finance these operations by charging the subjects to whom the supplies are destined, because the beneficiary has limited tax power[3] or because this would distort competition[4] and/or violate equity principles.[5]

For many transfers, financial illusion gives the impression that they are 'free of charge', whereas in actual fact a charge is imposed by some governments.

For instance, for the overwhelming proportion of citizens, pensions are not a 'free lunch', but correspond to contributions paid.

1.5 Should Public Services be Produced by the State?

In principle, the statement that the state should satisfy a given want does not imply that:

a.   the state should provide the service with its public expenditure;
b.   and that if the state acts through the supply of public goods, it should do so by means of its own production of such services.

The answer to this conundrum must be sought through an analysis of the efficiency of vertical integration as compared to outsourcing contracts that economists, after Coase, have developed with regard to the theory of the firm. The fundamental point consists in the 'transaction costs' and the associated costs of gathering information, and of the repeated bargaining procedures.

In actual fact, services directly provided by public bodies are often rather more extended than would be justified from the allocative point of view, because of the internal pressure every bureaucracy exerts to expand its sphere of influence.

1.6   'Trust' Goods, Transaction Costs, and Opportunistic Modes of Behaviour in Agency Relations

The fundamental reason for entrusting the public operator with direct provision of public goods other than in the area of wants that are genuinely public by nature is bound up with the question of 'trust goods' which, as their name indicates, embody certain particular trust characteristics.[6] Paying a subsidy to an enterprise in order to enable it to supply goods and services in cases where the market, left to its own devices, fails to give the right quantity (or quality), involves an assessment of the production achieved by this enterprise.

At times, it may be fairly easy to find a measurement criterion, and the subsidy procedure is simple and uncomplicated to set in place. But at other times this may not be the case, as can happen when there is a risk that the product may be of poor quality, if the parameter to which the subsidy is linked does not take into account some of the significant details required for quality evaluation of the product. This may occur, for instance, with regard to surgical services supplied by hospitals as for complex treatments, or in the case of the school-leaving examinations in the general education system, in contrast to the vocational schools, the quality tests for which are more easily devisable.

Some economists have vigorously defended an entirely private system of educational provision, in which the state simply pays the cost of the service, giving a voucher to be spent in whichever educational institution the parents or pupils prefer.

However, it is by no means certain that, if the educational system were entirely privatized, the services provided by schooling as for the compulsory education schools would be supplied according to the desirable principles of good quality which are of fundamental importance in this field.

If, on the other hand, private schools exist alongside state-run schools, it will be possible to draw comparisons, and those who do not wish to undergo discrimination have the option of attending the free state school system.

The flow of information concerning the principal–agent relation when state-run and private schools exist side by side can improve.

1.7   Classification of Goods and Public Transfers Utilized in Consumption and Investment and Final and Intermediate, that is Instrumental Goods

In the public economy, as in the market economy, resource utilizations can be distinguished into consumption and other current expenses, and investments. Intermediate utilizations are those which are instrumental to some other public or private production, while final utilizations are those consisting in consumption and investments. These two classifications interact (see Table 7.2).

The expenditure required to build a public road is an investment expenditure and at the same time it is an expenditure for an intermediate good, since the road serves consumers, enterprises and the public operator services as well, as goods instrumental to their circulating vehicles. Road maintenance expenses are a consumption expense and, at the same time, an intermediate expense, for precisely the same reasons. Medical treatment is a form of final consumption, and the hospitals in which some of the treatment is administered are a final investment. Current expenditure for state education is, at one and the same time, a consumption and production expenditure; schools, in turn, are a mixed investment, that is partly of consumption and partly instrumental to the production that avails itself of specific professional skills.

Table 7.2   Overview of public goods according to final and intermediate utilization

	Final goods	Intermediate goods
Current expenses	e.g. public medical treatment	e.g. road maintenance expenses
	Public education	
Investments	Hospitals	Ports, roads
	Schools	

Table 7.3   Classification of investment expenditure

	Financial investments	Real investments
Directly productive investments	e.g. financing enterprises that invest in depressed areas	Agricultural reclamation works
Investments playing an intermediate role in production (indirectly productive)	Financing of private research	Public research Industrial port
Consumption investments	Financing of private 'social' housing	Public hospital Municipal water mains
Investments playing an intermediate role in consumption	Financing of private urban waste treatment plants	Municipal wholesale market

Investments destined to be utilized for production are classified as 'productive investments'.

But at this point it should be recalled that public expenditure does not entirely take the form of 'transformations', that is of goods (including services): a large part consists of transfers. Thus we can make a second classification, concerning investment expenditure (see Table 7.3).

It is helpful to distinguish productive investments from other types of investments because there may be special arguments in favour of public debt financing of productive investments (see Chapter 6, subsection 1.14), provided that – obviously – they translate into a genuine future increase in GDP. However, this classification must be applied with caution, as asserting that 'all' educational expenses are a productive investment implies a twofold drift: from the concept of current expenses to that of expenditure for durable goods, and from the concept of a durable good for 'human capital' to expenditure to form 'productive factors'.

2   ANALYSIS OF EXPENDITURE BY FUNCTIONAL CLASSES: LAW, ORDER AND DEMOCRACY

2.1   The Ratio of the 'Functional Classification' of Public Expenditure in the Cooperative Model

The starting point for the 'rational' functional classification of goods, and thus of public expenditure, consists of a reference to the type of wants satisfied. Fundamentally, this involves the question of different fiscal 'prices' to be borne by the presumed beneficiaries.

With regard to the subjects to whom the goods are destined, predominantly allocative public expenditure can be subdivided into four sectors: the institutional sector, which concerns the demand for protection, government and democracy arising from the subjects of civil society organized into a *polis*; the demand for production, which in the cooperative model concerns the demand springing from operators involved in production of public goods and of services for productive activities, namely enterprises, workers and savers; and consumption demand, which in the cooperative model concerns the demand by private individuals for public consumption goods, or goods that are instrumental to private consumption. Expenditure for the fourth sector, the social sector, consists of goods and transfers to satisfy both allocative and distributive wants.

The wants of the first sector are experienced by all individuals inasmuch as they form part of politically organized society.

In the cooperative model, the wants of the second sector are those experienced by individuals, inasmuch as they are organized into, or intended for, productive activities on the market. The wants of the third sector are – again in the cooperative model – those experienced by citizens and other subjects residing in the *polis*, in their individual private, family or associative life. The wants of the fourth sector – in the welfare state of a cooperative type – are those experienced by the less favoured and also those experienced by normal subjects in their need for 'social insurance' (see Table 7.4).

2.2   Sector I.A: Expenses for Justice

In a state based on the rule of law, one aspect of the cooperative model is that it does not tolerate an excess of regulations and does not accept that a breach of administrative regulations should fall under the heading of a 'crime'. Therefore justice expenses cannot be elevated.

An expenditure amounting to 2–3 per cent of GDP implies a rather large judicial body, composed of judges and their technical and administrative assistants.

Table 7.4   The four sectors of public expenditure

Demand	Main beneficiaries		
Supply	Community as a whole	Enterprises	Families
Sector I			
Institutional expenses (Conflictual collective goods)	●		
Sector II			
Production expenses (Normal collective goods)		●	●
Sector III			
Expenses for civil society (Merit goods and normal collective goods)			●
Sector IV			
Social expenses (i.e. for 'social insurance') (Merit goods and redistributions)			●

The problem of Justice is to a large extent a qualitative issue: it depends on the simplicity and certainty of the procedures and of the laws, and on the working attitude of the personnel; however, the work cannot be organized along the lines of an enterprise, since its independence is of vital importance. A certain degree of X inefficiency therefore has to be accepted, as the necessary counterpart of the independence of the judges.

2.3   Sector I.B: Military Expenses

Military expenses, which in the cooperative model are conceived as 'defence expenditure' and denominated as such, are often one of the major items of public expenditure.[7]

To cope with technological progress increasingly costly and more powerful military equipment is required, and since each state seeks to procure weaponry and equipment for its defensive purposes, the increase in expenditure does not correspond to an increase in security.

According to a widespread economic-sociological belief, military expenses are underpinned above all by the so-called 'military-industrial complex'. This is due to the fact that military equipment is supplied by private industry, which

Table 7.5   Analysis of political-institutional expenditure (Sector I)

A.	Expenses for government and democracy	Expenses for elective assemblies, governments, the head of state and of the lower-level governments, for the Constitutional Court Expenses for general and administrative elections and referendums Public funding of political parties
B.	Justice	Expenses for personnel, offices, equipment, computerization and software Prison expenses Expenses for the Criminal Investigation Department (CID) (= investigations pursuant to court proceedings and trials) Legal aid expenses, witnesses, etc. Expenses for rehabilitation of former prisoners Redress for miscarriage of justice
C.	Military needs	Servicemen's salaries, disability pensions and disbursements for military honours Purchase and maintenance of military equipment Quarters, provisioning and welfare of military personnel Military material for current consumption (ammunition, fuel, etc.) Expenses for personnel recruitment and training Military prisons and tribunals Indemnity for 'military easements' (occupation of land for target shooting ranges, missile deposits, etc.) and for war-related damage Technical-scientific research and strategic and historical-military studies
D.	Public order	Personal expenses of the police force and compensation to victims of terrorism and for death in the line of duty Remuneration of police informants Scientific and technical laboratories Computerized archives and related services Barracks, technical means, current materials

Note: This table is a synthesis and remaking of that in Forte (1984) *Il Bilancio nell'Economia Pubblica*, vol I, pp. 218–19.

develops powerful pressure groups. However, according to another school of thought, the expenditure for defence is undervalued because the want of defence is a consolidated want which is felt in its real dimension only when the threat to security becomes dramatically real.

With regard to military goods, a problem of external economies emerges. Military defence (or potential offence) may be carried out over a vast area involving more than one state. Each one benefits from the overall result, but the individual 'allied' states may manage to contribute to the cost in proportion not so much to what could be seen as their interest but, rather, to what is effectively their 'strategic ability' in obtaining the full benefit of the 'collective game', even if they have been somewhat sparing in their participation in the common effort.

Whether a state has a military apparatus that makes substantial outlays for expensive equipment, or a military apparatus that spends on personnel (provisioning and salaries), in either case their military apparatus may tend to maximize its volume of activities measured in terms of expenditures (see Chapter 5, subsections 1.7 and 1.8, models of Niskanen and of X inefficiency). But the first type of apparatus will pursue maximization of the outcome, that is an elevated volume of 'output' evaluated in terms of military capacity, while the second type of apparatus will pursue 'maximization of numbers', in other words an elevated volume of inputs of staff, which means jobs for officers and undergraduates.

The latter model is more likely to be predominant if the 'defence demand' is weak, whereas the output maximization model tends to emerge in countries where there is a more pressing need for defence: the more intensely perceived the threat of the potential enemy, the more actively the policy of power vis-à-vis others is implemented.

2.4   Sector I.C: Expenses for Policing and Interior Defence

The demand for 'order and interior defence' springs not only from a widespread feeling among the population but also from specific individual wants of citizens and enterprises.

> Crime in one's local neighbourhood or talked about in the press, with gripping and dramatized descriptions (robberies, kidnapping, and so on), evoking fears of threats to people's property and citizens' safety, trigger a demand for 'law and order' services that can provide specific safeguards for individual users of such services, ensuring protection for their dwellings, their property, for people going about their daily business, as well as for enterprises and their trading activities and transportation of goods.

Preventive patrolling and defensive action by public law enforcement officers is unavoidably only partial. But a distinction should be drawn between prevention that cannot but be selective, versus repressive action, which should be generalized, albeit – in the less severe cases – limited.

Repressive action should cease when the cost of investigations exceeds the advantage of the desired positive result multiplied by the probability of achieving it. This should, however, be calculated taking into account the 'external effects' of deterrence. The higher the percentage of criminals captured and repressed, the lower the likelihood – as viewed by those intent on committing a crime – of obtaining the hoped-for benefit of the criminal action, and the greater likelihood of paying the penalty. According to a theorem proposed by Cesare Beccaria and Gary Becker, the deterrence of massive sanctions is less effective that the deterrence of accurate enforcement. Thus for the offender, a sanction of 100 with a 50 per cent likelihood of its application means a probability of paying 50, while a sanction of 80 with a 65 per cent likelihood of application means a probability of paying 52. Also obviously the years of imprisonment cannot be increased without limits.[8]

Utility of commiting crimes increases with increasing income levels and average wealth of the community, because the possible gain increases likewise.[9] Furthermore, the development of international communications makes it more difficult, *ceteris paribus*, to uncover and track down ill-gotten gains. Technological progress increases the means and thus the costs of deterrence and crime detection, but it also affects the costs of means used to commit crimes. The incidence of costs increases both in the sector of crime and also in that of individual and collective services for defence against crime. And the supply is often unable to assuage the demand for public order.

Consequently, private defence activity develops alongside the public service. This is by no means unreasonable if this activity is regulated so as not to damage public order, since in the cooperative model an intervention by the state is not warranted where private enterprise can operate effectively in its own interest while also pursuing a general interest.

3 ANALYSIS OF EXPENDITURE BY FUNCTIONAL CLASSES: PRODUCTION EXPENSES

3.1 Public Expenditure for Production in General

It is excessive to assume that all expenses in the cooperative model are productive factors, as maintained by De Viti De Marco (1934 [1936]).

Public civil expenses such as education are not merely useful for production but also for citizens as consumers of a superior good; defence expenses are of use for the whole community; social transfer payments have a redistributive function, and so on.

According to Röpke (1944 [1948]), a distinction can be made in the cooperative model between 'framework policy' and 'structural policy'. The second type of policy can be distinguished into 'market-conforming interventions', designed to favour competition in the economy and therefore conforming to the genuine market economy (such as investment in infrastructures and expenditure on research and professional training), and 'adaptation' policies to moderate the harshness and frictions of the shifts and disturbances in economic life.

Thus at times the state may decide to carry out productive expenditure of the adaptation type to achieve a more satisfactory balancing effect, thereby pursuing not just an allocative aim but also a 'distributive' aim, by aiding deprived communities, less developed areas that are distant from those considered as 'strong', and so on (see Chapter 3, subsections 1.13–1.14).

A large part of the benefit of production expenditure does lend itself to monetary measurement and thus to an analysis of allocative advantageousness and redistributive effectiveness. In many cases it is also possible to attempt to evaluate its contribution to employment. Finally, for many infrastructures, there is a technical, 'tangible' relation between supply and demand, so that even if measurement of the monetary value is lacking because the services cannot be sold, or is defective because of the difficulty of taking the external economies into account, the volume of use can still be measured by means of physical data. A typical case is that of roads, with truck usage that can be estimated in terms of tons/km of freight transported.

3.2   Sector II.A: Technical Assistance, Research, Professional Training, Promotion

This type of expenditure does not form part of the framework policies, and belongs instead to the category of 'structural policy'.

Professional training is, obviously, of use to those who receive it. But it also generates substantial specific and atmosphere-related 'external economies' for enterprises. However, personnel training may not always be advantageous for enterprises interested in employing specialized labour: the point is that since (luckily!) slavery does not exist, those who train a given person cannot be sure of making use of their services for a prolonged period of time in such a manner as to achieve the profit required to compensate the training costs.

This generates a vast area of intervention by the central and peripheral government, with favourable effects both on productivity and employment. Such an effect is particularly marked with regard to professions where there are no large enterprises that could shoulder the burden of training, even if they were willing to accept the risk of 'losing' some of the trained staff after a certain period of time. A typical case is that of crafts-manship in specialized forms of work.

> Tax relief and favourable conditions on social insurance contributions for apprenticeships may encourage professional and vocational training by private enterprises that generate external economies, thereby acting as a total or partial surrogate of public expenditure on professional training.

However, professional training sometimes also falls under the heading of 'adaptation policies'.

This is because the public operator also has a 'distributive' reason for considering professional training as a distributive want, so that the under-privileged and the less well-off can thereby be given a more favourable opportunity regarding economic and social competition. This enables the public operator to provide a buffer against unemployment rather more efficiently than with policies that foster a culture of dependence.

Similar observations can be made for expenditure on technological research, which can be viewed as a 'conforming intervention'. It is a mistake to adopt overly stringent patent protection measures, as this would give rise to a monopoly. Thus there are areas of research where collective action appears appropriate, given the substantial external economies.

3.3   Sector II.B: Infrastructures of Public Utility, that is for Satisfying Conditional Wants

> In part, the infrastructures in question (roads, city squares, ordinary bridges, street lighting) are 'intrinsically' indivisible Dupuit goods (see Chapter 3, subsection 1.10), and in part they are public goods which, in addition to divis-ible advantages, also produce external effects that cannot be divided (water works and land reclamation, firefighting and other fire prevention services). Additionally, there are Hotelling type (Chapter 3, subsection 1.11) public utility service enterprises for which prices are set that are supposed to cover the costs, provided the prices are appropriately discriminated. But often the goal of covering the costs is not achieved (railways, turnpikes and toll-paying interstates, tunnels, the postal service and telecommunications, sewerage, ports, aqueducts).

Almost all of the goods and services considered here have two char-acteristics: that of satisfying 'conditional' wants and that of enabling the suppliers to forge a monopoly, given that it is a question of activities that 'inherently involve a road'. The latter characteristic may give rise to a regime of concessions granted to 'public utility enterprises', either pri-vately or publicly owned (Einaudi, 1940 [1956]).

The first of the two above characteristics implies that the goods of this kind are indispensable for production of all other goods, for without them, there can be no organized economy.[10] Furthermore, if the market alone is unable to supply the required goods, then it implies public subsidy. However, it also involves control over tariffs and conditions of service, because in this case exploitation of monopoly positions may inflict particularly elevated damage on the users.

The fact that the 'public utilities' give 'conditional' services makes them crucial for purposes of aggregations among interdependent investments in new areas, and it also intensifies the problems that can arise in relation to monopolistic exploitation.[11]

3.4 Sector II.C: Financing of Enterprises

The main justifications for subsidies to private enterprises as well as public enterprises reside in the presence of infant industries, or the aim of encouraging technological progress or providing support for a distressed geographical area. As can be seen, this to some extent involves policies which, in the cooperative model, can be justified as 'conforming interventions' (infant industries, encouragement of technological progress), but it partly also involves (delicate) 'adaptation' actions.[12]

In order for policy measures to be in line with these principles, the aid should be of a temporary nature. If this is not the case, then the intervention is not market-conforming but 'merely protectionist' and the adaptation policy degenerates into a 'culture of dependence' (see Chapter 3, subsection 1.14).

Furthermore, in order to ensure that these measures are 'rational', they should be accessible to all public or private enterprises, with equal treatment.

4 ANALYSIS OF EXPENDITURE BY FUNCTIONAL CLASSES: CONSUMPTION EXPENDITURE

4.1 Expenditure for Civil Society in General

Collective expenditure for and of consumption endows civil society with well-being and quality of life.

> The inference Say drew from the concept that public finance is a consumption phenomenon was that the greater the restrictions on this form of expenditure, the better it would be for the public budget. This argument is unilateral if one

admits, as Say himself admitted, that the final goal of the economy is indeed not production, but consumption.[13] It can instead be considered as a question of determining the extent to which such 'consumption' is useful, in comparison to the private or non-subsidized consumption it replaces, and to what extent the state can levy charges in order to carry out public consumption without compromising production development.

Public expenditure of this type has gradually increased with the growth in national income, which has led to the rise of new wants. This is related in part to the complementarity of public consumption expenditure with private consumption. A typical case is that of road expenses in relation to the expansion of vehicle traffic with increasing prosperity of urban and rural communities.

However, the increase in expenditure of this nature partly also corresponds to the growth of higher wants such as education, culture, goods relating to the environmental, artistic and cultural heritage (museums, restoration of artworks, archaeological finds, and so on).[14]

It should also be noted that public consumption expenditure does not necessarily fall under the heading of current expenses. An important part is constituted by investment expenditure: housing infrastructures, school buildings, road and city square construction, the purchase and restoration of artworks all represent capital expenses which give future consumption utility flows.

Public expenditure for civil society does not lend itself so easily to monetary measurement as is the case with production expenditure, as it does not translate into a productive advantage but rather into final consumption satisfaction with notable 'external effects'.

If an entry ticket has to be purchased for going to a museum, a theatre, a public park, and so on, the resulting charge will cover no more than a part of the provision with a 'divisible' benefit, while the remainder concerns the overall community. Nevertheless the charge does play an important function in signalling the public's preferences and prompting a sense of responsibility in the supply.[15]

4.2   Sector III.A: Expenditure for Public Infrastructures

In part, as we have seen, this subclass of expenditure (see Table 7.6) appears in conjunction with that for satisfying production wants. Precisely for this reason, there are delicate problems of coexistence, associated not only with the fact that infrastructures provided free of charge do not have a fully indivisible character but also with the issue of how to ascribe the fixed costs to the various users of public utility services for which a charge is made.

This may give rise to allocative distortions.

Table 7.6   Analysis of public consumption expenditure (Sector III)

A.	Expenditure for public infrastructures	Expenditure associated with other kinds of spending of the same subclass in Sector II Public parks and outdoor recreation centres Drinking fountains and rest rooms Cemeteries
B.	Civil protection and environmental heritage goods	Civil disaster protection against earthquakes, flooding, volcanic eruptions, man-made disasters Environmental protection of fauna, flora, forests, the landscape, coasts, rivers, seas, lakes, underground bodies of water and irrigation channels, land, to safeguard against pollution
C.	Education	Compulsory schooling up to school-leaving age Secondary education Undergraduate and post-graduate university education University of the Third Age Lifelong education Study grants Provision of free transport, textbooks, school meals
D.	Artistic and cultural goods and services	Museums and exhibitions Botanical, zoological and astronomical centres Academies and art conventions Theatre, music and cinema shows Restoration, purchase and conservation of historic buildings and goods of the archaeological and historical heritage Subsidies to the world of publishing Pensions and prizes to artists, literary figures, philosophers, humanists etc.
E.	Leisure	Seaside holiday or mountain camps etc., sports pitches, gyms and fitness centres, spa establishments, care facilities for athletes preparing for competitions

4.3 Sector III.B: Civil Protection and Goods Forming Part of the Environmental Heritage

These free goods and in general the environment involve costs for the public operator with regard to prevention and protection against fire, flooding, landslides and man-created pollution. The latter should be limited or prohibited or the costs should be shouldered by the supplier or the consumers of the goods that caused the pollution (Coase (1960); Forte (2007) on the Coase theorem revisited).

4.4   Sector III.C: Education

This is the major class of expenditure for civil society in a developed economy and in a democratic society. Human capital is essential, both for the economy and society. Education can be seen as a good having productive aims that improve the income level of those who acquire education and also of society as a whole. At the same time, it is also a consumption good that allows greater enjoyment of higher goods of a cultural or artistic nature, and more significant participation in political and social life. Consumption of state education is fully divisible into units of sale, but a charge must not be imposed, except to a limited extent, in the form of school fees. If the entire cost had to be paid by users, the consumption of education would not necessarily continue up to the point where the marginal gain is equal to marginal costs, because:

1. part of the proceeds go to society in the form of 'technological' external economies, arising from the benefits that go to the advantage of productive processes and from the technological progress of the 'human capital' that is continuously enhanced through education;
2. part of the individual benefits are not adequately appreciated by those who should prompt the demand, due to 'short-sightedness' and also because only those who have received an education succeed in perceiving the advantage of being even more educated (see Chapter 3, subsections 2.6 and 2.8 on merit goods);
3. those who bear the costs are generally not those who benefit from the service, but rather the beneficiary's parents or whoever is entrusted with a young person's education, and this also involves an extensive band of compulsory schooling.

Public expenditure for education that is free (or almost free) of charge up to school-leaving age, and raising the school-leaving age to 16, belong to the class of conforming interventions (Röpke 1944 [1948]) for the co-operative model. Each individual thus achieves a genuine 'equality of starting points' and this is advantageous for them but also for the overall society.

Making education totally free of charge beyond the age of compulsory schooling raises a number of problems. It can be observed that those who make the greatest use of higher education generally – apart from exceptions, which are admirable – belong to medium or medium-high income families. Therefore, it can be argued that the absence of a charge for this type of education gives rise to a 'perverse' redistribution, except in the case of particularly meritorious subjects who generate particularly significant 'external economies' by virtue of the elevated quality of their human capital. A case can thus be made for an increase in fees with increasing educational steps, but allowing exemptions for high achievers and those from financially deprived backgrounds.

The fact that education is largely a public good does not, however, imply that it must necessarily be provided by the state or local public body. This is particularly true with regard to education beyond the compulsory schooling age, where the problem of quality control of private education is particularly delicate. It would be logical to provide 'school vouchers', especially for certain types of educational institutions such as those offering vocational training, and students could then use the vouchers to enrol at the school of their choice.

4.5 Sector III.D: Public Expenditure for Artistic and Cultural Goods and for Cultural Activities

This class of expenditure, in itself certainly meritorious[16] is subject to considerable distortions, while choice is rendered more difficult by the inevitable presence of value judgements (see Chapter 3, subsection 2.9).

These are, obviously, goods whose use allows divisible consumption.

Consider the case of artistic performances (music, theatre, exhibitions): the costs rise constantly, on account of 'Baumol's law' according to which there can be no development of labour productivity in these personal service sectors, but the remunerations must be made commensurate to the increase in per capita income generated by the growth in average productivity of the economy. Therefore, if the service is delivered at market prices, demand may decrease, as a result of the worsening price levels. Furthermore the costs of the cultural goods of archaeological, historical, or artistic value increase by another law similar to the one that applies to the health services in presence of an ageing population and of techonolgical developments (Forte, 'Introduction' to Mantovani, 2008).

Thus the arts, music, the cultural goods of museums and cities may deteriorate. On the other hand, we have seen that they form part of 'superior merit goods' (see Chapter 3, subsection 2.8). The action of the government – central and local – may be inadequate. The way out from this dilemma may consist in an increasing appeal to non-profit organizations and in a favourable tax policy for private support of these goods.

The fact remains that in order to correspond to the objectives of artistic and cultural freedom and pluralism of expression, there is good reason for

these forms of consumption to be made available more by non-profit associations and private individuals and enterprise and mixed private–public
insititutions acting in competition with one another, rather than by the
state (see Mantovani, 2008).

5   ANALYSIS OF EXPENDITURE BY FUNCTIONAL CLASSES: SOCIAL EXPENDITURE

5.1   Importance and Characteristics of the Welfare State

Expenditure for social insurance and social services, together with education expenditure, constitute the so-called 'welfare state'.[17]

As was pointed out earlier in the discussion on individual and collective welfare and on 'merit consumption' (Chapter 2, subsection 3.8 ff. and
Chapter 3, section 2) there are two conceptions of the 'welfare state': a
paternalistic approach, and the individualistic approach. The latter corresponds to the cooperative model. It should also be kept in mind that
there are two possible frameworks for the financing of social expenditure:
it can be achieved through the general system of public finance, or else on
the basis of specific contributions for the various classes of expenditure.
Furthermore, for each of these frameworks, two different paradigms can
be outlined: either a system composed of a single state-run management
for each large intervention sector (for instance, pensions or health care),
which gathers together all the contributions and from which all expenditure emanates, or else a system of bodies decentralized territorially or by
categories (for example industrial and commercial employees, craftsmen,
agricultural workers), with possible freedom of choice among competing
institutions. The latter paradigm most closely corresponds to the cooperative model in which, for normal citizens, the need for social insurance is
to be financed by the paradigm of 'Ulysses who ties himself to the mast'
(see Chapter 3, subsection 2.5), with expenses to be borne by the beneficiaries. But this paradigm should be kept separate from expenditure
designed to provide social assistance: the latter refers to the wants of
the less favoured, for whom financing cannot be carried out except by
transfers and public services, the expenses of which are borne by taxpayers in general. The other part of expenditure, namely social insurance
expenditure, is to be financed through the beneficiaries' contributions,
which should be commensurate with their personal income, and – broadly
speaking – the services delivered should correspond to the contributions,
with a mechanism based on the insurance principle (see Chapter 6, subsections 1.9–1.10). Since a certain portion of subjects who are entitled to be

covered by social insurance are unable to pay contributions (or can only pay a tiny amount) due to their low (or nil) personal income, the shortfall should be compensated by transfers from general taxation for a certain proportion of pension insurance, for which separate accounting records should be kept.

5.2 Analysis of the Details of Sector IV Expenditure A: Old Age Pensions

Among the large items of expenditure in the welfare state, this is the major aspect.[18] It rests on the assumption that social insurance and social assistance extend – as is normally the case in the present-day welfare state of industrialized countries – to all elderly citizens in order to guarantee them not merely a minimal pension but, additionally, a supplementary pension that is commensurate with their salary (or self-employed income), in relation to the contributions paid on their working income.

Generally (see Chapter 6, subsection 1.9) the so-called pay-as-you-go pension scheme is adopted, in which pensions are paid to pensioners with the contributions that are being collected from those who are actively in work. Thus this system does not require the contributions to be invested in order to fund a revenue, unlike the procedure that insurance companies have to adopt in order to guarantee their solvency (the latter being the so-called 'capitalization' system). This system of 'solidarity between generations' makes it possible to provide substantial pensions immediately, but it destroys savings, as it exempts current workers from saving for their own future, while failing to generate a corresponding provision set aside for reserves. It is thus a criterion that may not reflect the principle of 'conforming interventions' which should guide the cooperative model of the public economy, especially in cases where the public economy expands its expenditure enormously in order to solve the problems of the social insurance wants of the 'welfare state'.

The mechanism of 'obligatory contributions', detached from any relation with the pension it will give a right to, does not act as a guarantee that the part of public expenditure financed in this manner will not weigh on the ordinary fiscal system: rather, it is a mechanism that lends itself to generating a masked public debt, the fiscal burden of which will be manifested in the future (Peacock, 1992).

Therefore, to restore the concept of saving for one's old age, it appears appropriate to allow the development of freely chosen private 'supplementary pension' insurances, by exemption of their premiums from personal income tax. Since the same is done for the social insurance contributions, this cannot be regarded as a privilege.

5.3 Unemployment Allowance, Redundancy Benefit ('*Cassa Integrazione Guadagni*')

The overall 'social insurance' system does not consist only of provision for the wants of senior citizens. It also concerns wants that arise from gaps in income or family responsibilities or particular problems during normal periods of life (see Table 7.7).

Table 7.7   Analysis of social expenditure (Sector IV)

A.	Social insurance expenditure	Old age pensions Disability pensions Unemployment allowance and redundancy benefit (*Cassa integrazione guadagni*) Child allowance Sickness benefit Maternity allowance
B.	Social assistance expenses	Poverty allowance Old age assistance Assistance for emigrants and immigrants Disabled assistance Assistance for neglected children Drug rehabilitation programmes Former prisoners' assistance programmes Destitute or statutory funeral arrangements
C.	Health care expenses	Medical expenses Pharmaceutical expenses Outpatient and hospital expenses Preventive medicine Hygiene expenses Maternity and legal abortion expenses
D.	Social consumption and investment expenses for social public indemnities	Subsidized housing (social housing) Housing rent vouchers (for the poor and the evicted) Basic necessities distributed free of charge to the less favoured War pensions for widows and orphans Compensation payments for natural disasters
E.	Aid to poor countries	Subsidies to international agencies Credit aid Grants for direct interventions Financing of private non-governmental organizations

Naturally, the unemployment allowance should not be paid to those who 'refuse to work', for instance to anyone who has received three successive job offers and has rejected them. Even if the allowance is financed through labour contributions, the fund will go into deficit during periods of depression in which the number of unemployed increases. Therefore, the criterion of balancing the budget 'in the cyclical budget' should be applied here. The same holds true for redundancy benefit funds (*cassa integrazione guadagni*) in relation to 'prolonged crises', when the disbursement is a preliminary action prior to possible unemployment.[19]

5.4 Child Allowance

The child allowance is based on the solidarity principle according to which the income that gives the basic minimum living requirements should be commensurate not only with the product of labour but also with maintenance of family responsibilities that involve children under working age. This problem cannot be addressed by individual enterprises, because if it were established that the wage should include the upkeep of a family, then those who have a larger family would be the last to be hired and the first to be dismissed.

With the gradual rise in income from permanent employment and the greater availability of work, the 'social need' for child allowances diminishes. Naturally, with a decrease in the number of children the extent of the problem is further reduced, but this may generate external diseconomies. Thus instead of adopting the criterion of support for the less favoured, child allowances may be conceived as a structural intervention of demographic policy, to take into account the external economies generated for the community by families that have children and bring up the new generations, averting or inverting the adverse effects resulting from demographic decline.[20]

5.5 Disability Allowances for Accidents in the Workplace

In principle, disability allowances have the character of an insurance: they are granted to those who have suffered a permanent disability due to an accident on the job. Therefore they should be financed through compulsory contributions to be borne by enterprises and commensurate with the risk. But it can be argued that there is no reason for such a form of 'social insurance' to be managed by the public economy. If one assumes that an enterprise will be reluctant to insure the workers against accidents because this represents an additional cost, then it could be established that accident insurance is compulsory and is to be chosen on the market. Making it compulsory could be justified by the further assumption that workers themselves may be disinclined to contemplate insurance, because they are under pressure to provide for their immediate needs so that they prefer present utility and underestimate future risk, and would rather have better pay (or merely that job without any accident insurance). However, private insurance goes against the principle that cover is compulsory as a means to guarantee full protection and not a lesser degree of protection, which might be preferred because of 'improvidence'.

5.6   B: Social Assistance Expenditure

The principle of assistance both in monetary terms and also with provision of goods and personal services for the less favoured belongs to the great criteria of equity that the public economy based on the cooperative social contract can in no way dispense with (see Chapter 2, subsections 3.9–3.14).

However, there is a difference between the model that involves a number of different modes of action in relation to the multiplicity of different wants, and the model founded on automatic granting of a 'minimum income' to the needy – commensurate with their degree of need – that is a 'negative income tax', which the needy may then utilize as they see fit (see Chapter 3, subsection 3.2).

5.7   C: Public Health Care Expenditure Against Compulsory Health Care Insurance

It can be argued that the need for 'compulsory social insurance' in the sector of expenditure on health care could be satisfied by establishing that each citizen has an obligation to take out insurance cover, rather than by provision through the public health service.

But one can argue against such a solution by pointing out that demand and supply in the sphere of health care are particularly affected by problems of informational asymmetries and moral hazard.[21] Assuming that the insurance premium cannot vary in relation to any opportunistic behaviours, an individual with few scruples or lacking respectfulness may – once she is insured – feel no compunction about seeing a doctor over the slightest cold or headache, and asking for tests and diagnoses and hospitalization every time she fears there may be something wrong with her.

There is, however, a further informational asymmetry: the individual does not know, either exactly or approximately, which cases she should take seriously, that is which cases genuinely require making use of the health care provision and securing the services which are appropriate according to the present state of the art. If she turns to a private insurance arrangement, who can guarantee that the menu offered by the insurance company is truly in 'her interest'? On the other hand, there exist considerable economies of scale in some important segments of this service, and this suggests that coordination of supply is advisable. A mixed public–private supply system with competition among the various subjects appears to be preferable.

5.8   Health Care in the Paternalistic Model of the Public Economy

With regard to health care, the paternalistic model of the welfare state prescribes that the general system of taxation should provide the right for people to have whatever treatment is necessary for their health, in hospital or as out-patients, or medical and pharmaceutical treatment, on the basis of prescriptions issued by National Health Service doctors free from any economic influence. All treatment is provided at zero cost to the patient, and all patients are treated equally and have no possibility of choice among service providers.

The market is thereby completely eliminated. However, given the characteristics of the demand and the tendency of the supply to display strategic behaviour, in a monopoly regime, this model applied in its pure form faces an insurmountable financial crisis, quite apart from objections concerning freedom of choice and efficiency.

Moreover, with the above delineated construct, the 'sovereignty of the public health provision apparatus' cannot fail to translate into bureaucratic power that swells the expenses, while paying scant regard to the quality of the service.

5.9   Health Care in the Cooperative Model of the Public Economy. The Contributive System and Prescription Charges

The cooperative model cannot allow the suppression of freedom of choice, even if one sets aside the advantages in terms of important issues of efficiency. Freedom of choice can be accomplished both by having a multiplicity of operators and private and public services on the market, in competition with one another, and by setting up decentralized collective decision-making, and by supplementing compulsory public social insurance with complementary arrangements involving private insurance companies, and limiting public health care provision – for 'normal' persons – to essential medication, sickness and major operations, and fundamental tests.

This observation also prompts the suggestion that in addition to contributions for the overall health service, 'tickets' should be adopted (that is subsidized prices), for individual services that carry a relatively modest cost, with regard to which a non-risk-averse subject would be prepared to forgo insurance cover, if they were not protected by the National Health Service. It is obvious that someone who pays a price, however small, will avoid superfluous consumption.

> This notwithstanding, in Italy the 'tickets' for medication available only at pharmacies upon presentation of a prescription by a National Health Service physician were repealed in 2000, on the eve of general elections.

'Tickets' for hospital services could also be proposed with the aim of discouraging strategic behaviour by hospital staff, as a means of thwarting the tendency to prolong the duration of hospitalization in order to obtain more substantial funding, when funds are subsidized by the government in relation to output volume. However, considerations of vertical equity imply that 'life-saving' medication and treatment for very serious pathologies and states of need should be exempted from such charges.

Regionalization of the system may increase freedom of choice in collective decision-making concerning what services to provide, because each region can modify the contributions and prescription charges in relation to service efficiency and also in relation to the variety of additional services.

5.10   The Good Samaritan

It may be rational to give users the right to choose their preferred public health unit, even beyond the confines of the health care units of their own region. Naturally, this unit will have the right to claim back from the patient's own health care unit the cost for the various services provided.

> The suggestion has also been put forward of granting each citizen a sort of 'global yearly voucher' for the national health service, on the understanding that whatever remains unspent on the voucher by virtue of a citizen's thrift is hers to keep (or, say, roughly 70 per cent of the savings). But this proposal is dangerous because it prompts irrational choices that would tend to save on one's own health, and in any case it eliminates the 'guardianship' principle whereby the community as a whole, being more provident than the individual in everyday choices, 'binds' her to a mode of behaviour guided by far-sighted providence, and thus requires her to pay contributions which will grant her the right to treatment in relation to her state of 'need for health'.

5.11   The Problem of 'Tragic Choices' in the Health Care Sector

A physician or a surgical team cannot 'serve' more than a given number of users, at any given date or period of time.

A hospital only has a certain number of beds and the corresponding extent of equipment, and it has no interest in extending the number of beds, if demand is destined to be fluctuating. Furthermore, the number of specialists is limited. Organ transplant banks have a systematically lower supply compared to demand.

Therefore rationing systems will inevitably have to be adopted, but considerations of equity clearly rule out the hypothesis of selecting users of essential public health care facilities on the basis of their willingness to pay a price.

Two conflicting criteria can be discerned in this connection: that of awarding priority to residents, and that of awarding priority to the most serious cases and the most urgent operations. Reflections in the available literature on this issue suggest that cost–benefit analyses are particularly important in the health care sector (in the absence of significant monetary measures, this will often have to be performed with ordinal criteria, referring to a value ranking of the outcomes), and likewise also cost-efficacy analyses (see Kliemt, 2008).

NOTES

1. It derives from A.C. Pigou, *A Study in Public Finance*, in the various editions. For the 'transformations' Pigou, in the third edition (1947), employed the term 'non-transfer'. Initially he had employed the term 'exhaustive', which seemed to imply that they were always unproductive.
2. Examples of the first type include contracts awarded by the different public administrations to private enterprises for works and supplies of various kinds: supply of computerized facilities for services involving relations with the public such as the public registry of births, marriages and deaths, supply of ecology services, renting and leasing of fully-equipped schools and hospitals.

   Among examples of the second type, one can mention purchases of pharmaceutical drugs upon presentation of a National Health Service prescription at any pharmacy; or the so-called 'school voucher', that is the possibility granted to certain citizens having the appropriate prerequisites to avail themselves of certain educational services at designated institutions, which will then be refunded by the state; or also, the 'health voucher', which represents an analogous opportunity to avail oneself of medical treatment free of charge at authorized private clinics, or a 'culture voucher' for free museum trips, and so on.
3. The United Nations does not have any fiscal power. The European Union has extremely limited tax power.
4. This may be the case with regional or local consumption taxes that have different tax rates or which, having been levied by the producer, go to the benefit of the local government where the producer is located, rather than to the local government where the consumers who bear the actual incidence of the charge are located.
5. Transfers to the poor Regions and municipalities from an equalization fund financed by the affluent Regions and municipalities are meant to avoid unfair distribution of the tax burden between the different areas.
6. The term 'trust goods' was introduced by B. Blankart; see Chapter 3, subsection 2.7.

7. Military expenditure ranges, today, from 5 per cent of the *gross product* in countries like the USA and the UK, to 3 per cent in countries like Italy, which have a lower defence burden.
8. See Krohm (1973).
9. Similarly for tax evasion; Chapter 8, section 15.
10. Mazzola (1890). The theory of 'conditional goods' applies not only to production but also to consumption. Today nobody would like to live in a place lacking roads, water, sewerage, telephone facilities, electricity, street lighting, waste collection and postal services. Districts deficient in these services are considered to be 'blighted'. However, Mazzola's formulation which claims that all public wants are conditional upon consumption or upon the production of other goods appears excessive (see Chapter 3). Also many conditional wants may be satisfied by the market, without any need for public expenditure, as they are divisible into units of sale for which demand exceeds the costs (for instance, having a telephone line or being hooked up to the electricity supply in suburban areas, and so on).
11. See Chapter 3, subsection 1.13–1.14. The connection between the issues dealt with in the two paragraphs with regard to the reassurance theorem and the theorem of decreasing costs of industries and areas is also crucial.
12. See previous note.
13. Say (1803 [1841, 1867]). The position was mitigated in Say (1828–29 [1840]). Here Say introduces the distinction between expenses for productive consumption (such as expenditure on roads and other public works) and unproductive consumption, that is consumption properly speaking. In other words, he admits that part of public expenditure is not consumption-related but rather production-related. According to F. Forte and C. Magazzino (2010), the optimal size of the government (measured in size of public expenditure) in relation to economic growth, for Italy would be 37.68 per cent of GDP, against the effective rate of 51.52 per cent in 2009. For the UK the optimal size would be 43.50 against an effective rate of 51.17. For Germany it would be 41.99 against 47.64, for France 39.49 against 55.15, and for Denmark 38.63 against 55.41.
14. In any case, in Italy, this expenditure amounts to little more than 8 per cent of the gross product, a large part of which (6 per cent) is for education. Public expenditure for the artistic and cultural heritage is a small figure: 0.5 per cent of GDP, including the local authorities.
15. On the need to apply prices, to the greatest extent possible, for divisible consumption so that users can choose the goods they prefer and avoid taxes – which are also levied on what one dislikes – and avoid losing direct control over cost increases that come about when users are called upon to share in them, see Seldon (1977). For artistic and cultural goods see Forte and Mantovani (2000).
16. For the problems pertaining to this class, see Forte and Mantovani (2004).
17. Public expenditure for social insurance and social assistance, including health care, amounts to more than 20 per cent of GDP in Italy, that is about half of global public expenditure gross of interest.
18. In Italy this expenditure amounts to 13–14 per cent of GDP.
19. In Italy there is also a redundancy benefit fund (*'cassa integrazione guadagni'*) for temporary interruption of work. This is an illogical scheme for the public economy, as it is not logical for there to be a 'public want' in favour of enterprises which, by contract, have undertaken to pay a worker a monthly wage and then cannot maintain the payment because – for sudden unexpected reasons – utilization of the contracted workforce cannot be maintained.
20. It should be recalled that in the terminology adopted here, the expression 'structural policies' is used in the Röpke meaning, to designate action that respects the principle of allocational optimality under 'freedom of choice' which is proper to the welfare function of the cooperative model.
21. Clerico (1984) and bibliography therein.

8. Public revenue and the tax burden

1 INTRODUCTORY CONCEPTS

Public revenues (see Table 8.1) are generally the means utilized to finance public expenditure. However, they can also be conceived as a direct tool of public finance, to fulfil aims of economic and social regulation, and these objectives may at times be pursued independently of that of covering public expenditure.[1]

> In the cooperative model, however, the non-fiscal utilization of public revenue plays a limited role. This is partly because it is admissible only for 'conforming interventions', but partly also because a predominantly non-fiscal use of tax dues contrasts with the general principle of taxation, understood as the 'fiscal price' for public services or as a collective burden on whoever produces external diseconomies.
>
> The 'conforming interventions' that are in line with the model examined here include taxes designed to restrict what are regarded as forms of demerit consumption, on the basis of the principle of Ulysses tied to the mast (see Chapter 3, subsection 2.5), and also phenomena related to external diseconomies. Tax on tobacco and spirits can be cited as an example in which a levy is imposed on demerit consumption instead of prohibitions that deprive the consumer of freedom of choice.

Certain exceptions to the requirement that public expenditure be covered through *recurrent receipts* (Table 8.1, A and B) may be made, but they have a limited nature.

> Cases may arise where a government resolves to cover expenses by selling financial and real assets. But this form of funding should preferably be used to reduce the public debt, or for investment expenditure, in order to avoid inflicting damage on future citizens. Moreover, this method – although considerably effective for a certain period – cannot be used over a prolonged period of time to provide for the public expenses of a modern state. This is because the government's assets that can be privatized without compromising the provision of public services represent only a part of the overall national wealth, while public expenditure accounts for a considerable portion of the national income, which, in turn, stands in a particular relation with the national wealth (in developed countries with per capita GDP like that of Italy, this relation stands at 1 to 4).
>
> A state like Italy, which has accumulated a large volume of financial and real assets, either directly or indirectly in public bodies and public enterprises that

Table 8.1   Sources of public revenue

A. *Main recurrent receipts*
   a) Levies in the strict sense:
      1) taxes,
      2) special charges and obligatory social contributions.
   b) Prices for the public services and fees:
      1) quasi-private prices,
      2) public economic prices (covering the full costs),
      3) political prices (lower than the full cost),
      4) monopoly tax-prices (exceeding the full cost by monopolistic behaviour),
      5) fees.
B. *Secondary recurrent receipts*
   a) issue of banknotes (by debts with the central bank);
   b) issuance of public debt on the market within the limits allowed by a sustainable debt burden (see Chapter 13, section 10).
C. *Secondary non-recurrent or marginal receipts*
   a) public debt in excess of the limits under Bb),
   b) privatizations,
   c) revenue in nature without compensation or with partial compensation,
   d) fines, pecuniary penalties, compensations for damage, transfers from foreign states and private individuals to the government considered.

---

are part of the state or of the local governments, has an excellent reason for privatizing financial and real assets in order to redeem part of the public debt, especially when their private management promises greater effectiveness and efficiency than their public utilization.

However, there is a contrast between the interests of the 'bureaucratic Leviathan' that does not want to privatize anything at all and those of the politicians who want to pursue the interest of the state as the expression of the citizens.[2]

2   REQUISITIONING, WORK INJUNCTIONS AND EXPROPRIATION WITHOUT COMPENSATION

A second possible exception to recourse to current receipts (Table 8.1, A and B and Table 8.2) consists of direct procurement of factors, products and assets by the government, using coercive methods such as food product requisitioning, compulsory unpaid work, expropriation of property without compensation, and so on.

Unpaid or only part-paid individual work is a limited source of public revenue. First, there are sectors where services cannot be obtained with compulsory coercive action, on pain of low quality of work. But above all,

Table 8.2   Sources of public revenue and the tax burden

*(The example of Italy, Consolidated account of the 'General Government',
Year 2000, in percentage over GDP)*

Direct taxes	14.5%
Indirect taxes	15.6%
Social contributions	12.8%
Other current receipts	2.9%
Total current receipts	45.7%
Capital receipts	0.6%
Total receipts	46.3%
Tax burden	43.5%

Main taxes
(ITALY, State, in % over GDP = 1.000 billion euros)

Direct taxes		Indirect taxes	
Personal income tax	9.7	VAT	5.2
Corporate income tax	1.7	Other taxes on business transactions	0.6
Other	1.9	Vehicle tax	0.07
Total direct taxes	13.3	State television licence	0.1
		Mineral oils excise	1.5
		Spirit and miscellaneous excise tax	0.5
		Tobacco excise	0.5
		Lotto and lotteries	0.6
		Other	0.6
Total state tax revenue	23.2	Total indirect taxes	9.84

Notes
The table is purely indicative of the orders of magnitude and therefore it has not been
updated. Vehicle tax, if the share pertaining to the regional and local bodies is added,
amounts to 0.45% of GDP.
   The main direct local taxes are the property tax on immovable wealth (ICI), 0.83% of
GDP, and the Regional tax on production (IRAP) 2%.
   The municipal solid waste collection tax gives 0.35% of GDP.

the functioning of the market economy places a clear limit on direct coercive procurement of personal resources by the government, because such a
system would place all individuals at the mercy of the state power.

   To limit arbitrary action by the fiscal power, modern constitutions of
market economies rule out product, asset and personal service requisitioning unless compensation is awarded. Thus the incision of property rights

done by the government to meet its public finance needs can be done exclusively through the taxation. And in our legal systems expropriation, requisitioning and work injunctions involve a public expenditure not very different from the burden which would result from procuring such resources on the market.

3   THE CANONS OF TAXATION

Taxes (as well as the other compulsory contributions such as those of social security) are obligatory monetary levies collected by the fiscal power in favour of the public budgets as a means of financing public expenditure and/or secondarily for purposes of economic and social regulation.

Taxes are contributions that are not linked to the advantages or costs of specific items of public expenditure. Rather, they serve to cover expenses which it would be impossible or undesirable to divide, and at times, to tamper with the economic and social process.[3]

We can present an overview, based on F. Neumark (1970), of the major canons of taxation in a market economy system.[4] To a large extent, with the exception of those listed under I and IV, they represent a synopsis of the main aspects dealt with in previous chapters, in Chapter 10 on optimal taxation, and in Chapter 13 on fiscal policy.

I   *Fiscal and budget canons*
  1. Canon of the adequacy of the revenue obtained by the tax levy.
  2. Canon of the capacity of adaptation to budget requirements (suitability of revenue increase by increasing the considered taxes).
II   *Ethical-political canons*
  1. Postulate of justice:
  a) Canon of the generality of taxation;
  b) Canon of the equality of taxation;
  c) Canon of adaptation to conditions, that is the principle of the tax levy according to the individual capacity to pay of the various persons, partly also in relation to consumption of public goods (see section 6).
  2. Canon of fiscal redistribution towards the less favoured in relation to situations of particular need.
III   *Canons of fiscal policy*
  1. Principles of public policy pertaining to intervention in the economy:
  a) canon of '*non placet*' with regard to dirigisme;

b) canon of minimization of interference in the private sphere and in individual freedom to avail of one's disposable income;

c) canon of '*non placet*' with regard to tax levies that interfere with competition and which would lead to undesirable consequences (Neumark states that only 'conforming interventions' in the sense of Röpke (1944 [1948]) are acceptable, that is interventions that remove distortions and promote competition); (see the treatment of horizontal equity in Chapter 6, subsection 1.5).

2. Principles of macroeconomic fiscal policy:

a) canon of 'active' (or 'deliberated') flexibility of taxation;

b) canon of 'passive' (or 'incorporated') flexibility, whereby taxation has structural characteristics such that the tax revenue automatically decreases during the trough of the business cycle and rises during the cyclical upswing when there is a danger of inflation;

c) canon of the orientation of taxation towards a growth policy, in particular with tax relief for investment in technology and for research expenditure.

IV *Legal and technical canons*

1. Canon of (relative) simplicity, reciprocal non-contradictoriness and systematic coherence of tax laws, to reduce transaction costs in the process of application of tax levies.

2. Canon of transparency of fiscal measures.

3. Canon of practicability of tax laws.

4. Canon of stability of tax laws.

5. Canon of non-costliness, not only in the sense of 'no excess of burden' with respect to revenue of the tax (on which see Chapter 9 and 10), but also in the sense that the cost borne by the administration in levying taxes should not exceed a reasonable percentage of the revenue obtained.

6. Canon of ease of payment.

4 LIMITS ON THE POWER OF TAXING

The issue of limits on the power to tax has always existed, but for a certain period it was believed that it was sufficient to observe the principle holding that a tax should be laid down by the law and that such a law should be voted by the representative assemblies, in a universal suffrage regime. This is no longer sufficient. In order to avert exploitative domination by the majority over the minority it is necessary to set constitutional limits on the tax laws approved by majority voting.[5] Thus the principle that a tax is established by a law (already mentioned in Chapter 6, subsection 1.5 with regard to the generality of the rules *)* – essential though it is in a democratic system – is of no avail in setting a limit on taxation. However, it does serve to protect citizens against the exercise of arbitrary power in matters of taxation: the law is 'equal for everyone', and cannot vary from case to case. This means that the system of taxation does not depend on the discretion of whoever holds the reins of political power or of whatever body is concretely in charge of managing tax collection, whether it be the revenue service and the related bureaucracy, customs and excise officers and similar enforcement authorities, a tax law judge or an ordinary court judge.

Despite this, the complexity and ambiguity of tax legislation often result in circumstances where it appears difficult to eliminate the discretionary power of bureaucrats and of ministerial officers, a power which the Constitution excludes from determining the essential characters of taxation: the passive subject, the taxable base and the rate.

The intricacy of tax laws is often due to the fact that pressure groups have a specific interest in blurring their formulation in order to extort special dispensations and attenuations in their own favour. It is also because the halls of parliament are an inadequate venue for careful specialist framing of technical texts such as tax legislation, and additionally, because the bureaucracy prefers to retain a certain discretionary ascendancy.

That a tax should be endowed with certainty is, moreover, an essential prerequisite for it to be a market-conforming intervention, and to ensure that it does not contradict the 'need for security' which is the first reason why citizens accept to submit to the power of the state. From this point of view the principle of non-retroactive application of a tax is a highly relevant issue: a tax must be endowed with certainty at the moment when the subject has availability of the taxable base to which the tax refers.

The certainty of a tax requires simplification, but this involves relinquishing perfectionism both from the point of view of abstract equity, and from that of allocative optimality.[6]

5 THE RULE WHEREBY TAXES CAN BE LEVIED ONLY ON THOSE WHO BENEFIT FROM PUBLIC EXPENDITURE

The power to levy taxes – in a modern state respecting the individual rights of a free society, and particularly in the cooperative model – is conditional upon the individual duty to contribute to public expenditure. The state cannot expect to be able to tax whatever person, thing or activity comes within arm's reach, but must limit itself to demanding taxes from persons and goods that have a link with its public services. Therefore only *citizens*, or more convincingly *residents* (whether citizens or otherwise), as well as enterprises and industrial plants domiciled within its borders, the economic activities conducted within its territory and the assets located therein can be subjected to a tax levy.

6   THE CRITERION OF ABILITY TO PAY

Taxes cannot be imposed in total disregard of the individual economic situations affected, if the aim is for society to thrive and individual citizens to be able to bear the burden.

This leads to the emergence of the criterion of so-called 'ability to pay' (already mentioned in Chapter 6, section 1, with regard to the principle of the fiscal constitution). This criterion is rooted – *ideally* – in two considerations: on the one hand allocative arguments of economic tolerability and distributive equity with regard to subjects affected by the incidence of taxation, and on the other, criteria of global 'quid pro quo', and thus of allocative correctness, in relation to the overall benefits of public expenditure for the various classes and species of taxpayers and taxable elements.

> The criterion of ability to pay is stated in the Italian Constitution in a vague and tautological manner, as it is not easy to define by means of a formula. It has often been considered – by public finance scholars – to be an 'empty box', in reaction to the way this term has been abused, on occasion at the hands of utilitarian economists, on other occasions through the attempts of those who sought to offer some sort of justification for every new tax excogitated by politicians.

In essence, ability to pay consists of four basic elements: a relation, albeit generic, with public expenditure (by virtue of the principle of territoriality or residence or at least citizenship); the existence of an 'economic situation' consisting of economic capacity; the possibility of devolving a certain portion of this capacity to the government without severely compromising one's private choices; and 'monetization', that is the availability of 'liquidity' in order to pay. Taxes should not be levied on the increments of values of real and financial assets when such increases arise in the market evaluation but are not yet recorded in the balance sheets. They should be taxed only when the assets are sold or the capital gains are recorded in the balance sheet of the firm so that the taxpayer gets the liquidity from the transfer or from the increased capacity of obtaining credit on the market. The requisite of liquidity also involves a prohibition against retroactive taxes, as the taxpayer may no longer have the availability of the previous taxable matter. Similarly, the requirement of the 'capacity of devolving a certain portion of the taxable matter to the government without severely compromising one's private choices' likewise leads – among other things – to a prohibition on retroactive taxes: a taxpayer must be able to know her tax liabilities when she makes her choices, not *ex post*.[7]

From the point of view of both the first and the second aspect, income and consumed income and capital constitute the basic reference of capacity to pay. And since capital has value in terms of the physical or psychological income that can be derived therefrom, that is to say in relation to purchasing power (see Chapter 2, section I, the concept of economic welfare as capacity for choice), disposable income is the prime indicator of *ability to pay*. Disposable income can be defined in various ways, depending on whether reference is being made to the macroeconomic and global perspective or to the microeconomic and individual perspective. In the latter profile it can also be defined with reference to 'capacity for choice' and the other aspects of objective and subjective utility.

From the objective point of view of the overall economy, the income is the yearly national product plus the net receipts from abroad, minus those that are paid abroad without gainful purpose or to honour obligations entered into.

From the microeconomic point of view of the single enterprise or individual and in the profile of capacity for choice, income can be defined as every net *disposable* proceed obtained during the year, on the assumption that the value of one's estate and assets remains unchanged at the end of the tax year in comparison to the beginning of the tax year. Any variations achieved and therefore disposable are summed algebraically with net proceeds.

Thus if an asset of a private individual such as a home increases in value not as a result of a sale but only through a calculation concerning the variation in market prices, in a market-conforming system of taxation, then the increase in value does not affect the individual's capacity to pay, because she can hardly be expected to sell a room of her own home to settle a hypothetical resulting tax liability.[8]

There are many economists who argue that only consumed income is real income, because it is the only type of income that gives final satisfaction. But this goes back to the point of view of welfare as utility = pleasure, and not as 'capacity for choice', whereas 'capacity for choice' appears to be the only plausible measure of individual welfare. Also, if one conceives taxes as prices of public services, one cannot argue that the income saved has not been produced with the contribution of the public services. This is not to deny that consumption can indeed be a measure of capacity to pay, linked to public expenditure for consumption on the part of central and local governments.

7 THE TAX BURDEN

The overall amount of taxes imposed on a subject i, in relation to i's income, gives rise to what is known as the individual 'tax burden': $T_i/R_i = P_i$ the tax burden on i. Similarly, for the overall economy, T/R indicates the overall tax burden, that is the relation between *tax revenue* and the official *gross national income* or *gross domestic product* (GDP).

The tax burden tends to vary from subject to subject, and may – for the same individual i – change over time and in relation to the different choices she undertakes.

But this apparently simple concept becomes more complicated as soon as one conceives of T_i/R_i as the set of all the tax dues to which i is subject, multiplied by her taxable bases *ex ante* and then set in relation with her income as modified by the tax charge, or, alternatively, if we see T_i as the tax revenue that i pays as a result of these tax rates and taxable bases, whether directly, as a taxpayer nominally required to pay, or through a *withholding agent* (the employer) who pays on her behalf, or through a person who is legally responsible for payment of the tax but who has effectively passed the tribute on to her by means of economic shifting of the tax. Indeed because of taxes and to lighten their burden, taxpayers frequently modify their conduct and thus their taxable base.

> For example, i may decide to repair her own sink, she will transform part of her garden into a vegetable patch, she will redecorate the interior walls of her home by herself instead of hiring a painter, and will take on less paid work so as to manage her personal income tax return, her corporate income tax and her VAT accounts rather than pay an accountant. The incomes of i are thus reduced, after tax, on account of the taxpayer's *fiscal planning*, and the greater the period of time elapsed since this was introduced, the more their incomes will be reduced. That is to say, the individual *ex ante* tax burden is different from the *ex post* tax burden, after the tax has modified the taxpayer's choice (see Chapter. 9 on the income and formulation effects of taxes).

8 THE LAFFER CURVE

The national tax burden, which is measured as the relation between the revenue obtained from taxes and the Gross National Product, is therefore an *ex post* concept, and it is obviously influenced by this circumstance. Laffer expressed this concept with a curve that was already in use among economists but was considered of minor importance; it would thereafter be known as the 'Laffer curve'.[9]

On the x-axis in Figure 8.1 we place the *ex ante* tax burden, T/R, measured as the ratio between the tax rate T and the taxable base, *ex ante*,

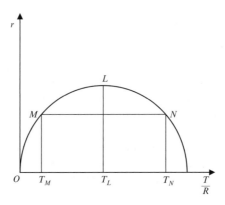

Figure 8.1   The Laffer curve

referring any taxable bases and all tax rates to the income R. On the y-axis
we place the tax revenue r. It grows as T/R rises, but not indefinitely. With
the tax rate T_L, a maximum point L is reached, after which the increase in
the tax rate induces a reduction in R, leading to a decreasing tax revenue r.

Thus the tax rate T_N at point N corresponds to $T_N/R > T_L/R$, but the
revenue r is less than in L and is equal to that given by the tax rate T_M, at
point M. This is particularly true if what is considered is not the revenue
r of a single year, but that of a longer period, because taxpayers with an
excessive tax burden increase their fiscal planning in order to pay less,
their evasion accumulates and they engage in a lower amount of business
activity and work less or go abroad, while the flow of investments from
abroad decreases. The process is symmetrical as well. When taxes and/
or social insurance contributions are reduced, individuals and enterprises
increase their level of employment, and they invest and save more in the
country where the lowering of the tax burden is carried out. This process
takes some time. Therefore the increase in taxable bases and revenue due
to lower taxes is manifested after a time lag (see Fedeli and Forte, 2009a).

However, since the national income R that is obtained with the tax rate
T_N is less than that obtainable with the tax rate T_M, what we will have, *ex
post*, is the paradoxical fact that under equal revenue, $T_M/R_M < T_N/R_N$,
that is to say, a lower tax rate can give a higher revenue with a lower tax
burden.

With T_N/R_N, private individuals' capacity for choice on the market has
decreased more than the increase in their collective capacity for choice;
thus even on the assumption that they may appreciate public goods somewhat more than the private goods, if this decrease is substantial then taxpayers feel they have been damaged. Hence the 'rational fiscal protest'.

The reduction in taxes and social insurance contributions can, on the basis of what was noted earlier in reflections on the Laffer curve, generate increases in revenue which partially or entirely compensate, or even exceed, those deriving from the previous tax rates. But this takes effect over time, as pointed out above. *Therefore the Laffer curve is not a static concept, but should be viewed within a time perspective.* Furthermore, it prompts the suggestion that the national tax burden *ex post* (the revenue/GDP ratio) can increase with taxes lower than the existing ones (Fedeli et al., 2008; Fedeli and Forte, 2008). Therefore it is not always a valid instrument for comparing the aggregate tax burden in the different economic systems.

9   PROGRESSIVE, PROPORTIONAL AND REGRESSIVE TAXATION

A tax system can be proportional, progressive or regressive with respect to the various classes of possessors of income or to GDP or per capita income, depending on whether the overall complex of taxes is a constant, increasing or decreasing percentage to GDP or to individual incomes. A similar argument holds in relation to GDP or individual incomes of the various regions or provinces of a given nation.

Finally, the proportional, progressive or regressive ratio of taxation with respect to GDP or individuals' incomes may be observed by examining taxation over time: a tax system which always collects the same share of GDP (or per capita income) as the latter rises is proportional, in the dynamic sense; if it collects a rising share, then it is a progressive tax system, and regressive if it collects a decreasing share.

But the three mathematical concepts of proportional, progressive and regressive ratio also hold in relation to the taxable base of the various taxes.

Any tax is said, in general, to be proportional if it always constitutes the same fixed percentage of the taxable base considered (for example if it is always 20 per cent), regardless of whether the taxable base increases or decreases.

A tax is progressive if it varies more than proportionally with variation in the taxable base: if, for instance, it is 10 per cent for low taxable bases and the first portion of medium-low taxable bases, then is 20 per cent, 30 per cent, and so on.

A tax is regressive if it varies less than proportionally with variation in the taxable base (for example 30 per cent for low taxable bases, 20 per cent for medium-low bases, and so on).

There are a number of different techniques for implementing progressivity, and these have different effects:

- by detraction or deduction;
- by tax brackets;
- by classes;
- with a continuous formula.

The first technique is implemented by a fixed detraction from the tax or a fixed deduction from the taxable base, and then with a constant rate above this allowance (for example the first 1000 euros are not taxed, but without this allowance the income is taxed at 20 per cent. Clearly, for a (gross) tax base of 2000 euros, which, after the allowance of 1000 euros, becomes a *net* tax base of 1000 euros, the overall tax rate is only 10 per cent, for a base of 5000 it is 16 per cent and for a base of 10000 it is 18 per cent).

Progressivity by tax brackets is implemented by subdividing each taxable base into successive brackets and applying to each one a different tax rate (for example 10 per cent on the first 1000 euros or fraction thereof, 15 per cent on the subsequent 1000 or fraction thereof, 20 per cent on the third 1000 or fraction thereof, and so on). This form of progressivity serves to implement vertical equity on all fractions of taxable base, as in the other two forms described below, but it is better suited to a moderately progressive cooperative model than is the case with the other forms in question (see Chapter 4, section 7).

A less refined and harsher method is progressivity by classes: taxpayers with taxable bases up to 1000 euros pay 10 per cent on their entire taxable base; those with no more than 2000 pay, let us say, 15 per cent on that entire taxable base; those with no more than 3000 pay 20 per cent on the entire base, and so on. This gives rise to large jumps in the tax rate when passing from one taxable base class to another.

As a consequence, after the tax, the income relations between income classes may be inverted, with a larger class ending up in the position of a previously smaller class. For example, if a 10 per cent tax is imposed on an income of 10000 euros and incomes up to 20000 are taxed at 20 per cent, then after tax an income of 11000 becomes 8800 and one of 10000 becomes 9000.

At the opposite extreme stands continuous progressivity, configured with perfectionism because applied with a mathematical formula, such that, for example, to each additional 100 euros there corresponds a slightly higher tax rate. This requires taxpayers to engage in complicated and bothersome minutiae of calculations.

Its mathematical perfection by no means makes up for the nuisance, given that progressivity, as we will see, is a concept that is hard to relate to rigorous concepts of justice. Furthermore, it harbours the risk that the formula may have no ceiling, beyond a certain income.

Usually, tax systems that contain progressive taxation are progressive over time because, at unchanged tax rates and detractions and deductions, the taxable bases tend to move up gradually towards the higher tax brackets on account of the real and monetary increase in GDP, in per capita real income and in monetary income.

Price increases considered close to monetary stability, at an inflation rate lower than 2 per cent per year may, within a few years, generate a sharpening of progressivity, even in an economy stagnant in real terms, thus making growth more difficult.

10   DISTRIBUTION OF THE TAX BURDEN AND THE PRINCIPLES OF TAX EQUITY: LIMITS OF THE MINIMUM SACRIFICE PRINCIPLE

The principle of the minimum sacrifice,[10] which holds in the welfare model founded on maximization of collective welfare as the algebraic sum of individual welfares, aims to minimize the loss of utility of the 'collective whole' to which the individual belongs, as a particle. The lowest amounts of utility should be sacrificed before those at a higher level, regardless of who possesses them. Moreover, those who suffer less hardship in generating utilities, inasmuch as they are more capable and better able to withstand strenuous physical and intellectual effort, will have to undergo the sacrifice of their utilities to a greater extent than those who are less capable and less well equipped to endure physical and intellectual exertions, because restoration of the utilities lost through taxation implies greater trials and tribulations for the latter group (see Chapter 2, subsection 3.14).

But this formulation is not valid as a criterion of justice, if reference is made to subjective utility strictly speaking, because the wealthy, the refined and the intelligent may experience greater pleasure on a high income as compared to the disabled and uneducated poor. Furthermore, it is an unacceptable formulation as a general criterion of justice, in a cooperative model or more generally in an individualistic framework, where what has to be considered is the relation between taxes and the individual advantages of public expenditure. Thus the aim should not be to pursue the welfare of society conceived as a whole but rather that of the individuals contained within society.

In principle, this criterion implies, *prima facie*, a levelling progressivity.

However, theoreticians adopting such a principle also consider the negative economic effects of this form of taxation, which give rise to a sacrifice in excess of the minimum. Therefore they put forward suggestions of reducing the progressivity. The distributive criterion is thus indeterminate.

11   THE PRINCIPLE OF UTILITY IN TERMS OF EQUAL SACRIFICE: VERTICAL AND HORIZONTAL EQUITY

The principle of equal sacrifice is theorized for models of the market-conforming public economy, when it is deemed impossible to share out taxes on the basis of consumption of public goods and an alternative criterion is thus sought. The criterion implies the view that every subject's utilities are measurable and can be compared with one another, at least roughly. Moreover, it is a principle that starts out from the individualist postulate that each subject counts for herself and that the state is concerned with the welfare of each subject. From this it has been inferred – under the hypothesis of isomorphism – that those who have a higher income and the same burden of family responsibilities and general state of health should pay a higher share to achieve *vertical equity*.

However, even if the trend of the utility curve is decreasing, this does not necessarily authorize progressivity for subjects who have different income levels.

Let us suppose that the decreasing marginal utility has the shape of an equilateral hyperbola, so that the product of the values marked on the ordinates and the abscissae is constant. We will place income on the ordinates and the marginal utility of money on the abscissae. On this basis, the 10 per cent levied from 200, which gives 20, will have the same utility as the 10 per cent levied on 100, which gives 10; consequently, the tax will have to be proportional.[11] Furthermore, in the individualist approach the principle under examination clashes against the postulate that it is legitimate to compare the utilities of different subjects, especially when the isomorphism hypothesis is adopted, so that similar subjects have similar utility curves: this is not a positive hypothesis, but one of normative economy.

12   THE PRINCIPLE OF PROPORTIONAL SACRIFICE AND THE MINIMAX OF CONCESSIONS PERTAINING TO OSFOB

The principle of proportional sacrifice may become a criterion for taxing in relation to the benefit, if it can be hypothesized that the advantage of public expenditure, as a first approximation, is proportional to the utilities the various subjects derive from their income and consumption, so that consumption of public goods increases more than proportionally with increasing income.[12] In effect, this principle necessarily leads to progressive taxation, since the principle does not require each individual to sacrifice the same utility, like the principle of equal sacrifice, but rather the same share of her own utility. Whoever has a greater utility will have to sacrifice a greater amount thereof in order to reach the same share. Comparison of utilities among different subjects is thus avoided.

13   THE DISTRIBUTION OF TAXATION AND CORRECTION OF MARKET RESULTS

Very high incomes may give the impression of being unfair in the sense of deriving from market imperfections. But quite apart from this observation, it can be argued that excessive concentration of incomes and wealth reduces economic efficiency by narrowing the opportunities for choice open to the greater part of the community and delaying competitive turnover. It may also adversely affect democracy and access to public office in civil life.

This may provide an argument for 'non-fiscal' utilization of the principle of progressivity on income and for a substantial inheritance tax on large estates, as well as differential taxation of massive capital gains.

On the other hand, this argument can be countered by arguing that such corrective action of taxation can be accepted only as a 'remedy of the last resort'. For if the market is not working properly, the appropriate move is to set it to rights, rather than taxing its 'defective functioning'. Also, it is doubtful that these 'corrective' high taxes are good taxes: if taxes are very high the taxpayers have high incentives to evade and elude them (see section 15 below).

14   TAX DISTRIBUTION AND FISCAL RENTS

The interest groups that not infrequently seek to exert leverage over the majority or the minority may succeed in wresting special tax concessions in return for their strategic backing of one or the other side. We can denominate these concessions as 'fiscal rents'.

In addition, taxpayers' 'tax planning' behaviour can often give rise to deviations from the distributive principles which are supposed to underpin the taxation system.

These derogations and deviations can be legal or illegal. If they are legal, they can be called 'fiscal erosion', while the illegal variants are known as 'tax evasion'. Mid-way between stand 'tax avoidance', which is on the border between lawful and unlawful behaviour, and which derives from astute interpretations of laws that lend themselves to the discovery of loopholes. A fiscal planning behaviour designed to sidestep taxes, either legally or through unlawful artifice, may also be termed 'tax avoidance'.[13] One can propose a theorem according to which the higher and the more progressive the tax rate scale, the greater the advantage – and therefore the probability – of illegal and legal violations that generate fiscal rents, which may be both the fruit and the cause of distortion of economic competition.

15 TAX EVASION

From the economic point of view, it can be stated that there is a constant specific cost ($C_{te}C_{te}$ in Figure 8.2) of evasion, which may be higher or lower depending on the technical means and the personal activities undertaken to engage in tax evasion.

For example, tax evasion by omission of entries or invoices in the account books, for purposes of taxation, involves a system of double counting and the

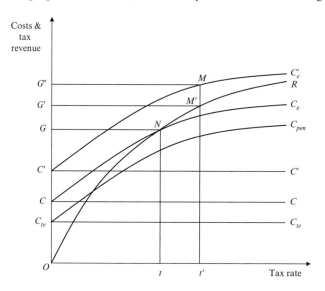

Figure 8.2   Costs and revenues of tax evasion

risk that some customer may not pay, or that some supplier may deliver unfit goods or deliver beyond the due date without it being possible to mount any form of suitable protest. Smuggling may involve the need to hire specific personnel and /or disguise the appearance of vehicles, camouflage the warehouses, fiddle the meters and /or work in secret or at night, or pay a higher amount to the persons hired to do the job.

The revenue obtained by the taxpayer through evasion OR (Figure 8.2) – consisting in the amount of tax saved – is dependent on two variables, namely the tax rate and the taxable base. Given the tax base, the potential revenue from evasion increases with increasing T of the tax. This increase is indicated on the abscissae, while the revenue is shown on the ordinates.

Tax evasion can be unmasked. The possibility of detection depends not only on the costs borne by the taxpayer, but also on the nature of the evasion mechanisms adopted as well as on the means – and thus the costs – available to the revenue service for verifying reported income and tax collection enforcement. Casual risk factors may also play a role.

Such penalties are generally commensurate with the extent of unpaid tax but also with the 'dangerousness' of the techniques employed to defraud the tax system, as well as with any previous history the taxpayer may have in terms of tax evasion or other violations of the law. There may also be 'moral' or 'professional' consequences of various types.[14]

The penalties are never proportional to the amount evaded, for there is a limit beyond which they cannot rise, due to lack of solvency of the evader, while prison sentences graduated according to the amount and type of evasion, are necessarily contained between a minimum and a maximum. Thus the curve of the 'penalties', indicated by $C_{te}C_{pen}$ (Figure 8.2) on the ordinates, composed of the penalties multiplied by the probability of being detected, increases with an increasing tax rate, indicated on the abscissae, which gives the curve OR.

For the sake of simplicity we will disregard the circumstance that risk aversion shows a decreasing trend with increasing income because the marginal utility of high incomes is lower and exhibits a less decreasing trend that that of low incomes. In fact this hypothesis, which lies at the base of the Allingham and Sandmo (1972) theorem, converges with the argument that penalties are less than proportional with increasing evaded incomes, and increases its robustness with regard to the greater probability of evasion when taxes on high-income subjects are involved, even under equal tax rates.

Given the *constant* cost curve $C_{te}C_{te}$, involved in organizing the activity of tax evasion, above it we may trace the *increasing* costs curve connected to the evasion given by $C_{te}C_{pen}$. But in addition to the constant cost curve

$C_{te}C_{te}$, an evasion cost curve referring to the moral costs should be taken into consideration. The line will be different from taxpayer to taxpayer, but as an average we can identify a constant value up to a certain point, which decreases beyond a certain tax rate, partly because the ethical duty of paying one's taxes tends to fade when the tax liability is high. Considering for the sake of simplicity only the constant-costs part of this line, by adding together the three curves we have CC_e, the global cost curve of evasion.

An increase in the tax rate to the value t, on the abscissae, gives rise to a value G of the revenue curve OR, for which the amount of the tax evaded equals the cost of tax evasion for the taxpayer. The two curves cross at point N.

From tax rate t onwards, given the revenue curve OR, it appears advantageous to evade, and the advantageousness increases gradually with an increasing tax rate. If all subjects engaged in evasion, the revenue lost by the state at the tax rate t' would amount to $G'G$, at point M$'$. A tax increase from t to t' would give zero yield to the Treasury. But if the revenue service increases the cost of administering the tax collection process from level CC to level $C'C'$, then it may raise the total cost for the taxpayer to, say, $C'C'_e$, in order to obtain the revenue OG' by means of tax t', at point M'. For the taxpayer, the cost of evasion now becomes OG', which exceeds the amount OG' that she owes to the revenue service. In this case, evasion is no longer an advantageous option.

Naturally, with regard to other taxes, the situation may appear less unfavourable. However, it should be borne in mind that if the revenue service raises the tax collection cost from CC to $C'C'$, it will not secure possession of the entire increase in revenue from G to G': it will have additional revenue given by $GC' - CC'$, both multiplied by Ot'. Clearly, for the revenue service it is no longer advantageous to enhance the battle against tax evasion when the cost of fighting evasion becomes equal to the proceeds of the battle itself.

As for the advantageousness of tax avoidance, since this is not a crime, the taxpayer will have no need to calculate the costs of 'being found out' and being prosecuted when evaluating whether or not it may be advantageous to evade. The cost curve of tax avoidance may become CC.

16 TAX DISTRIBUTION AND SHIFTING

The design of taxation, as conceived by the law, can be aided or, conversely, undermined by the fact that the economic burden of a tax may not rest with the person or business who has the statutory liability for paying the tax: rather, the incidence of the tax may, by means of tax *shifting* processes, pass forward to other subjects, that is to the *actual taxpayer* who bears the ultimate burden (see Chapter 11 on shifting).

Often, tax shifting is well recognized among policy makers who frame tax legislation, and in drawing up the tax laws they may favour the phenomenon by establishing the seller's *right to obtain relief*, or more frequently the *obligation to obtain relief*, from the purchaser in respect of the tax paid.

At times, shifting contradicts the policy maker's choice. This is the case with personal income tax, profits tax, or property tax, if the income holder succeeds in passing taxes forward to those who buy her goods and services, or backwards to those who supply production factors.

Therefore there exist economic limits on choices in matters concerning taxation. This is a strong constraint on fiscal power in modification of income and wealth distribution.

NOTES

1. Objectives other than procuring revenue are also known as 'extra fiscal objectives'. They are usually held to include income redistribution through taxation: but here the distinction between the fiscal and extra fiscal purposes of tributes is mistaken, as redistribution – if present – emerges from a comparison among the effects of public expenditure.

   A similar argument holds when the extra fiscal objectives include the aims of macroeconomic stabilization which refer to variation in the budget balance, reducing or increasing the deficit. Only in the case of taxes introduced – with the mere objective of macroeconomic stabilization – to generate a budget surplus, or of protection of domestic production like custom duties giving modest or zero revenue, can it be stated that these are cases of purely extra fiscal measures. See in general on the interlacing between fiscal and extra fiscal tasks in modern states, the 'classic' by M. Pugliese (1932). Lerner (1944, pp.302–22), claims that public revenue (or taxes, which are its major component) merely has the aim of combating inflation, in that if the system is facing underemployment, public expenditure can be carried out with the issue of non-inflationary money. But it is obvious that if such a formulation is taken to imply that tax revenue is only a potential necessity, then it is misleading. Given the size of the public sector, the possibility of financing public expenditure by issuing non inflationary money is very limited.
2. In the Bible the Leviathan is 'an enormous man-eating monster', taken by the English philosopher T. Hobbes (1588–1679) as the symbol of the omnipotence of the state over the individual. In an extended sense the term is used of a system, structure or apparatus that suffocates the individual.
3. Obviously this is the definition of the Austrian/Italian/Swedish economic school of public finance. The bibliography on the concept of taxation is immense and to a large extent it can be identified with, and overlaps, debate on the economy of public goods.
4. Neumark principles are adopted here because they are drawn from the principles of the Ordo school which basically coincide with those of the cooperative model of fiscal economy developed here.
5. The principle is different from that of the constitutional limit on the global tax burden which is criticized by A.T. Peacock (1985), in Forte and Peacock (eds) (1985), where it

is argued that it is not very effective with regard to the exaggerated burden placed by the tax system on individual taxpayers. See Chapter 6, subsection 2.16–2.17. On the constitutional limits on individual taxes, cf. Forte, in *Etica Pubblica E Regole Del Gioco* (1995).

6. The canon of taxes 'endowed with certainty' is the second among those stated by Adam Smith (1776), in *The Wealth of Nations*, Book V, Chapter II, Part II, 'Of taxes'.

7. The criterion of capacity to pay has been interpreted in many ways, starting from the eighteenth century. We have already noted the definition given by Smith, who links it to income enjoyed under the protection of the state, that is by whoever lives and spends in that state.

    According to Dalton (1957), this principle is to be considered as an empty box, in which everyone puts whatever they please as they see fit, and therefore it should be banished from scientific debate.

    However, Art. 53 of the Italian Constitution, by laying down that 'all citizens are required to contribute to public expenditure in the extent of their capacity to pay', placed a constitutional limit on taxes that exceed the capacity to pay them, which found important specific applications by the Constitutional Court.

8. The case is different for corporations and the other entities that have a balance sheet where they may valorize their capital gains.

9. The name of 'Laffer curve' has its origin in the name of the economic adviser to US President Ronald Reagan, who popularized the old principle that, from the microeconomic point of view, any excessive increase in a tax rate reduces instead of increasing the revenue thereby derived. From a macroeconomic point of view, a reduction in revenue, without a decrease in spending, may give rise to greater tax revenue by generating an expansion of global demand.

10. The first complete and rigorous formulation of this principle, with regard to the issue of taxation, was due to F.I. Edgeworth (1897 [1925]). It was subsequently taken up again by A.C. Pigou (1947), who adopted it as the basis for his theory on allocative and distributive optimality of the tax burden.

11. The demonstration can be found in Pigou (1947, Chapter VII).

12. For the demonstration, see Chapter 4, section 7 concerning cost-sharing in a cooperative game where, in order to share out the benefits among themselves, the players choose the principle of minimaximization of the concessions, that is OSFOB. Note that this criterion is subject to empirical verification regarding consumption of public goods.

13. In the context of evasion, 'simple' evasion should be distinguished from 'fraud', which consists in acts of evasion performed by means of 'artifices' designed to mask the situation (such as false accounting, invoicing of non-existent expenses, entering personal expenses as production expenses, concealing proceeds by non-issue of invoices, and so on). In the case of simple tax evasion, the task of the revenue service is to undertake 'ascertainment activities' in order to determine whether unlawful but in itself transparent behaviour has taken place. In the case of 'fraud', the matter becomes more complicated. It is not sufficient to increase such activities in order to acquire knowledge of tax omission behaviour that can be ascertained *prima facie*. It is necessary to undertake investigations – with the aid of trained personnel – to gather additional more complex information capable of disclosing the fraudulent action and demonstrating that it was performed deliberately.

    At times, the demonstration may be incomplete and the taxpayer may, if her position is investigated by the tax inspectors, be able to defend herself, with at least partial success. Tax investigation raises new problems of specialized technical personnel training and *overall* information costs. Thus the efficiency of investigations processed by the tax authority is crucial for fair and impartial tax enquiries and for the probity of taxpayers.

14. On the costs of tax collecting that weigh on the taxpayer, see Sanford (1981) in Peacock and Forte (1981).

9. Income effects and allocation effects of taxes

1 THE DISTINCTION BETWEEN ALLOCATIVE EFFECTS AND INCOME (AS PURCHASING POWER) EFFECTS OF TAXATION

Taxes interfere with individual consumption choices, with production, and so on.

They generally have allocative effects, which pertain to the allocation effects (or formulation effects) of taxes, and also income effects. The former consist in modifications of taxpayers' choices to the extent to which the choices depend on the way the tax is formulated. The latter consist in the effects exerted on such choices by the levy of a given sum through taxation, independently of how the contribution is formulated.[1]

2 ALLOCATIVE AND INCOME EFFECTS IN THE CASE OF TAXES ON UTILIZATION OF RESOURCES

We will begin to consider these effects by analysing a tax which is then spent. We will also consider taxation on employment in resources in consumption and savings or investment or in different types of consumption or various types of savings and investments.

Given two goods or two employments of a given resource, A and B, available to a citizen i, if the price of good (or employment) A increases as a result a tax, i will have to forgo a greater quantity of good (or employment) B in order to purchase a given unit of good A. Thus a change takes place in the exchange rate between the two goods, and this may lead the subject to modify her choice between the two goods. This is the allocative or 'formulation' effect of the levy.

Furthermore, if the price of good (or employment) A increases, this means that i's purchasing power has decreased: the amount of disposable money available to her has remained unchanged, but the quantity of goods (or employment of a given resource) A that i can obtain with that same amount declines, if *i*'s purchases (or employment) of *B* undergo no variation. Therefore *i* will have to reduce her purchases (or employment) of *B* or of *A* or possibly of both *B* and *A* or reduce her savings or her capital or try to increase her revenue.[2] This is the 'income effect' of taxation, as a purchasing power effect.

Very often, taxation generates a loss of welfare greater than that due to its negative effect on purchasing power, precisely because it also has distortive allocative – that is 'formulation' – effects.

> This will be discussed in particular in the next chapter on optimum taxation, in which we will not use indifference and transformation curves, as these are tools for 'ordinal' economic analysis and are thus designed to ascertain what is preferred and 'to what extent'. Rather, we will use demand and supply curves, as these lend themselves to analysis of a cardinal type that focuses on evaluation *of the quantity* of the advantages and of the damage, in terms of utility, resulting from the different alternatives.

The two effects, namely of income and of allocation, usually come into action at the same time, through individual *i*'s reaction to the variation in prices resulting from taxation. But here we will endeavour to examine them separately, by means of Figure 9.1, in the (simplified) hypothesis that prior to the tax the allocation of resources was optimal.

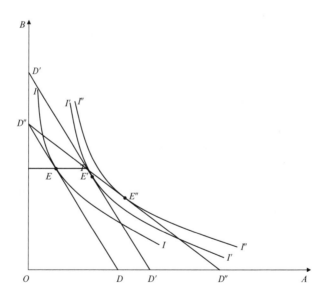

Figure 9.1   Income and allocation effects: analysis by compensatory variations

Let $D''D''$ be the budget straight line between the two goods or employment of a given resource, A and B (indicated, respectively, on the abscissae and the ordinate in Figure 9.1).

The indifference curve $I'I'$ meets the budget straight line $D''D$ ''at point E'', which is the point chosen by i. Then a tax is levied on A. The price of A (or the cost of employment of the given resource of i) increases, causing the budget straight line to move to $D''D$. The new point of equilibrium for i is $E < E''$. It is located on the indifference curve $II < I'I'$. To separate the two effects, namely the effect of variation in purchasing power and the allocative (or 'formulation') effect, we will consider the budget straight line which, passing through T on $D''D''$, restores to i the tax ET paid on A, and thus gives her the same purchasing power as does $D''D''$. The budget straight line coincides with $D''D''$ at a point T and it involves the same 'exchange rate' between A and B (or price ratio of A and B or the same relative prices of A and B) as is given by DD''. Therefore, it preserves only the allocative effect (or 'formulation') of the tax under examination, while it fully compensates the income effect, as purchasing power.

Obviously, this compensatory variation in purchasing power has a plausible practical sense if one assumes that the tax is spent in favour of i, with disbursements of sums of money to i (for example interests on public debt, salaries, pensions, various subsidies), independently of the allocation effects of this expenditure.

The displacement of the budget straight line as compared to $D''D''$, due to the 'restoration' of the sum of the tax to i, does not, however, enable i to purchase E'' on $I'I'$, but only to reach E' on $I'I'$.

The worsening from E'' to E' gives a monetary measure of the 'distortion' springing from the harmful allocative effect. It thus measures the loss of welfare incurred by i due to the tax and to its allocation net of removal of purchasing power (cancelled by moving the budget straight line from DD'' to $D'D'$).

By contrast, to measure the purchasing power effect resulting from the tax – unless it is restored to the taxpayer in question – all that is needed is to consider the difference between the budget straight line $D'D'$ and DD''. These lines are parallel and are therefore characterized by the same relative prices (that is the same terms of trade) between A and B, but they correspond to two different situations: that in which, after the tax, i has the same purchasing power as before by virtue of a compensation, and that in which i undergoes the tax on A without any compensation.

The sum of the income effects and the allocation effects gives rise to the 'welfare effects' of the tax. It is shown in Figure 9.1 that the welfare effects – if the tax is not 'restored' to the taxpayer – can be measured, for i, by the displacement of $I'I'$ to II and from E'' to E. It should be noted that we have assumed budget lines which, in the absence of taxes, are parallel to one another. This involves the hypothesis that the mean costs of the goods under consideration, and therefore of their supplies, are 'constant' (and thus equal to the marginal costs, which are likewise constant). If the costs of A and B have an increasing or decreasing trend, and the trend is different for A compared to B, then the reduction in demand generates supply price variations and consequently causes a modification of the budget lines net of tax. This complicates the picture. But, despite the additional complication, the result does not change with regard to the generation of allocation effects pertaining to the taxed good.

3   INCOME EFFECTS AND ALLOCATIVE EFFECTS OF TAXATION ON RESOURCE ACQUISITION AND POSSESSION, AND WEALTH EFFECTS

The case considered above concerns income effects as reduction in purchasing power and allocative effects in relation to the hypothesis of taxes levied on goods or *on alternative employments* of resources. But income effects involving purchasing power and allocative effects can also be induced by taxes that have an impact on production or possession of resources: production of income, possession of wealth or of given assets and so on.

We may now move on from the income effect to examination of wealth effects. The latter are represented by diminution in the value of assets or in capitalization of future purchasing power flows when the income point of view is adopted, and by the capitalization of expected lower utility flows when the subjective welfare point of view is adopted.

The wealth effect comes about, for permanent taxes, in relation to expected reduction in the amount of future flows of incomes from labour, capital or business, or in a reduction in the purchasing power of such flows (due to price increases deriving from taxes shifted into the price of goods) (see Chapter 11).

4   INCOME EFFECTS IN THE ABSENCE OF ALLOCATION EFFECTS: THE CLASSROOM CASE OF THE FIXED SUM TRIBUTE CONSISTING IN A SMALL CAPITATION (POLL) TAX

One may imagine the limit case of a tax devoid of allocative effects.

Let us consider a 'classroom case' of a levy consisting of a fixed sum, for example a small poll tax on residents, which remains unchanged independently of the taxpayer's behaviour in the sense that whatever she decides to do, she will always pay the same sum.

> The only possibility she has of avoiding the poll tax on her income involves her relinquishing her definition as a resident, and thus as a taxpayer, and additionally, not having children, in order not to generate other taxpayers. But since, by hypothesis, the tax is only a modest sum, she will surely not opt for such a change in her moral choice.

5   REAL AND MONETARY INCOME EFFECTS

An elevated customs duty which does not give tax revenue does not deprive the economy of money and therefore has no *monetary* income effects. But it may induce price increases for certain consumption goods in an amount roughly equal to the duty, and thus have an impact on consumers' purchasing power and real income. Indirectly, if it allows domestic industries that would otherwise have been left inactive to continue operations with resources that would not have been employed, then it might have some real positive income effects.

6   'ANNOUNCEMENT' EFFECTS

The monetary effects – both for taxes and also for public expenditure – may be delayed as compared to the real effects.

> Forthcoming tax measures can have major consequences even before they come into effect, due to the mere fact of having been announced.
>
> Precisely in order to avoid market turbulence induced by the 'announcement' of the proposed new tax legislation, which some learn of before others or regard as more reliable than others do, the technique of resorting to a decree which has the immediate force of law (*Decree-Law*) is often adopted for taxes that are likely to have the most substantial influence on the price of goods. This is because pre-announced measures can spark panic buying, which can trigger a run on certain products and also disrupt the securities market, whereas the Decree-Law is generally a surprise move.
>
> The time lag between the 'announcement' effect and the effect of the fact of the tax levy tends to shrink in more advanced economies where taxpayers arrange their lives around plans based on expectations. Thus for corporate taxes the time lag between the 'announcement' effects and the effects of the fact of the levy is less than is the case for individuals, assuming an identical lapse of time.

7   ALLOCATIVE AND INCOME EFFECTS OF TAXATION IN RELATION TO CHOICES BETWEEN PRODUCTION AND LEISURE TIME

Taxpayer *i* who is subject to a proportional tax on her income suffers an allocation effect that induces her to prefer leisure time over income. To gain greater insight into this situation it is necessary to abandon the hypothesis of budget lines corresponding to transformation curves among goods characterized by constant costs. Instead, we need to consider the 'transformation curves' between two goods, namely earned income and 'leisure' time, that is time available for free choices which do not give an income for tax purposes. Leisure time is not produced, but it must be relinquished in order to produce the good defined as 'income'. The transformation curves indicate the alternative results in terms of economic income or leisure time obtainable by the subject through the sacrifice of her leisure time, the loss of which has an increasing marginal utility. It is obvious that working a six-hour day is not exceedingly demanding, but working twelve hours a day is more tiring and the return tends to decline. Therefore the cost of transforming leisure time into work displays an increasing trend, and on the assumption that income per hour of work is constant, this indicates that the transformation curve has decreasing returns and at a certain point falls to zero. At a given point, it is no longer possible to transform leisure time into work because physiological laws of the need for pause and rest come into play. On the other hand, leisure time is a higher good, in the sense of the income elasticity greater than 1. Therefore, at low income levels, the preference for income is very high, because the marginal utility of income is elevated. But as income increases, the marginal utility of income declines, and a greater desire for leisure time is experienced, not so much because it gives a greater utility in absolute terms when an individual has a higher income, but, rather, because the income itself provides a lower utility (see Figure A.4 in the Appendix). With a high income, a marginal amount of income gives less satisfaction than a marginal amount of leisure time, in comparison to the situation faced by an individual on a medium-high or medium income. This also affects choices of weekly hours of work and leisure time.

It follows that taxation on low-paid employment and self-employment income does not generate a reduction in the supply of labour but rather – at times – an increase in the labour supply, because the taxpayer needs to work more in order to achieve the minimum of income she considers necessary for herself and her family, that is the 'minimum required for living'. But this does not occur when the income level increases. And if the tax rate is high, the supply of labour will decrease considerably, because leisure time will become comparatively more advantageous. This will be felt in particular if 'leisure time' includes not only time off from a regular taxed job but also the production of income in nature, which is not subject to taxation. For instance, taxed individuals may decide to spend some time on 'DIY', which they would have no time to do if they were at work, so that they would necessarily have to hire tradesmen – plumbers, painters and decorators. Also, by allowing themselves more time for leisure they can cook their own meals at home instead of going out to eat as they do when they face a gruelling day at work which leaves no time for home cookery.

8   THE CONCEPT OF COMPENSATED DEMAND CURVE[3]

The distinction between allocation effects and income effects described above enables us to consider so-called compensated demand curves: these are the demand curves of subjects that benefit from 'compensatory varia-tions' in the increase (or alternatively, decrease) in the price of the goods considered, compared to a given equilibrium point (see Figure 9.2).

The compensated demand curve, represented here by D_c, is net of nega-tive income effects of price rises compared to a given equilibrium price (E_0 in Figure 9.2). It is also net of the positive income effects deriving from price decreases compared to the same equilibrium price E_0. Therefore, in

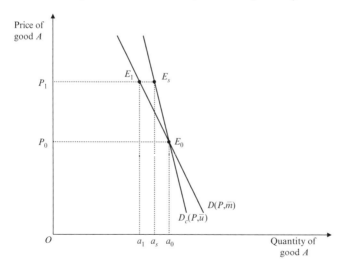

Figure 9.2   Compensated demand curve

comparison to the normal demand curve, the compensated demand curve is greater in the segment above E_0 in which the negative income effect of normal demand is compensated by an increase, and it is smaller in the segment below E_0 where the positive income effect of the price diminution that acts upon the normal demand curve is here compensated by a decrease. The compensated demand curve D_c exceeds DD above E_0. Therefore, at the point given by price E_s, the quantity demanded with the compensated demand curve is Oa_s; with the normal demand curve the quantity demanded for the same price is only Oa_1. In terms of utility, D_c is a function of the marginal utility curve $D_c(P, \bar{u})$ with constant income, whereas D is a function of the marginal utility curve $D(P, \bar{m})$ gross of variations in income that derive from price variations.

Assuming that the tax is small or the good itself is of trifling importance, the income effect due to reduction in welfare or real income – that is in purchasing power – following price rises will be negligible.[4] However, if the tax imposes a heavy burden and/or the good on which it is levied plays a major role in the consumer's budget, then the price rise will have a negative income effect which cannot be disregarded.

The above observations imply that if one seeks to examine the allocative effects of taxes separately from the income effects, in order to assess which effects are allocatively neutral and which ones are distortionary, it is helpful to have a demand curve that allows separate consideration of the reduction in demand caused by the rise in the relative price of the taxed good, in order to distinguish this reduction from that deriving from the diminution in the consumer's real income (that is purchasing power). This issue will be addressed in the next chapter.

NOTES

1. This definition goes back to Pigou (1947). Pigou employs the term '"announcement" effects' for the effects of the formula of taxation, which is improper because it refers to the allocative and income effects of announcing that a given tax has been instituted.
2. This phenomenon is known as 'tax removal'; see Chapter 11, section 5.
3. The compensated demand curve was proposed by the Nobel prize-winner M. Friedman in an early essay entitled 'The Marshallian demand curve' (1949, reprinted in 1953).
4. This is the hypothesis that led Marshall to neglect the income effect and concentrate only on allocative effects, with regard to price variations. He then demonstrated, by means of a reference to the loss of consumer's surplus, that indirect taxation has a distortive effect additional to the burden arising from the levy itself.

10. Optimal taxation in a public economy conforming to the market economy

1 OPTIMAL TAXATION AS TAXATION WHICH MINIMIZES DISTORTIONS

This chapter focuses on the model of taxation that conforms to the market economy, from the allocational point of view, developing what was investigated in the previous chapter, where the income and allocation (or formulation) effects of taxes were addressed. The present chapter likewise eschews an ordinal analysis based on indifference curves and budget lines, in favour of a cardinal analysis, as in the previous chapter. More specifically, it dispenses with indifference curves and budget lines that refer to transformation curves among goods hypothesized to have constant cost and supply trends, and replaces them with a supposedly quantitative analysis performed by means of algebraic sums, which are computed by considering the demand and supply curves of the various goods or alternative utilizations of resources. This is done by introducing cost and supply curves with an increasing or decreasing trend, in addition to those with a constant trend. We have seen that all taxes have allocation effects and this is true even of general income tax, which reduces the incentive to work and, in general, hinders the incentive to engage in activities that could produce personal income. General taxes on consumption can favour savings and self-produced goods in kind, devoted to production as well as to consumption for one's own personal use that does not translate into market exchanges and therefore is not subject to being taxed. Since there exists no such thing as a neutral tax, the best procedure will involve finding the form of taxation that minimizes undesirable distortions and leaves only the fully justified levies. This is a quest which, however, is only a first approximation. The benefits of public expenditure, which differ according to the various economic activities and situations, should also be taken into account. In particular, it cannot be stated that income tax always 'discriminates' in favour of leisure time. This does not hold to the extent to which this taxation is the price for the use of public goods instrumental to the production of income, while the leisure time is not, in itself, a good that is produced, and therefore no utilization of public goods cooperates in its creation.

2   OPTIMAL TAXATION AND THE AGGREGATION OF DISUTILITIES OF THE VARIOUS TAX CHOICES

Two different approaches to this subject can be pursued:

a.   the *axiomatic* approach according to which the welfare function to be maximized is given *a priori*, by means of the algebraic sum of the utilities of the various subjects. This means that optimum taxation is that which, for each revenue, minimizes the sum of the losses of utility inflicted on the various taxpayers;

b.   the individualistic approach, in which the public operator leaves each individual free to pursue her own welfare and creates the conditions for this to be possible, intervening only to correct dysfunctions and severe iniquities. Thus in this case, optimal taxation, in the perspective of allocative efficiency, is that which minimizes the distortions affecting an average subject, whether the subject be a person or an enterprise.

Current theory is, essentially, built around the first of the above approaches, and this – as seen earlier on numerous occasions – exposes it to severe criticism in a public choice individualistic approach such as that followed here, namely, criticisms advanced by the cooperative model of the public economy subsidiary to the market economy as a system of free choices.

Allocatively optimal taxation in the individualistic public choice approach, in terms of unanimity voting, will aim to minimize the distortion effects of taxation affecting an average individual or enterprise. The arguments will start out from plausible hypotheses on the trend of the utility curves and the elasticity or rigidity of demand and supply of factors and resources.

This minimization requires:

a.   minimization of distortion in consumption;

b.   minimization of distortion between monetary revenue and benefits 'in kind' (such as one's spouse helping with the housework);

c.   minimization of distortions in investments and in the combinations among production factors;

d. minimization of distortions of the labour supply and savings, with respect to consumption and future income more or less distant in time.

An analysis of the intricate problem of comparing the distortive effects of the above elements can be carried out by assuming compensated demand curves, depending on the various individual cases, with recourse to the so-called 'Harberger triangles', named after the author who developed the Marshallian analysis on deadweight loss of consumer's rents and extending it to the producer's rents, and to that of the worker and the saver on whom tax is levied.

> Underlying the minimization of the sum of Harberger triangles lost by taxpayers and not gained by the Treasury, as an allocative aim there is the assumption – of first approximation – that the utilities lost in the various cases, *prima facie*, are homogeneous and have the same weight if they refer to the same monetary amount, and can be compared cardinally with the tax revenue yield. Assuming that all the triangles pertaining to 'the consumer's rents' and to 'the supplier's rents' concern a given 'representative taxpayer' *i*, for whom the minimization calculation is made, then a rather implausible abstract hypothesis is being made.

The various subjects have different overall situations with regard to the various taxes as well as the 'rents' they sacrifice, on account of the distortions due to taxation. Rather than purely and simply a sum, what has to be imagined is a 'bargaining equilibrium', in which the optimal tax is that which minimizes the distortions affecting the different subjects on the basis of generally shared apportioning criteria, such as OSFOB, hypothesized for the costs and advantages of public action.

3 THE ALLOCATIVE DISTORTIONS OF A PRODUCTION TAX, IN A COMPETITIVE REGIME

Now we will examine the way the Harberger triangle minimization rules operate, starting from the simplest case, namely that of the distortive effects of a production tax on goods purchased by subject i.[1]

Let us consider the demand curve for a good X, with the supply curve BB (see Figure 10.1). The price is P and the quantity purchased is OQ. Tax is added to the cost BB, increasing BR to $B'B'$.

In principle, there are now two hypotheses: with the non-compensated demand curve DD and the compensated demand curve D_cD.

For the purposes of the present investigation, we will focus on the

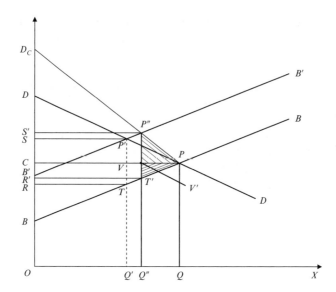

Figure 10.1   Allocative distortions of a consumption tax: case A

hypothesis of the compensated demand D_cD, which isolates the allocative distortions. The compensated curve D_cD will appear as a demand that is more upwardly rigid (or less elastic) than the non-compensated demand *DD*.

The levy commensurate to the quantity, which raises the costs from *B* to *B'*, moving away from the equilibrium point *P*, with the compensated demand PD_c, will be measured with respect to the new equilibrium point *P''*; it is, therefore, *P''T''*. The loss of rent incurred by the producer and the consumer – net of tax paid to the revenue service – is the entire amount indicated in the shaded area in Figure 10.1, namely *T'PP''*. This 'deadweight loss' is less than that incurred in the case of demand *DD in relation to the tax yield obtained from the levy*, as demand D_cP is more rigid, and consequently the quantity undergoes a smaller decrease (passing from *OQ* to *OQ''* rather than to *OQ'*), while the price increases by a greater percentage. In the limit case of absolutely rigid demand there is no distortion.

The deadweight loss of the producer's rent with D_cP is *PV'T'* and that of the consumer's rent is *PVP''*. The rigidity of demand reduces the loss of producer's rent.

In Figure 10.2, which in all other respects is identical to Figure 10.1, we have plotted a highly rigid compensated demand curve, in the relevant segment, and a supply curve CB_c at constant costs and a supply curve *BB*

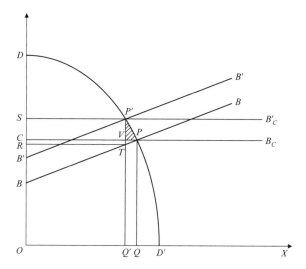

Figure 10.2 *More rigid demand curve and elastic supply curve (constant costs): case B*

at markedly rising costs. In the first hypothesis we have only the distortion $P'VP$ referring to the consumer. Let us turn now to rising costs. Since DD' is far more rigid than D_cP shown in Figure 10.1, there is only a very slight effect of loss of the producer's rent, represented as VPT (Figure 10.2).

In other words, tax on consumption tends to the allocative optimum for enterprises, when costs are constant or demand is rigid. For purchasers, it tends to the allocative optimum when demand is rigid.

4 ALLOCATIVE DISTORTIONS OF A CONSUMPTION TAX, IN A MONOPOLY REGIME

It is likewise easy to demonstrate that price will increase less than the tax under a monopoly regime versus price rises compared to tax under a competitive regime, and indirect taxation will – to a large extent – be borne by the monopolist.

For the sake of simplicity, let us assume constant prices, in order to highlight the monopoly rent (Figure 10.3). In a competitive regime, prior to the tax TP', the price would be P. In a competitive regime, the tax would modify the price from P to P', with a deadweight loss of the consumer's rent amounting to $P'PT$. In a monopoly regime, prior to tax, the price is P_M, given by the meeting point between the marginal return and

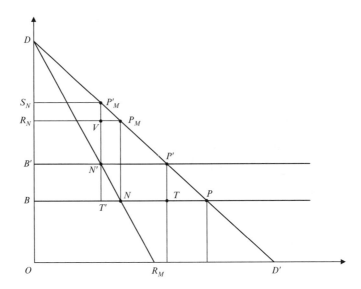

Figure 10.3   Distortive effects of the tax on consumption in a monopoly regime: case C

the marginal costs (which are equal to average costs, given the hypothesis of constant costs).

After application of the tax TP', the price rises to $P'M$, and the resulting deadweight loss of the consumer's rent is only P'_MP_MV. (Since the consumer is already exploited by the monopolist, her tax burden cannot be increased much further by the new tax.) But for the monopolist, the monopoly rent declines from BNP_MD to $B'N'P'_MSD$. The revenue yielded by the tax is $BB'N'T'$; of this amount, which is borne by the consumer, the monopolist recovers only $S_NP'_MR_NV$, and loses a further $NPMVT'$.

Therefore although the rent the consumer loses due to the distortion effect of the tax is much less than the amount she loses in a competitive regime (and the share of the tax levied on her is likewise lower), the monopolist suffers an additional burden above and beyond that of the tax itself (mainly borne by the monopolist), while the enterprise, in a competitive regime, has no loss of rent. On the assumption that the monopolist's rent is considered 'unfair', and is thus excluded from considerations on the individual welfare that the community as a whole can pursue, and given that the optimum regime is that of competition, then it can be stated that since a consumption tax in a monopoly regime minimizes the consumer's loss of welfare as compared to a competitive regime, it falls within the canons of optimal taxation.

5   SAVINGS AND LABOUR

We will now turn to examining the two hypotheses of labour income and savings income, using the available graphic representations. If the supply of labour is downwardly elastic, in other words if a 'price' reduction (the worker's gain) reduces the supply more than proportionally because the taxed individual prefers leisure time and/or less strenuous and less risky work, which she can easily procure for herself, and demand is not rigid because enterprises and families show a market reaction to price increases, then the distortion affecting the supply will be substantial. This should be taken into consideration in progressive taxation of medium and medium-high incomes, in cases when such incomes involve a notable presence of specialized, managerial and/or technological and entrepreneurial labour, both in terms of employment and self-employment income.

With regard to savings, in an open economy, one can readily formulate the hypothesis that its supply is likely to be very elastic, in relation to taxation in a given country, as savings can easily be transferred to another state and thereby be subject to a lower rate of taxation. Analogously, in an open economy the domestic supply is not very rigid, as enterprises can to some extent obtain financing on the foreign financial markets, and can delocalize their productive activities abroad. This results in a substantial accumulation of distortion effects on the supply side and also on the demand side. Such a situation explains why, in taxing personal income, it may be optimal to apply a moderate 'final withholding tax' on financial gain from unearned income, that is on savings income in various forms (shares, bonds, investment funds, bank and postal deposit accounts, futures, and so on).

6   ADDITIONAL REFLECTIONS AND OVERVIEW OF THE PRINCIPLES OF ALLOCATIVE OPTIMALITY

On the assumption of the theorem of allocatively optimal taxation, what is required is to minimize undesirable distortions while maximizing discriminations designed to combat (or counterbalance) distortions that are brought about on the market by defective or unacceptable individual decisions and external economies and diseconomies.

Setting aside the issue of market imperfections and individual choices, allocative optimality can be said to be achieved when:

a. losses in consumers' rents are minimized, taking into account that the more the goods and supplies subject to tax levies have an elastic demand, the greater the loss of consumer rents, under equal tax levy;

b. losses in producers' rents are minimized, taking into account that the more the incomes and goods subject to tax levies are supplied at decreasing and/or increasing cost (under equal demand elasticity), the greater the loss in producers' rents;

c. distortions are reduced, by also taxing goods complementary to those on which no tax can be charged and goods that are rivals of taxed goods. This involves taxing goods complementary to untaxed income in kind. And it involves favouring broad-based taxes proportional to incomes or only slightly progressive, when demand is elastic, as is the case for overtime work.

To reduce 'distortions' it will be necessary to avoid discriminating among rival goods and – *ceteris paribus* – to tax all goods that satisfy a certain want, with the same percentage on the price. In the case of activities that carry risk, which involve hazards and costs that are difficult to detract, it will be necessary to adopt reduced tax rates and exemptions.

Finally, since a subject has variable wants over time, her loss of consumer's rent is minimized if a tax levy takes effect at a moment when the relation between income and wants is more favourable (that is is more affluent), and this suggests taxing optional goods whose consumption increases with increasing consumer prosperity.

At this point the imperfections of the market and of individual choices come into play in the framework of allocative optimality. To correct such imperfections, what can be suggested (prudently), on the basis of the principle of 'Ulysses tied to the mast' (see Chapter 3, subsection 2.5) is to impose a (differential) levy on consumption that damages a person's health or which is in conflict – albeit not in absolute terms – with shared social ethics. A further suggestion would involve exemption or a lower tax rate on merit consumption, as well as a more favourable tax regime for goods complementary to personal savings, such as goods designed to enhance human capital.

However, in addition to allocative principles, aspects of basic freedom must also be addressed. What sense is there in taxing goods complementary to those on which it proves impossible to levy a tax because they form part of a small-scale informal economy, such as those of the family garden and 'do-it-yourself' home repairs?

7 THE THEORY OF THE OPTIMUM TAX AS A SIMPLE AND CERTAIN TAX

Perfection in the field of taxation, regarded as a goal leading to allocative optimality in the search for minimization of distortions, is just as dangerous as the enlightened dirigisme that seeks to manipulate taxes down to the minutest detail, in order to correct market imperfections.

> For instance, the idea of a high rate of tax on all forms of luxury consumption that exhibit rigid (compensated) demand means complicating the tax collection system, by increasing the array of value-added tax rates or of special levies on consumption (excise tax), especially if one takes into consideration goods with modest taxable bases, which give a very limited tax yield.

In general, if an excessive range of discrimination is allowed, there is the risk of arbitrary decision-making power, exploitation and lobbying that interferes with public choice, as well as uncertainty, complications, inequality of treatment and corruption in implementation of policy choices.

8 OPTIMAL TAXATION AND DIFFERENT ALLOCATIVE EFFECTS IN COMPARISON TO THOSE PERTAINING TO DISTORTED CHOICES

The picture of optimal taxation is incomplete if the focus purely on the allocative effects arising from choice distortions were to result in neglect of the dynamic effects associated with the process of accumulation.

> In this perspective, income effects translate into allocative effects: for instance, if companies tend to invest undistributed corporate profits, then in the long term a heavy tax on corporate profits leads to a decline in corporate investment.

In general, awareness of these effects reinforces the argument that in terms of medium-long period dynamics, it is more suitable to attenuate taxation of subjects that are particularly efficient in accumulation and in highly qualified work, as the income they achieve generates new savings, new qualified labour and entrepreneurial development. This confutes the hypothesis advanced by some scholars of optimal taxation theory (Mirrlees, 1982) who put forward the opposite argument by claiming that it is less penalizing for such taxpayers, in subjective terms, in a subjectivistic perspective, to rely on their drive and energy in order to restore the income of which they have been deprived by taxation.

If allocative optimality is considered in association with growth, this may prompt the view that taxation should be conceived in such a manner as to stimulate the supply of flexible labour, of qualified labour, of research and of investment in creative entrepreneurial activity, in such a manner as to increase the global product and employment. A greater product with greater employment generates greater income for every individual.

Therefore, from the dynamic point of view current theory on optimal taxation is a construct that still requires further elaboration.

NOTE

1. For an in-depth examination of optimal taxation theory, with regard to consumption tax and in direct taxes as opposed to direct taxation, see first De V. Graaff (1957, pp. 47 ff. and 66 ff), and, more recently, Bradford and Rosen (1976); Sandmo (1976).

11.   Tax shifting

1   PRELIMINARY DEFINITIONS

In the previous chapters we saw that as a result of market laws, taxes levied on certain taxpayers are often shifted to other subjects.

Tax shifting[1] means that the economic burden of a tax passes from those who are legally responsible for paying the tax, or who are in some way affected by the levy, to other subjects who stand in an economic relation with the original subjects. As a result of the tax, a change comes about in this relation. Shifting may concern different subjects who are in relation with the same object, as in the case of a tax on the seller shifted to the purchaser or in the case of a tax on the wage paid by the employer and shifted to the employee. But shifting may also concern the same subject for different objects, as in the case of a tax on capital transferred from capital to income, or in the case of a tax on a given production factor shifted to the product of which the factor forms part. This tax then may be shifted by the producer to the traders and the consumers so that the subject changes. But shifting may also concern the transfer of a tax from given subjects for given objects to different subjects for different objects. This may be the case of a tax on a given good produced by given firms that sell this good to other producers, who then use that good as production factors in other goods or services and shift the tax onto the consumers. Thus a high tax levied on the producers of petrol may be passed to the sellers and subsequently transferred to the users of trucks and cars. The tax then may be shifted to other subjects for different objects through increases in the prices of the goods transported and through profit reductions affecting car manufacturers.

The incidence of a tax is the fact of bearing its economic burden. The taxpayer on whom the incidence of a tax rests may in some cases be the entity legally responsible for payment of the tax; in many other cases it is a de facto taxpayer who is unable to pass on to other taxpayers the tax or a share of its burden. The object of the incidence is the one which incorporates the tax in question.

The incidence is in a certain sense the terminal phenomenon of shifting: shifting reaches its final point when the incidence of a tax is genuinely brought about. However, a word of warning is in order.

First, as mentioned above, this terminal phenomenon may hold only for a portion of the tax burden, so that even if a tax incidence is borne by a certain subject (and object), there may be shifting to another subject (or object). Secondly, the incidence does not necessarily consist in a tax burden that is equal to its nominal tax rate, and consequently it is perfectly conceivable that shifting of a greater (or smaller) sum than the tax itself may be shifted from a given taxpayer to other taxpayers and from a given object to another.

The process of tax shifting, by virtue of which the incidence of the tax comes to rest on a different entity from that which the law formally indicates, can be favourable or unfavourable to achievement of the objectives pursued by the tax policies, depending on the different circumstances. The process of shifting is favourable if the incidence of the tax formally imposed on certain subjects and on certain objects is genuinely intended by policy makers to rest on the other subjects or objects onto which it has been transferred. This is the case, for instance, with tax on tobacco or petrol and VAT on enterprises, which, by means of forward shifting, comes to bear on consumption. In contrast, the tax shifting process is unfavourable to the government's fiscal choices if the tax measures imposed on the given subject and object were truly intended to rest on them or if the government's aim is for the market forces to generate a different form of shifting.

Effectively, interest in the study of tax shifting is linked to awareness of the need for a careful analysis of the effects of the decision-making processes of the public choices. Although it is in itself a study in positive economics, the study of tax shifting acquires its full meaning in normative analysis.

2 DIFFUSION AND CAPITALIZATION OF TAXATION

The term *diffusion* refers to the dilation of the incidence and shifting of taxation, and it is generally taken to imply an amplification of the sphere of action of both phenomena to the entire economy. In addition to certain specific phenomena of shifting and incidence which can generally be circumscribed to particular sectors, factors or products, other more general circumstances can be observed. Deflation of consumer demand due to a tax is a typical 'diffusion' phenomenon. It is more closely linked to *income effects than to allocative effects.*

The term *capitalization*, or amortization of taxation, is much more rigorous: it refers to the transition of tax from the payment 'flows' pertaining to factors and products, forwards to the stock of capital and assets from which the flows derive. Capitalization is a form of incidence, to the extent to which capital value decreases and thereby induces 'amortization' of the levy, which is incorporated in the (lower) capital value of the good on which tax is imposed. Tax capitalization is also a shifting channel to the extent to which the decrease in capital value triggers further modifications in the prices of funds and flows, thereby leading to other economic burdens for their holders; it is a diffusion channel to the extent to which it appears appropriate to consider these other phenomena in a fairly undifferentiated manner, with highly aggregated references.

We will now examine how amortization or capitalization of taxation is determined quantitatively. Let us suppose that the ordinary market rate of return on goods is not influenced by a tax that has its incidence on the income from a good *B*. In this case, if market evaluations of good *B* depend only on the return it generates, and the latter is determined by the average market performance of goods in general, then the capital value of *B* will decrease by the same percentage as the income reduction brought about by the tax. Assuming that the tax on *B* has not (yet) been shifted forward onto users of *B* (which, for instance, is the residential housing sector), and that the tax rate in question is 20 per cent, then the capital value of the good is reduced by 20 per cent. If the tax rate is 10 per cent, the capital value of the good is reduced by 10 per cent. Capitalization of the levy, that is the transition whereby the tax on income passes from income to capital, increases as the net average market rate of return of the goods considered becomes lower, because the rate of capitalization through which an income is transformed into capital value is the inverse of the rate of return multiplied by 100. For example, if the rate of return is 5 per cent, the rate of capitalization is 20, since 5 per cent is 5/100 = 20. The inverse of 5 is 1/5, which gives 0.20, which, multiplied by 100, gives 20. Now let us consider a rate of return of 2 per cent. The rate of capitalization is 2/100 = 0.50 multiplied by 100, namely 50. Therefore, the lower the interest rate, the greater the passage of the income effect from income to capital; consequently, also, the lower the rate of return on the capital considered, the greater is the above-stated passage. But capitalization is not the end of the shifting process. Let us consider capital goods *B* that are investment goods produced and enduring over a span of, say, 50 years. Once the capital value of goods *B* has declined, on account of the new levy affecting their yield, by a percentage equal to the rate of the tax, then the profitability of producing goods *B* will also have declined. If the demand for new goods *B*, before the tax, is zero in the sense that demand for *B* is strictly limited to as many as are needed to replace existing *B*s, then every year, before the tax, the demand for *B* will on average be 2 per cent. If the production cost of these goods after the tax has remained unchanged and its capitalization is equal to the value that goods B had prior to the tax, it will now no longer be profitable to produce them. And supply will decline, let us say, by 2 per cent a year. Conceivably, this may not cause the market price of goods B to rise significantly, if their demand is elastic in that segment. But after a few years, once supply has decreased by – let us say – 10 per cent, the price will go up, unless demand is extremely elastic. For residential dwellings, a 10 per cent decrease in supply would be quite likely to cause house prices to rise by about 10 per, given the rigidity of demand. If B consists of bonds issued by joint-stock companies, the reduction in value of bonds already existing on the market will make it less advantageous for companies to issue new bonds. Companies will have greater recourse to issues of stocks and will engage in fewer investments. When the yield of domestic private bonds is determined by the international financial market, capitalization will take place in full because the interest rate gross of tax needs to rise to the level existing prior to the tax, which was dictated by the international market.

3   SHIFTING AND INCIDENCE: FORWARD, BACKWARD, OBLIQUE OR LATERAL

Shifting is defined as *forward* when it leads to a worsening of conditions for purchasers who buy from the taxpayer on whom the tax was imposed (see Figure 10.1 for the consumption tax, where the uncompensated D results in a price rise from P to $P'C$ with a burden for the purchaser amounting to $PCSP'$). It is defined as *backward* when it leads to a worsening of conditions for the suppliers of the taxpayer on whom the tax was imposed (in the same figure it can be seen that part of the tax falls on the supply, which is affected by $PCRT'P$). It is *oblique or lateral* when it leads to a worsening of conditions for products or goods associated with those on which it was imposed, in production or consumption.

Backward shifting comes about through a reduction in the price net of tax (from P to T for the supplier, in Figure 10.1), while forward shifting comes from a price increase.

Within this framework, amortization or capitalization is a backward shift, as it consists in a stock price reduction springing from a tax burden that weighs on the associated revenue (flows).

The word 'price' is used here in a broad sense, and includes not only prices *par excellence*, that is prices of goods, but also the remunerations of factors: wages, which are the price of labour; interest, which is the price for the use of capital and so forth.

Forward shifting refers to the rising price *gross* of tax. If the price net of tax also increases, as in the case of decreasing costs, and very rigid demand, then the shifting will be greater than the amount of the tax. Nevertheless, even a slight rise in the price gross of tax is sufficient for there to be some forward shifting. Forward shifting may be greater than the amount of the tax on goods that have an uncompensated demand curve that increases, as a result of the increase in the price of the good taxed. In effect, this happens with so-called inferior goods, that is those with regard to which consumption is greater when income is lower.[2] A very high tax on mass consumption of inferior goods generates a negative income effect on consumers, who increase their demand for such products.

Backward shifting, on the other hand, refers to the rising price *net* of tax. If the gross price after the tax is lower than the earlier price, it can be said that the backward shift is greater than the amount of the tax. This may happen for tax on labour, whether of subordinate workers or of self-employed, and on the labour of small businesses run by low-income subjects, if such subjects, affected by the tax that contracts their demand and their income, increase the units supplied in order to 'remove' the income effect of the tax (see further on in section 4).

Incidence can usefully be defined with regard to relative rather than absolute prices. Indeed, incidence emerges not only from the modifications occurring in the prices a given subject faces as a purchaser, but also in the prices that this subject achieves as a seller, in the attempt to likewise shift the tax forwards. Similarly, incidence also results not only from the modifications the subject finds herself faced with as a seller, but also in those she succeeds in achieving as a purchaser, in the attempt to shift the tax backwards.

> The factors–products–factors process is, as is known, a circular process: workers, enterprises and capitalists receive remuneration for the factors and present themselves – on the market – as purchasers of consumer and investment products. The gain achieved from these, in turn, feeds the yield from the factors. Thus forward shifting can follow the circuit from products to factors and return to the products, and backward shifting can follow the inverse circuit, and at each link in the chain there can be a certain incidence and a certain shifting.

4   FORWARD SHIFTING EQUAL TO THE TAX, LESS THAN THE TAX, GREATER THAN THE TAX: TAX ON THE VALUE OF GOODS AND SERVICES

Indirect taxes on individual goods and general taxation on all goods, such as the general taxes on sales as a percentage on the price of ceding goods and services, can be transferred forward with price increases equal to, lower

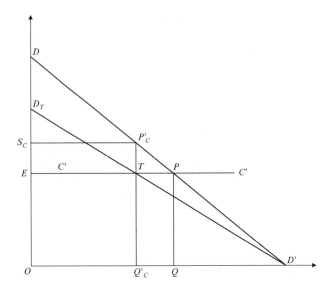

Figure 11.1   Tax shifting ad valorem: *case of constant costs*

or greater than the amount of the tax. These three different possibilities, which are indicated in Figures 11.1, 11.2 and 11.3 respectively, depend in a competitive regime on the trend of the cost curve (in a monopoly regime, as we saw in the previous chapter on optimal taxation, the tendency is for shifting to be lower than in a competitive regime, and this makes it unlikely, although not impossible, that shifting will be greater than the amount of the tax). Let us assume a sales tax of 33 per cent of the price. This can be represented as a one-third reduction in the demand curve, which implies a very high tax when the demand price is high; the tax gradually decreases in absolute value as the demand price gradually goes down, until it eventually becomes almost zero when the demand price tends to zero. The demand curve before the tax is DD', and after the tax it is D_TD'. In all three figures we maintain the same demand curve before the tax and the same levy and therefore the same demand after the tax. We will start from the simplest case, that of Figure 11.1, in which costs are constant and therefore the marginal cost curve for the market supply, in the sector of goods considered, appears as a straight line parallel to the axis of the abscissae. In our case this is $C'C'$, which intersects the demand curve before the tax at P, for the quantity OQ. Then the tax intervenes, generating the new demand curve D_TD'. It meets the cost curve at T, giving rise to the demanded quantity OQ'_C. As can easily be seen, the tax presents itself as an addition to the cost, giving rise to price P'_C which differs from price P as regards the segment TP'_C

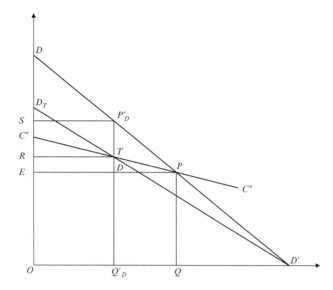

Figure 11.2 Tax shifting ad valorem: *case of decreasing costs*

which is exactly equal to the amount of the tax. And as can likewise easily be seen, this does not depend on whether demand is or is not fairly elastic, as demand elasticity merely results in a greater or lesser extent of reduction in the quantity demanded. It can readily be demonstrated that with more rigid demand, the reduction in demand is less marked, whereas with greater elasticity the reduction intensifies: but the price always increases more than the amount of the tax. Therefore it is correct to state that in a competitive regime with constant costs, the tax on the value of goods brings about a price increase equal to the amount of the tax, whatever the elasticity (or rigidity) of the demand curve. However, this proposition conceals a trap: namely the higher the demand price, the higher is the amount of the tax in absolute value, because the tax is a constant percentage of the price. With rigid demand, the price rise attributable to the tax is less than occurs with elastic demand, as there is a smaller reduction in the quantity demanded and therefore a smaller increase in the price, net of tax, to which the additional percentage price rise due to the tax has to be applied.

Now let us consider Figure 11.2, which shows the same demand curve and the same tax as that which reduces it in Figure 11.1, but the cost regime of the sector considered is now decreasing. Thus the reduction in demand leads backwards, onto a higher segment of the cost curve. And it can be stated that whatever the extent of the tax-induced contraction in quantity demanded, the price always increases more than the amount of the tax.

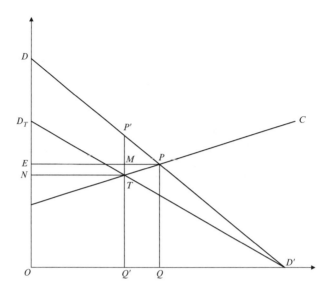

Figure 11.3   Tax shifting ad valorem: *case of increasing costs*

This is because, in addition to the higher price brought about by the tax, the greater cost due to the reduction in quantity demanded also has to be taken into account. In Figure 11.2, the price passes from P to P'_D with a reduction in quantity demanded from OQ to OQ'_D. The price rise is given by the segment $P'_D T$, which is equal to the tax, for the quantity $OQ'_D + TD$ which is the increase in cost due to the reduction in the quantity supplied, from OQ to OQ'_D. But it is also important to note that the tax is in any case shown to be greater than that which has to be paid in a regime of constant costs (Figure 11.1), having the same demand curve and the same tax rate.

Now the third hypothesis can be addressed without difficulty. This is the hypothesis that was mentioned, in Figure 11.3, in which the costs of the sector under consideration are increasing. This is the classical and neo-classical framework, for an economy based on a regime of competition, with small traditional enterprises (in the case of large and technologically advanced enterprises, as is found in the competitive global market, costs tend to be decreasing because fixed costs associated with technological and organizational progress play a major role). In this third hypothesis, prices increase less than the amount of the tax, because the reduction in the quantity demanded also involves a reduction in the marginal cost of the production sector considered.

Thus in Figure 11.3, the supply as influenced by the tax – which is again 33 per cent, as in the previous hypotheses – decreases from OQ to OQ'. The price goes up by $P'M$, which is a smaller amount than $P'T$, the amount of the tax. This is because the segment MT of the tax rate remains on the supply in the form of reduction in marginal cost. The decline in demand, under equal elasticity of the demand curve, is smaller than in the constant cost hypothesis and, *a fortiori*, smaller than in the decreasing cost hypothesis. Consequently, the absolute value of the tax is likewise smaller than in the first two cases. In the Appendix further comments on the revenue yielded by the tax *ad valorem* are offered, in connection with tax shifting, and on backwards shifting in relation to the cost regime.

5 REMOVAL AND LEGAL AVOIDANCE OF TAX

A subject is said to remove the tax burden from herself when she deals with it by increasing her productive activity or improving her efficiency, or more generally by intensifying her efforts towards wealth production.

A subject is said to avoid tax legally when and to the extent to which she does not fall under the purview of tax because she gives up the opportunity to engage in any business activity or to own a certain good or obtain a product that will be taxed, regardless of whether the tax will take the form of a levy on a subject legally responsible for paying the tax or incidence resting on a person.

It would be mistaken to imagine that by so doing the subject is able to escape absolutely any incidence of tax; for she would have to abstain from consumption, forgo ownership of any goods at all, or of gain from taxed income (and so forth), and this manner of proceeding would involve considerable sacrifice.

There is only one special case in which legal tax avoidance through sacrifice of a taxed activity (or good) implies total elimination of the incidence: namely, that in which the taxpayer manages to manipulate her activity in such a manner that, although it substantially continues just the same as before, and achieves a remuneration equal to the previously taxed income, it nevertheless becomes formally different. This legal 'tax avoidance' which is named 'tax elusion' is possible when the tax laws are badly constructed and lend themselves to being circumvented.

NOTES

1. Tax shifting long represented the part of financial economics which formed the greatest focus of attention among the most rigorous scholars. However, it can be stated – albeit, with due caution – that it is a sector in which economic research has by now reached

fairly general agreement. For a general overview see, among the vast literature on this topic, Seligman (1910); Fasiani (1951); Einaudi (1902 and 1941); Forte (1978); McLure (1975).

2. Marshall, in his *Principles of Economics* (1920 [1961]), writes 'As Mr Giffen has pointed out, a rise in the price of bread makes so large a drain on the resources of the poorer labouring families and raises so much the marginal utility of money to them, that they are forced to curtail their consumption of meat and the more expensive farinaceous foods: and, bread being still the cheapest food which they can get and will take, they consume more, and not less of it.'

12. Public prices

1   QUASI PRIVATE PUBLIC PRICES

Adopting – with a few adaptations – a classification introduced by Luigi Einaudi,[1] public prices, that is to say the prices for goods provided by the public economy either directly or through concession of a 'public service' to a market enterprise, can be distinguished into the four categories indicated here below:

a.   quasi private prices;
b.   monopoly public prices;
c.   economic public prices;
d.   political prices.

These different price categories reflect different relations with demand and cost, and therefore have different allocative and distributive characteristics.

Quasi private prices are the revenue the state obtains by ceding goods and services according to the laws of the market; this category refers to cases where the organization of provision according to market rules generates no appreciable contrast with the general aims pursued by the public economy.

> The classic example introduced by Einaudi is that of the sale of forest timber. The state possesses forests, not with the intention of drawing a financial gain from them, but in order to protect nature and enhance the landscape, ensure safeguards for the ecological balance and protect the soil. In pursuing this aim, the state carries out investments that are not based on calculating the profits likely to be obtained from the timber, but rather on the benefits deriving from the above-mentioned protective aims.
>
> The sale of timber *at market prices* will yield monetary proceeds which, however, may not be sufficient to cover the costs of investment and forest management. This is because the major benefits of this investment and forestry management programme consist of the ecological benefits and enhancement of the landscape. The price is 'quasi private' because it corresponds to the market price. It cannot be defined as 'private' *tout court* because the supply is not determined by calculations similar to those of the private sector but through choices of a different kind decided by the public operator.

When the public operator grants the use of government domain (destined to public ends, and inalienable, as broadcasting frequencies), and of its property, it should do so in accordance with competition as occurs on the market, by calling for tenders from subjects that aspire to the concession. (This would include, for instance, use of beaches for bathing establishments, use of the airwaves for television and cell phone telephony, of the subsoil for mining explorations.)

> This principle – consistent with the cooperative model, in which the public economy is 'market-conforming' – is a general rule of the European Economic and Monetary Union, aiming to ensure competition among enterprises in the various member states, in cases when such enterprises utilize public property. Within the European Union, tendering is compulsory.

It is also worth pointing out that the state and/or local authority that owns these goods forming part of the 'government domain' have no reason to privatize them, as it is important for them to retain their ownership in order to protect them against excessive utilization and render them accessible to all subjects under equal conditions of access.

2   MONOPOLY PUBLIC PRICES

Monopoly public prices are the monopolistic revenue the public operator obtains by exploiting the demand as privileged operator.

In an economic and monetary union they constitute a residual instrument.

> It is well known that a monopolist obtains a monopoly surplus deriving from the difference between the price that maximizes profits, based on the equality between marginal cost and marginal return, and the price an enterprise operating in a regime of competition should apply (based on the equality between average cost inclusive of the profit margin, and price).
>
> On the one hand the Treasury may need a tax revenue that is easy to collect. Thus goods with a rigid demand are singled out, such as tobacco and salt, and are subjected to a monopoly regime in order to collect the monopoly profit by a formal tax. But this is forbidden in the European Monetary Union, which requires competition in all markets wherever this is possible.
>
> Alternatively, the state may individuate goods whose widespread use involves an element of danger. The state may then exert control over them by means of a monopoly, in order to restrict demand. An example of this second type is that of the lotto game, casinos and lotteries. But within the European Union the exercise of gambling by a given enterprise can be established only by tenders, in order to avoid discrimination. It follows that the licence tax that the government thereby obtains is a monopoly revenue, as in order to be awarded a

concession – if there is competitive tendering – concessionaires must devolve to the grantor most of the 'monopolistic rent' which they expect to obtain.

However, in a genuine cooperative model there is no reason to suppose that the state here should operate according to the criterion of maximum monopolistic profit. If it is a case regarded as 'demerit' consumption according to collective preferences expressed at the constitutional stage in presence of adequate information, the state should adopt a more restrictive approach. If, as may be the case, the interference in the private preferences appears groundless, then the state should merely aim to apply a consumption tax following optimal taxation principles.

3 ECONOMIC PUBLIC PRICES

In the cooperative system, this category of prices represents the optimal system for the 'public utilities' that supply goods and services of public civil and/or productive interest. Despite being characterized by considerable external effects and decreasing costs (see Chapter 3, subsection 1.11, on Hotelling goods), these services can, according to the cooperative model, be managed as enterprises, either directly or via a concession, by means of discriminated tariffs, without global margins of monopolistic exploitation. A typical case is that of postal tariffs (mainly paid for by postage stamps).

The public price that is commensurate, globally, with the 'full cost', that is with the average cost plus a margin, which is roughly in line with that of a market enterprise operating in a competitive regime, can be defined as 'economic' because it imitates this market price.

> We know that prices below the average cost are allocatively better when costs are decreasing and the external economies are substantial (see Chapter 3, subsections 1.10–1.11). But price discrimination may allow public utility enterprises to achieve, as an average calculation, a public price comparable to the average full cost, even if in some cases the public utilities set their prices equal to the marginal cost or possibly even below the latter, to take into account the social return or particular aspects of merit or redistributive equity. Those who pay prices higher than the full cost, for purposes of balancing the budget, can be said to undergo taxation in favour of those who pay less than the cost.
>
> But if the principle of the deficit were to be adopted, someone would still have to pay it, through taxation.[2]

On the other hand, the constraint of having to balance the budget requires the public enterprise to make every effort to maintain efficiency, by containing costs and improving the service in order to acquire a greater number of users at the same price. In contrast, the possibility of being able to rely on deficit operation could open the floodgates to laxity of behaviour.

If the public enterprise is unable to balance the budget through price discrimination, this requirement can nevertheless be fulfilled in another two ways.

First, it can be done by establishing that certain fixed costs do not form part of the business costs. The burden of expenditure for the construction of a motorway can be lessened by means of favourable credit terms; railway investments can be partly carried out with grants. Secondly, pre-established subsidies could be set up, on the understanding that these, in a certain sense, form part of the business revenue.

> In an economic and monetary union favourable credit arrangements are ruled out because they distort competition in the single market. However, the public operator can build an infrastructure (for example the railway network or the motorway) and then grant the operating concession to an enterprise through the system of calling for tenders. This will ensure that the free supply of the good 'infrastructure' does not give rise to distortions of competition and of allocation of resources, even though coverage of the cost may be only partial.

Thus there is a grey area between economic public prices and political public prices. Prices below the true full cost may retain the character of economic prices because the regulated enterprise, which performs public utility services,[3] succeeds in balancing the total average cost either because it does not have the burden of interest and depreciation charges on the fixed capital but only that of its extraordinary maintenance and that of the operating costs, or else because it has only the latter.

When the prices set by regulated public utilities systematically give rise to a return lower than the costs of infrastructures which may not be considered as a public good, and *a fortiori* when the prices are below variable costs, then we are clearly dealing with political prices. The term *political* is to be understood as meaning that at this point the company ceases to be a market enterprise: its activity depends above all on government subsidies or on the system of taxation, and thus on non-market factors. Consequently, the enterprise in question is unable to have recourse to credit unless it receives guarantees from the government and/or the above-stated subsidies. In an economic and monetary union subsidies to public utilities can indeed be allowed, for special cases pertaining to specific 'public service' requirements, but given the budget constraints that imply rigorous public spending policies, such subsidies should be granted according to clearly defined formulas and not merely as a rescue operation for a loss-making enterprise.

Article 86 of the European Union Treaty establishes that the undertakings entrusted with the operation of services of general economic interest or having the character of a revenue-producing monopoly shall be subject to the rules contained in this treaty, in particular to the rules on competition, in so far as the application of such rules does not obstruct the performance, in law or in fact, of the particular tasks assigned to them. The development of trade must not be affected to such an extent as would be contrary to the interests of the Community. This formulation does allow extensive adoption of political prices. But it is clearly designed to limit the use of subsidies that lead to privileges for domestic enterprises compared to those of other member countries, if such a phenomenon would have a substantial impact on competition at the intracommunity level.

However, rather than subsidies hypothetically designed to cover the fixed costs inclusive of special maintenance, uncoupling the infrastructures from the public utilities would appear to be a more suitable solution, in a public choice perspective, as it would assign to the given enterprises a budget net of fixed costs, having a non-discretionary character. But it should be borne in mind that in order to cover the expense that both these alternatives involve, it is necessary to have recourse to taxes, and any taxation, as noted earlier, may generate distortions. In an economic and monetary union there are fiscal constraints that may render this solution particularly problematic. Therefore additional arguments are needed, above and beyond the mere Hotelling theorem, to allow solutions that lead to prices below the true full cost. Examples are the argument that the service under consideration generates *great* external economies as occurs with some types of public transport (for example urban public transport services, which may reduce road traffic congestion), or that it responds to important redistributive aims benefiting the less favoured (eg. some types of public services in favour of isolated low-income communities).

4 TAXONOMY OF POLITICAL PRICES: FROM PUBLIC ENTERPRISES TO NON-PROFIT UNDERTAKINGS

The principles of the cooperative model of public economy do not allow operation of enterprises that provide public utility services running *systematically* at a deficit, the latter then being financed by the public operator by *ex ante* or *ex post discretionary* transfer payments. The rationale for this prohibition is that it would generate a distortion of competition. Only in highly exceptional cases is this rule waived. Therefore, *for public utility enterprises*, political prices will be a residual problem.[4]

In the cooperative model, on the other hand, there may be some justifications for political prices, and similar justifications are admissible even within an economic and monetary union. Such cases would include provision of semi-public merit goods, distributive operations pursuing the ends of education, health care, and cultural, social and humanitarian goals (see Chapter 3, sections 2 and 3). These public political prices, however, should not concern enterprises but activities of the Public Administrations and of non-profit bodies which, in a broad sense, belong to the public finance because they provide public goods. A partial list is given below:

1. educational fees, for enrolment in universities and other educational institutions;
2. health care 'tickets', payable to the health care facilities for diagnostic tests, medical and surgical treatment, first aid and emergency care and in some cases for hospital stays in public treatment facilities;[5]
3. revenues of museums and similar institutions, through the fees charged for entry to a temporary exhibition or the permanent museum display;[6]
4. theatre and concert tickets, and entry charges for other cultural events organized by public operators;
5. below-cost prices of school meals;
6. rents from social housing, lower than the market level in favour of (supposedly) low-income tenants;
7. prices for state- or local authority-run crèches and daycare centres, and nursing homes for the aged, and funeral and cemetery services;
8. below-cost tariffs for goods and services in favour of the disabled and other subjects needing social and health care assistance.

The parameters of political prices should by no means be randomly determined, as often happens. But the exclusive link-up with economic conditions, as for instance happens by means of the so-called 'means test' (that is to say, checking on the income and personal estate indicators of those who wish to utilize the public services in question) may be irrational, as the subsidy implied by the political price may concern provision of specific services that refer to individual wants with a specific, humanitarian or merit character that justifies the supply of the service. Consequently, the dominant variable for deciding who is entitled to benefit from the service should be determined by the intensity of such wants that rationally justifies the subsidy.

Thus in the case of care and assistance for the severely sick, the severity of the illness should be taken into consideration; for crèches and daycare centres, it is not only the family income that should be considered but also the conditions of the mother and the family; for educational fees, an important parameter is that of merit,[7] and so on.

NOTES

1. L. Einaudi (1940 [1956]) Book One, Chapters 1, 2 and 3.
2. See in this regard Chapter 3, subsection 1.11, at the end and the bibliography cited therein.
3. The concept of an enterprise that conducts public utility services is distinct from that of a public enterprise. The concept of 'public utilities' is generally taken to mean regulated enterprises that have substantial fixed costs due to infrastructures that cannot be easily duplicated or which operate with a non-reproducible good or service (for example a port), and which therefore enjoy a natural monopoly or quasi monopoly position and supply goods and services that *condition* civil life and productive activities.
4. Our definition differs from that of Pantaleoni (1919), according to whom 'political' prices are those that arise if the same good can be bought and sold at different prices depending on whether the buyer or seller do or do not have certain prerequisites of a political, social, ethical, religious, national or physiological nature, and so on. Economic prices, according to Pantaleoni's definition, are those which are 'subject to the law of indifference. . .such that equal quantities of the same good, in the same place and time, are sold at the same price. . . This law is the effect of the indifference of choice by buyers and of the indifference of choice of the seller when faced with the buyers.' In our definition (which follows that of Einaudi), economic public prices admit discriminations designed to assure that the public utility enterprises have shares of the consumers' rents in order to be able to balance the budget, when the marginal costs at the meeting point with demand are lower than average costs.
5. Emergency room and hospitalization 'tickets' are not applied in Italy.
6. In a rational system public sale of so-called accessory goods and services such as refreshments and restaurant facilities, publications, postcards, slides, gift objects, and so on, should form part of quasi private prices because these are proceeds determined by the market pertaining to such goods and service.
7. Which in Italy is enshrined in the Constitution.

13.   Public debt and fiscal policy

1   THE PUBLIC DEBT AND THE PUBLIC DEFICIT

1.1   The Public Debt is the most Subtly Menacing Expression of the Powers of the Fiscal Leviathan

In appearance the public debt would seem to be a normal financial operation, carried out in the market economy, involving a request for money against interest and with the promise of repayment. But, on closer inspection, there is a major difference for the creditor. The subscriber has no need to exercise due diligence in examining how the funds are going to be used so as to assess whether the loan contract is likely be honoured with interest payments and capital repayment. Rather, it is vital to ascertain if the debt is genuinely public and if the fiscal Leviathan is endowed with good fiscal power[1] and, conceivably, has the power to finance itself with money.[2] Should the worst come to the worst, the credit will be eroded as a result of inflation triggered by the very circumstance of gathering the means to honour the credit itself, and by the risk that the heads of government may decide not to respect the commitment made to the creditors. In particular, the risk of default cannot be ruled out in the case of a foreign debt, which may be unsustainable for the balance of payments, especially if it was contracted at extortionate conditions which now appear iniquitous, even though they were accepted at the time.

In short, the public debt does not stand or fall depending on the principled use to which it is put, unlike the private debt of enterprises. Instead, it is contingent on the reliability of the fiscal-monetary power of whatever body has issued the debt. It generates a burden for the taxpayers and for investors operating on the market, reducing global growth or at least that of regions which do not benefit from the investment expenditure to which the public debt is supposed to be destined (efficiently and effectively, in the best of hypotheses),[3] without there being a public income to finance the debt service.[4] And the taxes by means of which it will eventually be paid generally bring about distortionary effects, as was seen earlier (Chapters 9 and 10), especially if the taxes are high.

1.2 The Neo-Ricardian Theory of Lucas and Barro, of Complete Present Capitalization

This proposition is, in actual fact, contested by authors such as Lucas and Barro, exponents of the so-called school of new classical macroeconomics, who maintain that citizens can in no way be deceived by a state that issues debts. When debts are issued, they contend, citizens immediately suffer the burden of the taxes they themselves and their descendants will have to bear in order to repay the debt. Accordingly, they reduce their consumption in order to have a greater quantity of capital available precisely to fulfil that onus. Admittedly, they will in part be content with simply saving less, but even if they were subjected to the tax at the present time, they would in part reduce their savings, and in part their consumption.

This theoretical approach appears to be flawed by the assumption of identity of interests between present and future selves and between present subjects and the descendants of the latter.

Even admitting the assumption of perfect information about the future, it still remains true that present subjects are inclined not to devote the same degree of care and attention to their own present and their own future, or to the futures associated with them.

Future selves and futures are less important for present individuals than their present selves (see Chapter 3, subsections 2.5–2.7). Therefore it is rational, from *their* point of view, although obviously not from the point of view of all selves in the temporal sequence, to award preference to a debt that will be paid in the future and which gives advantages in present time, as compared to a present burden designed to pay for present advantages, or present burdens intended to pay for future advantages, for which they do not have a differential compensation in present time.

As Tobin (1980) put it, Barro's contribution is to show how mortal households can have effectively infinite horizons. The condition is that each generation includes in its utility function, along with consumption at various stages of its lifetime, the *utility* of the next generation. The child's utility is a function – in indirect form – of his endowment plus the bequest received from the parent. Within a given present value of taxation, a shift in timing from one generation to the next leaves the parent facing the same budget constraint as before. He will make up for the heavier taxation in store for the child by providing a larger bequest. The chain of overlapping generations behaving in this manner makes the horizon of each generation effectively infinite.

1.3   Tobin's Critique

In addition to the criticisms already implicit in the above comment, Tobin also remarks that:

a. some households may be childless, and many of those who do have children are indifferent to their utility (or not as interested as they are in their own utility); to this I would add that children do not always survive their parents;
b. not all households save in order to provide a bequest for their children, and the 'chain of overlapping generations' may be broken.

Clearly, the fact that a person's descendants bear a greater burden does not lead to any greater propensity to save if the incentive underlying saving is quite independent of the overall utility of the future generations, and appears instead as a function of present income.[5]

On the other hand, there is one element Tobin does not consider: the uncertainty about who, in the future, is going to bear the deferred burden. This is a powerful tool exploited for manipulative ends by governments that take on debts.

It would be naive to assume that citizens are given crystal-clear information on the true extent of the public debt, or that efforts are made to ensure they have a clear understanding of whether politicians who have contracted the debt believe it can be financed with the flow of revenue generated by the increase of GDP, at unchanged tax rates. Misunderstandings and disinformation are particularly likely to arise with multi-party governments (cf. Holler, 1987a).

1.4   Public Debt in an Individual State of an Economic and Monetary Union (EMU)

In an EMU for the purposes of macroeconomic equilibrium and growth of GDP within the community, what is taken into account is the trend and balance of its 'general government' budget (see Chapter 6, subsections 1.2 and 2.9). A criticism of the theory on rational expectations of the future tax burdens that are likely to be associated with future payment of the debt was provided above; we may now add the argument that the debt taken on in an individual state generates a future burden that will affect all the citizens of the EMU. For while it may be true that the taxes pertaining to the debt of an individual state generate a burden only for the citizens of that state, the fact remains that the other states will have to contract fewer debts if the aim is to respect a given debt/GDP relationship for the entire

Union, in order to ensure safeguards with regard to issued share capital of the private sector.

1.5 The Public Debt as a Burden on the Current Generations of the Whole EMU

Furthermore, the burden for the future is not the same concept as the burden weighing on the future generations. It can be granted that the interest generated by the deficit may, to a large extent, be paid with new public debt. But this process has its limits.[6]

Once the debt has exceeded a certain ratio to GDP, the burden of servicing this debt, that is the burden of the interest and the prospect of having to issue new debts as soon as the previous short-term, medium-term and long-term debts come to maturity, creates serious problems that severely hamper the growth of GDP if the aim is to safeguard monetary stability and national solvency as well as that of the Union of which the state under consideration (possibly) forms part.

In short, the public debt is a 'deferred tax', but every generation is in time to bear the weight of a substantial part of the public debt it has voted for. Every generation passes on to future generations a portion of the burden of its own public debt, and receives a part of the debt from prior generations, which the latter did not pay. However, the greater the debt generated in the immediate present, the heavier the burden promises to be in years to come.

With the reduction in growth there emerges – in new and more persuasive terms – the (pseudo) Ricardian theme of a net reduction in wealth.

Now, if the public debt has not been destined to productive investments that have significance for citizens who bear the debt, then citizens who experience the debt as a negative 'wealth effect' have a lower income than they could have had if the circumstances had been different. In the EMU this burden concerns the entire area of the Union, because the financial market is a single market.

Having thus clarified in what sense the public debt is a tax deferred on the short term and, *pro quota*, a tax on the future and on the future generations in terms of reduced growth, which affects the entire Union, it should now also be noted that those who subscribe the debt do obtain the benefit of the interest, and that the reduction in growth occurs only if the public debt is not invested with an efficiency comparable to that of the market. Average growth may not decrease, and in fact it may even increase (if the public debt is invested efficiently in the market), but it increases above all in the state that issues the debt, whereas the others may experience lower growth due to the drainage of financial resources towards the aforesaid state, or they may have to make greater sacrifices in order to achieve the desired growth.

1.6 In the Absence of Full Employment, what Burdens are Generated by the Public Debt, and Who For

At times it may happen that the emission of public debt may enable the government to collect savings that would otherwise remain inactive, thereby increasing the economic resources available in the present and allowing them to be used in the present without withdrawing resources from the private investment sector to pass them on to the government. Alternatively, it may enable the government to gather savings that would otherwise not have been created, because preference would have been awarded to using the money for consumption or for investment in a more attractive employment.

In the first of these scenarios, it might appear better to sell the public debt to the Central Bank so that the Central Bank can expand the money supply rather than placing it on the market. Also, it is clear that the interest the Bank obtains from the state is a mere internal transfer of the public sector, because the Central Bank, in an economic perspective, is an integral part of the public economy. However, such a move is in any case precluded in the cooperative model (see below, subsections 2.1 and 2.4). With regard to monetary policy, in the cooperative model the excess of demand for money over supply is (theoretically) counterbalanced by an expansion of the money supply via a reduction in the interest rate, to the advantage of the credit system of the market economy.

If the public debt is placed on the market, in a situation of underemployment, while the burden for future taxpayers remains, there is also a greater income with which to pay it, as a result of the expansion generated by the debt. But at times the public debt generates an excess of demand for total domestic credit in relation to points of the Phillips curve, which concerns the ratio between rise in wages and the demand for labour, in an economy with a rigid labour market. This may come about even before full employment, with the consequence of inflationary pressure which causes, in the present, sacrifices for vast classes of subjects. The public debt is thereby transformed into a tax under the form of 'inflation' (see below, subsection 2.8).

On the other hand, contrary to the beliefs of post-Keynesian orthodoxy, it cannot be taken for granted that the expansion resulting from the deficit-based fiscal policy will, by virtue of the spontaneous increase in revenue associated with the growth of GDP, necessarily generate the means to pay the debt contracted to prompt this increase.

Let us suppose that a public debt amounting to a real 1 per cent of GDP of a given year t_0 causes a 2 per cent growth in GDP, by virtue of a very favourable interaction between the multiplier and the accelerator and a permissive money supply. If we also assume that the real interest on the debt is 5 per cent of GDP, then in the years after t_0 it will be necessary to levy taxes for 0.05 of GDP in order to service the above debt and redeem it.

Given a tax burden and a social security tax burden amounting to 40 per cent (25 per cent taxes and 15 per cent social contributions) of the greater GDP, it would appear that there is 0.8 per cent available – permanently – to finance the debt. Therefore, it would seem that there is ample scope to pay the debt burden without increasing the tax burden.

But further reflection leads to the realization that as GDP grows, the need for public expenditure also grows, above all for social insurance and local expenditure, which to a large extent constitutes a production cost and, to a lesser extent, is complementary to private consumption linked to the greater GDP. Consequently, only a part of the increased tax revenue linked to growth of GDP can be devoted to paying the interest on the new public debt.

1.7 Reduction of 'Crowding Out' under the Hypothesis of an Open Capital Market

If the economy is open from the financial point of view, at an equilibrium interest rate with regard to the supply of public debt by the state i of the EMU Z in the period t_0, there can be an inflow of capital from abroad: both for subscription of the public debt and also to collect the resources for the enterprises and banks of Z, whose financing is 'crowded out' by that of the state. Thus the 'overloading' on the private operators of Z present in t_0 is lower than in the hypothesis of an economy with a closed capital market, but the burden for the future periods of $t_f \ldots t_n$ increases in relation to the future loss of global disposable income of Z.

Indeed servicing the foreign debt, in the hypothesis of balance of payments equilibrium in all other respects, implies that the global income of Z, during the future period t_f, will be lower than its aggregate product by an amount equal to the outflow of disbursements for servicing the aforesaid debt.

If the debt was 'invested well' during the previous period t_1, then in a t_f all the citizens of the state i of Z will obtain an adequate compensation to offset this 'net loss' compared to the national product of $t_f \ldots t_n$ that would otherwise have been possible. But in the hypothesis that the debt was utilized for consumption, the benefit of debt-financed public expenditure will consist only in greater present-day welfare not counterbalanced by a corresponding greater GDP of i of Z. The consequences of such a situation will be made clear below.

1.8   The 'Crowding Out' Effect of the Public Debt through the EMU Interest Rate

As the economy approaches full employment, if it is desirable to avoid inflationary pressure deriving from inordinate expansion of 'total domestic credit', the Central Bank of the EMU will not be able to expand the demand for money and therefore the Treasury will have to establish a high interest rate for the public debt in order to 'crowd out' private demand for bank credit or for non-banking financial investment: up to a volume sufficient to reach equilibrium.

Naturally, it may be the case that the public debt is destined to productive investments and that such utilization is more advantageous, in the collective preference, than the 'crowded out' private investments. But often the opposite is true, especially if the investment has no market value, as happens when it is carried out with projects that do not give a monetary return but only collective benefits that are difficult to calculate. In any case, the 'crowding out' concerns the entire area of the EMU while the benefit of the expenditure is 'regional'. This benefit (directly) concerns the community of the state that has issued the debt.

1.9   The Increasing Cost Curve of the State's Demand for Saving

For a state that issues public debt, there is a law of decreasing returns, in terms of additional availability of savings as a response to successive increases in real interest. This is due to the fact that while the rise in the real interest rate at first attracts liquidity and funds that might otherwise go abroad, this 'contribution' to the dilation of the domestic supply of savings then little by little begins to fade, its place being taken, in the expansion of this supply, by the increased advantageousness of investing in public debt rather than in private investment and of saving versus consumption. But even this 'difficult' contribution to the dilation of supply of savings to the Treasury gradually dries up, and savings no longer respond to successive increases in the real interest rate. In any case, even the aggregate medium-long period domestic savings supply curve, in relation to the real interest rate, presents a markedly rigid segment after the initial elastic segment.

1.10   The Fundamental Theorem of Long-Term Sustainability of the Public Debt

To identify the route that leads to the 'debt crisis', it is necessary to explore the 'critical point' beyond which the crisis erupts. This critical point can be ascertained by means of the 'fundamental theorem on the sustainability of the public debt' which dictates the conditions within which a new issue of debt can be repeated without overstepping the critical point.

The theorem in question has the following threefold statement:

1. Debt issued for additional deficit expenditure or for tax reduction in a situation of deficit can take place without increasing the debt/ GDP ratio only when the interest rate is lower than the GDP growth rate;
2. If the interest rate is equal to the growth rate, no debt can be issued for additional expenditure or tax reduction in deficit if the debt/GDP ratio is to be maintained unchanged;
3. If the interest rate exceeds the growth rate, it is not even possible to issue debt to repay the entire amount of the interest on the old debt without increasing the debt/GDP ratio.

Note that 'additional expenditure' in deficit is to be understood here as referring to expenditure other than payment of the interest on the old debt.

Otherwise stated, the 'fundamental theorem' asserts that when a new debt is contracted in order to pay the interest on the old debt, the volume of the public debt gross of servicing the interest is maintained in a constant percentage over GDP as long as the growth rate of GDP equals the interest rate. It decreases percentagewise compared to GDP if the interest rate is lower than the growth rate of GDP, and increases in the opposite case.[7]

The demonstration is very simple.

Let D_{t0} be the volume of the public debt at time t_0, I_{t1} the interest rate in t_1; GDP_{t0} the volume of GDP in t_0 and C_{GDPt1} the growth rate of GDP from t_0 to t_1. Let I_{Dt1} be the volume of interest on the public debt in t_1 that results from Dt_0 for It_1.

Let Δ_{Dt0} denominate the increase in public debt from time t_0 to time t_1.

Now, assuming D_{t0}, if the entire servicing of the interest I_{Dt1} is covered by debt and no further debt is issued, then $\Delta_{Dt0} = D_{t0} \times I_{Dt1}$. On the other hand, the volume of growth of GDP of t_0 from t_0 to t_1, which is Δ_{GDPt0}, is equal to $GDP_{t0} \times C_{GDPt0}$. Now if $C_{GDPt1} = I_{t1}$, we will have that both D_{t0} and GDP_{t0} grow by the same percentage. And multiplying the numerator and the denominator of the debt/GDP ratio by this same identical percentage, which we write as C_{GDPt1}, we will have that the new debt always has the same ratio with GDP:

$$D_{t0}/GDP_{t0} = [D_{t0} + (C_{GDPt1} \times D_{t0})]/[GDP_{t0} + (C_{GDPt1} \times GDP_{t0})]$$
$$= D_{t1}/GDP_{t1} \qquad (13.1)$$

Obviously, when $C_{GDPtl} < I_{tl}$, we will have

$$D_{t0}/GDP_{t0} = [D_{t0} + ((C_{GDPtl} + K) \times D_{t0})]/[GDP_{t0} + (C_{GDPtl} \times GDP_{t0})] = D_{tl}/GDP_{tl} \quad (13.2)$$

in (13.2) we have inserted, in the numerator, on the right-hand side a rate K, which is summed with C_{GDPtl} to equal I_{tl}. Whereas when $C_{GDPtl} > I_{tl}$, then the result with the same corrective K which now has the sign –, will be

$$D_{t0}/GDP_{t0} = [D_{t0} + ((C_{GDPtl} - K) \times D_{t0})]/[GDP_{t0} + (C_{GDPtl} \times GDP_{t0})] = D_{tl}/GDP_{tl} \quad (13.3)$$

From these three elementary formulas the following precept can be obtained:

- given (13.1), then in order to avoid an increase in the percentage of public debt beyond a point considered to be dangerous, such as 110 per cent of GDP, which may be the 'critical point', it is necessary to balance the primary budget B_I, defined as the gap between revenue E and public expenditure net of the expense for the interest S_p, therefore:

$$B_I = S_p - E = 0$$

If on the other hand, (13.3) holds, then it is possible to have

$$B_I = S_p - E > 0$$

In other words B_I can have a deficit equal to the gap K between C_{GDPtl} and I_{tl} multiplied by D_{t0}, without there being an increase in the percentage of public debt over GDP.

But if (13.2) holds, which is the most typical case in a heavily indebted country, in a world characterized by high interest rates and poor economic growth, then the country will be faced with:

$$B_I = S_p - E < 0$$

which obliges generation of a *surplus* K times C_{GDPtl} in the primary budget. Here in order to move away from the 'critical point' it will in fact be necessary to have a *surplus* $K' > K$.

Therefore the recovery policies of a severely indebted country must act simultaneously on three fronts:

- low inflation and a stable exchange rate, in order to have an interest rate that does not exceed international levels and does not incorporate a differential for the risk of inflation and the exchange rate risk;
- a policy that does not depress the growth rate of GDP, in order to generate a tendency to equality between the interest rate and growth;
- a surplus of B_I amounting to $K' \times D_{GDPt1}$, in order to move away from the 'critical point' within a few years.

In an EMU, where only a country i is heavily indebted, where all countries are subject to a fiscal discipline and the central bank of the Union acts correctly, the first requirement may be the result of the overall policy of the Union.

2 THE ISSUING OF MONEY AND INFLATION

2.1 The Ways of Issuing Money in the Cooperative Model of the Public Economy

The power to issue money that is legal tender, devoid of real intrinsic content and not endowed with coverage or having only partial coverage in gold, silver or foreign currency is a power inherent in the sovereignty of the collectivist state and of the controlled economy state. This power is not acceptable within the cooperative model, in which money is an instrument of the market economy and should be appropriately managed in conformity to its optimal functioning, in such a way as to ensure its stability. Furthermore, its management should be run by an independent authority that can be controlled by public opinion, but is not subject to governmental or parliamentary interference (see below, subsection 2.4).

2.2 Issue of Divisional Currency by the State

On the basis of the rule stated above, the government is limited to issuing coin. This form of direct monetary financing of the state cannot but be extremely limited and concerns only coin made of base metal. Minting has a cost and therefore the financial gain of this type of issue is not given by the total value of the issue itself, but by the latter minus the cost of the metal summed with that of minting, transport and insurance: often the gain is zero or negative.

In the European EMU the Central Bank issues divisional currency as well, and the states have no monetary power.

2.3 Taxation of the Gains of the Central Banks in the Cooperative Model of the Public Economy for an EMU

But the fiscal Leviathan will not so easily be put to rest when faced with the prohibition on 'printing paper money' imposed in modern states. It resorts to indirect systems, which are no less effective. Indeed, in a regime in which the issuing institution is strongly independent of the government and in which, at the same time, 'forced circulation' has been brought into action – that is to say, there is no requirement for the money issued to be covered in hard currency or gold or securities – a most logical method is to introduce a tax either directly or indirectly on the substantial returns the Central Bank obtains by virtue of having the sole right to print bank notes. In the cooperative model, for an EMU a tax on the gain of the Central Bank in the individual states is allowed only in terms of the ordinary corporation tax, and this is justified by the fact that the Central Banks of the Sovereign States which are members of the Union are 'domestic banking subjects'. The Central Bank of the Union should be exempted from any domestic taxation of the member states, inasmuch as it is a supranational (banking) subject. In principle it should be subjected to taxation by the government of the Union with a tax similar to the corporation taxes of the member states.

This does not happen in the European Monetary Union: the ECB profits are exempted from any taxation.

2.4 Tax on Monetary Circulation Within the EMU

This could be a source of revenue for the government of the Economic and Monetary Union, through the Central Bank which holds the main monetary power, for the entire area. However, in the cooperative model this taxation is precluded by the principle that the rights of monetary seignorage belong to the individuals as members of the market economy.

2.5 The Prohibition on Treasury Credit Accounts at the Central Bank and the Prohibition of Sale of the Public Debt to the Central Banks in the EMU, in a Cooperative Model of Public Economy

The concession of a credit account by the Central Bank to the Treasury is the means through which the state indirectly makes use of its monetary power, in order to circumvent the principle of separation between government and the Central Bank. The system whereby the Central Bank purchases public securities and subsequently places them on the market is a less invasive method. If it wishes to refuse the purchase, the Central Bank can claim that while it can absorb the loan at the present time, it may have difficulty in placing it on the market in future if the loan itself should turn out to be disproportionate to the economy's capacity to absorb it.

In a cooperative model of public economy and *a fortiori* in an EMU, both of these methods are excluded because they imply that the deficit of a member state is passed on throughout the area of the Union, with the expansion of the money supply.

In the European EMU both methods are forbidden.

2.6 Sale of the Domestic Public Debt to the Banking System with Expansion of Credit is Dangerous

Such a method is truly the most consummately astute move by the fiscal Leviathan when it holds power over the monetary policy of the Central Bank. It consists in allowing the banks to issue new secondary money under the form of credit expansion (so-called M_2). This fills bankers with glee as their volume of business swells and groups linked to the banking system are enabled to utilize money that comes from the 'quantitative easing' and make a gain on these amounts by lending to the state. But this requires the acquiescence by the Central Bank in the directives of the Treasury, which in the cooperative model of public economy and *a fortiori* in an EMU cannot be the case, because the Central Bank of an EMU expands or decreases the money supply for the entire area of the Community with a single interest (or discount) rate, and not for the benefit of the government and particularly of the government of one of its sub-parts. The Central Banks of the member states in an EMU are supposed to be the mere executors of the monetary policy decided on the level of the Central Bank of the Union.

Within the European Monetary Union the Central Bank (ECB) cannot buy bonds of the member state governments, except on a purely transitory basis, and only if the state in question is endowed with an A 'rating' by the international rating agencies.

2.7 The Issue of Non-inflationary Money in an EMU

There are cases in which issuing money by printing bank notes (m_1) or credit expansion (m_2) is by no means an element of monetary inflation, and it is important to underline that these are quite normal, 'physiological' situations. More specifically, as is well known, in an economic system the demand for money tends to increase every year due to the increase in transactions, which goes hand in hand with the increase in domestic product and with the development of the subdivision of labour. Additionally, the increase in demand for money also stems from increase in the income of individuals and enterprises, which increases their need for liquidity.

In an EMU each Central Bank will issue money on the basis of the quantity required at the interest rate fixed by the Central Bank of the Union, and this in turn will be determined according to global parameters emerging in the Union. Operations conducted by the individual Central Banks of the Union will generate returns that will remain in their own hands, except for operations conducted between such banks and the Bank of the Union.

To the extent to which the gain achieved by a Central Bank of the Union with its monetary and financial operations is taxable, with the general corporation tax, it will flow into the individual state of the Union. However, the government of EMU, even in a cooperative model of public economy, could in principle deduct from this amount the tax described in subsection 2.4, given that the EMU holds 'monetary sovereignty', that is the so-called right to 'seignorage' over the issue of currency, in the interest of the market economy.

2.8 The Issue of Inflationary Money: In Particular in an EMU

We will now turn to the hypothesis of the issue of money as an inflationary public finance tool. Such a move is made possible by the permissive orientation of the Central Bank, which expands credit to banks in order to 'ease' the public debt or to enable enterprises to cope with sharp labour cost rises or to deal with emergencies such as a war, where military enterprises need easy access to credit in order to produce the weaponry indispensable for the nation's defence.[8]

It should, however, be stated straight out that there exists no absolutely clear-cut distinction between inflationary and non-inflationary issue of money and of credit, because the nature of bank notes and of the expansion of credit, that is to say m_1, m_2 and m_3, is identical in both cases. A discriminating element is given by the size of their effect on prices, which is linked both to the quantity of the emission and also, in a rather complex manner, to the quantity of public expenditure financed by the issue.

> According to the monetary stability criteria of the ECB, a price increase beyond 2 per cent is considered inflationary.

A further complication resides in the fact that, conceptually, a certain issue of money can be said to be inflationary both when it 'prompts' prices to rise and also when it 'enables' prices – that were rising under their own impetus – actually to develop that rise.

Now, one way of discouraging these price rises, if they are driven by wage costs, is to restrict the money supply in order to bring global demand down to levels below full employment by the higher interest rate. This policy, leading to job reductions, would counter the drive towards wage increases and induce a tendency towards price reduction or at least price containment, through a reduction in consumption demand.

> In the European EMU, monetary policy is implemented by the ECB, in both directions, without recourse to purchase or sale of the public debt of member states.

2.9   Inflation as 'the Most Iniquitous of Taxes'

Inflation can be defined as 'the most iniquitous of taxes', not so much on account of its distributive effects – which, as we will see, vary according to circumstances – as, rather, because of its distortion effects, which are extremely severe. As will be shown, the latter effects can be extremely severe if inflation exceeds a moderate percentage; furthermore, the perverse action of inflation as a tax is exacerbated by the arbitrariness both of the burden it imposes and its benefits.

> Basically, unlike taxation in a democratic state, in the case of inflation it is not the law that determines who has to pay and who stands to receive a benefit, but the push and pull of the state and the various groups involved in the inflationary process.

It is necessary to distinguish between 'unexpected' inflation and that which has become incorporated in the system. Inflation that arrives as a 'sudden thunderbolt' damages the creditors of fixed obligations, and consequently of those who are on fixed employment incomes and holders of loans with interest, as well as holders of bank notes (which are an 'interest-free' loan in favour of the Central Bank that issued the notes), whereas it provides a temporary advantage for employers in relation to wages, and for holders of debt (private individuals and the state) in relation to interest-paying loans.

The optimal situation for economic operators, in the case of unexpected inflation, is that they should be at one and the same time borrowers for loans in the domestic currency and owners of real estate and stocks of durable goods and commodities, because whereas the debt devalues, property and stocks maintain their real value intact. Commercial enterprises and real estate companies are thus among the subjects most favoured by unexpected inflation.

2.10   Why the Burden and Benefits of Unexpected Inflation do not Compensate Each Other

Since we have a creditor and a debtor for each loan, and a payee and a payer for each wage or other payment pre-established in nominal currency, it would be tempting to suppose that inflation does not give rise to any net burden for citizens, but that the burdens created for some subjects are exactly counterbalanced by benefits for the others. This assumption is mistaken. For bank notes, we do not have the creditor citizen i on the one hand and, on the other, the citizen j who owes the debt. Instead, we have on the one hand the creditor citizen and, on the other, the fiscal Leviathan that owes a debt, in the sense that it has issued (usually indirectly) the paper money, which depreciates through the effect of inflation. The Leviathan can then issue further paper money in order to maintain the volume of money unchanged, in real terms, with respect to the volume of the gross product.

> Thus in the end, even in a paper money regime, the inflation tax that is in favour of the fiscal Leviathan rather than of other private individuals consists in 'clipping' the money, that is to say, shearing the purchasing power of money held by private individuals, in favour of the Leviathan. However, the state will have to shoulder the task of issuing debt at higher interest rates, if citizens no longer believe that monetary stability is guaranteed.

In short, inflation is a tax on circulating money, whose rate is the inflation rate itself, and for which the taxable base is, specifically, the money supply.

2.11   Inflation as a Tax on Market 'Choices'

The 'distortion' effect of a tax of this kind clearly emerges if one considers that a tax on circulating money signifies taxing the means by which exchanges are undertaken in the market system, and more precisely, taxing the very means that satisfy the need to transport purchasing power over time, that is potential welfare, which is none other than 'capacity for choice'. The inflation tax is the form of taxation that has the greatest negative impact on capacity for choice. It can be defined as the *tax on market choices par excellence*.

However, when inflation comes to be part of the economic system, the distributive effects undergo modification and become increasingly uncertain and variable, while the system becomes distorted, in order to take into account its own reduced capacity for choice.

> This can be likened to the situation of a feudal economy in which travelling and engaging in trading exchanges was extremely difficult, and whoever ventured to make a journey with a money bag among her possessions was continually exposed to thefts and hold-ups by gangs of swashbuckling barons and buccaneers.

However, inflation disturbs the structures of the fiscal Leviathan as well. If the state is highly indebted, a bout of unexpected inflation gives it immediate relief. But it then finds itself facing the problem of updating the tax system, which is commensurate with old values such as land registry coefficients, excises stated in units of money per kilogram or litre, car tax stated in units of money per fiscal horse-power, and so on, and upgrading the old values to the new system, as well as the problem of having to collect the taxes on income of previous years in devalued money. Nor is it an easy task to engage in constant recalculation of taxable annual incomes in money that is progressively undergoing devaluation. Therefore a state that has no debts and only a small number of employees could in effect be damaged instead of obtaining an advantage from unexpected inflation, which, in any case, the state cannot eliminate at the same speed as it arrived on the scene.

2.12 Rationality of the Constitutional Limitation on the Production of Inflation

The constitutional limitation on the possibility for the fiscal-monetary authority to produce inflation is rational, since, as we have seen, although inflation generates substantial advantages for some social groups, it is nevertheless true that overall it creates more damage than advantages. Inflation acts contrary to the primary purpose of the state, to which the cooperative model of the public economy should conform, in a market economy free society: namely that of increasing capacity for choice and exchanges, supplying society with organization and certainty.

> Basically, then, inflation is the negation of the state. It is like the propagation of injustice and lack of security, which cast doubt on the very reasons for the existence of the modern state: namely, the task of assuring law and order and the related opportunities for trade and capacity for choice.

The major step in limiting the state's possibility of generating inflation is implemented by the obligation to balance or almost balance its budget.

Since the development of inflation is dependent, as a limiting condition, on the quantity of money, rules can be established in order to regulate the issue of money in relation to growth of the gross product and the objective of monetary stability. But often it is impossible to set a quantitative rule *a priori* in this regard, because secondary money (credit) and tertiary money (m_3: operations by other financial subjects) vary both in relation to demand originating from the economy and also in relation to international affairs.

Therefore it is important for the Central Bank to declare *what criteria it intends to follow,* as to the inflation rate and the parameters affecting it, thereby ensuring accountability, that is to say the possibility for its conduct to be subjected to assessment by domestic and international financial opinion.

NOTES

1. The crux of the theory of the public debt, from the point of view of the public economy in autonomous governments, consists precisely in the analysis of its differences and similarities vis-à-vis private debt. The theoretical literature on this issue has by now become almost boundless.

    A particularly important contribution to this literature has been made by Italian economists. The starting point, however, is represented by D. Hume, *Of Public Credit*, in *Essays Moral, Political, Literary*, 1742, which highlights its intrinsic arbitrariness, underpinned by the fiscal power, and warns that 'destroy the public debt or it will destroy you'. Subsequently, a major step forward was taken by the so-called Ricardo theorem (Ricardo, 1817) according to which the public debt should not be seen as a burden on the future but on the present, as the tax utilized to fund the service (which he believed to be a tax levied on income from property) is capitalized negatively in the value of present-day property. But note that Ricardo put forward this thesis with numerous reservations *in order to confute it*. He contended that the owner of property which is encumbered by indebtedness, in future years, feels better off than one who has to pay out in the present an amount corresponding to the capitalized value of the debt. Therefore the former will be induced to save less than the latter, in reaction to the (presumed) impoverishment due to the debt. De Viti De Marco (1893 [1992]) transforms the argument put forward by Ricardo (to confute it) into a theorem, asserting that the public debt, under the hypothesis of continuity among the generations, is always a burden for the present. Puviani (1903) maintains that for the government in power the public debt appears as a burden on the future, in contrast to taxation, or at least this is the illusion governments try to induce in their tax-paying electors.

    Against De Viti's theorem, B. Griziotti (1917) advanced mordant criticism, denying the continuity of the temporal horizon among generations and highlighting – as far as the present is concerned – that the interests of the holders of assets may prompt them to prefer a public debt and future general taxes that burden workers as well, for the service of the debt, rather than a present special tax that would place a burden on themselves. In the future generation, the offspring of the persons without property will have to pay more taxes to service the debt, without there being any increase in their income (assuming that the debt has been spent unproductively), while the heirs of the capitalists, faced with greater taxes, will have the bonds of the public debt. Thus the burden of the debt – according to Griziotti – is on the future, but with unequal distribution.

    After the period of Keynesian euphoria, in which the public debt was seen above all as a tool for promoting greater income which would then facilitate payment of the interest, J.M. Buchanan (1958 and 1960) took up again and further developed Griziotti's theory, within an extremely cogent logical framework. Buchanan separates the macroeconomic point of view, in which it *would appear* impossible to transfer to the future the burden of public expenditure made in the present, from the microeconomic point of view, in which, from an individual perspective, a saver who receives public bonds that finance present expenditure has no burden, whereas the future taxpayer who will have to pay for this past expenditure will indeed have a burden, and this burden may be greater or lower than the benefit transmitted to her through the above-mentioned expenditure.

Macroeconomists assume a somewhat sceptical approach towards this overall picture, preferring to underline the negative effects that an excessively high tax burden, designed to finance a public debt that grows more than the domestic product, can have on the growth itself. Particular attention is devoted to this issue in the (pioneering) studies by E. Domar (1944 [1955]; 1946). F. Modigliani (1983) clarifies the apparent paradox of the Griziotti–Buchanan theorem, observing that in the macroeconomic profile, the burden transferred to the future by means of the public debt is constituted by the failure to accumulate productive capital, which in turn results from the circumstance that the financing of market investments undergoes a 'crowding out' due to the placement of the public bonds. Against this formulation, R.J. Barro (1974; 1976 and 1979) spearheaded a counter-revolution in the 1970s, oriented towards reviving the so-called Ricardo theorem. Barro supports the hypothesis of integral present-day capitalization of the future burden of the debt, on the basis of the theory of rational expectations, arguing that given the complete interdependence between generations, the above-mentioned decrease in wealth automatically induces greater accumulation. The repartee and reservations advanced by various authors are displayed, either in the text or in the notes, during the development of this chapter.

2. This power is, however, generally not granted to the government in the fiscal constitution of the cooperative state and in the Maastricht Treaty of the European Monetary Union, not only in order to avoid an excessive public debt, but also to prevent the debt from being subsequently erased through soaring inflation.

3. As can be inferred from the survey given in note 1, there is a certain amount of confusion between the fact that the public debt is interpreted as a burden for the future and the fact that it is interpreted as a burden for the future devoid of benefit, or with a benefit lower than the cost, or, possibly, equal to or greater than the cost.

4. A distinction should be drawn between two types of situation concerning the difficulty of paying for the servicing of the public debt when this has been devolved to investments: namely, the situation pertaining to enterprises that have turned out not to be sufficiently profitable to repay the debt contracted to fund the investments, so that the state itself has had to shoulder these debts; and the situation pertaining to collective investments 'free of charge', the benefits of which never translate into monetary returns referring to the investment, which means that they must in any case be funded through taxes. In both situations, there arises a problem of 'debt sustainability'.

5. An incisive critical assessment of Barro can be found in F. Modigliani (1983). Basing his arguments on the laws he himself, as well as other scholars, had identified concerning the incentive toward accumulation of saving, Modigliani rejected Barro's theory because one can completely rule out the proposition according to which the amount of wealth a society desires to hold depends on the size of the public deficit, as a society's wealth is determined fundamentally by the income of the society itself. This, in turn, comes about not only because a large part of saving is the result of individuals' 'lifecycle' in which, first, there is accumulation, followed later by spending, but also because a large part of the 'bequests' are more a function of the income of whoever 'leaves' a bequest than a function of the aim of bequeathing a given wealth.

6. This question is addressed again further on, in subsection 1.10, with regard to the 'fundamental theorem' on 'new debt sustainability' in a non-stationary economy, in which the

new debt tends to become unsustainable once it has reached a substantial percentage of GDP and the interest rate systematically exceeds the growth rate of GDP.

7. The theorem according to which the public debt can become stabilized, in percentage over GDP, without the need to finance the interest with taxes but by having recourse, instead, to further debt (with the effect of transferring the burden onto the future) when the interest rate is equal to the growth rate of GDP, emerges implicitly from the analysis by Domar (1944). However, it has subsequently been highlighted by Diamond (1965), that with finite temporal horizons, in which the new public debt does not generate new accumulation to a corresponding extent, there is the possibility of an increase in the debt, to be serviced by means of additional debt, when the growth rate exceeds the interest rate.

8. This is a theme that formed the object of classical enquiries by Keynes.

14. Supranational, regional and local public finance

1 MORE THAN ONE PUBLIC ECONOMY GOVERNMENT THAT OPERATES WITHIN A SINGLE MARKET AND A GOVERNMENT THAT HAS JURISDICTION OVER MORE THAN ONE MARKET

So far we have considered mainly sovereign states which, alone or together with other sovereign states, form or participate in a unified market, in a context where the unified market communicates with other markets yet remains distinct, either because there exists a border which may be associated with some tariff or non-tariff barrier,[1] or because an independent monetary power is exercised within the unified market.

But this is not the only possible situation in which the public economy may operate. Indeed, in our era and within the framework we have been considering, the above scenario constitutes a highly partial representation of a far more complex situation.

In effect, within a state that governs a piece of the single market there are public economy powers distributed over the territory and operating on different levels of government. These powers belong to what can be roughly defined by the overall term of *regional* public economy. They concern, firstly, the grassroots units of local government, each of which exercises authority over a part of the national territory, without solution of continuity, namely the municipalities (equivalent to the British *local councils*); at the next higher level one finds the *lower intermediate units*, namely the provinces (comparable to the British *counties*), which gather together a multiplicity of municipalities under the control of a county capital and exert powers of coordination and common services; and finally, the *higher intermediate units*. The latter may – for some important functions, although not for all of the major functions – represent the primary source of public power, in which case we are dealing with a federal state or with a confederation of states; alternatively, they may have only derived power on specific matters, and this is the case of a unitary state (like France). In a (con)federal state, the higher intermediate units are '(con)federated states', while in an EMU there is a further government above them, ruling the Union'.[2] Other spheres of the intermediate-level public economy include the metropolitan authorities, which have a vast range of powers, not only over the territory of the county seat but also over that of the boroughs that ring the central municipality.[3]

2 GOVERNMENTS WITH JURISDICTION OVER MORE THAN ONE MARKET

In the case of regional governments, one finds a plurality of governments operating on a single market with a single currency, under the control of a single sovereign government. But in addition to this situation and to the one considered, in particular in the previous chapters, of sovereign states belonging to an EMU, there are also 'supranational' governments that rule on interdependent markets in which there is a plurality of states and different monetary authorities. As an example, one may cite the World Trade Organization (WTO) which has jurisdiction with regard to safeguarding the rules and commercial exchanges of international trade (including financial trade) for countries that are members of this organization.

The International Monetary Fund is a special kind of 'government', endowed only with monetary powers of the last resort, over all member countries (all those of the world, with few exceptions).

Given the picture outlined above, four groups of theoretical problems concerning governmental decision-making processes can be identified. First are those pertaining to the relation between the public economies of the central governments and the so-called regional and local public economies entrusted with providing for 'local public wants' by means of public revenue. In a framework of this kind, public choice is subject to the constraints imposed by the circumstance of operating within a single market, with a single monetary authority and a single political-military-judicial framework.

The second group of theoretical problems pertains to the public economies of 'prefederal' or 'quasi federal' governments, in other words to the public economies of Economic Unions such as the European Union prior to the European EMU set forth with the Maastricht Treaty. Here the public economy of the top government does not operate within the framework of a single central monetary power, nor is it endowed with any 'original' political power, even though the scope of its action ranges over the entire territorial extension of the member states, which forms a 'great market'.[4]

Thirdly, a group of problems can be outlined which arise in connection with the Economic and Monetary Unions among sovereign states belonging to an Economic Union such as the European EMU and the regional governments of member states.

Finally, the fourth group of problems involves international organizations which exercise power of coordination in the common interest of independent member states that belong to different monetary areas.

3   THE STATE WITH MORE THAN ONE LEVEL OF GOVERNMENT: CRITERIA FOR ASSIGNMENT OF FUNCTIONS AT THE DIFFERENT LEVELS

Five fundamental criteria for assignment of functions that involve provision of public goods and services at different governmental levels can be identified.

I.   *Homogeneity and dishomogeneity of preferences concerning 'intrinsically indivisible public wants'* concerning the fundamental issues of defence, justice and domestic law and order discussed earlier in Chapter 3, section 1. It was pointed out that subjects perceive these public wants individually in relation to a given community, identified in terms of a territory and, at times, a common language, an ethnic grouping or a shared religious affiliation, and they experience empathy towards the other subjects belonging to that same community. Generally this criterion makes it possible to satisfy the public wants in question on the level of the unitary or federal 'national' state; however, within this framework one also finds situations of a confederation in which there coexist different languages and ethnic groupings united by geographical and historical factors, as for instance in the case of Switzerland, Belgium or Canada. The European Economic and Monetary Union – which is not yet a state – is not yet endowed with its own army (which, however, it is striving to set up), or its own judiciary and its own federal police, because there is a lack of 'homogeneity' with regard to the intrinsically indivisible 'political' public wants of this nature.

II. *Efficacy, efficiency and equity of the agency relation between citizens and their elective representatives:* in itself, the informational asymmetry between the elected and the electors, together with the complications of decision-making processes involving large institutions, has as one of its consequences that decision-making processes tend to be passed on to a lower level. The diversity of preferences among citizens prompts the desire for a multiplicity of governments, of a lower level, allowing a broader spectrum of choice. Similar considerations can be put forward for the reduction in exploitation and for the greater efficiency made possible by a multiplicity of governments, acting at the same level or at different levels and competing with one another, allowing citizens a genuine possibility of choosing among alternatives or at least to assess their performances comparatively.

III. *The area of diffusion of wants and benefits of public goods, that is the positive and negative externalities (or 'spillover').* In many cases the provision of public goods has benefits that 'spill over' beyond the communities they spring from, especially if such communities are 'restricted' (a typical instance is that of scientific research). Likewise, empathy, or solidarity, which inspires redistributive policies, also has a dimension that exceeds the local community, partly because – in the cooperative model – it is linked to the principle which holds that the state assures to each individual the conditions to pursue their own welfare, in the market system, by means of equal opportunity factors and the guarantee of a minimum for the less favoured.

IV. *Economies and diseconomies of scale in provision of public goods*: scientific research on important projects cannot achieve substantial success unless it is conducted on an extremely vast scale (analogously, its results have a very wide-ranging circulation). Consequently it is generally appropriate for this function to be exercised at high levels of government, whereas a daycare centre for the pre-school age has an optimal dimension on a small scale, and centralization of its management by a higher-level government generates diseconomies of scale and leads to bureaucratic complexities.

V. *Network economies and diseconomies:* there are certain services whose provision should be assured by units coordinated into a network specifically designed for the purpose: such is the case, for instance, for roads in a city or metropolis, which call for a unitary design for planning and control of traffic flows, or the network of secondary roads, or primary A-roads and major international routes. For each of these networks there is an optimal dimension (that is an economic dimension) in terms of minimum cost that calls for its assignment to a given level of government as regards investment, management policy and control, by the public operator.[5]

4 EXTERNAL EFFECTS AND OPTIMUM DIMENSION OF THE HIGHER-LEVEL SUBJECT

One of the basic principles of the optimal territorial dimension of a government (public finance) (as discussed in point III above) is the absence of significant 'external effects' that go beyond its own territory and which arise from pursuit of collective goals, that is to say goals that concern a plurality of members of the community at the same time. In order for a government Z to make the best decisions on public expenditure, taxation and the public debt, it is helpful for a large part of the positive and negative effects produced by these three aspects to exert their effects on the territory that falls under the jurisdiction of government Z, so that the gains and costs of the government's policies coincide with the gains and costs of the community in which the aforesaid government Z operates, and whose members vote the government into power.

If this situation is not achieved, misallocation of the actions of the public economy may ensue.

Let us assume that the only collective problem arising in a given territory is that of the elimination of mosquitoes. Any mosquitoes hatching in an area Z of the territory can fly to the other areas Z', causing damage to the inhabitants. A rational government that has authority only over Z and which pursues optimization for the inhabitants of Z will engage in expenditure for the elimination of mosquitoes only up to the point where the costs to be borne by the inhabitants of Z in the form of taxation are equal to the return (satisfaction) for the citizens of Z deriving from reduction of the nuisance of the mosquitoes. If expenditure continues beyond this point, achieving a utility for the citizens of Z', the government of Z – under the democratic hypothesis that it pursues the welfare of its own inhabitants – regards this as totally irrelevant.

Therefore the expenditure undertaken in Z can cease at a lower level than that which would be desirable if the advantages for citizens of Z' were taken into consideration as well as those of the citizens of Z. But this problem does not arise if the perfectly rational government concerned only with the welfare of the persons residing within its own territory has a territorial jurisdiction that covers both Z and Z'.

Other examples on the optimum dimension at the higher level of government can be cited in connection with allocative interdependency.

Let us suppose that in addition to the mosquitoes that hatch in Z, other mosquitoes hatch in Z' and then reproduce in Z as well, but also mate partly with mosquitoes deriving from Z'. The mosquitoes can be eliminated from Z and Z' only if action is undertaken simultaneously in both areas: in other words, there are reciprocal external effects of Z on Z' and of Z' on Z, which can be combated only by means of reciprocal and opposite external effects of Z on Z' and of Z' on Z. The actions of Z and Z' form part of a 'system' and are not valid separately.

5 EXTERNAL EFFECTS OF REDISTRIBUTIVE POLICIES AND OF FULL EMPLOYMENT: THE HIGHER LEVEL IS OPTIMAL

We saw in section 3, item III that one of the important goals of higher-level public finance is that of improving income distribution in order to assure a minimum standard of living to all citizens. If there exist two distinct governments, one having authority over Z and the other over Z', with these two zones being contiguous, then the rational government operating on Z will engage in transfer payments to the poor of Z so that inequalities are reduced to reasonable proportions, but it will not be able to address the inequalities in Z' (nor would its citizens desire it to do so, since these are two different states).

However, if there is freedom of movement, the poor of Z' will move over to the territory of Z.

Even if the assumption may be made that the government of Z is altruistic, it would normally be unable to pursue its redistributive action up to the point at which the situation within Z is fully satisfactory. This is due to the fact that the government of Z cannot tax the citizens of Z'; and many of the rich of Z will emigrate to Z', given that the redistribution within Z in favour of the less favoured will have resulted in a worsening of the conditions of the wealthier citizens of Z as compared to that of the wealthy in Z'.

Only a government that operates simultaneously on Z and Z' would be able to enact a substantial and equitable redistribution policy that would provide fair treatment for both territories in their relations with each other.

6 CONSTANT COSTS AND OPTIMUM DIMENSION OF PROVISION ON THE HIGHER LEVEL

We saw in section 3, item IV, that fixed or constant costs represent one of the factors leading to choice in favour of assigning competences to government units with jurisdictions that extend over greater dimensions. Fixed or constant costs characterize some public services, the assessment of many taxes and, above all, the cost of the public administration and of the democratic organs.

> The existence of these fixed costs renders small municipalities anachronistic, in that their expenses per inhabitant are artificially increased by this burden while they have to abandon a considerable number of services that ought to be part of their provision, because the fixed costs constitute an obstacle.

Even if it is established that the local authority cannot be too small, provision of certain services is nevertheless inappropriate at the level of the local authority that serves only its own citizens, because such services cannot be run properly with the desirable level of efficiency, which is dependent on the fixed costs. A university, for example, generally cannot be run efficiently by the local authority, but must be governed at least at the regional level.

By the same token, certain types of public services could not be provided appropriately by states lacking an elevated per capita income or having a small population, because the unit cost to be borne by each citizen would be prohibitive. This can easily be seen with reference to expenses for scientific research in the field of space exploration.

7 OVERCROWDING, CONGESTION AND DISECONOMIES OF SCALE: OPTIMUM ASSIGNMENT TO THE LOWER LEVEL

In section 3, item IV, we also touched on the issues of diseconomies of scale springing from the increasing organization and information costs that arise in connection with excessive size of the units providing the services. Typical cases can be illustrated in reference to primary schools, or health care centres. Beyond a certain size, they display organizational dysfunctions and problems of poor service quality due to difficulties of supervision and assessment. This makes it difficult for control to be exercised at the managerial level and it also deprives electors of effective control over public action, because the very wide range of questions to be addressed leads to elevated information costs at the higher decision-making levels. Furthermore, only very rarely are public goods 'pure' in the Samuelsonian sense. Often they are Dupuit goods. Consequently, beyond a certain point the overcrowding of the numbers of usage units generates escalating external diseconomies that adversely affect all users, eventually translating into so-called 'congestion'.

8 USERS' TRANSFER COSTS AND THE OPTIMAL USER 'BASIN' AT THE LOWER LEVEL

Often, as service units expand, they experience economies of scale.

> Thus it is clear that in a school with a large number of pupils, the teachers can (theoretically, at least) be distributed more satisfactorily over the various

courses than in a small school. Likewise, if a single authority presides over a large number of schools, of various levels, staff can be deployed over a range of tasks – teaching, educational planning and management in conjunction with the local authority, and so forth – according to the experience they have acquired as well as on the basis of their various specializations, and this can be done much more satisfactorily than in the case of an authority that manages only one school of a single level.

But what needs to be considered now is the question of the transfer costs the user incurs in benefiting from the public goods and services that can be (entirely) utilized only in the place where they are actually supplied.

Ideally, in order to ensure allocative optimality for citizens, such public services should be distributed throughout the territory so that user 'basins' do not involve 'excessively' high transfer costs for citizens to reach the point of supply and that the fixed costs are 'properly utilized'.

9   MINIMIZATION OF THE 'TRANSACTION COST' BETWEEN THE PRINCIPAL-ELECTOR AND THE AGENT-MANAGER OF THE PUBLIC ECONOMY, AS AN ARGUMENT IN FAVOUR OF ASSIGNMENT TO LOWER LEVELS

Deeper reflection about the choice of governmental level at which services should be provided shows that neither the question of the user's transfer costs (mentioned in the above section 7), nor the diseconomies that arise when the providing unit is 'too large', lead conclusively to a decision in favour of government units established at a lower level. Rather, they simply suggest that decentralization of provision units within the public economy offers a more workable solution. Decentralization can in fact be implemented by the unitary state itself, by means of appropriate sizing and localization of its supply structures.

However, a new, specific argument in favour of local governments can be advanced, with regard to the principal–agent relation of the public economy.

The elector, as the 'principal' of those who manage the public economy, incurs transaction costs in the endeavour to achieve an effective and efficient relation with the agents. Such costs, which can at times be extremely high or indeed prohibitive, can be classified into three groups. The electors must:

●   be aware of the situation of public goods and have knowledge of the alternative costs and benefits relating to the various wants that may be satisfied through collective action;

- be able to transmit her own preferences to the potential and actual agents, both at the moment of electoral choices and also on subsequent occasions;
- have the possibility of knowing the agent-candidates and of exercising control over their operations and the outcomes.

In local finance of a city or a province, these three problems can be solved rather more easily than within the public finance of a nation as a whole. First, information concerning public goods and services of a local nature designed to provide collective advantages that are limited to the individual locality is considerably easier for a citizen to acquire as compared to the situation regarding goods and services operated at the national level.

> For instance, whenever a citizen steps outside her home she can judge the state of local road maintenance, and it does not take long for her to become aware of whether or not a new flyover would be helpful in solving the city's traffic problems; also, conversation with family members and friends is soon likely to touch on the question of whether it is really necessary to build a new primary school and whether the staffing is considered satisfactory in terms of staff numbers and quality, and so on.

Citizens' opinions on local services can more easily be conveyed to those who stand for local council elections, or who are in charge of local authority offices, than is the case for the opinions held by electors on matters concerning the way national public affairs are run. This is clearly due to the fact that within the local community, relations with the political agent are more immediate, the issues involved are more circumscribed and preferences are communicated more concretely, given the greater availability of specific information.

Finally, an elector can more easily gauge the quality and behaviour of a local administrator than that of a national member of parliament. Also, even if in both cases all resolutions in the various assemblies may be passed by roll call or show of hands, the fact still remains that openness on how motions are approved in parliament is not easy to achieve (and government officials often show considerable reluctance in disclosing the relevant information), whereas the action of the local council can be evaluated *de visu* and the news circulates very rapidly on the local level.

> Whereas debate within government circles is often shrouded in confidentiality, news on 'altercations' in local council meetings soon spreads throughout the local community, thanks to the 'local news' features in the media.

If government is 'close' to the citizens in terms of its organizational set-up and interaction with the local community, costs are reduced and there is substantial improvement in the outcome of action undertaken through forms of direct democracy such as opinion polls, referendums, neighbourhood assemblies, parent–teacher meetings, campaigns by users of public transport, and so forth.

NOTES

1. Non-tariff barriers are those constituted by administrative constraints and impediments, such as import and export licences, health and hygiene inspections, security checks, passports and passport control at borders, the obligation to pay domestic taxes and charges at the moment of entry from abroad rather than at the recipient's official location, and, in parallel, the obligation whereby the right to exemption of charges for exports does not consist in a duty-free exemption but rather in (slow) reimbursement procedures, and so forth.
2. These various levels of government naturally have different designations in the legal and political systems of the various states. For example, in Switzerland the primary units of government that make up the confederation, which is a less intense union than the federation properly speaking, bear the denomination 'Cantons' rather than 'States', in contrast to the USA where they are known as 'States'. In Germany, they are known as 'Länder'. There is nothing preventing the term 'Region' used in Italy (a quasi confederal state) for the higher-level intermediate governments.
3. In France the metropolitan municipalities such as Paris are actually composed of numerous smaller municipalities or boroughs, each exerting power over a part of the territory of the overall area of Paris. The mayor of the chief municipality is also the mayor of the entire metropolitan authority. A similar situation, as it is well known, holds for 'Greater London'.
4. Since 1993, within the EU (formerly EEC), all fiscal and non-fiscal frontier barriers have ceased to exist, as have a large part of the barriers against free circulation and against freedom of economic and business undertakings in another EU country, as well as the hiring of subjects of the various member states in each of the other states.
5. Which can either carry out these activities directly or contract them out to private operators.

Appendix

THE CIRCUIT OF THE NATIONAL PRODUCT BETWEEN FAMILIES, ENTERPRISES AND GOVERNMENT: CHAPTER 1, SUBSECTION 1.9

In Figure A.1, at the summit of the circuit of public finance in the national product one finds families and enterprises as 'principals' of the agency relation. They carry out their choice of agents (with regard to which, see the box immediately below), who, in turn, carry out their own decision-making processes pertaining to the public sphere, by voting in the parliamentary assemblies or the assemblies of the regional and local administrations, or by complying with the outcome of direct democracy referendums. This is the legislative and deliberative power. The decisions are translated into acts, partly by the application of regulations and partly through the provision of public goods and services of various kinds by the governments at the different levels (supra-national, central, regional, local). This constitutes the 'brain' of the 'executive power', which is indicated in the box immediately on the right of that referring to the assemblies, which has arrows going in both directions, as the government is accountable to the assembly, of which it is the agent, and in order to enact its decisions it avails itself of the bureaucracy, which is its agent. Thus below the box of the governments we find the box referring to the public bureaucracy, which constitutes the 'body' of the executive power. The arrow in the figure points downwards, as the bureaucracies are agents of the government rather than vice versa, although at times they wield greater power than the government itself, which may be in thrall to them. Part of the public goods consists of sums of money (transfers), such as pensions and subsidies, and therefore does not involve utilization of material or immaterial means. But in addition to this, the bureaucracy also provides public goods and services 'in kind', partly directly (with its value-added) and partly (and at times almost entirely) by availing itself of production factors that are supplied by the market. And all this has a cost. Therefore, three flows emerge from the bureaucracy box. One concerns the lower box, at the centre of the figure, and it refers to the market operators who supply goods and services denominated 'intermediate' for public consumption and investments. Here there are two arrows, one going from the bureaucracy

[Chapter 1, subsection 1.9. *The circuit of the national product between families, enterprises and government*

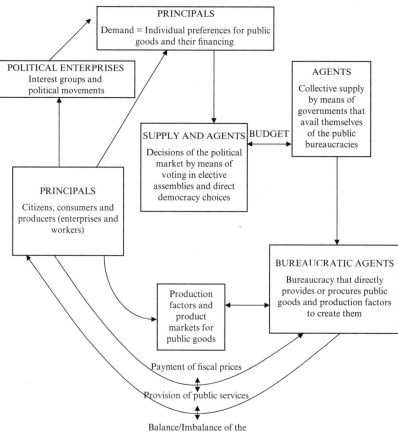

Figure A.1   Demand and supply of public goods in the model that tends towards the cooperative system

towards the market operators, who receive the orders commissioned by the bureaucracy and the payments by the latter, and the other going from these operators to the bureaucracy, which receives their goods or services. A second flow concerns the 'fiscal prices' (in the broad sense of the term, indicating all forms of public revenue, which acts as the compensating counterpart of public services and goods – in money or in kind – provided to the payer or to third parties, on the basis of the choices which, in a democracy, are made by taxpayers in accordance with voting rules and in the framework of constitutional principles that should safeguard them against extortions). The fiscal prices go from the 'principals' indicated on the left, half-way down the figure, to the bureaucracy, which receives them and spends them. In actual fact, part of the financial means are taken on the market as public debt. But in the picture under consideration, this is not taken into account, in order to avoid overcomplicating the picture. Debts have to be paid sooner or later, and therefore the fiscal means come back into play, in relation to financial equilibrium. The third flow that concerns the bureaucracy box likewise involves the 'principals' of the system and consists in public goods and services that are provided to the principals, part of which are provided officially free of charge or semi-free and covered by means of taxes, obligatory contributions, and fees, and part by means of quasi market or market payments. Therefore the arrow goes from the bureaucracy to the citizens and the enterprises, which are the final principals of the bureaucracy, in the cooperative model.

However, we find an intermediate box positioned between the box of the 'principals' as beneficiaries of public goods and services and the box of the principals themselves considered as electors. This intermediate box is occupied by the 'political enterprises', composed of parties and interest groups (among which it is worth mentioning the trade unions and the associations of economic operators) that act as intermediaries between the principals as the beneficiaries of the public activities and as decision-makers with regard to public choices. But there is also a flow of political decisions of the citizens that occurs outside of this intermediation. Therefore two lines emerge from the box of the principals, with two arrows, one going towards the political enterprises and the other towards themselves as a democratic decision-making body (whose choices do not make themselves felt exclusively through the voting process but also through response to opinion polls, the various forms of protest or of manifested consensus, in meetings, views aired via the media or even over coffee or drinks at the pub or in dining rooms and, sometimes, in the bedroom). One arrow goes from the political enterprises to the electors. We have omitted, for the sake of simplicity, the three arrows going from the political enterprises to I) the members of the elective assemblies, II) the members of the governments, III) the bureaucracies. The political enterprises bring pressure to bear by means of their power to exercise control over electoral choices and by real, albeit not (always) official, agency relations between themselves as political enterprises and the political representatives, the governments, the high-ranking public executives and officials. We have also disregarded the flow of pressures (and money) from the operators who work with the bureaucracy and the political enterprises.

OPTIMAL ALLOCATION OF PRODUCTION FACTORS AMONG THE DIFFERENT PRODUCTS AND FULL EMPLOYMENT: REPRESENTATION USING THE EDGEWORTH-BOWLEY (EB) BOX: CHAPTER 2, SUBSECTION 2.6

We have two subjects or economic areas or production sectors M and N, which produce two goods:

- subject (sector, economic area) M supplies good A, whose production, represented by the isoquants marked q and obtained by means of labour L and capital K, increases as we move rightwards and/ or upwards from the origin 0 at the bottom left-hand corner of the box;
- subject (sector, economic area) N supplies product B, whose production, represented by the isoquants marked Q, likewise obtained by means of labour L and capital K, increases as we move leftwards and/or downwards from the origin $0'$ at the top right-hand corner of the box, thus giving the opposite configuration.

If we rotate the sheet of paper on which Figure A.2 is represented, we can move the isoquants for good B into the position occupied by those for good A, and vice versa. Using the artifice of the box EB, it is possible to establish the level of full employment of factors L and K. This is because using the artifice of the box EB, we have indicated the total availability of L on the right-hand and left-hand side of the box, and of K on the lower side and the upper side. The quantity of factors that is not used to produce A can be used to produce B or else it can be left inactive. In effect, the isoquants Q_l of B and q_l of A involve considerable unemployment of the two production factors. But in a system that functions in an optimal manner, this will not come about. Assuming that Q_N is the maximum amount of B that we want to produce, we will have a production of A that will lead to exhausting the available capital and labour resources, and this will come about once the isoquants of B touch the isoquants of A. This is due to the fact that the segments of labour factor L and of capital factor K used by B, summed with those used by A, will by then have used up the total available. In our figure, this happens with the tangency of Q_N to q_M, at point E. This is the optimal point from the allocative point of view, not only because it assures full employment, but also because at this point the tangency between the two curves of Q and q assures that the marginal productivity is identical for the production factors employed in B and in A. The equilibrium point E indicates the

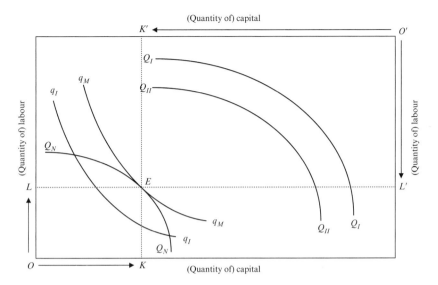

Figure A.2   Optimum equilibrium in production

potential exchange relation between the two goods *A* and *B*, as a function of their marginal costs, that is their relative price of full employment equilibrium.

X INEFFICIENCY IN THE STRICT SENSE (EXCESS OF PERSONAL AND OTHER PRODUCTION FACTORS) AND IN THE BROAD SENSE (EXCESSIVE PRICES FOR PRODUCTION FACTORS AND POOR ORGANIZATION AND TECHNOLOGICAL BACKWARDNESS OF THE PUBLIC ADMINISTRATIONS): CHAPTER 5, SUBSECTION 1.8

In Figure A.3, the marginal costs of the supply of public goods are not given by the curve *OC*, which concerns a situation of normal efficiency, but instead they rise to *C′ C′*, which involves an excess of costs compared to normal efficiency costs. This situation comes about when, in order to provide a certain service deemed to be useful, the public bureaucracy employs more resources than is necessary or pays more for them than would be possible. But excess capacity also comes about when the public bureaucrats produce nothing (useful) and survive by 'vegetating', as in

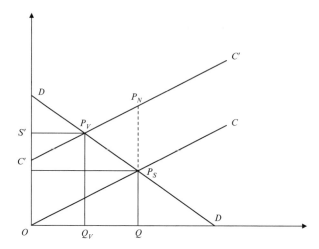

Figure A.3   Equilibrium with X inefficiency

so many pointless institutions (or 'quangos'). The consequence of such situations is not only genuine X inefficiency, but also X_P inefficiency, that is an excessive price of production factors, and additionally X_{OT} inefficiency, due to poor organization and technological backwardness (for instance, scant and bungling use of computerization). The result as regards public goods, at the equilibrium point concerning the citizen, is lower production than in conditions of maximum efficiency. This means that in Figure A.3 we have OQ_V rather than OQ, with consumer's and producer's rents that are (far) lower than would be the case with normal costs. Thus the rents are $C'DP_V$ instead of ODP_S, the latter being what would be expected in situations with costs characterized by normal efficiency. If the aim were to produce OQ, in accordance with the citizen's wishes, on the basis of estimates of normal costs, with the hypotheses shown in Figure A.3, then the global rent would not only be zero but it would actually be negative, as the negative gap between the marginal cost on the curve $C'C'$ and the demand curve P_NP_S is greater than DC'. Thus the triangle $P_VP_NP_S$ of the consumer's negative rent deriving from the production OQ is greater than the positive triangle of the producer's and the consumer's rent $DC'P_V$ which is present up to the production OQ_V.

ALLOCATIVE EFFECTS AND INCOME EFFECTS OF TAXATION IN RELATION TO THE CHOICE BETWEEN PRODUCTION AND FREE TIME: CHAPTER 9, SECTION 7

THE TAX BURDEN: CHAPTER 8, SECTION 7

THE LAFFER CURVE: CHAPTER 8, SECTION 8

The transformation curves BA, BA', BA'' and BA''' between free time, which we indicate on the y-axis, and income-earning labour (taken to mean only the fiscal income) that we indicate on the abscissae, for a subject J refer to different hypotheses which give J a different gain, depending on the level of taxation which may be higher or lower, leading to a different net income under equal gross income. The curves of the (four) different stylized situations presented here are naturally merely a selection of all the transformation curves that could be indicated in the figure for each slightest variation in net income, resulting from slight changes in the tax rate of each individual person. The transformation curves move leftwards on the abscissae, as far as net income is concerned, in relation to variations in the tax burden, but they all have the same maximum position on the ordinates, with regard to free time. This position is always given by the number of hours a person, physiologically, has available when she is not producing (fiscal) income, net of the need to sleep and to engage in other indispensable practices for her own bodily care. The free time considered here is not merely the time dedicated by J to mere idling or *dolce far niente* or unproductive activities. It is also time that J can devote to producing untaxable or untaxed economic utilities of the informal or underground economy, which may well translate into purchasing power but do not constitute income. This explains the trend of J's different equilibrium points, resulting from the different tax rates. Let us suppose that in the absence of taxation the equilibrium is in L, for income R and free time OT. Now let us examine what happens with 20 per cent proportional taxation, which involves movement towards a smaller transformation curve and the search for the highest possible new indifference curve that is compatible with this lesser return on the abandonment of free time. The plotting of our indifference curves is such that the equilibrium point will be identified at point L' on the transformation curve BA', which involves a 20 per cent gap between income gross and net of tax. Other points on BA' involve indifference between free time and income, but they do not give J sufficient gross income to pay the 20 per cent tax. At L', on the other hand, J has a lower net income than at L, and this allows her to pay the 20 per cent tax. Also,

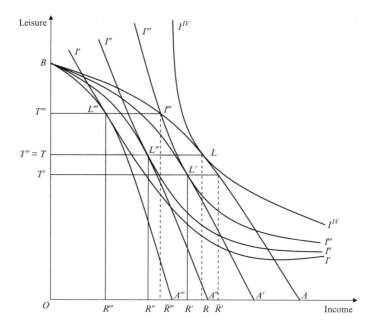

Figure A.4   Income effects and allocative effects in the choice between income from labour and free time as the income tax gradually rises, and possible Laffer effect

her income has gone down by only 10 per cent, not by 20 per cent, as compared to the income obtainable at *L*. This is because *J* has increased her hours of work, even though each hour of forsaking free time now produces less income. From the allocative point of view her labour is less advantageous for *J*, because it is less remunerative, but from the point of view of the (new) situation of a lower income that has come about, the lower income she draws from labour has a greater marginal utility. There is an income effect that exceeds the allocative effect. Free time can be classed as superior consumption: when income decreases, its utility becomes, comparatively, lower than that of goods which can be purchased with the income. But now, let us imagine that the tax rate, which for the sake of simplicity we will suppose to be proportional, has increased to 33 per cent. With our indifference curves, this involves a movement to *L*": the taxpayer now increases her free time, because although it is true that free time is a superior good, there is just as much truth in the concept that given a tax rate of 33 per cent, it no longer appears advantageous to forgo free time in order to produce income for all the hours that were previously devoted to it when the lower tax rate was in force. In our graph, the taxpayer now works as many hours as she would have worked in the absence of taxation, since L'' allows the same gross income as L. If the tax rate were 50 per cent, the taxpayer would move to the equilibrium point L''', which involves a gross income $\overline{R}'''$, that is to say a very elevated quantity of free time and a low income. It should also be noted that the 33 per cent tax rate of the example gives a greater revenue yield than the 50 per cent rate, because 50 per cent of $O\overline{R}'''$ which is $R'''\,\overline{R}'''$ in our graph is less than 33 per cent of OR, which is $R''R$. In effect, in our graph $R''R$ is 2 cm, while $R'''\,\overline{R}'''$ is 1.5 cm. Thus this diagram also constitutes the graphic demonstration of the (possibility of the) 'Laffer curve'.

ALLOCATIVE EFFECTS AND INCOME EFFECTS OF TAXATION IN RELATION TO THE CHOICE BETWEEN PRODUCTION AND FREE TIME: CHAPTER 9, SECTION 7

SAVING AND LABOUR: CHAPTER 10, SECTION 5

In the hypothesis we are considering in Figure A.5, the supply of labour $W'GTS$ is, after an initial segment, absolutely rigid, as the worker I in question desires to obtain a full-time contract, with normal working hours and all the additional advantages this brings, including overtime hours, and her choice does not vary in the relevant section of the curve. This is because the allocative effects of a reduction in the net wage of each hour of labour would be compensated by the income effect, and the latter would in turn derive from the fact that 'free time' is a superior good, in the sense clarified earlier. Thus when income decreases, there is an increase in the marginal utility that can be obtained from it, and if the marginal utility of free time remains unchanged, the result is a comparatively lower appreciation of the free time itself. So before tax, given the firms' labour demand curve, indicated by the letter S, the quantum of labour worked by I is OL, for a wage of LS. But now this is subject to a personal income tax of 25 per cent, reducing the wage of I by this percentage. Since it is withheld at source by the firm, it can be represented as proportional to the salary paid. As the labour supply is rigid, in the relevant segment, the quantity of labour supplied will remain unchanged and the tax will be borne entirely by the worker. The yield will be exactly the same as the tax percentage multiplied by the wage that existed prior to the tax. In our diagram, even a higher tax, up to the level SG, would not be shifted forwards by the workers, as their supply is rigid. Naturally, in real life, this is unlikely to happen for extremely high taxes that leave the workers with a very low

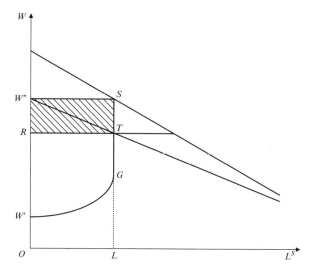

Figure A.5   Incidence of personal income tax on earned income in the case of rigid labour supply (for low-income subjects or subjects with numerous wants)

net wage, because such a situation would be bound to trigger trade union unrest and industrial action designed to recover part of their lost purchasing power by obtaining wage increases that the firms would have to agree to.

ALLOCATIVE EFFECTS AND INCOME EFFECTS OF TAXATION IN RELATION TO THE CHOICE BETWEEN PRODUCTION AND FREE TIME: CHAPTER 9, SECTION 7

SAVING AND LABOUR: CHAPTER 10, SECTION 7

Now we will turn to the hypothesis of workers A with rather high wages, whose labour supply L^S is fairly elastic. This can be explained by noting that since their fairly high income makes them comfortably off, allowing them to satisfy multiple wants, the A subjects are willing to go without additional amounts of free time only on condition of receiving an additional contribution to their income that will remunerate them in compensation for this renunciation. So the elastic labour supply curve may hold not so much in terms of number of hours worked, but instead in terms of

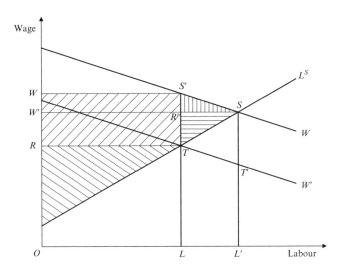

Figure A.6   *Incidence of personal income tax, for earned and business*
               income, in the case of elastic supply (of subjects with income
               higher than the indispensable)

quality of work performed: in conditions that involve a different degree of
fatigue, a different degree of risk, a greater or lesser degree of stress. This
may be the case for many self-employed professional activities, for managerial activities and highly specialized jobs, which require intensive training and the commitment to constant updating. Let the labour demand
curve of the A subjects be constituted by $S'SW$. The equilibrium point, in
the absence of taxation, is at S, for the supply of labour OL, with a wage of
SL. But now this is subject to personal income tax which, after withholding at source, can be represented, as in the previous case, by a reduction in
the demand curve, the reduction being equal to the tax rate.

Now, the equilibrium point will no longer be at S. It will be at S' in
which the labour demand curve of the A workers, net of tax, meets the
demand curve, inclusive of tax. Now the actual labour supply has declined
to OL' and the A workers receive a unitary wage $L'S' > LS$. But $L'T >
LS - S'T$. That is to say, the A workers have a net gain that is greater than
the gross gain decreased by the tax they are liable for: this is because their
gross unitary wage has increased as compared to the wage they earned in
the situation where taxation was absent. Part of their levy has been transferred onto the employers, who pay higher unitary wages than before, for
the amount $S'R'$. The triangle $S'ST$ indicates the loss of welfare caused
by the allocative distortion. $S'RS$ is a burden borne by the enterprises

and $R'ST$ is borne by the workers A. It should be noted that in this case there is no need to have recourse to compensated demand curves in order to evaluate the allocative distortion, because the firms' labour demand is presumably not significantly influenced by the income effects concerning their labour costs, provided the taxes in question do not massively increase these costs.

ALLOCATIVE EFFECTS AND INCOME EFFECTS OF TAXATION IN RELATION TO THE CHOICE BETWEEN PRODUCTION AND FREE TIME: CHAPTER 9, SECTION 7

SAVING AND LABOUR: CHAPTER 10, SECTION 5

The debtor who issued the securities pays $P'_M P'T'T$, while the saver pays $T'TZZ$.

Let the savings supply curve be S, while the demand curve is represented by DR. The equilibrium point between demand and supply of savings prior to tax is at P, with the saver obtaining compensation in the form of interest or dividends and capital gains, represented in the figure by PQ. Then the personal tax is imposed, and given the system of withholding at source, we can represent it as a reduction in the demand curve proportional to the

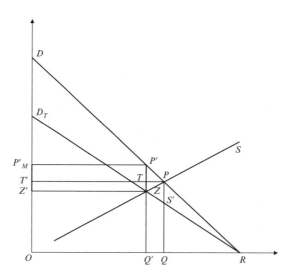

Figure A.7   Effect of personal income tax on savings income

amount of the tax, the latter being 33 per cent in our figure. The tax is $P'Z$. The gross return on savings rises to $Q'P' > QP$ but lower than $PQ + P'Z$, since a part of the tax remains on the savers. But in any case this part is small, given the pronounced elasticity of the supply curve, and given also that it is combined with the moderate elasticity of the demand curve. The greater portion of the tax is shifted forward to those who are demanding savings.

However, it should be noted that if the tax had not been shifted forward, its amount would have been $PS' < P'Z$. It should additionally be noted that $P'T$, the tax rate whose incidence rests on the demand for savings, is practically equal (in our figure, which reflects realistic situations) to the tax rate that the saver would have been subject to, with a supply of savings amounting to OQ, if she had not succeeded in transferring the greater portion of the tax onto the users of the savings.

Bibliography

INTRODUCTION

Blankart, B. (2008), *Öffentliche Finanzen in der Demokratie: Eine Einführung in die Finanzwissenschaft*, Munich: Vahlen, 7th edition.

Buchanan, J.M. (1960 [2001]), '"La scienza delle finanze": The Italian Tradition in Fiscal Theory', in J.M. Buchanan (1960), *Fiscal Theory & Political Economy: Selected Essays*, Chapel Hill: University of North Carolina Press; reprinted in *The Collected Works of James M. Buchanan* (1999–2002), vol. 15 (2001), *Externalities and Public Expenditure Theory*, Indianapolis: Liberty Fund.

Buchanan, J.M. (1988), *Economia y Politica*, edited by José Casas Pardo and Segundo Bru Parra, Valencia: Universitat de Valencia.

Buchanan, J.M. and G. Tullock (1962 [1999]), *The Calculus of Consent: Logical Foundations of Constitutional Democracy*, Ann Arbor: University of Michigan Press; reprinted (1999) as vol. 3 of *The Collected Works of James M. Buchanan* (1999–2002), Indianapolis: Liberty Fund.

De Viti De Marco, A. (1888), *Il Carattere Teorico dell'Economia Finanziaria*, Rome: Pasqualucci, English translation [The Theoretical Character of Public Finance].

Edgeworth, F.I. (1897), 'The pure theory of taxation', *Economic Journal*, 7(25), 46–70.

Einaudi, L. (1919), 'Osservazioni critiche intorno alla teoria dell'ammortamento dell'imposta e teoria delle variazioni nei redditi e nei valori capitali susseguenti all'imposta' [Critical observations on the theory of the amortization of tax and theory of income and capital value variation following taxation], in Einaudi (1941 [1958]).

Einaudi, L. (1938 [1959]), *Miti e Paradossi della Giustizia Tributaria* [Myths and Paradoxes on Justice in Taxation], Turin: Einaudi, 3rd edition, 1959.

Einaudi, L. (1940 [1956]), *Principi di Scienza delle Finanze*, Turin: Einaudi, 4th edition, 1956.

Einaudi, L. (1941 [1958]), *Saggi sul Risparmio e l'Imposta* [Essays on Savings and Taxation], Turin: Einaudi, 2nd edition, 1958.

Fasiani, M. (1951), *Principi di Scienza delle Finanze*, Turin: Giappichelli, 2 vols, 2nd revised and enlarged edition.

Forte, F. (1976), *Teoria Generale della Finanza Pubblica*, vol. 1, *Principi di Economia Finanziaria*, Turin: Boringhieri.

Forte, F. (1999), *Storia del Pensiero dell'Economia Pubblica*, vol. I, *Il Pensiero Antico Greco, Romano, Cristiano*, vol. II, *Dal Medioevo al Mercantilismo*, Milan: Giuffrè.

Forte, F. (2003), 'Economies internal and external, increasing returns and growth: the seminal contribution of Alfred Marshall revisited', *Rivista di Diritto Finanziario e Scienza delle Finanze*, **62**(2), 187–240.

Forte, F. (2005a), 'Giuseppe Ricca Salerno capostipite della scuola delle scelte economiche democratiche della finanza pubblica', *Rivista di Diritto Finanziario e Scienza delle Finanze*, **64**(1), 3–29.

Forte, F. (2005b), 'Sui contributi di Alexis de Tocqueville alla teoria dell'economia pubblica e delle politica economia' [On the contributions of Alexis de Tocqueville to the theory of the public economy and economic policy], in *Rivista di Politica Economica*, May–June, pp. 41–66.

Forte, F. (2007), 'La teoria politica della finanza pubblica di Benvenuto Griziotti', in Osculati (2007).

Forte, F. (2009), *L'Economia Liberale di Luigi Einaudi*, Fondazione Einaudi di Torino, Florence: Olschki.

Griziotti, B. (1909), 'I principi distributivi delle imposte moderne sul reddito e sugli acquisti di rendite e di incrementi di capitali' [The distributive principles of modern taxes on income and on the increases in rents and capital increases], in *Giornali degli Economisti*, November–December, series III, year xx, n. 11, pp. 455–505; republished in Griziotti (1956).

Griziotti, B. (1912), 'Considerazioni sui metodi limiti e problemi della scienza pura della finanza', Rome: Universelle; reprinted in Griziotti (1956), vol. I.

Griziotti, B. (1915), 'Crisi e tendenze negli studi finanziari' [Crises and tendencies in financial studies], in *Giornali degli Economisti*; republished in Griziotti (1956).

Griziotti, B. (1925), 'Programma scientifico dell'insegnamento a Pavia e problemi della ricostruzione finanziaria' [Scientific programme of course of lectures in Pavia and problems of financial reconstruction], in *Studi nelle Scienze Giuridiche e Sociali della Facoltà di Giurisprudenza dell'Università di Pavia* [Studies in the Juridical and Social Sciences of the Law School of the University of Pavia]; republished in Griziotti (1956).

Griziotti, B. (1935), 'Vecchi e nuovi indirizzi nella scienza delle finanze' [Old and new approaches in public finance], in *Annali di economia dell'Università Bocconi*, vol. x; republished with amendments in Griziotti (1953).

Griziotti, B. (1939), 'Brevi analisi e sintesi finanziarie' [Brief analyses and financial overviews], in *Rivista di Diritto Finanziario e Scienza delle Finanze*, September, Part I.

Griziotti, B. (1953), *Saggi sul Rinnovamento dello Studio della Scienza delle Finanze e del Diritto Finanziario* [Essays on the renewal of the study of public finance and financial law], Milan: Giuffrè.

Griziotti, B. (1956), *Studi di Scienza delle Finanze e Diritto Finanziario*, Milan: Giuffrè, 2 vols.

Keynes, J.M. (1936 [1980]), *The General Theory of Employment, Interest and Money*, London: Macmillan; reprinted in Keynes (1980), *The Collected Writings*, vol. VII, The Royal Economic Society, London: Macmillan.

Lindahl, E. (1919 [1958]), 'Die Gerechtigkeit der Besteugung: Eine Analyse der Steuerprinzipien auf der Grundlage der Grenznutzentheorie', Lund: Gleerupska Universitets–Bokhandelen; abridged English translation as 'Just taxation. A positive solution', in Musgrave and Peacock (eds) (1958).

Lindahl, E. (1928 [1958]), 'Einige strittige Fragen der Steuertheorie', in H. Mayer (ed.), *Die Wirtschaftstheorie der Gegenwart*, vol. IV, Vienna: Julius Springer, pp. 281–304; abridged English translation as 'Some controversial questions in the theory of taxation', in Musgrave and Peacock (eds) (1958).

Marshall, A. (1920 [1961]), *Principles of Economics*, 9th edition (1961), edited by C.V. Guillebaud, London: Macmillan.

Mazzola, U. (1890), *I Dati Scientifici della Finanza Pubblica*, Rome: Loescher; Chap. IX has been translated in English as 'The formation of the prices of public goods' and included in Musgrave and Peacock (eds) (1958).

Mill, J.S. (1848 [1871, 2006]), *Principles of Political Economy, with some of their Applications to Social Philosophy*, London: J.W. Parker; 7th and final edition (1871) reprinted (2006) in vols II and III of the *Collected Works of John Stuart Mill*, Indianapolis: Liberty Fund.

Montemartini, G. (1900 [1958]), 'Le Basi Fondamentali di una Scienza Finanziaria Pura', *Giornale degli Economisti*, **11**, 555–76; English translation as 'The fundamental principles of a pure theory of public finance', in Musgrave and Peacock (eds) (1958).

Müller, D. (2003), *Public Choice III*, Cambridge: Cambridge University Press.

Musgrave, R.A. (1959), *The Theory of Public Finance. A Study in Public Economy*, New York: McGraw Hill.

Musgrave, R.A. and A.T. Peacock (eds) (1958), *Classics in the Theory of Public Finance*, London: Macmillan (with texts by Barone, Cohen

Stuart, Edgeworth, Goldscheid, Leroy Beaulieu, Lindahl, Mazzola, Montemartini, Pantaleoni, Ritschl, Sax, Von Stein, Von Wieser, Wagner, Wicksell).

Osculati, F. (ed.) (2007), *La Figura e l'Opera di Benvenuto Griziotti*, Milan: Cisalpino.

Pantaleoni, M. (1883 [1938, 1958]), 'Contributo alla teoria del riparto delle spese pubbliche', *La Rassegna Italiana*, vol. 4; reprinted in Pantaleoni (1938), *Studi di Finanza e Statistica,* Bologna: Zanichelli; abridged English translation as 'Contribution to the theory of the distribution of public expenditure', in Musgrave and Peacock (eds) (1958).

Pareto, W. (1916 [1954, 1935, 1983]), *Trattato di Sociologia Generale,* with an 'Introduction' by N. Bobbio (1954), Milan: Comunità; English edition by A. Livingston and A. Buongiorno (1935) as *The Mind and Society; a Treatise on General Sociology*, New York: Harcourt, Brace & Co.; reprinted (1983), New York: Ams Press.

Pasinetti, L. (ed.) (1992), *Italian Economic Papers*, vol. I, Il Mulino, Oxford University Press, pp. 81–97.

Peacock, A.T. (1992), *Public Choice Analysis in Historical Perspective*, Mattioli Lectures, Cambridge: Cambridge University Press.

Pigou, A.C. (1920)*, The Economics of Welfare*, London: Macmillan.

Pigou, A.C. (1928 [1947]), *A Study in Public Finance*, London: Macmillan (1947), 3rd revised edition.

Puviani, A. (1903 [1973]), *Teoria dell'Illusione Finanziaria*, re-edited by F. Volpi (1973), Milan: ISEDI.

Ricardo, D. (1817 [1947, 2005]), *Principles of Political Economy and Taxation*; reprinted by P. Sraffa (1947) as vol. I of the *The Works and Correspondence of David Ricardo*, reprinted in 2005 by Liberty Fund, Indianapolis.

Ricca Salerno, G. (1888), *Scienza delle Finanze*, Florence: Barbera.

Sax, E. (1887), *Grundlegung der Theoretischen Staatswirthschaft*, Vienna: Hölder.

Say, J.B. (1841 [1848]), *Traité d'économie politique*, 6th edition, Paris: Guillaumin; English translation as *A Treatise on Political Economy*, Philadelphia: Grigg, Elliott & Co.

Seligman, E.R.A. (1925), *Studies in Public Finance*, New York: Macmillan.

Sidgwick, M.H. (1883), *The Principles of Political Economy*, London: Macmillan.

Smith, A. (1776), *An Inquiry into the Nature and Causes of the Wealth of Nations*; reprinted by W.B. Todd (ed.) (1982), with an Introduction by E. Cannan, Indianapolis: Liberty Fund.

Stiglitz, J.E. (2000), *Economics of the Public Sector*, New York: W.W. Norton, 3rd edition.

Wagner, A. (1883), *Finanzwissenschaft*, Leipzig: Winter.

Wicksell, K. (1896 [1958]), 'Ein neues Prinzip der gerechten Besteuerung', in *Finanztheoretische Untersuchungen*, Jena: Fischer; partial English translation (1958) as 'A new principle of just taxation', in Musgrave and Peacock (1958).

Wieser, F. von (1889 [1893]), *Der Natürliche Wert*, Vienna: Holder; English translation as *Natural Value*, London and New York: Macmillan.

CHAPTER 1

Alchian, A. (1950), 'Uncertainty, evolution, and economic theory', *Journal of Political Economy*, **58**(3), 211–21.

Aristotle, (324–320 BC), *The Politics*, translated by T.A. Sinclair and revised by T.J. Saunders, London: Penguin Books.

Arrow, K. (1951 [1963]), *Social Choice and Individual Values*, New Haven: Yale University Press.

Auerbach, J.A. and M. Feldstein (eds) (1987–2002), *Handbook of Public Economics*, vols I–IV, Amsterdam: North-Holland.

Axelrod, R. (1984), *The Evolution of Cooperation*, New York: Basic Books.

Banzhaf, J.F. (1965), 'Weighted voting doesn't work: a mathematical analysis', *Rutgers Law Review*, **19**, 317–43.

Bell, D. (1976), *The Cultural Contradictions of Capitalism*, London: Heinemann.

Black, D. (1958), *The Theory of Committees and Elections*, Cambridge: Cambridge University Press.

Black, D. (1969), 'On Arrow's impossibility theorem', *Journal of Law and Economics*, **12**(2), 227–48.

Blankart, B. (2008), *Öffentliche Finanzen in der Demokratie: eine Einführung in die Finanzwissenschaft*, 7th edition, Munich: Vahlen.

Boadway, R. (2002), 'The role of public choice considerations in normative public economics', in Winer and Shibata (2002).

Bowen, R. (1943), 'The interpretation of voting in the allocation of economic resources', *Quarterly Journal of Economics*, **58**, 27–48.

Brennan, G. and L. Lomasky (1993), *Democracy and Decision: The Pure Theory of Electoral Preference*, Cambridge: Cambridge University Press.

Breton, A. (1974), *The Economic Theory of Representative Government*, London: Macmillan.

Breton, A. (2002), 'Public and welfare economics under monopolistic and competitive governments', in Winer and Shibata (2002).

Breton, A. and G. Galeotti (1985), 'Is proportional representation always the best electoral rule?', *Public Finance/Finances Publiques*, **40**(1), 1–16.

Breton, A. and R. Wintrobe (1982), *The Logic of Bureaucratic Conduct: An Economic Analysis of Competition, Exchange, and Efficiency in Private and Public Organizations*, Cambridge: Cambridge University Press.

Brosio, G. (1986), *Economia e Finanza Pubblica*, Rome: NIS.

Buchanan, J.M. (1949 [1960, 1999]), 'The pure theory of government finance: a suggested approach', *Journal of Political Economy*, **57**(6), 496–505; reprinted in Buchanan (1960) and in *The Collected Works of James M. Buchanan* (1999–2002), vol. 1 (1999), *The Logical Foundations of Constitutional Liberty*, Indianapolis: Liberty Fund.

Buchanan, J.M. (1954a [1960, 1999]), 'Social choice, democracy, and free markets', *Journal of Political Economy*, **62**(2), 114–23; reprinted in Buchanan (1960) and in *The Collected Works of James M. Buchanan* (1999–2002), vol. 1 (1999), *The Logical Foundations of Constitutional Liberty*, Indianapolis: Liberty Fund.

Buchanan, J.M. (1954b, [1960, 1999]), 'Individual choice in voting and the market', *Journal of Political Economy*, **62**(4), 334–43; reprinted in Buchanan (1960) and in *The Collected Works of James M. Buchanan* (1999–2002), vol. 1 (1999), *The Logical Foundations of Constitutional Liberty*, Indianapolis: Liberty Fund.

Buchanan, J.M. (1959 [1960, 1999]), 'Positive economics, welfare economics and political economy', *Journal of Law and Economics*, **2**, October, 124–38; reprinted in Buchanan (1960) and in *The Collected Works of James M. Buchanan* (1999–2002), vol. 1 (1999), *The Logical Foundations of Constitutional Liberty*, Indianapolis: Liberty Fund.

Buchanan, J.M. (1960), *Fiscal Theory and Political Economy*, Chapel Hill: University of North Carolina Press.

Buchanan, J.M. (1966 [1999]), *Public Finance in Democratic Process: Fiscal Institutions and Individual Choice*, Chapel Hill: University of North Carolina Press; reprinted (1999) as vol. 4 of *The Collected Works of James M. Buchanan* (1999–2002), Indianapolis: Liberty Fund.

Buchanan, J.M. (1968 [1999]), *The Demand and Supply of Public Goods*, Chicago: Rand McNally; reprinted (1999) as vol. 5 of *The Collected Works of James M. Buchanan* (1999–2002), Indianapolis: Liberty Fund.

Buchanan, J.M. (2001), *Moral Science and Moral Order*, vol. 17 of *The Collected Works of James M. Buchanan* (1999–2002), Indianapolis: Liberty Fund.

Buchanan, J.M. and G. Tullock (1962 [1999]), *The Calculus of Consent: Logical Foundations of Constitutional Democracy*, Ann Arbor: University of Michigan Press; reprinted (1999) as vol. 3 of *The Collected Works of James M. Buchanan* (1999–2002), Indianapolis: Liberty Fund.

Casas Pardo, J. and P. Schwartz (eds) (2007), *Public Choice and the Challenges of Democracy*, Cheltenham, UK and Northampton, MA, USA: Edward Elgar.

Coase, R. (1937), 'The nature of the firm', *Economica*, **4**(16), 386–405; reprinted in Coase (1988).

Coase, R. (1960), 'The problem of social cost', *Journal of Law and Economics*, **3**(1), 1–44; reprinted in Coase (1988).

Coase, R. (1988), *The Firm, the Market, and the Law,* Chicago: University of Chicago Press.

Condorcet, Jean-Antoine-Nicolas de (1785 [1974]), 'Essai sur l'application de l'analyse à la probabilité des décisions rendues à la pluralité des voix', in Jean-Antoine-Nicolas de Condorcet (1974), *Mathématique et société*, selected writings edited by R. Rashed, Paris: Hermann.

Croce, B. and L. Einaudi (1957), *Liberismo e Liberalismo*, Naples: Ricciardi.

Dahl, R.A. (1963 [1990]), *Modern Political Analysis*, Englewood Cliffs: Prentice-Hall.

Dahl, R.A. (1998), *On Democracy*, New Haven: Yale University Press.

De Viti De Marco, A. (1934 [1936]), *Principi di Economia Finanziaria*, Turin: Einaudi; English translation (1936) as *First Principles of Public Finance*, London: Jonathan Cape; New York: Harcourt, Brace & Co.

Downs, A. (1957), *An Economic Theory of Democracy,* New York: Harper.

Downs, A. (1960), 'In defense of majority voting', University of Chicago, mimeoed essay for private use.

EC, IMF, OECD, UN and World Bank (1993), *System of National Accounts*, Brussels/Luxembourg: Commission of the European Communities; Washington, DC: International Monetary Fund; Paris: Organisation for Economic Co-operation and Development; New York: United Nations; Washington, DC: World Bank.

Einaudi, L. (1919), 'Osservazioni critiche intorno alla teoria dell'ammortamento dell'imposta e teoria delle variazioni nei redditi e nei valori capitali susseguenti all'imposta', in Einaudi (1941 [1958]).

Einaudi, L. (1940 [1959]), *Miti e Paradossi della Giustizia Tributaria*, Turin: Einaudi.

Einaudi, L. (1941 [1958]), *Saggi sul Risparmio e l'Imposta*, Turin: Einaudi.

Einaudi, L. (2006), *Luigi Einaudi: Selected Economic Essays*, edited by

L. Einaudi, R. Faucci and R. Marchionatti, New York: Palgrave Macmillan.

Eucken, W. (1952 [2004]), *Grundsätze der Wirtschaftpolitik*, Tübingen: Mohr Siebeck.

EUROSTAT(1995),*European System of Accounts: ESA 1995*, Luxembourg: Office for Official Publications of the European Communities.

Fedeli, S. and F. Forte (2001), 'Voting powers and the efficiency of the decision-making process in the European Council of Ministers', *European Journal of Law and Economics*, **12**(1), 5–38.

Felsenthal, D.S. and M. Machover (1998), *The Measurement of Voting Power: Theory and Practice, Problems and Paradoxes,* Cheltenham, UK and Lyme, NH, USA: Edward Elgar.

Fisichella, D. (1970), *Sviluppo Democratico e Sistemi Elettorali*, Florence: Sansoni.

Fisichella, D. (1982), *Elezioni e Democrazia. Un'Analisi Comparata*, Bologna: Il Mulino.

Forte, F. (1975), *Manuale di Politica Economica*, Turin: Einaudi, 4th edition.

Forte, F. (1982), 'The law of selection in the public economy as compared to the market economy', *Public Finance/Finances Publiques*, **37**(2), 224–45.

Forte, F. (1984), 'Democracy as a public good. Efficiency versus effectiveness', *Economia delle Scelte Pubbliche*, **3**.

Forte, F. (1986), 'La teoria dell'imprenditore politico di G. Montemartini e il suo socialismo riformista', in Various Authors (conference proceedings) (1986), *La Cultura delle Riforme in Italia fra Otto e Novecento: I Montemartini*, Milan: La Pietra.

Forte, F. (1995), *Etica Pubblica e Regole del Gioco*, Naples: Liguori.

Forte, F. (1997), 'The measurement of fiscal burden on GDP instead of on national net value added produced: a chapter in fiscal illusion', *Banca Nazionale del Lavoro Quarterly Review*, **202**, September.

Forte, F. (2000), *Principi di Economia Pubblica*, Milan: Giuffrè.

Forte, F. (2005a), 'Sui contributi di Alexis de Tocqueville alla teoria dell'economia pubblica e della politica economica', *Rivista di Politica Economica*, **XCV**(5–6), 41–66.

Forte, F. (2005b), 'Il pensiero di Leoni sulle decisioni di voto dei rappresentanti degli azionisti e degli elettori e sulla rilevanza della probabilità nelle decisioni individuali e collettive', in Masala (ed.) (2005).

Forte, F. (2009a), *Ezio Vanoni Economista Pubblico*, edited by S. Beretta and L. Bernardi, Istituto Bruno Leoni, Soveria Mannelli (CZ): Rubbettino.

Forte, F. (2009b), *L'Economia Liberale di Luigi Einaudi. Saggi*, Fondazione Einaudi di Torino, Florence: Olschki.

Forte, F. and J.M. Buchanan (1961 [1989, 2001]), 'The evaluation of public services', *Journal of Political Economy*, **69**(2), 107–21; reprinted in J.M. Buchanan (1989), *Explorations into Constitutional Economics*, compiled by R.D. Tollison and V.J. Vanberg, College Station: Texas A&M University Press, and in *The Collected Works of James M. Buchanan* (1999–2002), vol. 15 (2001), *Externalities and Public Expenditure Theory*, Indianapolis: Liberty Fund.

Forte, F. and D. D'Amico (2007), 'A theory of the democratic fiscal constitution', in Casas Pardo and Schwartz (2007).

Friedman, M. and R. Friedman (1980), *Free to Choose: A Personal Statement*, London: Secker & Warburg.

Galbraith, J.K. (1958), *The Affluent Society*, London and New York: Penguin Books.

Gauthier, D. (1986), *Morals by Agreement*, Oxford: Clarendon Press.

Giuffrè, G. and U. Villani (eds) (1988), *La Città Fraterna. Per il Quarantesimo Anniversario della Dichiarazione Universale dei Diritti dell'Uomo*, Milan: Giuffrè.

Goldschmidt, N. and M. Wohlgemuth (eds) (2008), *Grundtexte zur Freiburger Tradition der Ordnungsökonomik*, Tubingen: Mohr Siebeck.

Graham, G. (1988), *Contemporary Social Philosophy*, Oxford, UK and New York, USA: Blackwell.

Greenaway, D. and G.K. Shaw (eds) (1985), *Public Choice, Public Finance, and Public Policy: Essays in Honour of Alan Peacock*, Oxford, UK and New York, USA: Blackwell.

Grilli, D., V. Masciandaro and G. Tabellini (eds) (1991), 'Institutions and policies', *Economic Policy*, **6**(13), 342–92.

Griziotti, B. (1912), 'Considerazioni sui metodi limiti e problemi della scienza pura della finanza', Rome: Universelle; reprinted in Griziotti (1956), vol. I.

Griziotti, B. (1956), *Studi di Scienza delle Finanze e Diritto Finanziario*, Milan: Giuffrè (2 vols).

Grofman, B. and A. Lijphart (eds) (1984), *Electoral Laws and their Consequences*, New York: Agathon Press.

Hayek, F. (1982), *Law, Legislation and Liberty: A New Statement of the Liberal Principles of Justice and Political Economy*, London: Routledge.

Holler, M. (1987a), 'An introduction to the logic of multiparty systems', in Holler (1987b).

Holler, M. (ed.) (1987b), *The Logic of Multiparty Systems*, Dordrecht: Kluwer Academic Publishers.

Kelsen, H. (1920 [1929]), *Vom Wesen und Wert der Demokratie*, 2nd and enlarged edition (1929), Tübingen: Mohr.

Bibliography

417

Kelsen, H. (1924), *Das Problem des Parlamentarismus*, Vienna: Braumüller.
Kelsen, H. (1955), 'Foundations of democracy', *Ethics*, **66**(1), 1–101.
Kelsen, H. (2006), *Verteidigung der Demokratie: Aufsätze zur Demokratietheorie*, selected and edited by M. Jestaedt and O. Lepsius, Tübingen: Mohr Siebeck.
Kenessey, Z. (ed.) (1994), *The Accounts of Nations*, Amsterdam and Washington, DC: IOS Press.
Koslowski, P. (1987a), 'Market and democracy as discourse', with a comment by F. Forte, in Koslowski (ed.) (1987b).
Koslowski, P. (ed.) (1987b), *Individual Liberty and Democratic Decision-Making: the Ethics, Economics, and Politics of Democracy*, Tübingen: J.C.B. Mohr.
Laver, M. and N. Schofield (1990), *Multiparty Government. The Politics of Coalition in Europe*, Oxford: Oxford University Press.
Leoni, B. (1960), 'Political decision and majority rule', *Il Politico*, **25**(4), 724–33.
Leoni, B. (1961 [1991]), *Freedom and the Law*, Princeton: Van Nostrand, 3rd expanded edition (1991), Indianapolis: Liberty Fund.
Leoni, B. (1967 [2009]), 'Rappresentanza politica e rappresentanza dei partiti', *Il Politico*, **3**, 489–508; reprinted in Leoni (2009b).
Leoni, B. (1991), *Liberty and the Law*, 3rd expanded edition, Indianapolis: Liberty Fund.
Leoni, B. (2009a), *Law, Liberty and the Competitive Market*, edited and with an 'Introduction' by C. Lottieri and a 'Foreword' by RA. Epstein, London: Transaction Publishers.
Leoni, B. (2009b), *Scritti di Scienza Politica e di Teoria del Diritto*, with an 'Introduction' by M. Stoppino, Soveria Mannelli (RC), Rubbettino.
Lequiller, F. and D. Blades (2006), *Understanding National Accounts*, Paris: OECD.
Lijphart, A. (1990), 'The Political Consequences of Electoral Laws, 1945–1985', *American Political Science Review*, **84**(2), 481–96.
Lindahl, E. (1919 [1958]), 'Die Gerechtigkeit der Besteuung: Eine Analyse der Steuerprinzipien auf der Grundlage der Grenznutzentheorie', Lund: Gleerupska Universitets–Bokhandelen; abridged English translation as 'Just taxation. A positive solution', in Musgrave and Peacock (eds) (1958).
Lindahl, E. (1928 [1958]), 'Einige strittige Fragen der Steuertheorie', in H. Mayer (ed.), *Die Wirtschaftstheorie der Gegenwart*, vol. IV, Vienna: Julius Springer, pp. 281–304; abridged English translation as 'Some controversial questions in the theory of taxation', in Musgrave and Peacock (eds) (1958).
Lindblom, C. (1977), *Politics and Markets: The World's Political Economic Systems*, New York: Basic Books.

Luce, R.D and H. Raiffa (1957), *Games and Decisions: Introduction and Critical Survey*, New York: Wiley.

Marshall, A. (1920 [1961]), *Principles of Economics*, 9th edition (1961) edited by C.V. Guillebaud, London: Macmillan.

Masala, A. (ed.) (2005), *La Teoria Politica di Bruno Leoni*, Soveria Mannelli (CZ): Rubbettino.

Mattozzi, A. and M. Merlo (2007a), 'Political careers or career politicians?', *Journal of Public Economics*, **92** (3–4), 597–608.

Mattozzi, A. and M. Merlo (2007b), 'Mediocracy', *NBER Working Paper No. 12920*.

Mazzola, U. (1908), *I Dati Scientifici della Finanza Pubblica*, Rome: Loescher.

McLean, I. (1987), *Public Choice. An Introduction*, Oxford: Blackwell.

McNutt, P.A. (1996), *The Economics of Public Choice*, Cheltenham, UK and Brookfield, VT, USA: Edward Elgar.

Mill, J.S. (1861 [1963]), *Considerations on Representative Government*; reprinted in *The Collected Works of John Stuart Mill* (1963), vol. XIX, London: Routledge & Kegan Paul.

Montemartini, G. (1900 [1958]), 'Le basi fondamentali di una scienza finanziaria pura', *Giornale degli Economisti*, **21**, 555–76; English translation as 'The fundamental principles of a pure theory of public finance', in Musgrave and Peacock (1958).

Montemartini, G. (1902), *Municipalizzazione dei Pubblici Servigi*, Milan: S.E.L.

Morgernstern, O. (1963), *Spieltheorie und Wirtschaftswissenschaft*, Vienna: Oldenbourg.

Mosca, G. (1896 [1985]), *La Classe Politica*, reprinted in 1985, with an 'Introduction' by N. Bobbio, Bari: Laterza.

Müller, D. (2003), *Public Choice III*, Cambridge: Cambridge University Press.

Musgrave, R.A. (1959), *The Theory of Public Finance. A Study in Public Economy*, New York: McGraw-Hill.

Musgrave, R.A. and A.T. Peacock (eds) (1958), *Classics in the Theory of Public Finance*, London: Macmillan (with texts by Barone, Cohen Stuart, Edgeworth, Goldscheid, Leroy Beaulieu, Lindahl, Mazzola, Montemartini, Pantaleoni, Ritschl, Sax, Von Stein, Von Wieser, Wagner, Wicksell).

Nash, J. (2007), *The Essential John Nash*, edited by H.W. Kuhn and S. Nasar, Princeton: Princeton University Press.

Nelson, D. and E. Silberberg (1987), 'Ideology and legislator shirking', *Economic Inquiry*, **25** (1), 15–25.

North, D. (1990), *Institutions, Institutional Change and Economic Performance*, Cambridge: Cambridge University Press.

Ordeshook, P.C. (ed.) (1978), *Game Theory and Political Science*, New York: New York University Press.

Panebianco, A. (ed.) (1989), *L'Analisi della Politica: Tradizioni di Ricerca, Modelli, Teorie*, Bologna: Il Mulino.

Pantaleoni, M. (1883 [1938, 1958]), 'Contributo alla teoria del riparto delle spese pubbliche', *La Rassegna Italiana*, vol. 4; reprinted in Pantaleoni, M. (1938), *Studi di Finanza e Statistica*, Bologna: Zanichelli; abridged English translation as 'Contribution to the theory of the distribution of public expenditure' in Musgrave and Peacock (eds) (1958).

Pantaleoni, M. (1904), 'Tentativo di analisi del concetto di forte e debole in economia', in *Scritti vari di Economia. Serie prima*, Palermo: Sandron.

Pareto, W. (1906 [1909, 1971, 2006]), *Manuale di Economia Politica*, Milan: S.E.L.; French translation by A. Bonnet revised by the author (1909), *Manuel d'Economie Politique*, Paris: V. Giard & E. Brière; English translation (1971), *Manual of Political Economy*, New York: A.M. Kelley; critical edition (2006) by A. Montesano, A. Zanni and L. Bruni, Milan: Egea.

Pareto, W. (1916 [1954; 1935, 1983]), *Trattato di Sociologia Generale*, with an 'Introduction' by N. Bobbio (1954), Milan, Comunità; English edition by A. Livingston and A. Buongiorno (1935) as *The Mind and Society; a Treatise on General Sociology*, New York: Harcourt, Brace & Co., reprinted (1983), New York: Ams Press.

Peacock, A.T. (1979), *The Economic Analysis of Government, and Related Themes*, Oxford: Martin Robertson.

Peacock, A.T. (1992), *Public Choice Analysis in Historical Perspective*, Cambridge: Cambridge University Press.

Peacock, A.T. and H. Willgerodt (1989a), *Germany's Social Market Economy*, London: Macmillan.

Peacock, A.T. and H. Willgerodt (1989b), *German Neo-liberals and the Social Market Economy*, London: Macmillan.

Popper, K.R. (1945 [2006]), *The Open Society and its Enemies*, London: Routledge.

Razin, A. and E. Sadka (eds) (1987), *Economic Policy in Theory and Practice*, London: Macmillan.

Ricca Salerno, G. (1888), *Manuale di Scienza delle Finanze*, Florence: Barbera.

Rowley, Ch.K. and A.T. Peacock (1975), *Welfare Economics. A Liberal Restatement*, Oxford: Martin Robertson (now Blackwell).

Ruffini, F. (1946), *Diritti al Libertà*, edited by P. Calamandrei, Florence: La Nuova Italia.

Ruffini, E. (1976), *Il Principio Maggioritario. Profilo Storico*, Milan: Adelphi.

Samuelson, P.A. (1954), 'The pure theory of public expenditure', *Review of Economics and Statistics*, **36** (4), 387–9; reprinted in Samuelson, P.A. (1966 [1986]), *Collected Scientific Papers*, edited by J.E. Stiglitz, vol. II.

Samuelson, P.A. (1955), 'Diagrammatic exposition of a pure theory of public expenditure', *Review of Economics and Statistics*, **37** (4), 350–56; reprinted in Samuelson (1966 [1986]).

Samuelson, P.A. (1958), 'Aspects of public expenditure theories', *Review of Economics and Statistics*, **40** (4), 332–8; reprinted in Samuelson (1966 [1986]).

Samuelson, P.A. (1966 [1986]), *Collected Scientific Papers*, edited by J.E. Stiglitz, vol. II, Cambridge, MA: MIT Press.

Santagata, W. (1991), 'Ideologia, opportunismo, pluralismo', *Stato e Mercato*, **3**, 371.

Sartori, G. (1987), *The Theory of Democracy Revisited*, Chatham, NJ: Chatham House Publishers.

Sax, E. (1924 [1956, 1958]), 'Die Wertungstheorie der Steuer', *Zeitschrift für Volkswirtschaft und Sozialpolitik*, **4**, 191–240; reprinted in *Zeitschrift für Nationalökonomie*, **15** (3), 317–56; partial English translation as 'The valuation theory of taxation', in Musgrave and Peacock (eds) (1958).

Schmitt, C. (1927 [1932; 1976, 2007]), 'Der Begriff des Politischen', *Archiv für Sozialwissenschaft und Sozialpolitik*, **58**, 1–33; revised and enlarged text (1932), Munich: Duncker & Humblot; English translation (1996) by G. Schwab, *The Concept of the Political*, New Brunswick, NJ: Rutgers University Press; expanded edition (2007) with a 'Foreword' by T.B. Strong, Chicago: University of Chicago Press.

Schumpeter, J. (1942 [2006]), *Capitalism, Socialism, and Democracy*, New York and London: Harper & Brothers; London: Routledge.

Sen, A.K. (1999), 'Democracy as a universal value', *Journal of Democracy*, **10** (3), 3–17.

Sen, A.K. (2003), 'Democracy and its global roots', *New Republic*, **14**, 28–35.

Shapley, L.S. and M. Shubik (1954), 'A method for evaluating the distribution of power in a committee system', *American Political Science Review*, **48** (3), 787–92.

Smith, A. (1776), *An Inquiry into the Nature and Causes of the Wealth of Nations*, reprinted by W.B. Todd (ed.) (1982), with an 'Introduction' by E. Cannan, Indianapolis: Liberty Fund.

Spinoza, B. (1670 [2007]), *Tractatus Theologico-Politicus*, English translation by M. Silverthorne and J. Israel, *Theological-Political Treatise*, edited by J. Israel, Cambridge: Cambridge University Press.

Thurow, L.C. (1980), *The Zero-Sum Society. Distribution and the Possibilities for Economic Change*, New York: Basic Books.

Vanberg, V. (1994), *Rules and Choice in Economics*, London and New York: Routledge.

Van Doel, H. (1979), *Democracy and Welfare Economics*, Cambridge: Cambridge University Press.

Wicksell, K. (1896 [1958]), 'Ein neues Prinzip der gerechten Besteuerung', in *Finanztheoretische Untersuchungen*, Jena: Fischer; partial English translation (1958) as 'A new principle of just taxation', in Musgrave and Peacock (1958).

Williamson, E.O. (1985), *The Economic Institutions of Capitalism: Firms, Markets, Relational Contracting*, London: Collier Macmillan.

Winer, S.L. and H. Shibata (2002), *Political Economy and Public Finance: The Role of Political Economy in the Theory and Practice of Public Economics*, Cheltenham, UK and Northampton, MA, USA: Edward Elgar.

CHAPTER 2

Arrow, K. and M. Intriligator (eds) (1981), *Handbook of Mathematical Economics*, 4 vols, Amsterdam and New York: North-Holland.

Arrow, K.J. and T. Scitovsky (eds) (1969), *Readings in Welfare Economics*, London: Allen & Unwin.

Atkinson, A.B. and J. Stiglitz (1980), *Lectures on Public Economics*, London and New York: McGraw-Hill.

Auerbach, A.J. and M. Feldstein (eds) (1985–2002), *Handbook of Public Economics*, 4 vols, Amsterdam: North-Holland.

Axelrod, R. (1984), *The Evolution of Cooperation*, New York: Basic Books.

Barry, B. (1989), *Theories of Justice, Vol. I of A Treatise on Social Justice*, London: Harvester Wheatsheaf.

Bator, F. (1958), 'The anatomy of market failure', *Quarterly Journal of Economics*, **72**(3), 351–79.

Baumol, W.J. (1965) *Welfare Economics and the Theory of the State*, 2nd edition, Cambridge, MA: Harvard University Press.

Becker, G. (1976a), 'Altruism, egoism, and genetic fitness: economics and sociobiology', *Journal of Economic Literature*, **14**(3), 817–26.

Becker, G. (1976b), *The Economic Approach to Human Behaviour*, Chicago: University of Chicago Press.

Binmore, K. (1994), *Playing Fair: Game Theory and the Social Contract I*, Cambridge, MA: MIT Press.

Binmore, K. (1998), *Just Playing: Game Theory and the Social Contract II*, Cambridge, MA: MIT Press.

Binmore, K. (2004), 'Reciprocity and the social contract', *Politics, Philosophy & Economics*, **3**(1), 5–35.

Blaug, M. (2007), 'The fundamental theorems of modern welfare economics, historically contemplated', *History of Political Economy*, **39**(2), 185–207.

Brennan, G. and J.M. Buchanan (1985 [2000]), *The Reason of Rules: Constitutional Political Economy*, Cambridge: Cambridge University Press; reprinted (2000), as vol. 10 of *The Collected Works of James M. Buchanan* (1999–2002), Indianapolis: Liberty Fund.

Brousseau, E. and J.-M. Glachant (eds) (2002), *The Economics of Contracts: Theories and Applications*, Cambridge, MA: Cambridge University Press.

Buchanan, J.M. (1962 [1999]), 'Politics, policy, and Pigovian margins', *Economica*, New Series, **29**(113), 17–28; reprinted in *The Collected Works of James M. Buchanan* (1999–2002), vol. 1 (1999), *The Logical Foundations of Constitutional Liberty*, Indianapolis: Liberty Fund.

Buchanan, J.M. (1971 [1979b]), 'Equality as fact and norm', *Ethics*, **81**(3), 228–40; reprinted in Buchanan (1979b), pp. 231–52.

Buchanan, J.M. (1975 [2000]), *The Limits of Liberty: Between Anarchy and Leviathan*, Chicago: Chicago University Press; reprinted (2000) as vol. 7 of *The Collected Works of James M. Buchanan* (1999–2002), Indianapolis: Liberty Fund.

Buchanan, J.M. (1976 [2001]), 'A Hobbesian interpretation of the Rawlsian difference principle', *Kyklos*, **29**(1), 5–25; reprinted (2001) in *Moral Science and Moral Order*, vol. 17 of *The Collected Works of James M. Buchanan* (1999–2002), Indianapolis: Liberty Fund.

Buchanan, J.M. (1977), *Freedom in Constitutional Contract: Perspectives of a Political Economist*, College Station: Texas A&M University Press.

Buchanan, J.M. (1979a), 'Natural and Artifactual man', in Buchanan (1979b), pp. 93–112.

Buchanan, J.M. (1979b), *What should Economists do?* Indianapolis: Liberty Press.

Buchanan, J.M. (1986), *Liberty, Market, and State: Political Economy in the 1980s*, London: Harvester Wheatsheaf; Part Three, *Explorations in the Theory of Justice*.

Buchanan, J.M. (2001), *Moral Science and Moral Order*, vol. 17 of *The Collected Works of James M. Buchanan* (1999–2002), Indianapolis: Liberty Fund.

Buchanan, J.M. and G. Tullock (1962 [1999]), *The Calculus of Consent: Logical Foundations of Constitutional Democracy*, Ann Arbor:

University of Michigan Press; reprinted (1999) as vol. 3 of *The Collected Works of James M. Buchanan* (1999–2002), Indianapolis: Liberty Fund.

Caffè, F. (1956), 'Vecchi e nuovi indirizzi nelle indagini sull'economia del benessere', in C. Napoleoni (ed.) (1956), *Dizionario di Economia Politica*, Milan: Comunità.

Caffè, F. (1966), *Politica Economica*, Turin: Boringhieri.

Chiancone, A. and F. Osculati (eds) (1993), *Il Merito della Spesa Pubblica: la Natura e l'Offerta dei Beni non de Mercato*, Milan: Franco Angeli.

Coase, R. (1960), 'The problem of social cost', *Journal of Law and Economics*, **3**(1), 1–44; reprinted in Coase (1988).

Coase, R. (1988), *The Firm, the Market, and the Law*, Chicago: University of Chicago Press.

Cornes, R. and T. Sandler (1986), *The Theory of Externalities, Public Goods, and Club Goods*, Cambridge: Cambridge University Press.

Diekmann, A. and P. Mitter (eds) (1986), *Paradoxical Effects of Social Behavior: Essays in Honor of Anatol Rapoport*, Heidelberg: Physica-Verlag.

Dworkin, G., G. Bermant and P.G. Brown (eds) (1977), *Markets and Morals*, Washington: Hemisphere Pub. Corp.

Ellis, H.S. and W. Fellner (1943 [1952]), 'External economies and diseconomies', *American Economic Review*, **33**(3), 493–511; reprinted in Stigler and Boulding (eds) (1952).

Fedeli, S. and F. Forte (2001), 'Il "modus vivendi" all'interno di una società pluralista significato, costi, limiti e possibilità della tolleranza', in Mazzocchi and Villani (eds) (2001).

Fedeli, S. and F. Forte (2002), 'Minimizing frustration versus Median Voter's Equilibria', in M. Holler et al. (eds) (2002), *Power and Fairness*, Jahrbuch für Neue Politische Ökonomie, 20, Tübingen: Mohr Siebeck.

Fleurbaey, M. (2008), 'Economics and economic justice', *The Stanford Encyclopedia of Philosophy (Fall 2008 Edition)*, edited by Edward N. Zalta, available at http://plato.stanford.edu/archives/fall2008/entries/economic-justice/.

Forte, F. (1991), *I Diritti della Natura. Saggio di Economia Eco-Ambientale*, Rome: Nuove Edizioni del Gallo.

Forte, F. (1993), 'I beni meritori: scelte razionali, esternalità, paternalismo, preferenze sulle preferenze', in Chiancone and Osculati (eds) (1993).

Forte, F. (1995), *Etica Pubblica e Regole del Gioco*, Naples: Liguori.

Forte, F. (1996), 'Teoria della giustizia. Riflessioni su Nash, Harsanyi, Gauthier, Rawls e Barry', in G. Muraro and M. Rey (eds) (1996), *Ineguaglianza e Redistribuzione*, Milan: Franco Angeli.

Forte, F. (2003), 'Economies internal and external, increasing returns and growth: the seminal contribution of Alfred Marshall', *Rivista di Diritto Finanziario e Scienza delle Finanze*, no. 2, pp. 187–240.

Forte, F. and M. Mantovani (1954), *Economia e Politica dei Beni Culturali*, Soveria Mannelli: Rubbettino.

Forte, F. and G. Mossetto (1972), *Economia del Benessere e Democrazia*, Milan: Franco Angeli.

Freeman, S. (ed.) (2003), *The Cambridge Companion to Rawls*, Cambridge: Cambridge University Press.

Friedman, M. (1953), *Essays in Positive Economics*, Chicago: Chicago University Press.

Friedman, M. and L.J. Savage (1948), 'The utility analysis of choices involving risk', *Journal of Political Economy*, **56**(4), 279–304.

Gauthier, D. (1986), *Morals by Agreement*, Oxford: Clarendon Press.

Graaff, J. de V. (1957), *Theoretical Welfare Economics*, Cambridge: Cambridge University Press.

Graaff, J. de V. (1972), 'On making a recommendation in a democracy', *Economic Journal*, **72** (286), 293–8.

Graham, G. (1988), *Contemporary Social Philosophy*, Oxford, UK and New York, USA: Blackwell.

Granaglia, E. (1988), *Efficienza ed Equità nelle Politiche Pubbliche*, Milan: Franco Angeli.

Hare, R.M. (1976 [1982]), 'Ethical theory and utilitarianism', in D. Lewis (ed.) (1976), *Contemporary British Philosophy IV*, London: Allen & Unwin; reprinted in Sen and Williams (eds) (1982).

Hare, R.M. (1981), *Moral Thinking: Its Levels, Method, and Point*, Oxford: Clarendon Press; New York: Oxford University Press.

Harsanyi, J.C. (1955), 'Cardinal welfare, individualistic ethics and inter-personal comparisons of utility', *Journal of Political Economy*, **63**(4), 309–21.

Harsanyi, J.C. (1975), 'Can the maximin principle serve as a basis for morality. A critique of John Rawls' "Theory"', *American Political Science Review*, **69**(2), 594–606.

Harsanyi, J.C. (1977 [1982]), 'Morality and the theory of rational behaviour', *Social Research*, **44**(4), 623–56; reprinted in Sen and Williams (eds) (1982).

Harsanyi, J.C. (1985), 'Rule utilitarianism, equality and justice', *Social Philosophy and Policy*, **2**(2), 115–27.

Harsanyi, J.C. (1986), 'Utilities and utilitarian ethics', in Diekmann and Mitter (eds) (1986).

Hicks, J. (1939), 'The foundations of welfare economics', *Economic Journal*, **49**(196), 696–712.

Hicks, J. (1940), 'The valuation of the social income', *Economica*, New Series, **7**(26), 105–24.

Hochman, H.M. and G.E. Peterson (eds) (1974), *Redistribution through Public Choice*, New York: Columbia University Press.

Hochman, H.M. and J.D. Rodgers (1969), 'Pareto optimal redistribution', *American Economic Review*, **59**(4), Part 1, 542–57.

Holler, M., H. Kliemt, D. Schmiedtchen and M.E. Streit (eds) (2003), *Power and Fairness*, Jahrbuch für Neue Politische Ökonomie, 20, Tübingen: Mohr Siebeck.

Hume, D. (1740 [2003]), *A Treatise on Human Nature, Vol. III Of Morals*, Mineola, NY: Dover Publications.

Hume, D. (1751 [1998]), *An Enquiry Concerning the Principles of Morals*, edited by T.L. Beauchamp, Oxford: Clarendon Press.

Kaldor, N. (1939 [1960]), 'Welfare propositions and interpersonal comparison of utility', *Economic Journal*, **49**(195), 549–52; reprinted in Kaldor (1960).

Kaldor, N. (1960), *Essays on Value and Distribution*, Glencoe, IL: Free Press.

Kaplow, L. and S. Shavell (2002), *Fairness versus Welfare*, Cambridge, MA: Harvard University Press.

Little, I.M.D. (1950 [2002]), *A Critique of Welfare Economics*, Oxford: Clarendon Press; reprinted with a retrospective 'Preface' by I.M.D Little (2002), Oxford: Oxford University Press.

Mazzocchi, G. and A. Villani (eds) (2001), *Etica, Economia, Principi di Giustizia*, Milan: Franco Angeli.

Meade, J.H. (1952 [1969]), 'External economies and diseconomies in a competitive situation', *Economic Journal*, **62**(245), 54–67; reprinted in Arrow and Scitovsky (eds) (1969).

Myint, H. (1948), *Theories of Welfare Economics*, Cambridge, MA: Harvard University Press.

Nagel, T. (1988), *The View from Nowhere*, New York: Oxford University Press.

Nash, J.F. (1950 [2002]), 'The bargaining problem', *Econometrica*, **18**(2), 155–62; reprinted in Nash (2002).

Nash, J.F. (2002), *The Essential John Nash*, edited by H.W. Kuhn and S. Nasar, Princeton, NJ: Princeton University Press.

Pantaleoni, M. (1904), 'Massimi edonistici individuali e collettivi', in *Scritti vari di Economia. Serie prima*, Palermo: Sandron.

Pareto, W. (1906 [1909, 1971, 2006]), *Manuale di Economia Politica*, Milan: S.E.L.; French translation by A. Bonnet revised by the author (1909), *Manuel d'Economie Politique*, Paris: V. Giard & E. Brière; English translation (1971), *Manual of Political Economy*, New York:

A.M. Kelley; critical edition (2006) by A. Montesano, A. Zanni and L. Bruni, Milan: Egea.

Pareto, W. (1916 [1954; 1935, 1983]), *Trattato di Sociologia Generale,* with an 'Introduction' by N. Bobbio (1954), Milano, Comunità; English edition by A. Livingston and A. Buongiorno (1935) as *The Mind and Society; a Treatise on General Sociology,* New York: Harcourt, Brace & Co., reprinted (1983), New York: Ams Press.

Pigou, A.C. (1920), *The Economics of Welfare,* London: Macmillan.

Pigou, A.C. (1932 [2002]), *The Economics of Welfare,* 4th edition, London: Macmillan; reprinted with a new 'Introduction' by N. Aslanbeigui (2002), New Brunswick, NJ: Transaction Publishers.

Rawls, J. (1971 [1987]), *A Theory of Justice,* Cambridge, MA: Harvard University Press; French translation (1987) by C. Audard, *Théorie de la Justice,* with an 'Introduction' by J. Rawls, Paris: Le Seuil.

Rawls, J. (1982), 'Social unit and primary goods', in Sen and Williams (eds) (1982).

Rawls, J. (1993), *Political Liberalism,* New York: Columbia University Press.

Ricardo, D. (1817 [1947, 2005]), *Principles of Political Economy and Taxation,* re-edited (1947) by P. Sraffa as vol. 1 of *The Works and Correspondence of David Ricardo,* reprinted (2005), Indianapolis: Liberty Fund.

Robbins, L. (1932 [1935]), *An Essay on the Nature and Significance of Economic Science,* 2nd edition, London: Macmillan.

Röpke, W. (1944 [1948]), *Civitas Humana: Grundfragen der Gesellschafts- und Wirtschaftsreform,* Zurich: Eugen Rentsch Verlag; English translation (1948) by C.S. Fox, *Civitas Humana: Humane Order of Society,* London: W. Hodge.

Rowley, C.K. and A.T. Peacock (1975), *Welfare Economics. A Liberal Restatement,* Oxford: Martin Robertson (now Blackwell).

Ruffini, F. (1946), *Diritti di Libertà,* edited by P. Calamandrei, Florence: La Nuova Italia.

Salvatore, D. (2007), *International Economics,* New York: Wiley.

Samuelson, P.A. (1947), *Foundations of Economic Analysis,* Cambridge, MA: Harvard University Press.

Scanlon, T.M. (1975), 'Preference and urgency', *Journal of Philosophy,* **72**(19), 655–69.

Scanlon, T.M. (1977), 'Liberty, contract, and contribution', in Dworkin et al. (eds) (1977).

Scanlon, T.M. (1982), 'Contractualism and utilitarianism', in Sen and Williams (eds) (1982).

Scanlon, T.M. (1998), *What We Owe to Each Other,* Cambridge, MA: Belknap Press of Harvard University Press.

Scitovsky, T. de (1941), 'A note on welfare propositions in economics', *Review of Economic Studies*, **9**(1), 77–88.

Scitovsky, T. (1952), *Welfare and Competition: The Economics of a Fully Employed Economy*, London: Allen & Unwin.

Sen, A. (1970 [1982]), 'The impossibility of a Paretian liberal', *Journal of Political Economy*, **78**(1), 152–7, and *Reply*, JPE, n. 79, reprinted in Sen (1982).

Sen, A. (1971 [1982]), 'The impossibility of a Paretian liberal: reply', *Journal of Political Economy*, **79**(6), 1406–7, reprinted in Sen (1982).

Sen, A. (1982), *Choice, Welfare, and Measurement*, Oxford: Basil Blackwell.

Sen, A. and B. Williams (eds) (1982), *Utilitarianism and Beyond*, Cambridge: Cambridge University Press.

Simons, H. (1938), *Personal Income Taxation. The Definition of Income as a Problem of Fiscal Policy*, Chicago: University of Chicago Press.

Stigler, G.J. (ed.) (1988), *Chicago Studies in Political Economy*, Chicago: Chicago University Press.

Stigler, G.J. and G.S. Becker (1977), 'De Gustibus non est Disputandum', *American Economic Review*, **67**(2), 76–90.

Stigler, G.J. and K.E. Boulding (eds) (1952), *Readings in Price Theory*, London: Allen & Unwin.

Stiglitz, J. (2000), *Economics of the Public Sector*, 3rd edition, New York: W.W. Norton.

Vanberg, V. (1994), *Rules and Choice in Economics*, London and New York: Routledge.

Veca, S. (1989), *Etica e Politica*, Milan: Garzanti.

Villani, A. (1991), *La Giustizia secondo John Rawls*, Milan: ISU.

Von Neumann, J. and O. Morgenstern (1944), *Theory of Games and Economic Behavior*, Princeton: Princeton University Press.

Wolff, R.P. (1977), *Understanding Rawls: A Reconstruction and Critique of 'A Theory of Justice'*, Princeton: Princeton University Press.

CHAPTER 3

AA.VV. (1962), *Immigrazione e Industria*, Milan: Edizioni di Comunità.

Akerlof, G.A. (1970), 'The market for "lemons": Qualitative uncertainty and the market mechanism', *Quarterly Journal of Economics*, **84**(3), 488–500.

Alchian, A. (1950), 'Uncertainty, evolution, and economic theory', *Journal of Political Economy*, **58**(3), 211–21.

Alchian, A.A. and H. Demsetz (1972), 'Production, information costs, and economic organization', *American Economic Review*, **62**(5), 777–95.

Alchian, A.A. et al. (1973), *The Economics of Charity: Essays on the Comparative Economics and Ethics of Giving and Selling, with Applications to Blood*, London: Institute of Economic Affairs.

Alesina, A. (1987), 'Macroeconomic policy in a two party system as a repeated game', *Quarterly Journal of Economics*, **102**(3), 651–78.

Alesina, A. (1988), *Macroeconomics and Politics*, Cambridge, MA: MIT Press.

Alesina, A. and G. Tabellini (1988), 'Credibility and politics', *European Economic Review*, **32**(2–3), 542–50.

Andersen, T.M., K.O. Moene and A. Sandmo (eds) (1995), *The Future of the Welfare State*, Scandinavian Journal of Economics Series, Oxford: Blackwell.

Arrow, K.J. and T. Scitovsky (eds) (1969), *Readings in Welfare Economics*, London: Allen & Unwin.

Atkinson, A.B. (1975), *The Economics of Inequality*, Oxford: Clarendon Press.

Atkinson, A.B. and J.E. Stiglitz (1980), *Lectures on Public Economics*, London and New York: McGraw-Hill.

Bariletti, A. (1993), 'Paternalismo, Libertà Individuale, Beni di Merito', in Chiancone and Osculati (eds) (1993).

Barro, R. (1974), 'Are government bonds net wealth?', *Journal of Political Economy*, **82**(6), 1095–117.

Barro, R. (1976), 'Reply to Feldstein and Buchanan', *Journal of Political Economy*, **84**(2), 343–50.

Barro, R. (1986), 'Reputation in a model of monetary policy with incomplete information', *Journal of Monetary Economics*, **17**(1), 3–20.

Barro, R. (1996), 'Reflections on Ricardian equivalence', *NBER Working Paper no. 5502*, Cambridge, MA: National Bureau of Economic Research.

Baumol, W.J. (1965), *Welfare Economics and the Theory of the State*, 2nd edition, Cambridge, MA: Harvard University Press.

Baumol, W.J., J.C. Panzar and R.D. Willig (1982), *Contestable Markets and the Theory of Industry Structure*, New York: Harcourt Brace Jovanovich.

Becker, G.S. and K.M. Murphy (1988), 'A theory of rational addiction', *Journal of Political Economy*, **96**(4), 675–700.

Blankart, B. (2008), *Öffentliche Finanzen in der Demokratie: Eine Einführung in die Finanzwissenschaft*, 7th edition, Munich: Vahlen.

Boersch-Supan, A. and W.R. Ricter (eds) (2000), 'Public finance and transitions in social security', *International Tax and Public Finance*, **7**(4).

Bovenberg, A.L., B. Jacobs and R.A. de Mooij (eds) (2008), 'Reinventing the welfare state', *International Tax and Public Finance*, **15**(1).

Braithwaite, R.B. (1955), *Theory of Games as a Tool for the Moral Philosopher*, Cambridge: Cambridge University Press.

Brennan, G. and J.M. Buchanan (1985 [2000]), *The Reason of Rules: Constitutional Political Economy*, Cambridge: Cambridge University Press; reprinted (2000) as vol. 10 of *The Collected Works of James M. Buchanan* (1999–2002), Indianapolis: Liberty Fund.

Brittan, S. and S. Webb (1990), *Beyond the Welfare State: An Examination of Basic Incomes in a Market Economy*, Aberdeen: Aberdeen University Press.

Brosio, G. and W. Santagata (eds) (1992), *Rapporto sull'Economia delle Arti e dello Spettacolo in Italia*, with contributions by A. Peacock et al., Turin: Fondazione Giovanni Agnelli.

Brunetta, R. and C. Carraro (1990), 'Income policies as cooperative strategies: lessons from the Italian experience of the '80s', in Brunetta and Dell'Aringa (1990).

Brunetta, R. and C. Dell'Aringa (eds) (1990), *Markets, Institutions and Cooperation*, London: Macmillan.

Bryant, R.C. and R. Portes (eds) (1987), *Global Macroeconomics: Policy Conflict and Cooperation*, London: Macmillan.

Buchanan, A. (1991), *Secession: The Morality of Political Divorce from Fort Sumter to Lithuania and Quebec*, Boulder: Westview Press.

Buchanan, J.M. (1954a [1960, 1999]), 'Individual choice in voting and the market', *Journal of Political Economy*, **62**(4), 334–43; reprinted in *Fiscal Theory & Political Economy: Selected Essays*, Chapel Hill: University of North Carolina Press, pp. 90–104, and in *The Collected Works of James M. Buchanan* (1999–2002), vol. 1 (1999), *The Logical Foundations of Constitutional Liberty*, Indianapolis: Liberty Fund.

Buchanan, J.M. (1954b [1960, 1999]), 'Social choice, democracy, and free markets', *Journal of Political Economy*, **62**(2), 114–23; reprinted in *Fiscal Theory & Political Economy: Selected Essays*, Chapel Hill: University of North Carolina Press, pp. 75–89, and in *The Collected Works of James M. Buchanan* (1999–2002), vol. 1 (1999), *The Logical Foundations of Constitutional Liberty*, Indianapolis: Liberty Fund.

Buchanan, J.M. (1958 [1999]), *Public Principles of Public Debt: A Defense and Restatement*, Homewood, IL: R.D. Irwin; reprinted as vol. 2 (1999) of *The Collected Works of James M. Buchanan* (1999–2002), Indianapolis: Liberty Fund.

Buchanan, J.M. (1962 [1999]), 'Politics, policy, and Pigovian margins',

Economica, New Series, **29**(113), 17–28; reprinted in *The Collected Works of James M. Buchanan* (1999–2002), vol. 1 (1999), *The Logical Foundations of Constitutional Liberty*, Indianapolis: Liberty Fund.

Buchanan, J.M. (1965 [2001]), 'An economic theory of club', *Economica*, New Series, **32**(125), 1–14; reprinted in *The Collected Works of James M. Buchanan* (1999–2002), vol. 15 (1999), *Externalities and Public Expenditure Theory*, Indianapolis: Liberty Fund.

Buchanan, J.M. (1968 [1999]), *The Demand and Supply of Public Goods*, Chicago: Rand McNally; reprinted (1999) as vol. 5 of *The Collected Works of James M. Buchanan* (1999–2002), Indianapolis: Liberty Fund.

Buchanan, J.M. (1975a [2000]), *The Limits of Liberty: Between Anarchy and Leviathan*, Chicago: Chicago University Press; reprinted (2000) as vol. 7 of *The Collected Works of James M. Buchanan* (1999–2002), Indianapolis: Liberty Fund.

Buchanan, J.M. (1975b [1999]), 'The Samaritan's dilemma', in Phelps (1975); reprinted in *The Collected Works of James Buchanan* (1999–2002), vol.1 (1999), *The Logical Foundations of Constitutional Liberty*, Indianapolis, Liberty Fund.

Buchanan, J.M. (1976 [2001]), 'A Hobbesian interpretation of the Rawlsian difference principle', *Kyklos*, **29**(1), 5–25; reprinted in *The Collected Works of James M. Buchanan* (1999–2002), vol. 17 (2001), *Moral Science and Moral Order*, Indianapolis: Liberty Fund.

Buchanan, J.M. (1992), 'Perche dovremmo tutti risparmiare di piu la teoria economica dell'etica del risparmio', *Biblioteca della Libertà*, **27**(117).

Buchanan, J.M. (1999–2002), *Collected Works*, 20 vols, Indianapolis: Liberty Fund.

Buchanan, J.M. (2001), *Externalities and Public Expenditure Theory*, vol. 15 of *The Collected Works of James M. Buchanan* (1999–2002), Indianapolis: Liberty Fund.

Buchanan, J.M. and W. Craig Stubblebine (1962 [1999]), 'Externality', *Economica*, New Series, **29**(116), 371–84; reprinted in *The Collected Works of James M. Buchanan* (1999–2002), vol. 15, *Externalities and Public Expenditure Theory*, Indianapolis: Liberty Fund.

Camerer, C., S. Issacharoff, G. Loewenstein, T. O'Donoghue and M. Rabin (2003), 'Regulation for conservatives: behavioral economics and the case for "asymmetric paternalism"', *University of Pennsylvania Law Review*, **151**(3), 1211–54.

Chiancone, A. and F. Osculati (eds) (1993), *Il Merito della Spesa Pubblica: la Natura e l'Offerta dei Beni non di Mercato*, Milan: Franco Angeli.

Clapham, J.H. (1922), 'Of empty economic boxes', *Economic Journal*, **32**(127), 305–14.

Clerico, G. (1984), *Economia della Salute: una Analisi Introduttiva*, with an 'Introduction' by F. Forte, Milan: Franco Angeli.

Clerico, G. (1997), *Istituzioni, Incentivi ed Efficienza in Sanità*, Padua: Cedam.

Coase, R. (1946), 'The marginal cost controversy', *Economica*, New Series, **13**(51), 169–82; reprinted in Coase (1988).

Coase, R. (1960), 'The problem of social cost', *Journal of Law and Economics*, **3**(1), 1–44; reprinted in Coase (1988).

Coase, R. (1974), 'The lighthouse in economics', *Journal of Law and Economics*, **17**(2), 357–76; reprinted in Coase (1988).

Coase, R. (1988), *The Firm, the Market, and the Law*, Chicago: University of Chicago Press.

Colombatto, E. (ed.) (2004), *The Elgar Companion to the Economics of Property Rights*, Cheltenham, UK and Northampton, MA, USA: Edward Elgar.

Cornes, R. and T. Sandler (1986), *The Theory of Externalities, Public Goods, and Club Goods*, Cambridge: Cambridge University Press.

Culyer, A.J. (2005), *The Dictionary of Health Economics*, Cheltenham, UK and Northampton, MA, USA: Edward Elgar.

Culyer, A.J. and J.P. Newhouse (eds) (2000), *Handbook in Health Economics*, Amsterdam and New York: Elsevier.

D'Amico, D. (forthcoming), 'Merit goods, paternalism, and responsibility', *Quaderni del Dipartimento di Scienze Storiche, Giuridiche, Economiche e Sociali*, Università 'Mediterranea' di Reggio Calabria.

De Viti De Marco, A. (1888), *Il Carattere Teorico dell'Economia Finanziaria*, Rome: Pasqualucci.

De Voogd, J. (1992), *Guaranteed Minimum Income Arrangements in the Netherlands, Belgium, Denmark, France, Germany, and Great Britain*, The Hague: Dutch Ministry of Social Affairs and Employment, Department of Labour-Market and Education.

Diamond, P.A. (1965), 'National debt in a neoclassical growth model', *American Economic Review*, **55**(5), 1126–50.

Domar, E. (1944 [1955]), 'The "burden of the debt" and the national income', *American Economic Review*, **34**(4), 798–827; reprinted in Smithies and Butters (eds) (1955).

Dupuit, J. (1842–53), *De l'Utilité et de sa Mesure*, selected writings, reprinted (1933) by M. De Bernardi, with a 'Preface' by L. Einaudi, Turin: Edizioni de La riforma Sociale.

Eatwell, J., M. Milgate and P. Newman (eds) (1987), *The New Palgrave: A Dictionary of Economics*, London: Macmillan.

Einaudi, L. (1938 [1959]), *Miti e Paradossi della Giustizia Tributaria*, Turin: Einaudi.

Einaudi, L. (1942), 'Di alcuni connotati dello stato elencati dai Trattatisti Finanziari', *Rivista di Diritto Finanziario e Scienza delle Finanze*, **6**(4), 191–200.

Einaudi, L. (1949), *Lezioni di Politica Sociale*, Turin: Einaudi.

Ellis, H.S. and W. Fellner (1943 [1952]), 'External economies and diseconomies', in *American Economic Review*, **33**(3), 493–511; reprinted in Stigler and Boulding (eds) (1952).

Elster, J. (1979), *Ulysses and the Sirens*, Cambridge: Cambridge University Press.

Elster, J. (1982), 'Sour grapes. Utilitarianism and the genesis of wants', in Sen and Williams (1982).

Elster, J. (1983), *Sour Grapes: Studies in the Subversion of Rationality*, Cambridge: Cambridge University Press.

Elster, J. (2000), *Ulysses Unbound: Studies in Rationality, Precommitment, and Constraints*, Cambridge: Cambridge University Press.

Elster, J. (2006 [2009]), *Raison et Raisons*, Paris: Fayard; English translation (2009) by S. Rendall, *Reason and Rationality*, Princeton: Princeton University Press.

Fasiani, M. (1951), *Principi di Scienza delle Finanze*, Turin: Giappichelli, 2 vols, 2nd revised and enlarged edition.

Forte, F. (1967), 'Should "public goods" be public?', *Papers on Non-Market Decision Making*, later *Public Choice*, **3**(1), 39–47.

Forte, F. (1971), 'Le economie esterne marshalliane e la teoria contemporanea dello sviluppo economico', *Rivista Italiana di Scienze Economiche e Commerciali*, **2/3**, 117–60.

Forte, F. (1991), *I Diritti della Natura. Saggio di Economia Eco-Ambientale*, Rome: Nuove Edizioni del Gallo.

Forte, F. (1993), 'I beni meritori: scelte razionali, esternalità, paternalismo, preferenze sulle preferenze', in Chiancone and Osculati (eds) (1993).

Forte, F. (2003), 'Economies internal and external, increasing returns and growth: the seminal contribution of Alfred Marshall revisited', *Rivista di Diritto Finanziario e Scienza delle Finanze*, **62**(2), 187–240.

Forte, F. (2005), *Analisi Economica del Diritto*, vol. I, *Le Regole*, Reggio Calabria: Iiriti.

Forte, F. (ed.) (2008), *Money, Markets and Morals*, Munich: Accedo Verlagsgesellschaft.

Forte, F. and J.M. Buchanan (1961), 'The evaluation of public services', *Journal of Political Economy*, **69**(2), 107–21.

Forte, F. and H. Hochman (1969), 'Monetary and fiscal policy: ambiguities in definitions', in Haller and Rechtenwald (eds) (1969).

Frey, B.S. and W.W. Pommerehne (1989), *Muses and Markets: Explorations in the Economics of the Arts*, Cambridge, MA: Blackwell.

Friedman M. (1948), 'A monetary and fiscal framework for economic stability', *American Economic Review*, **38**(3), 245–64.

Friedman, M. (1962), *Capitalism and Freedom*, Chicago: University of Chicago Press.

Galbraith, J.K. (1958), *The Affluent Society*, London and New York: Penguin Books.

Gini, C. (1912), 'Variabilità e mutabilità', reprinted in Gini, C. (1955), *Variabilità e Concentrazione*, Rome: Veschi.

Graham, G. (1988), *Contemporary Social Philosophy*, Oxford, UK and New York, USA: Blackwell.

Granaglia, E. (1993), 'Il criterio del "functioning" e la ridefinizione delle politiche sociali come beni di merito', in Chiancone and Osculati (eds) (1993).

Griziotti, B. (1917), 'La diversa pressione tributaria del prestito e dell'imposta straordinaria', reprinted in Griziotti (1956), vol. I.

Griziotti, B. (1956), *Studi di Scienza delle Finanze e Diritto Finanziario*, Milan: Giuffrè (2 vols).

Haller, H. and H.C. Rechtenwald (eds) (1969), *Finanz- und Geld Politik im Umbruch*, Mainz: Hase & Köhler.

Hayek, F. (1982), *Law, Legislation and Liberty: A New Statement of the Liberal Principles of Justice and Political Economy*, London: Routledge.

Hobbes, T. (1651 [2002]), *Leviathan*, edited by A.P. Martinich, Peterborough, Ontario: Broadview Press.

Hochman, H.M. and G.E. Peterson (eds) (1974), *Redistribution through Public Choice*, New York: Columbia University Press.

Hochman, H.M. and J.D. Rodgers (1969), 'Pareto optimal redistribution', *American Economic Review*, **59**(4), Part 1, 542–57.

Hotelling, A. (1938 [1969]), 'The general welfare in relation to problems of taxation and of railway and utility rates', *Econometrica*, **6**(3), 242–69; reprinted in Arrow and Scitovsky (eds) (1969).

Hume, D. (1742 [1987]), *On Public Credit*, in *Essays Moral, Political, Literary*, edited by E.F. Miller, with an appendix of variant readings from the 1889 edition by T.H. Green and T.H. Grose, revised edition, Indianapolis: Liberty Fund.

Kaldor, N. (1955), *An Expenditure Tax*, London: Allen & Unwin.

Keynes, J.M. (1923 [1971]), *A Tract on Monetary Reform*, London: Macmillan; reprinted (1971) in J.M. Keynes, *The Collected Writings*, vol. IV, The Royal Economic Society, London: Macmillan.

Keynes, J.M. (1934 [1979]), *A Treatise on Money in Two Volumes*, London: Macmillan; reprinted (1979) in J.M. Keynes, *The Collected Writings*, vols V–VI, The Royal Economic Society, London: Macmillan.

Keynes, J.M. (1936 [1980]), *The General Theory of Employment, Interest and Money*, London: Macmillan; reprinted (1980) in J.M. Keynes, *The Collected Writings*, vol. VII, The Royal Economic Society, London: Macmillan.

Kliemt, H. (1993), 'On justifying a minimum welfare state', *Constitutional Political Economy*, **4**(2), 159–72.

Kliemt, H. (2008), 'On the health care that is and that might be. Projecting health care provision into the future in a Buchanan type constitutional political economy', in Forte (ed.) (2008).

Knight, F.H. (1924 [1951]), 'Some fallacies in the interpretation of social cost', *Quarterly Journal of Economics*, **38**(4), 582–606; reprinted in Knight (1951).

Knight, F.H. (1951), *The Ethics of Competition*, London: Allen & Unwin.

Leoni, B. (1961 [1991]), *Freedom and the Law*, Princeton: Van Nostrand, 3rd expanded edition (1991), Indianapolis: Liberty Fund.

Lerner, A.P. (1944), *The Economics of Control: Principles of Welfare Economics*, New York: Macmillan.

Lindahl, E. (1919 [1958]), *Die Gerechtigkeit der Besteugung Eine Analyse der Steuerprinzipien auf der Grundlage der Grenznutzentheorie'*, Lund: Gleerupska Universitets-Bokhandelen; abridged English translation as 'Just taxation. A positive solution', in Musgrave and Peacock (eds) (1958).

Lorenz, M.O. (1909), 'Methods for measuring concentration of wealth', *Publications of American Statistical Association*, **9**(70), 209–19.

Lucas, R.E. (1972), 'Expectations and the neutrality of money', *Journal of Economic Theory*, **4**(2), 103–24.

Lucas, R.E. (1981), *Studies in Business-Cycle Theory*, Cambridge, MA: MIT Press.

Lucas, R.E. and T.J. Sargent (1981), *Rational Expectations and Econometric Practice*, Minneapolis: University of Minnesota Press.

Maffettone, S. (1989), *Valori Comuni*, Milan: Il Saggiatore.

Marshall, A. (1920 [1961]), *Principles of Economics*, 9th edition (1961), edited by C.V. Guillebaud, London: Macmillan.

Martino, A. (ed.) (1977), *Un Reddito Garantito per Tutti?*, Turin: Biblioteca della Libertà.

Mazzola, U. (1890), *I Dati Scientifici della Finanza Pubblica*, Rome: Loescher; excerpts in Musgrave and Peacock (eds) (1958).

McLean, I. (1987), *Public Choice: An Introduction*, Oxford: Blackwell.

Meade, J.H. (1952 [1969]), 'External economies and diseconomies in a competitive situation', *Economic Journal*, **62**(245), 54–67; reprinted in Arrow and Scitovsky (eds) (1969).

Mill, J.S. (1863 [2001]), *Utilitarianism*, London: Parker, son, and Bourn; reprinted (2001), Kitchener, ON: Batoche Books.

Modigliani, F. (1983), 'Government deficits, inflation and future genera-tions', in D.W. Conklin and T.J. Chourcene (eds) (1983), *Deficits, How Big, How Bad*, Ontario: Ontario Economic Research Report.

Modigliani, F. (1987), 'The economics of public deficits', in Razin and Sadka (eds) (1987).

Modigliani, F. (1988), 'The role of intergenerational transfers and life cycle saving in the accumulation of wealth', *Journal of Economic Perspectives*, **2**(2), 15–40.

Morgenstern, O. (1963), *Spieltheorie und Wirtschaftswissenschaft*, Vienna: Oldenbourg.

Mossetto, G. (1992), *L'economia delle Città d'Arte. Modelli di Sviluppo a Confronto*, Politiche e Strumenti di Intervento, Milan: Etas.

Müller, D. (2003), *Public Choice III*, Cambridge: Cambridge University Press.

Musgrave, R.A. (1959), *The Theory of Public Finance. A Study in Public Economy*, New York: McGraw-Hill.

Musgrave, R.A. (1987), 'Merit goods', in J. Eatwell et al. (eds) (1987).

Musgrave, R.A. and P.B. Musgrave (1973), *Public Finance in Theory and Practice*, New York: McGraw-Hill.

Musgrave, R.A. and A.T. Peacock (eds) (1958), *Classics in the Theory of Public Finance*, London: Macmillan (with texts by Barone, Cohen Stuart, Edgeworth, Goldscheid, Leroy Beaulieu, Lindahl, Mazzola, Montemartini, Pantaleoni, Ritschl, Sax, Von Stein, Von Wieser, Wagner, Wicksell).

Nagel, T. (1988), *The View from Nowhere*, New York: Oxford University Press.

Nozick, R. (1974), *Anarchy, State, and Utopia*, New York: Basic Books.

Okun, A. (1975 [1990]), *Equality and Efficiency: The Big Trade Off*, Washington: The Brookings Institution; Italian translation (1990) with an 'Introduction' by F. Forte, Naples: Liguori.

Olson, M. (1965), *The Logic of Collective Action: Public Goods and the Theory of Groups*, Cambridge: Harvard University Press.

Parfit, D. (1984), *Reasons and Persons*, Oxford: Clarendon Press.

Peacock, A.T. (1979a), 'The limitations of public good theory: The light-house revisited', in Peacock (1979b).

Peacock, A.T. (1979b), *The Economic Analysis of Government, and Related Themes*, Oxford: Martin Robertson.

Peacock, A.T. (1991), 'Welfare philosophies and welfare finance', in Wilson and Wilson (eds) (1991).

Peacock, A.T. (1992), *Public Choice Analysis in Historical Perspective*, Mattioli Lectures, Cambridge: Cambridge University Press.

Peacock, A.T. and G.K. Shaw (1971 [1976]), *The Economic Theory of Fiscal Policy*, London: Allen & Unwin.

Peacock, A.T. and R. Weir (1975), *The Composer in the Market Place*, London: Faber Music.

Phelps, E.S. (ed.) (1975), *Altruism, Morality, and Economic Theory*, New York: Russell Sage Foundation.

Pigou, A.C. (1920), *The Economics of Welfare*, London: Macmillan.

Pigou, A.C. (1922), 'Empty economic boxes. A reply', *Economic Journal*, **32**(128), 458–65.

Pigou, A.C. (1947), *A Study in Public Finance*, 3rd revised edition, London: Macmillan.

Posner, R. (1986), *Economic Analysis of Law*, 3rd edition, Boston: Little Brown.

Puviani, A. (1901), 'La ragione dell'imposta', re-published in F. Volpi (1974), *Teoria della Finanza Pubblica*, Milan: Franco Angeli.

Razin, A. and E. Sadka (eds) (1987), *Economic Policy in Theory and Practice*, London: Macmillan.

Ricardo, D. (1817 [1947, 2005]), *Principles of Political Economy and Taxation*, re-edited (1947) by P. Sraffa as vol. I of the *The Works and Correspondence of David Ricardo*; reprinted (2005), Indianapolis: Liberty Fund.

Röpke, W. (1944 [1948]), *Civitas Humana. Grundfragen der Gesellschafts- und Wirtschaftsreform*, Zurich: Eugen Rentsch Verlag; English translation (1948) by C.S. Fox, *Civitas Humana: Humane Order of Society*, London: W. Hodge.

Samuelson, P.A. (1954), 'The pure theory of public expenditure', *Review of Economics and Statistics*, **36**(4), 387–9; reprinted in Samuelson (1966 [1986]), *Collected Scientific Papers*, edited by J.E. Stiglitz, vol. II.

Samuelson, P.A. (1970), *Economics*, 8th edition, New York: McGraw-Hill.

Sandmo, A. (1995), 'Introduction. The welfare economics of the welfare state', in Andersen et al. (eds) (1995).

Sax, E. (1887), *Grundlegung der Theoretischen Staatswirthschaft*, Vienna: Hölder.

Schmitt, C. (1927 [1932,1976, 2007]), 'Der Begriff des Politischen', *Archiv für Sozial-wissenschaft und Sozialpolitik*, **58**, 1–33, revised and enlarged text (1932), Munich: Duncker and Humblot; English translation (1996) by G. Schwab, *The Concept of the Political*, New Brunswick, NJ: Rutgers University Press; expanded edition (2007) with a foreword by T.B. Strong, Chicago: University of Chicago Press.

Schumpeter, J. (1942 [2006]), *Capitalism, Socialism, and Democracy*, New York and London: Harper & Brothers; London: Routledge.

Seldon, A. (1986), *The Riddle of the Voucher: An Inquiry into the Obstacles to Introducing Choice and Competition in State Schools*, London: The Institute of Economic Affairs.

Sen, A. (1967), 'Isolation, assurance and the social rate of discount', *Quarterly Journal of Economics*, **81**(1), 112–24.

Sen, A. (1973a), *On Economic Inequality*, Oxford: Clarendon Press.

Sen, A. (1973b), 'Behavior and the concept of preference', *Economica*, August, pp. 105–32.

Sen, A. (1985), *Commodities and Capabilities*, Amsterdam: North-Holland.

Sen, A. (1987), *The Standard of Living*, edited by G. Hawthorn, with contributions by Müllbauer, Kanbur, Hart, Williams, Cambridge: Cambridge University Press.

Sen, A. and B. Williams (eds) (1982), *Utilitarianism and Beyond*, Cambridge: Cambridge University Press.

Sidgwick, M.H. (1883), *The Principles of Political Economy*, London: Macmillan.

Sinn, H.W. (1995), 'A theory of the welfare state', in Andersen et al. (eds) (1995).

Smith, A. (1776), *An Inquiry into the Nature and Causes of the Wealth of Nations*, reprinted by W.B. Todd (ed.) (1982), with an Introduction by E. Cannan, Indianapolis: Liberty Fund.

Smithies, A. and J.K. Butters (eds) (1955), *Readings in Fiscal Policy*, Homewood, IL: R.D. Irwin.

Spinoza, B. (1991 [2001]), *Theological-Political Treatise*, edited by L. Chianese, 2nd edition, Indianapolis: Hackett Publishing.

Stigler, G.J. and G.S. Becker (1977), 'De gustibus non est disputandum', *American Economic Review*, **67**(2), 76–90.

Stigler, G.J. and K.E. Boulding (eds) (1952), *Readings in Price Theory*, London: Allen & Unwin.

Sugden, R. (2007), 'The value of opportunities over time when preferences are unstable', *Social Choice and Welfare*, **29**(4), 665–82.

Sugden, R. (2008), 'Why incoherent preferences do not justify paternalism', *Constitutional Political Economy*, **19**(3), 226–48.

Sunstein, C. and R. Thaler (2003), 'Libertarian paternalism', *American Economic Review Papers and Proceedings*, **93**(2), 175–9.

Thurow, L.C. (1980 [2001]), *The Zero-Sum Society: Distribution and the Possibilities for Economic Change*, New York: Basic Books.

Tirole, J. (1988), *The Theory of Industrial Organization*, Cambridge, MA: MIT Press.

Tittmuss, R. (1970), *Commitment to Welfare*, London: Unwin.

Tobin, J. (1980), 'Government deficits and capital accumulation', in J.

Tobin (1980), *Asset Accumulation and Economic Activity: Reflections on Contemporary Macroeconomic Theory*, Chicago: University of Chicago Press.

United Nations (1990), *External Debt Crisis and Development*, New York: United Nations.

Vicarelli, F. (ed) (1983), *Attualità di Keynes*, Rome: Laterza.

Villani, A. (1988), *Economia Politica dell'Arte e dei Beni Culturali*, Milan: ISU.

Viner, J. (1931 [1952]), 'Cost curves and supply curves', *Zeitschrift für Nationalökonomie*, **3**(1), 23–46; reprinted in Stigler and Boulding (eds) (1952).

Von Neumann, J. and O. Morgenstern (1944), *Theory of Games and Economic Behavior*, Princeton: Princeton University Press.

Von Weizsäcker, C.C. (1971), 'Notes on endogenous change of tastes', *Journal of Economic Theory*, **3**(4), 345–72.

Weber, M. (1922 [1976, 1978]), *Wirtschaft und Gesellschaft. Grundriss der Verstehenden Soziologie*, Tübingen: Mohr, 5th revised edition based on the critical text established by Johannes Winckelmann 1976; English translation (1978) as *Economy and Society. An Outline of Interpretive Sociology*, edited by G. Roth and C. Wittich, Berkeley: University of California Press.

Wilson, T. and D. Wilson (eds) (1991), *The State and Social Welfare*, London and New York: Longman.

CHAPTER 4

Atkinson, A.B. (1970), 'On the measurement of inequality', *Journal of Economic Theory*, **2**(3), 244–63.

Atkinson, A.B. (1975), *The Economics of Inequality*, Oxford: Clarendon Press.

Boadway, R. (2002), 'The role of public choice considerations in normative public economics', in Winer and Shibata (2002).

Bowen, R. (1955), 'The Interpretation of Voting in the Allocation of Economic Resources', *Quarterly Journal of Economics*, **58**(1), 27–48.

Breton, A. (2002), 'Public and welfare economics under monopolistic and competitive governments', in Winer and Shibata (2002).

Buchanan, J.M. (1949 [1960, 1999]), 'The pure theory of government finance: a suggested approach', *Journal of Political Economy*, **57**(6), 496–505; reprinted in Buchanan, J.M. (1960), *Fiscal Theory & Political Economy: Selected Essays*, Chapel Hill: University of North Carolina Press, and in *The Collected Works of James M. Buchanan* (1999–2002), vol. 1 (1999), *The Logical Foundations of Constitutional Liberty*, Indianapolis: Liberty Fund.

Buchanan, J.M. (1954 [1960, 1999]), 'Individual choice in voting and the market', *Journal of Political Economy*, **62**(4), 334–43; reprinted in *Fiscal Theory & Political Economy: Selected Essays*, Chapel Hill: University of North Carolina Press, and in *The Collected Works of James M. Buchanan* (1999–2002), vol. 1 (1999), *The Logical Foundations of Constitutional Liberty*, Indianapolis: Liberty Fund.

Buchanan, J.M. (1959 [1960, 1999]), 'Positive economics, welfare economics and political economy', *Journal of Law and Economics*, **2**, October, 124–38; reprinted in Buchanan, J.M. (1960), *Fiscal Theory & Political Economy: Selected Essays*, Chapel Hill: University of North Carolina Press, and in *The Collected Works of James M. Buchanan* (1999–2002), vol. 1 (1999), *The Logical Foundations of Constitutional Liberty*, Indianapolis: Liberty Fund.

Buchanan, J.M. (1960), *Fiscal Theory and Political Economy*, Chapel Hill: University of North Carolina Press.

Buchanan, J.M. (1966 [1999]), *Public Finance in Democratic Process: Fiscal Institutions and Individual Choice*, Chapel Hill: University of North Carolina Press; reprinted (1999) as vol. 4 of *The Collected Works of James M. Buchanan* (1999–2002), Indianapolis: Liberty Fund.

Buchanan, J.M. (1968 [1999]), *The Demand and Supply of Public Goods*, Chicago: Rand McNally; reprinted (1999) as vol. 5 of *The Collected Works of James M. Buchanan* (1999–2002), Indianapolis: Liberty Fund.

Buchanan, J.M. and G. Tullock (1962 [1999]), *The Calculus of Consent: Logical Foundations of Constitutional Democracy*, Ann Arbor: University of Michigan Press; reprinted (1999) as vol. 3 of *The Collected Works of James M. Buchanan* (1999–2002), Indianapolis: Liberty Fund.

De Viti De Marco, A. (1934 [1936]), *Principi di Economia Finanziaria*, Turin: Einaudi; English translation (1936) as *First Principles of Public Finance*, London: Jonathan Cape; New York: Harcourt, Brace & Co.

Einaudi, L. (1940 [1959]), *Miti e Paradossi della Giustizia Tributaria*, Turin: Einaudi.

Einaudi, L. (1941 [1958]), *Saggi sul Risparmio e l'Imposta*, Turin: Einaudi.

Fedeli, S. and F. Forte (2003), 'Minimising frustrations versus Median Voter's Equilibria', in Holler et al. (2003).

Forte, F. (2000), *Principi di Economia Pubblica*, Milan: Giuffrè.

Forte, F. (2009), *L'Economia Liberale di Luigi Einaudi*, Fondazione Einaudi di Torino, Florence: Olschki.

Gini, C. (1912), 'Variabilità e mutabilità', reprinted in C. Gini (1955), *Variabilità e Concentrazione*, Rome: Veschi.

Greenaway, D. and G.K. Shaw (eds) (1985), *Public Choice, Public Finance, and Public Policy: Essays in Honour of Alan Peacock*, Oxford, UK and New York, USA: Blackwell.

Holler, M.J., H. Kliemt, D. Schmidtchen and M.E. Streit (eds) (2003), *Power and Fairness*, Tübingen: Mohr Siebeck.

Lindahl, E. (1919 [1958]), 'Die Gerechtigkeit der Besteugung: Eine Analyse der Steuerprinzipien auf der Grundlage der Grenznutzentheorie', Lund: Gleerupska Universitets–Bokhandelen; abridged English translation as 'Just taxation. A positive solution', in Musgrave and Peacock (eds) (1958).

Lindahl, E. (1928 [1958]), 'Einige strittige Fragen der Steuertheorie', in H. Mayer (ed.), *Die Wirtschaftstheorie der Gegenwart*, vol. IV, Vienna: Julius Springer, pp. 281–304; abridged English translation as 'Some controversial questions in the theory of taxation', in Musgrave and Peacock (eds) (1958).

Lorenz, M.O. (1905), 'Methods of measuring the concentration of wealth', *American Statistical Association*, **9**(70), 209–19.

Mazzola, U. (1908), *I Dati Scientifici della Finanza Pubblica*, Rome: Loescher.

McLean, I. (1987), *Public Choice. An Introduction*, Oxford: Blackwell.

McNutt, P.A. (1996), *The Economics of Public Choice*, Cheltenham, UK and Brookfield, VT, USA: Edward Elgar.

Müller, D. (2003), *Public Choice III*, Cambridge: Cambridge University Press.

Musgrave, R.A. and A.T. Peacock (eds) (1958), *Classics in the Theory of Public Finance*, London: Macmillan (with texts by Barone, Cohen Stuart, Edgeworth, Goldscheid, Leroy Beaulieu, Lindahl, Mazzola, Montemartini, Pantaleoni, Ritschl, Sax, Von Stein, Von Wieser, Wagner, Wicksell).

Pantaleoni, M. (1883 [1938, 1958]), 'Contributo alla teoria del riparto delle spese pubbliche', *La Rassegna Italiana*, vol. 4; reprinted in M. Pantaleoni (1938), *Studi di Finanza e Statistica*, Bologna: Zanichelli; abridged English translation as 'Contribution to the theory of the distribution of public expenditure', in Musgrave and Peacock (eds) (1958).

Peacock, A.T. (1992), *Public Choice Analysis in Historical Perspective*, Cambridge: Cambridge University Press.

Ricca Salerno, G. (1888), *Manuale di Scienza delle Finanze*, Florence: Barbera.

Samuelson, P.A. (1954), 'The pure theory of public expenditure', *Review of Economics and Statistics*, **36**(4), 387–9; reprinted in P.A. Samuelson

(1966 [1986]), *Collected Scientific Papers*, edited by J.E. Stiglitz, vol. II.

Samuelson, P.A. (1955), 'Diagrammatic exposition of a pure theory of public expenditure', *Review of Economics and Statistics*, **37**(4), 350–56; reprinted in P.A. Samuelson (1966 [1986]), *Collected Scientific Papers*, edited by J.E. Stiglitz, vol. II.

Samuelson, P.A. (1958), 'Aspects of public expenditure theories', *Review of Economics and Statistics*, **40**(4), 332–8; reprinted in P.A. Samuelson (1966 [1986]), *Collected Scientific Papers*, edited by J.E. Stiglitz, vol. II.

Sax, E. (1924 [1956, 1958]), 'Die Wertungstheorie der Steuer', *Zeitschrift für Volkswirtschaft und Sozialpolitik*, **4**, 191–240; reprinted in *Zeitschrift für Nationalökonomie*, **15**(3), 317–56; partial English translation as 'The valuation theory of taxation', in Musgrave and Peacock (eds) (1958).

Sen, A. (1973), *On Economic Inequality*, Oxford: Clarendon Press.

Stiglitz, J.E. (1986 [2000]), *Economics of the Public Sector*, New York: W.W. Norton.

Tiebout, C.M. (1956), 'A pure theory of local expenditures', *Journal of Political Economy*, **64**(5), 416–24.

Wicksell, K. (1896 [1958]), 'Ein neues Prinzip der gerechten Besteuerung', in *Finanztheoretische Untersuchungen*, Jena: Fischer; partial English translation (1958) as 'A new principle of just taxation', in Musgrave and Peacock (1958).

Winer, S.L. and H. Shibata (2002), *Political Economy and Public Finance: The Role of Political Economy in the Theory and Practice of Public Economics*, Cheltenham, UK and Northampton, MA, USA: Edward Elgar.

CHAPTER 5

Alchian, A. and W.R. Allen (1973), 'The pure economics of giving', in A. Alchian et al. (eds) (1973).

Alchian, A.A. and H. Demsetz (1972), 'Production, information costs, and economic organization', *American Economic Review*, **62**(5), 777–95.

Alchian, A. et al. (eds) (1973), *The Economics of Charity. Essays on the Comparative Economics and Ethics of Giving and Selling*, London: Institute of Economic Affairs.

Axelrod, R. (1984), *The Evolution of Cooperation*, New York: Basic Books.

Baumol, W.J. (1959), *Business Behavior, Value and Growth*, New York: Macmillan.

Becker, G. (1976), *The Economic Approach to Human Behaviour*, Chicago: University of Chicago Press.

Becker, G.S. (1983), 'A theory of competition among pressure groups for political influence', *Quarterly Journal of Economics*, **98**(3), 371–400.

Becker, G.S. (1985), 'Public policies, pressure groups and dead weight costs', *Journal of Public Economics*, **28**(3), 329–47.

Bentley, A.F. (1908), *The Process of Government. A Study of Social Pressures*, Chicago: University of Chicago Press.

Boardman, A.E. (1996), *Cost-Benefit Analysis: Concepts and Practice*, Upper Saddle River, NJ: Prentice-Hall.

Bondonio, P.V. and F. Scacciati (1990), *Efficienza e Produttività negli Enti Locali: L'Introduzione degli Incentivi nel Pubblico Impiego*, Rome: NIS.

Breton, A. and R. Wintrobe (1982), *The Logic of Bureaucratic Conduct: An Economic Analysis of Competition, Exchange, and Efficiency in Private and Public Organizations*, Cambridge: Cambridge University Press.

Brosio, G. (1988), 'Perché esistono le burocrazie pubbliche? Elementi per una teoria positiva del settore pubblico', *Economia Pubblica*, **4–5**, 175–84.

Brosio, G. (ed.) (1989), *La Teoria Economica dell'Organizzazione*, Bologna: Il Mulino.

Brosio, G. (1993), *Economia e Finanza Pubblica*, 2nd edition, Rome: Carocci.

Brousseau, E. and J.-M. Glachant (eds) (2002), *The Economics of Contracts: Theories and Applications*, Cambridge, MA: Cambridge University Press.

Buchanan, J.M. (1965, [2000]), 'Foreword' to Gordon Tullock's *Politics of Bureaucracy*, reprinted (2000) in *Politics as Public Choice*, vol. 13 of *The Collected Works of James M. Buchanan* (1999–2002), Indianapolis: Liberty Fund.

Buchanan, J.M. (1980 [2000]), 'Reform in the rent-seeking society', in Buchanan et al. (1980), pp. 359–67; reprinted (2000) in *Politics as Public Choice*, vol.13 of *The Collected Works of James M. Buchanan* (1999–2002), Indianapolis: Liberty Fund, pp. 346–54.

Buchanan, J.M. (1999–2002), *Collected Works*, 20 vols, Indianapolis: Liberty Fund.

Buchanan, J.M., R.D. Tollison and G. Tullock (eds) (1980), *Toward a Theory of the Rent Seeking Society*, College Station: Texas A&M University Press.

Butler, S.M. (ed.) (1985), *The Privatization Option: A Strategy to Shrink the Size of Government*, Washington, DC: The Heritage Foundation.

Chakravarty, S. (1987), 'Cost–benefit analysis', in Eatwell et al. (eds) (1987).

Coase, R. (1937), 'The nature of the firm', *Economica*, **4**(16), 386–405; reprinted in Coase (1988).

Coase, R. (1988), *The Firm, the Market, and the Law*, Chicago: University of Chicago Press.

Congleton, R.D., A.L. Hillman and K.A. Konrad (eds) (2008a), *40 years of Research on Rent Seeking 1: Theory of Rent Seeking*, Berlin: Springer.

Congleton, R.D., A.L. Hillman and K.A. Konrad (eds) (2008b), *40 years of Research on Rent Seeking 2: Applications: Rent Seeking in Practice*, Berlin: Springer.

DiMaggio, P.J. (ed.) (1986), *Nonprofit Enterprise in the Arts: Studies in Mission and Constraint*, New York and Oxford: Oxford University Press.

Eatwell, J., M. Milgate and P. Newman (eds) (1987), *The New Palgrave: A Dictionary of Economics*, London: Macmillan.

Fedeli, S. (1992), 'Interesse personale, controllo e incentivi nelle imprese pubbliche', *Economia Pubblica*, 9/10, p. 431.

Fedeli, S. (1999), 'Competing bureaus and politicians: compliance approach to the diversion of public funds', *Public Choice*, **100**(3–4), 253–70.

Fedeli, S. and M. Santoni (2001), 'Endogenous institutions in bureau-cratic/compliance games', *Economics of Governance*, **2**(3), 203–29.

Forte, F. (1967), 'Should "public goods" be public?', *Papers on Non-Market Decision Making*, later *Public Choice*, **3**(1), 39–47.

Forte, F. (1983 [1984]), 'Monitoring the productivity of bureaucratic behaviour', in Hanusch (ed.) (1983); reprinted (1984) also as 'Controlling the productivity of bureaucratic behaviour', *Atlantic Economic Journal*, **12**(1), 32–40.

Forte, F. (1984), *Il Bilancio nell'Economia Pubblica*, Milan: Giuffrè.

Forte, F. and J.M. Buchanan (1961), 'The evaluation of public services', *Journal of Political Economy*, **69**(2), 107–21.

Forte, F. and A. di Pierro (1980), 'A pure model of public bureaucracy', *Public Finance/Finances Publiques*, **35**(1), 91–100.

Forte, F. and C.H. Power (1994), 'Applying game theory to the protection of public funds: Some introductory notes', *European Journal of Law and Economics*, **1**(3), 193–212.

Fuguitt, D. and S.J. Wilcox (1999), *Cost-Benefit Analysis for Public Sector Decision Makers*, Westport: Quorum Books.

Greffe, X. (1981), *Analyse Economique de la Bureaucratie*, Paris: Economica.

Hansmann, H. (1987), 'Economic theories of nonprofit organization', in Powell (ed.) (1987).

Hanusch, H. (ed.) (1983), *Anatomy of Government Deficiencies*, Berlin and New York: Springer.

Hochman, H.M. and G.E. Peterson (eds) (1974), *Redistribution through Public Choice*, New York: Columbia University Press.

Jenkins, B. and E.C. Page (eds) (2004), *The Foundations of Bureaucracy in Economic and Social Thought*, 2 vols, Cheltenham, UK and Northampton, MA, USA: Edward Elgar.

Kamerman, S.B. and A.J. Kahn (eds) (1989), *Privatization and the Welfare State*, Princeton: Princeton University Press.

Krueger, A.O. (1974), 'The political economy of the rent seeking society', *American Economic Review*, **64**(3), 291–303.

Leibenstein, H. (1978), *General X–Efficiency Theory and Economic Development*, New York: Oxford University Press.

Levin, H.M. and P.J. McEwan (2001), *Cost-Effectiveness Analysis. Methods and Applications*, Thousand Oaks, CA: Sage Publications.

Lindblom, C.E. (2001), *The Market System: What It Is, How It Works, and What to Make of It*, New Haven: Yale University Press.

Mantovani, M. (2008), *Lezioni di Economia Pubblica dei Beni Culturali*, with an 'Introduction' by F. Forte, Turin: Giappichelli.

McGuire, C.B. and R. Radner (eds) (1972), *Decision and Organization*, Amsterdam: North Holland.

Migué, J.-L. and G. Bélanger (1974), 'Toward a general theory of managerial discretion', *Public Choice*, **17**(1), 27–47.

Mishan, E.J. (1972), *Elements of Cost–Benefit Analysis*, London: Allen and Unwin.

Müller, D. (2002), 'Interest groups, redistribution and the size of government', in Winer and Shibata (eds) (2002).

Müller, D. (2003), *Public Choice III*, Cambridge: Cambridge University Press.

Musgrave, R.A. (1969), *Fiscal Systems*, New Haven: Yale University Press.

Nas, T.F. (1996), *Cost–Benefit Analysis: Theory and Application*, Thousand Oaks, CA: Sage Publications.

Niskanen, W.A. (1971), *Bureaucracy and Representative Government*, Chicago: Aldine.

North, D. (1990), *Institutions, Institutional Change and Economic Performance*, Cambridge: Cambridge University Press.

Olson, M. (1965 [1971]), *The Logic of Collective Action. Public Goods and the Theory of Groups*, Cambridge, MA: Harvard University Press.

Ostrom, E. (1990), *Governing the Commons: The Evolution of Institutions for Collective Action*, Cambridge: Cambridge University Press.

Ostrom, E. (2005), *Understanding Institutional Diversity*, Princeton: Princeton University Press.

Ostrom, E., R. Gardner and J. Walker (1994), *Rules, Games, and Common-Pool Resources*, Ann Arbor: University of Michigan Press.

Peacock, A.T. (1979a) 'The economics of bureaucracy: an inside view', in Peacock (1979b).

Peacock, A.T. (1979b), *The Economic Analysis of Government, and Related Themes*, Oxford: Martin Robertson.

Powell, W.W. (ed.) (1987), *The Nonprofit Sector: A Research Handbook*, New Haven: Yale University Press.

Rose-Ackerman, S. (ed.) (1986), *The Economics of Nonprofit Institutions: Studies in Structure and Policy*, New York: Oxford University Press.

Rose-Ackerman, S. (1996), 'Altruism, nonprofits, and economic theory', *Journal of Economic Literature*, **34**(2), 701–28.

Simon, H.A. (1957), *Models of Man, Social and Rational. Mathematical Essays on Rational Human Behavior in a Social Setting*, New York: Wiley.

Simon, H.A. (1972), 'Theories of bounded rationality', in McGuire and Radner (eds) (1972), pp. 161–76.

Tirole, J. (1988), *The Theory of Industrial Organization*, Cambridge, MA: MIT Press.

Tollison, R.D. (1982), 'Rent Seeking. A Survey', *Kyklos*, **35**(4), 575–602.

Tullock, G. (1965 [2005]), *The Politics of Bureaucracy*, Washington, DC: Public Affairs Press; reprinted (2005) in vol. 6 of *The Selected Works of G. Tullock*, edited and with an 'Introduction' by C.K. Rowley, Indianapolis: Liberty Fund.

Tullock, G. (1980a), 'Efficient rent-seeking', in Buchanan et al. (1980).

Tullock, G. (1980b), 'Rent-seeking as a negative-sum game and efficient rent-seeking', in Buchanan et al. (eds) (1980).

Weber, M. (1922 [1976, 1978]), *Wirtschaft und Gesellschaft. Grundriss der Verstehenden Soziologie*, Tübingen: Mohr, 5th revised edition based on the critical text by Johannes Winckelmann (1976); English translation (1978) as *Economy and Society. An Outline of Interpretive Sociology*, edited by G. Roth and C. Wittich, Berkeley: University of California Press.

Weisbrod, B.A. (1988), *The Nonprofit Economy*, Cambridge, MA: Harvard University Press.

Williamson, E.O. (1964), *The Economics of Discretionary Behavior: Managerial Objectives in a Theory of the Firm*, Englewood Cliffs, NJ: Prentice-Hall.

Williamson, E.O. (1985), *The Economic Institutions of Capitalism: Firms, Markets, Relational Contracting*, London: Collier Macmillan.

Winer, S.L and H. Shibata (eds) (2002), *Political Economy and Public Finance. The Role of Political Economy in the Theory and Practice of Public Economics*, Cheltenham, UK and Northampton, MA, USA: Edward Elgar.

Wolfe, J.N. (ed.) (1973), *Cost–Benefit and Cost-Effectiveness Studies and Analysis*, London: Allen & Unwin.

Zamagni, S. (ed.) (1998), *Non Profit Come Economia Civile*, Bologna: Il Mulino.

CHAPTER 6

Abrams, B.A. and W.R. Dougan (1986), 'The effects of constitutional restraints on government spending', *Public Choice*, **49**(2), 101–16.

Alchian, A. (1950), 'Uncertainty, evolution, and economic theory', *Journal of Political Economy*, **58**(3), 211–21.

Alesina, A. and R. Perotti (1999), 'Budget deficits and budget institutions', in Poterba and von Hagen (eds) (1999).

Backhaus, J.G. (ed.) (2005), *Essays on Fiscal Sociology*, Frankfurt-am-Main: Peter Lang.

Barry, B. (1989), *Theories of Justice*, vol. 1 of *A Treatise on Social Justice*, London: Harvester Wheatsheaf.

Baumol, W.J., J.C. Panzar and R.D. Willig (1982), *Contestable Markets and the Theory of Industry Structure*, New York: Harcourt Brace Jovanovich.

Blankart, B. (2008), *Öffentliche Finanzen in der Demokratie: Eine Einführung in die Finanzwissenschaft*, 7th edition, Munich: Vahlen.

Blejer, M.I. and A. Cheasty (1991), 'The measurement of fiscal deficits: Analytical and methodological issues', *Journal of Economic Literature*, **29**(4), 1644–78.

Brennan, G. and J.M. Buchanan (1980 [2000]), *The Power to Tax: Analytical Foundations of a Fiscal Constitution*, Cambridge: Cambridge University Press; reprinted (2000) as vol. 9 of *The Collected Works of James M. Buchanan* (1999–2002), Indianapolis: Liberty Fund.

Brennan, G. and J.M. Buchanan (1985 [2000]), *The Reason of Rules: Constitutional Political Economy*, Cambridge: Cambridge University Press; reprinted (2000) as vol. 10 of *The Collected Works of James M. Buchanan* (1999–2002), Indianapolis: Liberty Fund.

Brosio, G., M. Ferrero and W. Santagata (1982), 'Gli amministratori locali come politici. Un tentativo di verifica empirica del ciclo elettorale dei bilanci comunali italiani', *Quaderni di Sociologia*, 30.

Buchanan, J.M. (1975), 'The Samaritan's dilemma', in E.S. Phelps (ed.),

Altruism, Morality and Economic Theory, New York: Russell Sage Foundation.

Buchanan, J.M. (1999), *The Logical Foundations of Constitutional Liberty*, vol. 1 of *The Collected works of James M. Buchanan* (1999–2002), Indianapolis, Liberty Fund.

Buchanan, J.M. (2001), *Choice, Contract, and Constitutions*, vol. 16 of *The Collected Works of James M. Buchanan* (1999–2002), Indianapolis: Liberty Fund.

Buchanan, J.M. and G. Tullock (1962 [1999]), *The Calculus of Consent: Logical Foundations of Constitutional Democracy*, Ann Arbor: University of Michigan Press; reprinted (1999) as vol. 3 of *The Collected Works of James M. Buchanan* (1999–2002), Indianapolis: Liberty Fund.

Buiter, W.H. (1990), *Principles of Budgetary and Financial Policy*, Cambridge, MA: MIT Press.

Buiter, W., G. Corsetti and N. Roubini (1993), 'Excessive deficits: sense and nonsense in the Treaty of Maastricht', *Economic Policy*, **8**(16), 58–100.

Casas Pardo, J. and F. Schneider (eds) (1996), *Current Issues in Public Choice*, Cheltenham, UK and Brookfield, VT, USA: Edward Elgar.

Casas Pardo, J. and P. Schwartz (eds) (2007), *Public Choice and the Challenges of Democracy*, Cheltenham, UK and Northampton, MA, USA: Edward Elgar.

D'Amico, D. (2007), 'Buchanan on monetary constitutions', *Constitutional Political Economy*, **18**(4), 301–18.

Elster, J. (1996), 'The constitution making process', in Casas Pardo and Schneider (eds) (1996).

Forte, F. (1985a), 'The theory of social contract and the EEC', in Greenaway and Shaw (eds) (1985).

Forte, F. (1985b), 'Competitive democracy and fiscal constitution', *Atlantic Economic Journal*, **13**(3), 1–11.

Forte, F. (1991), 'Constitutions as contracts and as conventions. An economic analysis', *Contributi per la Discussione*, Politeia, Milan: Bibliotechne.

Forte, F. (1995), 'On the rationale and viability of the Maastricht fiscal and monetary constitution', *Notizie di Politeia*, 37–8.

Forte, F. (1997a), 'I bilanci pubblici Italiani alla luce della costituzione fiscale di Maastricht', *Economia Pubblica*, 4.

Forte, F. (1997b), 'The erosion of the rule of law principle in tax matters. Some reflections on the Italian case in a public choice perspective', *Economia delle Scelte Pubbliche/Journal of Public Finance and Public Choice*, **1**, 25–35.

Forte, F. (ed.) (1998), Le regole della costituzione fiscale, *Notizie di Politeia*, Special Issue no. 49–50.

Forte, F. (1999a), 'Government policies and the budget process', in Schiavo-Campo (ed.) (1999).

Forte, F. (1999b), 'The Italian post war constitution: reasons of a failure', *European Journal of Law and Economics*, **7**(2), 103–17.

Forte, F. (2001), 'The Maastricht excessive deficit rules and creative accounting', in Mudambi et al. (eds) (2001).

Forte, F. (2005), 'Fiscal and monetary illusion and the Maastricht rules', in Backhaus (ed.) (2005).

Forte, F. and D. D'Amico (2007), 'A theory of the democratic fiscal constitution', in Casas Pardo and Schwartz (eds) (2007).

Forte, F. and A. Peacock (eds) (1985), *Public Expenditure and Government Growth*, Oxford: Basil Blackwell.

Granaglia, E. (1988), *Efficienza ed Equità nelle Politche Pubbliche*, Milan: Franco Angeli.

Greenaway, D. and G.K. Shaw (eds) (1985), *Public Choice, Public Finance and Public Policy: Essays in Honour of Alan Peacock*, Oxford and New York: Blackwell.

Hagen, J. von and I.J. Harden (1995), 'Budget processes and commitment to fiscal discipline', *European Economic Review*, **39**(3–4), 771–9.

Hallerberg, M. and J. von Hagen (1999), 'Electoral institutions, cabinet negotiations, and budget deficits within the European Union', in Poterba and von Hagen (eds) (1999).

Hardin, I. (1993), 'Budget objectives, norms and procedures', in Wildavsky and Zapico-Goñi (eds) (1993).

Hayek, F. (1982), *Law, Legislation and Liberty: A New Statement of the Liberal Principles of Justice and Political Economy*, London: Routledge.

Hume, D. (1740 [2003]), *A Treatise on Human Nature*, vol. III of *Of Morals*, Mineola, NY: Dover Publications.

Maffettone, S. (1989), *Valori Communi*, Milan: Il Saggiatore.

Milesi-Ferretti, G.M. (1997), 'Fiscal rules and the budget process', *Giornale degli Economisti*, **56**(1–2), 5–40.

Modigliani, F. (1958), 'New developments on the oligopoly front', *Journal of Political Economy*, **66**(3), 215–32.

Mudambi, R., P. Navarra and G. Sobbrio (eds) (2001), *Rules and Reasons: Perspectives on Constitutional Political Economy*, Cambridge: Cambridge University Press.

Müller, D. (2001), 'On writing a constitution', in Mudambi et al. (eds) (2001).

Müller, D. (2003), *Public Choice III*, Cambridge: Cambridge University Press.

North, D. (1990), *Institutions, Institutional Change and Economic Performance*, Cambridge: Cambridge University Press.

Nozick, R. (1974), *Anarchy, State, and Utopia*, New York: Basic Books.

Organization for Economic Cooperation and Development (1995), *Budgeting for Results: Perspectives on Public Expenditure Management*, Paris: OECD.

Peacock, A.T. (1985), 'Macro-economic controls of spending as a device for improving efficiency in government', in Forte and Peacock (eds) (1985).

Persson, T. and G. Tabellini (eds) (1994), *Monetary and Fiscal Policy, vol. 2, Politics*, Cambridge, MA: MIT Press.

Persson, T. and G. Tabellini (2003), *The Economic Effects of Constitutions*, Cambridge: MIT Press.

Poterba, J.M. and J. von Hagen (eds) (1999), *Fiscal Institutions and Fiscal Performance*, Chicago: University of Chicago Press.

Roubini, N. and J. Sachs (1989), 'Political and economic determinants of budget deficits in the industrialized democracies', *European Economic Review*, **33**(5), 903–38.

Rubin, P.H. (2002), *Darwinian Politics: The Evolutionary Origin of Freedom*, New Brunswick: Rutgers University Press.

Schiavo-Campo, S. (ed.) (1999), *Governance, Corruption, and Public Financial Management*, Manila: Asian Development Bank.

Streit, M.E. and W. Mussler (1994), 'The economic constitution of the European Community. From Rome to Maastricht', *Constitutional Political Economy*, **5**(3), 319–53.

Vanberg, V. (2001), 'Constitutional order and economic evolution. Competitive and protectionist interests in a democratic society', in Mudambi et al. (eds) (2001).

Vanberg, V. (2007), 'Democracy, citizen sovereignty and constitutional economics', in Casas Pardo and Schwartz (eds) (2007).

Wicksell, K. (1896 [1958]), 'Ein neues Prinzip der gerechten Besteuerung', in *Finanztheoretische Untersuchungen*, Jena: Fischer; partial English translation (1958) as 'A new principle of just taxation', in Musgrave and Peacock (1958).

Wildavsky, A. and E. Zapico-Goñi (eds) (1993), *National Budgeting for Economic and Monetary Union*, Dordrecht and Boston: M. Nijhoff Publishers.

Willet, T. (ed.) (1989), *Political Business Cycles*, Durham: Duke University Press.

Wolfe, J.M. (ed.) (1973), *Cost–Benefit and Cost-Effectiveness Studies and Analysis*, London: Allen & Unwin.

CHAPTER 7

Aghion, P. and S.N. Durlauf (eds) (2005), *Handbook of Economic Growth*, Amsterdam: North-Holland/Elsevier.

Andersen, T.M., K.O. Moene and A. Sandmo (eds) (1995), *The Future of the Welfare State*, Scandinavian Journal of Economics Series, Oxford: Blackwell.

Aschauer, D.A. (1989), 'Is public expenditure productive?', *Journal of Monetary Economics*, **23**(2), 177–200.

Atkinson, A.B. (1975), *The Economics of Inequality*, Oxford: Clarendon Press.

Atkinson, A.B. and J.E. Stiglitz (1980), *Lectures on Public Economics*, London and New York: McGraw-Hill.

Balassone, F. and D. Franco (2000), 'Public investment, the stability pact and the "Golden Rule"', *Fiscal Studies*, **21**(2), 207–29.

Balassone, F. and D. Franco (eds) (2001), *Fiscal Rules*, Rome: Banca d'Italia.

Barr, N.A. (1989), *Student Loans: The Next Steps*, Aberdeen: Aberdeen University Press.

Barro, R. (1991), 'Economic growth in a cross section of countries', *Quarterly Journal of Economics*, **106**(2), 407–43.

Becker, G.S. (1964 [1993]), *Human Capital: A Theoretical and Empirical Analysis, with Special Reference to Education*, New York: Columbia University Press; 3rd edition (1993), Chicago: University of Chicago Press.

Becker, G.S. and W.M. Landes (eds) (1974), *Essays in the Economics of Crime and Punishment*, New York: Columbia University Press.

Becker, G.S. and G.J. Stigler (1974 [1988]), 'Law enforcement, malfeasance, and compensation of enforcers', *Journal of Legal Studies*, **3**(1), 1–18; reprinted in Stigler (ed.) (1988).

Berndt, E.R. and B. Hansson (1991 [1992]), 'Measuring the contribution of public infrastructure capital in Sweden', *NBER Working Paper No. 3842*; published (1992) in *Scandinavian Journal of Economics*, 94 Supplement, S151–S168.

Blaug, M. (ed.) (1968), *Economics of Education: Selected Readings*, Harmondsworth: Penguin Books, 2 vols.

Boardman, A.E. (1996), *Cost–Benefit Analysis: Concepts and Practice*, Upper Saddle River, NJ: Prentice-Hall.

Boersch-Supan, A. and W.R. Richter (eds) (2000), 'Public finance and transitions in social security', *International Tax and Public Finance*, **7**(4).

Bovenberg, A.L., B. Jacobs and R.A. de Mooij (eds) (2008), 'Reinventing the welfare state', *International Tax and Public Finance*, **15**(1).

Braithwaite, R.B. (1955), *Theory of Games as a Tool for the Moral Philosopher*, Cambridge: Cambridge University Press.

Brittan, S. and S. Webb (1990), *Beyond the Welfare State: An Examination of Basic Incomes in a Market Economy*, Aberdeen: Aberdeen University Press.

Brosio, G. (ed.) (1987), *La Spesa Pubblica*, Milan: Giuffrè.

Brosio, G. and W. Santagata (eds) (1992), *Rapporto sull'Economia delle Arti e dello Spettacolo in Italia*, with contributions by A.T. Peacock and others, Turin: Fondazione Giovanni Agnelli.

Brunetta, R. and C. Carraro (1990), 'Income policies as cooperative strategies: Lessons from the Italian experience of the '80s', in Brunetta and Dell'Aringa (1990).

Brunetta, R. and C. Dell'Aringa (eds) (1990), *Markets, Institutions and Cooperation*, London: Macmillan.

Bryant, R.C. and R. Portes (eds) (1987), *Global Macroeconomics: Policy Conflict and Cooperation*, London: Macmillan.

Buchanan, A. (1991), *Secession: The Morality of Political Divorce from Fort Sumter to Lithuania and Quebec*, Boulder: Westview Press.

Buchanan, J.M. (1965 [2001]), 'An economic theory of clubs', *Economica*, New Series, **32**(125), 1–14; reprinted in *The Collected Works of James M. Buchanan* (1999–2002), vol. 15 (1999), *Externalities and Public Expenditure Theory*, Indianapolis: Liberty Fund.

Buchanan, J.M. (1975a [2000]), *The Limits of Liberty: Between Anarchy and Leviathan*, Chicago: Chicago University Press; reprinted (2000) as vol. 7 of *The Collected Works of James M. Buchanan* (1999–2002), Indianapolis: Liberty Fund.

Buchanan, J.M. (1975b [1999]), 'The Samaritan's dilemma', in Phelps (ed.) (1975); reprinted in *The Collected Works of James M. Buchanan* (1999–2002), vol.1 (1999), *The Logical Foundations of Constitutional Liberty*, Indianapolis, Liberty Fund.

Buchanan, J.M. (1976 [2001]), 'A Hobbesian interpretation of the Rawlsian difference principle', *Kyklos*, **29**(1), 5–25; reprinted (2001) in *Moral Science and Moral Order*, vol. 17 of *The Collected Works of James M. Buchanan* (1999–2002), Indianapolis: Liberty Fund.

Buchanan, J.M. (2001), *Externalities and Public Expenditure Theory*, vol. 15 of *The Collected Works of James M. Buchanan* (1999–2002), Indianapolis: Liberty Fund.

Chakravarty, S. (1987), 'Cost–benefit analysis', in Eatwell et al. (eds) (1987).

Chiancone, A. and F. Osculati (eds) (1993), *Il Merito della Spesa Pubblica: la Natura e l'Offerta dei Beni non di Mercato*, Milan: Franco Angeli.

Clerico, G. (1984), *Economia della Salute: una Analisi Introduttiva*, with an 'Introduction' by F. Forte, Milan: Franco Angeli.

Clerico, G. (1997), *Istituzioni, Incentivi ed Efficienza in Sanità*, Padua: Cedam.

Coase, R. (1960), 'The problem of social cost', *Journal of Law and Economics*, **3**(1), 1–44; reprinted in Coase (1988).

Coase, R. (1988), *The Firm, the Market, and the Law*, Chicago: University of Chicago Press.

Conrad, K. and H. Seitz (1994), 'The economic benefits of public infrastructure', *Applied Economics*, **26**(4), 303–11.

Creedy, J. (1995), *The Economics of Higher Education: An Analysis of Taxes versus Fees*, Aldershot, UK and Brookfield, VT, USA: Edward Elgar.

Culyer, A.J. (2005), *The Dictionary of Health Economics*, Cheltenham, UK and Northampton, MA, USA: Edward Elgar.

Culyer, A.J. and J.P. Newhouse (eds) (2000), *Handbook in Health Economics*, Amsterdam and New York: Elsevier.

De Viti de Marco, A. (1934 [1936]), *Principi di Economia Finanziaria*, Turin: Einaudi; English translation (1936) as *First Principles of Public Finance*, London: Jonathan Cape; New York: Harcourt, Brace & Co.

De Voogd, J. (1992), *Guaranteed Minimum Income Arrangements in the Netherlands, Belgium, Denmark, France, Germany, and Great Britain*, The Hague: Dutch Ministry of Social Affairs and Employment, Department of Labour-Market and Education.

Devarajan, S., V. Swaroop and H. Zou (1996), 'The composition of public expenditure and economic growth', *Journal of Monetary Economics*, **37**(2), 313–44.

Easterly, W. (2005), 'National economic policies and economic growth: a reappraisal', in Aghion and Durlauf (eds) (2005).

Eatwell, J., M. Milgate and P. Newman (eds) (1987), *The New Palgrave: A Dictionary of Economics*, London: Macmillan.

EC, IMF, OECD, UN and World Bank (1993), *System of National Accounts*, Brussels/Luxembourg: Commission of the European Communities; Washington, DC: International Monetary Fund; Paris: Organisation for Economic Co-operation and Development; New York: United Nations; Washington, DC: World Bank.

Einaudi, L. (1940 [1956]), *Principi di Scienza delle Finanze*, Turin: Einaudi.

Einaudi, L. (1949), *Lezioni di Politica Sociale*, Turin: Einaudi.

Engelbrecht, H.J. (1997), 'International R&D spillovers, human capital and productivity in OECD economies: an empirical investigation', *European Economic Review*, **41**(8), 1479–88.

Erenburg, S.J. (1993), 'The real effects of public investment on private investment', *Applied Economics*, **25**(6), 831–7.

EUROSTAT (1995), *European System of Accounts: ESA 1995*, Luxembourg: Office for Official Publications of the European Communities.

Ford, R. and P. Poret (1991), 'Infrastructure and private sector productivity', *OECD Economics Department Working Papers*, no. 91.

Forte, F. (1967), 'Should "public goods" be public?', *Papers on Non-Market Decision Making*, later *Public Choice*, **3**(1), 39–47.

Forte, F. (1983 [1984]), 'Monitoring the productivity of bureaucratic behaviour', in Hanusch (ed.) (1983); reprinted (1984) also as 'Controlling the productivity of bureaucratic behaviour', *Atlantic Economic Journal*, **12**(1), 32–40.

Forte, F. (1984), *Il Bilancio nell'Economia Pubblica*, Milan: Giuffrè.

Forte, F. (1997), 'The measurement of fiscal burden on GDP instead than on national net value added produced: A chapter in fiscal illusion', *Banca Nazionale del Lavoro Quarterly Review*, **202**, September.

Forte, F. (2007), 'Coase theorem revisited', *Rivista di Diritto Finanziario e Scienza delle Finanze*, **66**(3), 348–63.

Forte, F. (ed.) (2008), *Money, Markets and Morals*, Munich: Accedo Verlagsgesellschaft.

Forte, F. and J.M. Buchanan (1961 [1989, 2001]), 'The evaluation of public services', *Journal of Political Economy*, **69**(2), 107–21; reprinted in J.M. Buchanan (1989), *Explorations into Constitutional Economics*, compiled by R.D. Tollison and V.J. Vanberg, College Station: Texas A&M University Press, and in *The Collected Works of James M. Buchanan* (1999–2002), vol. 15 (2001), *Externalities and Public Expenditure Theory*, Indianapolis: Liberty Fund.

Forte, F. and S. D'Eugenio (2005), *Il Bilancio dell'Operatore Pubblico e il Project Management*, Milan: Giuffrè.

Forte, F. and C. Magazzino (2010), 'Optimal size of governments and economic growth in European Union countries', Working Papers, CREI, Università di Roma 3, Roma.

Forte, F. and M. Mantovani (2000), 'Efficiency and effectiveness of museums' supply in an agency context', *Studi Economici*, **55**(71), 5–46.

Forte, F. and M. Mantovani (2004), *Economia e Politica dei Beni Culturali*, Soveria Mannelli (CZ): Rubbettino.

Forte, F. and A. Peacock (eds) (1985), *Public Expenditure and Government Growth*, Oxford: Basil Blackwell.

Frey, B.S. and W.W. Pommerehne (1989), *Muses and Markets: Exploration in the Economics of the Arts*, Oxford: Blackwell.

Fuguitt, D. and S.J. Wilcox (1999), *Cost–Benefit Analysis for Public Sector Decision Makers*, Westport: Quorum Books.

Gini, C. (1912), 'Variabilità e mutabilità', reprinted in C. Gini (1955), *Variabilità e Concentrazione*, Rome: Veschi.

Graham, G. (1988), *Contemporary Social Philosophy*, Oxford, UK and New York, USA: Blackwell.

Gramlich, E.M. (1994), 'Infrastructure investment: a review essay', *Journal of Economic Literature*, **32**(3), 1176–96.

Granaglia, E. (1993), 'Il criterio del "functioning" e la ridefinizione delle politiche sociali come beni di merito', in Chiancone and Osculati (eds) (1993).

Hanusch, H. (ed.) (1983), *Anatomy of Government Deficiencies*, Berlin and New York: Springer.

Hochman, H.M. and G.E. Peterson (eds) (1974), *Redistribution through Public Choice*, New York: Columbia University Press.

Johnes, G. and J. Johnes (eds) (2004), *International Handbook on the Economics of Education*, Cheltenham, UK and Northampton, MA, USA: Edward Elgar.

Kenessey, Z. (ed.) (1994), *The Accounts of Nations*, Amsterdam and Washington, DC: IOS Press.

Kliemt, H. (1993), 'On justifying a minimum welfare state', *Constitutional Political Economy*, **4**(2), 159–72.

Kliemt, H. (2008), 'On the health care that is and that might be. Projecting health care provision into the future in a Buchanan type constitutional political economy', in Forte (ed.) (2008).

Kling, H. (2006), *Crisis of Abundance: Rethinking how We Pay for the Health Care*, Washington, DC: Cato Institute.

Krohm, G. (1973), 'The pecuniary incentives to property crime', in S. Rottenburg (ed.), *The Economics of Crime and Punishment*, Washington, DC: American Enterprise Institute for Public Policy Research.

Lequiller, F. and D. Blades (2006), *Understanding National Accounts*, Paris: OECD.

Levin, H.M. and P.J. McEwan (2001), *Cost-Effectiveness Analysis. Methods and Applications*, Thousand Oaks, CA: Sage Publications.

Lorenz, M.O. (1909), 'Methods for measuring concentration of wealth', *Publications of American Statistical Association*, **9**(70), 209–19.

Mantovani, M. (2008), *Lezioni di Economia Pubblica dei Beni Culturali*, with an Introduction by F. Forte, Turin: Giappichelli.

Martino, A. (ed.) (1977), *Un Reddito Garantito per Tutti?*, Turin: Biblioteca della Libertà.

Mazzola, U. (1890), *I Dati Scientifici della Finanza Pubblica*, Rome: Loescher.

McMahon, W.W. (1999), *Education and Development, Measuring the Social Benefits*, Oxford: Oxford University Press.

Milbourne, R., G. Otto and G.M. Voss (2003), 'Public investment and economic growth', *Applied Economics*, **35**(5), 527–40.

Mill, J.S. (1848 [1871, 2006]), *Principles of Political Economy, with some of their Applications to Social Philosophy*, London: J.W. Parker; 7th and final edition (1871) reprinted (2006) in vols II and III of the *Collected Works of John Stuart Mill*, Indianapolis: Liberty Fund.

Mishan, E.J. (1972), *Elements of Cost–Benefit Analysis*, London: Allen and Unwin.

Morrison, C.J. and A.E. Schwartz (1996), 'State infrastructure and productive performance', *American Economic Review*, **86**(5), 1095–111.

Nas, T.F. (1996), *Cost–Benefit Analysis: Theory and Application*, Thousand Oaks, CA: Sage Publications.

Okun, A. (1975 [1990]), *Equality and Efficiency: The Big Trade Off*, Washington: The Brookings Institution; Italian translation (1990) with an 'Introduction' by F. Forte, Naples: Liguori.

Paradiso, M. (2000), 'Decidere per l'ambiente: il caso della valutazione contingente', *Rivista di Scienza delle Finanze e Diritto Finanziario*, **59**(1), 53–72.

Peacock, A.T. (1991), 'Welfare philosophies and welfare finance', in Wilson and Wilson (eds) (1991).

Peacock, A.T. (1992), *Public Choice Analysis in Historical Perspective*, Cambridge: Cambridge University Press.

Phelps, E.S. (ed.) (1975), *Altruism, Morality, and Economic Theory*, New York: Russell Sage Foundation.

Pigou, A.C. (1947), *A Study in Public Finance*, 3rd revised edition, London: Macmillan.

Posner, R. (1985), 'An economic theory of criminal law', *Columbia Law Review*, **85**(5), 1193–231.

Rey, M. (1990), 'Problemi di gestione dei rifiuti solidi urbani', *Economia Pubblica*, 1–2, 35–42.

Röpke, W. (1944 [1948]), *Civitas Humana. Grundfragen der Gesellschafts- und Wirtschaftsreform*, Zurich: Eugen Rentsch Verlag; English translation (1948) by C.S. Fox, *Civitas Humana. Humane Order of Society*, London: W. Hodge.

Sandmo, A. (1995), 'Introduction. The welfare economics of the welfare state', in Andersen et al. (eds) (1995).

Say, J.B. (1803 [1841, 1867]), *Traité d'Économie Politique*, Paris: Déterville, 6th edition, 1841, Paris: Guillaumin; English translation of 4th edition by C.R. Prinsep, *A Treatise on Political Economy*; new American edition by C.C. Biddle (1867), Philadelphia: J.B. Lippincott & Co.

Say, J.B. (1828–29 [1840]), *Cours Complet d'Économie Politique Pratique*, Paris: Rapilly, 2nd edition (1840), Paris: Guillaumin.

Schiavo-Campo, S. (ed.) (1999), *Governance, Corruption, and Public Financial Management*, Manila: Asian Development Bank.

Seldon, A. (1977), *Charge*, London: Smith.

Semmler, W., A. Greiner, B. Diallo, A. Rezai and A. Rajaram (2007), 'Fiscal policy, public expenditure composition, and growth theory and empirics', *World Bank Policy Research Working Paper* no. 4405.

Sen, A. (1973), *On Economic Inequality*, Oxford: Clarendon Press.

Sen, A. (1985), *Commodities and Capabilities*, Amsterdam: North-Holland.

Sen, A. (1987), *The Standard of Living*, edited by G. Hawthorn, with contributions by Müllbauer, Kanbur, Hart, Williams, Cambridge: Cambridge University Press.

Sinn, H.W. (1995), 'A theory of the welfare state', in Andersen et al. (eds) (1995).

Smith, A. (1776), *An Inquiry into the Nature and Causes of the Wealth of Nations*, reprinted by W.B. Todd (ed.) (1982), with an Introduction by E. Cannan, Indianapolis: Liberty Fund.

Stigler, G.J. (1970), 'The optimum enforcement of laws', *Journal of Political Economy*, **78**(3), 526–36.

Stigler, G.J. (ed.) (1988), *Chicago Studies in Political Economy*, Chicago: University of Chicago Press.

Teixerira, P., B. Jongbloed, D. Dill and A. Amaral (eds) (2004), *Markets in Higher Education: Rhetoric or Reality?*, Dordrecht and Boston: Kluwer Academic Publisher.

Thurow, L.C. (1980 [2001]), *The Zero-Sum Society: Distribution and the Possibilities for Economic Change*, New York: Basic Books.

United Nations Statistical Office (2008), *A System of National Accounts*, New York: United Nations.

Vanoli, A. (2002 [2005]), *Une Histoire de la Comptabilité Nationale*, Paris: Découverte; English translation (2005), *A History of National Accounting*, Washington, DC: IOS Press.

Villani, A. (1988), *Economia Politica dell'Arte e dei beni Culturali*, Milan: ISU.

Wilson, J.D. (ed.) (2008), *Special Issue on Education, International Tax and Public Finance*, **15**(2).

Wilson, T. and D. Wilson (eds) (1991), *The State and Social Welfare*, London and New York: Longman.

Wolfe, J.M. (ed.) (1973), *Cost–Benefit and Cost-Effectiveness Studies and Analysis*, London: Allen & Unwin.

CHAPTER 8

Allingham, M.G. and A. Sandmo (1972), 'Income tax evasion: a theoretical analysis', *Journal of Public Economics*, **1**(3–4), 323–38.

Andel, M. and H. Haller (eds) (1980), *Handbuch der Finanzwissenschaft*, Band II, Tubingen: J.C.B. Mohr.

Andreoni, J., B. Erard and J. Feinstein (1998), 'Tax compliance', *Journal of Economic Literature*, **36**(2), 818–60.

Beccaria, C. (1775 [1958]), 'Tentativo analitico sui contrabbandi', *Il Caffè*; reprinted in Beccaria (1958), vol. I.

Beccaria, C. (1958), *Opere*, edited by S. Romagnoli, Florence: Sansoni, 2 vols.

Becker, G.S. and W.M. Landes (eds) (1974), *Essays in the Economics of Crime and Punishment*, New York: Columbia University Press.

Brennan, G. and J.M. Buchanan (1980 [2000]), *The Power to Tax: Analytical Foundations of a Fiscal Constitution*, Cambridge: Cambridge University Press; reprinted (2000) as vol. 9 of *The Collected Works of James M. Buchanan* (1999–2002), Indianapolis: Liberty Fund.

Buchanan, J.M. (1966 [1999]), *Public Finance in Democratic Process: Fiscal Institutions and Individual Choice*, Chapel Hill: University of North Carolina Press; reprinted (1999) as vol. 4 of *The Collected Works of James M. Buchanan* (1999–2002), Indianapolis: Liberty Fund.

Buchanan, J.M. and D.R. Lee (1982a [2000]), 'Tax rates and tax revenues in political equilibrium: Some simple analytics', *Economic Inquiry*, **20**(2), 344–54; reprinted (2000) in *Politics as Public Choice*, vol. 13 of *The Collected Works of James M. Buchanan* (1999–2002), Indianapolis: Liberty Fund.

Buchanan, J.M. and D.R. Lee (1982b [1987]), 'Politics, time, and the Laffer curve', *Journal of Political Economy*, **90**(4), 816–19; reprinted in J.M. Buchanan (1987), *Economics: Between Predictive Science and Moral Philosophy*, compiled by R.D. Tollison and V.J. Vanberg, College Station: Texas A&M University Press.

Cassone, A. and R. Cugno (1987), 'Il comportamento dell'evasore fiscale: una rassegna critica della letteratura', *Rivista di Scienza delle Finanze e Diritto Finanziario*, **46**(2), 241–73.

Cremer, H. and F. Gahvari (1993), 'Tax evasion and optimal commodity taxation', *Journal of Public Economics*, **50**(2), 261–75.

Dalton, H. (1957), *Principles of Public Finance*, London: Routledge.

Dardanoni, V. and M. Marrelli (1988), 'Tax evasion and the intensity of auditing', *Rivista di Scienza delle Finanze e Diritto Finanziario*, **47**(2), 165–72.

De Viti De Marco, A. (1934 [1936]), *Principi di Economia Finanziaria*,

Turin: Einaudi; English translation (1936) as *First Principles of Public Finance*, London: Jonathan Cape; New York: Harcourt, Brace & Co.

Eatwell, J., M. Milgate and P. Newman (eds) (1987), *The New Palgrave: A Dictionary of Economics*, London: Macmillan.

Edgeworth, F.I. (1897 [1925]), 'The pure theory of taxation', *Economic Journal*, **7**(25), 46–70, reprinted in Edgeworth (1925).

Edgeworth, F.I. (1925), *Papers Relating to Political Economy*, London: Macmillan.

Einaudi, L. (1940a [1956]), *Principi di Scienza delle Finanze*, Turin: Einaudi.

Einaudi, L. (1940b [1959]), *Miti e Paradossi della Giustizia Tributaria*, Turin: Einaudi.

Einaudi, L. (1941 [1958]), *Saggi sul Risparmio e l'Imposta*, Turin: Einaudi.

Fasiani, M. (1951), *Principi di Scienza delle Finanze*, Turin: Giappichelli, 2 vols, 2nd revised and enlarged edition.

Fedeli, S. (1998), 'The effects of the interaction between direct and indirect tax evasion: the cases VAT and RST', *Public Finance/Finances Publiques*, **53**(3–4), 385–418.

Fedeli, S. and F. Forte (1999), 'Joint income-tax and VAT-chain evasion', *European Journal of Political Economy*, **15**(3), 391–415.

Fedeli, S. and F. Forte (2008), 'Deregolamentazione del Mercato del lavoro ed effetto Laffer. Evidenza empirica dall'Italia (1997–2001)', *Economia Internazionale/International Economics*, **61**, 313–38.

Fedeli, S. and F. Forte (2009a), 'The Laffer effects of a program of deregulation cum detaxation. The Italian reform of labour contracts in the period 1997–2001', *European Journal of Law and Economics*, **27**(3), 211–32.

Fedeli, S. and F. Forte (2009b), 'Models of cross-border VAT fraud', Working Paper no. 123, Dipartimento di Economia Pubblica, Università di Roma 'La Sapienza', available at http://dep.eco.uniroma1.it/docs/working_papers/WP123.pdf.

Fedeli, S. and F. Forte (2009c), 'EU VAT fraud', Working Paper no. 129, Dipartimento di Economia Pubblica, Università di Roma 'La Sapienza', available at http://dep.eco.uniroma1.it/docs/working_papers/WP129.pdf.

Fedeli, S. and F. Forte (forthcoming), 'The sociological theory, fiscal illusion and the Laffer curve. Reflections on an Italian case', in J. Backhaus (ed.) (forthcoming), *Essays on Fiscal Sociology*, Frankfurt-am-Main: Peter Lang.

Fedeli, S., F. Forte and E. Zangari (2008), 'An econometric analysis of the employment and revenue effects of the Treu reform in the period 1997–2001', *Rivista di Politica Economica*, **98**(1–2), 215–48.

Forte, F. (1953), 'Teoria dei tributi speciali', *Rivista di Scienza delle Finanze e Diritto Finanziario*, **12**, 330–98.

Forte, F. (1973), *Il Consumo e la sua Tassazione, Vol. I, Elementi di una Teoria Generale, Vol. II, Le Imposte sulle Vendite e sul Valore Aggiunto*, Turin: Einaudi.

Forte, F. (1987), 'The Laffer Curve and the theory of fiscal bureaucracy', *Public Choice*, **52**(2), 101–24.

Forte, F. (1995), *Etica Pubblica e Regole del Gioco*, Naples: Liguori.

Forte, F. (2008a), 'On the ethics of the Laffer Curve', in Forte (ed.) (2008b).

Forte, F. (ed.) (2008b), *Money, Markets and Morals,* Munich: Accedo Verlagsgesellschaft.

Forte, F. and A. Peacock (1981), 'Tax planning, tax analysis and tax policy', in Peacock and Forte (eds) (1981).

Forte, F. and A.T. Peacock (eds) (1985), *Public Expenditure and Government Growth*, Oxford: Basil Blackwell.

Frey, B. and P. Feld (2002), 'Deterrence and morale in taxation: an empirical analysis', *CESifo Working Paper*, No. 760.

Gordon, J.P.F. (1989), 'Individual morality and reputation costs as deterrents to tax evasion', *European Economic Review*, **33**(4), 797–805.

Griziotti, B. (1915), 'Crisi e tendenze negli studi finanziari', *Giornale degli Economisti*, **1**, 93–110; reprinted in Griziotti (1956), vol. II.

Griziotti, B. (1935), 'Vecchi e nuovi indirizzi nella scienza delle finanze', *Annali di Economia dell'Università Bocconi*, vol. X; reprinted with changes in Griziotti (1953).

Griziotti, B. (1938), 'Nuovi orientamenti nei sistemi tributari', reprinted in Griziotti (1956), vol. II.

Griziotti, B. (1939), 'Brevi analisi e sintesi finanziarie', *Rivista di Scienza delle Finanze e Diritto Finanziario*; reprinted in Griziotti (1956).

Griziotti, B. (1953), *Saggi sul Rinnovamento dello Studio della Scienza delle Finanze e del Diritto Finanziario*, Milan: Giuffrè.

Griziotti, B. (1956), *Studi di Scienze delle Finanze e Diritto Finanziario*, Milan: Giuffrè, 2 vols.

Hey, J.D. and P.J. Lambert (eds) (1987), *Surveys in the Economics of Uncertainty*, Oxford: Blackwell.

Laffer, A.B. (2004), 'The Laffer curve: past, present and future', *Backgrounder*, no. 1765, Heritage Foundation.

Lerner, A.P. (1944), *The Economics of Control. Principles of Welfare Economics*, New York: Macmillan.

Marrelli, M. (1984), 'On indirect tax evasion', *Journal of Public Economics*, **25**(1–2), 181–96.

Marrelli, M. (1987), 'The economic analysis of tax evasion: empirical aspects', in Hey and Lambert (eds) (1987).

Mill, J.S. (1848 [1871, 2006]), *Principles of Political Economy, with some of their Applications to Social Philosophy*, London: J.W. Parker; 7th and final edition (1871) reprinted (2006) in vols II and III of the *Collected Works of John Stuart Mill*, Indianapolis: Liberty Fund.

Monissen, H. (2008), 'Explorations of the Laffer Curve', in Forte (ed.) (2008).

Musgrave, R.A. (1959), *The Theory of Public Finance. A Study in Public Economy*, New York: McGraw-Hill.

Neumark, F. (1970), *Grundsätze Gerechter und Ökonomisch Rationaler Steuerpolitik*, Tübingen: J.C.B. Mohr.

Peacock, A.T. (1985), 'Macro-economic controls of spending as a device for improving efficiency in goverment', in Forte and Peacock (1985).

Peacock, A. and F. Forte (eds) (1981), *The Political Economy of Taxation*, Oxford: Blackwell.

Pestieau, P. and U.M. Possen (1991), 'Tax evasion and occupational choice', *Journal of Public Economics*, **45**(1), 107–25.

Pigou, A.C. (1947), *A Study in Public Finance*, 3rd revised edition, London: Macmillan.

Pugliese, M. (1932), *La Finanza e i suoi Compiti Extra-Fiscali negli Stati Moderni*, Padua: Cedam.

Puviani, A. (1903 [1973]), *Teoria dell'Illusione Finanziaria*, re-edited by F. Volpi (1973), Milan: ISEDI.

Reinganum, J.F. and L.L. Wilde (1985), 'Income tax compliance in a principal–agent framework', *Journal of Public Economics*, **26**(1), 1–18.

Ricardo, D. (1817 [1947, 2005]), *Principles of Political Economy and Taxation*, re-edited (1947) by P. Sraffa as vol. I of the *The Works and Correspondence of David Ricardo*; reprinted (2005), Indianapolis: Liberty Fund.

Röpke, W. (1944 [1948]), *Civitas Humana. Grundfragen der Gesellschafts- und Wirtschaftsreform*, Zurich: Eugen Rentsch Verlag; English translation (1948) by C.S. Fox, *Civitas Humana. Humane Order of Society*, London: W. Hodge.

Sandmo, A. (2005), 'The theory of tax evasion. A retrospective view', *National Tax Journal*, **58**(4), 643–63.

Sanford, C. (1981), 'Economic aspects of compliance costs', in Peacock and Forte (1981).

Smith, A. (1776), *An Inquiry into the Nature and Causes of the Wealth of*

Nations, reprinted by W.B. Todd (ed.) (1982), with an Introduction by E. Cannan, Indianapolis: Liberty Fund.

Steve, S. (1997), *Scritti Vari*, Milan: Franco Angeli.

Stigler, G.J. (1970), 'The optimum enforcement of laws', *Journal of Political Economy*, **78**(3), 526–36.

CHAPTERS 9, 10 AND 11; APPENDIX

Arrow, K. and M. Intriligator (eds) (1981), *Handbook of Mathematical Economics*, 4 vols, Amsterdam and New York: North-Holland.

Auerbach, A.J. and M. Feldstein (eds) (1985–2002), *Handbook of Public Economics*, 4 vols, Amsterdam: North-Holland.

Bishop, R.L. (1968), 'The effects of specific and ad valorem taxes', *Quarterly Journal of Economics*, **82**(2), 198–218.

Bradford, D.F. and H.S. Rosen (1976), 'The optimal taxation of commodities and income', *American Economic Review Papers and Proceedings*, **66**(2), 94–101.

Buchanan, J.M. (1999–2002), *Collected Works*, 20 vols, Indianapolis: Liberty Fund.

Buchanan, J.M. and F. Forte (1964 [2001]), 'Fiscal choice through time: a case for indirect taxation?', *National Tax Journal*, **17**, 144–57; reprinted in *Debt and Taxes*, vol. 14 of *The Collected Works of James M. Buchanan* (1999–2002), Indianapolis: Liberty Fund.

Due, J.F. (1940), 'Ad valorem and specific taxes', *Quarterly Journal of Economics*, **54**(4), 679–85.

Eatwell, J., M. Milgate and P. Newman (eds) (1987), *The New Palgrave: A Dictionary of Economics*, London: Macmillan.

Edgeworth, F.I. (1897 [1925]), 'The pure theory of taxation', *Economic Journal*, **7**(25), 46–70; reprinted in Edgeworth (1925).

Edgeworth, F.I. (1925), *Papers Relating to Political Economy*, London: Macmillan.

Einaudi, L. (1902), *Studi sugli Effetti delle Imposte. Contributo allo Studio dei Problemi Tributari Municipali*, Turin: Bocca.

Einaudi, L. (1941 [1958]), *Saggi sul Risparmio e l'Imposta*, Turin: Einaudi.

Fasiani, M. (1951), *Principi di Scienza delle Finanze*, Turin: Giappichelli, 2 vols, 2nd revised and enlarged edition.

Feldstein, M. (1983), *Capital Taxation*, Cambridge, MA: Harvard University Press.

Fisher, I. (1927), *The Nature of Capital and Income*, London: Macmillan.

Forte, F. (1973), *Il Consumo e la sua Tassazione, Vol. II, Le Imposte sulle Vendite e sul Valore Aggiunto*, Turin: Einaudi.

Forte, F. (1978), *Effetti delle Imposte, Strutture del Mercato ed Equilibrio Macroeconomico*, Milan: Giuffrè.

Forte, F. (2000), *Principi di Economia Pubblica*, Milan: Giuffrè.

Forte, F. (ed.) (2008), *Money, Markets and Morals*, Munich: Accedo Verlagsgesellschaft.

Friedman, M. (1949), 'The Marshallian demand curve', *Journal of Political Economy*, **57**(6), 463–95.

Graaff, J. de V. (1957), *Theoretical Welfare Economics*, Cambridge: Cambridge University Press.

Griziotti, B. (1918), 'Teoria dell'ammortamento delle imposte e sue applicazioni', *Giornale degli Economisti*, **56**(1); reprinted in Griziotti (1956), vol. I.

Griziotti, B. (1956), *Studi di Scienza delle Finanze e Diritto Finanziario*, Milan: Giuffrè (2 vols).

Harberger, A. (1974), *Taxation and Welfare*, Chicago: University of Chicago Press.

Marshall, A. (1920 [1961]), *Principles of Economics*, 9th edition (1961) edited by C.V. Guillebaud, London: Macmillan.

McLure, C. (1975), 'General equilibrium incidence analysis: the Harberger model after ten years', *Journal of Public Economics*, **4**(2), 125–61.

Mirrlees, J.A. (1981), 'The theory of optimal taxation', in Arrow and Intriligator (eds) (1981).

Mirrlees, J.A. (1982), 'The economic uses of utiliarianism', in Sen and Williams (1982), pp. 63–84.

Monissen, H. (2008), 'Explorations of the Laffer curve', in Forte (ed.) (2008).

Musgrave, R.A. (1959), *The Theory of Public Finance. A Study in Public Economy*, New York: McGraw-Hill.

Peacock, A. and F. Forte (eds) (1981), *The Political Economy of Taxation*, Oxford: Blackwell.

Pigou, A.C. (1947), *A Study in Public Finance*, 3rd revised edition, London: Macmillan.

Ramsey, F.P. (1927), 'A contribution to the theory of taxation', *Economic Journal*, **37**(145), 47–61.

Ricardo, D. (1817 [1947, 2005]), *Principles of Political Economy and Taxation*, re-edited (1947) by P. Sraffa as vol. I of *The Works and Correspondence of David Ricardo*; reprinted (2005), Indianapolis: Liberty Fund.

Sandmo, A. (1976), 'Optimal taxation. An introduction to the literature', *Journal of Public Economics*, **6**(1–2), 37–54.

Seligman, E.R. (1910), *The Shifting and Incidence of Taxation*, 3rd edition, New York: Columbia University Press.

Sen, A. and B. Williams (eds) (1982), *Utilitarianism and Beyond*, Cambridge: Cambridge University Press.

Steve, S. (1990), *Lezioni di Scienza delle Finanze*, 7th edition, Padua: Cedam.

CHAPTER 12

Arrow, K. and T. Scitovsky (eds) (1969), *Readings in Welfare Economics*, London: Allen & Unwin.

Bailey, S.J. and P. Falconer (1998), 'Charging for admission to museums and galleries: A framework for analysing the impact on access', *Journal of Cultural Economics*, **22**(2–3), 167–77.

Blomquist, S. and W. Christiansen (2005), 'The role of prices for excludable public goods', *International Tax and Public Finance*, **12**(1), 61–79.

Brown, S.J. and D.S. Sibley (1986), *The Theory of Public Utility Pricing*, Cambridge: Cambridge University Press.

Coase, R. (1946), 'The marginal cost controversy', *Economica*, New Series, **13**(51), 169–82; reprinted in Coase (1988).

Coase, R.H. (1974), 'The lighthouse in economics', *Journal of Law and Economics*, **17**(2), 357–76; reprinted in Coase (1988).

Coase, R. (1988), *The Firm, the Market, and the Law*, Chicago: University of Chicago Press.

Dupuit, J. (1842–53), *De l'Utilité et de sa Mesure*, selected writings; reprinted (1933) by M. De Bernardi, with a 'Preface' by L. Einaudi, Turin: Edizioni de La Riforma Sociale.

Eatwell, J., M. Milgate and P. Newman (eds) (1987), *The New Palgrave: A Dictionary of Economics*, London: Macmillan.

Einaudi, L. (1940 [1956]), *Principi di Scienza delle Finanze*, Turin: Einaudi.

Forte, F. (2000), *Principi di Economia Pubblica*, Milan: Giuffrè.

Forte, F. and C. Marchese (1984), *Prezzi Pubblici e Tariffe*, Milan: Giuffrè.

Hotelling, A. (1938 [1969]), 'The general welfare in relation to problems of taxation and of railway and utility rates', *Econometrica*, **6**(3), 242–69; reprinted in Arrow and Scitovsky (eds) (1969).

Marchese, C. (1991), 'Le prestazioni delle poste Italiane', *Economia Pubblica*, **3**, 121.

Mushkin, S.J. (ed.) (1972), *Public Prices for Public Products*, Washington, DC: Urban Institute.

Pantaleoni, M. (1911 [1919]), 'Considerazioni sulle proprietà di un sistema di prezzi politici', *Giornale degli Economisti*, **42**(2), 9–29 and 114–133; reprinted in M. Pantaleoni (1919), *La Fine Provvisoria di un'Epopea*, Bari: Laterza.

Peacock, A.T. (1979a), 'The limitations of public good theory: The lighthouse revisited', in Peacock (1979b).

Peacock, A.T. (1979b), *The Economic Analysis of Government, and Related Themes*, Oxford: Martin Robertson.

Peacock, A.T. (1989), 'The future of public service broadcasting', in Veljanovski (ed.) (1989).

Rees, R. (ed.) (2006), *The Economics of Public Utilities*, Cheltenham, UK and Northampton, MA, USA: Edward Elgar.

Sawkins, J.W. and R. McMaster (1997), *Quasi Markets for Water Services. Reviving the Auld Alliance?*, Hume Monograph no. 1, Edinburgh: The David Hume Institute.

Seldon, A. (1977), *Charge*, London: Smith.

Stigler, G.J. and K.E. Boulding (eds) (1952), *Readings in Price Theory*, London: Allen & Unwin.

Tollison, R.D. and T.D. Willett (1973), 'The university and the price system', *Journal of Economics and Business*, Spring–Summer, pp. 191–7.

Veljanovski, C. (ed.) (1989), *Freedom in Broadcasting*, London: Institute of Economic Affairs.

Vickrey, W. (1997), *Public Economics: Selected Papers*, edited by R. Arnott, A.B. Atkinson, K. Arrow, and J. Drèze, Cambridge: Cambridge University Press.

CHAPTER 13

Alesina, A. (1987), 'Macroeconomic policy in a two party system as a repeated game', *Quarterly Journal of Economics*, **102**(3), 651–78.

Alesina, A. (1988), *Macroeconomics and Politics*, Cambridge, MA: MIT Press.

Alesina, A. and G. Tabellini (1988), 'Credibility and politics', *European Economic Review*, **32**(2–3), 542–50.

Barro, R. (1974), 'Are government bonds net wealth?', *Journal of Political Economy*, **82**(6), 1095–117.

Barro, R. (1976), 'Reply to Feldstein and Buchanan', *Journal of Political Economy*, **84**(2), 343–50.

Barro, R. (1979), 'On the determination of the public debt', *Journal of Political Economy*, **87**(5), 940–71.

Barro, R. (1986), 'Reputation in a model of monetary policy with incomplete information', *Journal of Monetary Economics*, **17**(1), 3–20.

Barro, R. (1996), 'Reflections on Ricardian equivalence', *NBER Working Paper no. 5502*.

Baumol, W.J. (1965), *Welfare Economics and the Theory of the State*, 2nd edition, Cambridge, MA: Harvard University Press.

Buchanan, J.M. (1958 [1999]), *Public Principles of Public Debt: A Defense and Restatement*, Homewood, IL: R.D. Irwin; reprinted as vol. 2 (1999) of *The Collected Works of James M. Buchanan* (1999–2002), Indianapolis: Liberty Fund.

Buchanan, J.M. (1960), *Fiscal Theory and Political Economy: Selected Essays*, Chapel Hill: University of North Carolina Press.

De Viti de Marco (1893 [1992]), 'La pressione tributaria dell'imposta e del prestito', *Giornale degli Economisti*, **6**, 38–67, 216–31; English translation as 'Fiscal burden arising from taxation and public debt', in Pasinetti (1992).

De Viti de Marco (1898a), 'Contributo alla teoria del prestito pubblico', in De Viti de Marco (1898b).

De Viti de Marco (1898b), *Saggi di Economia e Finanza*, Rome: Editi dal Giornale degli Economisti.

Diamond, P.A. (1965), 'National debt in a neoclassical growth model', *American Economic Review*, **55**(5), 1126–50.

Domar, E. (1944 [1955]), 'The "burden of the debt" and the national income', *American Economic Review*, **34**(4), 798–827; reprinted in Smithies and Butters (eds) (1955).

Domar, E.D. (1946), 'Capital expansion, rate of growth, and employment', *Econometrica*, **14**(2), 137–47.

Forte, F. and H. Hochman (1969), 'Monetary and fiscal policy: ambiguities in definitions', in Haller and Rechtenwald (eds) (1969).

Friedman, M. (1948), 'A monetary and fiscal framework for economic stability', *American Economic Review*, **38**(3), 245–64.

Griziotti, B. (1917), 'La diversa pressione tributaria del prestito e dell'imposta straordinaria', reprinted in Griziotti (1956), vol. I.

Griziotti, B. (1956), *Studi di Scienza delle Finanze e Diritto Finanziario*, Milan: Giuffrè (2 vols).

Haller, H. and H.C. Rechtenwald (eds) (1969), *Finanz- und Geld Politik im Umbruch*, Mainz: Hase & Köhler.

Holler, M. (1987a), 'Introduction', in Holler (1987b).

Holler, M. (1987b), *The Logic of Multiparty Systems*, Dordrecht and Boston: Kluwer Academic Publishers.

Hume, D. (1742 [1987]), *Of Public Credit*, in *Essays Moral, Political, Literary*, edited by E.F. Miller, with an appendix of variant readings from the 1889 edition by T.H. Green and T.H. Grose, revised edition, Indianapolis: Liberty Fund.

Kaldor, N. (1955), *An Expenditure Tax*, London: Allen & Unwin.

Keynes, J.M. (1923 [1971]), *A Tract on Monetary Reform,* London: Macmillan; reprinted (1971) in J.M. Keynes, *The Collected Writings*, vol. IV, The Royal Economic Society, London: Macmillan.

Keynes, J.M. (1934 [1979]), *A Treatise on Money in Two Volumes*, London: Macmillan; reprinted (1979) in J.M. Keynes, *The Collected Writings*, vols V–VI, The Royal Economic Society, London: Macmillan.

Keynes, J.M. (1936 [1980]), *The General Theory of Employment, Interest and Money*, London: Macmillan; reprinted (1980) in J.M. Keynes, *The Collected Writings*, vol. VII, The Royal Economic Society, London: Macmillan.

Lerner, A.P. (1944), *The Economics of Control: Principles of Welfare Economics*, New York: Macmillan.

Lucas, R.E. (1972), 'Expectations and the neutrality of money', *Journal of Economic Theory*, **4**(2), 103–24.

Lucas, R.E. (1981), *Studies in Business-Cycle Theory*, Cambridge, MA: MIT Press.

Lucas, R.E. and T.J. Sargent (1981), *Rational Expectations and Econometric Practice*, Minneapolis: University of Minnesota Press.

Modigliani, F. (1983), 'Government deficits, inflation and future generations', in D.W. Conklin and T.J. Chourcene (eds) (1983), *Deficits, How Big, How Bad*, Ontario: Ontario Economic Research Report.

Modigliani, F. (1987), 'The economics of public deficits', in Razin and Sadka (eds) (1987).

Modigliani, F. (1988), 'The role of intergenerational transfers and life cycle saving in the accumulation of wealth', *Journal of Economic Perspectives*, **2**(2), 15–40.

Pasinetti, L.L. (ed.) (1992), *Italian Economic Papers*, vol. I, Bologna: Il Mulino/Oxford University Press.

Peacock, A.T. and G.K. Shaw (1971 [1976]), *The Economic Theory of Fiscal Policy*, London: Allen & Unwin.

Puviani, A. (1903 [1973]), *Teoria dell'Illusione Finanziaria*, re-edited by F. Volpi (1973), Milan: ISEDI.

Razin, A. and E. Sadka (eds) (1987), *Economic Policy in Theory and Practice*, London: Macmillan.

Ricardo, D. (1817 [1947, 2005]), *Principles of Political Economy and Taxation*, re-edited (1947) by P. Sraffa as vol. I of the *The Works and Correspondence of David Ricardo*; reprinted (2005), Indianapolis: Liberty Fund.

Smithies, A. and J.K. Butters (eds) (1955), *Readings in Fiscal Policy*, Homewood, IL: R.D. Irwin.

Tobin, J. (1980), 'Government deficits and capital accumulation', in J.

Tobin (1980), *Asset Accumulation and Economic Activity: Reflections on Contemporary Macroeconomic Theory*, Chicago: University of Chicago Press.
United Nations (1990), *External Debt Crisis and Development*, New York: United Nations.

CHAPTER 14

Ahmad, E. and G. Brosio (eds) (2006), *Handbook of Fiscal Federalism*, Cheltenham, UK and Northampton, MA, USA: Edward Elgar.
Ahmad, E. and V. Tanzi (eds) (2002), *Managing Fiscal Decentralization*, London: Routledge.
Bondonio, P.V. and F. Scacciati (1990), *Efficienza e Produttività negli Enti Locali: l'Introduzione degli Incentivi nel Pubblico Impiego*, Rome: NIS.
Breton, A. and A. Scott (1978), *The Economic Constitution of Federal States*, Toronto: University of Toronto Press.
Buchanan, J.M. (1965 [2001]), 'An economic theory of clubs', *Economica*, New Series, **32**(125), 1–14; reprinted (2001) in *Externalities and Public Expenditure Theory*, vol. 15 of *The Collected Works of James M. Buchanan* (1999–2002), Indianapolis: Liberty Fund.
Buchanan, J.M. (2001), *Federalism, Liberty, and the Law*, vol. 18 of *The Collected Works of James M. Buchanan* (1999–2002), Indianapolis: Liberty Fund.
Cornes, R. and T. Sandler (1987), *The Theory of Externalities, Public Goods and Club Goods*, Cambridge: Cambridge University Press.
Musgrave, R.A. and P.B. Musgrave (1973), *Public Finance in Theory and Practice*, New York: McGraw-Hill.
Oates, W.E. (1999), 'An essay on fiscal federalism', *Journal of Economic Literature*, **37**(3), 1120–49.
Romagnoli, G.C. (1984), *Nuove Politiche di Finanziamento degli Enti Locali in Italia: Confronti con l'Esperienza Nordamericana*, with an 'Introduction' by F. Forte, Milan: Franco Angeli.
Salmon, P. (2002), 'Decentralization and supranationality the case of the European Union', in Ahmad and Tanzi (eds) (2002).
Salmon, P. (2006), 'Horizontal competition among governments', in Ahmad and Brosio (eds) (2006).
Tiebout, Ch.M. (1956), 'A pure theory of local expenditures', *Journal of Political Economy*, **64**(5), 416–24.
Wellisch, D. (2000), *Theory of Public Finance in a Federal State*, Cambridge: Cambridge University Press.

Index